THE BLUE GUIDES

*Albrecht Altdorfer, The Resurrection (detail),
Kunsthistorisches Museum, Vienna*

BLUE GUIDE

AUSTRIA

Ian Robertson

A & C Black
London

W W Norton
New York

Third edition 1992

Published by A & C Black (Publishers) Limited
35 Bedford Row, London WC1R 4JH

© A & C Black (Publishers) Limited 1992

ISBN 0–7136–3383–6

Published in the United States of America by
WW Norton & Company Incorporated
500 Fifth Avenue, New York, NY 10110

Published simultaneously in Canada by
Penguin Books Canada Limited
2801 John Street, Markham, Ontario L3R 1B4

ISBN 0–393–30836–7   USA

The publishers and the author have done their best to ensure the accuracy of all the information in Blue Guide Austria; however, they can accept no responsibility for any loss, injury or inconvenience sustained by any traveller as a result of information or advice contained in the guide.

Maps and plans drawn by Thames Cartographic Services Ltd
Maps based on material supplied by Freytag-Berndt u Artaria

Ian Robertson was born in Tokyo and educated at Stowe. After spending some years in publishing and specialist bookselling in London he was commissioned in 1970 to re-write *Blue Guide Spain*. He has re-written and radically revised several editions of Blue Guides to *Ireland, Paris and Versailles*, and *Switzerland*, and has compiled Blue Guides to *Austria, Cyprus, France* and *Portugal*.

Typeset by CRB Typesetting Services, Ely, Cambs.

Printed and bound in Great Britain by
William Clowes Limited, Beccles and London

PREFACE

Several revisions and a number of additions have been incorporated in this third edition, and minor errors and infelicities corrected.

Although its accessibility was affected over several decades by the shadow of Germany in the 1930s and that of Russia in the early 1950s, Austria has since made a remarkable recovery in several fields. She has also done much to cater for the tourist, and can now provide the traveller with a quality of accommodation and service second to none, although in certain places the individual may be swamped by the pressures to satisfy the group. By avoiding the beaten track, which is not difficult, the visitor will soon find a great deal to interest and delight. The beauties of the landscape, in every season, hardly require commendation; the wealth of Baroque churches and monasteries will astonish; while the quality of its museums, and not only those of Vienna, will come as a surprise to the majority of travellers.

There is little need to emphasise the interest of Austria, particularly Vienna (and to a lesser extent Salzburg, the birthplace of Mozart) for the lover of classical music: Gluck, Haydn, Beethoven, Schubert, Brahms, Bruckner, Mahler, Hugo Wolf, Schönberg, Berg and the Strauss family all lived here, and these are only some of the more obvious names.

Less emphasis is placed in this guide on Austria as a country for the winter sports enthusiast, for which it provides very extensive facilities. Full and up-to-date information in this field is easily available from the Austrian National Tourist Offices and from organisations concentrating on such sports, although articles on Skiing and Mountaineering are included.

Following the conventional formula adopted for the Blue Guides, the country is described in a series of routes following its network of roads, *free autobahns* or motorways (although there are a few toll roads). It does not pretend to be a fast motorist's guide, but rather one intended for those who wish to take a closer look at the country, its architecture and monuments, the very diversity of which should satisfy the demands of the most enthusiastic tourist. Towns are described for sight-seeing on foot, almost always the most convenient way of getting about, and a complement of town plans, etc. has been incorporated.

A very considerable area of Austria has been covered in person, both in summer and winter, but in compiling so comprehensive a guide it is virtually impossible to visit every locality, every Baroque church and every waterfall. Therefore, the readers' assistance is solicited, and any constructive suggestions for corrections or improvements will be gratefully welcomed, and acknowledged by the author, who alone is responsible for all inexactitudes, shortcomings, inconsistencies, and solecisms. No one is better aware of the difficulty of avoiding errors both of omission and commission. Selection remains the touchstone by which guide books are judged, and an attempt has been made to provide a balanced account of most aspects of Austria without being so exhaustive as to leave no opportunity to discover additional pleasures.

The continuing practice of 'starring' the highlights may come in for some criticism, but although the system is subjective and inconsistent, such asterisks do help the hurried traveller to pick out those things which the consensus of informed opinion (modified occasionally by the author's personal prejudice, admittedly) considers should not be missed. In certain cases a museum has been starred, rather than individual objects among those described, when the standard of its contents is remarkably high.

Austria is tourist-conscious, for it relies to a considerable extent on this form of 'invisible export'. Each town and province attempts to vie with others in making the most of its numerous natural attractions, and the visitor will find that public services function well; that conveniences are clean ... civic pride is very often in evidence, and in general value for money is given in hotels and restaurants. The staff in local tourist offices are usually very helpful and well-informed, even if sometimes their knowledge is only local. There is, in general, more professionalism in the sensitive field of providing guidance and offering hospitality than in many other countries.

In addition to those who assisted in the compilation of the earlier editions of this Guide—several of whom have continued to give advice or suggest improvements—the author would like to express his obligation to the following: *Werner Fritz, Marion Telsnig, Ruth Kamml* and *Dr Zundritsch* in London; and in Vienna, Director *Norbert Burda; Walter Aichner,* Lienz; *Uli Sauerzopz,* Eisenstadt; *Helmut Auernig,* Feldkirch; and *Heidi Lukas,* Innsbruck; *Dr Hans Gschitzer, Dr Gert Ammann* and *Dr Franz-Heinze Hye* in Innsbruck; *Dr Renate Langenfelder,* Salzburg; *Dr Günter Düriegl, Dr Georg Kugler, Dr Herbert Haupt,* and *Dr Michael Krapf,* Vienna; the Director of the museum at Niedersulz; and *Dr Brigitte Reiffenstein, Dr Ernst Menhofer, Dr Peter Marginter, H. Hillerbrandt* (Secession Building), *Irene Montjoye, Franz Neuwirth, Elfriede Winter, Christian* and *Renée Nebehay, David Hermges, Mag. Prof. Reinolf Reisinger, Angelika Holler,* and *Wendy Hofmaier.*

Eva and Hubert Fiedler, and Arthur and Marion Boyars, have patiently indulged and hospitably accommodated the author on his travels, while my wife, indefatigably, has remained at the wheel. Paul Langridge has offered all editorial support during the preparation of this third edition, which was overshadowed by the death of John Beer, whose earlier encouragement is here belatedly recorded.

A NOTE ON BLUE GUIDES

The Blue Guide series began in 1918 when Muirhead Guide-Books Limited published 'Blue Guide London and its Environs'. Finlay and James Muirhead already had extensive experience of guidebook publishing: before the First World War they had been the editors of the English editions of the Germany Baedekers, and by 1915 they had acquired the copyright of most of the famous 'Red' Handbooks from John Murray.

An agreement made with the French publishing house Hachette et Cie in 1917 led to the translation of Muirhead's London Guide, which became the first 'Guide Bleu'—Hachette had previously published the blue-covered 'Guides Joannes'. Subsequently, Hachette's 'Guide Bleu Paris et ses Environs' was adapted and and published in London by Muirhead. The collaboration between the two publishing houses continued until 1933.

In 1933 Ernest Benn Limited took over the Blue Guides, appointing Russell Muirhead, Finlay Muirhead's son, editor in 1934. The Muirhead's connection with the Blue Guides ended in 1963 when Stuart Rossiter, who had been working on the Guides since 1954, became house editor, revising and compiling several of the books himself.

The Blue Guides are now published by A & C Black, who acquired Ernest Benn in 1984, so continuing the tradition of guidebook publishing which began in 1826 with 'Black's Economical Tourist of Scotland'. The Blue Guide series continues to grow: there are now more than 40 titles in print with revised editions appearing regularly and many new Blue Guides in preparation.

'Blue Guides' is a registered trademark.

EXPLANATIONS

Type. The main routes are described in large type. Smaller type is used for the majority of sub-routes and excursions, for historical and preliminary paragraphs, and (generally speaking) for descriptions of greater detail or minor importance.

Distances, total and intermediate, are measured in kilometers, and total route distances are also given in miles. Road distances along the routes themselves record the approximate distance between the towns or villages, etc. described, but it should be emphasised that with the re-alignment of many roads it is almost certain that these distances will vary slightly from those measured by motorists on their milometers. Measurements of buildings and **altitudes** are expressed in metres (m).

The **Population** figures (in round numbers) are taken from the last census, of 1981, with a few updated when available.

Anglicisation. For the sake of consistency, the personal names of emperors, archdukes, etc. have retained their German form; *Heinrich* (Henry); *Albrecht* (Albert); *Friedrich* (Frederick); *Carl* or *Karl* rather than Charles (although Charles V may be anglicised in certain cases). With the exception of Vienna (*Wien*)—and the *Danube* rather than *Donau*—placenames also retain their German form, although the provinces are usually given their English form; Tyrol (*Tirol*), Carinthia (*Kärnten*), Styria (*Steiermark*), and Upper and Lower Austria (*Ober-* and *Niederösterreich*), apart from Austria (*Österreich*) itself.

The hopes that he will be forgiven for the inclusion of certain pleonasms, such as the Inn*tal* valley or Kaiser*gebirge* range.

Abbreviation. In addition to generally accepted and self-explanatory forms, the following occur in this guide.

C   = Century
F&B = Freytag & Berndt
Hl. = *Heilige*, Saint
m   = metres
Pl. = Plan
R   = Room
Rte = Route

CONTENTS

Maps and Plans

INTRODUCTION TO THE HISTORY OF AUSTRIA

by *Ernst Wangermann*

Prehistoric Austria. The territory covered by present-day Austria has been settled by man since palaeolithic times. But the caves in which evidence of human occupation has been discovered (e.g. the Gudenus Höhle near Weissenkirchen), do not enjoy the fame of those in southern France or northern Spain, for little beyond the barest traces of human life and activities have been found there.

There is evidence of fairly general occupation, at least on the higher ground, in neolithic times (from about 5000 BC). Agriculture and stock raising now supplemented hunting, fishing and food gathering. It was sometime during this period that the territory now covered by Austria attained an exceptional degree of economic importance through the development of salt-mining. The oldest centre of this activity was Dürrnberg, near Hallein (Salzburg). Other salt-mines such as those at Hallstatt (Upper Austria) and Hall (Tirol) have also been in operation from late neolithic times.

The ethnic composition of Austria's prehistoric population is the subject of speculation. But there is general agreement that during the last centuries BC the Celts established a kind of ascendancy based on control of the salt trade, and later of the copper and iron trade as well. As far as we know, it was the Celts who established the first stable 'state' structure in this area, the Celtic kingdom of *Noricum*, which covered the territory of present-day Austria minus its western extremities. Some of the finest known examples of Celtic art, belonging to the cultural tradition of La Tène, were produced in Noricum, and were excavated near Dürrnberg. They display a striking combination of foreign influences and native originality. With the development of larger settlements (*oppida*), the production of bronze and glass objects became increasingly standardised.

Roman Austria. Relations between this Celtic kingdom and its Roman neighbour to the south were on the whole peaceful. Expanding trade was of mutual benefit. The main difficulty arose from the Celts' inability to prevent periodic incursions of marauding Germanic tribes across their territory and into northern Italy. Roman penetration into Noricum was probably part of the policy of improving the security of northern Italy. After Rome's civil wars ended with the battle of Actium (31 BC), the area was conquered and occupied and the Roman frontier moved forward to the line of the Rhine and the Danube. The territory of present-day Austria was divided between three Roman provinces: Vorarlberg and most of Tirol were part of *Rhaetia*; Salzburg, Carinthia, Styria, Upper and most of Lower Austria constituted the Roman province of *Noricum*. The Vienna basin and Burgenland were part of *Pannonia Superior*, the province which covered about half the territory of present-day Hungary.

Here, as elsewhere, Romanisation brought in its wake a century or so of peace and a notable development of urban life and long-distance communication. Legions to defend the Danube border were stationed at *Laureacum* (Enns/Lorch), *Vindobona* (Vienna) and *Carnuntum* (Petronell), and their camps provided the basis for the growth of a thriving urban economy. Other cities developed at

Brigantium (Bregenz), *Aguntum* (Lienz), *Juvavum* (Salzburg) and *Flavia Solva* (Leibnitz). The number of inhabitants in these cities ranged from about 2000 to 15,000. A road along the Danube provided the chief East-West line of communication. Traffic to and from Italy was carried by two roads over the Alps and one skirting the Eastern Alps via the Pannonian plain.

Though built primarily for the movement of troops, Italian traders used these roads to bring oil, wine, pottery and glassware into the Alpine region and to export its salt, metals, wool and livestock. With Roman produce came the Roman deities whose worship was deftly amalgamated with that of the earlier Celtic ones. Excavations have revealed evidence of Mithraic worship, probably brought in by soldiers. Legend from later Carolingian times provides some evidence of the early penetration of outlawed Christianity. It tells of *Florianus*, a Roman administrator, who refused to conform to the official Imperial worship, and was drowned in the river Enns near Laureacum. The abbey of St. Florian (Upper Austria) is supposed to stand on the site of the grave of Austria's first Christian saint and martyr, whose image still adorns many houses to safeguard them against the danger of fire.

Germanic and Slav Settlement. From about the middle of the second century the *Pax Romana* became increasingly fragile. Plans to secure the Danube frontier from the growing pressure of migrant peoples by further annexations beyond the Danube had to be abandoned. Archaeological remains testify to periodic destructive incursions followed by only partial and temporary recovery of prosperity. As the Imperial administrative and military machine crumbled, the Christian Church, officially legalised in the Roman Empire by Constantine early in the fourth century, stepped into the breach. It was the bishops and the first monks who directed the efforts to salvage something from the disintegrating structure of Roman organisation and civilisation, and to mitigate the conquerors' impulse of exploitation. In Noricum, this achievement is reflected in the history and legend of St. Severinus (died 482), written a few years after the events (511) by one of his disciples. *Severinus*, like Florianus a Roman administrator, helped to ensure the continuation of some kind of civilised, urban, Roman and Christian life throughout Noricum in this violent and unsettled period. But the removal of his body from its original resting place to be reburied in Italy, was seen to mark the final abandonment of Noricum by the Roman Empire.

During the following three centuries, two quite different kinds of change occurred in the territory of present-day Austria. The written evidence records the spectacular and often violent establishment of a succession of loose power structures over the Alpine region by migrant Germanic and Asiatic peoples—the Huns, the Goths, the Lombards, the Avars, and others. The main objectives of these peoples were the centres of Roman wealth which lay beyond the Alps, in Italy to the south and in Gaul to the west. Simultaneously with these constant armed migrations, however, a far more fundamental development was taking place, namely the permanent settlement of the land which had been either abandoned or left unsettled by the Celto-Roman population. The settler peoples were the Alamanni, who came from Swabia to settle the extreme west (now Vorarlberg), the Bavarians coming from Bohemia to settle the north and west (Lower and Upper Austria, Salzburg, and northern Tirol), and the Slavs, escaping Avar oppression and settling the south and east (Styria, Carinthia, and southern Tirol). Placenames give us a rough indication of the areas settled by each of these peoples. Lines of demarcation were often disputed, and there is evidence of the Slav population in Carinthia accepting a limited and conditional Germanic overlordship at an early date. Placenames ending in -heim and -ing(en) generally indicate a Bavarian settlement, those ending in -itz a Slav one. A few placenames indicate the existence of a Celto-Roman population, which may have survived on a larger scale than the written evidence suggests. Despite the bitter rivalry over territory and overlordship, the Germanic and Slav settlers had one important thing in common—the ability and technology to clear and cultivate the valleys and lowlands. For it was during these so-called 'dark centuries' that the territory of Austria was first fully opened up.

Christianisation and the Emergence of an Austrian Entity. The Germanic and Slav settlements marked a major setback for Christianity. Roman Christianity fought determined rearguard actions in its own defence, and managed to survive in a number of centres. But generally it made no attempt to convert the conquering and settling population. This arduous task was pioneered in the seventh century by Irish monks whose asceticism and missionary zeal were not directed solely towards the Anglo-Saxons. St. Columbanus was the first of these. He preached and founded monasteries and churches on the territory of present-day Austria. When the Irish missions had laid the foundations, a permanent superstructure of Church organisation was built by men sent in from Bavaria, which had become a dependency of the expanding Frankish Empire. The Bavarian dukes tried to establish a systematic control over the Alpine region, both on account of its strategic importance and because of its greater distance from the centre of Frankish power from which they tried to secure a certain degree of autonomy. In this period, the success of such a design depended largely on the co-operation of the Church. For even at this early stage of its history, the Church alone could provide the necessary organisational framework and ideological drive. The key figure in the ecclesiastical penetration from Bavaria was St. Rupert, a Rhenish noble, who selected the largely deserted Roman Juvavum, henceforth called Salzburg, as the base for his Austrian mission. There, about the year 700, he founded the abbey of St. Peter and the nunnery on the Nonnberg, both now Benedictine houses. Conversion made rapid progress in much of what is now Austria, as is indicated by the Pope's agreement to the elevation of Salzburg to a bishopric. From about 767, Salzburg had its own Cathedral, built next to the abbey of St. Peter and richly endowed by its Bavarian sponsors. In 798 it achieved primacy among the Bavarian bishoprics by its elevation to an archbishopric. Salzburg became something like Austria's ecclesiastical capital, and was to remain so for much of its history. Further monastic foundations followed under the Bavarian Duke Tassilo III (740–88), notably at Innichen in the Pustertal (now in Italy) and at Kremsmünster (Upper Austria), whose beautiful 'Tassilo chalice' still recalls its Bavarian-sponsored origins. The location of these two important foundations on the borderline between the Germanic and Slav areas of settlement suggests that the Bavarian bishoprics were competing with the Eastern Church in the work of Christianising the Slavs.

Tassilo's attempts at asserting his independence provoked a formidable reaction on the part of the most determined and successful of the Frankish rulers, Charlemagne. The latter's success in making good the Frankish claim to overlordship meant that from the late eighth century onwards the Alpine region was integrated into the most advanced power structure in the Germanic world. With Charlemagne's conquest of the Lombard Kingdom in northern Italy and his subsequent coronation by the Pope (800), the Frankish Empire claimed to have entered upon the inheritance of Imperial Rome. Of this far-flung realm, the Alpine region constituted an exposed frontier area, liable to invasion by the still unsettled peoples to the east. It was therefore organised, like other frontier areas, as border marches administered by a margrave (*Markgraf*). The dukes of Bavaria would probably have liked to assert a hereditary claim to this dignity and function in the south-eastern border marches. But the determination to curb Bavarian aspirations to greater autonomy from Frankish overlordship caused the Carolingians and their successors in the East Frankish or German Kingdom to keep these marches out of Bavarian hands. Thus, paradoxically, the resistance of the Frankish/German rulers to Bavarian independence promoted a distinctive political development of the exposed area of the south-eastern marches which was to become Austria.

In the tenth century, this area was overrun by the last incursion from a nomadic people originating in Asia, the Magyars. After their defeat by the German Emperor *Otto* 'the Great' in 955 at the famous battle of the Lechfeld, the border march was restored, and Leopold of Babenberg installed as margrave (976). At this time the region's distinctive development was already reflected in the new name *Ostarrîchi*, which occurs in a document of 996, referring to the lands governed by Margrave Leopold. Austria had emerged, and the survival of the house of Babenberg for nearly three centuries did much to ensure its continuing unity.

Austria under the Babenbergs (976–1246). The Babenbergs were not only long-lived; they also produced rulers of exceptional political and administrative ability. Their first achievement, perhaps the prerequisite for all others, was the stabilisation of the frontier dividing their territory from the Magyars to the east and the Slavs to the north-east. It was during the eleventh century that the river Leitha became the border between Austria and Hungary, which it was to remain until 1919. Behind the stabilised frontiers, the land, devastated and depopulated to some degree as the result of successive armed migrations, was resettled. Unlike the preceding land-settlement, this one was exclusively Germanic (Bavarian and perhaps Franconian as well), and in comparison with all the earlier settlements, it was intensive. From the evidence of placenames, we can tell that the majority of the villages now existing in Austria originated in the early Babenberg period, many of them wrested from the forests.

The Babenbergs first resided in Melk, on the Danube. With the stabilisation of the eastern frontier, they moved downstream, establishing residences successively in Tulln, Klosterneuburg and finally, at about the middle of the twelfth century, in Vienna. The territorial advantages they derived for themselves testifies to their political ability. At the height of the 'Investiture Conflict' between Empire and Papacy, Margrave *Leopold II* (1075–95) supported the latter. This opened his territory to the influence of some of the great reformers, who followed the lead of *Hildebrand* (*Pope Gregory VII*) in this struggle. The most important of these was *Altmann*, bishop of Passau, whose bishopric, with that of Salzburg, shared ecclesiastical control over the territory of the Babenbergs. In c 1083, Altmann founded a monastery overlooking the Danube opposite Krems, which, as the Benedictine abbey of Göttweig, became a model and centre for the Church Reform movement. Leopold's successor, *Leopold III* (1095–1136), later to be revered as Austria's patron saint, maintained a more neutral position, and increased his influence in Germany by marrying into the Imperial family. Yet he continued to support the Church Reform movement, and was responsible for two major foundations, Klosterneuburg, which became his residence, and Heiligenkreuz in the Wienerwald, the first of the Cistercian houses in Austria. Opposing the Emperor was a risky policy, but apart from one incursion by *Wratislaw* of Bohemia, the margraves managed to keep their territory free from fighting. This was in marked contrast to Salzburg, which became a major battleground, so much so that in 1077 Archbishop Gebhard, a leading supporter of the Pope, ordered the construction of a fortress above the city for his own protection, the Hohensalzburg, which still dominates the place.

In the much longer conflict between the German king/emperors and their overmighty subjects, the Babenbergs judiciously supported the former. Their loyalty was duly rewarded, and in 1156 earned them their elevation to the status of dukes with virtually sovereign powers over their Austrian duchy (*Privilegium Minus*). The first Babenberg Duke of Austria was Leopold III's son *Heinrich II Jasomirgott* (1141–77), who was also the first to establish his residence in Vienna. To add distinction to his new residence, in 1155 he founded the Benedictine *Schottenkloster* there, so called because it was inaugurated with the help of Irish and Scottish monks summoned from Regensburg in Bavaria.

Participation in the Crusades brought the Babenbergs into contact with Byzantium and made possible intermarriage with the East Roman Imperial family. Moreover, the Crusades considerably enhanced the economic importance of Austria, for the Danube now became one of Europe's main routes to the East. The constant passage of men, produce, and goods, which included exotic luxuries discovered in the Moslem world, increased Austria's prosperity, and provided the basis for the rise of the Danubian towns of Linz, Krems, and Vienna. The imprisonment of *Richard I* of England by *Duke Leopold V* (1177–94) in the fortress of Dürnstein, and his subsequent release for a huge ransom, exemplifies another and less creditable way of profiting from the trans-Austrian traffic engendered by the Crusades.

Austria's growing prosperity was reflected in the impressive number of buildings erected during the twelfth and early thirteenth centuries, especially those of the monastic foundations, the Stephansdom in Vienna, and the cathedral of Gurk, a new bishopric founded in Carinthia by Salzburg.

Under the last Babenbergs, *Leopold VI* (1198–1230) and *Friedrich II* (1230–46), Vienna became the centre of German courtly poetry, and the renowned *Minnesänger Neidhart von Reuenthal* and *Walter von der Vogelweide*, attended their court. Here, too, originated that pre-eminent German epic, the *Nibelungenlied*, the events of which, set in Babenberg Austria, are suffused with memories of earlier armed migrations.

As the Babenbergs were still subjects of the German king or emperor even after their elevation to a dukedom, some of their achievements were possible only in so far as they succeeded in becoming 'overmighty subjects'. They were virtually sovereign lords of their territory, *Landesfürsten*, and as such, they endeavoured to maintain maximum independence from their overlords, at the same time keeping a tight hold on their own most powerful subjects, the *Ministeriales*. In the end, this struggle on two fronts evidently overstretched their resources. The last Babenberg, the childless Friedrich II 'the Quarrelsome', had to fight, simultaneously, both the *Emperor Friedrich II* and his formidable and ambitious subjects, the *Kuenringer*. Possessions and toll-rights along the Danube had enabled the latter to exploit the growing wealth derived from the Danubian trade. This is presumably why these 'robber barons' of the popular tradition were increasingly difficult to control. To make matters worse, the stabilisation in the east which the Babenbergs had achieved was once again undermined by a new westward movement, that of the Mongols. The 'quarrelsome' Friedrich tried to turn Hungary's consequent preoccupation to his own advantage. Eventually, in 1246, having fought off a revolt led by his nobles, and lost his capital Vienna to the Emperor, he was killed in battle against the Magyars near the Leitha. Thus ended a period which some historians still regard as one of the most prosperous in the history of Austria.

Late-Medieval Austria. The extinction of the Babenbergs coincided almost exactly with that of the Stauffen dynasty, which resulted in a German *Interregnum*. This made a peaceful succession to the Babenberg inheritance practically impossible. The greater part inevitably fell to Austria's most powerful neighbour, the Bohemian king *Přemysl Ottokar II* (1252–78). He secured his position by a policy of supporting the towns and restraining the overmighty feudal lords. Vienna seems to have enjoyed his special favour. He extended its privileges, and commissioned an ambitiously conceived rebuilding of the church of St. Stephen, recently destroyed by fire. The leading burghers repaid these favours by their consistent support for Ottokar against his main rival, **Rudolf of Habsburg**, whose election as German king in 1272 had put an end to the *Interregnum*. Rudolf, claiming the reversion of the Babenberg inheritance, won the support of the nobility, and was thus able to occupy Vienna and to defeat his formidable opponent at the battle of the Marchfeld (1278).

Austria's Habsburg connection, which was to last until 1918, was not initially an unmixed blessing. The stimulating contact with progressive Bohemia was severed, and was succeeded by the domination of the Habsburgs' Swabian followers, who were resented in Austria as foreign intruders and unwelcome rivals. While the Habsburgs pursued a successful policy of territorial expansion, which led to the permanent accession to Austria of Carinthia (1335) and Tirol (1363), they were unable to agree amongst themselves an order of succession. As a result, there was a series of disputed successions, which allowed the nobility to achieve a political ascendancy, which helped to retard Austria's general development for more than a century. All sections of Austrian society, as well as her neighbours, were inevitably drawn into this conflict, which was particularly damaging and bloody in Vienna. In the urban centres, the only constructive development to be noted in this period is the establishment of the mendicant orders. Their pastoral and social work among the poor, however, did not significantly lessen the general urban *misère* and frustration, one symptom of which was the cruel persecution and massacre of Jews under *Albrecht V* (1404–39).

While Austria stagnated under the Habsburgs, Bohemia flourished under the Luxemburg dynasty, which defeated the Habsburgs in the rivalry for the elective German royal dignity in 1308. Thereafter, the Habsburgs had to struggle very hard not to be completely overshadowed by their Bohemian neighbours. This rivalry in the event produced some positive results for Austria. **Duke Rudolf IV** (1358–65) emulated the new university of Prague by founding one in Vienna (1365), and he strove to compete with Prague's St. Vitus's Cathedral by the reconstruction of St. Stephen's on a truly majestic scale. He was unable, however, to procure Vienna's elevation to a bishopric. The reputation of the new university was assured by Rudolf's successor **Albrecht III** (1365–95) and his Chancellor, who were quick to secure the services of some of the more eminent teachers at the University of Paris when they had to leave Europe's outstanding centre of learning because of the Papal schism.

By the early fifteenth century, Habsburg marital policy—soon to raise them to the position of Europe's leading dynasty—and the imminent extinction of the Luxemburg dynasty, created the prospect of a great union of Danubian territories including Austria, Bohemia, and Hungary. Though the growing threat from Turkish incursions fostered a widespread realisation of the desirability of such a union, the divided Habsburgs lacked the strength to assert successfully their hereditary claims in Bohemia and Hungary. The reign of the sickly young *Ladislaus the Posthumous* (1440–57) is strikingly reminiscent of the last phase of the Merovingian dynasty. For on his death, he was succeeded in Bohemia and Hungary by his guardians. The Austrian lands were once more fiercely disputed by two contenders for the succession, who, between them, brought the country as close to material ruin as had the barbarian invasions. Fortunately, one died in 1463, leaving *Friedrich of Styria*, who had already been elected German king and crowned as Emperor **Friedrich III** by the Pope, to succeed to all the Austrian Habsburg lands apart from Tirol. This marked the conclusion of Austria's 'wars of the roses'.

The purchase of the Adriatic port of Fiume (1471) may indicate that the country was at last strengthening her commercial position, but Friedrich III was neither powerful nor wealthy enough to maintain a really secure and lasting peace in his lands; for a time he even lost control of Vienna and Lower Austria to the Hungarians under their 'national king' *Matthias Corvinus*. But as Emperor he could bestow on his own lands the status for which his predecessors had vainly striven for so long—Austria became an Archduchy (1453) and Vienna a bishopric (1469). However, the results of his participation in international politics were detrimental rather than beneficial to Austria's progress and prosperity.

Reformation and Social Revolution. No sooner had the Habsburgs overcome their bitter internal dynastic conflicts than they became deeply involved in the mutual rivalries of the great European dynasties. For Friedrich III ultimately succeeded in his ambition to secure for his son **Maximilian I** (1493–1519) the hand of *Mary of Burgundy*, only child of *Charles the Bold* and heiress to the Duchy. The marriage took place in 1477. Thanks to their earlier acquisition of Flanders and Brabant, the economic power-house of fifteenth-century Europe, the Dukes of Burgundy were able to set a dazzling new standard of courtly culture and magnificence, and to overshadow the power of the kings of France.

The close links which Austria now had with one of the great centres of late-medieval and humanist civilisation, provided a creative stimulus to Austrian culture. Under Maximilian I, Vienna became a major centre of Renaissance humanism in its own right. The poet Konrad Celtis founded a society of scholars there, the *sodalitas litteraria Danubiana*; he did much to make the university renowned for its cultivation of humanist scholarship, and he laid the foundations of Vienna's distinctive theatrical tradition.

The fact that the all-pervading political message articulated by this many-sided cultural activity was the glorification of Maximilian and of Habsburg power did not detract from its intrinsic quality. But the fact that this power was now dedicated to the furtherance of the essentially Burgundian objective of eclipsing France, necessitating expensive campaigns in Flanders and northern Italy, was nothing less than a disaster for Austria with her still modest economic resources. For it was not from France that any threat to the life and prosperity of the people inhabiting the Austrian lands was forthcoming, but from the East, where tensions and pressures now prompted the Mohammedan Turks to push ever further westwards up the valleys of the Drau and the Danube. The Turks did not invade to expropriate land on which to settle so much as in search of tribute and slaves.

The challenge now confronting the Habsburg dynasty was the defence of Austrian lands from these incursions from the East. And indeed we can recognise a certain disposition to rise to the challenge. Representative assemblies, sometimes with peasant participation, were convoked to discuss and organise defensive strategy. The marriage alliance with the Jagellon dynasty ruling in Hungary and Bohemia (1515) brought the countries most directly threatened by the Turkish advance into a closer union. However, the continuing pursuit of Burgundian ambitions, to which the ambitions of Spain were added after Maximilian's son *Philip* unexpectedly found himself married to the only surviving offspring of the Catholic Kings, made impossible any consistent and effective defensive posture against the Turks. The Austrian population thus found itself subjected to vastly increased financial burdens, and yet deprived of the effective shield which alone would have justified these burdens in their eyes. In the autumn of 1529, Vienna itself had to withstand a Turkish siege.

The threat from without exacerbated an already acute internal crisis. The intensification of seigneurial and inter-state rivalries, and the increasingly ostentatious display of competitive power, involved a cost for society which was not in this period of declining feudalism met by a corresponding growth in its productive capacity. The only major innovations took place in the technology involved in mining the precious metals and the metals used in the production of weapons and armour, and the Habsburgs were lucky in being able to draw on deposits of silver in Tirol and of iron in Styria. Agriculture remained largely stagnant. The rising costs of government, war, and the conspicuous extravagance of the ruling-class were therefore defrayed by the subject population through currency devaluation, resulting in inflation, and through increased taxes and feudal impositions. The fact that the people of the Austrian lands resisted the consequent decline in their living standards, must be ascribed to the social and intellectual climate of the time, which was not conducive to fatalistic passivity. The critical spirit of enquiry and the appetite for authentic original texts stimulated by the humanist scholars gradually transcended the restricted circles of professional teachers and theologians, and influenced the rank and file of the clergy and some of their congregations. More and more people were examining and discussing the Scriptures simply because they were concerned about their earthly destiny and their prospects of eternal salvation. Reforming preachers made the vernacular Bible available to laymen. And in this new light many things seemed different. Long-accepted truths and authorities were now seen to lack scriptural sanction. There was, for example, no sanction in the Bible for tithes, serfdom and feudal dues. Subjects who resented the increased burdens imposed on them could now appeal confidently against the harsh justice of their overlords to the merciful justice of God. In this they were abetted by the more radical of the reforming preachers.

The widespread social revolution which resulted from these attitudes culminated in the so-called Peasants' War of 1525/26, which was not a series of *jacqueries* or desperate outbreaks of inarticulate violence. The religious reformation, the presence of preachers inspired by the writings of *Martin Luther* in Germany and *Huldreich Zwingli* in Switzerland, and the support provided by the urban population, gave the social revolution a political dimension. There is some evidence of organisational links embracing whole regions. Rebels mobilised behind programmes of reform in which demands for a return to the 'old law' were put forward alongside aspirations to which they considered themselves entitled under 'divine justice', and which anticipate modern democratic and socialist ideals. The eighth of the 'Twenty-Four Articles of the Common People of Salzburg' (1525) declared: 'It is clear and proven by scripture that we are all free by nature and by divine freedom and not enserfed nor subject to any man'. *Michael Gaismair's* 'New Order' for Tirol (1526) envisaged the transformation of monasteries into hospitals, the use of the tithe to support the poor, the destruction of castles and city walls, the abolition of internal tolls and the draining of marshland.

These revolutionary movements attracted sufficient support to prevail against the forces which an individual ruler, taken by surprise, could deploy against them. The archbishop of Salzburg, *Matthäus Lang*, was driven out of his residence in 1525 by an army of rebellious peasants wholeheartedly supported by the burghers of Salzburg. He took refuge in his impregnable fortress, Hohensalzburg, where he was besieged for several months before being rescued by troops from outside his territory. But such successes, though spectacular, were short-lived. The rebels could not hold their ground against a large concentration of professional mercenaries such as **Ferdinand I** (1521–64), Maximilian's successor in the Austrian lands, sent against them. The scale of the revolutionary movement, the radicality of its demands, and the devastation which followed in the wake of its temporary triumphs, provoked a strong reaction from those who felt threatened by it. The mercenaries were therefore explicitly encouraged to deal with the defeated rebels with the utmost harshness, and they did so. Feudalism was not to be overthrown by a peasant-led revolution. Nevertheless, the memory of such a revolution subsequently helped to check some of the abuses which had provoked it.

The Triumph of Confessional Absolutism. Under the terms of the religious settlement in the Empire (*Augsburger Religionsfriede*, 1555), the Austrian Habsburgs, firmly committed to the Catholic faith, were entitled to enforce conformity to the Catholic Church in their own territories. Ferdinand I persecuted, exiled and even executed Lutherans and Anabaptists both before and after this settlement. But his involvement in the Burgundian and Spanish conflicts of his elder brother, the *Emperor Charles V*, the continuing and not very successful wars against the Turks, and the weakness of his own dynastic position in the kingdoms of Bohemia and Hungary which he had 'inherited' as a result of the death in battle of the Jagellon king *Louis II* at Mohács (1526), made effective and consistent enforcement of confessional uniformity impossible.

The reformed religion therefore made rapid progress in Austria throughout the reign of Ferdinand I, and even more during that of his more tolerant successor **Maximilian II** (1564–76). The decay and corruption of the institutions of the Catholic Church were such that people of all social classes felt a strong attraction to the reformed religion. Appetite for Church property was not a significant factor in this attraction, for despite the fact that the monasteries were largely deserted and most of the remaining monks no longer followed a monastic way of life, there was no general plunder of monastic property. Indeed, the Reformation in Austria was remarkable for the evolution of a fairly peaceful and harmonious coexistence between the rival faiths. The Reformers' energy was channelled primarily into education. The emphasis on the written word as the principal vehicle of divine revelation implied a massive drive against illiteracy. The Protestant nobility took the lead in establishing schools through the organisation of the provincial Estates, which provided the curriculum laid down by Melanchthon and others for the Protestant schools of the Empire. Apart from German and Latin, Greek and Hebrew were also taught. The teachers were of a very high calibre. *Johannes Kepler*, the greatest astronomer of his time, was a teacher at the school in Linz. As Vienna University remained in Catholic hands, its student population declined drastically, the Protestant nobility sending their sons to Wittenberg and other reformed universities.

The Counter-Reformation began as a concerted effort by the Catholic Church to outdo the Protestants in the field of education. It was spearheaded by the Jesuit Order, Catholic Europe's principal weapon in the fight against heresy. The Jesuits reached Vienna in 1551, and established colleges in quick succession in Vienna, Krems, Graz, Laibach (Ljubljana), Olmütz (Olomuč), and other centres. Their curriculum, and the catechism of their most renowned preacher *Peter Canisius*, provided the basic texts for Catholic education in Austria until the 1770s. A distinctive characteristic of Jesuit education was the use of drama as a didactic form, which contributed to Austria's evolving theatrical tradition.

The Protestant-Catholic educational rivalry could have provided a great stimulus to Austria's intellectual and cultural development, if the harmonious coexistence between the competing faiths, characteristic of the third quarter of the sixteenth century, had continued longer. But powerful factors emerged to undermine this harmony. The religious disputes were, inevitably, closely intertwined with the major social and political conflicts of the time. We have already seen how rebellious peasants were invoking scripture in support of their attack on tithes and serfdom. Similarly, the nobility and the burghers felt the attraction of Protestantism not only as a renewed and reformed Church, but also because the emphasis which its doctrine put on individual judgement and independence seemed to accord well with the struggle in which they were engaged against the extension and concentration of monarchical power to which Ferdinand I aspired no less vigorously than did *Charles V* in Spain and *François I* in France. Catholic monarchs, therefore, especially after the outbreak of the Revolt of the Netherlands, tended to see

Protestantism as a religion which encouraged political recalcitrance and social rebellion.

The movement towards a showdown, as always in situations of this kind, developed simultaneously in both the rival camps, mutually provoking and stimulating each other. On the Catholic side, it was led by *Duke Maximilian I* of Bavaria, and it received its most consistent encouragement from Spain. The movement's ideological headquarters was the Jesuit university of Ingolstadt. It was from there that *Archduke Ferdinand*, a cousin of **Emperor Rudolf II** (1576–1612), and his Bavarian wife, brought the ideology of the extirpation of heresy and confessional absolutism to Austria. And it was Ferdinand who embarked on the forcible conversion of Styria and Carinthia as soon as he succeeded his father as governor of these provinces in 1595. So-called Reformation-Commissions, accompanied by armed mercenaries, travelled across the two provinces, closed and destroyed Protestant schools and churches, burnt heretical books, expelled preachers and erected scaffolds for the execution of any who dared to return.

While Archduke Ferdinand subjected the provinces under his control to an uncompromising policy of confessional conformity enforced by military execution, the Emperor Rudolf II and his brother and successor **Matthias** (1612–19) practised a more restrained policy of compromise pending conversion by persuasion and conviction. This was also the policy of *Cardinal Khlesl*, bishop of Vienna, the son of a Protestant baker and a convert to Catholicism. The future, however, belonged not to them, but to Archduke Ferdinand: for neither Rudolf nor Matthias produced an heir. This made Ferdinand heir apparent to all the Austrian Habsburg lands, and made forcible conversion—as exemplified in Styria and Carinthia—their imminent fate. In a desperate attempt to ward off this daunting prospect, the Protestant-led Estates of Bohemia, who still enjoyed some constitutional rights in relation to the succession, on Matthias' death in 1619, decided to reject Ferdinand's hereditary claims to Bohemia, and to elect *Friedrich of the Palatinate*, a Protestant, in his place.

Ferdinand II (1619–37) now launched his crusade. He arrested Khlesl and sent an armed force into Bohemia, reinforced by Bavarian and Spanish contingents, to assert his hereditary claims. He defeated his opponents at the *Battle of the White Mountain* just outside Prague (1620). His victory not only made the Habsburgs the unrestricted hereditary monarchs of Bohemia, but also laid the foundations for confessional absolutism and the extirpation of Protestantism in all the Habsburg lands. Where Protestantism, as in Upper Austria, could still identify with the endemic social discontent, and the rebellious peasants could throw up leaders of the calibre of *Stefan Fadinger*, formidable rearguard actions could be fought (1626/27). But the verdict of the White Mountain was not to be reversed. Except where international factors limited Habsburg power (as in Turkish-occupied Hungary and Silesia), all the Habsburg lands were forced to submit to monarchical absolutism and Catholic conformity. Those who refused—of whom there were many thousands in all walks of life—were put to death or exiled.

One result was a transfer of property to Catholic loyalists and camp-followers on a staggering scale. Another was the growth of those trends in Austrian society which were to retard its rate of development in relation to Dutch, French, and English society in this period, among them the decline of the urban economy, the erosion of the peasants' capacity to resist exploitation, and the intellectual and cultural isolation from the Protestant world. Under the tutelage of the Jesuits and other Catholic missionary orders, the majority turned back to the faith of their fathers. In some respects the Counter-Reformation became itself a popular movement. Fear and hatred of Protestant heresy became a deeply-rooted popular emotion. And with the proliferation of feasts and ceremonial, often associated with new places of pilgrimage such as *Maria Taferl* in Lower Austria, 'baroque piety' in Austria tended to reflect the people's need for gregarious worldly enjoyment more than the spiritual objectives of the Council of Trent.

Rise to 'Great Power' Status. The events which culminated in Ferdinand II's triumph over his opponents were but one act of a larger drama played out on the European stage. The religious contest became interlocked with the major secular confrontations of the period, such as the defence of the Estates' rights against the concentration of monarchical power, and inter-dynastic rivalries. Seen in this context, Ferdinand's success was merely an early phase in the wider struggle known as the *Thirty Years' War* (1618–48), from which his successor **Ferdinand III** (1637–57) was finally compelled to withdraw through sheer exhaustion, although he had not attained his objective of establishing absolutism, or at least reversing the progress of Protestantism in the Empire. This had been frustrated to a large extent by the intervention of the Swedish army on the Protestant side. The great striking power of this force had been repeatedly demonstrated, not least in 1644, when it penetrated as far south as Lower Austria and close to Vienna itself, demolishing every fortresses in its path. The ruins of Dürnstein on the Danube can still be seen today in the state the Swedish army left it.

The period following the Thirty Years' War is commonly described by historians as that of Austria's rise to the status of a 'great power'. If territorial extent is accepted as the principal criterion of power, then there is no questioning this assertion, for the area in which Austrian Habsburg sovereignty was internationally recognised had more than doubled between 1648 and 1718. They achieved this expansion by virtue of their victory over the Turks, who had been forced to abandon Hungary, and by their inheritance in 1700 of the Spanish Habsburg possessions in the Netherlands and Italy.

But this expansion also entailed prolonged, destructive and expensive warfare, notably against the Turks, who continued to enslave thousands in the areas they overran. In 1683, Vienna, for the second time in its history, was besieged by the Turks, whose army, commanded by the Grand Vizier *Kara Mustapha*, was much larger than in 1529, when they had made their previous incursion. The defenders, decimated by disease, were able to hold out for two months before a relieving army, consisting of Imperial, Polish and Austrian contingents, advanced down the slopes of the Kahlenberg to destroy the Turkish camp and disperse their demoralised troops.

One of the regimental commanders who distinguished himself in the relief of Vienna was *Eugene of Savoy* (1663–1736), and it could be argued that the greatest contribution made by the then reigning monarch, **Leopold I** (1658–1705), to Austria's emergence as a 'great power' was his decision to take the unheroic-looking Prince into his service. Not long after, Eugene was given command of Leopold's entire Eastern army, and his daring and brilliance both in strategic planning and on the battlefields of Zenta (1697) and Peterwardein (1716), were the decisive factors which turned the Turkish defeat into an historic rout, and which gave the Habsburgs control over the entire Hungarian Kingdom including the Principality of Transylvania.

Eugene also distinguished himself in Austria's war against Bourbon France in the struggle to secure some part of the Spanish Habsburg inheritance. His spectacular successes at Blenheim (1704), Turin (1706), and Oudenarde (1708), also revealed his ability to collaborate effectively with *Marlborough*, the equally brilliant British commander. After the Treaties of Utrecht and Rastadt (1713; 1714) with France, and those of Karlowitz and Passarowitz (1699; 1718) with Turkey, the Austrian Habsburgs, in addition to their heartland, ruled over the lands of the Crown of St. Wenceslaus (Bohemia, Moravia, and Silesia); of the Crown of St. Stephen (Hungary, Croatia, and Transylvania); the former Spanish Netherlands (Belgium); and most of the former Spanish possessions in Italy (Lombardy, Naples, and Sicily).

Leopold I did not live to witness this culmination of his labours: his sons, **Joseph I** (1705–11; who died prematurely of smallpox) and **Karl VI** (1711–40) reaped the harvest. They were able to turn their attention to the task of providing suitable symbolic representations of the power they had acheived. Extravagant plans, designed by *J.B. Fischer von Erlach*, for the summer palace of Schönbrunn reveal their intention of putting even Versailles into the shade and thereby proclaiming, in architectural terms, Habsburg pretensions to supremacy over Louis XIV. Fischer von Erlach's plan for Schönbrunn remained on paper, although his magnificent *Karlskirche* (with its unusual twin pillars signifying Karl VI's claim to Spain) was completed. Building on this kind of scale became fashionable amongst the rich and powerful. To this 'building craze' we owe the Baroque rebuilding of the great monasteries of Melk, Göttweig, and St. Florian, and of nearly all the noble palaces in Vienna. Much as we may admire these architectural achievements, at the time they reflected an internal condition not particularly conducive to the consolidation of the country's status as a great power. The nobility were compensating themselves for the loss of some of their political influence under absolutism by improving their economic position, and this could only be at the expense of both the subject peasantry and the towns. Those who acquired the confiscated estates of Protestants after the Battle of the White Mountain, treated their domains as conquered land. In Bohemia, the former legal rights of the peasants were abolished. If the demesne—the part of the estate farmed directly by the noble land-owner—was profitable, he could annexe to it peasant holdings, a process known as *Bauernlegen*. In the Austrian provinces, where security of peasant tenure was the rule, exploitation was intensified both by raising rents and dues and by exacting more days of labour service (*Robot*). When economic recovery set in, neither the peasants nor the towns—still weakened by the effects of Protestant expulsions and prolonged warfare—could profit from it in the way the larger noble and ecclesiastical landowners could, who had in effect transformed themselves from receivers of customary rent into agrarian entrepreneurs.

For a monarchy whose strength depended increasingly on its ability to finance a regular standing army, this was an ominous development, for such a force could be maintained only by revenues from taxation, and it was those who paid the bulk of direct taxes who were being impoverished, while those who were assessed more lightly, or enjoyed immunities from direct taxation, prospered.

Hungary, with its great potential, might have become a source of additional wealth, but again the objectives of confessional absolutism stood in the way of this. Indeed, Leopold I's attempt to impose confessional absolutism on Hungary—as it had been imposed on the Bohemian and Austrian lands by Ferdinand II—and the determination of his ecclesiastical advisers to combine this, as Ferdinand had, with the forcible conversion of the population to Catholicism, resulted in catastrophic disaster. Initially, it drove many Hungarians into alliance with the Turks, and then, when the country was reconquered from the Turks, the victors were confronted by a widespread rebellion. The Hungarian nobility leading the revolt were wary of getting involved in religious controversy, but won significant peasant support by promising them full ownership of their land and a reduction of impositions to all who rose up against their new masters. Irregular bands of armed peasants and vagabonds, the dreaded *Kuruzen*, roamed far and wide and even approached the suburbs of Vienna, spreading terror and destruction in districts only recently devastated by the Turks. The *Gürtel* marks the line of defence hastily thrown up to defend the capital from this new threat. By the terms of the *Treaty of Szatmár* (1711), which put an end to the rebellion, the Hungarians agreed to recognise the Habsburgs as hereditary sovereigns on condition that Karl VI confirmed the quasi-feudal privileges of the nobility. He had thus to accept the antiquated feudal order of the newly acquired country, and to give up any notion of taxing the latter or of developing the country's economy along modern lines.

Karl VI's vulnerable position, due to his failure to secure an adequate financial basis for the country's great power status, was further complicated by his wife's failure to bear him a male heir. Disputes regarding precedence among a number of Archduchesses compelled him to promulgate an order of succession known as the *Pragmatic Sanction* (1713), which introduced the principle of indivisibility and primogeniture, and provided for a female succession in case of the extinction of the male line. In 1717 Karl's wife bore him a daughter, Maria Theresia. Her succession to an undivided inheritance was, in the event, to depend more on the military forces at her disposal than on the many promises to recognise her right to it that had been solicited by her father at a considerable price.

Crisis and Reform. For a while the Habsburg monarchy succeeded in consolidating its recent territorial gains, but during the 1730s the situation deteriorated rapidly and dramatically, and was made worse by inadequacies both in the policies adopted by Karl and in the men chosen to carry them out. The marriages he planned for his own daughter, and for the daughters of his late brother, were politically unwise. The renunciations required from the latter on betrothal to the Electoral Princes of Saxony, and Bavaria, respectively, did not prevent them from contemplating claims to parts of the Habsburg inheritance; indeed the marriages were bound to encourage them to do so. And Karl's increasingly obvious intention of making Franz, the heir to the Duchy of Lorraine, his son-in-law was bound to be seen by France as a provocation, in view of that country's long-standing intention of gradually absorbing the duchy. Karl's decision may have been the result of paternal indulgence in favouring a love-match, but, whatever the motive, the consequences were the eclipse (at Versailles) of the old and peacefully inclined minister Cardinal Fleury, and the ascendancy of the 'war party' led by Chauvelin, who had little difficulty in finding a pretext for aggressive action and in drumming up support from the enemies of the Habsburg monarchy.

Karl's alliances were as inept as his marital policies. Prussia alone was prepared to offer effective military assistance in his war against France, but due to the latent Habsburg-Hohenzollern rivalry in the Empire, only a small contingent was accepted. Russia's help, as always, was too little and too late; nevertheless Austria felt obliged to repay it, and thus became involved in Russia's expansionist designs against Turkey at a most inopportune time. British diplomats consistently outwitted Karl's ministers, ensuring that Austria met the challenge of France where British rather than where Austrian interests most required it.

The wars which resulted from this incompetent diplomacy were equally incompetently conducted. Although Prince Eugene's generation of generals had outlived itself, Karl was either too loyal or too lacking in judgement to replace them, for when Mercy assumed command in Italy in 1733 he was almost blind and deaf, and indeed totally incapacitated on some occasions. Yet he had to be killed in action before Königsegg replaced him and he was not much younger. The latter failed disastrously against the French, and was nevertheless given another opportunity of disgracing himself—this time against the Turks in 1738. His colleague Seckendorff was not only incompetent but also of doubtful loyalty. When peace was concluded, Karl had to surrender substantial territories to France's allies and to Turkey, while his son-in-law had to give up his native Duchy of Lorraine (Lothringen) in exchange for Tuscany. Thus, just at the moment when the male Habsburg line was about to become extinct, the weakness of the Habsburg Monarchy was exposed for all to see.

When **Maria Theresia** (1740–80) succeeded her hapless father morale was so low in government circles that few believed that the partition of the Habsburg inheritance could be avoided; and when, only weeks later, *Friedrich II of Prussia* (1740–86) actually invaded the prosperous province of Silesia, the inexperienced 23-year-old queen was left without counsel by her leading ministers. As was to be expected, Friedrich II's rapid success encouraged other states, notably Bavaria and France, to advance claims to neighbouring Habsburg territories, backing these claims by military occupation. The very survival of the monarchy now depended largely on the queen and Franz, her husband, whose support and advice was more important than has sometimes been recognised. Vigorous measures to secure adequate supplies for her armies moving up to the fronts were frustrated by the reluctance of the nobility to make sacrifices for what they considered a lost cause. In those provinces actually occupied by the Bavarians and Prussians, the Estates eagerly submitted to their new masters; ministers who owned land there even asked for permission to do homage in writing. Paradoxically, the only nobles who responded with any enthusiasm to the queen's appeals were those of obstreperous Hungary, who for the last time called out the feudal levy. In the subsequent *War of the Austrian Succession* (1740–48), although her forces were able to save the inheritance from general partition (such as Poland was to experience later in the century), Maria Theresia lost her Italian territories, apart from Lombardy, to the allies of France. Silesia was not recovered from Prussia, and the queen could never reconcile herself to this loss. However, she realised that there would have to be a complete transformation in the form of government, and not only internally, in order to raise the additional force necessary to retake Silesia. In her foreign relations Maria Theresia was to effect what historians have described as a 'diplomatic revolution'. She began with the reform of the systems of taxation and administration. The Estates henceforth had to vote tax grants for ten years at a time; the nobility—except in Hungary—were compelled to accept a fairer share of direct taxation; the responsibility for collecting taxes, and provisioning armies, was transferred from the Estates to the central administration, which was adapted to carry out such routines. In the event, these reforms embarked on in the late 1740s did not produce the desired results. The enormous sacrifices made during the *Seven Years' War* (1756–63), did not lead to the retaking of Silesia, and created further administrative chaos and economic ruin.

Maria Theresia in her youth

Guided by *Wenzel Anton Kaunitz* (1711–94), her Chancellor of State from 1753, Maria Theresia changed course and issued the guideline that 'the increase of the monarch's power and revenues cannot be sought except in the furtherance of the common welfare and prosperity'. This reflected the recognition that it would serve no useful purpose to impose even heavier taxes on what was a stagnant economy, and that increased revenue from taxation could only be secured from a modernised and expanding one. Far-reaching changes would be necessary if the task was to be attempted seriously. Maria Theresia accepted this, and her son **Joseph II**, co-Regent from 1765 and sole ruler from 1780, pressed forward her policies, perhaps less cautiously but more consistently, realising only too well that it was imperative to reverse the economic trends of a century or more of confessional absolutism. The vast capital locked up in monastic possessions would have to be released; the requirement of religious conformity to be relaxed in order to attract skilled workers from the economically more advanced countries who would introduce new industries and colonise underdeveloped regions; the Jesuits would have to be ejected from their controlling positions in education, and their outmoded curriculum replaced by a modernised, more practice-orientated system: confessional absolutism would have to be replaced by reforming 'Enlightened absolutism'.

It is easier to describe objectives than to assess concrete achievements, not least because the effectiveness of the reforms differed from province to province. Probably the life of the poorest in the most backward regions did not change a great deal, but their burdens were much reduced, and industry revived. Protestants brought in new skills, and the essential foundations were laid for universal primary education (*Allgemeine Schulordnung*, 1774). If we ascribe these reforms to Enlightened absolutism, the term should not be understood to imply that their basis was primarily ideological, for as often as not practical considerations were decisive in their adoption. Neither Maria Theresia nor Joseph II had much sympathy for the attitudes then fashionable among 'Enlightened' intellectuals. But to realise their reforms and to overcome the formidable and well-articulated opposition to policies which cut across cherished customs, traditions and vested interests, they had to rely on ideological ammunition, and this could only be provided by those who shared the fashionable 'Enlightened' views.

The controversy stirred up by these reforms naturally generated an independent and vocal public, whose views were disseminated through the medium of the periodical press, and in pamphlets, which towards the end of Joseph's reign—he died in 1790—struck an increasingly critical note. Some advocated more radical reform; some demanded total freedom of the press; others called for more popular participation in the work of reform, the purpose of which, after all, was the promotion of the public good.

Defence of the Old Order. The emergence of political consciousness among the people in general seems to us today one of the more positive developments of the Josephinian period, but in governmental circles these unforeseen consequences of the reforms caused considerable alarm and provoked what we would now call a conservative backlash. Radical pamphleteers were reprimanded for their presumption in daring even to suggest alternative policies, and were accused of destroying the bonds which held society together by undermining traditional loyalties and subordination. It was also evident that there was a connection between the airing of independent political ideas and the advance of unorthodox religious concepts, and the conservative reaction to such 'dangerous thoughts' prompted Joseph to take restrictive measures. While it is generally known that he relaxed censorship at the outset of his reign in an attempt to make his subjects more receptive to the changes he intended to introduce, it is less well known that he later back-pedalled on this, having persuaded himself that the wider freedom of the press had damaged the fabric of authority in his states. More drastic restrictions were instituted under his successors **Leopold II** (1790–92) and *Franz II* (1792–1835; **Franz I** as Austrian Emperor from 1804). In 1795 'insolent criticism in public speech, writing or pictorial representation likely to provoke discontent with the forms of government, and the administration or the constitution' was made a criminal offence punishable by five to ten years imprisonment.

During these last years of Joseph's reign a Ministry of Police (*Polizeihofstelle*) had been established, but in addition to its overt duty of protecting the security of the citizen, the police were obliged by a 'secret instruction', first issued in 1786, to monitor what people were saying about the monarch and his government, and to report regularly on the general political mood of the public (*Stimmungsberichte*). The suspected ubiquity of large numbers of paid informers recruited by the police for this undertaking naturally affected the general atmosphere profoundly, particularly in the cities; and when considering the tensions caused by the flood of reforms that had been embarked on, and the opposition of the clergy and nobility to most of them (which caused some to be subsequently repealed, such as the *February Patent* of 1789 concerning land tax and feudal dues), it is not surprising that many reports indicated widespread discontent during the 1790s.

The greater the government's preoccupation with the enforcement of political and social stability, the more it came to rely on the Ministry of Police, which in 1801 took over from the Ministry of Education the task of censorship. The conservative establishment were convinced that the revolution which broke out in France in 1789 was the natural end-product of Enlightenment, and all those still holding liberal views after the events of that year were denounced as abettors of an international conspiracy to subvert all established monarchies and religions. In this highly charged atmosphere, political dissidents were prosecuted for sedition and high treason. As there was no system of trial by jury in Austria and Hungary, there was little chance of acquittal, and almost all of the accused were convicted. Although in fact there was no conspiracy, ten were executed and dozens were sentenced to long terms of solitary confinement in the fortresses of Kufstein and Munkács. The expansion of revolutionary France into Imperial territory was a direct challenge to Austria to assume the chief responsiblity for defending legitimate order and existing laws (*das alte Recht*), and together with Great Britain, she maintained the most determined opposition to both revolutionary France and its heir, *Napoleon Bonaparte*.

Nevertheless, in the course of this counter-revolutionary struggle, Austria was involved in a series of disastrous and humiliating events. The reason was that she could not match French patriotic fervour in mobilising for war with any broadly-based manifestation of defiance; that was impossible in a state where feudalism was still entrenched. Her armies were defeated in Italy in 1797, at *Ulm* and at *Austerlitz* in 1805, and Vienna was twice occupied by Napoleon. *Archduke Johann* organised a people's militia (*Landwehr*), and although the soldiers fought better in the 1809 campaign (*Aspern* and *Wagram*), **Clemens Metternich**, for some time Austria's ambassador in Paris, who became State Chancellor in 1810, indulged in a policy of appeasement, even persuading Franz to agree to Napoleon marrying his daughter *Marie Louise*. The French had encountered stiff popular opposition only in the Tyrol, where *Andreas Hofer* led a rising fought by a *free* peasantry, with political rights entitling them to send representatives to the provincial diet. In Vienna, some former supporters of Josephinian reform secretly admired Napoleon (whose rise to greatness was in no way based on inherited advantage but on his own capacities), and perhaps expected from him some great act of liberation. One publisher took advantage of his occupation of Vienna in 1809 to bring out the first uncensored editions of the great German classics.

Though Austria's contribution to the final defeat of Napoleon was overshadowed by that of Great Britain and Russia, Metternich and the Emperor Franz were able to host the peace congress of 1814/15, better known as the *Congress of Vienna*. As one of the victorious allies, Austria was rewarded with valuable territorial gains, including the former archi-episcopal state of Salzburg and the former Republic of Venice. With these acquisitions adjacent to her heartland, Austria was prepared to relinquish the more distant Netherlands, which were later to become the kingdom of Belgium. The defunct Empire was replaced by a loosely-knit *German Confederation* (of almost 40 principalities), of which Austria was accorded the presidency.

The internal system evolved by Metternich and his colleague at the Ministry of Police, *Joseph Sedlnitzky*, was such as was thought to promote most effectively the long-term stability of the existing social and political order. For stability, the total prohibition of independent political activity and the strictest censorship of all political matter were considered essential. The management of censorship by Sedlnitzky's Ministry made Austria a by-word for petty and hide-bound reaction in this period. It stifled and demoralised writers like *Franz Grillparzer* and *Nikolaus Lenau*. Germany seemed by comparison a haven of freedom and fresh air.

For all the apparent stagnation, however, profound changes were taking place in Austrian society. The population was expanding rapidly, railways brought people closer together (*Nordbahn*, Vienna-Brünn, 1836; *Südbahn*, Vienna-Gloggnitz, 1841), and modern industry tended to concentrate the expanding population. In 1845, opposition to Metternich's system emerged into the open with a writers' petition against the censorship. Veiled calls for freedom and oblique political allusions on the public stage were now demonstratively applauded. There was a widespread feeling that the system could not survive much longer, because the people had come of age.

Revolution and Reaction. The moment of truth arrived, as it did in most other countries of Europe, in the spring of 1848. A combination of economic depression and political crises brought the people into the streets demanding the abolition of censorship, and constitutional government—demanding, that is, the recognition of their political maturity. At the same time, the existence of a political crisis paralysed the governments' will and ability resolutely to face up to the revolutionary challenge. In Austria, the imbecility of the reigning monarch, **Ferdinand I** (1835–48), contributed significantly to the political crisis by intensifying the rivalries between his archiducal uncles and ministers. Metternich's resignation was compelled as much by the jealousy of his ministerial rivals as by the threatening attitude of the revolutionary crowd. In the new ministry, committed to basic freedoms and constitutional rule, liberal officials like *Franz Pillersdorf* and even lawyers and business men were able to take the political initiative. But, more important, the revolution enabled the urban masses, fully exposed by now to the stresses and insecurities of modern industrialisation, to articulate their democratic aspirations. In this they were joined, encouraged, and led by the university students. Thus, while the citizens' *Nationalgarde* supported the liberal ministry in its efforts to restore law and order, the students of Vienna University, organised in the *Academic Legion*, helped to keep revolutionary agitation on the boil (*Sturmpetition*, May 1848), until the ministry conceded the election of a fully sovereign constituent assembly. This assembly, the *Konstituierende Reichstag*, represented all the non-Hungarian lands of the monarchy (the Hungarians having been granted national autonomy at the outset of the revolution), and contained a large number of peasant deputies. After settling the procedural problems arising from its multi-lingual composition, the *Reichstag* passed a resolution moved by the democratic student *Hans Kudlich*, proclaiming the emancipation of peasant land from all feudal burdens (*Grundentlastung*). In the event, this overdue abolition of feudalism was to be the one major direct achievement of the revolution.

All the other revolutionary aspirations for democratic self-government and national autonomy were frustrated by the bitter divisions between liberals and democrats, and by the conflicts between the different ethnic communities, which were rooted either in the old feudalism (e.g. Magyar lord *versus* Croat peasant), or in the new industrialism (e.g. German artisan *versus* Czech labourer). The defenders of Habsburg absolutism were not slow to take advantage of these conflicts. Already in June 1848, *Alfred Windischgrätz*, who had had to withdraw his troops from Vienna in March, was able to suppress a Czech democratic rising in Prague with tacit German support. When the democrats rose in Vienna in October 1848 to prevent reinforcements being sent to the loyalist Croats fighting the Hungarians (*Oktoberaufstand*), Windischgrätz's brutal reconquest of Vienna was demonstratively applauded by the wealthier citizens. No doubt they were hoping that their 'kind' Emperor (he was affectionately referred to as *Ferdinand der Gütige*) would abide by his constitutional promises. In reality, however, the reconquest of Vienna at the end of October 1848 was the beginning of a resolute counter-revolutionary strategy masterminded by *Archduchess Sophie* of Bavaria, the wife of Ferdinand's younger brother. The kindly imbecile Ferdinand, who had 'conceded everything' in March, was an obstacle to this strategy. The counter-revolutionary *Camarilla* therefore staged an abdication (December 1848), and put Sophie's son, the 18-year-old **Franz Josef** (1848–1916) on the throne.

Windischgrätz, for all his single-minded brutality, was unable to put down the revolution in Hungary, and the reign began with the humiliation of having to call in the troops of *Tsar Nicholas I*—the 'policeman of Europe'—to defeat the rebels at the Battle of Világos in August 1849. With the collaboration of *Prince Felix Schwarzenberg* (brother-in-law of Windischgrätz), *Karl Kübeck*, *Alexander Bach*, and *Othmar Rauscher* (archbishop of Vienna), Franz Josef now imposed on his Empire a tightly centralised neo-absolutist system, which was precariously sustained by those three well worn pillars of the Establishment: army, police and Catholic Church. The price for the Church's support was the *Concordat* of 1855, which reversed much of the liberal legislation of Joseph II in the ecclesiastical, matrimonial and educational sectors.

Dualism versus Pluralism. The emperor's authoritarian 'neo-absolutist' system had to be abandoned when his foreign policy failed disastrously. He forfeited the indispensable Russian alliance and antagonised half of Europe by remaining neutral during the Crimean War, and Austria's subsequent isolation made certain the defeat of his armies in later conflicts (at *Magenta* and *Solferino* against Napoleon III in 1859; and in 1866 at *Königgratz* or *Sadowa*, in Bohemia, against Bismarck's Prussians). Lombardy, and later Venetia went to form part of the newly united Kingdom of Italy; the German Confederation was replaced by a German Empire dominated by Prussia.

Under duress, Franz Josef conceded constitutional government on liberal lines, and in 1867 a *Bürgerministerium* (led by *Karl Auersperg*) promulgated a declaration of fundamental civil rights (*Staatsgrundgesetze*); the Concordat was abrogated and civil marriage restored; state jurisdiction over schools (*Reichsvolks-schulgesetz*) was instituted in 1869. The *Compromise* (*Ausgleich*) with Hungary in 1867 conceded so wide an autonomy that it virtually amounted to separate statehood, for only three ministries, those of Foreign Affairs, Finance, and War remained in common and the monarchy was renamed Austria-Hungary. This transformation to a dual monarchy gave some reprieve, but each problem resolved during this brief 'liberal era' gave rise to another bigger and more complex. The Compromise with Hungary may have satisfied the Magyars, but such concessions were not extended to the other provinces constituting the empire. Thus it exacerbated the griev-ances of the Czechs, and of the South Slavs. Further tension was created after the occupation of the Turkish provinces of Bosnia-Hercegovina (sanctioned by the *Congress of Berlin* in 1878), which added geatly to the South Slav population of the monarchy. Repeated attempts were made to reconcile these grievances, among them *Karl Hohenwart*'s 'Fundamental Articles' in 1871, which would have given Bohemia the same status as Hungary, and *Kasimir Badeni*'s 'Language Ordinances' in 1897, which would have made Czech-German bilingualism compulsory for all state officials in Bohemia; they all foundered on the rock of German, or Magyar, national chauvinism.

Bickering between the nationalities constituting the monarchy (*Nationalitätenhader*) became so endemic that it paralysed the legis-lature, and prevented the enactment of social and economic reforms, which the new political party of the workers, the Social Democrats, might otherwise have been able to push through. This party, united by *Viktor Adler* in 1889, on the basis of a Marxist programme of objectives, among them direct manhood suffrage and the abolition of capitalist property, adopted a programme of complete cultural auto-nomy for each nation at the party Congress at Brünn in 1899. It is conceivable that its quick implementation might have enabled the multi-national empire to survive; but the Social Democrats were not yet strong enough—even after their achievement of manhood suf-frage in 1907—to get such a controversial measure through Parlia-ment. Hence the break up of the Empire seemed merely a matter of time.

Dissolution. The problem which caused the greatest anxiety to the government was that of the South Slavs, for across the monarchy's southern border stood independent Serbia, to which they could look for protection and leadership. Serbia had long been the champion of the Slavs oppressed by the Turks, and was potentially a champion of Austria-Hungary's Slavs. With the progressive disintegration of the Turkish Empire in the Balkans after their defeat by Russia in 1877/ 78, Serbia's prestige grew; moreover, after the depression of the 1880s, intensified competition between Serb and Magyar agriculturalists further embittered relations, and with the expiration of a commercial treaty in 1906, a full-scale tariff war, known as the *Pig War*, broke out. Relations reached crisis point after the Balkan Wars of 1912 and 1913, from which Serbia emerged triumphant. *Leopold Berchtold*, the Austro-Hungarian foreign minister, anxious to contain Pan-Slavism, attempted to secure a greater share of the spoils for her rival, Bulgaria, but was only successful in blocking Serbia from an outlet to the Adriatic by insisting on an independent state, Albania. Meanwhile, *Archduke Franz Ferdinand* (heir presumptive since 1890, when *Rudolf*, the Emperor's only son, committed suicide at Mayerling) was attempting to build up a rival South Slav nationalism based on the traditionally loyalist and Catholic Croats, raising their hopes by hinting that on his succession he would broaden the Dualist basis of the monarchy to a tripartite one. In this tense situation, Franz Ferdinand's ostentatious attendance at the summer manoeuvres in Bosnia in June 1914 was little short of a provocation for Serbian nationalists, and on 28 June a member of one of their underground groups chose to assassinate him. This action was seized upon by Vienna as an opportunity to solve the South Slav problem once and for all by destroying any prestige and attraction Serbia might have had for them. That was the purpose of the aggressive *Ultimatum* to Serbia of 23 July, charging the country as a whole with total responsibility for the assassination. It transformed what in origin was a local conflict into a world war, for any humiliation of Serbia would reflect on her principal ally, Russia, which, having been humiliated herself as recently as 1908 over Austria-Hungary's 'annexation' of Bosnia-Hercegovina, was willing to go to war rather than allow this to happen.

Paradoxically, the subsequent fighting demonstrated that the government had exaggerated the extent of disaffection among the South Slavs. Serbia's heroic attempt to defend her territory might have been expected to strengthen anti-Habsburg feelings, but the Bosnian units actually fought with conspicuous bravery, and it was only among the Czech and Ruthenian units, fighting along the extensive Russian front in 1915, that disaffection became apparent on a significant scale. The failure of the campaign along this front in the following year was largely due to these units either refusing to fight or to their wholesale surrender to the Russians. And this encouraged the Romanians to enter the war on Russia's side. The desertions encouraged the group of Czech nationalist exiles, led by *Thomas Masaryk*, to launch a propaganda campaign in Britain and France, which resulted in the allies adopting independent Czech statehood as one of their war aims. With Italy's entry into the conflict on the side of the Allies, Austria-Hungary was, like Germany, compelled to fight on two fronts, which over-stretched her resources, already reduced as the large surplus-producing areas in the east were under Russian occupation. Acute food shortages, and the lack of other essentials, inevitably undermined civilian morale, and the gloom was intensified in November 1916 by the death of the octogenarian Franz Josef, seen by many as a symbol of the impending demise of the empire.

The new Emperor, **Karl** 'the Last' (1916–18; as King of Hungary, 1916–19), made an eleventh-hour attempt to save his monarchy by trying to negotiate a separate peace; but it came to nothing. The rapidly deteriorating condition of the civilian population—significantly worsened by official corruption—was hardly alleviated by the expedient of digging allotments around the main cities. The traditional anti-militarist tenets of the socialist labour movement, swept aside in the patriotic hysteria of July 1914, now rapidly gained credit. The internal political truce had been shattered dramatically in October 1916 with the assassination of *Karl Stürgkh*, the Prime Minister, by *Friedrich Adler*, the son of the Social Democrats' leader. The Russian Revolution of 1917 was also to make a profound impression, reflected in widespread industrial strikes in January 1918 and a naval mutiny at Cattaro the following month. Both the civil and military administration of the Habsburg Empire were rapidly disintegrating, and in the absence of any functioning central government, its component parts went their own way.

In Vienna, those members of Parliament representing the German-speaking regions met separately in October 1918 under *Karl Renner* and announced themselves as the 'provisional national assembly of the independent German-Austrian state'. On 11 November Karl withdrew from the government of the Empire without actually abdicating, and on the following day the provisional national assembly proclaimed the *Republik Deutschösterreich* to a huge crowd gathered in front of the Parliament Building.

First Republic and Third Reich. This Republic was seen by most Austrians as a provisional political structure. The German-Austrian democrats (including the Social Democrats) had envisaged a future in the context of either a democratised multi-national empire (the principle of self-determination having been invoked), or a democratic *Gross-Deutschland*, flanked by other democratic national states. But with the prospect of a multi-national empire evaporating, *Otto Bauer*, now leading the Social Democrats, vigorously worked for the union with the *Weimar Republic* until this was prohibited by the *Treaty of St. Germain* in 1919. This and the inclusion of the whole of the former provinces of Bohemia and Moravia, with their ethnically German regions (the *Sudetenland*), in the republic of Czechoslovakia was considered an intolerable violation of self-determination.

The new republic thus had independence imposed on it. It was compelled to remove the epithet 'German' from its official designation. To that extent, it rested on precarious foundations. However, though the Social Democrats, now the biggest single party, rejected independent statehood for Austria, they strongly supported democratic republicanism through which they were confident of achieving majority support and full political power in the foreseeable future. As they had so far made little headway among the peasantry who cherished their private property and Catholic faith, both of which the Social Democrats were thought to be threatening, this confidence was not really well founded. Nevertheless, it alarmed the opponents of socialism organised in the Catholic Christian Social, and the German-nationalist *Grossdeutsche*, parties. These were quite prepared to reject democracy, if democracy made it possible for socialists to become as powerful as the Austrian Social Democrats had become since 1918, especially in their stronghold of 'Red Vienna'.

The idea of adopting a more authoritarian structure of government, and of challenging the socialist workers on their own territory 'in the street', rapidly gained ground in these parties; for the instruments required for its realisation were to hand in the form of the paramilitary organisations which had sprung up in the period of anarchy at the end of the war. The strongest of these was the *Heimwehr*, originating in a Carinthian stampede to defend 'German soil' from the Slovenes. By the late 1920s, the *Heimwehr* was eager to respond to a call from the government to challenge the socialists, as can be seen from their numerous provocations. Otto Bauer, more radical in words than in deeds, instructed the *Schutzbund*, the paramilitary organisation of the Social Democrats, to keep their powder dry, while he negotiated an orderly but for his followers demoralising retreat with his right-wing opponent, the Chancellor *Ignaz Seipel*.

The climax came, as in Germany, with the onset of the Great Depression and mass unemployment which followed the collapse of the Viennese bank *Credit-Anstalt* in 1931. The government, wedded to the economic orthodoxies of the time, insisted on deflationary policies and an end to the 'extravagance' of the socialist municipality of Vienna, which was rehousing the Viennese workers in modern, well-designed blocks of flats like the famous *Karl-Marx-Hof*, and was well on the way to eliminating the scourge of tuberculosis in the city. When negotiating a League of Nations loan, Seipel's successor, *Engelbert Dollfuss*, had to give assurances that he would enforce deflation by whatever means might prove necessary. In March 1933, he took advantage of a procedural wrangle in parliament to prevent it from meeting, and embarked on government by authoritarian decree. Even now, Otto Bauer hesitated and offered further negotiations. But a rank-and-file movement in the *Schutzbund* decided on its own authority to resist the government's move to disarm them. Their action (February 1934) led to four days' bitter fighting between the army and the *Schutzbund*, which ended in the latter's defeat and disarmament, and the suppression of the Social Democrats and their trade unions. Democracy had survived in the new Austrian republic for only fifteen years.

The deflationary policies of Dollfuss merely retarded economic recovery, and left the problem of unemployment unsolved. There was a growing conviction that it was virtually no longer viable for a relic of a once extensive empire, and with a disproportionately large capital, to survive economically as an independent unit. Annexation to Germany therefore attracted growing support, despite Hitler's accession to power there in January 1933. By his suppression of the Social Democrats and the labour movement Dolfuss deprived himself of an important body of support which might have helped him to resist more positively any possible aggression on the part of Nazi Germany. He turned to *Mussolini* in Italy, with whom Fascist elements in the *Heimwehr* were hand in glove, and whose regime was regarded by them as a model to be followed in Austria.

After Dollfuss's assassination by a group of Nazi putschists in July 1934, Mussolini demonstratively took his widow and children under his wing. But already in 1936, Mussolini had come to an accommodation with Hitler. After this, Austria had little in the way of defence against Hitler's ever more openly proclaimed aim of annexation. *Kurt Schuschnigg*, who succeeded Dollfuss as Chancellor, temporised and hoped that Hitler might be satisfied with the allocation of one or two ministries to Austrian Nazis and the cessation of anti-Nazi propaganda (*Juliabkommen*, 1936). All too soon, however, it became clear that Hitler was only holding his hand until he had secured his control over the German army. In February 1938 he believed that his control was assured, and Schuschnigg was summoned to Berchtesgaden, where he received peremptory orders to hand over the key Ministry of State Security to the Austrian Nazi leader, *Artur Seyss-Inquart*. No one could be in any doubt that his task would be to prepare the country for a speedy annexation.

After returning from Berchtesgaden, Schuschnigg made an eleventh-hour attempt to broaden the basis of his regime, to legalise the socialist parties, and to construct a broad alliance to defend Austrian independence. He announced a plebiscite for 13 March, by which the new alliance's desire for independence could be proclaimed to the world. The Nazis, he must have hoped, would hesitate to invade in the face of such a public declaration of the people's will to resist their demands.

It was of course too late, even for token resistance. Schuschnigg's sudden conversion to democracy as the prerequisite for an independence struggle only made Hitler put forward his invasion plan sufficiently to prevent the plebiscite taking place. On 12 March 1938 Hitler's forces entered the country, and a few days later he came in person to Vienna to declare that Austria had 'returned home to the German Reich'. Another plebiscite was now fixed for 10 April to sanction the *Anschluss* after it had been completed and Nazi power was firmly established everywhere. It resulted in the almost unanimous affirmative to be expected under these circumstances. The Austrian Nazis were a minority, but a large majority acquiesced in the annexation, if only for its supposed economic implications.

Austria was now integrated into the Third Reich. Even the name of Austria was abolished and changed to *Ostmark*. Leaders of all the anti-Nazi parties were sent to the concentration camps; Jewish property was 'arianised', a process in which many Austrians cooperated and from which they profited. Most of the Jews emigrated: those who did not, perished. The unemployed were absorbed into arms production and other German war industries, and in September 1939 Austria entered the Second World War as an integral part of the Third Reich. By doing so, and she had no option, she was to share the catastrophic losses of life, limb, wealth and heritage, which was the price Germany paid under Hitler's dictatorship.

The Second Republic. Experiencing this tyrannical regime, the majority of Austrians came to recognise what their history had made it difficult for them to appreciate before: that they *were* a nation distinct from the Germans. This was also reflected in the growing resistance to the Nazi occupation, a subject not yet fully researched. The existence of this movement and the political activity of the Austrian emigrants contributed to the decision in November 1943 to issue the *Moscow Declaration*, in which the Allies stated their intention of restoring Austrian independence once hostilities had ceased. Eastern Austria became a battlefield during the last weeks of the war, and the destruction was considerable. Vienna was liberated on 13 April 1945, and by the 27th the belligerents had been driven from her territory. The devastated country had then to support four armies of occupation. Both the country and its capital were divided into allied zones. The Russians occupied Lower and Upper Austria north of the Danube and Burgenland; the British most of Styria, Carinthia and East Tyrol; the rest of Upper Austria and Salzburg was under American control, while French forces occupied the rest of the Tyrol and Vorarlberg.

On 27 April a provisional government was installed by the Russian commander, and headed by Karl Renner, the veteran Social Democrat who had been Chancellor immediately after the First World War, and his administration was approved by the Allied Council later that year. A month later a General Election was held and a Coalition was the outcome, with the People's Party winning a majority of seats and its leader, *Leopold Figl* succeeding as Chancellor. The People's Party and the Socialists, who between them represented more than 80 per cent of the electorate, joined in a coalition government which made good use of Marshall Aid to rebuild the economic infrastructure, financing investment rather than consumption. National monuments that had been largely destroyed by bombing, like the Stephansdom and the Vienna Opera, were rebuilt in an amazingly short time. The *Sozialpartnerschaft*, an institution unique to Austria, was eventually to form the framework for settling the competing claims of capital and labour, and secured for the workers a modest but steady rise in real living standards.

For some time it was thought that the country, like Germany, would remain divided, with the Russian zone being absorbed into the Soviet sphere of influence. However, in May 1955 the *Austrian State Treaty* or *Staatsvertrag* was signed, by which it was agreed to withdraw the occupying forces in return for a constitutionally guaranteed and permanent neutrality. After independence the climate of pessimism traditional in Austria gave way to one of relaxed optimism. After the death of *Julius Raab*, the Chancellor who had negotiated the Staatsvertrag, the People's Party appeared unable to find a leader of comparable stature, and support for it declined just at a time when the Socialists were winning an increasing number of votes among the rural constituencies. In 1970, the Socialists, for the first time in their history, gained an absolute majority in Parliament, and formed a government on their own, headed by *Bruno Kreisky* (1911–90), who remained Federal Chancellor until 1983. Its greatest achievements were probably the maintenance of a high level of employment even after the onset of the world recession, and the liberalisation of the country's intellectual and cultural life.

Despite these achievements, optimism gave way to a more pessimistic mood again during the 1970s and 1980s, with a feeling that recession would catch up with Austria sooner or later, and an awareness that in the pursuit of economic growth and rising living standards, too much damage was being done to the environment. A plebiscite on the question of whether to start production at the newly built nuclear power-station at Zwentendorf (Lower Austria) resulted in a small majority against nuclear energy; and more recently, growing opposition has been expressed towards other similar projects. While environmental questions have come to the fore as political issues, the great debates of the past, as to whether Austria was economically viable and whether Austrians are a nation in themselves, seem to have been settled for good.

Chronological Table

Rulers of Austria

House of Babenberg (Margraves)

976–94	Leopold (or Liutpold) I
994–1018	Heinrich I
1018–55	Adalbert
1055–75	Ernst
1075–95	Leopold II
1095–1136	Leopold III (canonised 1485)
1136–41	Leopold IV
	(Dukes, from 1156)
1141–77	Heinrich II (Jasomirgott)
1177–94	Leopold V ('the Virtuous')
1195–98	Friedrich I
1198–1230	Leopold VI
1230–46	Friedrich II ('the Quarrelsome')
1246–72	(Interregnum)
	(Marguerite von Babenberg married Přemysl Ottokar II of Bohemia in 1251, who took possession of the dukedom)

House of Habsburg (pron. Hapsburg)

1273–91	Rudolf of Habsburg
1291–1308	Albrecht I, elected king of Germany in 1298
1308–30	Friedrich I ('the Handsome'), king of Germany in 1314 as Friedrich III
1330–58	Albrecht II
1358–65	Rudolf IV ('the Magnanimous' or 'the Founder' — der Stifter)
1365–95	Albrecht III, who divided the Habsburg possessions with his brother Leopold III
1395–1404	Albrecht IV
1404–11	(Tutelary regime)
1411–39	Albrecht V, elected Emperor as Albrecht II in 1438
[1440–57	Ladislaus ('the Posthumous')]
1440–93	Friedrich III (descended from Leopold III; see above), elected Emperor of Germany (as Friedrich III) in 1452

German Emperors

1493–1519	Maximilian I
1519–21/2	Karl V, who in 1521 transferred the German possessions of the Habsburgs to his brother Ferdinand
1521/2–64	Ferdinand I, Emperor from 1556, on the abdication of Karl V
1564–76	Maximilian II
1576–1612	Rudolf II
1612–19	Matthias
1619–37	Ferdinand II
1637–57	Ferdinand III
1658–1705	Leopold I
1705–11	Joseph I
1711–40	Karl VI

1740–80	Maria Theresia (with Franz I von Lothringen or Lorraine as consort until 1765)
1780–90	Joseph II, who ruled with his mother from 1765
1790–92	Leopold II
1792–1835	Franz II (also known as the Emperor Franz I of Austria, from 1804)
1835–48	Ferdinand I
1848–1916	Franz-Josef I
1916–18	Karl I (King of Hungary, 1916–19)

The *Austrian Republic* (First)

	Presidents
1920–28	Michael Hainisch
1928–38	Wilhelm Miklas

	Among Chancellors were:
1918–20	Karl Renner
1922–24 and	
1926–29	Ignaz Seipel
1932–34	Engelbert Dollfuss
1934–38	Kurt Schuschnigg
[1938–45	[under Nazi occupation]

Second Republic

	Federal Presidents
1945–50	Karl Renner
1951–57	Theodor Körner
1957–65	Adolf Schärf
1965–74	Franz Jonas
1974–86	Rudolf Kirchschläger
1986–	Kurt Waldheim

INTRODUCTION TO THE ARTS AND ARCHITECTURE OF AUSTRIA

by *Nicolas Powell* and *Ian Robertson*

One of the earliest recorded artefacts of Western Art (variously, estimated to date from c 15,000 to 25,000 BC) is the *Venus of Willendorf*, a fubsy fertility goddess discovered in loess outcrops of the Wachau, that stretch of the Danube valley between Melk and Krems. More recently, her precedence has been contended by the 'Dancing Venus' of Galgenberg, carbon-dated to c 30,000 BC. However, the first civilisation of any importance for its artistic productions is that known as the *Hallstatt*, an Early Iron Age culture (c 750–400 BC), named after the site of burial grounds N of the Dachstein range, which derived its wealth from salt mining. It has left numerous finely worked artefacts, both in gold and bronze, which are displayed in the museum at Hallstatt, at Hallein (not far S of Salzburg), and also in the Natural History Museum, Vienna. Remarkable too is the toy-like *Strettweger Wagen*, a cult chariot of bronze supporting a crowd of armed men and a larger female figure carrying a bowl, to be seen at Graz.

Roman Period. Notable are the extensive remains of the Roman occupation excavated at *Carnuntum*, E of Vienna, where a camp stood at the intersection of the Amber Road (from the Baltic to the Adriatic) with the river traffic on the Danube (from the Rhine to the Black Sea). Other important sites were Vienna itself; Enns, at the confluence of that river (flowing from the Erzberg) and the Danube; and Magdalensberg (NE of Klagenfurt), where the life-size bronze known as the Youth of Magdalensberg was found in 1502. It was probably brought there from Italy, where it was cast in the early 1C BC after a Greek original of the 5C BC.

Romanesque and Gothic periods. Among the earliest extant examples of Romanesque art are two exceptional works of foreign origin. The *Tassilo Chalice*, possibly of Anglo-Saxon workmanship, was presented to the abbey of Kremsmünster between 769 and 788 by Duke Tassilo III of Bavaria, where it may still be seen. It is the only chalice known in the West dating prior to the 12C to include figurative decoration. The second import of outstanding interest is the *Verdun Altar*, a masterpiece of Romanesque enamel-work, commissioned in 1181 from *Nicolas of Verdun* by Abbot Werner of Klosterneuburg, where it has since remained. In addition to the panels of champlevé enamel on copper gilt are four painted panels— the oldest panel paintings in Central Europe—which were incorporated into the back of the altar during the 12C.

The Austrian contribution to Romanesque architecture consists principally of several ecclesiastical foundations, foremost among which is the cathedral at *Gurk* in Carinthia, with its remarkable crypt containing the tomb of the Blessed Henna (1174). There are reliefs of 1225 on the W vestibule, and frescoes in the W gallery dating from c 1220, a rare example of such painting remaining in situ. The Bishop's chancel also displays a cycle of paintings by the same artist, *Master Heinrich*; but the oldest surviving wall-paintings in Austria are those discovered at *Lambach* in 1960, which date from c 1080. The figures in these paintings are distinguished by their severity and have an air of portraits from life. The murals at *Pürgg* in Styria are also notable. Other part-Romanesque buildings of interest include those foundations at *Seckau, Schöngrabern, Heiligenkreutz, St. Paul im Lavanttal,* and *Millstatt.*

Painters in the 'International Style' of the mid 15C include the *Master of the Albrechts Altar* (at Klosterneuburg), the *Master of the Schottenstift,* and *Konrad Laib* (fl. 1448–57), and—in the provinces— *Thomas von Villach,* and, in the Tyrol, *Michael Pacher* (see below) and *Marx Reichlich* (fl. 1489–1520). These were followed by the so-called **Danube School,** or *Donauschule,* foremost among whom were *Lucas Cranach the Elder* (1472–1553), who established himself in Vienna for several years; *Albrecht Altdorfer* (c 1480–1538), from Regensburg, whose remarkable Sebastians Altar (1509–18) may be seen at St. Florian; the *Master of Pulkau* (fl. 1515–25); *Jörg Breu the Elder* (c 1480–1537); *Rueland Frueauf the Younger* (fl. 1497–1545); and *Wolf Huber* (1490–1553). Representative examples of their work are displayed in the Lower Belvedere, Vienna.

The *Stephansdom,* at Vienna, with its early 14C choir, although preserving several Romanesque portals and the Riesentor (c 1240) of the Romanesque cathedral, is among the finest examples of Gothic architecture extant in Austria. Good vaulting can be seen in the entrance of the *Landhaus* in Vienna (1516), and in the church at *Königswiesen* in Upper Austria, which compares well with the best geometric Bohemian work, and elsewhere. At *Feldkirch* in the Vorarlberg, the double vault of the parish church, supported by a central row of pillars (1478) may be compared, for example, with that of the Jacobin Church at Toulouse, among other French buildings.

Austria's most influential Gothic artist is *Michael Pacher* (fl. 1467– 98), whose altar at *St. Wolfgang* in the Salzkammergut, completed in 1481, is considered the most beautiful among surviving winged altars in Central Europe. Both its sculpture, with its remarkably rich carving, and the painting of the retable, are the work of Pacher. Among other notable altars of the period are those at *Kefermarkt* (NE of Linz), probably from a Passau workshop, and those at *Maria Elend* (originally conceived by Pacher), in Carinthia, and at *Heiligenblut.* The work of *Anton Pilgram* (fl. 1495–1515), whose pulpit and organ-tribune in the Stephansdom, Vienna, are characteristic, should not be overlooked.

Renaissance. The first Renaissance building of note in Austria is the so-called *Goldenes Dachl* (or Golden Roof) at *Innsbruck,* commissioned by Maximilian I to commemorate his marriage to Maria Blanca Sforza of Milan, and erected c 1497–1500 by *Nikolaus Türing,* his court architect. At Innsbruck too, the *Hofkirche,* designed by *Andrea Crivelli,* was built as a mausoleum for the Emperor, who in the event was buried at Wiener Neustadt, although the larger-than-life bronze figures which form part of the extensive sculptural ensemble around the empty sarcophagus (including 'King Arthur', after a design by Dürer), and which makes such an impression, remind one that Innsbruck was his chief residence. At neighbouring *Ambras,* to the SE of Innsbruck, is the so-called 'Spanish Hall' of its *Schloss,* when built, by the Archduke Ferdinand II of Tyrol in 1564– 89, the largest Renaissance hall in Central Europe. Here the Archduke's collection of curiosities can be seen, while in the old castle the Austrian 'National Portrait Gallery' has been installed.

Although built significantly later (1625–35), *Schloss Eggenberg,* in the W suburbs of *Graz,* is another important Renaissance edifice. As in many buildings of the period, among them the great abbeys and the palaces in Vienna, the reception rooms are in the upper floors. Also in Graz is the Italianate *Mausoleum of the Emperor Ferdinand II*, after plans by *Pietro de Pomis* (1614), responsible for several other churches in the area, but completed by *Peter Valnegro* in 1638. In style it points towards the Baroque. In Graz one may visit the *Landeszeughaus*, the armoury of 1643–45, preserving the extensive collection of arms and armour it was built to house. *Schloss Porcia* at *Spittal an der Drau* is another splendid Renaissance palace.

There are certain distinctive types of building which are a feature of Austrian architecture, among them the KARNER—charnel houses or ossuaries—of which there are some 110 in Lower Austria alone. They are usually two storeys high, and among the more notable are those at *Pulkau, Tulln, Petronell, Bad-Deutsch-Altenburg, Mauthausen*, and *Mödling* (c 1250), the last surmounted by an onion-dome. This type of dome, which probably originated further E, is widespread N of the Alps. In Austria, it is a particular feature of the pilgrimage churches, or WALLFAHRTSKIRCHE. Most provinces have at least ten of these churches, although there are many more in Lower Austria and Styria, and particularly in Carinthia. The majority of them are dedicated to the Marian cult. Notable is that of *Maria Saal* (NE of Klagenfurt; incorporating Roman sculptures); some, such as *Maria Taferl* (NE of Ybbs, on the Danube), and *Maria Trost*, near Graz, are spectacularly sited; while *Mariazell*, in the mountains S of St. Pölten, long patronised by the Habsburgs, is still the principal object of pilgrimage by the pious. Most of them, as with the great abbey churches, have been heavily baroquised: see below.

CASTLES, or their ruins, are a common sight. Several, such as *Hardegg*, may be seen along the Czechoslovak frontier, previously that of Bohemia; others, like that at *Riegersburg* (E of Graz), were bastions against Turkish incursions; while *Hochosterwitz*, NE of Klagenfurt, its hill-top keep approached by no less than 14 gates and five drawbridges, would appear to be the original 'fairy-tale castle'. A few towns and villages retain their original enceinte of fortifications, notable being those of *Freistadt*, NE of Linz; *Friesach*, on the border of Carinthia; and *Drosendorf*, on the Thaya.

It is hard to over-estimate the historical and cultural importance of the MONASTERIES of Austria in the furthering of education, the patronage of arts and music, and in the pursuit of scientific study. They also exercised immense influence on the surrounding communities through their pastoral activities, and indeed have long occupied a central position in Austrian life. As the individual buildings are described in the text, only a few of the major figures responsible for their rebuilding in the Baroque era are listed here. Almost all of them are of much more ancient foundation, such as *Zwettl*, founded in 1137, with its cloister of 1227.

Among the more influential architects in the ecclesiastical field were **Jacob Prandtauer** (1660–1726), responsible for reconstructing *Kremsmünster* (*C.A. Carlone* built the entrance gate). Prandtauer also began the rebuilding of *Melk* (1702–26), which was continued by Abbot Dietmayr between 1736 and 1739, while **Josef Munggenast** (died 1741) restored the onion-domes. Prandtauer worked on *Klosterneuburg* (planned in 1706, but unfinished), and *St. Florian*, completed by C.A. Carlone. Munggenast was responsible for work at *Altenburg, Zwettl*, and *Dürnstein. Johann Lukas von Hildebrandt* (see below), worked on the rebuilding of *Göttweig*, but the plans to baroquise it were only partly carried out. Among other monasteries reconstructed in the Baroque style during this period were *Lambach*; *Admont* (with its great library by *J.G. Hayberger*; 1745); *Wilten*, by *Christoph Gumpp* (1656); *Stams*, by *Georg Anton Gumpp*, grandson of the former; *Wilhering*, just W of Linz; *Vorau*, in Styria; *Lilienfeld*, S of St. Pölten, and several others. Among the outstanding buildings of this period are also the small Servite church at *Volders* (1620–54; E of Innsbruck); and that of *Stadl-Paura*, near Lambach, a triangular votive church of 1714–24 dedicated to the Trinity, built by **Johann Michael Prunner** (1669–1739).

One of the first churches in Vienna to be baroquised, after damage during the Turkish siege of 1683, was that of the Servites, originally by *Carlo Carnevale*, and restored by *Francesco Martinelli*, its oval plan influenced by the Baroque churches of Italy. Its towers were added in the mid 18C. As is confirmed by the number of Italians working in the capital at the time, Italian Baroque was a crucial influence in the development of Austrian 17C art and architecture. *Andrea Pozzo* (1642–1709), who had established his reputation with the staggering illusionistic ceiling of S. Ignazio in Rome, was also active in Vienna. He was responsible, among other works, for the high altar and ceiling-fresco of the *Franziskanerkirche* (1707), and the ceiling painting of the *Jesuitenkirche*, of the same date. In the *Piaristenkirche*, or *Maria Treu*, built after the designs of *Lukas von Hildebrandt* (1716), and later by *K.I. Dientzenhofer*, we find a variation on the centralised plan, in which there are two oval chapels on either side of the crossing, at the diagonals of which niched altars are set into the convex walls, the whole ensemble, containing frescoes by *Maulbertsch*, providing a superb example of this type of profusely decorated and colourful church.

The vigour of Baroque architecture in Austria is in many ways a direct consequence of the cultural reaction of the Counter-Reformation. Following the Council of Trent, several of the religious orders, led by the Jesuits (who established a number of colleges—the earliest (1551) in Vienna; the last in Steyr, in 1631), and including the Capuchins, Franciscans, and Servites, etc., set about erecting new churches and baroquising existing buildings. The new style fused architecture, painting—particularly fresco—and sculpture, which when complemented by the music of their Baroque organs, formed a magnificent *Gesamtkunstwerk*. Another spectacular extension of their radical programme was the re-housing of the monastic libraries, notably at *Melk*, with its gorgeous decoration, and at *Altenburg, Vorau*, and *Admont* (with its superb statues by *Stammel*), among several others; but the culmination of Austrian Baroque stucco-work and splendour may be found in the *Hofbibliothek* in Vienna, an impressive symbol of the Enlightenment as sponsored by the House of Habsburg.

An essential element in the flowering of the Baroque is the contribution of sculpture, and the three greatest Austrian masters at this period were Moll, Donner, and Messerschmidt, the work of the last two approaching the subsequent neo-Classical style. *Raphael Donner* (1693–1741) worked mainly in lead, and left fine examples of his art in Hungary. His most important work in Vienna is the 'Providentia Fountain' of 1737–39 in the Neuer Markt, although the lead original, preserved in the Lower Belvedere, has been replaced by a bronze copy. His 'Andromeda Fountain' stands in the courtyard of the Altes Rathaus, and dates from 1740–41; another important work is a *Pietà*, at Gurk, cast in the year of his death. His artistic heir was *Balthasar Moll* (1717–85), responsible for several monuments in the Stephansdom apart from the Imperial sarcophagi in the Kaisergruft, and a rather dull equestrian statue of Franz I in the Burggarten at Vienna. *Franz Xaver Messerschmidt* (1716–83) produced a number of fully Baroque sculptures, among them a statue of Maria Theresia as Queen of Hungary (1766), but he is probably best known for his 'character heads', grimacing busts which combine a Baroque penchant for the bizarre with neo-Classical severity. Examples may be seen in the Lower Belvedere and in the Historisches Museum in Vienna.

A form of sculptural decoration typically Austrian was the PESTSÄULE or plague column, seen in a great number of town squares throughout the country, and erected as thank offerings for deliverance from epidemics. They were often dedicated to the Trinity (*Dreifaltigkeitssäule*), or the Virgin (*Mariensäule*), and fine examples stand at *Petronell, Vorau, Zwettl,* and *Heiligenkreuz,* although perhaps the most splendid and historically interesting one is that rising up in a billow of clouds in the centre of the *Graben* in *Vienna.* More local objects of devotion were the image columns or BILDSTÖCKE, often seen by the wayside and frequently set up as the result of a vow. They are usually four-sided, and are roofed.

Baroque architecture in Austria after 1683 (the year Vienna was freed from Turkish pressure) was dominated by some of her greatest architects. The Habsburgs sought to rival the splendour of the court of Louis XIV by similarly ambitious building programmes, and were well served. The career of **Johann Bernhard Fischer von Erlach** (Graz; 1656–1723) was highly productive. From 1683 he was working for the Archbishop of Salzburg, whose *Cathedral,* by *Santino Solari* (1575–1646), was a notable Italianate composition only recently completed. Fischer von Erlach was responsible for both the *Kollegienkirche* and the *Dreifaltigkeitskirche,* among others, both imprinted with his characteristic style. He was then summoned to Vienna as Imperial Architect and Engineer, where he planned the *Karlskirche* (1716–22), completed by his son *Joseph Emanuel.* He was also responsible for the *Bohemian Chancery;* the *Winter palace of Prince Eugene* (centre block and staircase); the alterations of the *Lobkowitz palace;* plans for *Schönbrunn* (altered and completed by the more neo-Classical *Nikolaus Pacassi*); the exterior of the *Palais Schwarzenberg* (the interior completed by his son); and the *Palais Trautson,* among several other remarkable buildings. But it is the *Karlskirche,* built as a votive offering after the plague of 1713, and dedicated to St. Charles Borromeo, with its squat towers and flattened helms, and with its Roman façade broken by two 'Trajan columns', which is his masterpiece. The grand and austere interior was decorated after 1725 by *Rottmayr,* referred to below.

The other very influential architect was **Johann Lukas von Hildebrandt** (1668–1745), born of German parents in Genoa, a pupil of Carlo Fontana in Rome, and a fortress engineer during the Italian campaigns of Prince Eugene. His style is less contrived than Fischer von Erlach, and more ornamental. His greatest work is the *Belvedere,* the summer palace of Prince Eugene, rising on a gentle slope just beyond the former walls of Vienna, and he completed the latter's winter palace. He was also responsible for the staircase of the *Kinsky Palace* (1713–16), a successful solution to the problem of fitting an elaborate formal stair into a narrow site, and—in Salzburg—he built the main staircase of *Schloss Mirabell* (1720–27), straddled with putti sculpted by *Donner.* Among his churches is the splendid *Peterskirche,* just off the Graben in Vienna, with a simple oval plan, and containing a grandiose pulpit by *Matthias Steinl*, and a ceiling painted by *Rottmayr*. His staircase at *Göttweig* is also a remarkable achievement.

Baroque painting in Austria is perhaps seen at its best in fresco. One of the earliest and finest exponents of this art was **Johann Michael Rottmayr** (1645–1730), whose work is characterised by swirling figures in bright clouds, and by its cheerful colouring. He first worked at Salzburg, decorating the *Residenz*, and both the *Kollegienkirche* and *Dreifaltigkeitskirche*. From 1696 he was painting the *Gartenpalais Liechtenstein* at Vienna, the *Peterskirche*, and *Karlskirche*, and he was also working at *Melk*.

Another master during this period was **Daniel Gran** (1694–1757), who had been sent to train in Italy by his patron, Prince Schwarzenberg. Perhaps his most important work is the ceiling of the *Hofbibliothek* at Vienna, although he also painted the *Marmorsaal* at *Klosterneuburg*, among several other decorative projects. He shared his supremacy with **Paul Troger** (1698–1762), who had also studied in Italy, and worked mainly in the abbeys of Lower Austria, including *Altenburg*, *Melk*, and *Göttweig*, where his strong contrasts of colouring, and notable illusionist painting, are characteristic. **Martino Altomonte** (Naples, 1657–1745) painted several ceilings in the *Lower Belvedere*, in the *Residenz* at Salzburg, and also the *Grosser Saal* at *St. Florian*, but perhaps his most astonishing work is to be found in the remote abbey church at *Spital am Pyhrn*, with its illusionist perspective by **Bartolomeo Altomonte**, his son (1702–83), who worked mainly in the vicinity of Linz.

Franz Anton Maulbertsch (1724–96), was possibly the greatest master of Austrian Baroque painting; his self-portrait can be seen in the Lower Belvedere, together with his St. James of Compostela, a colourful sketch for the sadly destroyed frescoes at Schwechat. His work in the *Piaristenkirche* (1752–53) has already been mentioned, while other examples may be seen in a side chapel of the *Kirche am Hof*, and elsewhere in the vicinity of the capital. The work of **Martin Johann Schmidt** (1718–1801), better known as 'Kremser Schmidt', contains neo-Classical elements. He produced over a thousand altarpieces and other devotional paintings, and a good selection of his work can be seen in the Baroque Museum at the Belvedere, and in the museum at Krems itself.

Baroque art and architecture continued to be dominant in Austria throughout the second half of the 18C, overshadowing the NEO-CLASSICAL, although the few exponents of this style cannot be dismissed. An outstanding example of sculpture is the pyramidal *Memorial to the Archduchess Maria Christine* in the Augustinerkirche, Vienna, designed by *Antonio Canova* (1757–1822), who also carved the colossal Theseus fighting the Centaur now on the landing of the Kunsthistorisches Museum. Among architects were *Nikolaus Pacassi* (1716–90), who completed *Schönbrunn*, and two Frenchmen, *Jean-Nicolas Jadot*, imported by Maria Theresia's consort from Lunéville to design the *Old University* in Vienna (1733), although he had later to make way for Pacassi, and *Louis de Montoyer*, who built its oval hall, and designed an imposing palace for *Prince Rasumofsky*, the Russian ambassador, and Beethoven's patron. Local talent included *Josef Kornhäusel* (1782–1860), responsible for the library of the Schottenstift in Vienna.

The **Romantic Age**. Individual artists are well represented in the *Österreichische Galerie* in the Upper Belvedere in Vienna. Of importance among them was **Ferdinand Georg Waldmüller** (1793–1865), painter of numerous portraits, landscapes, and charming genre scenes. The influence of his naturalistic charm is seen in the work of **Emil Jakob Schindler** (1842–92; father of Alma Mahler) and *Tina Blau* (1845–1916), who carried her easel and palette into the Prater on a pram. Also representative of this period were *Leopold Kupelwieser* (1796–1862), who was influenced by the so-called 'Nazarenes' in Rome, and **Friedrich von Amerling** (1803–87), who taught in London, Paris, and Munich, and was a successful portrait painter with a clarity and richness comparable to Lawrence. Other names which should be mentioned are *Thomas Ender* (1793–1875), *Franz Eybl* (1806–80), *Johann Peter Krafft* (1780–1856), *J.B. Lampi* (1751–1830), *Rudolf von Alt* (1812–1905), *Josef Danhauser* (1805–45), and *Adalbert Stifter* (1805–68), the last better known as a poet.

Biedermeier. Wieland Gottlieb Biedermaier (sic) was the *nom de plume* adopted by two young German poets in the early 1850s, and the term 'Biedermeier' came to be used for the more intimate style of art and the simple forms of furniture and decoration that emerged as a reaction to the grandeur of the Empire style. Nowhere was it more favoured or better suited to the bourgeois temperament than early 19C Vienna, where it was adopted with enthusiasm by Franz II, whose Romantic inclinations had been satisfied with the *Franzenburg* at *Laxenburg*, S of Vienna. A curious Romantic conceit of military grandeur may be seen at the *Heldenberg* near *Kleinwetzdorf* (NW of Stockerau, in Lower Austria), a Valhalla constructed by an army contractor. Here some 142 cast-iron and zinc-pewter busts of war heroes stand in a garden, and marshals Radetsky and Wimpffen also lie buried.

The **'Ringstrassen era'** or **'Historicism'**. One of the first acts of Franz Josef—brought to the throne after the Revolution of 1848—was to order the demolition of Vienna's fortifications, which had served well to defend its rioting citizens from the army. With this 'peace-keeping' end in view (as with Haussmann's town-planning projects in Paris), the bastions surrounding the inner city were razed, and the glacis beyond them provided a wide swathe of land on which to lay out the Ringstrasse, which was to be flanked by grandiose edifices to typify the new Imperial Capital. At either end of the ring great barracks were placed, to avoid a repetition of the revolt. S of the city rose an extensive *Arsenal*, which now contains the Military Museum (the *Heeresgeschichtliches Museum*), erected in 1850–56 by *Leopold Förster* (1793–1863), and the Danish architect, *Theophil Hansen* (1813–91). The first building on the Ring itself was the *Votivkirche* (1856–79), built in the form of a 13C French cathedral by *Heinrich von Ferstel* (1828–83), raised in thanksgiving for the young emperor's escape from an assassination attempt, but paid for by the private subscription of his subjects. Adjacent to it reared the new *University* building (1873–84), also by Ferstel, this time in the style of a French Renaissance town hall. Further S the new town hall or *Rathaus* was erected (1872–73)—in the style of a Flemish cloth-hall—by *Friedrich Schmidt* (1825–91), from Wurtemberg. Opposite it was the new *Burgtheater* (1874–88), based on plans by the Hamburger *Gottfried Semper* (1803–79), in which *Karl Hasenauer* (1833–94) incorporated important ceiling-paintings in the staircase wings, some by young Gustav Klimt.

To the W stood the new *Parliament* (1872–73), by Hansen, in the

Classical style; while to the S of the last rose two sumptuous buildings, also planned by Gottfried Semper, which were to hold the Imperial Natural History collection and Art collection respectively, both completed by 1881. To the E of the latter (the present *Kunsthistorisches Museum*) was erected the S wing of the *Neue Hofburg*, built between 1881 and 1913 as part of a grandiose project to enclose a huge square, but which was never completed. Some distance S of the Neue Hofburg was the *Opera-house* (1861–69), built by *Eduard van der Nüll* (1812–68) and *August von Siccardsburg* (1813–68), designed in an ornate Italianate style, but so badly received that the former committed suicide, and Siccardsburg died broken-hearted shortly after.

Towards a New Architecture. Understandably, there was a strong reaction against the 'architecture' of the Ringstrasse, exemplified by several remarkable buildings by **Otto Wagner** (1841–1918), notably his *Post Office Savings Bank* of 1904–06, the main hall of which, with its air ducts and concealed devices for removing snow and ice from its glass roof, is still impressive. He was also responsible for several other outstanding buildings in the *Jugendstil* taste, among them his majolica-clad apartment block at Linke Wienzeile 40, and the decorative neighbouring corner building (1898–99), the distinguished *Kirche am Steinhof* (1904–07), in the W suburbs, and a number of stations for the *Stadtbahn* (1895–1902).

Among his pupils were **Josef Hoffmann** (1870–1956), who built numerous private houses, and was an influential designer; and **Josef Maria Olbrich** (1867–1908), the architect of the '*Secession*' building, crowned by its 'golden cabbage', completed in less than a year, in 1899. Another very individual architect was **Adolf Loos** (1870–1933). His finest work is perhaps the 'eyebrowless' 'Looshaus' on the Michaelerplatz, which caused general astonishment. The '*Loosbar*', off the Kärntnerstrasse, a mirrored box of 1907, is in his intimate style.

Hoffmann, with **Kolo Moser** (1868–1918) and Fritz Wärndorfer, a banker, founded in 1903 the *Wiener Werkstätte*, which had an immense influence on design during the early decades of the century, and which had itself many points of contact with the Glasgow School and Charles Rennie Mackintosh. Almost every designer and artist of merit in Austria worked for the craft workshop at some time, but it should not be forgotten that the now ubiquitous bentwood chair was originally designed by **Michael Thonet** (1796–1871), who had been brought to Vienna by Metternich.

The Secession and Modern Times. Foremost among the artists connected with the Ringstrasse and president of their headquarters, the Künstlerhaus, was *Hans Makart* (1840–84), who painted many huge theatrical canvases, extremely popular at the time. It is hardly surprising that in 1897 **Gustav Klimt** (1862–1918) reacted against the academic stranglehold on art, and with several like-minded artists (including the venerable Rudolph von Alt), formed an autonomous establishment, which was to provide the city with numerous successful and influential exhibitions in the newly constructed 'Secession' building; see above. Much of Klimt's art was colourful and voluptuous in its variation of the 'art nouveau' style, and very different from the sensual realism of his younger contemporary, **Egon Schiele** (1890–1918).

Associated with them, and encouraged by Klimt, was **Oskar**

Kokoschka (1886–1980), an exponent of an individual expressionist manner, while among other important early 20C artists were *Albin Egger-Lienz* (1868–1926), who made many studies of peasants; *Anton Kolig* (1886–1950), known for his sensual nudes and vivid portraits; his contemporary *Richard Gerstl* (1883–1908), a somewhat tormented figure who committed suicide; and *Herbert Boeckl* (1894–1966). A later generation includes Boeckl's pupil *Georg Eisler* (born 1928), and the Viennese 'fantastic realists', formed in 1958, among them *Ernst Fuchs* (born 1930), and *Rudolph Hausner* (born 1914); *Anton Lehmden* (born 1929) produces work of some individuality.

Among the sculptors of recent decades, the better known are *Fritz Wotruba* (1907–75), *Alfred Hrdlička* (born 1928), and *Joannis Avramidis* (born 1922).

In the field of architecture, it should be remembered that the city of Vienna was an innovator in community housing in the 1920s. *Karl Ehn's Karl-Marx Hof* (1927–30), with its 1300 apartments, was widely admired throughout Europe, even if it was soon after shelled by political reactionaries. Also of interest to the town-planner was the *George-Washington Hof*, designed by *Robert Oerley* and *Karl Krist*, perhaps the first modern 'neighbourhood unit'.

Among contemporary architects *Clemens Holzmeister* (1886–1983) is probably the best known outside Austria, although *Friedensreich Hundertwasser* (born 1928) has made a colourful impact. There have been several mammoth projects in the form of hospitals, and buildings to house United Nations' functionaries, but few of them have met with critical approval.

INTRODUCTION TO MUSIC IN AUSTRIA

by *Peter Branscombe*

When *Louis Spohr* arrived in Vienna in 1812 he called the city 'without doubt the capital of the musical world'. That opinion would surely be supported by innumerable people, visitors and residents, musicians and non-musicians alike, at many different periods. But there is another, and less agreeable, side to the coin—Vienna is also the city in which patrons, publishers, and public alike lost interest in Mozart, and failed to appreciate such composers as Schubert, Bruckner, Schönberg, Berg, and Webern. Taste has tended to be conservative in Vienna, with audiences preferring the familiar to the new and challenging. Yet even those who are critical of the Viennese public will have to admit that the city acted as a magnet to the legion of composers who made their careers there wholly or in part, drawn from Italy, north Germany, the Netherlands, France, Spain, Bohemia, Moravia, and Hungary. Apart from Schubert, none of the greatest Viennese composers was actually born there; they were attracted by its reputation, and if many of them suffered bitter disappointment, they chose to stay on.

Music in Salzburg. Though the emphasis in this study is bound to fall on Vienna, other Austrian cities and the numerous monastic founda-tions have also played a very important part in the history of Austrian music. Salzburg has a double importance. In its own right it is one of the leading centres; and it was here that Wolfgang Amadè Mozart (generally and wrongly named Amadeus) was born.

The history of Salzburg reaches back into the early eighth century, when St. Rupert founded the abbey of St. Peter; while later that century St. Vergil founded the cathedral. Surviving documents indicate that a lively tradition of music-making soon sprang up that included congregational singing of hymns in addition to the chant of the monks. Bell-founding and other musical activities are attested for the twelfth and thirteenth centuries. Some of the Minnesingers, including *Neidhart von Reuental*, had connections with Salzburg, and it is clear that from an early date learned and popular music existed side by side. Sacred but non-liturgical performances became established in celebration of the great feasts of the church year. By the late fourteenth century, under Archbishop Pilgrim von Puchheim, we already find the pre-requisite for polyphonic church music, a chapel choir. This was the period too of *Hermann*, the Benedictine Monk of Salzburg, the earliest poet-composer to write polyphonically in German as well as in Latin; his surviving works, secular and sacred, original and translations, homophonic and polyphonic, show an unusually broad melodic catchment-area: Gregorian chant, Latin hymns and sequences, folksong, but also new features like the use of major modality. A notable organ was constructed in Pilgrim's time; it was not replaced for two centuries.

During the fifteenth century, Salzburg's importance as a musical centre grew; *Oswald von Wolkenstein* (died 1445), one of the last and finest of the poet-musicians of the Middle Ages, was at the court of Salzburg in 1424. In the fields of church and ceremonial music it was a period of entrenchment; there was also an increasing number of instrument-makers, and demands on their skills came not only from the church but also from the increasing number of wealthy citizens who took a keen interest in music.

In the sixteenth century the Renaissance reached Salzburg. Under Cardinal Matthäus Lang (1519–40), a noted humanist and statesman, polyphonic music reached new heights; among his musicians were masters of the prominence of *Heinrich Finck* (c 1444–1527) and *Paul Hofhaimer* (1459–1537). A series of distinguished but less well-known musicians contributed, especially in organ music. Fresh impetus came from Archbishop Wolf Dietrich (1587–1612) who, apart from supervising the development of modern Salzburg, founded the Hofkapelle in 1591 and a few years later re-organised the cathedral choir. His musicians were drawn from Germany, the Netherlands, and especially from Italy (he had studied in Rome). By 1612 the music establishment had grown to nearly 80, and under his successors Archbishops Marcus Sitticus (1612–19) and Paris Lodron (1619–53) the new musical form of opera was introduced to transalpine audiences: a Hoftragicomedia was given in the archiepiscopal residence in February 1614, and by the end of the decade operas were being performed in the theatre hewn out of the rock at Hellbrunn. The foundation of the Benedictine Gymnasium and then of the University (1617 and 1622 respectively) gave new impetus not only to education but to music too: the operatic and other staged productions at key points of the academic year soon became a firm tradition, lasting to Mozart's time and beyond. A further gain in the early years of Lodron's reign was the completion of the splendid new cathedral in 1628—even if it is now accepted that the 53-part 'Missa salisburgensis' was written not by Orazio Benevoli for the festivities of 1628, but perhaps by Biber, and probably for the 1100th anniversary (1682) of the foundation of the Archbishopric.

It is a fine testimony to the growing international reputation and prosperity of the city that two of the greatest musicians of their day were engaged at the Salzburg court at the same time: *Georg Muffat* (1653–1704; from Alsace), was active there from 1678 to 1690, and *Heinrich Biber* (1644–1704; from Bohemia), from 1670 to the year of his death. With the local master, *Andreas Hofer* (from 1653), they brought church music to a very high level, but they were also active in opera and oratorio. Biber and Muffat wrote a quantity of excellent instrumental music too. Another indication of the attention paid to music in the Salzburg of the late-seventeenth and early-eighteenth centuries is the gift of a 'Gloggenspiel oder Carillon' at a price of 6000 gulden by Prince-Archbishop Johann Ernst von Thun in 1702; the instrument is still to be heard—one of the features of Salzburg for the visitor. In the following year a large new organ was built above the main entrance of the cathedral—the sixth in that superbly endowed building.

The early eighteenth century was a time of less distinction, though Biber's son *Karl Heinrich* was a talented composer of church music. For operas, Salzburg now looked to Vienna, obtaining at least 19 scores from *Antonio Caldara* (1670–1736), one of the masters of the age. The next generation marks the transition from high Baroque towards rococo and early Classical style, with *Johann Ernst Eberlin* (1702–62) proving himself a fine all-round composer; he was court organist from 1726 and Hofkapellmeister from 1749. Another stalwart was *Anton Cajetan Adlgasser* (1729–77), who wrote oratorios and school dramas, a quantity of instrumental music, and many church works which continued to be performed well into the following century. He is probably best remembered for his collaboration with the eleven-year-old Mozart and Michael Haydn on the oratorio 'Die Schuldigkeit des ersten Gebotes' (1767).

Leopold Mozart (1719–87) deserves to be honoured in his own right—he was a fine composer, an excellent violinist and theorist, and a talented teacher. He joined the Salzburg establishment in 1743, advancing to the rank of court and chamber composer in 1757 and to deputy Kapellmeister in 1763. Although quite prolific in every branch of composition except opera, he virtually ceased composing around 1762 to devote himself to the careers of his children. The other major figure in Salzburg music, again a man overshadowed by a more famous relative, was **Michael Haydn** (1737–1806). After an upbringing like his brother's in Lower Austria and Vienna, he became Kapellmeister to the Bishop of Grosswardein in Hungary (now Oradea, Romania) in 1757; in 1763 he took up an appointment as Konzertmeister at Salzburg, and there, apart from one or two periods of absence, he remained until his death. He wrote a large number of liturgical works, including a number of German settings, but also many splendid orchestral and chamber works, and numerous semi-dramatic scores (German oratorios and Singspiels rather than Italian operas). He was also a distinguished teacher—the young *Carl Maria von Weber* spent two periods of study with him, and *Neukomm* and *Diabelli* were with him for longer spells.

Wolfgang Amadè Mozart (1756–91) was already a widely travelled virtuoso and composer by the time of his appointment as Konzertmeister to Prince-Archbishop Schrattenbach in autumn 1769, just before he and his father set out on their first Italian journey— doubtless the ruler wished to secure the boy's loyalty to Salzburg even more than to give him a title with which to impress the Italians; Mozart was not actually paid for his services until 1772, but from the time of his advancement to organist (at the court chapel and the cathedral) in 1779 he actually drew quite a respectable salary. By then he had returned from Mannheim and Paris with an enhanced reputation and a growing list of masterpieces behind him. Nevertheless, Mozart's dissatisfaction with life and conditions in Salzburg is plain from his letters. He found his personal position even more irksome, when after the successful production of 'Idomeneo' in Munich in 1781, instead of returning to Salzburg, he was summoned to Vienna to join the Archbishop's entourage at the celebrations for the accession of Joseph II. The famous kick from the Archbishop's steward on 9 June 1781 finally ended Mozart's official association with the town of his birth (when Mozart took his wife to Salzburg in 1783, he feared he might be arrested because of his quarrel with his princely employer).

It would hardly be going too far to suggest that the city of Salzburg has lived off (but also enhanced) Mozart's reputation ever since his departure from it—the Mozarteum was founded in 1841, there was a large-scale festival in 1856 to celebrate the centenary of his birth, the Internationale Mozart-Stiftung (from 1880 known as the Internationale Stiftung Mozarteum) was founded in 1870, and from 1875 it began publication of the first complete edition of Mozart's works; in 1931 the Zentralinstitut für Mozartforschung came into existence, by which time the Salzburg International Festival, with the emphasis firmly on the music of its most famous son, had been in existence for a decade. Since 1956 there has been an additional smaller festival in January (Salzburg Mozart Week), which has seen the performance (and, importantly, the recording) of a number of Mozart's less familiar works.

Innsbruck, Graz, and some smaller musical centres. Vienna and Salzburg are merely the best-known musical centres in Austria—festivals from Mörbisch in the east to Bregenz and Hohenems in the west, cities from Linz in the north to Graz in the south-east and Innsbruck in the south-west, have traditions of various durations, but all contribute to the artistic life of the nation.

Until the Tyrolean line of the Habsburg royal house died out in 1665, **Innsbruck** was an independent court and capital—Duke Friedrich moved his residence there in 1363, from Meran. The principal church, St. Jacob's, dates from 1180 or earlier; it remained the focus of music until the court chapel was built in the middle of the sixteenth century. This chapel had a fine (and often enlarged and restored) organ by Jörg Ebert; it is also the burial-place of the Emperor Maximilian I. Adjoining it is the Silver Chapel, which also has a fine organ, a positive dated 1614. *Paul Hofhaimer* was Kapellmeister to Duke Sigmund from 1478, and he also served Maximilian in a similar capacity. The music establishment was particularly large and distinguished under Ferdinand II in the second half of the sixteenth century, with *Jacob Regnart*, the *Floris*, and *Tiburtio Massaino* among its composers; and from the 1620s Innsbruck was important in the establishment of opera north of the Alps. Little is definitely known about the music performed for the marriage of Emperor Ferdinand II with Eleonora Gonzaga in 1622, but a series of Habsburg marriages to Italian princesses can only have encouraged the beginnings of opera in Innsbruck, and around 1630 a tennis court was converted into a theatre. From the mid 1650s dates the first proper opera-house in German lands, and, with *Sbarra* as court poet and *Pietro Cesti* (1623–69) as court Kapellmeister, a series of operas were performed which established the pre-eminence of the Habsburgs as patrons, and drew Queen Christina of Sweden to Innsbruck at least twice. A final flowering of opera occurred there in the early eighteenth century under the governorship of Duke Karl Philipp of the Palatinate, with operas by *Jakob Greber*, *Alessandro Scarlatti*, and others. After Karl Philipp's departure for Germany in 1717, musical life lacked special distinction, though in 1765 *Johann Adolf Hasse*'s 'Romulo ed Ersilia' was commissioned for the wedding of Archduke Leopold and the Infanta Maria Ludovica. Thereafter, the theatres were leased, and Innsbruck gradually assumed the cultural identity of a moderate-sized city, with a quite lively theatrical and musical life, in which amateur choirs have played a leading part. The University dates from 1669, the printing of music goes back more than a century earlier, and an Institute of Musicology was established shortly after the end of the First World War.

Graz, capital of Styria and Austria's second city, has an even longer musical tradition than Innsbruck—a late-thirteenth-century chronicle lists some of its musicians. During the Reformation, Graz was largely Protestant, with a lively musical life; a hymn-book was published in 1569. However, the Counter-Reformation rapidly re-established Roman Catholicism, and from 1572 the Jesuits were active in Graz. Under Archduke Ferdinand (1595–1619) firm links with Italian music were established, but the departure of Ferdinand to Vienna following his accession to the throne entailed the removal of most of the musicians from the Kapelle. Thereafter, although there were some noblemen who kept small musical establishments, music in Graz was mainly a middle-class concern. In the mid eighteenth century Italian opera was briefly established, and in the first half of the nineteenth century the Styrian Music Society, directed by

Schubert's friend *Anselm Hüttenbrenner*, brought a number of distinguished artists to the city. Among those born in and near Graz were *Johann Josef Fux* (1660–1741), and the conductors *Ernst von Schuch*, and *Karl Böhm*; while many other musicians, including *Hugo Wolf* and the Wagnerian tenor *Joseph Tichatscheck*, the soprano *Amalie Materna*, and the conductors *Carl Muck, Franz Schalk*, and *Clemens Krauss*, studied or gained valuable experience there.

Most of the religious foundations dotted over the Austrian countryside have also had an important part in Austrian musical life. Their libraries contain rich treasures of both sacred and secular music, manuscript and printed; their chapels contain some of the most beautiful organs in German lands. The great Bruckner organ (Krismann, 1774) at the Augustinian monastery of St. Florian, near Linz, is because of that association perhaps the most famous, but the mid-seventeenth-century choir organ at Wilten in Innsbruck, or the lovely rococo instrument at the Cistercian Stiftskirche of Wilhering, near Linz, and the slightly later choir organ at the Cistercian monastery of Stams in the Tyrol, are wonderful examples of older instruments that survive in excellent order. The discovery of long-lost autograph scores in church organ-lofts has become part of post-war musical history (or legend); more important still are the collections of music in the libraries of monastic foundations, large and small. To cite examples almost at random, there are the manuscript symphonies by Leopold and Wolfgang Mozart which they presented to the Benedictine abbey of Lambach as a thank-offering for hospitality during their journeys between Salzburg and Vienna, or the Haydn Violin Concerto in A, known after the resting-place of its one extant source as the 'Melk' Concerto, or the remarkable collection of early Schubert editions and manuscripts at the Benedictine abbey of Seitenstetten, or the perhaps more widely known treasures of the ancient Benedictine monastery of Göttweig, which in 1983 celebrated with great splendour the 900th anniversary of its foundation. Then there are all the Bohemian and Moravian sacred foundations and castles, many of them once owned by or under the patronage of Austrian aristocratic families, the libraries and manuscripts of which are being brought together and catalogued in Prague; and the rich documentation of life and music under the Esterházys, of crucial importance for Haydn studies, which has been centralised in Budapest.

Music in Vienna: the Early Centuries. The history of music in pre-Renaissance Vienna is perhaps surprisingly incomplete. It must be taken for granted that the churches, the oldest of which are those dedicated to Saints Ruprecht, Peter, and Stephen, were important centres of liturgical music in the Middle Ages; probably the Schottenstift, and certainly the abbey and town of Klosterneuburg (which until the mid-twelfth century was the seat of the margraves of Babenberg), had wider significance. Some of the leading Minnesinger performed at court, including *Walther von der Vogelweide, Neidhart von Reuental, Ulrich von Liechtenstein, Tannhäuser*, and *Hugo von Montfort*. There is evidence that the musicians of Vienna were well organised before the end of the thirteenth century—the Nicolaibrüderschaft lasted from before 1288 until the reforms of Joseph II in the 1780s, and courtiers were appointed to supervise entertainments from the same period. The foundation of the University of Vienna in 1365 gave fresh impetus to the music-schools already established at the principal churches, and to the growing tradition of dramatic performance. French influence was strong in the late fourteenth century, and in the mid fifteenth century Friedrich III brought British and Flemish musicians to Austria. This was by no means a one-way movement—minstrels from Vienna are recorded as far afield as Spain, France, Switzerland, Burgundy, and Brabant.

Even under Maximilian I (reigned 1486–1519), the court was anything but sedentary—he was almost constantly on the move through his vast domains, usually accompanied by the majority of his musicians (they included major foreign composers like *Heinrich Isaac* and *Ludwig Senfl*, as well as the native *Paul Hofhaimer*). Polyphonic song became popular and widespread, and instrumental music also flourished. The division of the Habsburg lands following the death of Ferdinand I in 1564 led to an increase in the number of courts; the pre-eminence of Vienna is however indicated by the example of the native *Wolfgang Schmeltzl*, who around 1550 stressed the musical stature of Vienna in a treatise, published a valuable collection of songs, and introduced vernacular school drama. The sixteenth century was also a period of marked Netherlandish and Flemish dominance in musical life, though by the second half of the century Italian influence was beginning to radiate from Graz—the closest to Italy of the major Austrian courts; by the beginning of the following century Italian influence, centred on Vienna, was to prove decisive.

Opera and Theatre. The origins of opera in Vienna are disputed. It is unlikely that the Italian musical performance in the new Imperial residence on 15 June 1625 was an opera, and far from certain that the celebrations of a great Habsburg wedding in 1631 included an opera. However, two years later *Bartolaia*'s 'Il Sidonio' was performed in the Great Hall of the Hofburg on 9 July; opera had definitely reached Vienna. It was 1651–52, however, before a theatre was constructed specially to accommodate stage performances; it was built on the Tummelplatz, on the site of the present Redoutensäle, at the command of Ferdinand III and to the designs of Giovanni Burnacini. This wooden structure soon proved neither stable nor large enough, and the new emperor, Leopold I, commissioned Ludovico Burnacini (Giovanni's son) and Jacopo Torelli to build a splendid new house in preparation for his forthcoming wedding to the Infanta Margarita. The new house, however—its site was between the National Library and the Burggarten—was not ready until some 18 months later; it was inaugurated in 1668 with one of the most grandiose and, thanks to the survival of Burnacini's magnificent set-designs, best-documented Baroque operas, the *Cesti/Sbarra* 'Il pomo d'oro'. Even this 'Theater auf der Cortina' (the 'Cortina' being the defensive wall) had a short life; it was pulled down in 1683 because it presented too great a fire-risk during the Turkish siege.

After the expulsion of the Turks, dramatic performances were held in the courts of the Hofburg, or in the Stallburg; the Palais Trautson, in the Augarten, was also used for operatic performances. It too had fallen victim to the Turks, but Leopold re-built the 'Alte Favorita' as a grace and favour residence for his mother. Confusingly, many operatic performances were also given in the 'Neue Favorita', the royal palace now known as the Theresianum, the Diplomatic Academy. Its spacious gardens were used for open-air operatic performances from about 1695, often of the greatest splendour and scenic extravagance—as readers of Lady Mary Wortley Montagu's letters from Vienna (1716) will recall. After Karl VI's death at the Neue Favorita in 1740 his daughter Maria Theresia had the palace of Schönbrunn built; its orangery was occasionally used for operas, but the fine little theatre at Schönbrunn was—and remains—far more important. The Habsburg country seat at Laxenburg, to the south of Vienna, also had a theatre suitable for operatic performances.

All the theatres mentioned in the previous paragraph, except for the one at Schönbrunn, were more or less temporary structures. Between 1705 and 1708 *Francesco Galli-Bibiena* erected a solid new opera-house on the Tummelplatz; it actually had two stages, a small one for opera buffa and Italian plays, and a large one for full-scale opera performances. This was used for the last time in January 1744 at the marriage of Archduchess Maria Anna to Duke Karl of Lorraine, when the work performed was *Hasse*'s 'L'Ipermestra'. The building was dismantled in 1747, and the Redoutensäle were erected in its place.

Until the early-eighteenth century the populace at large had to make do with troupes of strolling players in the streets and squares for their theatre. In 1708–09, a public theatre was built near the Carinthian Gate, approximately on the site of the Hotel Sacher, solidly constructed of stone. By 1710 it had become the home of the troupe of *Josef Anton Stranitzky (1676–1726)*, known as 'Hanswurst' from his clown's role, the founder of the old Viennese popular theatre tradition. His repertoire consisted of farces constructed on the framework of blood-and-thunder dramas, with much improvisation and songs. Hanswurst, along with other male and female comic types loosely derived from the Italian comedy, became the mainstay of popular drama; after Stranitzky's death, *Gottfried Prehauser* became the new Hanswurst; his company lasted into the 1760s. Following a fire in 1761 the Kärntnertor-Theater was rebuilt as the principal opera house of Vienna, though until 1810 it shared the operatic and dramatic repertory with the Burgtheater. It was demolished in 1870, the year after the opening of the Hofoperntheater am Ring, the present State Opera building.

The Burgtheater was founded early in the reign of Maria Theresia, when the tennis court on the Michaelerplatz was rebuilt as a theatre. In 1760 a further enlargement took place. This 'Royal and Imperial Theatre by the Burg' was in its early years used mainly for French plays; from 1776 it was given over to the German repertory, and from 1778 until 1783 it was the home of Joseph II's 'German National Singspiel' venture, during which Mozart's 'Die Entführung aus dem Serail' was first performed. Concerts were frequently given in the Burgtheater, especially in Lent, and it was here, in the 1780s and early 1790s, that Mozart's three settings of libretti by Lorenzo da Ponte were heard. From 1810 the Burgtheater housed the Court Theatre company. It closed on 13 October 1888, the day before the ceremonial opening of the new—and present—Burgtheater on the Ringstrasse. Both State Opera and Burgtheater were virtually destroyed in the closing weeks of the Second World War. It was a matter of national pride to rebuild them as closely as possible to their original designs; both were ready for splendid state re-opening ceremonies within three weeks of each other in the autumn of 1955.

The Suburban Theatres. Apart from the court theatres, Vienna had a number of theatres outside the walls of the inner city. Until the mid-1770s the court maintained a firm hold on public spectacles, but from 1776, the year of the official foundation of the National Theatre, regulations were relaxed to permit the erection of new theatres under licence. From the early 1760s the extemporisations of *Hanswurst Prehauser* and his colleague *Kurz-Bernardon* were banned from the Burgtheater, and for a few years the ordinary people were deprived of vernacular theatrical entertainment.

As well as several more or less ephemeral undertakings there were three new suburban theatres built in the 1780s which are of abiding importance. The oldest was the Theater in der Leopoldstadt (Jägerzeile, later Praterstrasse), which *Karl Marinelli* opened on 20 October 1781. With the actor *La Roche* at the core of a versatile company (his role, Kasperl, was a descendant of Hanswurst), *Hensler, Perinet* and others to provide a string of lively and often vastly successful plays, and *Wenzel Müller* and *Ferdinand Kauer* to compose the scores and direct the performances, this ensemble soon became one of the most famous in Europe. After Marinelli's death the company was run by Hensler, and later by another of the dramatists, *Huber*. In the third decade of the nineteenth century the Leopoldstädter-Theater reached a new peak, with *Ferdinand Raimund* and *Ignaz Schuster* rivalling each other for comic excellence, and many other talented players. The entrepreneur *Karl Carl* took over the theatre in 1838, and rebuilt it as the Carltheater in 1847. He coarsened the repertoire, but his acumen in securing the services of *Wenzel Scholz*, and especially of *Nestroy*, who, like Raimund, was outstanding both as actor and as dramatist, ensured the continued triumph of the theatre. Although it ceased to be the home of traditional popular drama after Nestroy's retirement in 1860, the theatre continued in use until 1929; it was bombed in 1944.

The second of the suburban theatres was the Theater auf der Wieden. In spring 1787 the theatre director *Christian Rossbach* was granted permission to erect a theatre in the recently re-built housing-complex of Prince Starhemberg; it was opened on 14 October 1787. Soon Rossbach moved elsewhere, and the theatre was taken over by *Johann Friedel*, novelist and actor, and *Eleonore Schikaneder*, estranged wife of *Emanuel Schikaneder*. Friedel died suddenly in March 1789, whereupon Emanuel Schikaneder was summoned to take over the theatre. From the time of his arrival that summer the Theater auf der Wieden became important. He was a man of many parts—actor (his Hamlet was widely admired in his younger years), dramatist, composer (he wrote at least two Singspiel scores), singer, and theatre director; and as the librettist of 'Die Zauberflöte' he has gained a kind of immortality. He had a fine ensemble, and his performances of operas and ballets, as well as of comedies, were widely admired. No other work in Schikaneder's repertory came near to rivalling 'Die Zauberflöte' in popularity, but it is a sign of his dramatic skills that of the twelve most-performed works in the theatre's history, eight were written by him.

Towards the close of the eighteenth century, Schikaneder's incipient megalomania led him to replace the solidly built but rather small theatre in the Wieden suburb with the splendid new Theater an der Wien—in 1801, when it opened, it was probably the most lavishly equipped in the world, and it continues in use to this day. *Beethoven*'s 'Fidelio' was written for it; *Grillparzer*'s 'Die Ahnfrau', *Kleist*'s 'Das Käthchen von Heilbronn', and several of Nestroy's best-known plays had their first performances there; and so did a majority of Viennese operettas, from 'Die Fledermaus' via 'Die lustige Witwe' to *Ralph Benatzky*'s 'Axel vor der Himmelstür'. Innumerable concerts were given there by instrumentalists and singers of world renown;

yet the most distinguished years of all for this theatre were surely 1945 until 1955, when it was home to the Vienna State Opera during the legendary post-war years of that company.

The third of the permanent suburban theatres—third, since the Theater auf der Wieden and the Theater an der Wien are two manifestations of one company—is the Theater in der Josefstadt, built in 1788. For a dozen years before that, the director *Franz Scherzer* had been giving performances in a hall in the same suburb. The theatre is still in regular use today, though it has often been rebuilt. Its early years were undistinguished, but in 1822 Hensler, the former dramatist in the Leopoldstädter-Theater, took over its direction, and Beethoven's overture 'The Dedication of the House', specially commissioned for the occasion, ushered in a new era. Raimund made a series of guest appearances in 1833, culminating in the première of his last play, 'Der Verschwender', in 1834. *Conradin Kreutzer* was musical director at this time (his opera 'Das Nachtlager in Granada' also had its first performance there), and there were a number of important operatic events. For lengthy periods in the later nineteenth century the theatre again lacked distinction, but after the First World War *Max Reinhardt* became director, and *Hofmannsthal's* comedy 'Der Schwierige' had its world première there in 1924. Reinhardt's widow maintained the association after 1945. It is a beautiful little theatre, highly regarded for its performances of classics of the German and Austrian theatre.

The Eighteenth Century. During the eighteenth century there was a gradual weakening of the hold of the Viennese court over music in Austria. The divisions remained tolerably clear: operas, ballets, and other musical occasions at the royal and imperial court; sacred music at the cathedrals, churches, and in the monasteries which, since the Counter-Reformation, had regained much of their earlier importance; and, as the century progressed, an increase in musical activity at the palaces and castles of the aristocracy. By the last quarter of the century there was—in Vienna especially—much lively public musical activity. Less well documented is the musical life of the common people—dances, part-songs, folksongs; the importance of this area is indicated by the frequency and naturalness with which serious musicians absorbed features of popular music.

By the mid 1740s the pre-eminence of the court chapel was less marked. Following the deaths of Karl VI in 1740 and of his Hofkapellmeister, Fux, in the next year, musicians of competence rather than of international standing were in charge; under *Georg Reutter the Younger*, who was Court Kapellmeister from 1751, the establishment dropped alarmingly in size (there had been around 140 musicians under Karl VI; by the time of Reutter's death in 1772 there were a mere 20). True, Maria Theresia had more pressing priorities than for musical splendour, yet important posts were left unfilled, and geniuses were ignored; Gluck had to wait in the wings, Haydn to go elsewhere. Reutter was no more than an epigone in his own works, which included numerous operas and much church music, often imaginatively scored, but rather predictable. Far livelier, more forward-looking music was being written by the more unregarded composers of the era—*Mathias Georg Monn*, and *Georg Christoph Wagenseil*; *Starzer, Asplmayr, Gassmann, Albrechtsberger, Ordoñez*; the prolific and often unjustly belittled *Karl Ditters von Dittersdorf*, and *Leopold Hofmann*.

The one composer of genius available in Vienna before Mozart settled there was **Christoph Willibald Gluck** (born Erasbach, Upper Palatinate, 2 July 1714; died Vienna, 15 November 1787). He was strictly more a German/Bohemian composer than Austrian, and by the time he settled in Vienna he had a fine reputation in Italy, France, Bohemia, and Germany, where he had spent much of his time. As early as 1748 he was commissioned to write 'La Semiramide' for the re-opening of the Burgtheater on the Empress's birthday. Despite its success, it was six more years before Gluck received another court commission, and another 20 before he received a court appointment. However, his marriage into an influential Viennese family, and a post as Kapellmeister to the Prince of Saxe-Hildburghausen, helped to keep him in the forefront of attention, and from 1754 he supplied the court with a series of mainly French operas. They were largely conventional, yet startlingly prophetic touches occur; and Gluck's instrumental mastery in the ballet 'Don Juan' (1761), as well as his return to older patterns even after 'Orfeo ed Euridice' (1762), help place his operatic reforms in context: he was by no means always his own master, and when deprived of the support of Count Durazzo, director of the court theatres, and his favoured librettist *Calzabigi* ('Orfeo', 'Alceste', 'Paride ed Elena'), he resorted to familiar procedures.

Gluck's crucial importance lies in the new simplicity, power, and sublimity he was able to create through concentration on the essentials of the action: the seamless movement between narrative and lyrical expansion, strikingly forceful use of ballet and chorus (here the choreographer *Angiolini* lent invaluable support), effective and often startlingly original orchestration, a noble melodic sense, and command of dramatic irony—all these endow Gluck's greatest operas with a vitality which for long kept them among the earliest operas in the repertory. Durazzo's dismissal led Gluck to accept commissions from Paris which produced not only the revised versions of 'Orphée' and 'Alceste' but those splendid tragédies lyriques, the two Iphigenia operas and 'Armide'. After the failure of what was to be his last opera, 'Echo et Narcisse' (Paris, 1779), he finally returned to Vienna. Despite failing health (he suffered several strokes) he was able to revise as a German opera (with the poet *Alxinger*) 'Iphigenie auf Tauris' for the Burgtheater (1781). He died at what is now Wiedner Hauptstrasse 32 at the age of 73; his remains lie near those of other distinguished composers in the Zentralfriedhof.

Mozart's early years have been outlined in the section on Salzburg. When he finally freed himself from what he considered demeaning drudgery in the early summer of 1781, his prospects seemed bright. He was 25, and at the height of his powers. It must have seemed only a matter of time before he would be offered a worthy and well-paid appointment. But he was not his own best advocate; he made enemies, became the object of cabals; above all, and despite immensely promising beginnings, the fickle taste of the Viennese turned away from him. In Lent 1784, Mozart was able to send his father a list of the wealthy, aristocratic and influential patrons who signed the subscription-list for his concerts; when he last tried to mount a subscription series, he found he had no audience. The fragility of his hold on the public is suggested by the comments frequently encountered that his music was too learned, 'difficult'; 'Le nozze di Figaro' was well liked when it was staged on May Day 1786, yet ten weeks later the public fell for Dittersdorf's amiable but essentially trivial 'Doktor und Apotheker'.

One work about which there was never any doubt in the hearts

Mozart: a boxwood relief by Leonhard Posch, 1789

and minds of the public was 'Die Zauberflöte', which had its first performance in the closing weeks of Mozart's life. This was his only commission for the Volkstheater—Schikaneder was an old family friend, he knew what the public wanted, and in his libretto for Mozart he created a work which strikes a fine balance between the farcical and the potentially tragic, the simple and the spectacular. One of Mozart's pleasures in the late autumn of 1791 was to attend, and sometimes to take a mischievous hand in, performances of 'The Magic Flute' at Schikaneder's theatre, where the opera quickly began to run up record performance-figures.

But that is to anticipate: the Viennese years were also a period of personal happiness—his marriage to Constanze Weber, friendship with Haydn, dancing, merry-making, and billiards. When he needed money he could always turn out some popular compositions (and later, in his near-penury, borrow from his masonic friend, Puchberg). But despite public successes with his first Viennese opera, 'Die Entführung aus dem Serail' (1782), and the mighty series of piano concertos which he performed in public, having his own instrument carried from his dwelling to the venue, the hoped-for openings did not materialise. His appointment as Imperial and Royal Chamber Musician in December 1787 carried a small salary, and imposed the obligation only to compose dances (and what marvellous dances they are!) for the court's masked balls. Two of his three Italian operas to libretti by *Lorenzo da Ponte* were also court commissions ('Don Giovanni', like 'La clemenza di Tito', was written for Prague, though Mozart received a further fee when it was staged in Vienna). Most of the symphonies, concertos, and many of the chamber works, were written out of inner compulsion, and for personal use, rather than in response to commissions. Mozart's casual, happy-go-lucky attitude meant that he was not good at planning his activities or his family budget (his frequent changes of residence reflect this uncertainty). He could be very generous, but also hasty and ill-tempered. He must have been a difficult man to live and work with. But he was perhaps the greatest musician the world has ever known.

Joseph Haydn (born Rohrau, Lower Austria, 31 March 1732; died Vienna, 31 May 1809) is one of the greatest, and one of the most influential, composers in the history of music. From modest rural beginnings—his father was a wheelwright, his mother in service at the local Harrach schloss—he developed slowly and surely to become in his last years the most famous musician in Europe, and a man of means. His good treble voice took him via the town church at Hainburg to the cathedral choir in Vienna. When his voice broke (luckily, at later than average age) he had to make his own way—playing in churches and in small ad hoc groups for serenades, taking pupils, and studying (he seems to have worked his way through the treatises of Mattheson, Fux, and C.P.E. Bach, and to have studied the last-named's sonatas). He had an attic room in the Michaelerhaus, in the very middle of Vienna; all his life he remembered with gratitude the people who helped him then. In the same house lived the dowager Princess Esterházy, the court poet *Metastasio*, and the talented Martinez family. Haydn met, and was much helped and encouraged by, *Nicola Porpora* (1686–1768), the composer and singing-teacher; and he also met influential aristocrats through performing at soirées.

In the late 1750s he was invited to take part in, and write music for, the musical gatherings of Baron Fürnberg at his estate of Weinzierl, near Ybbs; tradition has it that the earliest string quartets were written for these occasions. From about 1759 Haydn was Kapellmeister to Count Morzin, whose summers were spent at Lukavec, in Bohemia; Haydn's first symphonies date from this period, and so too (unless they are slightly earlier) do his first keyboard concertos and church music. From 1 May 1761 Haydn was in the employment of Prince Paul Anton Esterházy, initially as vice-Kapellmeister under the elderly *Gregor Joseph Werner*, and after Werner's death in 1766 with absolute responsibility for the princely music. His residence was at Eisenstadt, some 48km from Haydn's birthplace, and close to what is now the Hungarian border at the Neusiedlersee.

The death of Prince Paul Anton in 1762 brought to power his brother Nikolaus. 'Nikolaus the Magnificent', he was called, and the splendour of his court, and his love of music, make the name entirely appropriate. From the mid 1760s, his principal seat was the elegant, newly enlarged palace of Eszterháza, out on the Hungarian plain. Haydn wrote a mighty series of symphonies, operas, and chamber compositions of every kind for his new patron (who was himself a talented player of the baryton, a viola d'amore with sympathetic strings). Haydn's operatic activities used to be little known and even less regarded; thanks largely to the efforts of scholars and record companies, the significance of Haydn's operatic music is now properly appreciated.

Haydn served Prince Nikolaus until the latter's death in autumn 1790, nominally a servant, but increasingly respected and honoured. His fame spread throughout Europe, as is attested by the innumerable manuscript copies of his works, and printed (frequently pirated, and spuriously attributed) editions. Commissions came from Spain, Bohemia, and France, as well as from closer at hand; and then, when the new Prince, Anton, released most of the musicians, Haydn was free to accept the most important foreign invitation of all, and accompany the violinist and impresario Salomon to London. The two London visits, in 1791–92 and 1794–95, mark the high point even in that long and brilliant career. The 'London' symphonies have to this day maintained their pre-eminence, and the chamber works are also of a wonderfully high standard. England made Haydn rich as well as celebrated; honours in profusion came his way. Though he was well into his sixties when he settled in Vienna after his return from London, there was no decline in his powers—indeed, the six great masses which he wrote for the name-day of Princess Maria Hermenegild, wife of Nikolaus II, the fourth Esterházy prince to whom Haydn was Kapellmeister, are among his grandest achievements. To them must be added the last string quartets, the 'Emperor's Hymn', and the two great oratorios, 'The Creation' (1798) and 'The Seasons' (1801).

Haydn's last years produced little music, but his renown grew still higher. He conversed with Griesinger and Dies, whose records provided the source for their invaluable biographies; and Haydn's copyist, Elssler, helped to compile the so-called 'Haydn Catalogue' of his works. The old man refused to take refuge in the inner city during Napoleon's bombardment of 12–13 May 1809. He died peacefully on 31 May, and despite the troubled times, his memorial service on 15 June, at which his friend Mozart's Requiem was performed, was attended by a great concourse of people.

The Nineteenth Century. Apart from the aging Haydn, and Beethoven in his early maturity, there was little depth of talent in Vienna around 1800. *Antonio Salieri* (1750–1825), Court Kapellmeister from 1788 until less than a year before his death, was a conscientious administrator and dedicated teacher, but he achieved little as a composer after the success in the year of his court appointment of 'Axur, re d'Ormus'. His deputy was *Georg Spängler*; his vice-Kapellmeister and eventual successor was *Joseph Eybler*. There was some talent among the court composers, who included *Anton Teyber* and the Bohemians *Leopold Kozeluch* and *Franz Krommer*; but all of them were essentially second-rate. Of higher quality were the opera-composers *Joseph Weigl* (1766–1846) and *Adalbert Gyrowetz* (1763–1850).

Tangible evidence of the success these composers hoped to achieve in Vienna—most of them came from elsewhere, and indeed many of them did achieve ephemeral success—is provided by the flourishing state of the music-publishing industry at this time. Foreigners set the pattern—Huberty from Paris, Torricella from Switzerland, the brothers Artaria from northern Italy. And Austrians and Bohemians rivalled them—Diabelli from Salzburg, Traeg, Hoffmeister, Kozeluch, Thaddäus Weigl, Steiner, Mollo, many of them composers too; later, Spina, Doblinger, and Haslinger cornered much of the market.

Just as there was much activity among a comparatively large number of mainly rather small publishing-houses, so too was Vienna's musical life spread over a large number of venues. The theatres, which held large audiences, were often available for concerts in Lent and Advent. Otherwise, the palaces and town houses of the aristocracy and wealthy middle-class citizens were frequently the scene for private concerts of considerable size and splendour—Haydn's last oratorios were first performed in the old Schwarzenberg Palace on the Neuer Markt, and several of Beethoven's works were first performed in the Palais Lobkowitz (to give perhaps unfair prominence to two patrons). In Mozart's day, the 'Mehlgrube' Casino (Mehlmarkt), the Trattnerhof (Graben), and the Augarten were often used; the old University and the premises of the Gesellschaft der Musikfreunde 'Zum Roten Igel' (Tuchlauben) are among halls that were important later.

Ludwig van Beethoven (born Bonn, baptised 17 December 1770; died Vienna, 26 March 1827) is in many ways the antithesis of Haydn, and indeed of Mozart too. Beethoven was in Vienna briefly in spring 1787, and probably took a few lessons from Mozart, but his mother's illness and death took him back to Bonn, and it was late 1792 before he returned to Vienna, to study with Haydn. Haydn's relations with his pupil were often strained, and it was convenient for Beethoven that when Haydn returned to London, he was able to study with *Schenk*, and *Albrechtsberger*, without causing direct offence. Beethoven soon evinced a markedly different attitude from that of Haydn, who had never lost his early circumspection and respect towards social superiors; Beethoven, the fiery young virtuoso and composer, tended to regard the aristocracy in terms of their usefulness to him and his career. They certainly showed him great generosity and understanding, which he repaid with dedications and appearances in their salons. As the century neared its close, a series of brilliant compositions, most of them incorporating the piano, appeared. By spring 1800, when he promoted his first benefit concert (it included the First Symphony and the Septet), he was the leading younger musician on the scene, with a growing reputation abroad as well.

The first years of the new century were a time of triumph for Beethoven, with a run of outstanding successes: the ballet 'The Creatures of Prometheus' (1801), the Second and Third Symphonies, and Third Piano Concerto, and the first version of 'Fidelio', on the grand scale, and in chamber music several more piano sonatas and other works. But on the personal level, this was the period when he first admitted to friends (far-away friends, in letters) the stark fact, which he had probably been facing for some time, that he was going deaf. By nature solitary, he now had to come to terms with this shattering disability. For years he would continue to appear in public as pianist and conductor, increasingly unable to control the performance, but enabled by his formidable will-power to continue to advance in his art. Prince Nikolaus II Esterházy commissioned a mass for his wife's name-day in 1807 (the Mass in C), thus challenging Beethoven to follow the superb series of masses which Haydn had written for the same annual event a few years earlier. The Razumovsky Quartets, Violin Concerto, Fourth Piano Concerto, and Fourth Symphony had all been performed in the previous months, and even the completion of the mass was followed by no slackening

Beethoven in 1812, by Franz Klein

of output—between autumn 1807 and Christmas 1808 the Fifth and Sixth Symphonies, two Piano Trios, the Choral Fantasy, and several chamber works were completed, the large-scale works being performed at the great concert Beethoven put on at the Theater an der Wien, along with the slightly older Fourth Piano Concerto and parts of the mass.

The financial outcome of that concert is not known; and artistically it cannot have been an unambiguous success. But within a matter of weeks Beethoven had achieved what no composer before him had achieved: complete financial independence for life. He committed himself only to remaining in Vienna (a generous offer from Kassel could thus be advantageously mentioned, and declined). From 1 March 1809 he was guaranteed 4000 florins per year by Archduke

Rudolph (patron, pupil, and friend), Prince Kinsky, and Prince Lobkowitz. The French occupation of Vienna, and a period of poor health, were doubtless in part responsible for some falling-off in the quantity of works Beethoven wrote. The quality (apart from occasional cheerful lapses like the Battle Symphony of 1813) remained of course wonderfully high, with the 'Emperor' Concerto, 'Harp' Quartet, 'Archduke' Trio, Seventh and Eighth Symphonies, and the last two Cello Sonatas among the high points of the period up to the Congress of Vienna.

The next years were unhappy, and comparatively barren. Beethoven's deafness was becoming increasingly hard to bear, he realised he would never marry, and his struggle for guardianship of his nephew Karl was both time-consuming, emotionally exhausting, and demeaning. The song-cycle 'An die ferne Geliebte' and the Piano Sonata in A (op. 101) were written in 1816, but it was autumn 1817 before Beethoven began to move into a new creative period, which produced the last four Piano Sonatas, the 'Missa solemnis', and the Diabelli Variations. By early 1824 the Ninth Symphony was completed, and Beethoven responded to the persuasion of his friends in promoting a concert (the last full-scale public event of his life) at the Kärntnertor-Theater on 7 May. The programme contained the Overture 'The Dedication of the House', three movements from the 'Missa solemnis', and the Choral Symphony. Beethoven had to be turned round to witness, and acknowledge, the applause of the audience— by now he had been completely deaf for some time, obliged to rely on the famous 'Conversation books' for the written questions of his visitors.

The final outburst of creative inspiration (and sheer hard work) gave birth to the incomparable series of six string quartets which are the summation of his life's work and the grandest achievement of the entire chamber music repertory. In the autumn of 1826, following his nephew Karl's attempted suicide, Beethoven visited the country for the last time; he and his brother Johann, with the convalescent Karl, stayed nearly ten weeks in Johann's house near Krems. Though already seriously ill, the composer managed to complete the F major Quartet and the alternative finale to the Quartet in B flat, op. 130. When he returned to Vienna in December he was suffering from jaundice and dropsy; a liver complaint supervened. Little could be done for him beyond alleviating his pain. In a will drawn up a few days before the end he left everything to Karl; he died in the afternoon of 26 March, and was buried three days later at the Währing cemetery after a funeral procession witnessed by an immense concourse of people.

Beethoven, like Mozart and Schubert, seldom lived for long in one apartment—it has been estimated that he had well over 40 changes of address during his 35 years in Vienna (by comparison, Mozart moved 17 times in 16 years, and Schubert 20 times in his 31 years). Beethoven liked to spend the winters in Vienna, favouring houses with a view over the glacis (the defensive plain between the city walls and the suburbs); in summer he liked to be in the suburbs (Heiligenstadt, Nussdorf, Grinzing, Hetzendorf) or the country (Mödling, the Helenental, Baden). In 1888 Beethoven's remains were reinterred in the Zentralfriedhof; they lie near those of Schubert and Mozart.

Of all the great Viennese composers, only Schubert was actually born in Vienna—and even he was the son of a schoolmaster who had emigrated from Moravia, and a mother from Austrian Silesia. **Franz**

Schubert was born on 31 January 1797 in the house now numbered Nussdorferstrasse 54 and carefully restored since the Second World War as a Schubert museum. The boy Schubert showed early talent, and at the age of ten he was accepted as a chorister at the famous Stadtkonvikt, or boarding-school for commoners, where he had ample opportunities. He was soon leading, and composing for, the school orchestra; he made good friends; he had the opportunity to conduct; and he had lessons from Salieri (whose pivotal position in Viennese music is indicated by his friendly relations with Haydn, his rivalry with Mozart, and by his short-lived position as pupil of Gluck and teacher of Beethoven).

Schubert, by Wilhelm August Rieder

Schubert's earliest surviving works date from 1810. They show how well he absorbed the achievements of his great predecessors, and the String Quartet in E flat, D 87, already shows glimpses of the mature composer as well as a firm grasp of the medium—Schubert, his brothers and father played quartets together. By the age of 17 Schubert had composed a quantity of songs, piano and chamber music, and had abandoned one and completed another opera. Schubert's hopes for a successful career as a theatre composer—

evinced by his love of the operas of Gluck, Weigl, Beethoven, Weber, Rossini—form what is arguably the most tantalising, even the most destructive, thread in his career. For he failed to learn from his mistakes, indeed hardly had the chance to, so seldom was any of his operatic music actually performed. Yet he persisted in tackling nearly 20 operatic projects, none of them very successful then or since, despite the beauty (and occasional dramatic effectiveness) of much of the music.

Autumn 1814 marks the decisive breakthrough from talented boy to outstanding genius. At the same time as he was starting to work as assistant teacher in his father's school he was completing the Mass in F, D 105, which was performed in two churches with much acclaim, and wrote 'Gretchen am Spinnrade'. 1815 was a miraculous year— four operas and Singspiels, two symphonies, two masses, a quantity of piano music, a string quartet, and no fewer than 145 songs, including 'Heidenröslein' and 'Erlkönig'. He also gained the friendship of the poet Johann Mayrhofer, and of Franz von Schober (in whose rooms the famous 'Schubertiads' were to take place, with the composer at the piano and Vogl or Baron Schönstein singing).

The course of Schubert's life was now established. For a little longer he put up with teaching, but he would soon be sustained by a growing circle of appreciative friends, occasional public acclaim, a mere trickle of mainly quite small fees for commissioned works, and a stream—now and again broadening into a flood, and sometimes almost drying up—of masterpieces in almost every field of composition. In July 1818 he left Vienna for a while, to act as music-teacher at Zseliz in Hungary to the daughters of Count Johann Esterházy; in summer 1819 he accompanied Johann Michael Vogl—a famous operatic baritone now almost at the end of his stage career, and then already beginning to earn a more durable niche in music history as the singer of Schubert's songs—to Vogl's birthplace, Steyr. The beauty of the countryside, and the relaxed atmosphere with much music-making, delighted Schubert; he began to write the 'Trout' Quintet, and whenever possible he returned to this region. Despite disappointments, of which Goethe's rejection of the proffered dedication of a collection of settings of his lyrics was perhaps the most severe, Schubert was gaining in confidence and esteem, thanks in part to a number of favourable notices in the Austrian and German press. His one-act Singspiel 'Die Zwillingsbrüder' was staged at the Court Opera in summer 1820, followed by his melodrama 'Die Zauberharfe'.

Throughout his life Schubert left works unfinished. Sometimes he wrote only a few bars, or sketches; others of the incomplete works— the oratorio 'Lazarus', the so-called 'Quartettsatz' (1820), and the B minor Symphony (1822)—are among his grandest achievements. He probably intended to return to these works after a more pressing task had been dealt with. Certainly it cannot often have been the pressure of a commission that led to the abandonment—Schubert received few commissions. Nor did he easily find publishers for his works, despite the fact that he wrote widely in the then-popular fields of solo and duet piano music, songs and concerted vocal music, and that he was gaining recognition for works performed in public concerts and private gatherings. The pictures that survive by Leopold Kupelwieser, and especially by Moritz von Schwind, create a delightful and nostalgic atmosphere of gaiety with friends, pretty ladies, and music. The harsher side of this life is revealed in Schubert's contracting venereal disease in 1822, which in his remaining years caused him much misery. Who knows, though, perhaps the increased poignancy of his songs, the sublime radiance of the later chamber works, the power of the Symphony in C (written mainly in 1825, on some of the same manuscript paper which Beethoven used for his A minor Quartet in the same year), the intense originality of the last piano sonatas, may all owe something to his determination to rise above the pain and shame brought about by his illness.

Certainly the last five years saw an astonishing outpouring of compositions of every kind, and in a profusion which even Mozart and Haydn hardly matched. Yet all this music brought him scant financial reward. He survived as an independent composer, thanks largely to generous friends; but only just. He lacked the toughness, even cussedness, that helped Beethoven; and he lacked interpretative skills and sheer charisma; and of course, Schubert died at an age when Beethoven was only just beginning to emerge in his true stature. He passed his final weeks with his brother Ferdinand, in what is now the Kettenbrückengasse. He had recently finished 'Schwanengesang', the last sonatas, the String Quintet, the Mass in E flat, and that haunting song 'Der Hirt auf dem Felsen'; he read the proofs of part II of 'Winterreise' on his deathbed. His last known request, in a note to Schober, was to borrow novels by Fenimore Cooper. Some friends came to see him, others stayed away (probably frightened of catching what was diagnosed as typhoid). He died on 19 November 1828 at 3 pm. He was buried two days later at the Währing cemetery, close to Beethoven. Two years later, a monument was erected, inscribed with an epitaph by Austria's greatest poet, Franz Grillparzer: 'The art of music entombed here a rich possession, but yet far fairer hopes.'

Popular Music: the Operetta. The deaths of Beethoven and Schubert within the space of 20 months left a gap that could never be filled; into the vacuum, however, were drawn a large number of foreign musicians—most notably *Franz Liszt* (1811–86), and *Thalberg* (1812–71), but also many other composers and virtuosos from both sides of the Alps. Public and private concert-giving was on the increase—the splendid new building of the Gesellschaft der Musikfreunde on the Karlsplatz was opened in 1831, the Philharmonic Concerts were inaugurated, and the great era of choral singing was boosted by the growing popularity of the male-voice choir.

Perhaps the most interesting phenomenon of the age after Beethoven and Schubert is the creation of a dividing-line between 'classical' and 'light' music. Haydn and Mozart, like their great successors, wrote a quantity of dance music; after the 1820s a gradual divergence of paths can be discerned. Of course many of the great composers of the last seven decades of the century wrote dances—Chopin, Brahms, and Dvořák, are obvious examples. But theirs were not pieces for dancing so much as reflective recreations of melodic and rhythmic figures which have their origins in the dance. For true dance-music one turns to the first great specialist composers, Lanner and the Strausses.

Joseph Lanner (1801–43) was at twelve already a violinist in Michael Pamer's orchestra; **Johann Strauss the Elder** (1804–49) was a viola-player in the group at an even younger age. While still in his teens Lanner had his own ensemble, which he built up until it was quite a large orchestra. For a time Strauss directed half of the orchestra, which was divided into two because of the amount of work they were invited to undertake. Lanner's dances—waltzes, galops, ländler, mazurkas—are elegant and pleasingly lyrical, with deft creation of mood and witty thematic allusions. Strauss is more robust, both in the bold rhythmic élan of his music and in his career as executant—in his mid-20s he was music director at the place of entertainment 'Zum Sperl', and before he was 30 he was already taking his 28-strong orchestra on extended, and highly successful, European tours. In 1838 he played at Buckingham Palace during the celebrations of Queen Victoria's coronation; in 1846 he secured a Viennese court appointment. His compositions were often linked to, but the best of them have far outlived, particular occasions. Apart from waltzes he wrote many galops, quadrilles, marches (including the ever-famous 'Radetzky-Marsch'), polkas and potpourris.

His son **Johann Strauss the Younger** (1825–99) was even more successful, not only in developing characteristic dance-forms, but also in writing almost 20 stage works which include the ever-popular 'Die Fledermaus' (1874) and 'Der Zigeunerbaron' (1885). His melodic piquancy and charm make him the waltz-composer par excellence— and also the admired friend or exemplar of many of the great classical composers of his own and later ages, including Wagner, Brahms, and Schönberg. Although Viennese operetta is often thought to have originated with Strauss, its beginnings lie earlier. The native theatre songs of *Adolf Müller* and others are one strand; another is *Offenbach*'s brand of operetta, which was illegally imported in the late 1850s during Nestroy's final years as director of the Carltheater—Offenbach's one-acters were orchestrated by *Carl Binder* and others from pirated vocal scores.

The decisive turning-point was the première of 'Das Pensionat' (1860) by the highly experienced theatre-composer **Franz von Suppé** (1819–95), who moved on to greater triumphs with 'Die schöne Galathea', 'Fatinitza', and 'Boccaccio', and to become music-director at the Kaitheater, and Carltheater. His overtures, for long favourites of the military band repertoire, have kept his name alive, though at least in Austria revivals of his operettas prove popular. The dominance of Johann Strauss and Suppé lasted into the early 1880s, by when they had been joined by *Carl Millöcker* ('Gräfin Dubarry', 1879; the still popular 'Der Bettelstudent', 1882; 'Gasparone', 1884). Another feature of light music at this time was the foundation of the *Schrammel* Quartet—two violinist brothers who, with a bass-guitar and later a G clarinet, accompanied popular Viennese songs in the Heurigen (the village wine-houses). By the mid-1890s, accordion had replaced clarinet, and the Wiener Lied had attained its classic form: sentimental, nostalgic, yet piquant too.

The next generation of operetta-composers was that of *Carl Zeller* ('Der Vogelhändler', 1891; 'Der Obersteiger', 1894) and *Richard Heuberger* ('Der Opernball', 1898)—Heuberger is also remembered as a choral conductor and music critic, and as the author of a biography of Schubert (he was related by marriage to the Schubert family).

Franz Lehár (1870–1948) ushered in, and dominated, the 'Silver Age' of Viennese operetta. 'Die lustige Witwe' was first heard in that mecca of the genre, the Theater an der Wien, in 1905. A succession of memorable scores followed—'Der Graf von Luxemburg' (1909), 'Zigeunerliebe' (1910), 'Paganini' (1925), 'Der Zarewitsch' (1927), 'Friederike' (1928), and 'Das Land des Lächelns' (1929)—the last three were first performed in Berlin, which had replaced Vienna as the operetta centre). Lehár's last work was 'Giuditta', commissioned for the Vienna State Opera (1934), an interesting score that lies between the normal dividing-lines of opera and operetta. Thanks above all to *Richard Tauber*, the tenor songs of Lehár have established a special place in the affections of three generations of music-lovers. *Oscar Straus* ('Ein Walzertraum', 1907) and *Leo Fall* ('Die Dollarprinzessin', 1907) provided strong rivalry, and *Ralph Benatzky* and *Robert Stolz* also enjoyed many successes. But the most resilient of all the final generation of operetta composers was *Emmerich Kálmán* (1882–1953), Hungarian by birth and often in musical style and setting, whose 'The Gay Hussars' (1908), 'Die Csardasfürstin' (1915), and especially 'Gräfin Mariza' (1924), have an appealing vitality and melodic freshness.

The Later Nineteenth Century. Having pursued the course of light music, we must return to some major figures in Austrian music history in the second half of the nineteenth century. **Anton Bruckner**

Anton Bruckner

(born Ansfelden, near Linz, 4 September 1824; died Vienna, 11 October 1896) is a totally distinctive phenomenon. From lowly origins in the Upper Austrian countryside he developed slowly, with many self-questionings and retracing of footsteps, towards the highly individual mastery of symphonic form achieved in his later works. His formative years were spent in the Augustinian monastery of St. Florian, first as chorister, later as organist and school-teacher. This eternal student studied harmony and counterpoint with *Simon Sechter*, professor at the Vienna Conservatory and once Schubert's teacher, from 1855, mainly by correspondence, and even when he had graduated with his diploma in 1861 (and had been cathedral organist at Linz for six years), he took lessons from *Otto Kitzler*, cellist and conductor at the Linz Theatre, in practical orchestral technique. Bruckner's experience of *Wagner*'s 'Tannhäuser', at the age of nearly 40, was crucial, and to be measured less in terms of thematic quotation and use of Wagnerian formulae than in harmonic boldness and formal adventurousness.

Bruckner's maturity can be dated to the three masses of 1864 to 1868. By 1868 too he had been finally persuaded to move to Vienna, to take up Sechter's post with a better salary, and also with the reversion of the post of organist at the imperial chapel. He also appeared with outstanding success at organ festivals in France and England (1869, 1871). Yet his ingrained humility and lack of self-confidence left him prey not only to personal doubts (for all that he was deeply religious) but also to the damaging advice of well-meaning, misguided friends, at whose behest Bruckner spent many months revising and re-writing earlier compositions, usually to their detriment. Nevertheless, the last 25 years of his life witnessed an extraordinary broadening and deepening of his musical language and symphonic mastery. Over those years he produced in two great waves Symphonies Nos 2 to 5 (1871–76) and 6 to 9 (1879 to his death), a single-minded progress interrupted only by a few vocal works and the String Quintet—and by increasing problems with his health. In his lifetime he met with limited success or understanding; his time has come in the second half of the twentieth century.

Johannes Brahms (born Hamburg, 7 May 1833; died Vienna, 3 April 1897) knew abundant success in his lifetime. He was 29 when, in autumn 1862, he settled in Vienna. He was already renowned as a pianist, and as a composer had the First Piano Concerto, the orchestral Serenades, B flat Sextet, Handel Variations, and a number of songs to his credit. He was well connected, with *Joachim*, and *Clara Schumann* among his friends. He soon made an impact in Vienna, both as composer (with the Piano Quartets in G minor, and A major) and as executant—though an official post as conductor of the Singakademie did not prove very happy, and he gave up a later appointment as director of the Gesellschaftskonzerte after three seasons. As pianist he continued to enjoy great success, and indeed he toured often and widely with his own works, still hoping for the call to a distinguished post in his home town or elsewhere in Germany.

From 1875, when he withdrew from conducting on a regular basis, he had more time for composition. By now the Variations on a Theme by Haydn (actually not by Haydn at all) were completed, as well as the German Requiem, and the First Symphony was approaching completion. From the late 1870s date many fine songs, the Second Symphony, and the Violin Concerto, and he was fêted wherever he went—the adulation of his lady admirers even caused him to find

Brahms in December 1896

alternatives to his favourite summer retreat of Pörtschach on the Wörthersee. During the 1880s the spate of new compositions continued, with two overtures, the Second Piano Concerto, the last two symphonies, the Double Concerto, various chamber works, and a number of songs and other vocal pieces. *Hans von Bülow* generously placed the Meiningen Court Orchestra at Brahms's disposal as a rehearsal orchestra, and he also toured with them and gave several concerts. After so much creative activity, a lull was not surprising; but Brahms's meeting with the clarinettist *Richard Mühlfeld* led to a renewal of vigour in summer 1891, with the Trio, and Quintet, both featuring the clarinet; the pair of Clarinet Sonatas followed three summers later. In between, Brahms wrote the lovely sets of late piano fantasias, intermezzos and pieces, and in the last complete year of his life he wrote the Four Serious Songs and the set of organ preludes. He was unwell that summer, suffering from jaundice, he thought. In fact—though it was kept from him—he had cancer of the liver; he grew progressively weaker, and died on 3 April 1897. He was buried at the Zentralfriedhof three days later, mourned by music-lovers from all over Germany and Austria.

Of an altogether younger generation, but inevitably drawn to take sides in the controversy which separated Brahms and the musical establishment on the one side, and Bruckner and the Wagnerians on the other, are two powerful individuals whose paths diverged after youthful friendship: Hugo Wolf and Gustav Mahler. **Hugo Wolf** (1860–1903) is one of the outstanding specialists in musical history. He came to Vienna from southernmost Styria in 1875, but his formal studies did not proceed smoothly, and much of his short life was spent in elegant, slightly bohemian society, encouraged and cared for by generous friends. He swung between elation and despair, periods of intense creativity alternating with periods of utter sterility. He began to find his calling as a Lieder composer while still in his teens, but he cherished larger-scale ambitions as well; and for a period in the 1880s he was a lively, passionately committed, music-critic. His fame rests mainly on the extraordinary outpouring of songs in a three-year spell either side of his thirtieth birthday: 53 settings of Mörike (mainly composed between March and September 1888), 20 of Eichendorff (mainly written in September 1888), 51 Goethe songs (mainly of November/December 1888 and January 1889), and the two collections of translations from Italian and Spanish poets made by Heyse and Geibel: the 44 settings of the 'Spanish Songbook' of 1889–90, and the 46 of the 'Italian Songbook' (part 1 mainly written in 1891, part 2, after a sterile period, in 1896). In the second creative period of his maturity he also wrote the seldom-performed opera 'Der Corregidor', and the three Michelangelo settings of 1897. Thereafter,

Mahler

he was committed to an asylum; there were brief periods of remission, but he never recovered his sanity. His songs are still a minority taste; to the growing number of devotees, they are even more perceptive, penetrating and precise than the songs of Schubert—near whom he lies buried in the Zentralfriedhof in Vienna.

Gustav Mahler (1860–1911) came from Bohemia to study at the Vienna Conservatory in 1875; he also studied rather haphazardly at the University. In 1880, by which time he had written his huge cantata 'Das klagende Lied', part of an opera, and some songs to his own texts, he was appointed conductor at the theatre at Bad Hall. From this time on he was busy pursuing a double career as conductor and composer, the main stages of his conducting career being Laibach, Olmütz, Kassel, Prague, Leipzig, Budapest—all for brief periods during his steady rise to eminence; and Hamburg, where he became first conductor in 1891. In 1897, having been baptised into the Roman Catholic church in an attempt to overcome anti-Semitism, he was appointed director of the Vienna Court Opera. His decade there is regarded as one of the most splendid in its history, with artistic integrity, careful preparation, and close attention to the visual aspects of the performance, among the virtues. All through these years Mahler devoted what time he could, especially during his summers, to composition; by the time he left Vienna for New York at the end of 1907 he had completed the first eight symphonies and all the song-cycles. The years of frenetic activity were taking their toll; Mahler was already suffering from a heart condition, and his conducting activities at the Metropolitan Opera, and later with the New York Philharmonic, in the winter seasons, and his composing and conducting of his own works in Europe in the summers (the triumphant première of the Eighth Symphony took place in Munich in September 1910), must have weakened him further. He fell ill in New York in January 1911, from a bacterial infection, and died in Vienna soon after his return in May.

The Twentieth Century. The end of the nineteenth century and beginning of the twentieth was a period of intense artistic activity in Vienna, with public taste largely aligned behind the upholders of tradition, and a probably unparalleled profusion of fresh stimuli calling the old order into question. Freud, and Adler, in psychology; Klimt, and Schiele, in painting; Schnitzler in drama; Hofmannsthal in the lyric; Mahler, and Schönberg in music,—all were powerful innovators. Further, they helped break down the barriers between disciplines—Schönberg was also active as a painter, Mahler's innovatory work at the Opera owed much to the brilliant stage designer Alfred Roller, Schnitzler's plays and prose fiction reveal the doctor and student of psychology, Oskar Kokoschka wrote Expressionist plays as well as being one of the great painters; for all the differences between them, Karl Kraus, and Hofmannsthal were both profoundly aware of the crisis of language—as, later, was Paul Wittgenstein (architect and teacher as well as philosopher).

Yet it was the language of music that was to change most startlingly, and **Arnold Schönberg** (born Vienna, 13 September 1874; died Los Angeles, 13 July 1951) was the chief architect of that change—though anyone hearing his Brahms-influenced early piano pieces or D major String Quartet, or the vast 'Gurrelieder' from his Wagnerian phase, would not have expected it. The young Schönberg, initially self-taught, was greatly helped and encouraged by *Alexander von Zemlinsky* (1872–1942; whose own compositions are

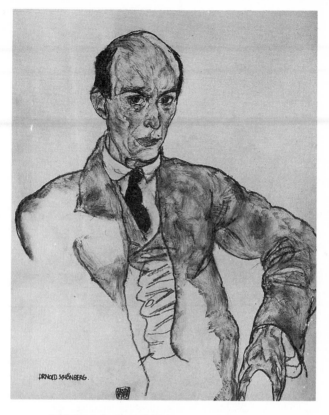

Schönberg, by Egon Schiele

now receiving welcome and overdue acclaim), and the successful hearing of the String Quartet at a concert of the Tonkünstlerverein in 1898 seemed to promise a break-through. The String Sextet 'Verklärte Nacht' was turned down the next year, however, and Schönberg had to undertake conducting and the orchestration of operettas to make ends meet. He married Zemlinsky's sister in 1901 and the couple tried their fortunes in Berlin. They returned to Vienna 18 months later with the score of the symphonic poem 'Pelleas und Melisande' complete, and *Richard Strauss*'s approval of it and 'Gurrelieder' a boost to Schönberg's confidence. He was able to find temporary employment teaching harmony and counterpoint, and in the autumn of 1904 Berg and Webern joined the group of pupils.

Given the conservative taste of Viennese audiences, public performances of their music were to be infrequent and seldom successful, so they began to organise private performances, and artists of the calibre of Mahler and his brother-in-law *Arnold Rosé* (leader of the Vienna Philharmonic Orchestra and of his String Quartet) lent their support. The works that Schönberg now completed—the first two numbered String Quartets, First Chamber Symphony, the song-cycle

'Das Buch der hängenden Gärten', the Five Orchestral Pieces opus 16 and the Piano Pieces opus 11—were greeted with more or less chilling incomprehension as Schönberg moved away from traditional tonal definition and towards the atonality of some movements in the last two of those works (1909). The opera 'Erwartung' dates from the same year. A period of retrenchment followed, with the theoretical 'Harmonielehre', and completion of the orchestration of 'Gurrelieder'. In 1911 Schönberg returned to Berlin, tired of the hostility of the Viennese, and began to make some headway, both there and internationally (Sir Henry Wood gave the Five Orchestral Pieces in London in 1912, and in 1913 'Gurrelieder' was performed with startling success in Vienna).

During the war years Schönberg's poor health restricted his military involvement; he returned to Vienna, worked at the oratorio 'Die Jakobsleiter', taught, and from shortly after the end of the war, was the guiding spirit behind the Society for Private Musical Performances. The early to middle 1920s were also the decisive years in the formulation of serialism: the Piano Pieces opus 23, Serenade, and Wind Quintet (1920–24) are the first fruits of dodecaphony (though *Josef Matthias Hauer*, 1883–1959, had independently, and somewhat earlier, reached similar if less far-reaching conclusions). In 1925 Schönberg went to Berlin for the last time; his second wife (his first wife had died in 1923) and some of his pupils went with him. He was in charge of the composition master-class at the Prussian Academy of Arts, and favourable circumstances encouraged a new creative period in which he wrote some of his most famous works: the Suite, the Variations for Orchestra, Third String Quartet, and the unfinished opera 'Moses und Aron'. In 1931 he moved into exile—his asthma was the prime cause of his move to Spain, but growing anti-Semitism made a return to Germany impossible, and in 1933 he and his family moved to America. Schönberg spent most of his last 17 years in Hollywood and Los Angeles, teaching, and above all composing the series of late masterpieces. His music has yet to be taken up seriously into the concert and operatic life of his native land, though the 1973 Vienna Festival staging of 'Moses und Aron', and the fine exhibition held there in summer 1974 (the catalogue of which is an essential documentary source), have gone some way towards making amends for three-quarters of a century of near-neglect.

Of Schönberg's two most famous pupils, **Alban Berg** (1885–1935) is the better known and more popular—in the limited sense that his operas 'Wozzeck' and 'Lulu', the Altenberg Songs, Lyric Suite, Chamber Concerto, and Violin Concerto are quite often performed, and give more pleasure to the average music-lover than do any of the works of the other two masters of the Second Viennese School. Apart from three years' war service (mainly a desk job, as he suffered from poor health), Berg's life was fairly uneventful, and he seldom left his native Vienna for long. He was not a performing musician, which limited his income but gave him leisure for composition; he often attended performances of his own and Schönberg's music, as well as meetings of the ISCM, wherever in Europe they were held. He loved the Carinthian countryside (as had Brahms), and in 1932 he purchased the 'Waldhaus' near Velden (though he could hardly afford it). It was there, in the summer of 1935, that what is believed to have been an insect-bite led to the blood-poisoning from which he died on Christmas Eve of that year. The combination of intellectual rigour and Romantic warmth in Berg's music has helped keep it before the public; his two operas reveal a mastery of the stage, as well as a compassion and musical beauty, that have kept them at least on the verges of the repertoire; *Friedrich Cerha's* realisation of the incomplete Act III of 'Lulu' in 1979, three years after Berg's widow's death had removed the obstacle to its release and performance, has given fresh impetus to Berg's cause.

The most enigmatic, and perhaps to prove the most influential, of the 'big three' of the Second Viennese School, is **Anton (von) Webern** (1883–1945). After a childhood spent in the provinces he studied at Vienna University, gaining a doctorate in musicology (significantly, in view of his own mastery of polyphonic devices, for a thesis on Heinrich Isaac). By then he had been Schönberg's pupil for two years and become a close friend of his fellow-pupil, the later expert on Byzantine music, and powerful symphonist, *Egon Wellesz* (1885–1974). The earliest work which Webern himself acknowledged was the Passacaglia for orchestra, opus 1 (1908). From that year he eked out a living by conducting in various Austrian and German towns, whilst continuing to compose, soon shaking off the influence of Wagner and Brahms, and ultimately developing his own brand of atonalism. Poor eyesight limited his military service in the war years; after, he settled near Schönberg at Mödling, sharing the work involved with the Society for Private Musical Performances, and directing several choirs. His fame as a conductor grew, but his music was rarely performed and seldom appreciated, and his impeccable Aryan ancestry was not enough to save him from accusations of decadence when the Nazis came to power; during his last years he had to resort to menial tasks to make a living. As is well known, his death a few weeks after the end of the war in Europe was a tragic accident—he was shot outside his son-in-law's house at Mittersill (cf.) by an American soldier. The extraordinary concision of his oeuvre is neatly indicated by the fact that his 31 completed and numbered works, plus a representative selection of his early pieces, are easily accommodated on four long-playing records. Music is here reduced to its bare essentials, yet in a committed performance these richly varied works come over with a precision and power that enable us to appreciate their seminal force in post-war musical developments.

Epilogue. Any historical survey is bound to be incomplete. Readers may, like the author, regret the absence of composers as distinguished as *Franz Schreker* (1878–1934), whose 'Der ferne Klang', and 'Die Gezeichneten', either side of the First War, are distinguished operas; and *Ernst Křenek* (born 1900), whose 'Jonny spielt auf' enjoyed phenomenal success following its première in 1927; *Franz Schmidt* (1874–1939), *Hans Gál* (1890–1987), and *Franz Salmhofer* (1900–75) are others of an older generation whom it would have been nice to include; of a more recent generation, *Gottfried von Einem* (born 1918) has proved a versatile and successful composer of stage works in particular; of younger contemporaries, *Friedrich Čerha* (born 1926), *Roman Haubenstock-Ramati* (born 1919), and *György Ligeti* (born 1923) have already built up strong international reputations. Yet the three masters of the Second Viennese School form a convenient as well as a crucially important stopping-point.

Skiing in Austria

by *Mark Heller*

Skiing and Austria have become synonyms. An impartial observer in the 1920s could never have predicted that 60 years later Austria would be able to promote more than 400 skiing villages and have served as the prototype for the modern, purpose-built resorts in North and South America, Australia, and New Zealand.

This same impartial source would have found the ski hills and mountains of Austria to be short, small, unchallenging and lacking any great peaks or ranges worthy of publicity. Paradoxically it is precisely these non-features and the unchanged small-village atmosphere which has proved to be the attraction. Possibly tired and disillusioned by the great, soulless skidromes, visitors find in these gentle hills and old farming villages the very charm which first attracted the holiday skiers of the 1920s and 1930s. As those skiers reported, it was quite simply 'good skiing ground'.

To generalise, Austrian skiing is based on a farming village with easy and rapid access to the valley meadows which are the ideal nursery ground and which lead without any impossibly steep slopes through the lightly forested upper slopes. These upper slopes have, after a thousand or more years of farming by the original immigrant Rhaetian and Walser peasants, been transformed into summer grazing. It is this gently contoured hillside that made the construction of the skiers' transport—the drag lift and chair—cheap to install and easy to maintain. At the same time, parish politics and rivalry has kept these villages, often close enough to be almost contiguous, as individual centres in their own right, refusing obstinately to link up with neighbours and share their skiing visitors. Slowly, however, this ancient pattern is being blurred by economic necessity. The visiting skier, conditioned by the long, linked runs of the modern French resorts and the ever-extending ski networks in Switzerland, expects to find neighbours such as Söll, Ellmau and Going one continuous ski resort. It took more than 20 years for this to become reality.

The history of skiing in Austria makes this hesitant development more comprehensible. The undisputed father of Austrian skiing—and alpine skiing world-wide—was *Mathias Zdarsky* (1856–1940). Failed poet, indifferent artist, fanatic gymnast, he acquired, by post, a pair of Norwegian skis with which he taught himself to ski on far steeper slopes than those for which these boards had been designed. He perfected techniques for steep alpine ground—later called the Stem and Stem Christiania—and, settling in *Lilienfeld*, not far W of Vienna, founded in 1896 the first Alpine Ski School. Among his many pupils was a certain *Viktor Sohm* who, in turn, founded his own school on the Arlberg Hospiz, *St. Christoph*. Among his pupils were the three *Schneider* brothers from Stuben. Of these Hannes, after teaching in St. Anton, founded the **Arlberg Ski School** in *St. Anton, Stuben, Zürs,* and *Lech*. It was the cornerstone of the dramatic impact of Austrian skiing.

A German film maker, Dr Arnold Fanck, gave the Arlberg school the publicity which led to its world-wide fame. 'Das Wunder des Scheeschnuhs', the film he made in 1920–21, and the subsequent book published in 1926 of still photographs culled from the film, amazed the non-skiing world for whom the sport was little more than an eccentricity. Quite incidentally it also gave the Arlberg and its four settlements an international reputation and guest list. St. Anton, St. Christoph, Stube, Zürs, and Lech became the mecca for all serious skiers and their followers.

Kitzbühel, conveniently located on the Arlberg rail line to Vienna, and already a well-known summer resort, became the fashionable destination during the 'gay twenties'. The ski mountaineers, summer mountaineers who had taken to skis, rediscovered the ski pleasures of the Oetztal, Stubai, and Silvretta while the Swiss and German railways ran special excursion trains for them from Zürich, Basle, Bern, and Munich.

The final step to popularity was the invention by *Erich Konstam* of Zürich of the T-bar drag lift in 1934. These installations provided even the smallest village with easy, cheap and simple transport to the treeless upper slopes, and literally overnight, numerous sleepy villages awoke to the economic advantages of tourism.

In the early 1930s *Erna Low* and *Major Ingham* inaugurated the first popularly priced package tours from England to a limited list of villages in the Vorarlberg and Arlberg. They depended on proximity to a main railway line, and this automatically limited their initial choice. In actual numbers it was a very limited operation and was completely overshadowed by the German and Austrian skiers who, with much shorter distances to travel, flooded the villages.

After the Second World War, when the occupying allied troops had vacated their carefully chosen mountain resorts, the French had their headquarters in the Zürserhof in Zürs, the Americans occupied the Gasteiner Tal and, arguably, installed the first chair-lift in Europe from Bad Gastein to the Graukogel—a very temporary structure. The great lift-off to winter tourism was almost fortuitous. The Marshall Aid Plan, designed to restore destroyed industry and commerce, saw no objection to subsidising the reconstruction and creation of the infrastructure necessary for a ski holiday resort. In this manner hundreds of tiny Tirolean hamlets installed a basic ski-lift, refurnished and enlarged the village inn, and offered themselves for sale to the tourist industry. In addition to Ingham and Erna Low, among the first to take this bait were the new British tour operators, the Clarksons, Lunn-Polys and SkiPlans. Between them they introduced the holiday-hungry British to what are now virtually household names—Mayrhofen, Westerndorf, Brand, Alpbach, Schruns and Gargellen—to list but a few. It was the beginning of apparently irreversible growth.

Today skiing in Austria is centred on the Vorarlberg, the Tirol, and Salzburg, and, to a lesser extent, in East Tirol, and Carinthia. Within these boundaries one can class the kind of skiing available into five general categories.

The single mountain, single village resort is the backbone of the Austrian skiing industry. The villages are low-lying by ski standards—below the 1000m level and mostly around 700m. The ski terrain extends, theoretically, up to about 2000m, but very few of the villages can claim slopes of that height. The lower reaches of these ski fields are lightly forested and well cleared, with easy access to the treeless summer grazing. Ski transport is rarely more than a basic lift—chair or drag—to a main assembly area and restaurant from where one or more lifts service the highest point suitable for skiing. This arrangement is essential in view of the low altitude of the resort where snow may vanish long before the upper meadows are made unskiable. Examples of this kind of village are *Alpbach* in the Wildschönau, one of the prettiest villages in the Tirol, or *Westerndorf* near Kitzbühel. The Tirol alone can list more than 200 such villages. But newcomers should be careful not to choose one which is too small and limited, with little more than a nursery lift on a village meadow, because even this will be listed as a 'ski resort'.

A second category is the village complex of linked ski resorts. *Kitzbühel*, the world's first ski 'circus', links *Jochberg*, *Aurach*, and *Kirchberg* with the main centre of Kitzbühel itself. Slightly less prestigious, but more far-ranging, are the villages of *Söll*, *Going*, *Ellmau*, and *Brixen im Thale*. Rather more exciting skiing will be found in the steep complex of *Hinterglemm*, *Saalbach*, and *Leogang* in Salzburg. The longest such linkage is the so-called *Salzburg Schaukel* which loosely combines *St. Johann*, *Wagrain*, *Flachau*, *Altenmark Dienten*, and *Maria Alm*, a total ski distance of 120km.

Thirdly, and unique, is the ski-bus linked chain of resorts surrounding *Innsbruck*. From this centre, with a minimum of travel, the skier can visit *Seefeld*, *Igls*, *Tulfes*, *Mutters*, *Götzens*, and *Axams*, with options along the Brenner Pass of *Oberperfuss*, *Steinach*, and the resorts of the Stubai valley.

Fourthly, there are the so-called summer ski areas, the glacier ski resorts where skiing is possible for 12 months in the year. Unlike similar skiing in France, Switzerland, and Italy, access to the ski-fields is easy, and distances are short, though for the most part the actual skiing, as is the case over most glaciers, is also simple and short. The 'Europe Sport Region' *Zell am See* offers the Kitzsteinhorn from the resort of *Kaprun*; an underground funicular provides access. The *Stubai Valley* has quite extensive skiing above the Dresdener Hut, reached by gondola from the end of the valley above Neustift. The *Oetztal* has developed skiing on the Rettenbach glaciers, reached by road from Sölden. The best of Austrian glacier skiing is to be found on the Tuxer glaciers, culminating at the summit of the Gfrorene Wand 3260, and is reached by gondola from Hintertux, at the end of the *Zillertal* where there are no less than seven ski resorts, including the British-dominated resort, *Mayrhofen*.

And then there is St. Anton and the Arlberg, where it all began over 60 years ago and, today, still one of the better ski regions of Europe. The day Zürs and St. Anton are lift-linked will be the culmination of a remarkable ski success story.

Austrian ski slopes have been in the forefront in providing excellent facilities for Nordic, Cross Country skiers, and there is hardly a resort, major or minor, which has not excellently maintained 'loipes'. Notable among these are those bordering the Wilder Kaiser mountains, Going, Ellmau, Söll and St. Johann. But Seefeld, close to Innsbruck and one of the foremost resorts, focuses entirely on all aspects of the Nordic disciplines. It has been the site for two Winter Olympics and one World Championship, and the trails available for every skier cover the entire range, from simple teaching ovals to day-long 30km trails extending deep into the picturesque Mieminger plateau.

Although the Austrian ski resorts are essentially 'ski-only' centres, many also advertise extensive winter walks and other entertainments such as hang-gliding, hot-air ballooning, etc. Most of the larger resorts also promote natural ice-rink skating, though the surface offered is often small and ill-prepared. A few centres have built extensive indoor ice facilities, mainly for curling, and Innsbruck and Kitzbühel have competition-sized rinks. Apart from the Olympic runs at Innsbruck, proper luge-runs are rare; on the other hand, nearly every village has a suitable country road which on given evenings is barred to traffic and opened to lugers for races and snow-games.

The Ski Club of Great Britain. As in all the Alpine countries, the SCGB maintains a number of representatives in selected resorts. Their function is to provide an advice and skiing service for their members. The location of these representatives varies from year to year and also during the course of the winter season. Snow-state reports from these centres are sent regularly to their London head-quarters and are reprinted in *The Times, Telegraph*, and *Guardian*. In addition, the Club headquarters at 118 Eaton Square, London SW3 (tel. 071-245 1033), maintains a library of information on most of the Austrian ski resorts. See also p 98.

Mountaineering in Austria

by *Geoffrey Pearson*

There is no better place for the novice to become acquainted with the Alps, than in Austria. About 70 per cent of the total area is covered by the mountains and foothills of the Eastern Alps, and there is a comprehensive network of well-marked paths which link up more than 700 mountain refuges or huts run by various Alpine organisa-tions. Hut-to-hut touring is, therefore, very popular and is the best way of getting to know any particular region. This may be done at many levels of altitude and difficulty. To begin with there are the straightforward marked paths from the valley bases to the huts, which are continued either along the sides of the valley or over a pass to the next hut. Sometimes there is an alternative rougher track, usually marked on the map with red dots and labelled 'Nur für Geübte'; this is the scrambler's route and requires a steady gait and occasional use of the hands. Then there are the climber's routes which involve glaciers, snow slopes, and rock ridges, and take in the principal peaks of the district. Generally the climbing is in the easier or middle grades of difficulty. The peaks are not so high as those in the Western Alps and the climbs tend to be shorter and difficulties not so sustained. They provide an excellent training ground for the young and are well suited to the middle-aged mountaineer who may find the 4000-metre peaks of Switzerland a little too demanding. However, they should not be underestimated, for to be caught out in bad weather is always a serious matter in the Alps and an expedition which is perfectly easy in fine weather may become difficult and even dangerous if the weather deteriorates.

Mountain Huts. Austria is fortunate in having such a wide-spread system of huts. In fact the word 'hut' is misleading and for many 'mountain inns' would be a more appropriate description. The hut wardens provide food and drink at all times and sleeping accom-modation either in mixed dormitories with blankets and pillows, or in bedrooms for which linen is provided. Charges are reasonable, but in the higher huts visitors must not expect to pay valley prices as provisions may have to be brought up by mule, goods lift, or even helicopter. The food varies from hut to hut. Some give a full restaurant service whilst at others the choice is more limited. Hot water (*Teewasser*) is always available to make hot drinks and most huts serve a cheap, high-calorie meal, originally intended for impecunious students, called *Bergsteigeressen*. Self-cooking facilities are not available. Many huts are owned by either the *Österreichischer Alpenverein* (ÖAV) known to English-speaking members as the *Austrian Alpine Club*, and the *Deutscher Alpenverein* (German Alpine Club). In these huts members are entitled to reductions of up to 50 per cent in accommodation charges and are given preference over non-members up to 7 pm. English visitors, if they intend staying long in the huts and are not already members of another Alpine Club which enjoys reciprocal rights, may wish to join the Austrian Alpine Club and this may easily be done through the United Kingdom Branch. Full details may be obtained from the Secretary, 13 Longcroft House, Fretherne Road, Welwyn Garden City, Herts. AL8 6PQ. All huts are open from the middle of June until the end of September. Many open for longer periods, especially during the Spring skitouring season, and a few stay open all the year. When huts are closed or unwardened, members may still use, them but a master key has to be obtained prior to the visit. Details are given in the '*AAC Hut Book*'.

Guides. Officially authorised mountain guides are available in most mountain villages in Austria and can often be obtained in huts below popular peaks. There is a fixed maximum daily fee for hire of a guide, provided the tour does not exceed grade 3 in difficulty. Harder climbs are subject to negotiation. If more than one tourist is taken, the guide's fee is increased for each additional tourist by 25 per cent for rock tours and 10 per cent for glacier and snow tours. The guide pays for his own food and accommodation. Members of the Austrian Alpine Club are entitled to a 10 per cent reduction in guide fees within the Federal Republic of Austria. The UK section of the AAC organises courses and tours with Austrian guides; details of these may be obtained from the Secretary.

Equipment. A pair of comfortable boots is essential. These should be large enough to take a thin inner sock and a thick outer sock of wool, and the sole should be rigid enough to take crampons if hard snow or ice is to be met. Breeches should cover the knee and not be too heavy. Jeans are quite unsuitable. Woollen shirts are best, with tails long enough to stay tucked in. Gortex *cagoules* with gaiters provide protection from wind, snow, and rain. Other necessities are a sweater or fibre-pile jacket, gloves or mittens, a woollen hat or balaclava, a sun hat, and sun glasses or goggles. Ropes are now made of synthetic materials and 30m is sufficient for a party of three. They are attached to the body by means of a climber's belt or harness. Shorter metal ice-axes are ousting the old-fashioned wooden walking-axe. A map, guidebook (see below), compass, torch, glacier cream, and lip salve complete the list of the bare minimum required. Every party should carry a first-aid kit and a polythene bivouac bag. If a camera is carried, it should have a UV filter.

Insurance. Some accident insurance is advisable for those climbing in Austria, although the voluntary rescue and helicopter services are free, which is not the case in other alpine countries where rescue can be very expensive.

Where to climb. The mountaineer has such a wide choice in Austria that in a short review it is only possible to mention a few of the better known peaks. There are always more difficult routes. Many snow peaks have north walls which are the playground of the ice specialist, and there are rock climbs of a high order in the *Karwendel* and the *Kaisergebirge*, but these are best left to the expert.

The climbing season runs from July to September, although very pleasant walking can be had below the snowline in June and October. Conditions vary from year to year. Sometimes snow is deep in early July and this makes progress slow and laborious. Later, one is more likely to meet ice on the higher peaks, especially if the summer has been warm. In all excursions involving the crossing of glaciers an early start is recommended.

In Austria it is rarely necessary to start in the dark, but climbers should be prepared to leave the hut at first light. The hut warden will be able to advise you as to starting times for peaks in the vicinity. Do not forget to sign the hut book and record where you are going. The following well-known peaks are, in good weather, within the scope of a party of moderate experience.

The **Grossglockner** (3797m), situated in the *Hohe Tauern*, is the highest summit in Austria and was first climbed in 1800. It is a fine mountain and in the words of that indefatigable Victorian pioneer John Ball, 'no true mountaineer can behold that beautiful peak without longing to attain its summit'. This is made comparatively easy by the existence of the *Erzherzog Johann Hut* at 3454m on the *Adlersruhe*. This hut can be reached either from *Kals* up the *Ködnitztal* or from *Heiligenblut* via the *Salm Hut* or the *Hofmannsweg*. From the Adlersruhe the summit can be reached in 1½ hours over gradually steepening snow slopes to the *Kleinglockner* summit, from where a steep descent is made to the *Glocknerscharte* before reaching the summit rocks. Not difficult, for there are plenty of belaying spikes, but care is needed if the rocks are icy or the ridges are corniced. Alternatively, a harder ascent can be made from the *Stüdl Hut* up the *Stüdlgrat*, a grade 3 rock climb.

The **Grossvenediger** (3674m). An easy snow peak, which is usually climbed from the *Neue Prager Hut* or the *Defreggerhaus* in about 3 hours. Often just a question of following tracks in the snow but there are some crevasses to be negotiated.

The **Grosse Mösele** (3478m) is the most important of the *Zillertal Alps* although the *Hochfeiler* is slightly higher (3510m). Both are situated on the Italian frontier. The former is regularly climbed from the *Berliner Hut* via the *Waxeck Kees* and the *Östliche Mösellscharte* in 6–7 hours. The latter is best approached from the Italian side.

The **Olperer** (3476m) is one of the finest summits of the *Zillertal Alps*, with far-ranging views. The usual ascent is by the rocky N ridge via the *Wildlahnerscharte* from the *Geraer* or *Spannagelhaus huts* in about 5 hours. It is also often climbed by the ESE ridge on the *Schneegupfgrat* from the *Olperer Hut*.

The **Zuckerhütl** (3505m), the highest summit in the *Stubai Alps*, is climbed without difficulty in good conditions from the *Hildesheimer*, *Dresdner*, or *Sulzenau Huts* via the *Pfaffensattel*, from where a steep snow slope leads to the top.

The summit of the **Ruderhofspitze** (3474m), in the *Stubai Alps*, can be reached easily from the *Franz Senn Hut*, 4½ hours from *Neustift*; in about 5 hours via the *Holltalscharte*; or from the *Neue Regensburger Hut* in slightly less time.

The **Wildspitze** (3774m), an Ötztal peak, ranks second only to the Grossglockner in height. It rises imposingly from its glacier basin and claims more annual ascents than any other major mountain in the Alps. It has twin summits, a N and a S peak. The latter carries a large metal cross, but the N peak is two metres higher. The traverse between the two is an exposed snow ridge, easy enough, but demanding caution if corniced or icy at the end of the season. Ascents may be made from the *Taschachhaus, Brauschweiger, Breslau* or *Vernagt Huts*. The shortest route is from the Breslau Hut (3½ hours), while the more interesting are from the Taschachhaus or Braunschweiger, which both traverse some magnificent glacier scenery. All these routes are technically easy, but good visibility is needed, and there are many large crevasses to avoid.

The **Similaun** (3606m) is a beautiful snow pyramid at the southern end of the Ötztal, on the Italian frontier. The *Martin Busch Hut*, 2½ hours from *Vent*, is the usual base, and the mountain may be climbed by its W ridge in 3½ hours, or its E ridge in 4½ hours. The traverse makes a fine expedition for an experienced party. The ascent of the W ridge, the easier of the two, may be shortened by starting from the *Similaun Hut*, just over the Italian border.

The **Weisskugel** (3739m), the second highest summit in the Ötztal Alps, is a very fine mountain set amid impressive glaciers. The normal routes via the *Hintereis Joch* and the S ridge can involve a long approach but are relatively straightforward. The nearest starting points are the *Bellavista* and *Weisskugel Huts* (4½ hours) on the Italian side of the frontier, but the climb is frequently done from the *Brandenburgher Hut* and the *Hochjoch Hospiz* (6 hours). The final part of the easy S ridge is a scramble over sometimes icy rocks. A slightly harder alternative is the ENE ridge via the *Weisskugel Joch*, from where the summit is reached in 1½ hours. The finest route of all is by the N ridge (7 hours from the *Weisskugel Hut*), one of the great rock and ice ridges of the Alps, and a serious undertaking of increasing difficulty: Grade 3+.

Maps. The *Alpenvereinskarten* at 1:25,000 are excellent maps showing great detail. The *Kompass Wanderkarten* (1:50,000) are useful, and adequate for walkers and climbers. The *Freytag & Berndt Touristenkarten* (1:100,000) cover a larger area, but are not so detailed. All these can be obtained from the United Kingdom section of the Austrian Alpine Club or from Stanfords, 12 Long Acre, London WC2.

Useful reference books: Climbers' guidebooks are published in English by West Col Productions, 1 Meadow Close, Goring, Berks., for the following regions: Glockner, Kaisergebirge, Zillertal, Karwendel, Stubai, and Ötztal. Guidebooks in German covering other areas are published by Rudolf Rother of Munich. Tallantyre Philip–Felix Austria Guides (obtainable from the Austrian Alpine Club (UK) Section) are: 1, Venediger Region; 2, Zillertal Alps; 3, Niederen and Hohen Tauern (includes Grossglockner); and 4, Pitztal, East and West.

The following books provide a mine of interesting, but mostly non-technical, information: *F.J. Smythe,* 'Over Tyrolese Hills' (1936); *W. Pause,* 'Salute the Mountains' (1962; translated from the German); *W.M. Conway,* 'The Alps from End to End'; *J.N. Walker,* 'Walking in the Alps' (1951); more practical is *Cecil Davies,* 'Mountain Walking in Austria' (1986; Cicerone Press, 2 Police Square, Milnthorpe, Cumbria.

Geographical Introduction

The Republic of **Austria** (*Österreich*), in central Europe, is bounded by six countries: Germany to the NW; Czechoslovakia to the N and NE; Hungary to the E; Yugoslavia to the SE; Italy to the SW; and Switzerland to the W (plus Liechtenstein). Its total area is 83,850 square km (32,376 square miles), and it consists of nine *Bundesländer* or autonomous provinces: **Vorarlberg** (2601 square km; capital *Bregenz*), abutting Switzerland; to the E of which is the **Tyrol** (*Tirol*; 12,648 square km; capital *Innsbruck*); **Salzburg** (7254 square km; capital *Salzburg*); to the S of which is **Carinthia** (*Kärnten*; 9533 square km; capital *Klagenfurt*); this is abutted to the NE by **Styria** (*Steiermark*; 16,386km²; capital *Graz*); to the NW of the latter, and NE of Salzburg, is **Upper Austria** (*Oberösterreich*; 11,978 square km; capital *Linz*); to the E of which is **Lower Austria** (*Niederösterreich*; 19,170 square km; its capital in the process of being transferred from Vienna to *St. Pölten*); with the state of **Vienna** itself (*Wien*; 415 square km) to the E of its centre. To the SE of Lower Austria, abutted to the W by Styria, is **Burgenland** (3965 square km; capital *Eisenstadt*).

The extent of the Austro-Hungarian Empire in 1918 was 677,000 square km, with a population of c 53,000,000. The present population of Austria, according to the census of 1981, is 7,555,000 (in round figures, estimated at 7,623,000 in mid 1989), with an average density of 90 per square km (varying between 46 per square km for the Tyrol, and 3690 per square km for Vienna). Vienna alone accounts for one-fifth of the total, while the larger provincial capitals make up about another fifth. This uneven distribution is caused largely by the physical structure of the country, over 60 per cent of which is Alpine in character. The population for the same area a century ago was 4,963,000.

German is the mother tongue of 99 per cent of the population; the rest being made up of ethnic groups of Croat, Slovak, or Czech speakers. Some 88 per cent is stated to be Roman Catholic, although many fewer practice.

Extending E from Switzerland, from which it is in part divided by the upper Rhine, the high Alps form the S frontier of the *Vorarlberg* with Switzerland, here known as the RÄTIKON and SILVRETTA ranges, the latter rising to 3399m at the *Fluchthorn*, E of which is the valley of the *Inn*, flowing NE. This main ridge, largely crystalline, is continued to the E by the ÖTZTALER ALPS, among them the *Wildspitze* (3774m), with its summit N of the present frontier between *Tyrol* and *S Tyrol*. Further E, the range is broken by the *Brenner Pass* (1370m), before being extended by the ZILLERTALER ALPS and rising to the HOHE TAUERN massif, with the *Dreiherrn* (3499m), *Grossvenediger* (3674m), and the *Grossglockner* (3797m), the highest peak in Austria. To the W of the latter, the range is pierced by the *Felbertauerntunnel*; to the E it is crossed by the high-lying *Grossglockner road* (B107), rising to 2505m at the *Hochtor*, and further E the rail-tunnel or *Tauerntunnel*, passes between *Badgastein* on the N flank, and *Mallnitz*. This main barrier ridge is extended by the NIEDERER TAUERN (under several names), pierced by the transverse autobahn A10, and further E, crossed by the B99. The next main crossroad (B113) follows the valley between *Liezen* and *Leoben*, beyond which the range veers NE as the HOCHSCHWAB, RAXALPE, and *Schneeberg* (2076m; the nearest peak to Vienna over 2000m). Beyond are the thickly wooded slopes of the lower *Wienerwald*, immediately to the W of *Vienna* itself.

Parallel to, and some distance S of this main mountain chain, and bearing SE from the Dreiherrn, is the subsidiary limestone range forming the frontier with Italy, and known as the KARNISCHE ALPS. Beyond the main border crossing SW of *Villach* the range is called the KARAWANKEN, with *Yugoslavia* on its S slopes. The range can be crossed at several points and a tunnel is being built SE of Villach. There are of course several intermediate ranges between this and the Tauern, among them the, transverse KORALPE (rising to 2140m), forming the border between *Carinthia* and *Styria*. Several valleys converge on Villach, long an important centre of communications, to the E of which are the Carinthian lakes, and the reservoirs formed by the river *Drau*, later the Drava. On the S side of the Lower Tauern is the valley of the *Mur*, providing one of the main highways SW from Vienna towards Italy. The autobahn driving S from *Vienna*, past *Graz*, and *Wolfsberg*, is being extended towards *Klagenfurt*, which is already connected by autobahn with *Villach* and Italy.

To the N of the main barrier of High Alps is another limestone range, together with intermediate ridges such as the LECHTALER ALPS (with the ALLGÄUER ALPS to the N on the German frontier), and KITZBÜHLER ALPS. Between the two lies *Innsbruck*, overlooked to the N by the KARWENDEL RANGE. The valley of the Inn provides the main highway between *Munich* and the Brenner, and also for the autobahn (which briefly passes through Germany) to *Salzburg*.

N of *Kitzbühel* is the impressive KAISERGEBIRGE, and to the NE is the German enclave formed by the mountains surrounding *Berchtesgaden*. These may be crossed from *Lofer*, to the SW, via the *Steinpass*, or circled to the S via *Zell am See*, there turning E prior to following the *Salzach* valley N from *Bischofshofen* to *Salzburg*.

Some 25km E of Bischofshofen is the long valley of the *Enns*, dividing the LOWER TAUERN range from the DACHSTEIN MASSIF to the N (2995m). The river Enns, after descending beyond *Liezen* and *Admont* through the attractive GESÄUSE, winds N round the ENNSTALER ALPS and lower ranges through *Steyr*, to enter the Danube near *Enns* itself. To the S of the Gesäuse rise the pinnacled EISENERZER ALPS, with further E, the ferriferous *Erzberg*, beyond which rises the HOCHSCHWAB; see above.

Some 20km E of Salzburg is the *Fuschlsee*, one of the smaller lakes in the district known as the SALZKAMMERGUT, named after its salt-works, exploited since prehistoric times. Its geological structure is complicated, resulting in several charmingly sited lakes—the main ones being *Mondsee*, *Attersee*, *Traunsee* and the *Wolfgangsee*, to the E of which lies *Bad Ischl*, at a junction of narrow valleys. To the S of this famous spa, surrounded by high mountains and rising steeply from the S towards the Dachstein range, is the *Hallstätter See*, and *Hallstatt* itself. To the E of Hallstatt are the high-lying lakes of *Altausseer See*, and the *Grundlsee*, N and NE respectively of *Bad Aussee*, with the TOTES GEBIRGE rising further NE to a height of 2523m. An extensive tract of broken country extends NE, forming the lower foothills of this range of alps, with the *Ötscher* (1894m) among them. The range later descends towards the *Danube* valley to the N.

To the N of Salzburg is another region of small lakes to the E of the river *Salzach*, which here forms the frontier with Germany until it enters the Danube at *Passau*. Most of the intervening area is rolling country known as the *Innviertel*, while to the N of the Danube where the hills are higher it is called the *Mühlviertel*. Beyond are the spurs of the Bohemian massif, the whole comprising *Upper Austria*, with *Linz* as its capital. Apart from the old main road between Salzburg and Linz, the two cities are now connected by the A1 autobahn. The autobahn is extended E above the S bank of the Danube and into *Lower Austria*, bearing away from the river at *Melk* and by-passing *St. Pölten* before dividing to provide alternative approaches to *Vienna*. At several points along this route there are good views, S towards the alpine foothills, and N towards the *Waldviertel*, a gneiss and granite tableland forming part of Lower Austria between the Danube and the Czech border. Further E is the *Weinviertel*, partly devoted to the cultivation of the vine, and also with a number of oil-wells, connected by pipe-lines to the main refinery at *Schwechat*, between Vienna and its airport.

Immediately E of the capital, from the left bank of the Danube to the Czech frontier formed by the *March* or *Morava*, is the flat alluvial plain known as the *Marchfeld*, frequently a battlefield. The main road E from Vienna to *Bratislava* follows the right or S bank of the Danube, passing the important Roman settlement of *Carnuntum* at *Petronell*. An autobahn is also under construction to join Vienna and Budapest. Some 20km S of Petronell, in the N part of the frontier province of *Burgenland*, is the extensive but shallow *Neusiedler See*, the S end of which is in *Hungary*. Some 15km W of the lake lies *Eisenstadt*, and a further 25km W is *Wiener Neustadt*, on the old main road—now largely an express-way—later climbing SW over the *Semmering pass* to *Bruck an der Mur* and to *Graz* or *Villach*. Weiner Neustadt is also on the direct road to Graz; the new A2 autobahn runs very roughly parallel to it, shortly climbing S to cross the *Styrian hills*. To the SE, these hills extend into the S part of Burgenland before reaching the Hungarian border and the Hungarian plain or *puzta*.

Glossary

Abendessen, supper
Abfahrt, descent
Alt, old
Altstadt, old centre of town
Apotheke, chemist's shop (drugstore)
Ausgang, exit
Autobahn, motorway

Bach, stream or brook
Bad, spa or bath
Bahnhof, railway-station
Bastei, bastion
Berg, hill or mountain
Bezirk/e, municipal district/s
Bildstöcke, wayside shrine, usually set up as the result of a vow

Brücke, bridge
Brunnen, fountain or well
Burg, fortified site

Chor, choir
Chorjoch, chancel

Denkmal, monument or memorial
Dom, cathedral
Doppelsesselbahn, double chair-lift
Dorf, village
Dreifaltigkeitssäule, Trinity Column
Durchgang, passage

Einbahnstrasse, one way street

Eingang, entrance; also
Einfahrt
Eis, ice
Eisenbahn, railway
Erzherzog/in, Archduke/
Archduchess

Fähre, ferry
Fahrkarte, ticket
Fahrplan, timetable
Ferner, glacier; also *Kees*
Filial Kirche, chapel of ease
Firn, snowfield
Flugelaltar, winged altarpiece
Flughafen, aerodrome
Fluss, river
Forst, forest
Freiherr/in, baron, baroness
Friedhof, cemetery
Frühstuck, breakfast
Funkhaus, broadcasting station
Fürst, prince
Fussgängerzone, pedestrian
precinct

Garten, garden
Gartensaal, garden room, often
grottoed
Gasse, lane or street
Gasthaus, inn
Gasthof, hotel or restaurant
Gebirge, mountain range
Geboren, born
Geburtshaus, birthplace
Gelb, yellow
Geöffnet, open
Geradeaus, straight ahead
Geschlossen, closed
Gesperrt, road closed
Gestorben, died
Glatteis, black ice
Gletscher, glacier
Glockenturm, belfry
Graben, moat or small valley
Grabstein, gravestone; also
Grabmal
Graf, earl; *Gräfin*, countess
Gross, large
Gruft, mausoleum, cenotaph or
tomb
Grün, green
Gymnasium, grammar school

Hafen, harbour
Hauptplatz, main square
Heilige, saint (*Sankt*)
Heimatmuseum, local museum
Herzog/in, Duke, Duchess

Himmelfahrt, Ascension
Hoch, upper or high
Hof, court or courtyard
Höhe, height
Höhenweg or *Höhenstrasse*,
mountain road
Höhle, cave
Hütte, hut or mountain
refuge

Insel, island

Jagdhaus or *Jagdhütte*,
shooting-box
Jahrhundert century

Kachelofen, tiled stove or pöele
Kanzel, pulpit
Kapelle, chapel
Karner, charnel-house or
ossuary; see p 43
Kaserne, barracks
Keller, cellar
Kellergasse, a street of cellars
Kirche, church
Klamm, gorge or ravine
Klein, small
Kloster, convent or monastery
Kogel or *Kofel*, dome-shaped
mountain
Kopf, head
Krankenhaus, hospital
Kreuz, cross
Kreuzgang, cloister
Kurhaus, pumproom of spa
Kuppel, dome or cupola

Land, province
Lauben, arcades
Lawine, avalanche
Links, left

Mariensäule, Column
surmounted by an image of the
Virgin
Markt, market-place
Mauer, wall
Maut, toll
Mesner, sacristan
Mittagessen, lunch
Mittelschiff, nave
Mühle, mill

Nieder, lower

Ober, upper
Offen, open
Orgelbühne, organ-loft
Ortsende, end of town or
village

Pestsäule, plague column, see p 45
Pfarrkirche, parish church
PKW, private cars (*LKW*, lorries)
Platz, place or square

Querschiff, transept

Rat, counsellor (*Hofrat*, etc.)
Rathaus, town hall
Rechts, right
Rot, red

Saal, hall or large room
Sattel, saddle or pass
Sackgasse, dead end
Säule, column
SB, Selbstbedienung, self-service
Scheitelstein, keystone
Schiff, nave, or ship
Schlechte Wegstrecke (or *Fahrbahn*), road in bad condition
Schlepplift, T-bar lift
Schloss, palace, castle or country-house
Schlucht, gorge or ravine
Schlüssel, key
Schnee, snow
Schule, school
Schwarz, black
Schwimmbad, swimming-pool
See, lake; or *Weiher*, small lake
Seilbahn, funicular
Seilschwebebahn, cable-car
Sessellift, chair-lift
Spital, hospice
Spitz, peak or summit
Stadt, town
Stausee, reservoir
Stauwerk, dam
Steig, path

Stein, stone
Sterbehaus, place of death
Stiege, steps or stairs
Stift, conventual or monastic foundation
Stock, floor or level in a building
Strand, beach
Strasse, road or street
Strassenbahn, tramway

Tal, valley
Tor, gate or gateway
Toreinfahrt, porte cochère
Treppe, stairs or steps
Treppenhaus, staircase
Turm, tower

Umleitung, deviation
Unter, under or lower

Verboten, forbidden
Vierung, crossing in a church
Vorrang, priority
Vorsicht, caution

Wald, wold; wooded or forested district
Wallfahrtskirche, pilgrimage-church
Wasser, water
Wasserfall, waterfall
Wechsel, exchange
Weg, path
Weiss, white
Wölbung, vaulting

Zentrum, the centre
Zeughaus, arsenal
Zimmer, room
Zoll, Customs
Zug, train
Zum, at the sign of
Zwiebeltürme, onion-tower, helm, or steeple

Maps

Map references are given at the head of each route in this Guide, using the following abbreviations: F&B = **Freytag & Berndt** *Grosse Strassen Karten* 1, 2, 3, at 1:300,000, or 4, at 1:250,000; and BEV = **Bundesamt für Eich-und Vermessungswesen** (the equivalent of the Ordnance Survey or *Landesaufnahme*) 47/9, etc., referring to the sheet of their maps at 1:200,000. *Der Grosse ÖAMTC-Städteatlas Österreichs* (Hölzel) contains numerous town plans.

The following maps are useful for general planning: *Michelin*'s Austria (426) at 1:400,000; or the F&B Autokarte Austria at 1:500,000, while BEV produce 'Übersichtskarte von Österreich' at 1:500,000. The general maps published by *Kümmerley and Frey*, and *Reise-und Verkehsverlag* (Stuttgart) are also good.

A useful map of Northern Europe, which covers the area from Dunkerque to Bratislava, with Dijon and Bern on its S border, is *Michelin* 987 (Benelux; Germany; Austria) at 1:1,000,000, while on a large scale (1:400,000) is *Michelin* 413 (Bayern, Baden-Württemberg), covering southern Germany and Bavaria. Those entering Austria from the S of France or Italy will require *Michelin* 988. Those travelling through Switzerland may prefer *Michelin* 427. Alternatively, F&B publish *Central Europe* at 1:2,000,000, which covers all routes to Austria. They also publish for the ÖAMTC (Austrian Touring Club) a double-sided map of the Alps (Alpen), the reverse including SE France and N Italy at 1:600,000.

Slightly more detailed are the F&B *Grosse Strassen Karten*, covering the country in three sheets at 1:300,000, plus No. 4, of the Salzburg/Salzkammergut area at 1:250,000, if necessary. The former are also available in atlas form, including in the same volume Central Europe in 12 double-page spreads, and 33 town plans, entitled *Grosser Auto Atlas Österreich*. F&B also produce a convenient paperback called *Österreich Touring*, comprising 24 double-page maps of the country at 1:250,000. *Ed. Hölzel* cover the country in four maps at 1:200,000.

F&B almost cover the country in two series of **Hiking Maps** or *Wanderkarten* (WK) at either 1:50,000 or 1:100,000, two of the former being available in atlas form (Wienerwald; and the Mountains further SW). F&B also produce a series of *Canoeing Maps*, etc.

BEV are in the process of covering the country in several series of maps at 1:200,000; 1:100,000; 1:50,000; and 1:25,000; and air-photographs at 1:10,000; apart from other more specialised maps.

Another important series is the *Alpenvereinskarten*, published by the *Oesterreichischer Alpenverein*, Wilhelm-Greil-Strasse 15, A-6010, Innsbruck. These cover most of the mountainous areas of Austria, the majority at 1:25,000, and several are also available in a form showing Ski routes (*Skirouten*).

F&B produce several town plans. Particularly useful are those for the province of **Vienna**, available as a map with index at 1:25,000; or of the city, also in atlas form (*Buchplan*) at 1:20,000. BEV publish maps of Vienna and its environs at 1:50,000, and 1:25,000. A map of *Public Transport in Vienna* is available at Tourist Offices and some Underground Stations (Karlsplatz, and Stephansplatz).

It is essential to use the latest editions of all maps. Most of the general maps listed should be readily available, or may be ordered through Stanfords, 12–14 Long Acre, London WC2; Robertson McCarta, 122 Kings Cross Road, London WC1X 9DS, etc.; Michelin maps can also be obtained from The Michelin Tyre Co., Ltd, Davy House, Lyon Road, Harrow, Middx. HA1 2DQ.

Freytag & Berndt's shops at Kohlmarkt 9, Vienna, or Wilhelm-Greil-Strasse 15, Innsbruck, are recommended. Both their own publications and a fine collection of other topographical and cartographical material, and guide books in various languages, are for sale, although there should be little difficulty acquiring them throughout the country. The address of BEV is Krotenthallergasse 3, A-1080 Vienna, with a retail department on the other side of the building.

Bibliography

The following brief list of books (mostly in English) does not pretend to be more than a compilation of works that might be useful for reference or in providing general background. Most of the titles have been published during recent decades, and contain comprehensive bibliographies for further reading.

Among bookshops in London catering specially for travellers are: *The Travel Bookshop*, 13 Blenheim Crescent, W11 2EE; *The Travellers' Bookshop* 25 Cecil Court, WC2N 4EZ; and *Daunt, Books for Travellers*, 83 Marylebone High Street, W1M 4AL.

Among the booksellers in Vienna who keep a range of English books in stock—although not always as wide a range of books on aspects of Austria as might be expected—the following may be mentioned: *The British Bookshop*, Blumenstockgasse 3 (parallel to and S of Weihburggasse, leading E from the Kärntner Strasse); *Prachner*, Kärntner Strasse 30; *Frick*, Graben 12; *Gerold*, Graben 31; *Shakespeare & Co.*, Sterngasse 2 (leading W from the Ruprechtsplatz); *Buchhandlung in der Hofburg*, Burg Durchgang 6; *J. Berger*, Kohlmarkt 3; and—for maps and topographical material—*Freytag & Berndt*, Kohlmarkt 9.

Topographical and general: *H.* and *M. Garland* (eds), the Oxford Companion to German Literature; *Stella Musulin*, Austria; *Stephan Zweig*, The World of Yesterday; *Ilsa Barea*, Vienna; *Edward Crankshaw*, Vienna, Portrait of a City in decline; *Robert Musil*, The Man without Qualities; *Arthur Schnitzler*, My Youth in Vienna; *John Lehmann*, Down River; and *John Lehmann* and *Richard Bassett* (eds), Vienna: a Traveller's Companion.

The first of a series of annual volumes of academic essays and reviews covering a wide field of interest—mainly literary—entitled 'Austrian Studies', is being published by the Edinburgh University Press.

In **German**: *Reinhardt Hootz* (ed.), Kunstdenkmaler in Österreich (4 vols; profusely illustrated); *Reclams* Kunstführer Österreich (2 vols) and Archäologie Führer; *Peter Pleyel*, Das Römische Österreich; *Otto H. Urban*, Wegweiser in die Urgeschichte Österreichs; *Georg Dehio* Handbooks, Die Kunstdenkmaler Österreichs (new editions in process of publication in several volumes); *Andreas Lehne*, Jugendstil in Wien; Handbuch der Historichen Stätten Österreich (2 volumes; Alfred Kröner Verlag), and *N. Nemetschke* and *G. Kugler*, Lexikon der Wiener Kunst und Kultur. There are many other good volumes on areas of Austria, and individual towns, etc.

Among earlier **Travels**: *Edward Browne*, An Account of Several Travels through a great part of Germany (1677); *Charles Patin*, Travels through Germany ... (1696); *Mary Wortley Montague*, Letters; *J.G. Keysler*, Travels (2nd ed. 1756–57); *William Hunter*, Travels in the year 1792 (1798); *William Wraxall*, Memoirs (1779); *John Barrow*, Tour in Austria ... in 1840 (1841); *Martha Wilmot*, More Letters: Impressions of Vienna 1819–1829 (1935); *Richard Bright*, Travels from Vienna through Lower Hungary, with Remarks on the State of Vienna during the Congress of the year 1814 (1818); *Charles Sealsfield* (Karl Anton Postl), Austria as it is (1828); *J. Russell*, Tour in Germany (2nd ed. 1825); *Basil Hall*, Schloss Hainfeld (1836); *Peter Evan Turnbull*, Austria (1839); *Anon*. [W. Blumenbach], Austria and the Austrians (1837); *Frances Trollope*, Vienna and the Austrians (1838); *William Robert Wilde*, Austria and its Institutions (1843); *J.G. Kohl*, Austria (1843). Of interest is the abridged version of Johann Pezzl's 'Sketch of Vienna in 1786–90' included in 'Mozart and Vienna', ed. H.C. Robbins Landon.

Art and Architecture: *E. Hempel*, Baroque Art and Architecture in Central Europe; *Fritz Novotny*, Painting and Sculpture in Europe, 1780–1880; *Nicolas Powell*, From Baroque to Rococo, and The Sacred Spring: Arts in Vienna, 1898–1918; *Sacheverell Sitwell*, German Baroque Art (1927); *John Bourke*, Baroque churches of Central Europe; *Peter Vergo*, Art in Vienna, 1898–1918, and Vienna 1900

(Catalogue of the Exhibition held at the National Museum of Antiquities of Scotland, 1983); *Robert Waissenberger*, Secession, and Vienna 1815–1848; *Werner J. Schweiger*, The Wiener Werkstätte; *Manfred Liethe-Jasper, Rudolf Distelberger*, and *Wolfgang Prohaska*, The Kunsthistorisches Museum, Vienna; *C.M. Nebehay*, Vienna 1900: Architecture and Painting; *Österreichische Gesellschaft für Architektur*, Architektur in Wien (concentrating on the 20C); and the Catalogue Vienna 1880–1938 (1986); *Franco Borsi* and *Ezio Godoli*, Vienna 1900; *K. Varnedoe*, Vienna 1900: Art, Architecture, Design.

History: *A.W.A. Leeper*, History of Medieval Austria; *R.J.W. Evans*, The Making of the Habsburg Monarchy, 1550–1700; *John Stoye*, The Siege of Vienna; *William Coxe*, History of the House of Austria; *Christopher Duffy*, The Wild Goose and the Eagle (Marshal von Browne); *Friedrich Heer*, The Holy Roman Empire; *John P. Spielman*, Leopold I of Austria; *Dereck McKay*, Prince Eugene of Savoy; *T.M. Barker*, Double Eagle and Crescent; *C.A. Macartney*, The Habsburg Empire, 1790–1918 (1971 ed.), and The House of Austria; *T.C.W. Blanning*, Joseph II and Enlightened Despotism; *Derek Beale*, Joseph II; *F.L. Petrie*, Napoleon and the Archduke Charles; *Edward Crankshaw*, The Fall of the House of Habsburg, and Maria Theresa; *P.G.M. Dickson*, Finance and Government under Maria Theresia, 1740–1780; *A.J.P. Taylor*, The Habsburg Monarchy; *Alan Sked*, The Decline and Fall of the Habsburg Empire, 1815–1918; *R. John Rath*, The Viennese Revolution of 1848; *J. Blum*, Noble Landowners and Agriculture in Austria, 1815–1848; *Arthur J. May*, The Habsburg Monarchy, 1867–1914, and The Passing of the Habsburg Monarchy; *Barbara Jelavich*, Modern Austria: Empire to Republic, 1815–1986; *A.B. Zeman*, The Break-up of the Habsburg Empire, 1914–1918; *Victor-L. Tapié*, The Rise and Fall of the Habsburg Monarchy; *Elisabeth Barker*, Austria 1918–1972; *G.E.R. Gedye*, Fallen Bastions (1938); *C.A. Gulick*, Austria from Habsburg to Hitler; *Carl Schorske*, Fin-de-Siècle Vienna; *Karl R. Stadler*, Austria (Nations of the Modern World series); *J. Gehl*, Austria, Germany, and the Anschluss, 1931–38; *Steven Beller*, Vienna and the Jews, 1867–1938; *Robert S. Wistrich*, The Jews of Vienna in the Age of Franz Joseph; *G. Brook-Shepherd*, The Last Habsburg, and Anschluss: the Rape of Austria; *Robert Pick*, Empress Maria Theresia; *Kurt Steiner* (ed.), Modern Austria; *F.C. Springell*, Connoisseur and Diplomat; the Earl of Arundel's Embassy to Germany in 1636; *Ludwig Pauli*, The Alps; Archaeology and Early History; *Gerhard Benecke*, Maximilian I; *Géza Alfoldy*, Noricum; *András Mocsy*, Pannonia and Upper Moesia; *D.F. Good*, The Economic rise of the Habsburg Empire, 1750–1914; *F.R. Bridge*, The Habsburg Monarchy among the Great Powers, 1815–1918; *S.R. Williamson*, Austria—Hungary and the Origins of the First World War.

Music: Numerous aspects of music in Austria are covered in volumes of the *New Oxford History of Music*, and *The New Grove Dictionary of Music* (from which several biographies have been extracted and published separately); and also in *The New Grove History of Opera*. Among other general studies are: *Louise Cuyler*, The Emperor Maximilian I and Music; *Hans Gál*, The Golden Age of Vienna; *Marcel Brion*, Daily Life in the Vienna of Mozart and Schubert; *Luigi Rognoni*, The Second Vienna School.

Books on individual composers include: *B.A. Brown*, Gluck and the French Theatre in Vienna; *H.C. Robbins Landon*, Mozart: the Golden Years, Mozarts' Last Year, (ed.) The Mozart Compendium: a Guide to

Mozart's Life and Music, Haydn, Chronicle and Works (5 vols), and with *D. Wyn Jones*, Haydn, his Life and Music; *Eric Blom*, Mozart; *Otto Erich Deutsch*, Mozart, A Documentary Biography; *Emily Anderson* (ed.), The Letters of Mozart and his family; *Maynard Solomon*, Beethoven; *Emily Anderson* (ed.) The Letters of Beethoven; *Martin Cooper*, Beethoven, the Last Decade; *Otto Erich Deutsch*, Schubert, A Documentary Biography, and (ed.) Schubert: Memoirs by his Friends; *Maurice Brown*, Schubert, a Critical Biography; *John Reed*, Schubert, the Final Years; *Frank Walker*, Hugo Wolf; *Alfred Einstein*, Gluck; *Hans Gál*, Johannes Brahms, his works and personality; *Michael Musgrave*, The Music of Brahms; *Malcolm MacDonald*, Brahms; *Donald Mitchell*, Gustav Mahler (3 vols); *Henri-Louis de La Grange*, Mahler, a Biography; *Deryck Cooke*, Gustav Mahler, an Introduction to his Music; *H. Blaukopf* (ed.), Gustav Mahler—Richard Strauss: Correspondence, 1888–1911; *H.F. Redlich*, Bruckner and Mahler; *H.H. Schönzeler*, Bruckner; *Dika Newlin*, Bruckner, Mahler, Schoenberg; *Willi Reich*, The Life and Work of Alban Berg; *H.F. Redlich*, Berg, the Man and his Music; *Douglas Jarman*, The Music of Alban Berg; *H.H. Stuckenschmidt*, Arnold Schoenberg, his life, world, and work; *Willi Reich*, Schoenberg, a critical biography; *Friedrich Wildgans*, Anton Webern.

PRACTICAL INFORMATION

Formalities and Currency

Passports are necessary for all British and American travellers entering Austria. *British Visitors' Passports* (valid one year), available from Post Offices in the UK, are also accepted. No visa is required for British or American visitors.

Custom House. Except for travellers by air, who have to pass customs at the airport of arrival, or those travelling by international expresses, where their luggage is examined in the train, luggage is still liable to be scrutinised at the frontier (apart from intermediate frontiers). Provided that dutiable articles are declared, bona fide travellers will find that the Austrian customs authorities are courteous and reasonable. Check in advance with Austrian Consulates or Tourist Offices for the latest regulations on the importation of firearms, whether sporting or otherwise.

Embassies (*Botschaftskanzlei*) and **Consulates** in Vienna. *British*, Jauresgasse 12 (with honorary consuls at Innsbruck, Bregenz, Graz and Salzburg); *Ireland*, Hilton Center, 16 Stock; *Australia*, Mattiellistrasse 2–4; *New Zealand*, Lugeck 1; *Canada*, Dr-Karl-Lueger-Ring 10; *S Africa*, Sandgasse 33; *USA*, Boltzmanngasse 16 (with a consulate at Gatenbaupromenade 2, and at Salzburg).

The addresses of **Austrian Embassies** in English-speaking countries are: 18 Belgrave Mews West, *London* SW1X 8HU (with the *Austrian Institute* at 28 Rutland Gate, SW7 1PQ); 91 Ailesbury Rd, *Dublin* 4; 107 Endeavour Street, Red Hill, *Canberra* (also for New Zealand); 445 Wilbrod Street, *Ottawa*, Ontario; 405 Church Street, *Pretoria*; and 2343 Massachusetts Ave, NW, *Washington* DC 20008, with consulates at Chicago, Los Angeles, and New York (and with the *Austrian Institute* at 11 East 52nd Street, New York, NY 10022).

Medical Advice. British travellers in Austria can get medical advice and attention by producing a current UK passport. In-patient treatment only is covered by reciprocal agreement with the NHS, although there may be a small payment during the first 28 days. See also p 114.

Security. No objects of any value should be left visible in cars parked in underground car-parks, or overnight near hotels. Valuables should be deposited with the manager of your hotel, and a receipt given. Contact the police in case of any trouble.

Currency Regulations. There are no restrictions on the amount of sterling the traveller may take *out* of Great Britain, nor any limit to the amount of *foreign* currency which may be brought into and taken out of Austria (provided proof is shown that the visitor entered with such an amount), but no more than 100,000 Austrian Schillings may be taken out of the country without special permission.

Money. The monetary unit is the Austrian *Schilling*, which is divided into 100 *Groschen*. Coins are issued by the Austrian National Bank of 2, 5, 10, and 50 Groschen, and 1, 5, 10, 20, 25, 50, 100, 500, and 1000 Schillings; and notes of 20, 50, 100, 500, 1000, and 5000 Schillings.

Exchange (*Wechsel*). Banks are normally open from 8.00–12.30, and 13.30–15.00 Monday to Friday, and (in Vienna) until 17.30 on Thursday. At other times, including weekends, money can be exchanged at main railway stations, at airports, and at certain Tourist Information Offices.

Tax refunds. Visitors may get a considerable tax refund on a variety of articles bought and exported, and a U34 form should be requested when applicable. The value must exceed 1000 Schillings.

Approaches to Austria; transport and motoring in Austria

There are several rapid rail and ferry services from London to the Channel ports, and beyond (see below), while the quickest means of transit is by air—often providing some remarkable alpine views en route—for which see p 98. Car-hire facilities are available at airports, main railway stations in Austria, and elsewhere.

Travel Information. General information may be obtained gratis from the *Austrian National Tourist Office* at 30 St. George Street, London W1R 0AL (just N of Conduit Street). They can provide information on accommodation, admission to museums, entertainments, festivals, and winter sports, etc., and are very efficient.

The Austrian National Tourist Office has branches in the *USA* at 500 Fifth Ave, 20th floor, Suite 2022, New York, NY 10110; Suite 2480, 11601 Wilshire Blvd, Los Angeles, California 90025; Suite 1950, 500 N Michigan Ave, Chicago, Illinois 60611; and Suite 500, 4800 San Felipe Street, Houston, Texas 77056.
  Also at Merrion Hall, Strand Road, Sandymount, PO Box 2506, Dublin 4, *Ireland*; 19th Floor, No. 1 York Street, Sydney 2000 NSW, *Australia*; Suite 3330, 2 Bloor Street E, Toronto, Ontario M4W 1A8, *Canada*, and Suite 1410, 1010 Sherbrooke Street W, Montreal PQ H3A 2R7, and also Suite 1220–23, Vancouver Block, 736 Granville Street, Vancouver BC V6Z IJ2; 11 Eton Road, The Galaxy, 2193 Parktown, Johannesburg, *S Africa*, and in most capitals and other important centres throughout the world.

In Vienna its offices are at Margaretenstrasse 1, A-1040, a short distance down the Wiedner-Hauptstrasse (itself a S extension of the Kärntner Strasse).

The addresses of the **Provincial Tourist Boards** (*Verkehrsvereine*) are listed below. That for *Vienna* itself is Obere Augartenstrasse 40, A-1025 (with several branches), while that for *Lower Austria* is Hoher Markt 3, A-1010 Vienna.
  Burgenland; Schloss Esterházy, A-7000 Eisenstadt
  Carinthia (*Kärnten*); Halleggerstrasse 1, A-9201, Krumpendorf
  Upper Austria (*Ober Österreich*); Schillerstrasse 50, A-4010 Linz
  Salzburg; Alpenstrasse 96, A-5033 Salzburg
  Styria (*Steiermark*); Herrengasse 16, Landhaus, A-8010 Graz
  Tyrol (*Tirol*); Bozner Platz 6, A-6010 Innsbruck
  Vorarlberg, Römerstrasse 7/1, A6901 Bregenz
  It should be emphasised that these offices are responsible for the provinces concerned in general, and are not the local town or municipal tourist offices.

Numerous and frequent **Passenger and Car Ferry Services** between England and the Continent are operated by British and French Railways, etc., and for the latest information on services, contact your

your local travel agent. *Hovercraft* services may be erratic in adverse weather conditions.

The *Austrian Federal Railways* or ÖBB (enquire at the National Tourist Offices) can provide full details of the variety of services available, together with their cost, and information on kilometric tickets, 'Austria' tickets, Motorail (car-carrier) expresses, etc. The network of railways throughout Austria is remarkably good considering its topography, and they are a reliable form of transport when climatic conditions might inhibit drivers not used to Austrian winters. For details of the InterRail cards for those under 26 and for InterRail Plus 26 contact British Rail International, International Rail Centre, Victoria Station, London SW1V 1JY (071-834 2345), Eurotrain, 52 Grosvenor Gardens, London SW1W 0AG (071-730 8518) and Wasteels Travel, 121 Wilton Road, London SW1V 1JZ (071-834 7066).

Motorists driving to Austria will save much trouble by joining one of the automobile associations, which can provide any necessary documents, as well as information about rules of the road abroad, restrictions regarding caravans and trailers, and arrangements for delivery of spare parts, insurance, etc. (The Automobile Association, 30 The Haymarket, London SW1, tel. 071-930 9059; the Royal Automobile Club, 130 St Albans Road, Watford, Herts WD2 4AH, tel. 0923 33573; the American Automobile Association, 8111 Gate House Road, Falls Church, Virginia.) Motorists who are not the owners of their vehicle should possess the owner's permit for its use abroad. The two main Austrian Automobile Associations are ÖAMTC, with offices at Schubertring 1–3, A-1010 Vienna, and ARBÖ, Mariahilfer Strasse 180, A-1150 Vienna, providing emergency breakdown services on dialling 120 or 123 respectively.

The insurance facilities offered by either *Europ Assistance* or the *AA* should be considered.

The speed limit in Austria on motorways is 130km per hour (81mph), but 50kmph (31mph) in built-up areas betweeen the place name signs. On all other roads it is 100kmph (62mph). The wearing of seat-belts is obligatory, while children under 12 must be in the back seats. The use of dipped headlights (or fog-lamps in conjunction with side-lights) is compulsory in bad visibility. Converter lenses are required under Continental regulations. The motorist must also possess a red breakdown triangle, and should carry a first-aid kit. Between approximately 15 November and 4 April studded tyres are permissible, and during the winter it is *advisable* to use snow tyres and to carry chains, although the latter may be hired from the Austrian automobile clubs. Black ice can be a hazard. Flashing white or yellow lights at unguarded level-crossings indicate that the signals are working, and that one may cross; a red light means STOP. Drivers not used to steep gradients should engage a low gear in good time when descending mountain roads; vehicles ascending always have priority. Several roads are closed to caravans, and it is not recommended to attempt crossing certain passes with them. Most motorways or *autobahns* in Austria are free, but some charge a toll, as do certain other roads (*Mautstrassen*). Information on road and weather conditions may be obtained in Austria by telephoning 711997.

The **Bus** network *in* Austria is extensive, and *Post-buses* will transport one to the remotest districts. Detailed timetables are available from railway stations and main bus stations, etc.

There are several regular **Bus or Coach services** from the UK to various destinations on the continent, and details may be obtained from *Victoria Coach Station*, London SW1, British Rail Travel Centres, etc.

Parking in the centres of the larger cities is limited, and although there are no obtrusive meters, a charge is made for parking vouchers, which can be obtained in banks, some petrol stations, and most Tabak-Trafik kiosks. The limit is usually 90 minutes between 8.00–18.00 on Monday–Friday, and until 14.00 on Saturday. Parking may be forbidden in certain streets, but normally one will be allowed to stop or park briefly—for a maximum of ten minutes. In Vienna, parking is forbidden in streets with tramways.

Travellers approaching Austria via France should equip themselves with a good, recently published map; see p 89. The most direct and fastest roads from the Channel ports to Austria are outlined below. Those preferring to use motorways should note that there are tolls to pay on those of France, Switzerland (one fee per annum), and Italy, although at present in Germany, and in Austria itself, they are *free*, apart from a few short stretches or when going through alpine tunnels.

Motorways, *autoroutes* in France (which can become expensive), may be entered near *St. Omer* from Boulogne, at *Calais*, and at *Dunkerque* (see below). From a point just E of *Arras*, the former A26 has been extended to *Reims*, where you can join the A4 from Paris, by-passing *Metz*. At 40km E of Metz one can either bear NE to enter Germany and make for *Karlsruhe*, or veer SE towards *Strasbourg*. Crossing the Rhine from the latter, one may either turn NE on the *autobahn* towards Karlsruhe, there following the A8 past *Stuttgart*, *Ulm*, *Augsburg*, and *Munich* (see below); or turn S to cross Switzerland via *Basle*, *Zürich*, and *St. Gallen*, to enter Austria at *Bregenz*; Bregenz may also be approached directly from Strasbourg by travelling through the Black Forest, and then skirting the N bank of the *Bodensee* (Lake Constance) via *Friedrichshafen*.

Another route, from Paris, is that following the A6 to *Beaune*, there turning onto the A36 for *Mulhouse*, some 30km NW of *Basle*.

From Dunkerque or Ostend one may cross Belgium on the E40 past *Liège* towards *Cologne*, but before reaching Cologne turn SE to follow the A61 towards *Mannheim* and bear S to *Karlsruhe*; see above. An alternative autobahn from Cologne is the A3, bearing SE past *Frankfurt* and *Nuremberg*; one can either take the A9 to *Munich*, or continue to follow the A3 past *Regensburg* to enter Austria S of *Schärding*.

From Munich one may follow the A8 SE, and then E past *Rosenheim* to enter Austria immediately W of *Salzburg*. Those in a hurry to reach *Vienna* directly from this Salzburg entry should follow the autobahn A1 to the E; see Rtes 14A and 21A. If entering Carinthia at *Villach*, from Italy, follow the recently completed A23 *autostrada* skirting Udine, which bears N c 100km NE of Venice.

Transport in Vienna. While most important monuments and museums are within easy walking distance of the centre, visitors are recommended to buy a *24 or 72 hour ticket*, available at the Opernpassage Tourist Office, the Tourist Information Office at Kärntner Strasse 38, the Vienna Public Transport Information Centres at Karlsplatz, and Stephansplatz, and other advance sales offices, at Vienna airport, Information Offices at the Westbahnhof and Südbahnhof railway stations, and at many tobacconists. The ticket is valid for an unlimited number of rides on the Vienna Transport System—Underground (*U-Bahn*), most buses, the *Stadtbahn*, and on trams (*Strassenbahn*; or street-cars).

Alternatively, you can buy a quantity of tickets from an advance booking-office or any *Tabak-Trafik* kiosk by asking for *Fahrschein-vorverkauf*. Weekly, monthly, and annual tickets are also available.

Much of the system has been sensibly automated, and most entrances to platforms and on buses have a ticket-punching machine, which must be used on entering. The same ticket may be used on any municipal transport between the start of the journey and one's destination, *in any one direction* (no back-tracking or use on the return journey permitted). If a reasonable time is allowed for the journey, it is possible to break the journey up and to visit places en route.

N.B. Care must be taken in crossing streets where trams run, for in certain places they travel in the opposite direction to other traffic.

Regular **Air Services** between England and Austria are maintained by **Austrian Airlines** (*Österreichische Luftverkehrs AG*), working in conjunction with **British Airways**. Full information on flights from London (Heathrow) to Vienna's *Schwechat* airport may be obtained from *Austrian Airlines*, 50 Conduit St, London W1R 0NP (just around the corner in Savile Row), and from *British Airways*, 75 Lower Regent St, SW1.

Austrian Airlines, refounded in 1957, has a well-equipped fleet of medium-range jets, and provides impeccable service. Their offices in *Vienna* are at Kärntner Ring 18 (a short walk SE from the Opera-house); the City Air-terminal is just behind the Hilton Hotel (Land-strasse Underground). The telephone number at Schwechat airport is (0222) 711 10-0.

The main offices of Austrian Airlines in Austria are Makartplatz 9, A-5020 *Salzburg*; Schubertstrasse 1, Am Hessenplatz, A-4020 *Linz*; Adamgasse 7A, Raika Passage, A-6020 *Innsbruck*; Herrengasse 16, A-8010 *Graz*; and 8 Mai-Strasse 17, Domgasse, A-9020 *Klagenfurt*.

In the USA they have offices at *New York* (15 W 50th St, NY 10020), *Chicago* (444 N Michigan Ave, Suite 3540, IL 60611), and *Los Angeles* (4000 MacArthur Blvd, Suite 740, Newport Beach, CA 92660). There are also offices in most capitals and important centres in Europe, and in many non-European cities, notably in the Near East, from which there are regular flights.

Austrian Airlines connects 46 cities in 35 countries in Europe, the Middle East, and N Africa. *Internal or domestic services* are also maintained by *Austrian Air Services* between Vienna, Salzburg, Linz, Graz, and Klagenfurt, and by *Tyrolean Airways* between Innsbruck and Vienna, Zürich, and Frank-furt. Reservations may be made through all Austrian Airline offices. They also provide *Charter flights* both to and from Austria.

Both international and domestic flights frequently provide outstanding views of the snow-clad alpine ranges en route.

There are bus services from airports (*Flughafen*) to town terminals, and vice versa, while taxis will also meet planes, and many car-hire firms have offices at airports. Austrian Airlines also have a comput-erised reservation service (OSCAR), and electronic hotel-reservation system (HOST), and own *Interconvention*, a firm organising con-gresses, together with a 50 per cent interest in *Touropa Austria*, the leading Austrian tour operator.

Apply to offices of Austrian Airlines for detailed information about fare reductions for infants, children, young people and students, group travel, accompanying spouse, etc.

For flight facilities from Gatwick available through the **Anglo-Austrian Society**, apply to 46 Queen Anne's Gate, London SW1H 9AU. It should be emphasised that these are *limited to members of at least six months' standing*. The **Ski Club of Great Britain**, 118 Eaton Square, London SW1W 9AF, is also able to provide Club flights. Charter flights also operate between London and Innsbruck and Klagenfurt.

Holiday Facilities. Austrian Airlines offer several interesting combinations in the way of package tours and sporting holidays—usually of a week's duration, including accommodation, board or half-board, transport, etc., during differing periods of the year—details of which may be found in brochures available from their offices and Austrian National Tourist Offices.

Among the facilities currently offered are tours of Baroque abbeys; and also ornithological, and wine-tasting tours, etc. Sporting holidays include mountain-walking, fishing, riding, sailing, etc. Details of flights during the winter-sports season and further information on holiday facilities is available from Austrian Airlines, or any travel agent. Other tour companies offering package tours to Austria are Austrian Holidays (tel. 071-439 7108), Austro Tours (tel. 0727 38191), GTF (tel. 071-792 1260), and Martin Randall Travel (for art and architecture tours) (tel. 081-994 6477), or contact your local travel agent.

By **Danube Steamer**. The *Donau-Dampfschiffahrts-Gesellschaft*, or DDSG (see p 321), provides a regular service from Passau, on the German frontier, to Linz, and thence via Krems to Vienna, and vice versa, together with several excursions. These include 'Rundfahrten' in Vienna itself, and there are also hydrofoil ferries from the capital to Bratislava, and on to Budapest, while a Russian company provides an excursion from Passau to the Black Sea. Full details can be obtained from Austrian National Tourist Offices, or from DDSG offices at Handelskai 265, A-1021 Vienna; Regensburgerstrasse 9/1, PO Box 9 A-4020 Linz; or Postfach 1424, Im Ort 14a (Dreiflusseck), 8390 Passau, Germany. The landing-stage for departures for boat trips in Vienna is at the Schwedenbrücke on the Donaukanal.

Postal and Other Services

Most *Post Offices* are open from 8.00–12.00 and 14.00–18.00 from Monday to Friday, and in the larger centres they are also open from 8.00–10.00 on Saturday. The main post offices in the cities and at the main railway stations are usually open round the clock. Correspondence marked '*poste restante*' or '*Postlagernd*' (to be called for) may be addressed to any post office, and is handed to the addressee on proof of identity (passport preferable).

The main post offices in the principal towns are: Fleischmarkt 19, A-1010 *Vienna*; Residenzplatz 9, A-5010 *Salzburg*; Maximilianstrasse 2, A-6010 *Innsbruck*; Domgasse 1, A-4010 *Linz*; Neutorgasse 46, A-8010 *Graz*; and Dr Hermanngasse, A-9020 *Klagenfurt*.

Stamps (*Briefmarken*) are also available at tobacconists (*Tabak-Trafik*); letter-boxes are painted yellow.

Telephones are to be found in most post offices, apart from public booths, etc. All places in Austria, and most places elsewhere in Europe, may be reached by automatic or STD dialing. Trunk calls within the country are approx. 33 per cent cheaper between 18.00 and 8.00 on weekdays, and from 18.00 on Friday until 8.00 on the following Monday. Hotels usually charge an additional fee. In the case of fire, dial 122; for Police, 133; for First Aid or Ambulance, 144.

Information Bureaux. Most towns, and many villages have a *Tourist Office*, often providing useful information on accommodation, local events, sporting facilities, times of admission to museums and Schlösser, etc. Staff have a very professional approach to their work, and most will speak English.

Hotels and Restaurants

The availability of accommodation is not indicated in this Guide. All types and categories of accommodation can be found throughout Austria, and both National, Provincial, and local or municipal Tourist Offices can provide lists of hotels, etc. (apart from information on camping sites, etc.). The usual European star system of categorisation is followed, charges varying according to the season. As tourism is such an important item in the economy, the general quality of Austrian hotels is high, and the service provided is remarkably good.

It is advisable to book in advance if visiting a town during a festival or festive season, and it is sensible to check on the exact situation of the hotel, as it may be further from the centre than expected. There are any number of *Gasthofs* outside the main towns, usually providing simpler but more hospitable, and spotlessly clean accommodation, while lodging may also be had at any house displaying *Zimmer frei* (room available). While language difficulties may arise, in areas frequented by English-speaking travellers, such as the Vorarlberg and Tyrol—but also elsewhere—a surprising number of people speak sufficient English to come to an understanding. The term *garni* indicates 'Bed and Breakfast'.

Food and Wine

by *Ingrid Price-Gschlössl*

To most people the mention of Austrian food conjures up visions of sumptuous cakes with lashings of whipped cream, but there is much more to Austrian cooking than Sachertorte and Salzburger Nockerl. Because of its diverse roots, Austrian cooking is one of the most varied in Europe. Under the Austro-Hungarian Empire, countries such as Bohemia, Silesia, Galicia, Moravia, Hungary, Slavonia, Croatia, Serbia, and parts of Northern Italy, all contributed dishes which, in the course of time, became an integral part of Austrian cuisine. It is therefore possible to eat goulash in Vienna that is just as authentic as the goulash you will get on the steppes of Hungary, or *cevapcici* that can compete with anything you will be served in Yugoslavia.

An Austrian's gastronomic day consists of:

Breakfast (Frühstück): coffee with *Semmeln* (bread rolls) or *Schwarzbrot* (brown bread), butter, jam or honey.

Mid-morning: a snack, which can be anything from a sandwich to a small goulash (*ein kleines Gulasch*) for those who start work very early.

Lunch (Mittagessen): at approx. 12.30. Most Austrians have their main meal, which consists of soup, main dish, and dessert, in the middle of the day. Coffee is generally taken mid-afternoon (with cake, if not figure-conscious).

Supper (Abendessen): early evening. It generally consists of a cold dish, i.e. a platter of meats, cheese, etc. with bread, wine or beer. Very often, whole families go out to eat in the late afternoon at one of the many small inns or 'Heurigen', where they will have a cold meal.

Among individual dishes are:

Suppe (soup): this is generally a clear soup, but will often contain either pasta, *Griesnockerl* (semolina gnocchi), *Leberknödel* (liver dumplings), *Fritatten* (shredded pancakes), rice, or *Fleischstrudel* (meat strudel). Often, particularly if the main course is not very substantial, thick soups are served, such as *Gemüsesuppe* (vegetable soup), *Hühnercremesuppe* (chicken soup), *Fischsuppe* (fish soup), *Gulaschsuppe* (goulash soup), *Linsensuppe* (lentil soup) or *Erbsensuppe* (pea soup), while a *Mehlspeise* (hot sweet dish), is often eaten on Fridays as a substitute for fish.

Vorspeise (entrée): served less frequently than soup, and mainly included on more important occasions. It often consists of hard-boiled eggs with different sauces or in aspic, patés, cold meats, etc.

Hauptspeise (main dish): generally a meat, fish, or even a sweet dish. Here you will find a great variety, as every type of meat is used. One of the great classics is 'Wiener Schnitzel', traditionally made with veal but very often replaced by pork escalopes and then served as 'Schweinsschnitzel'. There is also *Kalbsbraten* (roast veal), *Gefüllte Kalbsbrust* (stuffed breast of veal), *Kalbsvögerl* (paupiettes of veal), *Eingemachtes Kalbfleisch* (blanquette of veal), *Kalbsgulasch* (veal goulash), and *Naturschnitzel* (escalope of veal in a creamy sauce).

The beef dishes are as varied as the veal. Here the classic is *Tafelspitz*, a boiled fillet, served with chive sauce (*Schnittlauchsauce*) and chopped roast potatoes (*geröstete Kartoffeln*). Another is *Gulasch* (or *gulyas*) in all its many varieties. *Rostbraten* (braising steak in onion sauce) and its several variations, *Rindsbraten* (roast beef in a cream sauce), *Rindsrouladen* (paupiettes of beef) and all kinds of *Rindsragout* (beef stew), are also very popular.

The classic among the pork dishes is *Schweinsbraten*, a succulent roast, traditionally served with *Semmelknödel* (bread dumplings) and *Krautsalat* (cabbage salad—boiled warm cabbage made into a salad). A lot of ham is eaten, which is less salty than the English variety, and normally served with *Knödel* and *Sauerkraut*, or in a *Bauernschmaus*, which consists of boiled ham, roast pork cutlets, sausages, Sauerkraut and dumplings. There is also a *Schweinsgulasch* (pork goulash), *Szegediner Gulasch* (a pork goulash made with Sauerkraut and boiled potatoes), *Gefüllte Schweinsbrust* (stuffed breast of pork), *Krenfleisch* (boiled pork with horseradish sauce), *Serbisches Reisfleisch* (pork stew with rice cooked in the sauce), and there are many varieties of *Schweinsragout* (pork stew).

Mince is usually a mixture of different meats, i.e. beef, pork, and veal, and it is used for *Gefüllte Paprika* (stuffed green peppers in a rich tomato sauce) which, in summer, will be found on most menus, *Faschierter Braten* (meat loaf, which sometimes contains boiled eggs and carrots), or *Faschierte Laibchen* (rissoles). Lamb is eaten much less frequently in Austria than in Britain and then, as in France, more as mutton in a variety of stews.

Game is frequently on the menu, prepared in several ways, notably as *Wildragout* (venison stew with red wine sauce), or a *Hasenjunges* (a stew made with hare's blood), *Hirschgulasch* (venison goulash), and *Hasenrücken* (roast saddle of hare in a cream sauce). You may even be offered *Wildschwein* (wild boar), still found in parts of Austria and Hungary. *Fasan* (pheasant), one of the favourite game birds, is served roast, stuffed, or in a cream sauce.

There are endless varieties of poultry dishes, such as *Brathuhn* (roast chicken), *Gefülltes Brathuhn* (roast stuffed chicken—usually with a bread stuffing), *Backhendl* (chicken fried in breadcrumbs), *Paprikahuhn* (chicken paprika), and *Suppenhuhn* (chicken pieces in noodle soup). Roast goose is one of the traditional dishes for St. Martin's day (11 November), and at Christmas, although in recent years turkey has taken its place.

As Austria has no access to the sea, the choice of fish dishes is very much limited to fresh water fish, i.e. *Forellen* (trout), *Hecht* (pike), *Fogosch* or *Zander* (perch), and *Karpfen* (carp), which is also served at Christmas. In the Salzkammergut there is a delicious fish called *Saibling*, with a slightly pink flesh and well worth savouring. The fish are generally fried in breadcrumbs (*gebacken*), in a batter made with beer (*im Bierteig*), or stuffed (*gefüllt*).

Most menus will include some offal, for example *Beuschel* (lung stew), *Gebackene Leber* (liver in bread crumbs), *Geröstete Leber* (liver in onion sauce), *Geröstete Nieren* (kidneys in onion sauce), *Gespicktes Herz* (heart with bacon strips in a cream sauce). Sausages often feature on the menu, i.e. *Bratwurst* (smooth white sausage, fried), *Blutwurst* (black pudding), and *Leberwurst* (a type of sausage-shaped haggis, fried).

Beilagen (accompaniments): most main dishes are accompanied by a salad, which is generally either *grün* (plain lettuce) or *gemischt* (mixed). But often there is a choice of vegetables, such as *Erbsen* (peas), *Karotten* (carrots), *Fisolen* or *grüne Bohnen* (French beans), *Karfiol* (cauliflower) and *Kohlsprossen* (Brussel sprouts). The more substantial accompaniments are either *Knödel* (dumplings), *Kartoffel* or *Erdäpfel* (potatoes), *Nudeln* (pasta) or *Nockerl* (a type of gnocchi). There is a large variety of Knödel, e.g. *Semmelknödel* (white bread dumplings), *Serviettenknödel* (a richer version, made in the shape of a loaf), *Leberknödel* (with liver, usually served in clear soup), *Speckknödel* (with bacon filling), *Kartoffelknödel* (potato dumplings), etc. Kartoffeln are usually served either as *Salzkartoffeln* (plain boiled potatoes), *Kartoffelpüree* (puréed potatoes), *Petersilkartoffeln* (boiled potatoes with parsley), *Geröstete Kartoffeln* (sliced boiled potatoes fried with onion), or as *Kartoffelsalat* (potato salad).

Mehlspeisen (hot puddings): these are either eaten at the end of a meal or, more commonly, as a main course. The most famous is, undoubtedly, *Apfelstrudel*. Strudel, of Turkish origin, comes with a variety of fillings (some savoury), but the most usual amongst the sweet fillings are apples (*Apfelstrudel*), cream cheese (*Topfen-* or *Milchrahmstrudel*) and cherries (*Kirschenstrudel*). Another favourite is the fruit dumpling, usually made of potato dough filled with fruit, boiled, and then turned in fried sugared breadcrumbs. During summer, *Marillenknödel* (apricot dumplings) and *Zwetschkenknödel* (plum dumplings) will be on most menus, and should be sampled. Also to be recommended is *Kaiserschmarren*, which, despite the simple ingredients (pancake batter), is delicious, and is usually served with *Zwetschkenröster* (stewed plums). The *Salzburger Nockerl* is another favourite dish; but beware, for one portion of this sweet soufflé easily feeds two! Pancakes are called *Palatschinken* in Austria, and are often filled with apricot jam. *Topfenpalatschinken* are hot pancakes filled with cream cheese. For those with a smaller appetite, most menus offer a selection of *Kompott* (stewed fruit).

Torten (cakes) are often served as a dessert at the end of a meal, but are also available in *Konditoreien* (pastry shops) and coffee houses. It needs a lot of will-power to resist these tempting confections, of which the most well known is the *Sachertorte* (named after the Hotel Sacher in Vienna), a dark chocolate cake served with whipped cream. Other torten include *Dobos-Torte* (with a caramelised top), *Linzer Torte* (made of hazel nuts, and with a typical trellis top), *Malakoff-Torte* (similar to a charlotte Malakoff), *Nusstorte* (made with walnuts and filled with whipped cream), *Punschtorte* (a sponge cake with a filling made of biscuit crumbs soaked in punch and with a pink rum icing—rather potent, but delicious—and *Topfentorte* (a cheese cake, which is either baked or prepared cold with a setting agent).

Coffee and Coffee-houses. The founder of the Viennese coffee-house is said to be a Franz Georg Kulcycki (Kolschitzky) who, on 27 February 1684, shortly after the raising of the Turkish siege, opened the first coffee-house in the Schlössergasse. However, according to more recent investigation, coffee was originally introduced to the Viennese by Lodovico Conte di Marsigli, a young officer, who, as a prisoner of war to the Pasha in Temesvar, was apprenticed as a coffee cook. He arrived at Vienna with the commissariat, eventually becoming quartermaster in the Austrian army, and in 1685 he wrote a book called 'De bevenda asiatica'. (A 'Coffe-house' was referred to in Paris some 20 years earlier, and there the beverage was already fashionable.)

Soon the coffee-houses supplied their guests with newspapers and—quite a sensation—introduced billiards, which until then had been a game played only by the aristocracy. Aesthetes and intellectuals, men of letters, politicians, and their hangers-on, made coffee-houses their regular meeting-place.

The 19C and 20C saw the development of new types of coffee-house, e.g. the café-restaurant (*Kaffeerestaurant*), the coffee-house patisserie (*Kaffeekonditorei*) and the espresso (*Espressostube*). But even the modern Italian espresso was soon turned into something quite typically Viennese, with all the amenities the Viennese have come to expect of such an establishment.

Over the years certain coffee-houses developed very individual atmospheres; some have facilities for playing billiards, chess, and dominoes, or even have their own bridge room.

Coffee may be ordered in a variety of forms:

grosser or *kleiner Mokka*, large or small mocca

grosser or *kleiner Schwarzer*, large or small black coffee
grosser or *kleiner Brauner*, large or small coffee with a dash of milk or cream
Melange, half coffee and half milk in a large cup
eine Portion Kaffee, separate pots of coffee and hot milk
Einspänner, black coffee with whipped cream served in a glass
Teeschale licht, milk with a little coffee added
Teeschale gold, milk with slightly more coffee added
ein Kurzer, very small concentrated espresso
ein Gestreckter or Verlängerter, diluted espresso
Kaffee mit Schlag, coffee with whipped cream
Mokka gespritzt, black coffee laced with rum
Mazagran, cold coffee with lumps of ice and rum
Eiskaffee, cold coffee with vanilla ice cream and whipped cream

It is also possible in most coffee-houses to get a *Wiener Frühstück* (Viennese breakfast) which consists of coffee, or tea, or chocolate, with rolls and butter, jam or marmalade and an egg, if wanted.

Books. *Gretel Beer*, Austrian Cooking; *Rosl Philpot*, Viennese Cookery; *Lotte Scheibenpflug*, The Best of Austrian Cooking; *Elisabeth Mayer-Browne*, The Home Book of Austrian Cookery; *S.F. & F.L. Hallgarten*, The Wines and Wine Gardens of Austria.

Wine

Austrian wines, like those of Germany and Hungary, are predominantly white; red wine is produced in much smaller quantities. There are approx. 40,000 hectares of vineyards altogether, mainly in Lower Austria, Burgenland, Styria, and in the neighbourhood of Vienna. Although wine has been produced in Austria for at least a thousand years, Austrian wines are not as well known abroad as they should be.

There was a temporary setback in their sale of red wines after the scandal of 1985, when it was found that some had been adulterated with diethylene glycol, after which the government passed stringent legislation to protect the consumer and to control both the quality and quantity produced. The label must now give the quality grade, e.g. *Tafelwein* (table wine), *Landwein*, or *Tischwein and Qualitätswein, or Prädikatswein*, and the letter T, Q, or P must appear before the six-figure number on the band running over the cork top. The label must give the name and address of the producer or bottler, the alcohol content, and the sugar content (*trocken*, dry; *halbtroken*, medium dry; *suss*, sweet). The vintage year and grape variety must be specified on Spätlese and Auslese types. Only superior wines may be sold in the slim 0.7 litre bottles.
  Among terms one is likely to come across on wine labels are:
gerebelt, hand-picked
Eigenbaugewächs, from the maker's own vineyard
Naturwein, wine without added sugar
Originalabfüllung, estate bottled
reinsortig, only this particular type
Ried, vineyard (as in French *clos*)
Weingarten, *Weingut*, wine estate

Wine Regions

Lower Austria. Prevailing grape varieties: *white*—Rheinriesling, Grüner Veltliner, Neuberger, Riesling-Sylvaner, Welsch-Riesling, Müller-Thurgau, Zierfandler, Muscat-Ottonel, Traminer; *red*—Rotgipfler, Blauer Portugieser, Blauburgunder, Blaufränkisch, and Sankt Laurent.
  The wine regions lie N (*Weinviertel*) and S (*Wienerwald Steinfeld*) of the Danube, the former producing the Grüner Veltliner, a fresh

and fruity wine best drunk straight from the barrel, in the open air, with a sandwich.

Another important wine-producing region is the *Wachau*, well known outside Austria as the area where 'Schluck' (mainly made from the Sylvaner) is produced, although the local Rhine Riesling can be a really great wine. Krems is the main centre of the Wachau, with large vaults for bulk storage, a school of viniculture, and a wine museum.

The *Wienerwald Steinfeld* district, also known as the *Südbahn*, has some excellent vineyards on the slopes skirting the Vienna Woods. The best known is Gumpoldskirchen with its fine late-gathered wines made from Veltliner, Riesling, and Gewürztraminer. From Baden and Traiskirchen come fiery, spicy wines, while Bad Vöslau is better known for its dark, dry and pleasant red wine.

Burgenland. Prevailing grape varieties: *white*—Welsch-Riesling, Muscat-Ottonel, Furmint (Mosel), Traminer, Weissburgunder, Rüländer, Müller-Thurgau, Neuburger, and Bouviertraube; *red*—Blaufränkisch, Blauburgunder, Portugieser, and Sankt Laurent.

The Burgenland, like Hungary, specialises in sweet wines. *Rust*, on the shores of the Neusiedlersee, is the centre, and the Ruster Ausbruch, from late-picked grapes, is a very fine wine. Some of the best Auslesen and Beerenauslesen come from the far side of the lake. The sandy soil of the *Seewinkel* protected the original vines from the phylloxera louse, and this is one of the few places in Europe where wine is still made from ungrafted vines.

Styria. Prevailing grape varieties: *white*—Furmint, Riesling, Sylvaner, Traminer, Weissburgunder, Rüländer, Morillon, Müller-Thurgau, Muscat-Ottonel, and Sauvignon; *red*—Blauer Portugieser, Blaufränkisch, and Sankt Laurent. The blue Wildbacher is of local importance as it is the basic grape for a wine of special character and subtlety—the Styrian Schilcherwein.

The main districts are the *Schilcher* for reds (including the fresh, spicy Schilcherwein), the *Sausal-Leibnitz*, where the vineyards are planted to a height of 580m, the *Leutschach-Ehrenhausen*, where the wines are stronger and fuller, the *Klöch*, which produces wines of quality, some of them sparkling; and *East Styria*, which is the least important area.

Vienna. Prevailing grape varieties: Grüner Veltliner, Riesling, and Weissburgunder. No other capital city is so much associated with wine as Vienna. The wine villages of Grinzing, Sievering, and Nussdorf now lie within its suburbs, and both Viennese and tourists flock there to sample the new wine, known as **Heuriger**. The term 'heuriger' means either the new wine (*heuer*, this year) or the tavern in which it is served. If a grower has new wine—and by law it should have been produced in his own vineyards—he hangs out a green bough announcing that the wine of the year is ready for drinking.

Most of the Heuriger is Veltliner or Sylvaner, but Riesling and Traminer are also produced. A Heuriger should not be too dry and at its best is a vivacious, sprightly wine, and can go straight to one's head.

Wine is usually ordered by *ein viertel*, served in a glass holding 1/4 litre or 1/8 litre (*ein Achtel*). *Süss* is sweet, *mild* is mild, and *resch* or *herb* is dry.

Beer is often sold *vom Fass*, on tap from a keg. It is served in 1/2-litre (*Krügel*) or 1/3-litre (*Seidel*) glasses.

Most, a drink typical of Upper Austria, is a rather tart form of cider.
Ein G'spritzter is a glass of wine mixed with soda water; very refreshing on a hot day.

Menu

The following list includes many of the more common foods, with their English equivalents.

Suppen, Soups

Klare Suppen, clear soups
Hühnersuppe, chicken broth
Rindsuppe mit Ei, consommé with egg
Wildsuppe, game soup
Gebundene Suppen, thick or cream soups; *Püreesuppen*, purée soups
Gemüsesuppen, vegetable soups

Kalte Vorspeisen, Cold hors-d'oeuvres and entrées

Salate, salads
Pasteten, patés
Aufschnitt, cold meats
Warme Vorspeisen, hot entrées
Eier, eggs
Omeletten, omelettes
Rühreier, scrambled eggs
Pochierte Eier, poached eggs
Spiegeleier, fried eggs
Hartgekochte Eier, hard-boiled eggs
Kernweiche Eier, 4-minute eggs
Weiche Eier, soft-boiled eggs
Speck mit Ei, Bacon and eggs
among other terms are: *in Bierteig gebacken*, or *in Backteig*, deep fried
gebraten, fried, roast
gedünstet, braised
gekocht, boiled
gërostet, sautéed
gratiniert, au gratin
grilliert, grilled, or *am Grill*
gebacken, fried in breadcrumbs or baked
geselcht, salted
geräuchert, smoked
platte, richly garnished grilled meats
Müllerin Art (*in Butter gebraten*), meunière
Knödel, dumplings
Nockerl, small dumplings
Nudeln, noodles
Teigwaren, pasta dishes

Fische, Fish

SÜSSWASSERFISCHE, fresh-water fish
Aal, eel
Barsch, perch
Fogosch, fogas
Forelle, trout
Hecht, pike
Karpfen, carp
Lachs, salmon
Lachsforelle, salmon-trout
Saibling, char
Schill, or *Zander*, pike-perch
Wels, or *Waller*, catfish

SEEFISCHE, salt-water fish
Dorsch, hake
Goldbarsch, sea bream
Heilbutt, halibut
Hering, herring
Kabeljau, cod
Makrele, mackerel
Meeraal, conger eel
Räucherlachs, smoked salmon
Sardellen, anchovies
Schellfisch, haddock
Scholle, plaice
Seebarsch, perch
Seezunge, sole
Steinbutt, turbot
Thunfisch, tunny
Weissfisch, whiting
Gebackene Meeresfrüchte, seafood in breadcrumbs

Schalen-und Krustentiere, Shellfish

Austern, oysters
Hummer, lobster
Krebse, crayfish
Languste, spiny lobster
Meerkrebse, scampi
Muscheln, mussels
Schnecken, snails

Fleisch, Meat

Faschiertes, meat balls, or mincemeat
Rind, beef
Rindsschnitzel, steak
Rostbraten, roast loin
Rindszunge, ox-tongue
Hammel, mutton
Herz, heart
Hirn, brains
Innereien, offal
Kalb, veal
Kalbsbries, sweetbreads
Kalbskopf, calf's head
Lamm, lamb
Leber, liver
Nierndl, kidneys
Schinken, ham
Schwein, pork
Speck, bacon
Surbraten, salt pork
Wurst, sausage

Geflügel, Poultry

Ente, duckling
Gans, goose
Hühn, chicken
Hühnerleber, chicken livers
Indian or *Truthahn*, turkey
Kapaun or *Masthahn*, capon

Wild, Game

Fasan, pheasant
Hasen, hare
Hirsch, deer
Rebhuhn, partridge
Reh, venison
Schnepfe, woodcock

Wachtel, quail
Wildente, wild duck
Wildschwein, boar

Gemüse, Vegetables

Artischoken, artichokes
Bohnen, broad beans
Champignons, mushrooms
Chicorée, endives
Eierfrüchte, aubergine or egg-plant
Eierschwammerl, chanterelles
Erbsen, green peas
Fisolen, French beans
Gurken, cucumbers
Karfiol, cauliflower
Karotten, carrots
Kartoffeln (or *Erdäpfel*), potatoes; *Bratkartoffeln*, fried potatoes
Knoblauch, garlic
Kohl, cabbage
Kohlrüben, swede
Kohlsprossen, Brussel sprouts
Kukuruz or *Maiskolben*, corn-on-the-cob
Kürbis, pumpkin
Lauchgemüse or *Porree*, leek
Linsen, lentils
Morcheln, morels
Paradeiser, tomatoes
Pilze, mushrooms
Prinzessbohnen, haricot beans
Reis, rice
Rettich, radish
Rotkraut, red cabbage
Salate, salads
Schwarzwurzeln, salsify
Sellerie, celeriac
Spargelkohl, broccoli
Spargel(spitzen), asparagus (tips)
Spinat, spinach
Steinpilze, boletus
Trüffeln, truffles
Weisse Bohnen, haricot beans
Weisskraut, white cabbage
Weisse Rüben, turnips
Zucchini, courgettes
Zwiebel, onions

Süssspeisen, Sweets; *Mehlspeise* indicates hot sweet desserts in general

Aufläufe, soufflés
Salzburger Nockerl, sweet soufflé baked in the oven
Kücherl, fritters
Schmarren, omelettes broken into pieces
Strudel, strudels, of infinite variety, made of thinly rolled pastry, stuffed
Omelette nature, süss, sweet omelettes
Palatschinken, pancakes with a filling, often apricot
Topfenpalatschinken, cottage-cheese pancakes
Kleine Palatschinken, small pancakes or crêpes
Knödel, dumplings
Nudeln und Tascherl, noodles and turnovers, among them *Bröselnudeln*, breadcrumb noodles; *Griessnudeln*, semolina noodles; *Mohnnudeln*, poppy-seed noodles; *Nussnudeln*, noodles filled with nuts; *Powidltascherl*, turnovers filled with plum jam; and *Topfentascherl*, filled with cottage cheese
Torten, gâteaux; *Küchen*, cakes

Früchte, Fruit

Ananas, pineapple
Apfel, apple; *Apfelsaft*, apple-juice
Birnen, pear
Erdbeeren, strawberries
Heidelbeeren, bilberries
Himbeeren, raspberries
Kirschen, cherries
Mandeln, almonds
Marillen, apricots
Nuss, nuts or *Nüsse*, nuts
Pfirsiche, peaches
Pflaumen, or *Zwetschken*, plums
Ribisel, redcurrants
Walnüsse, walnuts

Miscellaneous

Getränkekarte, wine list
Rotwein, red wine
Weisswein, white wine
Sekt, sparkling wine
Wasser, water
Milch, milk
Kaffee, coffee; see p 103
Schlag, whipped cream
Schokolade, chocolate
Brot, bread
Honig, honey
Käse, cheese
Salz, salt
Pfeffer, pepper
Marmelade, jam
Olivenöl, olive-oil
Essig, vinegar
Senf, mustard
Zucker, sugar
Eis, ice cream
Semmel, bread roll
Gebäck, rolls

Visiting Churches, Museums, Monasteries and Schlösser

Much has been done in recent years to modernise and reform the provincial **Museums** of Austria. Although many will have heard of the great collections of the *Kunsthistorisches Museum* in Vienna, few realise that this is merely the tip of the iceberg, and that in the capital alone there are several other outstanding collections which bear comparison with the finest in Europe, for example the *Albertina* and the *Belvedere* ... but see p 237–39. In the provinces there are the *Landesmuseums* at *Graz* (Joanneum), and *Linz*; the Folk Museum, and *Ferdinandeum* at *Innsbruck*, and the collections at adjacent *Ambras* (in fact part of the Kunsthistorisches collection); the *Residenzgalerie*, and *Museum Carolino Augusteum* at *Salzburg*, the museums at *Krems*, and *Hallein*; the *Harrach collection* at *Rohrau*; and the *Open-air museum* just N of Graz, apart from numerous others, among them some of specialist interest (such as the *Josephinum* at Vienna), and without taking into consideration the several *Stiftmuseums*, such as those of *Klosterneuburg*, or *Kremsmünster*.

While the author has visited a high proportion of the museums of Austria in the service of this guide, it is quite possible that he may have overlooked a smaller museum of quality—particularly among the local or *Heimatmuseums*—or may not have given sufficient notice of others. Some important works may not have been listed because under restoration or on exhibition elsewhere.

Several important temporary exhibitions are regularly organised in some of the larger Schlösser—for instance at *Halbturn*, or *Schallaburg*—apart from those taking place at the *Künstlerhaus* in Vienna.

Unfortunately many of the monasteries may only be visited in groups, and in the case of *Melk*—for instance—too often at a rapid rate and in the company of coachloads ... but by no means all have been attacked by tourist blight. Most of the long-suffering guides of these tours are well informed, and obliging if additional details are requested. Usually churches are open until dusk, but several are not opened and may only be squinted at through grilles. Although Melk and *Göttweig* are impressive buildings, and should be seen, many will find a visit to some of the less ostentatious or less accessible more rewarding. Some indeed—in addition to their obvious architectural features—preserve remarkable Baroque libraries, as at *Admont* or *Vorau*; or outstanding collections of paintings, such as the Altdorfers at *St. Florian*; or such curiosities as the 'Mathematical tower' and Fish-tanks at *Kremsmünster*. Most of the monasteries restored in recent years are of architectural interest—*Zwettl, Lilienfeld, Altenburg, Millstatt, Herzogenburg, Vorau, Wilhering, Seitenstetten, Schlierbach*, and *Stams* may be cited as examples.

Numerous examples of the **Schloss**, either a country seat or castle, are found throughout the country; some remain in good condition or have been restored; others deserve restoration. Some are now owned by provincial or municipal authorities; others remain in private hands. Many have been converted into museums of varying quality; some are remarkable for their situation, for example *Riegersburg, Hochosterwitz*, and *Forchtenstein*; others for their size, as at *Schlosshof*, and *Eggenberg*; or for their historical associations, as at *Ambras*, or *Mirabell* (Salzburg).

In Austria a number of towns, large and small, have also preserved or restored their picturesque and colourful central squares or *Hauptplatz*, although often little more than wide streets. Visitors are indebted to the strenuous efforts of the *Federal Office for the Protection of Monuments* (Bundesdenkmalamtes) to conserve Austria's architectural heritage, and to restore damaged or derelict buildings. Among the smaller towns—or at least their centres—the Editor calls to mind *Krems, Steyr, Freistadt, Feldkirch, St. Veit an der Glan*, and *Kitzbühel* ... to mention a mere half-dozen at random.

A torch and a pair of binoculars are useful for exploring the darker recesses of churches.

Language

The German spoken in Austria is much softer and more musical than that spoken in Germany itself. There are also strong dialectical differences within Austria, but in principle the same basic rules of German grammar and pronunciation apply.

The traveller with only a little knowledge of German will get along perfectly well in Austria, and so will those with no German at all, for most Austrians learn English at school and are pleased to practice it on their guests, although any attempt by the visitor to speak German is always appreciated.

VOWELS: there are five vowels—a, e, i, o, u—in addition to which there are the combinations ai (pron. as in pie), au (cow), ei (pie), eu (boy), and ie (bee). Of the above, a, o, u, and au may modify, i.e. change their sound. They are written and pronounced: ä (eight), ö (feu), ü (sur), äu (boil). The two 'dots' above the letter concerned are referred to as the *Umlaut*, indicating a change in sound.

DIAGRAPHS OR TRIGRAPHS: these are groups of two or three consonants with a single sound, i.e. ch, pron. c as in back or ch, as in Bach; ck, pron. k; ph, pron. f; ss, pron. s; sch, pron. as in Schweppes; and th, pron. t.

Double s or ß (sz): a double s is written as ß at the end of a word or a syllable (when this syllable is not an integral part of the whole word, but merely a prefix) and also after a long vowel and before a consonant.

VOWEL SOUNDS: a (long as in father); a (short as in apple); e (long as ai in fair); e (short as e in bed, net, sent); e (long as ee in deep); e (short as in the preceding, but shorter); i (always short, as i in bit); i (long, also as ee in deep); o (always short, as o in not); o (always long, as aw in lawn); u (long u, as oo in ooze); u (short u, as oo in good); ö (always short, as ur in fur—the r not being pronounced); ö (always long, with no equivalent sound in English, but similar to the French eu in feu); ü (long, like the French u in sur); ü (short, like the French tu); e (pron. a as in ago); and er, as in fur*th*er.

CONSONANT SOUNDS: b (b as in bad); b (p as in put); c (ts, pron. as one sound, as in tha*t's* it—this is the sound of c before e, i, ö, or ä); c (k, the sound of c otherwise, although this has largely given way to k, ch in words from the Greek, as *ch*aracter); ch (as h in huge); ch (as the Scots loch); d (as in dead); d (as t in tomb); g (as in go); g (as s in casual); g (k, at the end of a word or syllable except when preceded by n, as Tag); g (as in -ig, except when followed by -lich: sonnig (pron. sonnigch), but kön*ig*lich (-ig); h (as in hand); j (as y in yes); l (as in lump); ng (as in sing); ph (f, in words from the Greek); qu (kv); r (r, trilled more than in English, although scarcely heard in the ending -er); s (as in soap); s (as in zeal); s (sh, as in sharp); ss/ˈ (s as in hi*ss*); sch (sh as in sharp); v (as f in far); w (as in vat); y (as y in yes); and z (tz, pron. as ts).

There are no silent letters as in English. So, unlike the English knave, the Germans say Knabe (kna:be), pronouncing both the k and e. H is not pronounced between two vowels unless it is part of the following syllable, i.e. sehen (zean), but Hoheit (hohait). Chs, when part of the word itself (the s not being added for some grammatical reason) is pronounced ks, i.e. sechs (zeks), Ochs (oks), wachsen (vaksan), etc.

STRESS: the German spoken language is strongly stressed.
1. The stress is laid on the stem of the word; i.e. geh'-en, Mäd'chen.
2. In compound words the stress is usually on the first part; i.e. Turm'-uhr, eis'-kalt, but not with the adverbial particles hin-ein, da-mit, etc.
3. Separable prefixes take the main stress; i.e. aus'-gehen, hinauf'-klettern.

4. The negative prefix un- is always stressed; i.e. un'-artig, Un'-sinn, etc.

There are several differences in vocabulary—notably in the culinary field—between Germany and Austria, largely due to differing cultural influences, and to the extent of the former Austro-Hungarian Empire. Among examples may be cited *Zwetschken* (plums), from Bohemian *svestka*; *Palatschinken* (pancakes), from the Hungarian *palacsinta*; *Ribisl* (red currants), from the Slavonic *ribezla*; and *Nockerl* from the Italian *gnocchi*. Another influence on Austrian German was the French language, that of the Court and aristocracy in the 18C, even if occasionally the spelling was slightly changed, such as *Kafetier* for the owner of a coffee-house. The use of the word *Schlag* (literally a *slap*) in conjuction with coffee or those delicious cakes, derived from *Schlagrahm*, meaning *whipped* cream, has caused amusement.

Travellers without a knowledge of German should acquire a good phrase-book and pocket-dictionary and they will soon pick up a number of everyday expressions, formulas, and words, such as *Grüss Gott*, the more usual and traditional greeting (God bless you) for *Guten Tag*, or good day; *bitte* (please), used on numerous occasions, when requesting (*bitte schön*), thanking, or excusing, etc.; also *danke schön*, thank you; *ja*, and *nein*; yes and no; *Gute Nacht*, good night; *Guten Abend*, good evening; *auf Wiedersehen*, goodbye; *gute Fahrt*, have a good journey; *warum?*, why; *Sprechen Sie englisch?*, Do you speak English?; *Ich spreche nicht deutsch*, I don't speak German; *Wo ist die* (*der, das*)..., Where is the...; *Herr, Frau*, and *Fräulein* (Mr, Mrs, and Miss) should always be followed by the surname, except when the latter is used to attract the attention of a waitress or shop-assistant, for example.

In some respects the Austrians are more formal than the people of some other European countries; there is the formality of hand-shaking on meeting and parting, while they are great sticklers for the use of their honorific academic and other titles, which they consider to be part of their name, perhaps a left-over of the Monarchy, when the hierarchy of civil servants administrating the Empire at all levels were thus categorised. Some people may still take exception if they are not addressed respectfully, although foreigners will be forgiven for their ignorance. In some fields almost everyone is a *Doktor* (having taken his doctorate, whatever the subject), *Magister* (equivalent to M.A.), or *Professor*, etc., apart from any variety of *Räte* (meaning councillor), of which there are *Hofräte* (equivalent to a Privy Councillor), *Oberäte, Kulturräte, Obermuseums-räte, Bibliotheksräte, Archivräte, Ministerräte*, etc., etc.

Although a pocket dictionary and/or phrase book is recommended, listed below are the German for the days of the week, and numerals. See also p 87 for a general Glossary, mostly of topographical and simple architectural terms, etc., and under Food and Wine, p 100.

Monday, *Montag*
Tuesday, *Dienstag*
Wednesday, *Mittwoch*
Thursday, *Donnerstag*
Friday, *Freitag*
Saturday, *Samstag*
Sunday, *Sonntag*
Holiday, *Feiertag*
Weekend, *Wochenende*
Month, *Monat*

1 *eins*	16 *sechzehn*
2 *zwei*	17 *siebzehn*
3 *drei*	18 *achtzehn*
4 *vier*	19 *neunzehn*
5 *fünf*	20 *zwanzig*
6 *sechs*	21 *einundzwanzig*
7 *sieben*	22 *zweiundzwanzig*, etc.
8 *acht*	30 *dreissig*
9 *neun*	40 *vierzig*
10 *zehn*	100 *hundert*
11 *elf*	110 *hundertzehn*
12 *zwölf*	200 *zweihundert*
13 *dreizehn*	1000 *tausend*
14 *vierzehn*	1500 *funfzehnhundert*
15 *fünfzehn*	

General Information

Climate. Most of Austria enjoys a Continental climate, with temperatures in the height of summer rising to 30°C (90°F), and in winter occasionally dropping to –20°C (–5°F). Vienna experiences biting winds in winter, and it is sensible to go out well muffled. A characteristic climatic phenomenon is the *Föhn*, a warm S wind, which in certain areas sends the temperatures up rapidly and produces nervous tension in some people. It is most frequent in the Upper Rhine, Inn, and Salzach valleys.

Crossing streets. Care should be taken when crossing streets, particularly those in which trams or streetcars run contrary to the expected direction. There is generally more discipline shown than in other countries; streets are crossed at street-crossings, and jay-walking is frowned upon.

Entertainment. Although several commercial brochures are produced, such as 'Hallo Wien', the Vienna Tourist Board publishes a monthly leaflet entitled 'Wien: Programm', which lists forthcoming concerts, operas, plays, etc. The provincial capitals provide similar information.

Health, etc. Information on emergency medical services (Ärztedienst) is available from local police stations; mountain resorts have a mountain rescue service (*Bergrettungsdienst*).

Ticks (*Zecken*). Travellers intending to go on a walking or camping holiday in certain areas of Austria are warned that there has been an increase in the tick population in recent years, and these can transmit a viral infection called 'tick-borne encephalitis'. The areas most affected are (in Lower Austria) around Baden, Wiener Neustadt, Klosterneuburg, St. Pölten, the Wachau, and parts of the Waldviertel; in Upper Austria, along the Danube valley between Passau and Linz, parts of the Mühlviertel, and Innviertel, and around the Traunsee; also in certain areas of Styria, and Carinthia. As the districts affected are liable to change, it is advisable to enquire in advance from Tourist Offices or Embassies. You should be vaccinated at least a fortnight before departure. Anyone who happens to be bitten by a tick while *in* Austria, and who has not been vaccinated, should go immediately to a doctor, who will inject the necessary antibodies.

Lifts (elevators). Many in older blocks of apartments are locked, and may only be entered by a key-holder; others require a 1 Schilling piece in the slot to obtain entrance, and a small supply of such coins should be carried.

Lost Property. Apply at local police stations, or, after a few days, in Vienna, at Wasagasse 22, not far N of the Schottenpassage.

Music Festivals, etc. Travellers wishing to plan a tour to take in such festivals should make enquiries well in advance to Austrian National Tourist Offices, who will provide information about booking procedures, etc. Accommodation should also be booked in good time.

Press; Radio, etc. Some foreign newspapers may be found at kiosks in the tourist centres. In Vienna the yellow-coated news-vendors in the streets are a syndicate of Egyptian origin.

At 8.05 each morning *Austrian Radio* broadcasts a news bulletin in English. The so-called 'Blue Danube Radio' also broadcasts programmes in English intermittently during the day in the Vienna area.

Public Holidays. The main public holidays (when many museums are closed) are: 1 January, 6 January (Epiphany), Easter Monday, 1 May, Ascension Day, Whit Monday, Corpus Christi, 15 August, 26 October (National Holiday), 1 November (All Saints), 8 December, and 25–26 December.

Shoes. Suitably strong, or rubber-soled shoes or boots should be worn in winter, particularly in towns, where leather shoes are likely to get ruined by the grit thrown down on the streets and pavements.

Shops are normally open from 8.00–18.00 Monday to Friday, and until 12.00 on Saturday; many will close for an hour or two at midday. Chemists' shops (*Apotheken*), which operate a night and Sunday rota system, will when closed display a notice giving the address of the nearest open.

Symbols. The national flag of the Republic is a tricolour of red, white, and red (often seen in the form of hanging banners); its emblem is a single-headed eagle with a mural crown, with its shanks bearing broken shackles (symbolising its independence in 1945), while its talons grasp a hammer and sickle.

Tipping; *Trinkgeld*. Although a sufficiently high service charge is usually included in the bill, it is the custom to reward good service—which it usually is even if occasionally slow—by 'rounding up' the bill.

Useful addresses: The Anglo-Austrian Society, 46 Queen Anne's Gate, London SW1H 9AU (with an office at Stubenring 24, Vienna); the Ski Club of Great Britain, 118 Eaton Square, London SW1W 9AF; the Austrian Institute, 28 Rutland Gate, London SW7, and at 11 East 52nd Street, New York; the Jewish Welcome Service, Stephansplatz 10, A-1010, Vienna.

Winter-sports; see p 78. Keep your distance from the skier walking along the street carrying his or her skis, who might suddenly turn!

1   Bregenz To Innsbruck

A.   Via Feldkirch and St. Anton

Total distance, 201km (125 miles). B190. 12km *Dornbirn*—7km *Hohenems*—18km **Feldkirch**—21km *Bludenz*—40km **St. Anton am Arlberg**—B316. 28km *Landeck*—B171. 19km *Imst*—56km **Innsbruck**.

Maps: F&B 3; BEV 47/9–11.

Travellers driving directly to Innsbruck are advised to take the *Arlberg Tunnel* (fee), entered 25km E of Bludenz, with an exit c 4km beyond St. Anton. The alternative route over the Arlberg Pass is very steep in places. It is virtually obligatory to use the tunnel throughout the winter. The A14 autobahn may be followed from just S of Bregenz to Bludenz. This can be entered with ease by those crossing the Swiss frontier. It can also be approached from the N bank of the Bodensee (Lake Constance). From near Landeck, the motorway runs parallel to the B171 along the Inn valley to Innsbruck.

BREGENZ (24,500 inhab.; 398m), the capital of the **Vorarlberg**, lies at the E end of the Bodensee, backed by a range of hills rising steeply from its shore to the *Pfänder* (1063m), pierced by a tunnel through which runs the A14 autobahn from the German frontier (Customs), 6km N of Bregenz on the lakeside road; *Lindau* (26,500 inhab.), on the German bank, is in itself a town of some character. The *Rhine*, which enters the lake 12km SW of Bregenz, here forming a small delta, marks the frontier with Switzerland, and can be crossed at several points (Customs) from the Swiss N1 or N13 autobahns, approaching from St. Gallen.

The present upper town is built around the strategically sited Celtic oppidum, which, when under Roman occupation, was an important trading post named *Brigantium*. The town was first documented in 1249, and in 1523 was sold by the counts of Montfort to the Habsburgs, who had already—in 1451—acquired the county. It was captured and pillaged by the Swedes in 1647; and in 1861 the first meeting of the Landtag of Vorarlberg took place here.

Roads entering the town converge on the KORNMARKT, parallel to the Seestrasse (Tourist Office), the railway line, and harbour. Here is the landing-stage for excursions on the **Bodensee** (541 sq km), the third largest of the European lakes, after Balaton, and Léman.

Also known as *Lake Constance*, the Bodensee was the Roman *Lacus Brigantinus*. It lies 369m above the sea level, and has a maximum depth of 252m. It is some 67km long (from Bregenz to the head of the Überlingen See, its NW arm); its greatest breadth is 13.7km. The lake is subject to sudden rises and falls of obscure origin, apart from normal seasonal variations, and its surface is sometimes rough. The fishing is good, and the *Blaufelchen* is a species peculiar to it. Traces of lake-dwellings have been discovered on its banks.

Some distance to the W is the well-equipped lakeside *Festspiel-und Kongresshaus* (1980), which has an open-air theatre and floating-stage moored to the shore, and is the venue of Summer Festivals.

In the Kornmarkt is the entrance to the **Vorarlberger Landesmuseum**.

The FIRST FLOOR is devoted to the archaeology of Brigantium, with Bronze Age ceramics, etc. from Altenstadt (Feldkirch); arms of the Hallstatt period, and other artefacts; also a reconstructed building from Rankweil. There are also several mosaics; a collection of jewellery; a bronze legionary's helmet; terra sigillata, and glass; murals; statuettes; and cult objects, etc.

The SECOND FLOOR contains several carved beams, furniture, and collections of glass, ceramics, pewter, wood and metalwork, arms, etc.; and musical instruments, including a 16C carved portative organ from Hohenems. Also a number of reconstructed rooms, blue and white tiled stoves, and collections of ex-votos, cult objects, and colourful costumes, together with 19C portraits depicting such costumes and accessories (lace, and gold and silver thread hats).

16C Flemish tapestries from Hohenems are displayed on the stairs. On the THIRD FLOOR: Carved and gilt altarpiece, and painted statues and panels by *Wolf Huber* (Feldkirch; 1485–1553); *Angelica Kauffmann* (1741–1807), five panels and several portraits, including one of Lady Henrietta Williams-Wynn. Part of a sandstone altar of c 830 from Lauterach; Calvary of 1500; *Jörg Frosch*, Adoration (Feldkirch; 1574); a collection of Baroque paintings and sculpture; paintings by *Wendelin Mossbrugger* (1760–1849), among others of the period, and a few late 19th and 20C works.

Adjacent to the E is the *Theatre*, installed in 1954 in a building of 1838, previously a wheat warehouse. Just beyond is the circular *Nepomuk-Kapelle* of 1757.—The Schillerstrasse, a few paces further E, leads right to approach the lower terminus of the cable-car to near the summit of the *Pfänder*.

From the W end of the Kornmarkt turn up the Rathausstrasse, passing (left) the *Seekapelle* (1696), which has a Renaissance retable. Then follow the Maurachgasse, climbing towards the upper enceinte (the site of the Celtic settlement), where there are several characteristic half-timbered houses, including the old Town Hall of 1662, by Michael Kuen, a local architect. Steps ascend to the 16C gate, and the adjacent ***Martinsturm**, with its huge bulbous onion-dome, built in 1599–1602, with a chapel of 1362 containing contemporary frescoes.

From the S end of the neighbouring *Ehregutaplatz* steps descend into a small valley and climb to the church of **St. Gallus**. Referred to as early as 1097, but rebuilt in the 14–15C and in 1672 attractively baroquised by Michael Kuen. It contains several well-carved statues, good walnut stalls from the former abbey church of *Mehrerau*, and a rococo organ-case; the organ is by Josef Gabler, who died in Bregenz in 1771.

From here cross a footbridge and descend towards the centre by the Kirchstrasse.—Conspicuous to the NE are the twin spires of the *Herz-Jesu-Kirche* (1908), which is not of any great interest.

To the S rises the *Gebhardsberg* (598m), with a restaurant built into the ruins of a castle (view), destroyed by the Swedes in 1647.

The main road leads due S from Bregenz after crossing the *Bregenzer Ache* at *Lauterach*, bearing across the motorway towards (12km) Dornbirn, 3km prior to which the B200 turns left; see Rte 1B. Unfortunately the valley here is spoilt by a rash of power-pylons.

Dornbirn (38,650 inhab.), lying at the foot of the BREGENZERWALD, is the main manufacturing and textile town of the province, in the centre of which is a neo-classical *Church* of 1839, and the so-called *Rotes Haus* of 1634. At Marktstrasse 33 is a museum of natural history. A local chemist is said to have been the first Austrian to drive an automobile, in 1893.

Driving S, and passing (right) a small airfield, at 6km **Hohenems** (12,650 inhab.) is entered. The town is dominated by the *Schlossberg* (733m), on which are castle ruins, and *Schloss Glopper* (1343), below which is the *Schloss* of 1562–73, once the residence of Marcus Sitticus von Hohenems, Prince-archbishop of Salzburg, who commissioned the Milanese architect Martino Longo to rebuild the castle, which later belonged to Count Waldburg-Zeil. The far wall of its courtyard, abutting the abrupt cliff, is a façade only. Since 1976, the *Rittersaal*, with its coffered ceiling, has been the venue for Schubertiads, a festival of better quality than many, held during the second half of June. Here, in 1755 and 1778, parts of the MS of the Nibelungenlied were discovered.—The *Pfarrkirche* of 1350, rebuilt in 1797, contains a notable altarpiece depicting the Coronation of the Virgin (1580).

On leaving the town, you pass (left) near a *Jewish cemetery* established in 1617. The Villa Heimann-Rosenthal contains a *Jewish Museum*. To the SE rises the *Hohe Kugel* (1645m). The road runs through (5km) *Götzis*, a small town of ancient origin, overlooked by rugged cliffs, with the ruins of a 14C castle, and churches of the mid 14C and 17C.

To the W rises a ridge, the *Kummenberg*, passed by the main road as it approaches (10km) *Feldkirch* (see below), which by-passes Rankweil, 3km to the E.

A minor road from Götzis passes through several old villages, among them *Röthis*, with a church of 1476. To the E of Röthis is a monastery founded in 1383, with a 15–18C church.—8km **Rankweil** stands at the foot of a precipitous crag surmounted by a pilgrimage *Church* by the site of an earlier castle (restored) preserving a cylindrical keep and parapet walk which provides extensive views towards the *Alpstein* range in Switzerland, and S towards the *Schesaplana* (2965m) in the RÄTIKON MASSIF. The Baroque *Church* contains a remarkable Romanesque crucifix, and a Virgin of c 1600. In the lower town is 13C *St. Peter's*, later baroquised. Relics of a Roman villa have been excavated not far to the W in the hamlet of *Brederis*.

The B193 leads S and then SE from RANKWEIL to BLUDENZ (23km), passing through or near several villages with interesting churches, among them *Satteins*, and *Schlins*, where the *St. Anna-kapelle* (c 1500) contains three Gothic altarpieces and an interesting landscape in which is depicted the Crucifixion.— *Bludesch* has a *Pfarrkirche* by Johann Michael Beer (1650) which contains a notable organ, and the neighbouring church of *St. Nikolas* has a Romanesque nave with frescoes of 1320, and a stone spire. Bludesch was the birthplace of the sculptor Nikolaus Moll (1676–1754).—Neighbouring *Ludesch* has a good 17C church, 1km SE of which is *St. Martin*, founded c 800 and rebuilt in the 15C, with a large Gothic altarpiece of 1629, and early 16C frescoes. Approaching *Bludenz* (see below) is *Nüziders* (Roman *Nucis Terra*, on the site of a Celtic settlement), near which are the ruins of the 13C fortress of *Sonnenberg*. The *St. Vinerus-kapelle* is 12–13C; the *Pfarrkirche* late 17C, with a choir of 1485.

At *Thüringen*, adjacent to Ludesch, (George) Norman Douglas (1868–1952) was born. He lived here for six years, in a house called 'Falkenhorst'. His father, John Sholto Douglas, managed cotton mills at Bregenz which had been established by his own father, the 14th Laird of Tilquhillie. Norman Douglas's mother was Vanda, daughter of Baron Ernest de Poelnitz. 'Together' describing a later visit to the Vorarlberg, was published in 1923.

7km **FELDKIRCH** (23,750 inhab.), an ancient town—perhaps the most interesting in the Vorarlberg—stands on the N bank of the river Ill, guarding the entrance to the Walgau valley, and retains several typical arcaded streets.

It was probably a Celtic settlement conquered by the Romans, but the earliest record of the town is from the mid 9C, when it is known as *Veldkirichum*. On the death in 1390 of the last Montfort count it was sold to Austria, and apart from a brief period in the early 15C it has remained in Austrian possession. It was pillaged by the Swedes in 1647 and ravaged by fire in 1697. Its Jesuit College, founded in 1658, the 'Stella Matutina', has long provided the Vorarlberg with its clerks and administrators. Wolf Huber (c 1490–1553), the artist, was born here.

It is dominated to the E by the 12C *Schattenburg*, a fortress enlarged by the Swiss counts of Toggenburg in 1416–36, and later by Maximilian I. It now contains a local museum, and the main road tunnels beneath its crag. From just below it, the Neustadt, off which is the

Rathaus (1493; reconstructed after 1697; with a notable Ratssaal), leads N to the **Domkirche**, at the NE side of the old enceinte. It was completed in 1478, with two naves divided by a line of lofty columns supporting reticulated vaulting. The pulpit, and the altarpiece of St. Anne (1521), by Wolf Huber, are remarkable; the modern glass is unfortunate.

A short distance to the W stands the *Katzenturm* (or Cat's Tower; late 15C), named after the lions' heads which decorated its defensive cannon. Near by is the former *Liechtenstein palace* (rebuilt after the fire of 1697), and the Tourist Office at No. 12 in the neighbouring Herrengasse. Further W is the *Churertor* (1491, and enlarged a century later), with its stepped gable; and beyond, guarding the river crossing, is the *Wasser-Turm* (1482).

The Montfortgasse leads back to the long MARKTPLATZ, its houses built over 12–14C arcades, at the S end of which is *St. Johannes*, dating from 1218, but several times modified. It was once that of the monastery of the Knights of St. John of Jerusalem, who formerly guarded the route through the Arlberg. A short distance beyond, nearer the river, is the 16C *Mühlertor*, and 15C *Pulverturm*.

A road leads 3km SW from the Wasser-Turm to the frontier of the anachronistic principality of **Liechtenstein** (capital, *Vaduz*), which although long a dependency of Austria, chose to enter into a Customs union with Switzerland in 1920.

The main road, autobahn, and railway, bear SE along the WALGAU to (21km) the turning (left) for **Bludenz**, also by-passed. This small textile town (12,900 inhab.), the fortifications of which were largely demolished in the mid 19C, retains several characteristic arcaded houses in its old centre, dominated by the *Schloss Gayenhofen*, 13C but reconstructed in the mid 18C. The *Pfarrkirche* (St. Lorenz; 1514) is approached by a covered stair. Adjacent is the *Oberes Tor* (1491), containing a local museum.

A minor road climbs to the SW up the BRANDNER TAL, settled by Valaisians in the mid 14C, to (15km) the *Lünersee*, a small lake below the *Schesaplana* (2965m), the highest peak of the RÄTIKON RANGE, here forming an amphitheatre, and marking the Swiss frontier.

BLUDENZ TO LANDECK VIA THE MONTAFON AND THE SILVRETTA STAUSEE (94km; toll; usually closed from mid October to late May). The B188 forks right off the B190 2km S, climbing up the valley of the Ill, the upper part of which is known as the MONTAFON, its pastures grazed by a local breed of tan-coloured cow.— 9km *Tschagguns*, with a 14C church enlarged in 1812, contains an organ of 1815 by J. Bergöntzle, a pupil of Silbermann. Another organ by Bergöntzle (dated 1792) can be seen at neighbouring *Bartholomaberg*; its church of 1732, with an onion-dome, has three Baroque altars by Georg Senn, and a processional cross of c 1150.—**Schruns**, 1km left of the road, the main centre of the valley, has a regional museum installed in a 17C house. Ernest Hemingway spent the winters of 1924–25 and 1925–26 at the Madlernerhaus and Hotel Taube here, where he completed 'The Sun also Rises' (or 'Fiesta'), as described in 'A Movable Feast'. To the E rises the *Hochjoch* (2520m).

The road continues SE through (8km) *St. Gallenkirch*, with a richly decorated church of 1474, enlarged in 1780.—9km to the SW lies *Gargellen* (1480m), dominated by the *Madrisahorn* (2826m) on the Swiss frontier (not far S of which are *Klosters* and *Davos*). The road climbs past *Gaschurn* to (11km) *Partenen* (1027m), with its hydro-electric power-stations, beyond which it ascends the *Silvretta-Hochalpenstrasse* in hairpin bends to the *Vermunt* reservoir before climbing E to (16km) the watershed at *Bielerhöhe* (2036m). Here, beyond the *Silvretta lake*, rise the gneiss summits of the SILVRETTA MASSIF, the *Gross Litzner* (3109m; SW); the *Silvrettahorn* (3244m); *Piz Buin* (3312m; to the S), and the *Tirolerkopf* (3095m) and *Augstenberg* (2191m) to the SE, while to the E rises the *Fluchthorn* (3401m). Bearing NE, the road descends past (left) the higher *Kops-Stausee* (reservoir) to (9km) *Galtür* (1582m), its church with similarities to that at St. Gallenkirch. The road descends the PAZNAUNTAL, watered by the Trisanna, and flanked by the VERWALLGRUPPE (*Kutchenspitze*; 3148m) to the N, and the SAMNAUNGRUPPE (with the *Vesulspitze*; 3089m) to the E, to (10km) *Ischgl*, a ski resort at 1377m, and the main centre of the valley, to meet, at 23km the B316 6km W of *Landeck*; see below.

2km beyond Bludenz, bear left up the KLOSTERTAL, watered by the Aflenz, to reach after 21km the W end of the **Arlberg Tunnel** (13,980m long; toll), opened in 1978. It runs parallel to the rail tunnel completed in 1884 (during its construction, 4000 workers were employed under the direction of Julius Lott). An exit is provided (at 16km) beyond its E end, to approach St. Anton.

The ARLBERG PASS is approached by climbing steeply past *Stuben*, the birthplace of Hannes Schneider (1890–1955), the pioneer of modern skiing techniques. Until 1825, when a road suitable for wheeled traffic was constructed over the pass, the Vorarlberg was virtually isolated from the rest of the country. Its church records state that 65 people died in avalanches between *Klösterle* and the top of the pass between 1666 and 1855, prior to the building of a defensive wall in 1848.—At 6km the *Flexenstrasse* turns left to (5km) **Zürs**; see Rte 1B. Another 3km brings you to the watershed between the Rhine and the Danube at 1793m, below (left) the *Valluga* (2811m), and you pass **St. Christoph**, the site of a hospice founded in 1386 by Heinrich the Foundling, destroyed by fire in 1957 and rebuilt in 1959 as a modern luxury Hospice-Hotel.

The Brotherhood of St. Christoph, a charitable organisation, was re-established in 1961. Opposite it are the buildings of the *Austrian Federal Sports Centre* for the training of government-approved ski instructors.

The road winds down below protective snow barriers to (7km) St. Anton in the Tyrolean ROSANNA TAL. To the S rises the VERWALL MASSIF, with the *Patteriol* (3056m) and the *Kuchenspitze* (3148m). **St. Anton am Arlberg** (1287m; 2150 inhab. out of season) was, with adjacent *St. Jakob*, one of the earliest winter sports centres in Europe.

Hannes Schneider (see above) started demonstrating the Arlberg method in 1909, and by 1928, in conjunction with Sir Arnold Lunn, introduced the downhill run and slalom race for the Arlberg-Kandahar Cup, the major skiing trophy, competed for here and elsewhere since. The run was c 3500m long, with a drop of 1022m. Stephan Kruckenhauser developed the 'wedeln' technique here after the Second World War, since when St. Anton has remained the home of an important ski school (founded 1912), with several hundred instructors.
The *Arlberg Ski Club* was actually founded at St. Christoph in 1901, and the whole area has been provided with extensive facilities (including cable-cars, a funicular railway, chair-lifts, and T-bars) for the winter-sporting enthusiast, apart from being a pleasant centre for mountain excursions in summer, details of which can be obtained from the helpful Tourist Office in the village centre.

A short distance E, off the main street, is an early wooden *Customs warehouse*, where salt-carriers were obliged to pay a tax and where in winter they might store their goods until able to cross the Arlberg pass. To the NW, beyond the railway (which of course provides easy access to the resort for non-motorists) is the *Museum*, containing an interesting collection of early skiing equipment, and photographs depicting the history of the sport, and of the construction of the railway tunnel, etc.

For the non skier, an ascent by cable-car to the summit of the **Valluga** (2811m; to the NW, with its TV antenna) is recommended. The Valluga normally provides a magnificent view of the surrounding peaks, whose position and heights are marked on the observation platform. Another ascent is that from just W of the village to the *Brandkreuz* (2050m S), overlooked to the SE by the *Vordere Rendlspitze* (2816m), while further S rises the *Madaunspitze* (2961m), and to the S, the MOOS TAL is closed by the *Saumspitze* (3039m).

The road, which after 6km rejoins the B316, descends the valley, passing through several short tunnels and through several minor villages, with the *Hohe Riffler* (3168m) rising to the S, and the ruined castle of *Burgfried* at the *Trisannabrücke*, to meet the Silvretta road (see above) at (17km) *Pians*. Well-sited at a junction of wooded gorges, Pians has a 14C chapel with 15C frescoes; to the S is the restored *Schloss Wiesberg* (13C).

6km **Landeck** (7300 inhab.), also by-passed by a recently completed stretch of the autobahn, is the main town of the Upper Inn valley (OBERINNTAL). It has a 13C fortress, now containing a folk museum; a *Pfarrkirche*, with fine vaulting of 1471, and a large altar of 1520; and a *Pestkirchlein* of 1650, with an impressive contemporary altarpiece.

Best approached from Landeck is *Grins*, 5km W, but N of the main road, rebuilt since a fire in 1948; and *Stanz*, N of Landeck, the birthplace of Jakob Prandtauer (1660–1726), architect of St. Florian and Melk. Its church has a Romanesque belfry. The ruins of *Schloss Schroffenstein*, to the NE, date from the 12C.

LANDECK TO NAUDERS (44km) or MARTINA. The B315 leads SE up the OBERINN-TAL past several castle ruins and the *Pontlatzerbrücke*, the scene of skirmishes both in 1703 and 1809, and then S to (13km) *Prutz*, from where a track up a side valley, the KAUNERTAL, leads 21km SE and S to the *Gepatsch reservoir*. Beyond this is the huge *Gepatschferner* (glacier) in the ÖTZTAL ALPS, here rising to 3532m at the *Weisseespitze* (S) and the *Glockturm* (2256m; W). There are also several other peaks of the KAUNERGRAT RIDGE to the E, the highest of which are the *Watzespitze* (3533m) and the *Hochvernagtspitze* (3531m).—Continue SW from Prutz, later passing below *Ladis*, an old village with castle ruins, and then (right) the church of *Serfaus* (1332, but founded c 804), with remains of exterior frescoes of the late 16C and a carved and polychromed Virgin and Child (12–13C).—The church at (9km) *Tosens* contains 15C murals.—8km *Stuben*, with a church of 1470 preserving a high altar and frescoes of interest. That of **Pfunds** (left), of 1474, contains contemporary murals and a carved altarpiece of 1513, while several houses retain characteristic features.—At 3km a track leads W to *Spiss*, with a fine 17C organ in its church.—Another road leads 4km to the Swiss border at *Schalkl*, and into the UNTER-ENGADIN.

The main road forks left, above the *Finstermünz* defile, with its early 16C fortified *Bridge*, to (11km) *Nauders*, known as *Inutrion* in Ptolemy's 'Geography', where the apse of the tiny *Kapelle St. Leonhard* has 12C frescoes. Another Swiss border crossing lies over a ridge (views) at *Martina*, 8km W of Nauders.— The main road climbs S to the Italian frontier at (4km) the *Reschenpass* (*Passo di Resia*; 1507m; Customs), the watershed between the Inn and the Adige, before descending the VINTSCHGAU (Val Ventosta), part of S Tyrol, and Austrian territory until 1919. *Merano*, in Italy, lies 85km to the SE.

The new autobahn leads NE from Landeck, while the B171 follows the Inn valley through *Zams*, later passing the ruins of the castle of *Kronburg* (1380), with a view ahead of the pyramidal *Tschirgant* (2372m) rising beyond (19km) *Imst*. Friedrich Augustus II of Saxony met with a fatal accident near here in 1854. In the upper town of **Imst** (6700 inhab.), the spired Gothic *Pfarrkirche*, rebuilt after a fire in 1822, has exterior frescoes; the *Kalvarienbergkirche* has murals of 1370 in its Romanesque apse, and there are several interesting fountains.—The geographer and topographic artist Georg Matthäus Vischer (1628–96) was born at *Wenns*, 13km to the S.

The B314 leads 12km NE to meet the road from Füssen to Innsbruck at *Nassereith*; see Rte 2.

The B171 continues E down the narrow INNTAL past *Karres*, with the slender spire (1506) of its church of 1493, with a Baroque interior.

FROM THE INN VALLEY TO OBERGURGL (51km). At 11km the B186 turns right to ascend the ÖTZTAL past (5km) *Oetz*, with a notable church (reached by a stiff climb, but it has been spoilt by tasteless restoration), and the *Gasthof zum Stern*, with its exterior decoration of 1573 and 1615.—8km from *Umhausen*, an unsophisticated village, just left of the road, a track leads E to the *Stuiben Falls*.—The valley, down which tumbles the Ötztaler Ache, narrows to a gorge, and *Langenfeld*, with its painted churches, is passed before reaching (23km) *Sölden*. A cable-car ascends from here to the *Geislacherkogel* (3058m), providing a panoramic view of the surrounding mountains, the highest peak of which (and the second highest in Austria after the Grossglockner) is the **Wildspitze** (3774m), rising to the SW.—At (3km) *Zwieselstein* a minor road climbs 13km SW to *Vent* (1895m), dominated to the NW by the *Wildspitze*, and almost encircled by other summits of the range, among which, to the SW, is the *Weisskugel* (3726m). Much devastation was caused in the VENTERTAL by the bursting of the Vernagtglacial lake in 1599, 1680, 1771 and 1845.—The main road climbs steeply into the GURGLTAL, at the head of which (9km) lies **Obergurgl** (1907m), a small resort, to the S of which the *Hohe Mutt* (2853m) provides panoramic views of the surrounding mountains. Prof. Piccard landed near here on the Gurgler glacier on 27 May 1931 after his first balloon ascent, 16,000m into the stratosphere.—From 2km N of the village the road (toll beyond Hochgurgl) ascends to the *Windeck belvedere*, and beyond—by a road completed in 1959—to the *Timmelsjoch pass* (2474m; closed early October–mid June) and the frontier (Customs) with S Tyrol.

Andreas Hofer (1767–1810), the Tyrolese patriot, was born near *San Leonardo in Passiria* (688m), which lies in the valley, 29km SE of Obergurgl, and 20km N of *Merano*.—The S44 climbs steeply in zigzags over the *Passo di Monte Giovo* (*Jaufenpass*; 2099m) and down to (37km) *Vipiteno* (*Sterzing*) to join the A22 motorway 15km SW of the **Brenner Pass**; see Rte 5.

The main road continues down the Inn valley (view ahead) past (right) *Haiming*, with the conspicuous Baroque spire of its 14C church, to (12km) **Stams**.

To the right of the road rise the twin onion-domed towers of the Cistercian *Abbey, a notable 17C building, with a white and ochre façade, entirely restored in the 1960s.

It was founded in 1273 by Elisabeth of Bavaria (widow of Conrad IV Hohenstaufen), in memory of her son, Conradin, executed at Naples by Charles d'Anjou in 1268, and built by her second husband, Count Meinhard II of Tyrol. The Romanesque church was consecrated in 1284, its crypt intended as a mausoleum for Tyrolean princes. The medieval abbey was sacked during a peasant revolt in 1525, and again in 1552 by the Protestant Maurice of Saxony; while in 1593 a ravaging fire destroyed most of its dependencies.

The present *Church* was erected in 1690–99 and baroquised between 1729–34 by Georg Anton Gumpp, its long nave (81.5m) flanked by chapels replacing the former side aisles.

Notable are the wrought-iron screens by Bernard Bachnitzer and Michael Neurauter separating the porch from the church; the brilliantly coloured frescoes in the vault of 1730–34 by Johan Georg Wolker (1700–66); the gilded pulpit of 1740 by Andreas Kölle; and the stucco-work by Franz Xaver Feichtmayr and Josef Vischer. A balustrade provides a view of the *Princes' Crypt*, guarded by 12 carved and gilded statues, by Andreas Thamasch (died 1697 at Stams), in a somewhat naive style. The statues are of those buried here and include Blanca Maria Sforza (died 1511), the second wife of Maximilian I; Eleonore Stuart (1433–80), daughter of James II of Scotland, who in 1449 married the Archduke Sigmund der Münzreiche (died 1496), also buried here. Remarkable is the *High Altar* (1613), by Bartholomäus Steinl and Wolfgang Kirchmayr, in the form of a Tree of Life, with richly carved ramifications framing images of saints and of the Virgin and Child. In the 18C it was backed, in questionable taste, by a stucco curtain drawn aside by putti.

To the right of the church is the *Heiligblutkapelle*, rebuilt by J.M. Gumpp, its screen embellished with roses. The same architect was responsible for the *Fürstensaal*, decorated with frescoes by Michael Hueber and Anton Zoller (1722).

A short distance W of the abbey is the 14C *Pfarrkirche of St. Johann*, tastefully baroquised in 1755, and containing delicate stucco-work; frescoes by Franz Anton Zeiler; and altars of 1764 by Hans Rindl.

At 8km *Telfs* (see Rte 2) is by-passed, and after 13km an exit for *Zirl* is reached; see Rte 3. To the S, at a higher level, is the notable church of *Ranggen* (1775), by Franz Singer, approached by a turning onto a side road and then after c 4km turning W again.

12km **Innsbruck** W; see Rte 4, and also for the church at *Götzens*, 6km SW.

B.   Bregenz to St. Anton via Warth

Total distance, 101km (63 miles). B190. 9km—B200. 65km *Warth*—B198. 7km **Lech**—5km *Zürs*—5km B197, 10km **St. Anton**. **Reutte** is 60km NE of Warth on the B198.

Maps: F&B 3; BEV 47/9–11.

This road is likely to be closed to the W and S of Warth between November and March, when travellers should approach Lech and Zürs via the *Klostertal*; see Rte 1A.

The B200 turns left off the Dornbirn road (see Rte 1A), climbing into the **Bregenzerwald*, with fine views just beyond *Alberschwende*. At 18km it crosses *Müselbach*, from which a minor road forks left to (7km) *Hittisau*.—The main road continues to climb S through several villages, among them *Egg*, and past (right) *Schwarzenberg*, where the church contains an altarpiece by Angelica Kauffmann (1741–1807; born at *Chur*, in the Grisons), whose parents lived here.—At 15km a road turns left for *Bezau*, and *Reuthe*, with a church of 1419 containing frescoes of c 1500.—3km *Mellau* is skirted, beyond which the road ascends E and then SE to (9km) **Au** (791m), with the *Diedamskopf* (2090m) rising to the NE, and the *Kanisfluh* (2044m) to the W, to the SW of which is the impressive bulk of the *Damülser Mittagspitze* (2095m).

10km up the valley to the SW is the high-lying hamlet of *Damüls* (1428m); its remarkable church of 1484 has contemporary frescoes. From here a minor road crosses the mountains to the W before descending to *Rankweil*; see Rte 1A.

Continuing SE from Au, you climb past the resort of *Schoppernau*, with a number of old wooden houses, to (13km) *Schröcken* (1296m), with the *Braunarlspitze* (2649m) rising to the SW, there ascending in steep curves on an improved section of road (good retrospective views) to (5km) the *Hochtannbergpass* (1679m). The road then descends steeply, with the *Widderstein* (2533m and 2536m) to the N, and the *Biberkopf* (2599m) further NE, to (5km) **Warth** (1494m).

To the N of the pass lies the KLEINWALSERTAL, a mountain-girt enclave of Austria, but much isolated from it, and only accessible by road from *Oberstdorf* in Germany. It was settled in the early 14C by emigrants from the upper Valais in Switzerland. Its main village is *Mittelberg*; its currency is Deutschmarks, and it remains in the German Customs area.

WARTH TO REUTTE (60km). The B198 descends the widening valley of the Lech, with the summits of the ALLGÄUER ALPS forming the frontier to the N, through (12km) *Holzgau*, with houses embellished with exterior murals.—8km *Elbigenalp*, with restored frescoes of 1676 by J.J. Zeiller in its *Pfarrkirche*, and earlier examples in the cemetery chapel, which also contains a naive Dance of Death by Anton Falger (1840). Elbigenalp was the birthplace of the artist Josef Anton Koch (1768–1839). The retrospective views are imposing.—27km *Weissenbach am Lech*.—From here the B199 crosses the TANNHEIMERTAL to the NW, later skirting the *Haldensee*, to reach the German frontier (Customs) after 23km. 3km beyond the frontier lies *Oberjoch*.—*8km* **Reutte**; see Rte 2.

From Warth the B198 turns S, with the *Rappenspitze* (2472m) rising to the E, to (7km) **Lech** (1444m; 1300 inhab. out of season), a well-sited and equipped ski-resort, dominated to the SW by the *Omeshorn* (2557m). Its 14–17C church contains frescoes of 1490.—The road continues S, with the *Rüfispitze* (2632m) rising to the E, to (5km) **Zürs** (1717m), also an important and flourishing ski centre, much developed since the road over the *Flexenpass* (1773m) was opened.—The B197 is met after 5km, above *Stuben*, and 10km W of **St. Anton**; see Rte 1A.

2 (Ulm) Füssen to Innsbruck

Total distance, 105km (65 miles). B314. 14km *Reutte*—20km *Lermoos*—20km *Nassereith*—B189. 25km *Telfs*—15km *Zirl*—11km **Innsbruck**.

Maps: F&B 3; BEV 47/10–11.

The A7 autobahn from *Ulm* to beyond (86km) *Kempten*, which at present is continued by the 'Alpenstrasse' via *Pfronten* to (41km) *Füssen*, is to be extended to pass to the W of Füssen and E of Reutte.

An ALTERNATIVE, minor road, is that from Pfronten to meet the main road SW of Füssen and 10km NW of Reutte, and passing through *Vils*, home of the Rief family of violin-makers in the 18C–early 19C. In 1735 a peace treaty was signed at the post-house at Füssen between Maria Theresia and the Elector Maximilian III of Bavaria.

At *Neuschwanstein*, 4km E of Füssen is the 'fairly-tale' Schloss conceived by Ludwig II of Bavaria, his residence until 1886, when deposed; he was drowned in the *Starnberger See* shortly after.

After crossing the frontier (Customs) the road shortly bears S between the *Tannheimer Berge* (W) and the *Ammergebirge* (E), at this point both rising to over 2000m.—**Reutte**, a market town of 5150 inhab., lies in the wide valley of the Lech, and retains several old houses, notably No. 7 Obermarkt (Das Grüne Hause, 16C, with decoration of 1700, recently restored), and the so-called 'Zeillerhäuschen' (Untergsteig 1). Wernher von Braun, who had developed the German V2s, fled here in 1945, where he was captured by the Americans. The town was damaged by bombing in February of that year.—At *Breitenwang*, just E of the town, is an attractive 16–17C church containing a fine organ-case, and frescoes by Johann Jakob Zeiller (1708–83), born at Reutte, as was the artist

Franz Anton Zeiller (1716–94). In 1137 the Emperor Lothaire III died here on his way back from Italy.

Continuing S, the road threads the EHRENBURGER DEFILE, dominated by the ruins of a 13–18C castle, to (9km) *Heiterwang*, from which this lake and the adjacent *Plansee*, further E, can be visited. You cross the district known as the AUSSERFERN to skirt (right) **Bischlbach**, with two churches: *St. Laurent*, rebuilt 1736, with frescoes by members of the Zeiller family; and *St. Joseph* (1710), built to the design of Johann Jakob Herkomer, the architect of Innsbruck cathedral.—The *Blattberg* (2247m) rises to the NE as you approach (13km) the village of *Lermoos*, well-sited among these limestone ranges, its church of 1751 with rococo decoration.

The B187 leads NE to (25km) *Garmisch-Partenkirchen* in Germany, reaching the frontier (Customs) at 12km. After 2.5km a right-hand turning leads to the resort of *Ehrwald* and the lower station (passport necessary) of a cable-car to near the summit of the **Zugspitze** (2968m), which is actually in Germany—the country's highest peak, and commanding a wide view.

The main road—an ancient trading route—bears S just before Lermoos to pierce a ridge and climb SW past two small lakes to (10km) the FERNPASS (1216m). It then descends past (right) *Schloss Fernstein* (1540), and left, another small lake, where, on an island, are the ruins of *Sigmundsburg* (1460). Beyond rises the *Wanneck* (2495m).— Passing through (10km) *Nassereith* (13km NE of Imst; see Rte 1A), with a small local museum, you climb E in zigzags to the *Holzleiten Sattel* (1126m; views), descending parallel to the *Mieminger Gebirge* (and shortly passing a road climbing over the ridge to the S to *Stams*; see Rte 1A) to (25km) **Telfs**, in the Inn valley, a small textile town of 7750 inhabitants at the foot of the *Hohe Munde* (2592m).

Here a road climbs steeply to the NE towards (13km) *Seefeld* (see Rte 3), off which another turns left directly to the German frontier at *Mittenwald*. At *Pfaffenhofen*, just S of Telfs, the church is built on the site of its 7C predecessor.

From Telfs you can take the motorway to Innsbruck or follow the old road E, below the church of *Pettnau* and through (14km) *Zirl*, burnt by the Bavarians in 1703, lying on the direct road from *Seefeld* (see Rte 3) and below the Nordkette range rising abruptly from the valley floor. Continuing E you approach the outskirts of **Innsbruck**, first passing its airport (right); see Rte 4.

3   (Munich) Garmisch to Innsbruck

Total distance, 59km (36 miles). 28km *Scharnitz*—B313. 10km **Seefeld**—10km *Zirl* crossroads—B171. 11km **Innsbruck**.

Maps: F&B 3; BEV 47/11.

The A95 autobahn from *Munich* leads to (88km) *Garmisch-Partenkirchen*, from which the E6 bears E and then S to by-pass *Mittenwald*, to reach the Austrian frontier at the *Scharnitzpass* (955m; Customs).

Claudia de Medici, widow of the Archduke Leopold V, built a fort here known as the Porta Claudia, in an attempt to defend the pass against Swedish incursions during the Thirty Years' War. It was later reconstructed after being sacked by the Bavarians in 1703, but was assaulted and razed by Marshal Ney in 1805, when its defenders were commanded by Col. Swinburne, an English officer in the Austrian service (and an ancestor of the poet).

There are slight relics of Roman *Mansio Scarbia* at adjacent *Scharnitz*. To the E is a mountainous area separated by three valleys known as the KARWENDAL, now a *Nature Reserve*.

At 8km fork right off the road, here crossing a high-lying plateau, with the WETTERSTEIN RANGE to the NW, to **Seefeld in Tirol** (1180m; 2500 inhab. out of season), a flourishing summer and winter resort, twice the venue of Winter Olympic Games. Its *Pfarrkirche* (dedicated to St. Oswald, the martyr of Northumberland) dates from 1319, but was enlarged in the 15C, when its S portal was built, and again in 1604. The spiny groining of its vault is notable, and also the 15C statues preserved in its neo-Gothic high altar. Stairs ascend to the Heiligblutkapelle of 1572, baroquised in 1724.

To the SW of the centre is the *Seekapelle* (1628), a round church erected by Leopold V and Claudia de Medici (see above), beyond which the road continues to (c 3km) a belvedere providing a fine view over the Inn valley, which forms the background to Dürer's Self-portrait of 1498 in the Prado Museum, Madrid. The road—an alternative to the direct descent; see below—may be continued via *Mösern*, before climbing down steeply to *Telfs*; see Rte 2. Hermann Broch (1886–1951), the author, lived at Mösern in the early 1930s before his arrest and later emigration to the USA.

The main road from Seefeld descends as steeply to the SE past the *Zirlberg belvedere* to the *Zirl* crossroads, 11km due W of **Innsbruck**; see last paragraph of Rte 2, and Rte 4.

4 Innsbruck

Maps: F&B 3 (also their WK 333); BEV 47/11.

INNSBRUCK, the capital of the *Tyrol*, with 117,300 inhab. (32,150 in 1880; 81,700 in 1939), is situated largely on the right bank of the river Inn, at 574m above sea level, and at a point just N of the *Sill gap*, the main route S to the Brenner Pass and Italy. To the W it is dominated by the steep slopes of the *Nordkette*, rising to between 2300 and 2700m. It contains the unique Mausoleum of Maximilian I; the Tyrol Folk Museum, one of the finest of its kind; and just beyond its SE outskirts, the three important collections at Schloss Ambras, which—apart from the beauty of its site—make a visit to Innsbruck memorable.

Tourist Information Offices (for hotel bookings, etc.) are open near the W, S, and E entrances to the town, in addition to the main office at Burggraben 3.

Its *Airport*, just W of the town, is the base of the *Tyrolean Airlines*, providing regular flights to and from Vienna, Graz, and Salzburg; and Zürich, Paris, Amsterdam, Rome and Frankfurt; also excursion flights; and an alpine ambulance service; but see p 98.

The Celtic settlement at a natural crossing of trade routes was occupied by the Romans, who established a castrum at *Veldidena*, which later gave its name to the medieval abbey of Wilten, S of the present town. *Insprugg* or *Insprucke*, on the right bank of the Inn, bridged before 1180, was the name given to the market moved here by the counts of Andrechs. The area was surrounded by a wall in 1234. It became a Habsburg property in 1363 under Duke Rudolf IV, when inherited from Margaret de Görz-Tirol. In 1390 it was ravaged by fire, but in 1420 Duke Friedrich IV, who governed the Tyrol from 1404 to 1439, made it his capital. In 1493 it passed to Maximilian I, who established his Imperial residence here, and it remained the principal seat of the Habsburgs until 1665. It continued to flourish under the Archduke Ferdinand II, who reconstructed Schloss Ambras.

Innsbruck, lying near a geological fault, suffered from earth tremors in 1572, 1670, and 1689, which accounts for its so-called 'earthquake buttresses', which were constructed against several houses at this time. In 1669 Leopold I founded its University. Here in 1718–19, Maria Clementina Sobieska, betrothed to James Edward, the Old Pretender, was held under arrest for several months while en route to join her future husband, and only escaped in disguise with the help of a Jacobite rescue party led by Charles Wogan, who whisked her rapidly over the Brenner into Venetian territory.

It grew as a commercial centre during the 18C, but after the Peace of Pressburg (December 1805) it passed into Bavarian hands, which precipitated the insurrections led by Andreas Hofer in 1809, when a number of combats took place on Berg Isel, just S of the town, but by the Treaty of Paris (1814) the Tyrol was returned to Austria. With the extension of railway lines, it further expanded in the later 19C, becoming formally the capital of the Tyrol in 1849, although Meran (Merano; now in S Tyrol) had previously retained that title. It was to Innsbruck that the Court exiled themselves during the Vienna Revolution of 1848. The line along the lower Inn valley was completed in 1858; that from Munich across the Brenner Pass to Verona in 1867; and that across the Arlberg in 1884.

A centre of communications between the Axis powers during the Second World War, it was bombed several times. The German 19th Army surrendered here on 5 May 1945. In recent decades it has grown rapidly. It has been the venue of the Winter Olympic Games on two occasions (in 1964 and 1976), and continues to be one of the more flourishing winter-sports centres of Austria.

Among natives were the Emperor Friedrich III (1415–93); Balthasar Ferdinand Moll (1717–85), the sculptor; Christoph, Johann Martin, and Georg Anton Gumpp (1600–72, 1643–1729, and 1682–1754 respectively), architects; and the artist Jakob Plazidus Altmutter (1780–1819). Hermann Keyserling (1880–1946), the philosopher, died here, as in 1662 did the English composer and viol player William Young, when in the service, from 1652, of the Archduke Ferdinand Karl. Johann Stadlmayr (c 1575–1648), the composer, lived from 1607 at Innsbruck, as Kapellmeister to Archduke Maximiliam II, and then to Leopold V.

The river Inn is spanned by the *Alte Innbrücke* just W of the Herzog Otto Strasse.

To the W, in the transpontine suburb of *Hötting*, is the beautifully domed **Mariahilfkirche**, built by Christoph Gumpp in 1648–89, with a circular nave, frescoes of 1689 by Kaspar Waldmann (1657–1720), an altar-painting by Egid Schor (1627–1701), a wrought-iron grille of 1731, and statues by Josef Kluckner (1800).

A short distance S of the E end of the bridge is the restored *Ursulinen Kirche* (1700–05), by J.M. Gumpp and his sons.—Further SE stands the characteristic **St. Johanneskirche am Innrain** (1729–35), by Georg Anton Gumpp, now restored. The heavy portico was added in 1750; the frescoes of 1794 are by Josef Schopf.

The MARKTGRABEN leads E from the riverbank to the N end of the broad Maria Theresien Strasse; see Rte 4C below. Beyond this junction is the BURGGRABEN, also marking the site of its medieval moat, which continues round the S side of the enceinte to the *Hofkirche*; see Rte 4B below. No. 3, now the *Tourist Office*, formerly the court stables and later a guard-house and officers' barracks, preserves its vault supported by eight columns.

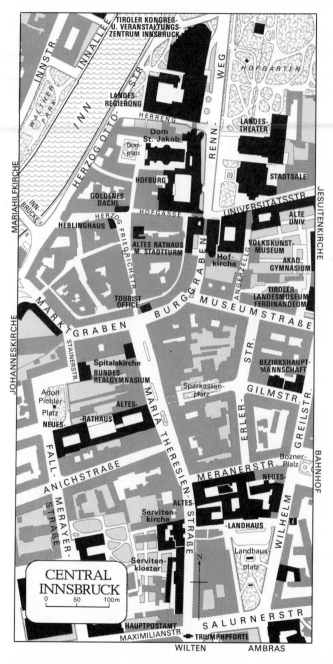

CENTRAL
INNSBRUCK
0   50   100m

A. The Altstadt

Turning into the old town opposite the Maria Theresien Strasse,
follow the Herzog-Friedrich Strasse, flanked by arcades ('*Lauben*'),
first passing (No. 39) the '*Golden Rose*' inn, where Montaigne lodged
in 1580; No. 35 is the *Kohleggerhaus* (15–16C); No. 31, the '*Weisses
Kreuz*' or White Cross inn, where Mozart and his father stayed in
1769; and No. 22, the 15–16C *Trautsonhaus*.

The 'Goldenes Dachl' (Golden Roof)

No. 21 is the *Altes Rathaus*, of various dates prior to 1450, with an adjacent 56m-high belfry or **Stadtturm**, which in 1560 received its octagonal upper storey, surmounted by angle-turrets, and with a bulbous dome replacing an earlier spire; the clock dates from 1602. Climb the tower for a good view of the city.

At the N end of the street, here broadening to form a small platz, is the so-called *°**Goldenes Dachl** (Golden Roof), a richly decorated Gothic loggia built over an oriel window and protected by a crocketed roof composed of fire-gilt copper tiles. It was constructed in 1494–96 as part of the *Neuer Hof* or *Fürstenberg*, a palace previously built by Duke Friedrich of Tyrol, and drastically modified in 1822.

The lower frieze consists of armorial blasons; the upper, forming a balustrade, is decorated with copies of sculptures by Nikolaus Türing the Elder (also the architect of the structure); the originals, of 1500–08, may be seen in the *Ferdinandeum Museum*. They represent morisco dancers on either side of the two central panels, which depict Maximilian I with his two wives: on his left, Mary of Burgundy (died 1482; a daughter of Charles the Bold and Margaret of York—a sister of Henry VIII of England), and Bianca Maria Sforza; and also between his chancellor and jester. The frescoes which embellish it are by Jörg Kölderer (1500).

No. 16 in the street is the *Katzunghaus*, with reliefs of 1530; while No. 10, on the corner, is the *Helblinghaus*, Gothic in origin, but c 1732 provided with a richly decorated rococo façade. To the W is the *Tänzlhaus*, baroquised by Johann Martin Gumpp in 1692.

No. 6 is the '*Goldener Adler*' (Golden Eagle) inn, of ancient origin.

Its illustrious guests have included Joseph II (in 1777), Goethe (in 1786 and 1790), Marshal Masséna, Metternich, Paganini, Kotzebue (in 1816), Heine (in 1828; who did not much care for either Innsbruck in particular, or the Tyrol in general), the early 19C 'travel-writer' Henry David Inglis, Andreas Hofer, and Ludwig I of Bavaria among several other crowned heads.

Opposite, and further W is the *Ottoburg*, a relic of the 14–15C fortifications.

The Pfarrgasse leads N from just E of the Goldenes Dachl to the domed **Pfarrkirche St. Jakob** (now with cathedral rank), built in 1717–24 by Johann Jakob Herkommer and Johann Georg Fischer, with an exuberant interior decorated with copies of frescoes by Cosmas Damian Asam (the originals of which were damaged during 1944), and with stucco-work by his brother Egid Quirin.

Notable are its *Pulpit* (by Nikolaus Moll), and *Organ-case* (by P. Trolf), both of 1725, and the painting by Lucas Cranach the Elder above the richly gilt high altar. Remarkable also is the funerary *°**Monument of the Archduke Maximilian III** (1558–1618), a grand master of the Teutonic Order, raised on Salomonic pillars and designed by Kaspar Gras and Hubert Gerhart. The archduke is shown praying, accompanied by St. George and his dragon. Note also the crested helmets and shields on the walls of this transept, that on the W being the funerary shield of the Teutonic Order.

Its apse abuts the *Hofburg*, perhaps best approached by turning along the Hofgasse (leading E from the Goldenes Dachl), in which No. 3 is the mid 15C *House of the Teutonic Order*, and No. 12 the *Burggriesenhaus* (1490), built to house the court giant Niklas Haidl, with his statue by Nikolaus Türing the Elder.

The W side of the Rennweg, which is shortly reached (once the site of tournaments and races, hence its name), is flanked by the **Hofburg**, with its two domed towers. The former rambling Imperial palace dating from the 15–16C (two water-colour sketches of which

—now in the Albertina, Vienna—were painted by Dürer in c 1494) was virtually rebuilt in 1756–76 by Johann Martin Gumpp the Younger and Konstantin Johann von Walter.

Groups are conducted round a series of rooms of comparatively slight interest, few of which contain any notable furniture or fittings (except for one finely carved candelabra). The room in which Franz I died in 1765 was later converted into a chapel. Among numerous Habsburg family portraits hanging in several rooms are Maria Theresia wearing the Hungarian crown; Maria Antonia, the latter's youngest daughter, better known as Marie-Antoinette; and a copy of Winterhalter's portrait of the Empress Elisabeth. The 'Chinese Room', the *Riesensaal*, with ceiling frescoes by Maulbertsch (1775–76), and the *Audience Chamber* are also crossed before the exit is reached.

Further N is the *Kongresshaus* of 1973, on the site of an old theatre destroyed in 1944, while opposite the palace is the grey *Theatre* of 1864, modernised in the 1960s.—For the *Rotunda* at 39 Rennweg, see p 140.

B.　The Hofkirche and Museum of Folk Art

To the S is the **Hofkirche** or *Franziskanerkirche* (combined ticket with Folk Museum), built by Ferdinand I in 1553–63 from the designs of Andrea Crivelli, to contain the tomb of his grandfather, Maximilian I (1493–1519); its construction was undertaken by Nikolaus Türing the Younger (grandson of the architect and sculptor of the 'Golden Roof'). The porch is by Heironymus Longhi, but the church is entered from the W side of the adjacent cloister. Its reticulated Gothic vaulting, sustained by ten tall red marble columns, is masked by Baroque stucco-work of c 1692.

The lofty nave is dominated by the ****Monument of the Emperor Maximilian I**, who was buried at Wiener Neustadt; see Rte 32B. It was begun in 1502, but not completed until 1584. The general design is due to *Gilg Sesselschreiber* of Munich, succeeded in 1518 by *Stefan Godl* of Nuremberg, and after 1548 by *Gregor Löffler* of Innsbruck. The notable *Organ*, by Jorg Ebert of Ravensburg, restored in 1970, dates from 1555–60. The Annunciation on its wings was painted by Domenico Pozzo of Milan.

The *Cenotaph* of black marble, sculpted in 1561–83, is surrounded by a wrought-iron grille of 1570 by *Jörg Schmeidhammer* of Prague, following the design of Paul Trabel of Innsbruck. At the angles of the cenotaph are bronze figures of Justice, Prudence, Temperance, and Fortitude, by Hans Lendenstreich, while Alexander Colin designed the kneeling statue of the Emperor in his coronation robes and facing the altar, cast in 1584 by *Lodovico de Duca*, a Sicilian sculptor.

The 24 reliefs which surround it, the majority carved by *Alexander Colin* after the designs of Florian Abel of Prague, illustrate episodes from the Life of Maximilian, and are of historical interest for the costumes and arms of the period depicted. However, the grille placed in front of the marbles makes close study difficult.

On either side of the cenotaph, between the columns, stand the unique 28 larger-than-life bronze **Statues** representing mourning figures of the Emperor's relations and ancestors, including some ideal rulers of the past (40 were originally planned). Many of them were designed to carry funerary torches. Although impressive in mass, they vary in artistic quality. The finest are by *Peter Vischer*, after drawings of 1515–18 by Albrecht Dürer (Nos 21 and 24), although several others are remarkable.

The initials G, S, V, PL, and GL before the following indicate that they were sculpted by *Stefan Godl*, or *Gilg Sesselschreiber*—who between them were responsible for the majority—or *Peter Vischer*, *Peter Löffler*, and *Gregor Löffler*. The numbering starts with the statue nearest the entrance.

1 G The Emperor Albrecht II (1397–1439). His wife was Elisabeth of Hungary.
2 G The Emperor Friedrich III (1415–1493), father of Maximilian.
3 G Leopold III (1095–1136), Margrave of Austria, canonised c 1485.
4 G *Albrecht IV von Habsburg (died 1239/40, when crusading), father of Rudolf I. After a drawing of Dürer's.
5 G Duke Leopold III (1349–1386), killed at the Battle of Sempach).
6 G Duke Friedrich IV, 'of the empty pockets' (1382–1439). Father of the Archduke Sigismund
7 G Duke Albrecht I (1248–1308, assassinated), Emperor in 1298. His wife was Elisabeth von Görz-Tirol
8 G Godefroy de Bouillon, King of Jerusalem (1061–1100).
9 G Elisabeth of Hungary (1396–1443), wife of the Emperor Albrecht II.
10 S Marie of Burgundy (1457–1482), first wife of Maximilian and daughter of Charles le Téméraire.
11 S *Elisabeth von Görz-Tirol (1263–1313), wife of Albrecht I; had 21 children.
12 S Kunigunde of Bavaria (1465–1520), Maximilian's sister.
On either side of the entrance to the choir, stalls of 1563.
13 G Ferdinand the Catholic of Aragón (1452–1516), husband of Isabel of Castile and father of
14 G *Juana of Spain ('la Loca', the Mad; 1479–1555), wife of Philip the Handsome.
15 G Philip the Good of Burgundy (1396–1467), father of
16 G Charles le Téméraire of Burgundy (1433–1477, killed at the Battle of Nancy), father of Marie of Burgundy.
Returning along the other aisle, we pass
17 S Zimburgis von Masovien (died 1429), wife of Ernst der Eiserne.
18 G Archduchess Margaretha (1480–1530), daughter of Maximilian.
19 G Blanca Maria Sforza (1472–1511), second wife of Maximilian.
20 G Archduke Sigismund of Tyrol (1427–1496), son of Duke Friedrich IV.
21 V *King Arthur of England (died c 542), with his visor up.
22 S & PL *Fernando of Portugal (1345–1383), grandfather of Maximilian's mother, Leonor of Portugal (1437–1467). She is buried in Wiener Neustadt.
23 S Duke Ernst der Eiserne (1377–1424), husband of Zimburgis von Masovien, and grandfather of Maximilian. He was buried at *Rein*, near Graz.
24 V *Theodoric, king of the Ostrogoths (454–526).
25 G Duke Albrecht II, the Wise (1298–1358), son of Duke Albrecht I and grandfather of Ernst der Eiserne.
26 S *Rudolf I of Habsburg (1218–1291), founder of the dynasty.
27 S Philip the Handsome of Castile (Felipe el Hermoso; 1478–1506, died at Burgos), Maximilian's son by Marie of Burgundy, and father of Charles V and Ferdinand I. His wife was Juana of Spain.
28 GL Clovis (Klodwig in German), king of the Franks (465–511).

Steps climb to the tribune, where there are 23 smaller bronze statues of saints, princes, and nobles, by Stefan Godl (originally intended for Maximilian's cenotaph, but not normally on view). Ascend to the so-called **Silberne** (Silver) **Chapel**, named after the silver image of the Virgin on the altar, to the left of which is an organ of 1614, under restoration. Here also is the armour of the Archduke Ferdinand II (died 1595), placed in a kneeling position. Adjacent is his *Tomb*, by Alexander Colin, with his armed effigy in marble, and with four plaques depicting scenes from his life. Near by, also by Colin, is the *Tomb* of *Philippine Welser* (died 1580), the duke's wife, who he had

Arthur of England, Fernando of Portugal, Ernst der Eiserne and Theodoric, king of the Ostrogoths

been obliged to marry secretly (in 1557), as she was a commoner, and the Emperor Ferdinand I barred their children from the succession.

On returning to the entrance of the church we pass (left) the *Tomb of Andreas Hofer* (1767–1810), the Tyrolese patriot, shot at Mantua on Napoleon's orders, whose remains were brought here in 1823. The tomb, by J.N. Schaller, dates from 1834. Here, in 1654, Queen Christina of Sweden, daughter of Gustavus Adolphus, was received into the Roman Catholic church.

The ****Museum of Tyrolean Folk Art** (*Volkskunstmuseum*), which should on no account be overlooked, is entered by turning left in the cloister and ascending to the FIRST FLOOR. Here are displayed numerous models of Tyrolean houses and numerous reconstructed rooms with panelling and carved wooden ceilings, some domed, saved from houses being demolished (mind your head on entering some): among them here and on the upper floor are those from

Niederdorf and Issing (Pustertal); and Villanders (Eisacktal); three from Sulzberg (Trentino); from Tiersburg (Gnadenwald), Ladis and Fiss. Notable are the collection of stoves or *öfen*, frequently green-tiled; collections of kitchen utensils; moulds; rollers; cutlery; flasks; pewter; ceramics; metal-work; basket-work; yokes; pump-handles; bells and bell-collars; painted brides' chests from the Zillertal; sections devoted to carding, spinning and weaving; a stocking-machine of 1773; carpentry and modelling; carved and painted figurines; machines; hand-printing; watch-holders; razor-boxes; axes, planes, and other implements; sleighs; brass weights and measures; strong-boxes; harnesses; pewter cows and other objects; powder-horns; games; musical instruments, including a Jacob Steiner violin; engraved bone objects; masquerades; tiles; firebacks; lanterns, and candlesticks, etc.

On the SECOND FLOOR are some remarkable examples of carved and painted furniture; clothes-presses; cradles; locks and handles; vestments; costumes and accessories (leather belts, braces, combs, and pins, etc.); cult objects; moulds for ex-voto candles, etc., and ex-votos (including animals); scapularies, rosaries, etc.

On the GROUND FLOOR are a number of Christmas cribs, with their numerous carved figurines, some very baroque.

Further E in the Universitätsstrasse is the *Alte Universität*, preserving in its W wing (1572) the former Jesuit College, while its E wing (1672) is by Johann Martin Gumpp the Elder. Next door is the octagonally domed **Jesuit Church** of 1627–46, by Christoph Gumpp the Younger, following the design of Carlo Fontana, with a façade and towers only completed in 1901, and the whole recently restored since serious bomb damage in 1943–44. In the crypt is the mausoleum of the Archduke Leopold V (died 1632) and his wife Claudia de Medici (died 1648).

About 1km further E, approached by the Dreiheiligenstrasse, is the entrance to the **Tiroler Landeskundliches Museum**, installed in the former *Zeughaus*, or *Arsenal*, of Maximilian I, and formerly moated. In 1517 it possessed sufficient arms to equip a force of 30,000 men. It now contains mineralogical and natural history collections; several relief models; sleighs; old fire engines; models of machinery; musical instruments; clocks; ex-votos, and naive paintings of Tyrolese (1703); arms and armour, including the arms of Andreas Hofer; and a section devoted to the local 'battles' of 1809. It also houses an important cartographical collection, including several mid 18C maps of the Tyrol by Peter Anich (1723–66), together with earlier examples by Wolfgang Lazin (1561) and Matthias Burgklechner (early 17C); globes and instruments.

C. The Landesmuseum Ferdinandeum and Maria Theresien Strasse

At No. 15 Museumstrasse, parallel to and S of the Universitätsstrasse, is the renovated *Tiroler Landesmuseum Ferdinandeum*, founded in 1823 and named after its patron, the Emperor Ferdinand. The exhibits include a *Maquette of the Tyrol*, constructed by the late Fritz

Ebster, at 1:20,000, covering the N and E Tyrol and the German-speaking areas of S Tyrol (Italian territory since 1919).

To the right on the FIRST FLOOR is a series of rooms devoted to the Archaeology of the Tyrol, with artefacts of the Hallstatt period and of the La Tène culture, among them fibulas, helmets, figurines, arms, implements, terra sigillata, glass, ceramics, and a huge reconstituted coffin of the 7C, with its original iron-work.

Among notable medieval paintings and sculpture are: *Marx Reichlich*, Adoration of the Magi (1489); *Habsburg Master of 1500*, Virgin and Child with St. Anne and St. Christopher; *Michael Pacher*, St. Catherine; carved plaques by *Nikolaus Türing the Elder* from the Goldenes Dachl (see p 125); a carved Crucifix of 1170; carved funerary monuments, escutcheons, and epitaphs, etc.; *Master of Bruneck of 1448* (Ulm, c 1400–67), Martyrdom of St. Ursula; *Sebastian Schel*, The Annenberger altarpiece (1517); *Bernhard Strigel*, Portraits of Maximilian I in 1508, and of Bianca Maria Sforza; *Hans Baldung Grien*, The Holy Family; *Jakob Seisenegger*, Portraits of Hans and Anna Kleplat; *Pieter Brueghel the Younger*, Rustic scene; Portraits by *Amberger, Marc Reichlich* and *Jörg Brue the Elder*; *Hans Maler von Schwaz*; Portrait of Anna von Ungarn; several statues by *Hans Multscher*, including a Christ with Mary and St. John.

SECOND FLOOR. Paintings: *Mabuse*, Christ on the Mount of Olives; *anon. Dutch*, Female portrait (1640); *Lucas Cranach the Elder*, St. Jerome; *Rembrandt*, Portrait of his father (1630); *Aelbert Cuyp*, Interior of the church at Dordrecht, and Three children with a lamb; *Gerhard ter Borch*, Male portrait; *Willem van Mieris*, two small portraits; *Jan Blom*, The hunters; *Momper*, Winter scene, and numerous works by minor Dutch and Flemish artists. Also *Jacob Denys*, Portrait of F. Gonzaga (1673); *Pietro Longhi*, Portrait of Christofor Migazzi (1760); and *Bernard Strozzi*, Portrait of Claudio Monteverdi in 1630. The altarpiece of 36 Limoges plaques by *Pierre Raymond* is very fine. Also displayed are: *Martin T. Polak* (1570–1639), Virgin and Child, and Self-portrait; *Philipp Haller*, Portrait of Grafin Herberstein (1740); *J.B. Lampi the Elder*, Self-portrait; *Mengs*, Portrait of Joseph Schopf; *Michelangelo Unterberger*, Death of the Virgin; *Franz Anton Leitensdorffer*, Portraits of Graf Spaur and his wife; *Heinrich Hintze*, Ambras in 1828; *Paul Troger*, Self-portrait (1730); *Martin Knodler*, Karl Graf Firmian and his courtiers; *Hendrik Vroom*, Sea battle (possibly depicting the Spanish Armada); *Franz von Defregger* (1834–1921), Tyrolean genre scenes; Landscapes by *Josef Anton Koch* (1768–1839); *Andreas Einberger* (1878–1952), Self-portrait; *Gerstl*, Self-portrait; *Kolo Moser*, Portrait of Professor Ceschka; *Klimt*, Portrait of Josef Pembaur; *Max Oppenheimer*, Portrait of Adolf Loos; *Kokoschka*, Portrait of Ludwig von Ficker; and several paintings by *Albin Egger-Lienz* (1868–1925).

From the W end of the Museumstrasse, the Burggraben and the MARIA THERESIEN STRASSE are regained. On the W side of the latter is the *Spitalskirche*, rebuilt in 1701–05 by Johann Martin Gumpp. Opposite the *Rathaus* stands the *Annasäule*, a column by Cristoforo Benedetti erected in 1706 to commemorate the retreat of the Bavarian forces commanded by the Elector Max Emmanuel in the face of a sortie from Innsbruck during the War of the Spanish Succession (on St. Anne's Day; 26 July 1703).—No. 38 in the street is the 17C *Trapp palace*.

Opposite is No. 43, the **Altes Landhaus** (1725–28), the seat of provincial administration, built by Georg Anton Gumpp, with a notable staircase and sculptures by Nikolaus Moll, and council-room with frescoes by Cosmas Damian Asam.—Adjacent (No. 45) is the *Fugger-and Taxis palace* (1679; remodelled 1784).

On the E side of the street a short distance further S is the restored *Servite Church* of 1616, beyond which is the **Triumphpforte**, a triumphal arch erected in 1765 for the state entry of Maria Theresia and her consort Franz I on the occasion of the marriage of their son, the future Leopold II, with the Infanta Maria Ludovica of Spain. The Emperor died before the conclusion of the festivities, hence the emblems of mourning in the ornamentation of its N side, added by Balthasar Moll in 1774.

Alpinists will want to visit the **Alpenvereinsmuseum**, at Wilhelm-Greil-Strasse 15 (also with an Information Office in its courtyard), not far E of the Landhaus. It contains numerous relief models of the Austrian mountains, paintings of alpine scenery by Ernst Platz, R. Reschreiter, and others; early maps of the Zillertal (1530), and of Kitzbühel (c 1620); and sections devoted to the development of skis and skiing, etc. For the maps produced by the *Österreichische Alpenverein*, see p 90.

D.   Wilten and Schloss Ambras

These two excursions can be made by car, or by tram No. 1 from the Railway Station to Wilten, and the No. 6 to Ambras.

About 1km S of the Triumphal Arch, at the end of the Leopold Strasse, stands—to the W of the railway—the *Pfarrkirche, or Wilten Basilika*, with its twin towers, founded in 1140. It was rebuilt in 1751–55 to the designs of Franz Xaver de Paula Penz, and its richly decorated but delicately coloured rococo interior contains remarkable stucco-work by Franz Xaver Feichtmayr, notable frescoes by Matthäus Günther, and a carved Virgin of the 14C.

To the E is the **Stiftskirche**, that of an abbey founded in the 9C and a Premonstratensian abbey since 1138. It was built in 1651–65 by Christoph Gumpp the Younger, its single tower being completed in 1667, and its façade and porch remodelled in 1716 by Georg Anton Gumpp. The whole has been restored since extensive bomb damage. Its portal is flanked by colossal statues of its legendary founding giants, by Nikolaus Moll. The somewhat heavy Baroque interior, with copied frescoes, preserves a fine wrought-iron grille by Johann Adam Neyer (1707), a high altar of 1665 by Paul Huber, with a painting by Ägid Schor, and a notable 18C organ.

A short distance N is the *Glockengiesser Grasmayer*, a bell-foundry dating back to the 15C.

On a height further S is the **Ski Ramp** (*Skisprungschanze*), erected for the Olympic Games on the *Bergisel* (with autobahn tunnels below). This was the site of the gallant skirmishing of Tyrolean marksmen (Schützen) commanded by Andreas Hofer and Josef Speckbacher against the Franco-Bavarian troops commanded by Marshal Lefebvre, Duc de Dantzig (among others), during the summer of 1809. (See also the first paragraph of Rte 6.)

From the Stiftskirche, the Klostergasse leads SE under the autobahn. Turning left beyond this, and 1.5km further E, is *Schloss Ambras*, also reached by tram No. 6, which continues up to Igls.

Schloss Ambras (also *Amras*) was a favourite residence of the Archduke Ferdinand II of Tyrol (1529–95), and of his wives:

Philippine Welser of Augsburg (1527–80) and Anna Katharina
Gonzaga of Mantua (whom he married in 1582). He was Governor of
Bohemia from 1547, and Regent of Tyrol from 1565. It was after his
second marriage that the schloss became an important cultural
centre, when his collections were systematically arranged with a
view to public exhibition.

Among these were numerous fine suits of *Armour*, several of
which, from the original collection, are displayed in a series of rooms
in the lower castle or *Unterschloss*, to the left of the entrance.
Unfortunately, the collections here and elsewhere at Ambras are
normally only open from May to September inclusive, except
Tuesdays.

The exhibits include tournament armour made for the archduke
himself, and other suits belonging to Maximilian I and Philip the
Handsome; also the fluted armour of Ludwig II of Hungary
(Innsbruck; 1515). Cupboards built for their display are still extant.
Among curiosities are suits made for Thomerle, the court dwarf, and
for the court giant, Giovanni Bona; two suits of Japanese armour, and
several Turkish pieces. The ceiling of the dining-hall should be noted.

To the right of the entrance is a second wing, in which is the
Archduke Ferdinand's *Cabinet of Curiosities*, known as the *Kunst-
und Wunderkammer*. Eighteen showcases hold a variety of objects
made of silver filigree, coral, wood, ivory, precious metals, stones,
and glass, together with several Oriental pieces, chessmen, clocks,
and scientific instruments, etc., and also portraits of several members
of the ducal family, and freaks (such as a hirsute man), among other
paintings. Adjacent is the *Antiquarium*, in which 22 bronze busts of
Roman emperors (1509–17; replicas from the foundry of Jörg Muskat
of Augsburg), originally planned to adorn Maximilian's tomb, but
moved to Ambras in 1570, and *copies* of antique sculptures, among
them some originals, are displayed in niches.

On approaching the upper castle, you pass (right) the so-called
Spanish Banqueting-hall of c 1572, by Giovanni Lucchese (restored),
with framed portraits and a coffered ceiling, and preserving its
original plasterwork frieze. In recent years it has been the venue of
Summer Festivals of Early Music.—Continuing the ascent, you
shortly reach the *Hochschloss*, dating from the 10–12C, with restored
Renaissance frescoes in its courtyard, and containing the **Portrait
Galleries**.

The extensive collections of c 275 *Portraits of members of the House of Austria
(and some others), form part of the Kunsthistorisches Museum, Vienna. The
guided tour takes approx. 1½ hours, and a detailed catalogue in German (with
family trees explaining the several branches of the House) is available. Only
some of the more remarkable portraits are listed below, with their catalogue
numbers. Also of interest are several restored murals, some of the original
panelling, and the so-called Baths of Philippine Welser. Unfortunately the view
N is less attractive than it once was.

5, Ladislaus Postumus and Magdalena of France; 9, the Emperor
Friedrich III, by *Hans Burgkmair the Elder*, and (174), his wife
Eleonore of Portugal, by the same artist; 190, Philippe le Bon of
Burgundy (a copy of a portrait by *Roger van der Weyden*); 193, 194,
Marie of Burgundy, by *Niklas Reiser* ?; 266, 267, Bianca Maria Sforza
(*studios of Ambrogio de Predis*, and *Bernard Strigel*, respectively);
18, Archduchess Margarete; 17, Philip the Handsome of Spain, and
(172) Juana 'la Loca' (the Mad), his wife; 170, Ferdinand II of Aragón;
171, Catherine of Aragón, by *Michiel Sittow*; 19, Triple portrait of Karl
V as a child, with his sisters Eleonore and Isabella; 179, Ludwig II

of Hungary, by *Hans Krell*; 55, 56, the Archduchess Anna, by *Jakob Seisenegger*, and *Hans Mielich*; 37, the Infanta Anna, by *Pantoja de la Cruz*; 84, the Archduke Wenzel, by *Sánchez Coello*; 23, Karl V, by *Francesco Terzio*; 176, Isabella of Portugal; 26, 27, Ferdinand I, by *Jan Vermeyen*, and *Johann Bocksberger the Elder*; 203, Duke Ludwig X of Bavaria, by *Christoph Amberger* ?; 215, Duke Christoph von Württemberg, by *Abraham de Hel* ?; 224, Lazarus von Schwendi; 223, Sebastian Schärtlin von Burtenbach; 51, Maximilian II, ascribed to *Guillaume Scrots*; 54, the same, by *Nicolas Neufchatel*; and 52, with his family, by *Giuseppe Arcimboldo*; 61, Mary of England, by *Anthonis Mor*; 106, Elizabeth I of England, by *Nicholas Hilliard* ?; 168, James I of England, *after John de Critz* ?; 68, 69, the Archduke Karl II; 64, the Archduchess Magdalena, by *Francesco Terzio*; 173, Eleonore de Toledo, duchess of Tuscany, by *Bronzino*; 29, Philip II of Spain, by *Sánchez Coello*; 31, Juana of Portugal, by the same; 123, 124, the Archduchess Maria Leopoldine, the latter by *Lorenzo Lippi*; 221, Duchess Sibylle von Jülich-Cleve-Berg, by *Lucas van Valckenborch*; 77, the Emperor Matthias, by the same; 105, the Archduchess Maria Magdalena, by *Pourbus the Younger*; 100, the Archduchess Eleonore, by the same; 101, the Archduke Maximilian Ernst, by *Joseph Heintz the Elder*; 108, the Archduke Johann Karl as a child; 180, Sigismund III of Poland, by *Martin Kober*; 106, the Archduchess Konstanze, by *Pourbus the Younger*; 86, the Archduchess Anna, by the same; 241, 242, Eleonore Gonzaga, both by *Justus Sustermans*, and (240) as a child; 43, the Infanta Maria Anna with her son Ferdinand, by *Friedrich Stoll*; 181, Wladislaw IV of Poland, by *Frans Luyex*, and 113, the Archduchess Cäcilia Renata, by the same; 183, Gustavus II Adolphus of Sweden; 109, 110, 111, Ferdinand III, the last by *Frans Luyex*; 217, Friedrich Wilhelm von Brandenburg, by *Frans Luyex*; 227, Johann Philipp Schönborn, by *Kneller*; 112, the Archduchess Maria Anna of Bavaria, by *Joachim von Sandrart*; 169, Charles I of England, from the *studio of Van Dyck*; 249, Catarina de Medici, by *Valore Casini*; 252, Claudia de Medici, by *Frans Luyex*; 257, Mattias de Medici, by *Justus Sustermans*; 260, Anna de Medici, by the same; 272, Galileo Galilei; 119, the Archduke Ferdinand Karl, by *Frans Luyex*; 121, the Archduchess Isabella Clara; 47, the Infanta Margarita Teresa; 138, Joseph I as a child, by *Benjamin von Block*; 229, Maria Karolina Gräfin Fuchs, by *Martin van Meytens*; 198, 199, Franz I, by the same, and by *Zoffany*; 142, the Archduchess Maria Amalie, by *David Richter the Elder*; 149, the Archduchess Maria Christine; 268, Isabella of Parma, by *Nattier*; 143, Maria Theresia in her youth, by *Andreas Möller*; 155, Prince Ferdinand III of Tuscany, by *Joseph Dorfmeister*; and 271, Marie Louise of Naples, by the same; 218, 219, Ferdinand and Therese Natalie von Brunswick-Wolfenbüttel, both by *Anna Rosina de Gasc*; 269, Prince Ludwig of Parma and his sisters, by *Zoffany*; 150, Leopold II and his family, by *Wenzel Werlin*; 154, Franz II, by *Joseph Hickel* ?; 216, Elisabeth Wilhelmine von Württemberg, by *J.B. Lampi the Elder*; 184, Gustav III of Sweden, by *Lorenz Pasch*; 157, Catherine II of Russia; 164, Louis XVI of France, by *François Callet*; 152, Marie Antoinette, by *Elisabeth Vigée-Lebrun*; 165, Napoleon I as King of Italy, from the *studio of Andrea Appiani*; and 156, the Sultan Suleiman II, by a Venetian artist.

Recent additions to the items on display at Ambras are several Gothic sculptures, and the Georgs altar, by *Sebastian Scheel* (died Innsbruck 1554) and *Sebald Bocksdorfer* ? (died 1519).

E.   Igls and Götzens

The right-hand turning at the above-mentioned junction ascends to the ski-resort of **Igls**, also reached with ease by the half-hourly bus **J** from Innsbruck railway station. It is a comparatively unspoilt village on a plateau to the S of the town, from which the recommended excursion is by cable-car ascending S above the bob-sleigh run to its upper station at 1952m, some 295m below the summit of the **Patscherkofel**. A viewing platform near this provides an imposing panorama N over Innsbruck towards the KARWENDEL RANGE, and both up and down the Inn valley.

Another excursion is that to *Götzens*, c 6km from the centre, reached by following the Volser Strasse (the continuation of the Innrain, leading SW from the Marktgraben and passing the modern University buildings). After passing under the autobahn fork left for **Götzens**, with an imposing Baroque *Church* of 1772–75 by Franz Singer, with frescoes by Matthäus Günther (1705–88), his last important work. The painting of the high altar is by Maulbertsch, while several statues are by Johann Schnegg. (The modern glass is an unfortunate addition.)
     For another excursion, take the tram No. 6 from the Maria-Theresien-Strasse N to the Hungerburg terminus, from which the *Hafelekar* (2334m) can be ascended by funicular and gondola for the *view*.

5   Innsbruck to the Brenner Pass, for Bolzano (or Lienz)

Total distance, 38km (23½ miles) on the B128; slightly more on the autobahn (toll).

Maps: F&B 3; BEV 47/11.

It is as well to check in advance during the summer months concerning the density of traffic on these roads, which can cause delays of several hours.

NB. The growing problem of heavy transit traffic from Germany to Italy skirting Kufstein and crossing the Brenner Pass has necessitated the planning of a trans-Alpine transporter railway from Munich to Verona, which will run through tunnels between Wattens and S Innsbruck, and to the E of the Brenner autobahn.

This short route is described for the convenience of people entering Italy from Innsbruck, along one of the most frequented crossings of the Eastern Alps, or for those entering Austria from Verona. The S Tyrol is described in detail in *Blue Guide Northern Italy*.
     Driving S, at 4km the *Sonnenburghof* provides a retrospective panorama of Innsbruck, and shortly after you get a view up the valley ahead on approaching (6.5km) the *Europabrücke*, or *Europe Bridge*, completed in 1965, a remarkable feat of modern engineering, in fact a viaduct 800m long and 190m above the valley at one point,

while several sections are built out from the valley on stilts. The old road (B128) is a pleasant alternative, preferably when entering Austria from the S.

At 4.5km the B183 turns right up the STUBAITAL, an attractive valley containing several interesting churches, many built or modified by Franz Xaver de Paula Penz (1707–72), a secular priest at adjacent Telfes. He also designed that of *Schönberg*, which is entered first, with frescoes by Anton Zoller. That at (7km) *Fulpmes* (right) contains rococo stucco-work, and an organ-case by the architect Clemens Holzmeister (1886–1983), who was born here.—7km *Neustift im Stubaital* has a wide-naved church by Penz, his last but not his best work, completed in 1774, with frescoes by J.A. Zoller and Franz Keller. The narrowing valley continues to ascend to (17.5km) *Mutterbergalm* (1728m), surrounded by peaks and glaciers. Among the former are the *Ruderhofspitze* (3474m; N), the *Schrankogel* (3797m; NW), the *Windacher Daunkogl* (3351m; SW), and the *Zuckerhütl* (3507m; S).

7km **Matrei am Brenner**, Roman *Matreium*, but of Celtic origin, and probably the earliest settlement in the Wipptal, was damaged by air attacks in 1945, but its church preserves some details of interest. It is overlooked by the 18C *Schloss Trautson*, partly restored after 1945.— There is a carved pietà by Jakob Pacher in the baroquised chapel of *Mützens*, 1km NW, beyond the autobahn.

5km **Steinach**, rebuilt after a destructive fire in 1853, has a twin-towered church by Penz, tastelessly decorated, but containing a remarkable high altar of 1765 by Johann Perger, with paintings by Martin Knoller (1728–1804), born at Steinach.—A track leads NE to the chapel of St. Katharina at *Aufenstein*, which has 14C frescoes and sculpture.

3km at *Schmirn*, c 6km E in a side valley, the church contains frescoes of 1757 by Anton Zoller.

3km at *Obernberg*, 6km SW, are a picturesque church founded in 1379 and rebuilt in 1761, and a typical MARKTPLATZ.

At 5km the **Brenner Pass** (Customs) is reached at a height of 1374m, dominated to the SE by the *Wolfendorn* (2776m) in the ZILLERTALER ALPEN. This range bears away to the E forming the boundary between the N and S Tyrol, the latter since 1919 being occupied by Italy, although a high proportion of its population remains German speaking.

A Roman road leads across the pass, the broad flat saddle of which, the lowest of the great alpine passes, forms the watershed between the Black Sea and the Adriatic. It was first mentioned with the crossing of Augustus in 13 BC, and was later one of the main routes of the Barbarian and later medieval invaders entering Italy from the N. The pass was illustrated in 'Travels through the Rhaetian Alps in the year 1786' by Sir Albanis de Beaumont. The Brenner railway was constructed in 1863–67 by the engineers Karl von Etzel and A. Thommen. It included the oldest existing spiral tunnels. This, together with the road, the main channel of communication between Germany and Italy, was heavily attacked from the air during the Second World War.

For the road descending S to (37km) *Bressanone* (*Brixen*) and *Bolzano* (*Bozen*), 47km beyond, see *Blue Guide Northern Italy*.— *Vipiteno* (*Sterzing*) lies 17km SW on the S12; see p 121. At 24km SE of Vipiteno, the S49 turns E out of the VAL ISARCO or EISACKTAL, and follows the Roman road along the valley of the Rienza (Rienz) to (31km) *Brunico* (*Bruneck*) and on to *Lienz*, in the E Tyrol. The Austrian frontier (Customs) is regained 39km E of Brunico, before descending the PUSTERTAL, in which there are a number of interesting monuments, to (35km) **Lienz**; see Rte 40B.

6   Innsbruck to Salzburg

A.   Via St. Johann (for Kitzbühel) and Lofer

Total distance, 164km (102 miles). B171. 10km **Hall**—18km **Schwaz**—9km *Wiesing* crossroads—24.5km *Wörgl*—1.5km B312—31km *St. Johann*. **Kitzbühel** lies 10km S.—27km **Lofer**—27km *Bad Reichenhall* (in Germany)—17km **Salzburg**.

Maps: F&B 3 and 4; BEV 47/11–12, 48/12–13.

Driving N along the Rennweg from central **Innsbruck** (see Rte 4), you pass (left), before crossing the Inn and bearing right, a rotunda, the *Bergisel-Riesenrundgemälde*. It contains a panorama painted in 1896 by Zeno Diemer depicting the skirmishes fought in the vicinity of Innsbruck in 1809.

10km *'Hall in Tirol* (12,600 inhab.), once walled, retains several streets flanked by quaint old houses in its centre. It previously flourished as the mint of the Tyrol, and as its main deposit of salt. To the N it is dominated by the *Grosser Bettelwurf* (2726m); to the S rises the *Glungerzer* (2677m).

In the lower town (where the salt evaporation houses operated until 1967) is the *Münzerturm* (1480), the tower of the old mint, twelve-sided in its upper part, adjacent to the *Schloss Hasegg* of 1280, with its chapel of 1515.

Turning right on ascending into the upper town, follow the Eugenstrasse past the *Damenstift*, built in 1567, but later baroquised, part of a convent of noble ladies; and then the early *Jesuit Church* (1608–84), with its Italianate gabled façade. The heavily decorated interior was visited by Montaigne in 1580. The Rosengasse, among other characteristic lanes, leads left to the central square, at the NW corner of which is the *Rathaus* of 1460 and 1536. To the SW is *St. Nikolaus*, hemmed in by other buildings, dating from 1281, with a later choir, and enlarged in the mid 15C. The Baroque tower replaced its predecessor after an earthquake. The unbalanced interior, tastelessly baroquised after 1752, is of slight interest.

To the N is the old village of *Absam*, birthplace of the violin-maker Jakob Stainer (c 1617–83).

The road shortly crosses the A12 autobahn (see Rte 6B) to (5km) **Volders**. Just before Volders, and close to the motorway, is the remarkable red and white *'Church of St. Karl Borromäus*, that of the adjacent Servite convent. A doctor of the convent, Hippolyt Guarinoni, was the amateur architect of the church. It dates from 1620–54, but several alterations were later made, and a tower added (completed 1735), while in 1765–66 the dome was surmounted by a lantern, and the interior stucco-work replaced. The central fresco is by Martin Knoller. It has recently been tastefully restored. A hurtling boulder, which miraculously braked to avoid crushing passing peasants, is preserved where it fell.

Above Volders itself stands *Schloss Friedberg* (1268), with mid 15C Gothic rooms preserving contemporary frescoes.

At 2km you reach *Wattens*, a small industrial town largely devoted to producing crystal-glass objects, the manufacture of which may be watched.

11km *Schwaz (10,950 inhab.), an ancient place on the right bank of the Inn, here commanded to the SE by the early 12C castle of *Freundsberg*, where the keep and chapel may be visited.

Schwaz formerly flourished owing to its silver and copper mines, largely in the hands of the Fuggers of Augsburg, whose fortified residence survives near the bridge. The town suffered severely in a fire in 1809 and by bombing in 1944. Kaspar Gras (1590–1674), the sculptor and medallist, died here.

Next to the *Fuggerhaus* is the *Franciscan Church* (completed 1515), in the cloister of which are the drastically restored relics of contemporary murals, while the interior of the church was baroquised in the 1730s.

The copper-tiled **Pfarrkirche** *'Unsere Lieben Frau'* is a large Gothic hall-church of four aisles, its reticulated vaulting supported by three rows of massive columns; its Baroque embellishments were removed in the 1900s. Founded in 1337, and altered in the later 15C, it received its belfry in 1508–13. It retains a late Gothic organ-loft, together with another of 1730; also the bronze funerary monument of Hans Dreyling, by Alexander Colin, the Epitaph of Ulrich Fugger, and several late Gothic statues of note. The *Totenkapelle* contains a well-carved altarpiece by Christof Scheller (1510).

You can see several stretches of the town *Walls*, notably by the *Stadtgraben*, on the N side of the enciente.

2km N, overlooking the motorway, is the abbey church of *Fiecht* (1741–44) on the site of an early Benedictine foundation, containing stucco-work by F.X. Feuchtmayr, and frescoes by Matthäus Günther. Its earlier furnishings were destroyed by a fire in 1868. It has been restored since 1945.

A silver-mine can be visited some 3km E of Schwaz, beyond which the small industrial town of *Jenbach* is by-passed. To the W, dominating the valley, is well-preserved **Schloss Tratzberg**; one of the rooms here is embellished by a rambling Habsburg family tree.

THE WIESING CROSSROADS TO THE ACHENPASS (for Munich: c 32km to the border). At 2km the *Wiesing* crossroads are reached. The B181 (a good road) climbs NW, later turning N (views) past *Eben*, with a richly decorated church, to skirt the *Achensee reservoir*, 9km long, above which (right) rises the *Hochiss* (2289m), and to the W, the KARWENDELGEBIRGE, above the growing resort of **Pertisau**. At its N end the lake is dominated by the *Schreckenspitze* (W; 2022m), and right, by the *Vorderunutz* (2078m). The road later descends to approach (left) the German frontier (Customs) near the *Sylvenstein Stausee*, and 29km S of *Bad Tölz*. A right-hand turning climbs to the ACHENPASS (941m). After skirting the *Tegernsee*, the A8 autobahn may be entered 44km N, 31km from *Munich*, and 37km W of the *Rosenheim* junction; see Rte 6B.

FROM THE WIESING CROSSROADS TO MAYRHOFEN (30km). From just E of the crossroads, the B169 turns up the ZILLERTAL from the village of *Strass*, passing at *Fügen* a church of 1495 with interesting frescoes, to (21km) **Zell am Ziller**, from which a road leads E to *Mittersill*; see below.—The valley was a centre of peasant revolt in 1645–47 against taxation and other impositions, and c 450 of its Protestant inhabitants were forced to migrate to Silesia as late as 1837 because of religous intolerance.—Conspicuous is the spire of the octagonal *Pfarrkirche* by Andrä Hueber, with its huge interior dome (1772–78), frescoes by Franz Anton Zeiller (1716–94), and the notable tomb of Johann Schoner (died 1451).—9km further S lies **Mayrhofen** (3300 inhab.), another attractively sited resort at the junction of several valleys, and dominated to the SE by the pyramidal *Ahornspitze* (2973m). Beyond rise the ZILLERTALER ALPEN, the frontier range, with the *Hochfeiler* (3509m) to the SW at the head of the ZEMMTAL. Just E is the *Grosser Möseler* (3480m). At the head of the ZILLERGRUND VALLEY to the SE is the *Rauchkofel* (3251m), with several other peaks over 3300m between the two.—To the W of Mayrhofen opens the TUXERTAL, which later veers SW towards the *Olperer* (3476m).

ZELL AM ZILLER TO MITTERSILL (70km), via the Krimml Falls (toll). The B165 at first climbs steeply in zigzags up the GERLOSTAL past the curiously domed mid 17C church of *Maria Rast* at *Hainzenberg*, and provides several retrospective views. It is overlooked to the N by the *Kreuzjoch* (2558m), and later skirts the *Durlassboden reservoir*, to reach (25km) the *Gerlospass* (1507m). An alternative road descends to the left; the main (toll) road leads ahead. This, the Gerlosstrasse, winds down from the *Fitzsteinalpe* (1628m) and provides distant glimpses of the upper and lower *Krimml Waterfalls*, where the *Krimmler Ache*, formed by its glacier, is precipitated in several falls and cascades into the valley below, an overall depth of c 400m. For a closer view, follow a path leading from the car-park. The road descends through the village of *Krimml*, and down the OBERPINZGAU VALLEY, beyond *Rosental* providing a good view S of the **Grossvenediger** (3674m), with its glaciers, the second highest peak in the HOHE TAUERN RANGE after the Grossglockner. The road continues down the widening valley, passing (right) the *Habachtal*, once reputed for its emeralds, to *Mittersill*, near the junction of the B161, B168, and B108; see Rtes 7 and 8A.

The Krimml waterfall

From the Wiesing crossroads, the B171 continues NE along the Inn valley, passing several castle ruins of the 12–13Cs, to reach (5km) **Brixlegg** (2600 inhab.).

Hugo Wolf composed much of his only opera, 'Der Corregidor', in the solitude of a hunting-lodge of neighbouring *Schloss Matzen* during the summer of 1895 (first performed at Mannheim in June the following year). The Schloss itself was the residence of W.A. Bailie-Grohman—author of 'Sports in the Alps', etc.— from 1893 until his death in 1922.

At *Kramsach*, just to the N, is the *Bauernhöfemuseum*, a collection of about 20 reconstructed farm-buildings from throughout the Tyrol.

A minor road climbs SE from Brixlegg to (9km) *Alpbach*, a village which has been the summer venue of a European University Forum in recent years.

3km **Rattenberg**, a village first referred to in 1074, and once of greater consequence, retains a number of characteristic 15–16C houses in its HAUPTPLATZ, and a *Rathaus* dating from 1535. Covered steps ascend to its 15C *Pfarrkirche*, baroquised in 1733–37, and containing remarkable statues by Johann Meinrad Guggenbichler on either side of the high altar.—The frescoes by Johann Josef Waldmann (1711) in the cupola (by F.D. Carlone) of the *Servite Church*, further N, are said to be notable, together with the vaulting in its cloister. It was in the ruined castle here that Wilhelm Biener, the chancellor of Claudia de Medici, was executed on a false charge in 1651.

At c 5km the pilgrimage church of *St. Leonhard* (1512) is passed. Founded in 1012 by Heinrich II, it has a Gothic organ-loft and good vaulting.—9km **Wörgl**, a small industrial town of 8600 inhab. is entered (but see below). Just beyond Wörgl crossroads are reached, where the B312 turns right, while the B171 continues ahead to (12km) **Kufstein**; see Rte 6B.

A lane climbs S from Wörgl to (6km) *Niederau*, 4km W of which is *Oberau*, in the WILDSCHÖNAU VALLEY, where the octagonal *Kapelle St. Antonius* of 1706 contains a remarkable carved high altar.—The B170 may be regained 6km E of Niederau.

WÖRGL TO KITZBÜHEL (30km). The B170 bears SE to (9.5km) *Hopfgarten*, with a rococo church of 1758–64 by Andreas Huber and Kassian Singer. The road continues up the BRIXENTAL, passing below (left) the *Hohe Salve* (1827m) to the village of *Kirchberg in Tirol*, providing a view S towards the *Grosser Rettenstein* (2362m) before entering (6km) *Kitzbühel* (see below). The small lake of *Schwarzsee* is skirted to the N.

The B312 shortly bears NE after c 6km passing a turning for *Itter*, where in its Schloss were confined several distinguished Frenchmen during the last war, among them Edouard Daladier, Paul Reynaud, and Generals Maurice Gamelin and Maxime Weygand.—At 4km the main road skirts **Söll**, an increasingly popular ski resort. Its *Pfarrkirche* of 1361, baroquised in the 1760s, has a good rococo interior and frescoes by Christof Anton Mayr. To the S rises the *Hohe Salve* (1827m). The road from *Kufstein* (12km NW) is shortly met. Ahead are the rugged limestone peaks of the KAISERGEBIRGE, rising to 2344m.

19km **St. Johann in Tirol** (6500 inhab.), with a small airfield, stands at the junction of three valleys, and contains a number of characteristic Tyrolean houses, and two churches—domed *St. Antonius* (1671–74), and *St. Johannes* (1723–28), with its two towers.

For the road to *Lofer*, see below; for that to *Saalfelden*, Rte 8B; for the B176, leading N, p 146.

To the S rises the *Kitzbüheler Horn* (1996m; panoramic views), to the W of which the B342 circles to (10km) ***Kitzbühel** (7850 inhab.), a charmingly sited summer and winter resort, standing at an altitude of 782m.

Formerly a Celtic site, it was fortified by the early 12C and in 1271 received its municipal charter. It flourished in the 16C owing to the copper and silver mines in the vicinity: a cross-section of the latter is shown in the local museum.

The medieval town lies on a slight ridge. It retains several gabled houses in the Hinterstadtstrasse and parallel Vorderstadtstrasse, at the S end of which is the 15C *Jochbergtor*, the only surviving gate.

Further N, beyond a stream, is the steeply roofed **Pfarrkirche St. Andreas** (1435–1506), baroquised c 1750, with a slender belfry. Its numerous statues, paintings, and carved tombstones, some of which are by members of the local Faistenberger family of artists, are its main decorative features.

At a higher level to the N is the two-storeyed **Liebfrauenkirche**, with an imposing mid 14C belfry. The lower church dates from 1373; the upper, with an attractive pink, yellow, and eau-de-Nil interior, contains good plasterwork, and frescoes of 1739 by Simon Benedict Faistenberger (1695–1759); the high altar has a copy of Cranach's Virgin and Child in the cathedral at Innsbruck. The ex-votos are notable.

For the road S see Rte 7.

From *St. Johann* the B312 bears NE away from the KAISERGEBIRGE through (8km) *Erpfendorf*, with a modern church (1957) by Clemens Holzmeister, and past (right at 7km) *Waidring*, with a church of 1764 preserving its Gothic belfry, and with a rococo interior containing statues by Georg Faistenberger. To the N, on the German frontier, rises the *Schebelberg* (1465m).—Some 6km S, near the N end of the *Pillersee*, the chapel of *St. Adolar* contains unusually colourful frescoes of c 1440 in its vaulting.

Leave the Tyrol at the PASS STRUB (704m) and descend steeply to (11km) **Lofer**, an attractively sited market village preserving numerous characteristic houses. It lies at the junction of three valleys, and is almost encircled by mountains, to the SW being over-looked by the *Loferer Steinberge* (*Grosse Ochsenhorn*; 2511m).

For the road SE to *Saalfelden* and *Zell am See*, see Rte 8B.

The SAALACH VALLEY is descended to the NE, with the REITER ALP massif to the E (*Grosse Hauselhorn*; 2284m), and to the N, the *Sonntagshorn* (1961m). At 12km the STEINPASS (558m; Customs) is reached, the border crossing of the so-called *Deutsches Eck* or *Bavarian Salient* or *Corner*, also known as the *Rupertiwinkel*. Here on 17 October 1809 the Tyrolese under Speckbacher suffered their first defeat by the Bavarians. After 6km turn right, and then left after a further 2km.

The right-hand fork here leads 23km to **Berchtesgaden** (22,000 inhab.), a beautifully sited market town, whose name is unfortunately and irrevocably associated with Adolf Hitler, who after 1934 used the 'Berghof' at Ober-Salzberg, an eyrie E of the town, as a retreat. It was here on 12 February 1938 that Schuschnigg, summoned by the Führer, was informed of German demands—the so-called 'Berchtesgaden Agreement'—a month before the Anschluss. Neville Chamberlain visited Hitler there the following September. It was largély destroyed by American bombs on 25 April 1945 and the site was captured nine days later. From here the main road may be regained 18km N at *Bad Reichenhall*, or one may cross back into Austria 11km NE at a point some 12km S of Salzburg.—5km S of Berchtesgaden is the picturesque *Königssee*, encircled by mountains rising abruptly from its shores, among them the *Watzmann* (2713m; W), painted by Adalbert Stifter in 1837, and to the E, the *Kahlersberg* (2350m), the latter marking the Austrian frontier.

After 7km the road skirts *Bad Reichenhall* (18,500 inhab.); 8km beyond join the autobahn just W of the frontier (Customs), or, alternatively, take the right-hand turning to cross back into Austria (Customs) to follow the B1.—**Salzburg**, or rather its hilltop castle, is conspicuous ahead; see Rte 9.

B.   Via the A12, A93, and A8 autobahns

Total distance, 178km (110 miles). A12. 59km *Wörgl* crossroads— 11km *Kufstein* crossroads—4km German frontier—A93. At 26km turn right onto the A8—68km Austrian frontier—10km **Salzburg**.

Maps: F&B 3 and 4; BEV 47/11–12, 48/12–13.

This is the fastest road between the two provincial capitals, from which most of the places mentioned in Rte 6A may be reached with ease. By-roads from *Kufstein* are described, but all these later go through Germany briefly.

Some 94km of the motorway also lie within Germany, and it is as well to top up with petrol while still in Austria. This also provides a fast road to or from **Munich** and *Rosenheim*, 62km NW, and 5km N, respectively of the junction of the A93 and A8, which is 26km N of the border crossing at Kufstein. See note at the head of Rte 5.

For the old main road (B171) from Innsbruck to the Wörgl crossroads (for *St. Johann* and *Kitzbühel*), see Rte 6A. After crossing this at *Volders*, the A12 runs parallel to and N of it.

From the Wörgl crossroads you veer N, with a view NE towards the rugged KAISERGEBIRGE, and shortly pass (left) the mid 14C keep of *Maria Stein*, with a two-storeyed chapel, which may be approached from the next exit.

At 11km the Kufstein exit is reached, with the *Pendling* (1563m) rising to the W, the strategically sited fortress, on the far bank of the Inn, dominating and guarding the valley.

*Kufstein (13,100 inhab.), in Bavarian hands in the 13–14C, was taken by Maximilian I in 1504, but was re-occupied by the Bavarians in 1703–04 and again in 1805–14. In 1703 its commander burnt the town at the foot of the castle hill to provide an exposed glacis. It was the birthplace of Johann Wolfgang Baumgartner (1712–61), the artist.

From the riverside UNTERER STADTPLATZ, on the E bank, you pass the late Gothic *Pfarrkirche St. Veit*, baroquised in 1707. Inside, on the S wall, is the tombstone of Hans Baumgartner (died 1493). The adjacent two-storeyed chapel preserves numerous tombstones and a rococo high altar.—Covered steps climb past the so-called *Helden-orgel* (originating, in 1931, as a war memorial), which is the 'local lion', giving resounding if not roaring recitals at midday and also at 18.00 in the summer. A lift from near the riverside promenade also ascends to the castle.

This **Fortress**, also known as that of *Geroldseck*, dates from the 12C. It was enlarged in 1415 and again in 1518–22, when the cylindrical *Kaiserturm*, with its vaulted gallery, was erected around a colossal central pillar. Further building took place in the early 18C under Johann Martin Gumpp the Younger, and a small museum illustrates the history of the citadel, etc. It was occasionally used as a state prison; in 1794–95 the future Duc de Bassano, Napoleon's minister, was held here.

The motorway can be regained just N of the town, near the frontier crossing (Customs).

KUFSTEIN TO NIEDERACHEN (28km), for St. Johann, or Salzburg. The B175 leads NE to (10km) **Ebbs**, with a massive church of 1748–56 by Abraham Millauer, with its interior entirely frescoed by Josef Adam von Mölk, and with attractive gilt scultpures.—Beyond, fork right, passing near the 15C *Schloss Wagrein*, and turn right onto the B172, dominated to the S by the *Pyramidenspitze* (1997m) in the ZAHMER KAISER RANGE. The N bank of the *Walchsee* is skirted, and we continue E, to approach *Niederachen*.—The B176 turns S here to (20km) *St. Johann*, from which at 10km a track climbs W up a valley between the two massifs of the KAISERGEBIRGE. The B312 is followed NE from St. Johann to *Salzburg*; see Rte 6A.

An ALTERNATIVE road is that crossing the frontier (Customs) 5km E of Niederachen, to *Reit im Winkl*, there following the **'Deutsche Alpenstrasse'** E through some very attractive country, to meet the A8 autobahn after 33km, some 6km S of *Traunstein*, and 24km W of the Austrian frontier near Salzburg.—Another route is that running N through *Kössen* and the picturesque KLOBENSTEIN PASS (Customs), descending the TIROLER ACHE to meet the autobahn at 27km, just S of the *Chiemsee*; see below.

The A93 autobahn (in Germany), entered just N of *Kufstein* (Customs), follows the left bank of the Inn to meet the A8 5km S of **Rosenheim** (52,000 inhab.), where you bear E, after 23km skirting the S bank of the **Chiemsee** (80 sq km), the largest of several lakes in the area. (On an island towards its W end is the extraordinary late 19C *Schloss Herrenchiemsee*, an uncompleted pastiche of Versailles by Georg Dollmann, commissioned by mad Ludwig II of Bavaria.) The motorway continues E, by-passing (left) *Traunstein* (17,000 inhab.). After 30km there is a good view NE towards the river Salzach, there forming the Austro-German frontier. The road then veers and descends SE, with the mountains ahead, some rising picturesquely to over 2500m, surrounding *Berchtesgaden*, and forming the *Deutsches Eck* or *Bavarian Salient*; see p 144.

At 14km the Austrian frontier is regained (Customs), with the hill above **Salzburg**, crowned by the castle of *Hohensalzburg*, conspicuous to the NE; see Rte 9.

7 Kitzbühel to Lienz, for Villach

Total distance, 94km (58 miles). B161. 29km *Mittersill* crossroads—B108. 65km **Lienz**.

Maps: F&B 3 and 4; BEV 47/12.

From **Kitzbühel** (see p 143), the road ascends the valley to the S, with attractive retrospective views of the KAISERGEBIRGE in the distance.—Beyond (9km) *Jochberg*, with a church of 1748–50 containing frescoes by Simon Benedikt Faistenberger, the road climbs through the KITZBÜHELER ALPES to (10km) the PASS THURN (1274m), descending (views) to the SE, later in zigzags, to (10km) crossroads just NE of **Mittersill**.

It was in this small town (5000 inhab.), at the home of his son-in-law (Haus Markt 101), that the composer Anton (von) Webern (1883–1945; see p 77) was shot dead by an American soldier. Webern was suspected—when stepping out for a smoke—of trying to escape from the house, which was apparently being visited by possible black-marketeers sought by the army of occupation. He lies in the local cemetery.

For the road (B165) ascending to the *Krimml Falls*, 32km W, see p 141, in reverse; for the B168 leading E along the PINZGAU VALLEY, see Rte 8A.

The B108 continues due S, shortly bearing SE up the deserted AMERTALER ÖD, with the *Schrottkopf* (2774m) rising to the left, to enter at 16km the *Felbertauerntunnel* (5304m long; toll, the return ticket may also be used for the Grossglockner road; see Rte 8C). Its S exit provides a view W towards the *Grossvenediger* (3674m); to the SE rises the *Muntanitz* (3232m), beyond which looms the *Grossglockner* (3797m); see Rte 8C.

The road descends to (16km) **Matrei in Osttirol** (1000m), a village of ancient origin on an old trading route. The *Pfarrkirche St. Alban*, founded in 1170, and rebuilt to the design of Wolfgang Hagenauer in 1768, retains its Gothic belfry of 1326. Several of its sculptures are by Johann Paterer (died 1785), a local artist; the frescoes are by F.A. Zeiller (1783).

In the hamlet of *Gans*, just W of the village, ask for the key to the church of *St. Nikolaus*, part Romanesque, part Gothic, preserving frescoes of c 1340 and c 1530 and, in the upper choir, others of c 1265.

7km further up the VIRGENTAL lies *Virgen*, with other churches of interest in the vicinity, notably that of *Obermauer*, of 1456, with remarkable late 15C frescoes, including a huge St. Christopher, and marble sculptures from an earlier period.

9km *Huben*.

Two minor roads turn off here: one to the NE to (13km) *Kals* (1325m), below the *Grossglockner*; and another to the W up the DEFEREGGENTAL to (15km) *St. Veit*, its church containing early 15C frescoes. This latter road continues, with the *Hochgall* (3426m) rising ahead, to (20km) the STALLER SATTEL (2052m; Customs), providing a little used entry into S Tyrol.

The B108 veers SE down the ISELTAL, with the *Hochschober* (3240m) to the E, to approach (19km) **Lienz**, overlooked to the W by the *Schloss Bruck*, and with the rugged LIENZER DOLOMITEN picturesquely rising ahead (*Grosse Sandspitze*; 2772m); see Rte 40B.

8   Kitzbühel to Badgastein

A.   Via Mittersill and Bruck

Total distance, 101km (63 miles). B161. 29km *Mittersill* crossroads—B168. 24km **Zell am Zee** lies 3km N—B311. 3km *Bruck* crossroads, for the *Grossglockner* road—20km *Lend*—B167. 25km **Badgastein** (for the *Tauerntunnel*).

Maps: F&B 4; BEV 47/12–13.

For the road to the *Mittersill* crossroads see Rte 7.

The B168 leads due E along the PINZGAU VALLEY past (3km) *Schloss Lichtenau* (16C), and several small villages.

Two roads climb S, from *Uttendorf* and *Fürth* respectively, towards the reservoirs and dams of *Limberg*, *Mooser*, and *Drossen*, etc. on the N flank of the HOHE TAUERN MASSIF, in which the pyramidal *Kitzsteinhorn* (3203m) is conspicuous; its highest peak is the *Grossglockner* (3797m).

At 21km crossroads are reached 3km S of **Zell am See** (see Rte 8B), but bear SE and continue ahead at (3km) the *Bruck* crossroads, where the *Grossglocknerstrasse* turns S; see Rte 8C.

At 10km a minor road (right) ascends the mountain-flanked RAURISTAL and HÜTTWINKLTAL valleys to (30km) *Kolm Saigurn*, dominated by the *Hocharn* (3254m), the *Hoher Sonnblick* (3105m), and the *Schareck* (3122m). Gold-mines were in operation here until the turn of the century. The old road is undergoing improvement and some remarkable viaducts are being built.

10km *Lend*, now by-passed, just beyond which fork right through a tunnel into the GASTEINTAL; the left-hand fork leads 17km NE to *St. Johann im Pongau* and *Bischofshofen*, 9km beyond; see Rte 10.

The B167 ascends the Gasteintal parallel to the railway, and at 16km by-passes (left) *Bad Hofgastein* (858m), which flourished in the 15–16C with the exploitation of the gold-mines of the Radhausberg (see below), one of the main sources of income of the Prince-bishops of Salzburg. The church of 1498–1507 contains several tombstones of interest. Medicinal baths were established here in 1785, with water piped down in wooden conduits from Badgastein, the baths of which later superseded them.

The road climbs steadily to enter the W suburbs of (9km) ***Badgastein** (1002m; 5600 inhab.), previously known as *Wildbad Gastein*. It is romantically sited at a cleft in an amphitheatre of mountains, although its charms have been marred by over-exploitation. To the W rises the *Stubnerkogel* (2246m), and beyond, the *Tischkogel* (2409m); while to the E is the *Graukogel* (2492m) and the *Feuersang* (2468m).

Its mineral springs were known in the 7C, and in 1436 the site was visited by Friedrich III. In 1496 a hospital was founded, and its reputation as a spa was promoted by Theophrastus Bombast von Hohenheim (1493–1541), the quack physician, better known as Paracelsus.

In August 1825 Schubert, in the company of the singer Vogl, spent three weeks here, 'where the country surpasses the wildest imagination'. Here he composed his D Major Piano Sonata (Deutsch 850). Coincidentally, Mozart's widow, Konstanze von Nissen, was at Badgastein at the same time; by then the town had become a fashionable resort. Several crowned heads of Europe visited the place, among them, from 1863 to 1887, Kaiser Wilhelm I, and it became correspondingly expensive. It was here in August 1863 that Franz Josef had fruitless conversations with the Prussian king prior to the German Assembly at Frankfurt. With the completion of the railway as far as Badgastein in 1905, when it was inaugurated by the aging Emperor, the resort became increasingly accessible; and by 1909 the line was open as far as Trieste.

In recent decades it has developed as a winter sports station, being the venue of the World Alpine Skiing Championships in 1958, while *Sportgastein* (1588m), reached by a toll road from *Böckstein* (4km SW) is also well equipped.

Its main points of interest—apart from its remarkable site—are the cascading **Gasteiner Ache**, well seen from the *Steinbrücke* in the main street spanning the narrow valley; and the small early 15C church of *St. Nikolaus*, vaulted from a central column and containing frescoes of 1480. The church stands c 700m NE, on the road descending towards *Badbruck*.

The resort of *Böckstein*, 4km SW, originally owed its importance to the neighbouring *Radhausberg* gold-mines; it is now the N terminus for the *Tauerntunnel*, a railway tunnel 8552m long, which pierces the range, here rising to 2832m. The S terminus is at *Mallnitz* in Carinthia, 9km N of *Obervellach*; see Rte 40A.

Vehicles and their passengers (toll) are loaded onto and unloaded from car-carriers at either end; the time taken to go through the tunnel is c 10 minutes. The winter service on this *Autoverladung* is every hour; in summer every half-hour, or every 20 minutes if traffic is heavy.

B.   Via Saalfelden and Zell am See

Total distance, 124km (77 miles). B342. 10km *St. Johann*—B312. 26km **Lofer**—B312. 24km *Saalfelden—13km* **Zell am See**—6km *Bruck* crossroads—20km *Lend*—B167. 25km **Badgastein**.

This may be shortened by 11km by taking the cross-route St. Johann—Saalfelden, which is described first.

Maps: F&B 4; BEV 47/12–13.

For the road from *Kitzbühel* to *St. Johann*, and *Lofer* see Rte 6A.

ST. JOHANN TO SAALFELDEN (39km). The B164, following the railway, leads SE up the valley of the *Pillersee* to (13km) *Fieberbrunn*, where the *Johann-Nepomuk Kapelle* of 1760 contains rococo plasterwork and frescoes by Matthäus Günther. The road later descends from the GRIESSENPASS (963m), with the LEOGANGER STEINBERGE (*Birnhorn*; 2634m) rising steeply to the N, and with a fine view ahead and to the NE of the STEINERNES MEER range (*Schönfeldspitze* or *Selbhorn*; 2653m), before reaching the B311 at *Saalfelden*; see below.

At *Lofer* turn SE through (2km) *St. Martin bei Lofer*, birthplace of Anton Faistauer (1887–1930), the artist.—2km W is the pilgrimage church of **Maria Kirchenthal** (1694–1701), designed by J.B. Fischer von Erlach, with a somewhat stark interior.

The road now passes along a narrows of the flat-bottomed valley, with the LOFERER STEINBERGE (*Grosses Ochsenhorn*; 2511m) to the W. Ahead is the limestone massif of the STEINERNES MEER (rising further SE, E of Saalfelden, to the *Schönfeldspitze* or *Selbhorn*; 2653m), and right, the LEOGANGER STEINBERGE (Birnhorn; 2634m). You shortly pass the *Schloss Saaleck*, and the entrance to the cave of *Lamprechtsofenhöhle*.

The SAALACH VALLEY later opens out as you approach (22km) **Saalfelden** (11,400 inhab.), a market town and summer and winter resort of slight interest in itself.

5km. SE is the steep-roofed and lofty-spired pilgrimage-church of *Maria Alm*, of 1508, with frescoes of 1757 by Christoph Anton Mayr.—A narrow mountain road (B164) climbs E over a 1291m pass prior to (15km) *Dienten*, overlooked to the NE by the *Hochkönig* (2941m), 15km N of *Lend*; see below.

The B311 climbs S, with a view ahead of the HOHE TAUERN RANGE, at 9km passing (left) *Maishofen*, 14km W of which, in the GLEMM-TAL, lies the resort of *Saalbach*.—After 2km you reach the *Zeller See*, and enter **Zell am See** itself 2km beyond. This lake-side resort of 7950 inhab., threaded by a busy main road, and with a railway-line skirting the lake, was formerly described by Baedeker as 'situated on a mound of débris formed by the Schmittenbach'. D.H. Lawrence stayed here in 1921. The *Pfarrkirche*, which stands a short distance from the lake, has some curious Gothic features, and restored frescoes in its Romanesque apse. To the E rises the *Hundstein* (2117m), while the town is overlooked to the W by the *Schmittenhöhe* (1965m), providing panoramic views.

A road junction is reached 2km S, and 3km beyond, the *Bruck* crossroads. For the road to **Badgastein** see Rte 8A.

C.   Bruck to Winklern: the Grossglockner road

Total distance, 70km (43 miles), without deviations.

Maps: F&B 4, and also their map of the road at 1:50,000; BEV 47/ 12–13.

The road is usually open from mid May until early November, but it can get crowded during summer months. The return part of the toll ticket (from Ferleiten, 13km S of the Bruck crossroads, to 4km above Heiligenblut) may be used for the *Felbertauerntunnel* (see Rte 7), etc. Vehicles are prohibited from stopping except at the parks provided.

The upper road, or *Hochalpenstrasse*, was engineered by Franz Wallack (1887–1966) from 1930–35. Parts of it followed a Roman track across the Hohe Tauern.

The *'**Grossglocknerstrasse**' leads due S from the Bruck crossroads, following the FUSCHER TAL to (7km) *Fusch* (811m), ascending to (7km) *Ferleiten*, and then climbing steeply in a series of hairpin bends up the E flank of the valley to (13km) the *Fuscher Törl* (2428m).

A side road turns left for 2km, climbing to a *Viewpoint* at the *Edelweiss-Spitze* (2571m), providing a superb *'Panorama* of some 35 peaks over 3000m high.

The main road continues S, later threading two short tunnels, the second of which after 6km pierces the *Hochtor* (2575m), marking the provincial frontier between Salzburg and Carinthia. The road reaches its highest point here, at 2506m. Its exit provides a view of the SCHOBERGRUPPE (*Roter Kopf*; 2381m, and *Petzek*; 3283m), and of the LIENZER DOLOMITEN in the distance; and to the W, the *Grossglockner* itself; see below.—Several zigzags bring you down to (7km; 1859m) the *Posthaus Guttal*.

Here the *Gletscherstrasse* turns off to the right. This deviation (constructed from Heiligenblut in 1900–08) leads 8km along the N side of the upper valley of the MÖLL to the *Franz-Josefs-Höhe* (2369m), given this name after the Emperor visited the site in 1856. On the debris-strewn slope of the *Freiwand*, it commands a splendid *'View* at the **Grossglockner** (3797m; some 12,460ft), the highest peak in Austria, and the 9km-long *Pasterzen glacier*, the largest in the E Alps, its upper end dominated by the *Johannisberg* (3460m) to the NW. The *Gletscherbahn* descends to the crevassed glacier.

The double-peaked *Grossglockner* was first ascended on 28 July 1800 by pastor Horasch of Döllach (see below), although the Klein-Glockner had been climbed by a party, championed by Franz Salm-Reifferscheid, Bishop of Gurk, the previous August. No other attempts were made for several decades. It was only regularly ascended after 1852.

The main road continues the descent to (8km) **Heiligenblut** (1288m), a beautifully sited village providing a fine view of the slender snow pyramid of the *Grossglockner* to the NW. Gold- and silver-mines were formerly exploited in the region, but these have understandably given way to other profitable expedients.

The *Pfarrkirche St. Vinzenz* (1430–83) preserves as a relic a phial said to contain 'Holy Blood' brought from Constantinople in 914, which gave the village its name. It also houses the remarkable polychromed and gilded *'High Altar*, carved in 1520 by Wolfgang Asslinger, a pupil of Michael Pacher.

The B107 descends the MÖLLTAL, passing several waterfalls, and at 10km the village of *Döllach*, 12km beyond entering *Winklern* (965m), attractively sited at an elbow of the valley.

For the road NE from here to *Obervellach* and on to **Spittal**, see Rte 40A in reverse, and for that to **Lienz**, 16km SW in the Drau valley on the far side of the *Iselsberg pass* (1204m); see Rte 40B.

9   Salzburg and Environs

The picturesquely sited provincial capital of 139,400 inhab. stands on both banks of the turbid *Salzach* at a height of 424m (near the Dom). It is dominated to the W by the abruptly rising dolomitic crag of the Mönchsberg, with its SE prow, the *Nonnberg*, crowned by a fortress and ancient convent. Below rise the domes and towers of its many churches, which, interspersed by imposing palaces and theatrical squares, among other charming features, make it a delightful town to wander through, and it also has a number of important museums. Salzburg is the venue for several festivals, particularly of opera, and you are not allowed to forget its association with Mozart, now its favourite son. It is a lively town, and being on a main route from the nearby German frontier it is often rather crowded. Salzburg has grown rapidly during recent decades, its population having increased by over 30,000 since 1960. In 1869 it was 27,850; in 1939 only 77,200. There is a project to build a Guggenheim Museum, designed by Hans Hollein, in Salzburg.

Long a Celtic settlement, exploiting the salt-mines of neighbouring Hallein, and at a junction of trading routes, it came under Roman control as *Juvavum*, being raised to the status of a municipality in c AD 50. In 477 it was sacked by Barbarians and virtually abandoned. In 700 the Franconian bishop of Worms, Rupert, later canonised, founded the abbey of St. Peter's, and the Benedictine convent of Nonnberg, the first abbess of which was Ehrentrude, Rupert's niece. Around these foundations the town, known as *Salzpurch*, revived, and became the seat of a bishopric. St. Virgil, an Irishman (once abbot of Aghaboe), bishop in 745–84, and canonised in 1233, built its first cathedral, rebuilt in 845–6 after a fire.

He was succeeded by Arno (785–821), a cleric of unusual culture, who in 798 was raised to the dignity of archbishop. By 946 the town, capital of a growing ecclesiastical principality, was also of commercial importance, with its own mint, and a fortress to protect its temporal interests. However, in 1167 it was sacked by supporters of Frederick Barbarossa, after which the cathedral was reconstructed in the Romanesque style. The town was virtually destroyed by a fire in 1200. Several late 13C church councils fulminated against the 'wandering scholars' of the time, who infested Salzburg and would 'lie in bake-ovens, frequent taverns, games, harlots, earn their bread by their vices, and cling with inveterate obstinacy to their sect, so that no hope of their amendment remaineth'.

In 1228 Rudolf of Habsburg created the archbishop and his successors princes of the Holy Roman Empire, but their accumulation of worldly riches brought them into conflict with the equally materialistic citizens, who were given several privileges as a reward for taking the side of Friedrich III in his quarrel with Archbishop *Bernhard von Rohr*. An attempt to consolidate their position by making the place a free Imperial city was crushed by the autocratic Archbishop *Leonhard von Keutschach* (1495–1519), who intransigently drove out its Jews.

He was followed by *Matthäus Lang von Wellenburg* (1519–40), during which period both the composers Heinrich Finck (in the early 1520s) and Paul Hofhaimer (from 1519 until his death in 1537) were working in Salzburg. Among later Prince-archbishops of consequence was *Wolf Dietrich von Raitenau* (1587–1612; a great-nephew of the Medici pope, Pius IV), who after a fire in 1598 invited Vincenzo Scamozzi (1552–1616; a pupil of Palladio) to lay out—in the Italian taste—several squares with fountains, and palaces, including the Residenz; he also designed the original Altenau-Mirabell palace. A somewhat salacious prelate, Wolf Dietrich later came into conflict over a matter of salt

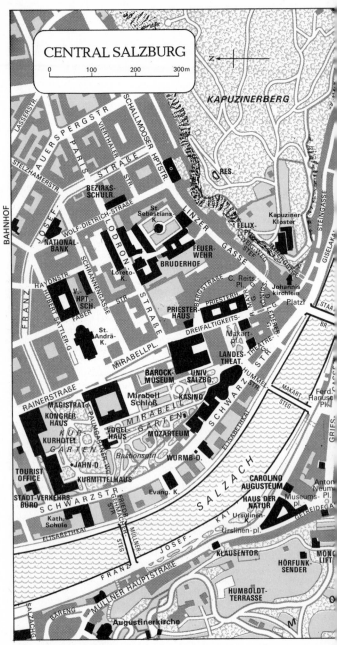

CENTRAL SALZBURG

0   100   200   300m

KAPUZINERBERG

BAHNHOF

LASSERSTR.

AUERSPERGSTR

SCHALLMOOSER HPTSTR.

VIERTHALER STR.

PARIS

STELZHAMERSTR.

STRAßE

BEZIRKS-SCHULR.

WOLF-DIETRICH-STRAßE

LODRON

St. Sebastians-K.

LINZER GASSE

RES.

Kapuziner Kloster

FELIX-PF.

WEGWEG STEG

PREBERGGASSE

STEINGASSE

GISELAKAI

NATIONAL-BANK

JOSEF

SCHRANNENGASSE

STRAßE

FEUER-WEHR

BRUDERHOF

HAYDNSTR.

FRANZ

HUBERT SATTLER G.

V.-HPT.-SCH. FABER

Loreto-K.

BERGSTRAße

C. Reits. Pl.

R. MAYR. G.

PRIESTERG.

PRIESTER-HAUS

KÖNIGS- STEG

SCH LEDERER G.

Johannis-kirchlein

Platzl

STAA

BR.

St. Andrä-K.

MIRABELLPL.

DREIFALTIGKEITS-

Makart-pl.

THEATRE- STR.

LANDES-THEAT.

HUMBE STR.

HUMBOLDTSTR

RAINERSTRAßE

BAROCK-MUSEUM

UNIV SALZBG

Mirabell Schloß

KASINO

SCHWARZ

MAKART STEG

Ferd. Hanusc Pl.

MAGISTRAT

KONGREß-HAUS

PAUNGARTNER WEG

MIRABELL GARTEN

SCHWARZ

ELISABETHKAI

GRIES-

KUR KURHOTEL GARTEN

VOGEL-HAUS

MOZARTEUM

TOURIST OFFICE

JAHN-D.

Bastionsgtn

WURMB-D.

SALZACH

CAROLINO AUGUSTEUM

Anton Neum

STADT-VERKEHRS-BÜRO

KURMITTELHAUS

SCHWARZSTR.

FRIEDRICH

Evang. K.

HAUS DER NATUR

Museums-Pl.

GETREIDEGA

Kath. Schule

ELISABETHKAI

MÜLLNER STEG

Ursulinen-K.

Urslinen-pl.

MON LIFT

FRANZ

JOSEF-KAI

KLAUSENTOR

HÖRFUNK-SENDER

M

MÜLLNER HAUPTSTRAßE

BÄRENG

SALZACHG

HUMBOLDT-TERRASSE

Augustinerkirche

), to the left of which ascends the im

low steps.

hann Jakob von Kuen-Belasy (1560
s to the earlier structure, his succes
ly the main walls, set about a more dra
e cathedral cemetery to give himself n

rly 17C buildings, to which the NW wings
e headquarters, and apparently in a deplor
thly decorated apartments, among them the b
aal, and *Rittersaal*. A number of the rooms
Rottmayr or Martino Altomonte; also with Brus
shops and emperors; and several *copies* of pe
hat Monteverdi's 'Orfeo' was performed in 1
in Mantua; and in the Guard-room that Moz
e' was first produced, in 1769. Numerous o
during his early years in Salzburg were perfor
r wrote, there was in Salzburg 'no stimulus for
ny of my compositions are performed, it is just
and chairs…'. Concerts take place here during

RD FLOOR, and the **RESIDENZGALEI
d in 1923 and reconstituted in 1975, is ba
e archbishops, dating back to 1612. Sev
in recent years, the more important of wh
hönborn-Buchheim collections. Its catalo

's Hall, displaying the arms of Wolf Dietr
erger, four paintings of The Flood; *Joos* (
raying; anon. *Master of the Donausch
ait of Cardinal Matthäus Lang von Well
1519–40), showing the fortress and the for
ground; *Jan van Hermessen*, Christ on
ration of the Magi (Antwerp ?; early 16
f the Sea; *Jakob Grimmer*, Landscape w
egger*, Portrait of Magdalena, daughter

A collector's gallery; *Caspar de Crayer*, Vir
rtzius*, Male portrait, and Portrait of Eberh
randt*, Portrait of his mother praying; *Ger
d Gambling by candle-light; *Ruisdael*, S
es, one of Norway; *Adrien Brouwer*, Ava
Lievens, Male portrait; *Ferdinand Bol*, Ha
and van der Eeckout*, Jude and Thamar; *P
o pasture; *Van Ostade*, two Tavern scenes;
yp*, and *Van Goyen*.
he Post-station, and Return from the hu
e on a terrace; *Gerrit Adriaensz Berckhey
-pond at the Hague; *Emanuel de Witte*, Inter
at Delft; *Bonaventura Peeters I*, Storm at s
unger*, Interior of Antwerp cathedral; *Dirk
a Renaissance palace; *Salomon van Ruysd
Jacob Gerritsz Cuyp, Male portrait; *Nicol
e with figures; *Elias van den Broeck*, Still life w
eer the Elder*, Woodland scene.—**R6** *Rube
V, Satyr with a basket of fruit; *Cornelis de V
rik van Balen*, Diana the hunter; *Anthonis M
van Thielen*, Virgin and Child surrounded

rights with the Elector of Bavaria, who brought pressure to bear on Pope Paul V. The pope deposed Wolf Dietrich, who died a prisoner in the Hohensalzburg castle in 1617.

He was succeeded by his cousin, *Marcus Sitticus von Hohenems* (1612–19), who commissioned Santino Solari to rebuild the cathedral and construct Schloss Hellbrunn. *Paris Lodron* (1619–53) ordered Solari to strengthen the city's fortifications as part of his policy of armed neutrality, which enabled Salzburg to survive the worst excesses of the Thirty Years' War. In 1622 a University was established (which was dissolved in 1810, and refounded in 1962). Lodron was in turn followed by *Guidobaldo Thun* (1654–64), and from 1668–87 by *Max Gandolph von Kuenburg*; during this period the witch-hunt known as the 'Zauberjackel' affair (1675–81) took place.

Among later prelates of note were *Johann Ernst Thun* (1687–1709), during whose encumbency J.B. Fischer von Erlach built four churches and the Schloss Klesheim; *Franz Anton von Harrach* (1709–27), who invited J. Lukas von Hildebrandt to modify and embellish a number of buildings, and Antonio Caldara (1670–1736) to supply him with new music; and *Leopold Anton von Firmian* (1727–44), who expelled the Protestant peasants of the principality in 1731, much to its detriment, as described in Goethe's 'Hermann und Dorothea'.

In 1737 Leopold Mozart (1719–87; born in Augsburg) established himself in Salzburg. In 1743 he entered Von Firmian's service as violinist, and was appointed court composer in 1757 and deputy Kappelmeister in 1763. In 1753 *Sigismund von Schrattenbach* succeeded to the archiepiscopal throne, and under his patronage Wolfgang Amadè Mozart (born 27 January 1756) entered the court chapel in 1769, although both before and after this date he was frequently travelling abroad. It was with *Hieronymus Colloredo*, the last Prince-archbishop (1772–1812), that in 1781 the young composer severed any bonds he may have had with the ecclesiastical hierarchy of Salzburg, after Count Karl Arco, son of the prelate's chamberlain, unceremoniously ejected him from his apartment in Vienna.

By the Treaty of Paris (26 December 1802), the principality was secularised and given to the Archduke Ferdinand, brother of Franz II, in compensation for his loss of Tuscany. Briefly in Bavarian hands from 1810, it reverted to Austria in 1816, becoming a duchy, and in 1850 a crown province. In the 1820s grass grew between the paving-stones of its streets, so few were its inhabitants after the dispersal of its court and university, but it was also being discovered during the Biedermeier period by the Romantic traveller.

Schubert, who visited the place in 1825, 'could not help feeling amazed at the number of wonderful buildings, palaces, and churches', but he was not alone in finding dull weather gave it 'a rather gloomy impression', and, he added, 'unfortunately it began to rain immediately after our arrival, which is very often the case here...'. The following year David Wilkie, with his artist's eye, compared Salzburg to 'Edinburgh Castle and the Old Town brought within the cliffs of the Trossachs, and watered by a river like the Tay'.

During the 1870s most of its defensive bastions were razed, particularly on the right bank, allowing its suburbs to expand. By 1863 it had been connected by railway to Vienna and Munich, and several other lines later converged on it, including the important line to Badgastein (1905), and through the Tauern range to Trieste (1909). From 1920 it has been the venue for music festivals, originally under the aegis of Hugo von Hofmannsthal, Richard Strauss, Alfred Roller, and Max Reinhardt. In 1925 the music festival was held in the old court riding-school, transformed by Clemens Holzmeister, also the architect of the new Festival Hall, inaugurated in 1960. Several buildings, including the cathedral, were severely damaged in air-raids in 1944–45, after which Salzburg was the HQ of the American zone of occupation.

Other natives were Franz Anton Danreiter (1695–1760), the topographical artist; Christian Doppler (1803–53), the physicist; Hans Makart (1840–84), the artist; the poet Georg Trakl (1887–1914); and the conductor Herbert von Karajan (1908–89), under whose autocratic regime many fine musicians were black-balled. Theophrastus Paracelsus died here in 1541; the composer Heinrich Biber (1664–1704) worked in Salzburg from 1670, and died there, as did Michael Haydn in 1806, and the composer Hans Pfitzner in 1949. From 1953 to 1963 Kokoschka taught at the Summer Academy for Visual Arts here, which he founded on returning to Austria from London, his home after 1938.

An autobahn circles round the W side of the town, from which there are four exits, that from the adjacent German frontier passing a tourist post before tunnelling beneath the Airport and crossing the W

flowers; *Theodor Rombouts*, Cardplayers; *Jan Brueghel the Elder*, Village scene.

R7 *Sebastian Stosskopf*, Still life; *Claude Vignon*, Flora; and works by *Le Sueur*.—**R8** *Jacques Blanchard*, Portrait of François Duquesnoy, the sculptor; *Gaspard Poussin*, Heroic landscape; *Robert Tournières*, Male, and Female portraits; *Joseph Vernet*, Bathers; *Pater*, Paddling; *Pierre-Nicolas Huillot*, Still life with musical instruments.

R9 *Guercino*, Doubting Thomas; *Pietro della Vecchia*, Armed warrior; *Titian*, Portrait of Giovanni da Castaldo.—**R10** *Caravaggio*, Lute-player; *Mateo Cerezo the Younger*, Magdalen praying; *Pedro de Moya* (?), Male portrait; *Pietro Ricchi*, Tancred and Erminia; *Barocci*, Self-portrait; *Bernardo Strozzi*, Sleeping child; the stuccoed ceiling in this and in the following rooms should be noted.

R11 *Paul Troger*, Healing of Tobias, Young Moses and Pharaoh; *Johann Heinrich Schönfeld*, Portrait of Guidobaldo Thun; *J.M. Rottmayr*, Mourning of Christ; *Maulbertsch*, The Last Supper, and Assumption; and works by *Martino* and *Bartholomeo Altomonte*.—**R12** *G.D. Tiepolo*, Male portrait; *Agostino Beltrano*, Sacrifice of Isaac; *Francesco Solimena*, Bath of Bathsheba; *Alessandro Magnasco*, Stormy landscape; works by *Salvator Rosa*, and *Zuccarelli*.

R13 *Johann Michael Neder*, Coffee-house; *Friedrich Loos*, unfinished View of Salzburg, and of the Rauris valley; and Views of Salzburg by *Franz Xaver Mandl*, and *Johann Fischbach*; and of Badgastein by *Thomas Ender*.—**R14** *Friedrich von Amerling*, Self-portrait, and of a Young girl; *Josef Feid*, The Traunsee with Schloss Orth; *Anton Hansch*, The Grossvenediger; *Ferdinand Georg Waldmüller*, Children at the window; *Heinrich Bürkel*, St. Peter's churchyard in winter.

R15 *Anton Romako*, Portrait of Dr. Johann Frank, and of a Young man; *Rudolf von Alt*, Appletrees at Goisern; *Hans Makart* (born in the Residenz, in 1840), Portraits of Clothilde Beer, his cousin, and of his first wife, Amalie Roithmayr, and of his Mother; *Gustav Klimt*, At Attersee.

Turning right on leaving the Residenz, we reach an arcade joining it to the **Dom St. Rupert**, or *Cathedral*.

Of slight interest are the adjacent excavations, although they have uncovered part of the former cathedral, devastated by fire in December 1598, and razed shortly afterwards. This five-aisled building, started in the late 12C, and replacing an earlier church, lay slightly N of the present building, and with its apse oriented more towards the NE, as shown on the plan in the crypt; see below.—To the W in the Domplatz rises the *Mariensäule* of 1766–71 by Wolfgang and J.B. Hagenauer.

Archbishop Wolf Dietrich commissioned Vincenzo Scamozzi to design a new cathedral, but its dimensions were excessive, and in 1610 work began on a less elaborate structure. However, on the prelate's deposition in 1612, his successor had the foundations re-dug to accommodate another even less ambitious plan provided by Santino Solari, and this edifice, complete except for its towers (of 1655) was consecrated in September 1628. The cupola was damaged by fire in 1859, and one of the crossing arches was destroyed by an American bomb in 1944. The restored Dom was reconsecrated in 1959. Its W front has been the scene of performances of Von Hofmannsthal's play 'Jedermann' ('Everyman') from 1920–37, and since 1946, during the Festival.

The most obvious features of the building are its octagonal cupola, the rounded apsidal transepts, and the heavy façade of white and rose Untersberg marble, flanked by four-storeyed towers surmounted by cupolas. The central gable displays the arms of Archbishop Markus Sittikus (a goat; an emblem perhaps more suited to Wolf Dietrich), and his successor, Paris Lodron; on either side are statues of Moses and Elijah, while on the balustrade below are the evangelists; flanking its porch are SS. Peter, Paul, Rupert, and Virgil. The bronze doors are modern confections.

The *interior* (99m long; 68m wide at the transepts; with a nave 31m high, and with a cupola rising to 71m) is in the early Italian Baroque style. While spacious, it is not satisfying; its stucco-work, by Josef Bassanio, is good but heavy, and neither its frescoes nor paintings are notable. The original organ of 1702, by Christoph Egedacher, with a case of 1706, has been enlarged and modernised several times. To the left of the entrance is a bronze font of 1321 (with 12C lions), a survival from the earlier church, in which Mozart was baptised Johannes Chrysost Wolfgang Theophilus in 1756; his nickanme Amadè, popularly Amadeus, was used only after 1777.

The ornate sculptured frames to the monuments and paintings in both transepts should be noted. From the S transept steps descend to the *Crypt*, dating only from 1959, cleverly displaying the foundations of the former cathedrals and of the projected structure planned by Scamozzi; here also are several tombs of former Prince-archbishops.

Steps below the S tower ascend to the **Dommuseum**, and the *Kunst-und Wunderkammer* (cf. Ambras). The latter is on the 1st floor and contains the curiosities collected by successive acquisitive archbishops and assembled by Archbishop Guidobaldo Thun. It includes shells, ivories, rosaries, scientific instruments and Baroque sculpture. Among other works displayed here and on the 2nd floor, reached by a spiral staircase, are *Simon Fries*, St. George and the dragon, and an Angel; an Angel by *Meinrad Guggenbichler*; paintings by *Troger*, and attributed to *Rottmayr*; several remarkable monstrances, crucifixes, and other cult objects; 12C Arab caskets; and vestments.

On turning left through another arcade on making your exit, the KAPITEL-PLATZ is entered, providing a view of the castle, and embellished by a large willow-sheltered *Horse-pond* of 1732, with sculpture by J.A. Pfaffinger and B. Opstal.

A lane leads from near its SW corner to the terminus of the funicular ascending to the *Hohensalzburg* fortress; see Rte 9C.

From here, cross the picturesque **Petersfriedhof**, the cemetery of the adjacent church. It is surrounded by arcades of 1626, with family tombs, etc.; arcade 31 contains that of Santino Solari, architect of the cathedral; 36 that of Sigmund Haffner von Imbachhausen, to whom Mozart dedicated his so-called 'Haffner Symphony' (K.385). Adjacent are *early Christian catacombs*, cut into the conglomerate rockface; in the middle of the cemetery is a late 15C chapel.

To the left on passing through an arch is the old-established *Stiftskeller*; to the right, the **Stiftskirche St. Peter**, replacing an earlier church destroyed by fire in 1127. Its first abbot, in 745, was John the Scot. During recent excavations here the foundations of 3C Roman villas and two sarcophagi were discovered. The present building is Romanesque, altered in the early 17C, and radically remodelled in the rococo taste in 1770. The portal and tympanum of the Romanesque church are preserved within the tower-porch surmounted by a Baroque helm of 1756. The grille of 1768 by Philipp Hinterseer, incorporates the arms of Abbot Beda Seeauer (1753–85).

The eau-de-Nil and white *interior*, with its comparatively narrow nave flanked by altars (several containing paintings by 'Kremser'

Schmidt), and with its upper walls covered by paintings, among them works by Kaspar Memberger (Carrying of the Cross), and Ignazio Solari (a Crucifixion), is remarkable, as is the green and gilt organ-case of 1620 and 1763, surmounted by statues by Hans Waldburger. 13C frescoes have been uncovered towards the E ends of both aisles. Beyond the crossing, with an octagonal cupola above, is the high altar of 1778 by Johannes Högler.

Several notable tombstones will be seen in the right transept and aisle, together with monuments in side chapels to Michael Haydn (died 1806; monument erected in 1821), and Marianne von Berchtold zu Sonnenburg ('Nannerl', Mozart's sister; 1751–1829), both of whom were buried in the communal grave. Mozart's C minor Mass (K.427) was first performed in this church, in 1783, with Constanze singing the soprano part.

Bearing right past a *Fountain* of 1673 by Bartholomäus Obstal, pass through an arch to reach the Franziskanergasse, between the Domplatz (right) and an entrance (left) to the steepled tower (begun 1486) of the *Franziskanerkirche, recently thoroughly restored.

Of ancient foundation, it was largely rebuilt in the early 13C, with a remarkable *Choir*, its vault sustained by five lofty columns, added in the first half of the 15C. Its Baroque high altar, designed by J.B. Fischer von Erlach in 1709, incorporates a Virgin with grapes by Michael Pacher (the Child is 19C), which is all that remains of the original Gothic altar. Behind the high alter, in one of the several baroquised chapels, is a marble altar of 1561 from the former cathedral. The child's tomb and the lion below the pulpit are noteworthy, as is the monument of Balthasari de Ravnach.

The Romanesque lion in the passage of the Sigmund-Haffner-Gasse 16, adjacent, is probably also from the old cathedral. At No. 12 lived Nannerl Mozart from 1801 until her death in 1829.

Opposite the church is the back-door of the *Rupertinum, preferably entered from the Wiener-Philarmoniker-Gasse 9, further W, where the museum of 20C painting, graphic art, sculpture, and photography has been installed in a 17C building, constructed around a narrow courtyard, which has been imaginatively modernised by G. Garstenauer. It also contains an important art library, and since 1980, when it was inaugurated, has been the venue of exhibitions of note.

To the SW is the **Festspielhaus**, in fact a complex of ingeniously placed auditoria, etc. built behind the facade of the former court stables of 1607. They comprise a small hall or *Theatre* of 1924, remodelled in 1962, its foyer retaining frescoes of 1926 by Anton Faistauer; the *Winter Riding-school* of 1660, with a ceiling fresco of 1690 by Rottmayr; the *Felsenreit-Schule*, with its three storeys of galleries cut into the adjacent conglomerate cliff, designed by J.B. Fischer von Erlach in 1693; and the main *Festival Hall* (1956–60), designed by Clemens Holzmeister. The latter is also partly hewn into the Mönchsberg to provide space for the stage and wings, and preserves on its W façade a portal by Fischer von Erlach. The complex may be visited in a group, except during the Festival, by previous application.

To the S is the entrance of the **Neutor tunnel** (128m long) cut through the ridge in 1764–67 and widened in 1915. Opposite is the *Hofstallschwemme* or *Pferdeschwemme*, the archbishop's monumental horse-trough, with the 'Horse-breaker' group of 1695 by Michael Bernard Mandl, behind which, concealing a disused quarry, is a wall embellished by equestrian frescoes by F.A. Ebner. For the

Universitätsplatz, leading E from the Sigmundsplatz to the Kollegienkirche, see below.

Adjacent to the W is the attractive arcaded courtyard, partly rebuilt after war damage, of the **Bürgerspital** (mid 16C almshouses), accommodating in its S wing the *Spielzeugmuseum*, a remarkable collection of toys. Beyond is the Gothic *St. Blasiuskirche*, the former hospital church, preserving some good ironwork.—Continuing NW past (right) a *Bakery* dating back to 1429, you pass through the *Gstättentor* (rebuilt 1618) to enter the ANTON-NEUMAYR-PLATZ.

On its W side is the *Mönchsberg lift*, which ascends to the *Cafe Winkler*, with plunging views over the town. Adjacent to the café is a circular *Panorama of Salzburg*, painted by Friedrich Loos (landscape), J.M. Sattler (monuments), and J. Schindler (figures), in 1825–29.

The Gstättengasse forks left to the **St. Markuskirche** or *Ursulinenkirche* (1705), replacing its predecessor destroyed by a rock-fall in 1669. Its architect was J.B. Fischer von Erlach, who was obliged to plan the church on a narrow trapezoid site. Its frescoes of 1756 are by Christoph Anton Mayr. One tower is damaged, due to subsidence.

A few steps beyond rises the *Klausentor*, a gateway marking the N extremity of the old town.

The road ascends to the suburb of *Mülln*, with the mid 15C *Augustinian church* (with rococo decoration of 1738), built on the flank of the Mönchsberg, but of no great interest.—The *Church* of the *Landeskrankenhaus*, further NW, was built by in 1699–1704.

By briefly following the main road SE from St. Mark's, and turning through an archway (right) we reach the MUSEUMSPLATZ, with (right), partially accommodated in the former Ursuline convent, the *Haus der Natur*, a natural-history museum more original than most, containing numerous dioramas.

Opposite is the *Museum Carolino Augusteum, so-called to flatter Caroline Augusta, the Bavarian fourth wife of Franz I, whom he married in 1816.

Steps descend to a BASEMENT displaying Roman mosaics and other relics of that period, and ascend past a marble Tympanum (1180) from the old cathedral to the FIRST FLOOR. Here are numerous artefacts of the Iron Age, and Hallstatt period, including a bronze Pitcher from Hallein-Dürrnberg. Also several good examples of Gothic sculpture, and altarpieces, notable among which are, by the Master of St. Leonhard, SS. Catherine, Barbara, and Apollonia (1462); *Rueland Frueauf the Elder*, The Virgin in a blue robe (1490); *Master of the Halleinaltar*, carved Crucifixion (1515); and parts of an altarpiece by the *Master of the Irrsdorfer altar; Master I.P.*, carved plaques of c 1520; five panels of the Aspacher altar; The Nativity by the *Master of the Virgo inter Virgines altarpiece*; a carved figure of St. Elisabeth von Thüringen (1450); the 13C Silver Treasure found in 1978 at Judengasse 10, and other gold and silver hoards; jewellery; and Christmas cribs, of all periods.

SECOND FLOOR, with a Portrait of Archbishop Sigismund Graf Schrattenbach, in a Baroque frame, and several Miniatures on the landing by Johann *Michael Sattler* (1786–1847); also a Salzburg street scene by the same artist; several works by *Rottmayr; Barbara Krafft* (1764–1825), Self-portrait, and others; *Friedrich Loos*, Views of Salzburg; and Portrait of Franz von Braun; *Johann Fischbach*, Self-portrait; a section devoted to the Biedermeier period; and another to the art of *Hans Makart*, including a Self-portrait, and portraits of Henriette Gomperz, the opera-singer, and of Freifrau von Waldburg; *Joseph Mayburger* (1814–1908), View of Salzburg in 1881; *Luca Giordano*, Lot and his daughters; *Anton Kolig*, Man reading; paintings by *F.X. König*; *Mengs*, Portrait of Don Pedro de Campomanes; *J.B. Lampi the Elder*, Portrait of Ignaz Holzhauzer; paintings by *Rosa Hagenauer* and of her husband *Johann Baptist Hagenauer*; and by *Paul Troger*. Also collections of Musical instruments; 17C Furniture; reconstructed panelled rooms; carved ceilings, etc.

Turn E from the Anton-Neumayr-Platz to follow the Griesgasse, where, at No. 23, a small collection of traditional Salzburg costumes is housed. A passageway leads to the **Getreidegasse**, one of the oldest thoroughfares in the town (with its numerous shop-signs, including too many ugly modern examples), off which open several attractive courtyards.

No. 9, towards its E end, is ***Mozart's Geburtshaus**, in which the composer was born on 27 January 1756. It was turned into a museum in 1880. Of its furnishings, only a cupboard on the landing of the apartment on the 3rd floor is original, but Mozart's Hammerklavier (by Anton Walter; Vienna; c 1780), and Clavichord of 1760, and several other instruments, may be seen, in addition to numerous other associated objects, many of them passed on to the Cathedral Musical Society by Mozart's widow and sons in 1841. The family portraits were given to the society after Constanze's death in the following year.

These include the unfinished portrait of Mozart by Joseph Lange (1751–1831; the actor husband of Aloysia Weber), and a boxwood relief by Leonhard Posch (1750–1831)—both early 1789—and among the best likenesses (see p 60). Lange also painted a not-very-flattering portrait of Constanze. In the autumn of 1773 the family moved to the present Makartplatz; see below.

Passing through the adjacent courtyard you reach UNIVERSITÄTSPLATZ, often the site of an animated fruit and flower market, or '*Grünmarkt*', dominated by the **Kollegienkirche** (1696–1707), with its convex façade, dome, and ornate towers with their statuary and parapets, an original but not very satisfying building by J.B. Fischer von Erlach. Its high altar of 1735 is by J.A. Pfaffinger, and it contains statues by Guggenbichler and paintings by Rottmayr.

Turning E through an archway, the Sigmund-Haffner-Gasse is regained a few paces S of the Rathaus.

B.   The Right or East Bank

At the N end of the *Staatsbrücke* is the PLATZL, a busy junction of streets. The narrow Steingasse leads right to the *Steintor*, a 17C defensive gate. At No. 7 in the street, steps ascend to the Kapuziner Kloster, providing an alternative approach to it; see below.

The Linzergasse, a narrow thoroughfare and once the main entrance from Linz, bears NE.

At No. 14 (right) a lane leads through an archway, climbing to the *Kapuziner Kloster* (1599–1602), conserving a door of 1450 from the old cathedral, which gives its name to the thickly wooded hill here, the *Kapuzinerberg* (views), on which there are relics of 17C fortifications.

On the left of the Linzergasse, a few minutes' walk beyond, is the **Sebastianskirche** (1512; baroquised in 1749, but damaged in the fire of 1818 which devastated much of this district). The tomb of Theophrastus Paracelsus (1493–1541) abuts the vestibule of the church. Adjacent is its *Cemetery*, an arcaded quadrangle of 1600, in the centre of which is the domed *Gabrielskapelle* (completed 1603; by Elia Castello), the mausoleum of Archbishop Wolf Dietrich (died 1617), its interior tiled, and containing ornately framed statues of the Fathers of the Church.

A few steps SE of the chapel lie the graves of, and monuments to, several members of the Mozart and Weber families, among them Mozart's maternal grandmother, Eva Rosina Pertl (died 1755); Leopold Mozart (1719–87); Nannerl's eldest daughter, Jeanette (died 1805); Constanze, his wife (1762–1842); her second husband, Georg Nikolaus von Nissen (1761–1826), and her aunt, Genoveva (died 1798; mother of Carl Maria von Weber); also Constanze's sisters Aloysia (died 1839), and Sophie (died 1846; in 1895 transferred to the communal grave).

The Dreifaltigkeitsgasse forks N from the Platzl, shortly reaching (right) the **Dreifaltigkeitskirche** (that of the *Holy Trinity*; 1694–1702), the first essay in Salzburg of J.B. Fischer von Erlach, with twin towers (later heightened), a concave façade, and a drum dome of oval plan, containing frescoes by Rottmayr in the dome, and sculptures by B.M. Mandl.

On the S side of the adjacent MAKARTPLATZ is the so-called **Tanzmeisterhaus**, the Mozart family home after they moved from

View over the Rudolfskai from the Kapuzinerberg by
Friedrich Loos, 1835

the Getreidegasse (see above) in the autumn of 1773 until Leopold
Mozart's death in 1787. Most of the building was destroyed in an air-
raid in October 1944, and the adjacent block was tastelessly erected
on the site of the ruins. It was possible to restore the vestibule and
Music-room, which now contains a permanent exhibition of musical
instruments of the period and Mozart autographs, etc. It also has
Johann Nepomuk della Croce's family portrait of 1780/81, in which
Wolfgang and Nannerl are playing a duet, while their father holds
his violin; the portrait on the wall is that of the composer's mother,
who died in Paris in 1778. The room is occasionally used for recitals.

It had once been the residence of dancing-masters, who also let it out for fancy-
dress parties and balls. In 1767 it was inherited from her cousin Spöckner by
Maria Anna Raab (c 1710–88), 'Mitzerl' to her friends, and it was here that
Michael Haydn celebrated his marriage to Maria Magdalena Lipp in August
1768. Spöckner had been a witness at Leopold Mozart's wedding in 1747, and
eventually, when their previous home had become too small, Mozart's father
was able to rent the apartments from Mitzerl. When not travelling, Mozart lived
and composed here until he left Salzburg in November 1780, and after that he
only spent a few weeks here with his wife during the summer of 1783. Nannerl
left the house in August the following year after her marriage to Johann Baptist
von Berchtold zu Sonnenberg, moving to St. Gilgen, her mother's old home.

From the NW corner of the square enter the charming ***Mirabell
Garten**, with tree-lined walks, terraces, and a central fountain of

1690, surrounded with sculptured mythological groups by Ottavio Mosto (and with a Pegasus of 1661 by Kaspar Gras), the whole laid out by Fischer von Erlach, and providing good retrospective views.

On its E side are the new *Mozarteum studios*, completed in 1977, and the entrance to the *Barockmuseum, installed in a dependence of the former walled *Orangery*, adjacent.

It is based on a remarkable collection, mostly of smaller Baroque sketches, paintings, models, and sculptures, accumulated by Kurt Rossacher. Among the more notable works are: *Bassano*, Portrait of Vincenzo Scamozzi, the first architect of the cathedral; *Bernini*, Models for a Transfiguration, and for a Bust of a youth, and a Portrait of Bernini by *Carlo Maratta*; *Johann Baptist Hagenauer* (1737–1810), Model for a Pietà; *Georg Raphael Donner* (1693–1741), Model for a group of Lot and his daughters; *Domenico Gargiulo* (1612–79), The House of Cards; *Balthasar Permoser* (1651–1732), The Magdalen; and *Houdon*, Model for a statue of George Washington. Also several works by *Martino Altomonte* (1657–1745), *Cosmas Damian Asam* (1686–1739), *Johann Wolfgang Baumgartner* (1712–61), *Carlo Innocenzo Carlone*, *Pietro da Cortona*, *Luca Giordano*, *Franz Anton Maulbertsch* (1724–96), *Johann Michael Rottmayr* (1654–1730), *Johann Martin, or 'Kremser' Schmidt* (1718–1801), *F. Solimena*, *G.B. Tiepolo*, *Paul Troger* (1698–1762), *Thomas Christian Winck* (1738–97), and *Jannarius Zick* (1730–97).

The present **Schloss Mirabell**, known as such since its name was changed in 1612, is largely a reconstruction by Peter von Nobile after the destructive fire in 1818, its predecessor having been rebuilt by J. Lukas von Hildebrandt in 1721–27 on the site of the Altenau palace. This had been erected by that vigorous prince of the Church, Wolf Dietrich, in 1606 to set up his Jewish mistress, the seductive Salome von Alt (born 1568), who reputedly had provided the prelate with a dozen children. King Otho of Greece (1815–67) was also born here.

The remarkable marble *Staircase of the 18C palace survived the fire, and may be seen by entering its W wing, its balustrades embellished by putti sculpted by Georg Raphael Donner. It ascends to the *Marmorsaal*, the occasional venue of chamber-concerts. A model of the earlier edifice is displayed in the vestibule; the present building has been the seat of the Bürgermeister or mayor of Salzburg since 1950.

In the upper gardens to the NW (with its aviary, rosery, 'Hedge-theatre', and sculpted dwarfs) is a relic of the ramparts needlessly demolished in the 1870s to make way for the Franz-Josef-Strasse, which circles to the E to meet the Linzergasse.

N of the Schloss is the *Kurgarten*, and beyond, the *Kongresshaus* (1956) facing the Auerspergstrasse, at the W end of which, at No. 7, is the *Municipal Tourist Office*.

From just below the bastion (not far W of which is the *Müllnersteg*, a footbridge spanning the Salzach providing a fine view S) follow the Schwarzstrasse S.—This later passes (left) the **Mozarteum** (1910–14, with an extension of 1940), the Conservatory of Music, containing two concert halls and an important library of Mozartiana. Some MSS are occasionally on display. In its gardens is the so-called 'Zauberflötenhäuschen', a much restored wooden summer-house in which composed part of 'The Magic Flute' in Vienna. It was dismantled in 1874 and brought to Salzburg.

Adjacent is the *Marionettentheater* (puppet theatre), established by Anton Aicher in Salzburg in 1913, and manipulated since by his descendants.

The *Landestheater* of 1892 (enlarged in 1938) is passed on regaining the Makartplatz.

C.   Hohensalzburg and Stift Nonnberg

The recommended approach is by the funicular (1894; recently modernised), the lower terminus of which is a few paces from the SW corner of the Kapitelplatz.

This brings you to an entrance to the ***Fortress of Hohensalzburg**, which dominates the older town, and provides several extensive views over it, and over the surrounding countryside.

The first stronghold was built c 1077 on the site of a Roman castrum. This was enlarged over the centuries, notably by Archbishop Leonhard von Keutschach, who added chapels. During the 1520s it resisted the revolts of peasants, and several bastions were constructed or strengthened during the 17C. It was used as barracks from 1861 until 1945, but survived relatively unscathed.

The state apartments may be visited in a conducted tour. The so-called *'Golden Room'*, with its ceramic stove of 1501, and the *Fürstenzimmer*, have features of interest, while collections of arms and armour, and a museum devoted to the local Erzherzog Rainer regiment, may be seen. An early 16C barrel-organ, the 'Hornwerk' or 'Stier' is pointed out, if not heard.

Descend the interior ramp and cross the courtyard flanked by the *St. George's Chapel*, on the exterior wall of which is the red marble funerary Monument to Archbishop von Keutschach (died 1519; his emblem, a turnip) by Hans Volenauer. The *Reisszug*, a winching device, once turned by horses, enabling supplies to be hauled up to the castle, can also be seen.

Before leaving the main gate, descend E and climb down an exterior ramp, turning right along a footpath to approach, after some minutes, the dependencies of **Stift Nonnberg**, a Benedictine convent since its foundation in the early 8C.

The present priory *Church* is entered from the S, and dates from 1464–1507, although parts of its Romanesque predecessor, destroyed by fire in 1423, survive and should be noted. The restored frescoes of c 1150 at the rear of the nave are remarkable. The well-carved columns near the entrance, the *Crypt*, and several tombs of abbesses, are of interest. An altarpiece of 1598 from the old cathedral may be seen in the adjacent *Johanneskapelle*, by the priory entrance, if the bell brings any response.

A long flight of steps descends N of the Nonnberg to the Kaigasse (see below), but it is suggested that you follow a footpath (the Nonnberggasse) leading SW which eventually reaches steps climbing down to the Nonntaler Hauptstrasse. Here turn left, to reach after a few paces the portico of domed *St. Erhardkirche*, by Giovanni Gaspare Zuccalli, of 1685–89, containing paintings by Rottmayr and stucco-work by Francesco Brenno.

Continue N before turning left along the Schanzlgasse (Alexander von Humboldt lived at No. 14 in 1797–98), flanked (right) by *Law-courts*, to enter the KAJETANER PLATZ. On its N side is the stone and ochre façade of the **Kajetanerkirche**, with its curiously gabled wings,

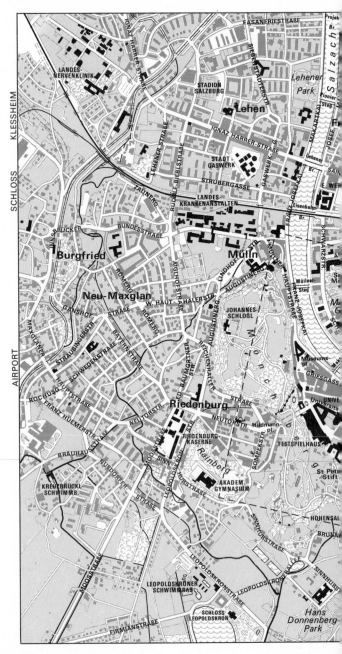

MARIA PLAIN

SALZBURG GENERAL

0   200   400   600m

Elisabeth-
Vorstadt

ERZHERZOG EUGENSTR.

ROBINIGSTRASSE

PLAINSTRASSE

ST. JAHNSTRASSE

-hheim

F.V. LEIMERSTR.

ELISABETHSTRASSE

RAINERSTRASSE

-EN-STRASSE

GNIGLER STR.

VOGELWEIDER STRASSE

GNIGLERSTR.

BAYERHAMERSTR.

HAUPTBAHNHOF

PLAINSTRASSE

LASTENSTRASSE

STR.

RÖCKLBRUNN-

Schallmoos

WEISER

GABELSBERGERSTRASSE

PERGSTR.

FRANZ

JOSEFSTRASSE

AUERSPERGSTR.

STERNECKSTR.

VOGELWEIDERSTRASSE

ROBINIGSTR.

STERNECKSTRASSE

LINZER BUNDESSTR.

RAINERSTR.

PARIS LODRON-

SCHALLMOOSER

HAUPTSTRASSE

FÜRBERGSTR.

akart-
pl.

BRUDERHOF

LINZER GASSE

Kapuzinerberg

Äußerer Stein

EBERHARD FUGGERSTR.

Platzl

Kapuziner-
Kloster

INSET PAGE 164-5

Staats

Br.

RUDOLFSKAI

GISELAKAI

IMBERGSTRASSE

ARENBERGSTRASSE

GAISBERGSTRASSE

Res.
pl.

Mozart
pl.

RUDOLFSKAI

Nonntl.
St.

Dr. Fr. Rehrl-
Pl.

UNFALL-
KRANKENHAUS

Bürglstein

Dom

Kapitel
pl.

Rudolfspl.

BÜRGLSTEINSTRASSE

Franz

AIGNER STRASSE

HOFEGGASSE

Stift
Nonnberg

Josef

Park

Salzach

ASSE

NONNTALER HAUPTSTRASSE

SPORT-
ANLAGE
UNION

PETERSBRUNNSTR.

HELLBRUNNER STRASSE

HELLBRUNNER STRASSE

IGNAZ-RIEDER-KAI

Nonntal

ERZABT KLOTZSTRASSE

ALPENSTRASSE

PÄDAGOGISCHE
AKADEMIE

ALLEE

HELLBRUNN

also built by Zuccalli, in 1685–97. The frescoes in its conspicuous transversally set oval dome are by Paul Troger, as is the painting in the right-hand altar; that of the Holy Family, on the left, is by Rottmayr.

The adjacent Pfeifergasse passes the *Chiemseehof* (originally built in 1305), of 1700, which has been the seat of provincial administration since 1861, to reach the Mozartplatz; see p 155.

An alternative approach is by following the Kaigasse W, which then veers N, off which a lane turns left to the Kapitelplatz; or by continuing ahead, the Mozartplatz.

D. The Environs: Schloss Hellbrunn; Schloss Leopoldskron; Schloss Klessheim; Maria Plain

These short excursions are best made by car, although Schloss Hellbrunn may be reached by the bus 'H' from the Rudolfskai.

The Stadtplan or City Map provided by the Tourist Offices may be found useful.

After following the B341 SE, fork right along the Hellbrunner Strasse, extended by the Hellbrunner Allee (see below) to **Schloss Hellbrunn**. The ochre-coloured building, designed by Santino Solari for Archbishop Markus Sittikus between 1613–19, has none of the heaviness apparent in the same architect's cathedral, a sketch of which, in its unfinished state, is seen in the portrait of the prelate hanging in the dining-room. Another painting depicts the archbishop's home at Hohenems; see Rte 1A. The walls and ceiling of the *Ball-room* are covered with trompe l'oeil paintings by Donato (Arsensio) Mascagni, who also decorated the octagonal *Music-room*, and painted the huge sturgeon in the so-called *Fischzimmer*.

The Italian Baroque *Gardens*, also laid out by Solari, are embellished by numerous obelisks, statues, grottoes, goats (the archbishop's emblem), theatres, pools, and fountains (trick, trickling, and jetting), etc., in the taste of the time. In the park stands the *Monatsschlössl*, containing a *Folk Museum*, and the *Steintheater*, a former quarry, which occasionally serves as a background to operatic performances. A zoo can also be visited.

Several other mansions may be seen on the return journey, among them the *Schloss Frohnburg* (1670), to the E of the Hellbrunner Allee, and the moated *Schloss Freisal* (1549; modified in the 19C), to the right of the Freisaalweg, forking left as the Allee bears right. Also in the vicinity are the *Schloss Emsburg* (1616) and *Schloss Emslieb* (1618), both built by Archbishop Markus Sittikus for a certain Frau von Mabon, and his nephew Jakob Hannibal, respectively.

From just S of the Schloss Freisaal, the Hofhaymer Allee leads W. Follow the Sinnhubstrasse, forking left, and then turn left into the Leopoldskroner Allee to approach **Schloss Leopoldskron**.

This rococo Schloss was built in 1736 by Bernard Stuart, a Scottish Benedictine mathematician of some taste, for Archbishop Firmian. From 1919–38 it was the property of Max Reinhardt, the stage-designer, and was later owned by the Salzburg Seminar in American Studies. A good view of it may be had from the lakeside road further SW.

Following the Leopoldskronstrasse NW, you pass the *Rainberg* hill (right) to meet the Neutorstrasse (not far W of the *Neutor tunnel*), where, by turning left and following the Maxglaner Haupstrasse circling N, and later the Klessheimer Allee, veering NW, you approach, between the autobahn and the Saalach river, **Schloss Klessheim**.

Now used for official receptions and as a residence for visiting VIPs, it was built in 1700–09 by J.B. Fischer von Erlach for Archbishop Johann Ernst Thun, but its interior was not completed until 1732. Archbishop Firmian added the porch and entrance ramp embellished by stags, his emblem, carved by J.A. Pfaffinger. The plan of the *summerhouse*, of 1694, to the N, will interest the architect.

Maria Plain is best approached by following the Rainerstrasse N from Schloss Mirabell, and then the Elisabethstrasse and its extension to a point just prior to the autobahn, there turning right along the Plainbergweg. The pilgrimage-church of **Maria Plain**, with its conspicuous twin belfries, designed by Giovanni Antonio Dario, dates from 1671–74, and contains altarpieces by Thomas Schwanthaler. It provides a wide view towards the S.

The *Robinighof*, Robinigstrasse 1, a turning off the Schallmooser Haupstrasse, the eastward extension of the Linzergasse, is a rococo mansion of some charm. It belonged to the Robinig family, friends of the Mozarts, for whom the Divertimento in D Major, K334, was composed in the summer of 1779.

10 Salzburg to Badgastein

Total distance, 88km (54 miles). B159. 17km **Hallein**—11km *Golling*—25km **Bischofshofen**—B311. 22km *Lend* crossroads—B167. 23km **Badgastein**.

Maps: F&B 4; BEV 48/13, 47/13.

The A10 autobahn provides a faster route. You take the exit to Hallein not far beyond Bischofshofen.

The old main road leads S past moated *Schloss Anif*, rebuilt in the mid 19C, where King Ludwig III of Bavaria was living in 1918, and then passes under the motorway to skirt the German frontier, here formed by the UNTERSBERG MASSIF rising dramatically to the right, dominated by the *Zeppezauer haus* (1853m; panoramic views). Its summit is reached by cable-car from *St. Leonhard*, on the direct road from Salzburg towards *Berchtesgaden*, with Customs 2km S of the village.

*Hallein** (461m; 15,400 inhab.), an ancient town of importance for processing salt from the adjacent Dürrnberg mines, retains several streets and squares of 17–18C houses, and a remarkable Celtic Museum; it has improved since described by Schubert in September 1825 as a 'curious but extremely dirty and horrid town'. It was the home of Franz-Xaver Gruber (1787–1863), composer of 'Silent Night, Holy Night' ('Stille Nacht, Heilige Nacht'). Its industry has been diversified in recent years.

The riverside *Museum** (unfortunately closed in winter) in the former administrative buildings of the Saltworks (1754), facing the PFLEGERPLATZ, contains one of the most important collections of Celtic artefacts in Europe, a high proportion of which were excavated in the vicinity. Even a cursory visit will give a general idea of their advanced culture. Some 25 rooms are devoted to an outstanding display of Celtic jewellery, arms and armour, metal flasks and urns, implements, pottery, plaques, coins, etc., while a section concerns the salt-mines in the Dürrnberg.

Both a road and cable-cars (Salzbergbahn) ascend steeply to the **Dürrnberg** (796m), with an open-air museum displaying reconstructed dwellings of the Celtic epoch, and the entrance to the *Salt-mines* (*Salzbergwerk*; open in summer). A visit to the salt-mines involves negotiating several underground galleries and slides.

The village church (early 17C) is constructed of the local pink marble.

Crossing to the far bank of the Salzach on leaving Hallein, the road continues S, with the *Hoher Göll* (2522m) rising to the W, at 6km reaching *Kuchl*, Roman *Cucullae*, with a late Gothic church and a small regional museum.—5km **Golling**, with an attractive main street, Schloss, and church preserving a Gothic belfry, is better known for its *Waterfall*, approached by road and path to its lower cascade.

On leaving Golling the road tunnels below the *Pass Lueg* (554m) between the TENNENGEBIRGE (2431m) and the HAGENGEBIRGE to the W, rising to 2363m on the German frontier, and referred to frequently during the 1809 campaign. Bear W through a narrows of the Salzach valley and below the motorway, before turning S towards (16km) the imposing mass of *Schloss Hohenwerfen*. Dating from c 1077, it was rebuilt in the 16C, and served as a prison for those protesting against the Prince-bishops' regime. It was restored after a fire in 1931.

Werfen itself, with a characteristically wide main street, is also the point of departure for the excursion in summer to the labyrinth of ice caves—the most extensive in Europe, and at a height of 1641m—known as the *Eisriesenwelt*. They were discovered in 1878; explored by Alexander von Mörk; and opened to the public in 1920. Enquiries about admission and access should first be made in the village.

The road shortly passes W of *Pfarrwerfen*, its 14C church with a tall spire. Just beyond Pfarrwerfen the narrow B99 (largely superseded by the motorway) turns left to thread the gorge of the Fritzbach, meeting the motorway after c 14km; see Rte 11.

After 8km **Bischofshofen** (9500 inhab.) now by-passed by the main road, is reached by turning right. A minor road and rail junction in a district known as the PONGAU, this small industrial town lies at a height of 585m, with the copper mines of *Mitterbergalpe* (in operation since the Bronze Age) not far to the SW. Its most interesting monument is the *Pfarrkirche* at the S end of the town, and the lowest sited of the three. Its choir dates from the 14C, while on the N side of the nave are 16–17C murals. Decorated processional staves may also be seen here, while the mid 15C tomb of Bishop Silvester Pflieger of Chiemsee should be noted.—Some Romanesque murals are preserved in the *Georgskapelle*, at a higher level.

To the W rises the *Hochkönig* (2841m). To the S, in the distance, is the HOHE TAUERN RANGE.—At 6km **St. Johann im Pongau** (7700 inhab.), rebuilt after a fire in 1852, lies to the left (from which you can ascend the *Grossarltal*), as the road veers SW through (7km) *Schwarzach im Pongau*, where in 1729 the leaders of the Protestant peasants of the area (some 30,000), chose to abandon their country rather than their faith.

From SE of the station a lane leads S up the *Liechtensteinklamm*, a narrow gorge, at the head of which is an imposing waterfall.

The main road continues SW, off which a turning shortly forks right below *Schloss Schernberg* (12th and 16C) to (4km) *Goldegg im Pongau*. Its *Schloss*, begun 1323, has interesting frescoes of a later date.—After 9km, just before *Lend*, turn left, through a short tunnel, and follow the GASTEINER TAL to (23km) **Badgastein**; see Rte 8A.

11 Salzburg to Villach via the Tauern and Katschberg tunnels

Total distance, 192km (120 miles).

Maps: F&B 4, and 2; BEV 48/13, 47/13–14.

Follow the A10 autobahn S past (17km) *Hallein* (see Rte 10), beyond which you cross the B159 and pass between *Golling* (left), its waterfall, and the *Hoher Göll* (2523m) before travelling through the first of several short tunnels. The road provides a fine view as it skirts the steep W slope of the TENNENGEBIRGE, of the craggy HAGENGEBIRGE range rising to the German border, and of the dramatically sited castle of *Hohenwerfen*, before reaching (27km) the exit for *Bischofshofen*; see Rte 10. The motorway then veers almost due E and then S to (20km) the exit for *Radstadt*, 6km E; see Rte 12B.

RADSTADT TO MAUTERNDORF (39km). The old main road (B99), ascending S up the TAURACH VALLEY, shortly narrows, and, after a tunnel, climbs E through *Obertauern*, with a Baroque church by Santino Solari (1621) to reach at 22km the RADSTÄDTER TAUERNPASS (1739m), passing en route the remains of a Roman road (on which a number of milestones have been set up), and several waterfalls. After crossing the TWENGER TALPASS (1382m) the B99 descends SE to (17km) **Mauterndorf**, an attractive village with several 15–17C houses, overlooked by its 13C castle, restored in 1894, and preserving 14C frescoes in its chapel. It was left to Marshal Hermann Goering in 1939 by Hermann von Epstein, his Jewish godfather, and Goering was captured here in 1945. Altogether some 72,000 German soldiers and several thousand refugees were surrounded and made prisoner in this mountain-girt valley during the last weeks of the war.

For the road to *Tamsweg* and *Scheifling*, see below.

The A10 may be regained by bearing S from Mauterndorf, after 6km reaching a turning (left) for *Schloss Moosham* (13C; enlarged in the 16C, and restored at the end of the 19C). It contains a museum devoted to the Lungau region, and is notable for its covered exterior passageways. In the vicinity is the Roman road-station of *Immurium*, with a mithraeum.—The main road passes through *St. Michael im Lungau*, its church preserving mid 13C frescoes, etc., before reaching the fork (right) to meet the motorway and later the *Katschberg-Tunnel* (toll), the recommended alternative to crossing the steep KATSCHBERG PASS (1641m), to which the left-hand fork ascends.

Continuing S from the Radstadt exit, the A10 ascends the FLACHAU towards the RADSTÄDTER TAUERN RANGE to approach the N entrance of the **Tauerntunnel** (6401m; toll), passing just E of the summit of the *Mosermandl* (2680m). From its S end, the road veers SW down the ZEDERHAUS VALLEY, after 45km reaching the exit to (12km) *Mauterndorf* and *Tamsweg*, 18km E; see above, and below.

MAUTERNDORF TO SCHEIFLING (70km). The B95 leads due E, after 4km passing below (left) *Mariapfarr*, its church containing Romanesque and Gothic frescoes of some importance.—7km **Tamsweg** (1021m; 5200 inhab.), the 'capital' of the LUNGAU region, to which it devotes a small museum. The MARKTPLATZ preserves some characteristic houses, while the *Rathaus* dates from 1570. The early 15C fortified pilgrimage church of *St. Leonhard*, above the town, has several features of interest, including fine contemporary glass.—The road turns S and then E down the MUR VALLEY—also followed once a week by the *Steiermärkische Murtalbahn*, with a steam locomotive— to (15km) *Predlitz*.—From here a minor mountain road climbs through the GURKTALERALPEN, crossing the range at the TUR-RACHERHÖHE PASS (1763m) before descending very steeply to meet the crossroad from *Radenthein* to *Feldkirchen in Kärnten* after 34km.

From Predlitz, just in Styria, the B97 leads down the valley to (23km) **Murau**, an ancient town retaining two of its medieval gates and stretches of wall, and dominated by the castle of *Obermurau*, built in the mid 13C by Ulrich von Liechtenstein. In 1628 it passed to the Schwarzenberg family, the 28-year-old Count Georg having married the 82-year-old Anna Neumann von Wasserleonburg. The *Pfarrkirche Hl. Matthäus*, just below, dating from 1296 and retaining frescoes of 14–16C, is approached by a lane climbing W from the Schillerplatz. Of the several churches in Murau this is the most interesting, but they all have noteworthy features. Hugo Wolf stayed some months at No. 43 in the characteristic ANNA-NEUMANN-GASSE, in 1886. This is an extension of the wider RAFFALTPLATZ, with the *Altes Rathaus*. The 16C *Rathaus* is passed (right) further E before entering the SCHILLERPLATZ, with its *Mariensäule* of 1717, beyond which, on the far bank of a stream, stands 12C *Hl. Ägydius*.

After 16km a right-hand turning leads 11km to *St. Lambrecht*; see Rte 37.—At (2km) *Niederwölz*, **Oberwölz**, a tiny walled village with old houses and two churches, lies 9.5km NW.—After 3km you reach, at *Scheifling*, the road from *Judenburg* (25km NE) to *St. Veit* (52km S); see Rte 37.

From just S of the Mauterndorf exit of the A10, the motorway enters the **Katschberg-Tunnel** (5439m; toll), at its S end descending into Carinthia and the valley of the LIESER, and by-passing several small villages, at 26km reaching an exit for **Gmünd in Kärnten**.

This ancient town (2600 inhab.), preserving its medieval enceinte, guarded the trade route from Venice to Salzburg and on to Nuremberg, and retains a characteristic HAUPTPLATZ with fortified gates at either end; a *Rathaus* with a restored 16C façade; and a 14C church containing the imposing tomb of Philipp von Leobenegh of 1572, and a *Crucifixion* of 1450 from Nöring. At the NE end of the platz is the *Neues*, or *Lodron'sches Schloss*, dating from 1651; to the NW is the *Altes Schloss* (15–17C), left as a ruin after being gutted by fire in 1886. Adjacent is the *Maltator* of 1504. A collection of Porsche cars may be seen in the *Auto-museum*, immediately NW of the walled town.

5km NW in the MALTATAL lies *Dornbach*, with a well-sited 15C castle and church of 1461 containing contemporary frescoes and paintings, and a notable Gothic statue of St. Rupert.—A minor road leads up the valley (toll) for c 25km to approach the *Speicher Sameralm*, a huge reservoir surrounded by mountains. To the E rises the *Grosser Hafner* (3076m), to the W, the *Ankogel* (3246m); while to the S is the *Hochalmspitze* (3360m).

The A10 now veers S, with the *Tschiernock* (2088m) rising to the SE, and the *Reisseck* (2965m) to the W, while ahead, beyond Spittal, stands the *Goldeck* (2142m). At 10km from the Gmünd exit you reach a junction for the road to (5km) Spittal, off which the more interesting but slower B98 leads towards Villach via *Millstatt*; see below.

Spittal an der Drau (554m; 14,750 inhab.), well sited at a junction of valleys, but of slight interest in itself, probably replaced Roman *Teurnia*, 5km NW (see Rte 40A): the town was founded around a hospice (Spital) in 1191.

Its main monument is the *Schloss Porcia*, a four-square edifice built by Gabriel von Salamanca (died 1539), secretary of Archduke Ferdinand, and later the residence of Hannibal Alfons Porcia (1698–1738). Notable are the portal of 1703, and the arcaded Renaissance *Courtyard*, while the main salon preserves a ceiling from the Schloss at Millstatt. A regional museum is housed on upper floors.

A cable-car ascends from Spittal to the summit of the *Goldeck* (2142m), dominating the town to the SW.

The B100 leads SE down the wide DRAU VALLEY together with the railway and the completed A10 motorway to approach (38km) **Villach** (see Rte 40A), with a view ahead of the KARAWANKEN RANGE, forming the frontier with Yugoslavia, and later of the *Landskron*, overlooking Villach from the E; see below.

SPITTAL TO VILLACH VIA MILLSTATT (49km, plus c 10km if the ascent to *Landskron* is also made). By following the B99 N under the motorway and turning right through *Seeboden*, the N bank of the **Millstätter See** is followed to (9km) *Millstatt* itself, a charmingly sited lakeside resort of 3150 inhab., sheltered from the N by a range rising to 2091m. The lake, the second largest and the deepest in Carinthia, is 12km long and c 1.5km across.

The town grew up around a Benedictine **Monastery** from c 1088 to 1469, and a fortified priory of the military order of St. George (founded by Friedrich III to combat the Turks) until 1598, although the property was bought by Christoph von Khevenhüller, governor of Carinthia, in 1542. From 1602 until 1773, when it was suppressed, it was in Jesuit hands.

It contains a number of notable features, among which are the Romanesque W door of its church, and its Romanesque cloister, but its dependencies were later put to commercial use, and from 1901 the Lindenhof hotel has been established in the former residence of the Grand Master of the Order. By passing through an archway next to the hotel, you reach a picturesque courtyard in which stand two ancient lime trees. Turn right to enter the *Cloister*, preserving remarkable capitals, and Gothic vaulting. At the NE corner, near steps leading to the chapterhouse, are several curious sculptures. There is a small museum.

On leaving, turn right through a passage (note reliefs) and right again, to reach the W front of the *Church*, with its Baroque towers. The *W porch* (1170), one of the finest of its period extant in Austria, has in its tympanum a representation of an early abbot dedicating the abbey, while the curious details of the colonettes, with their sculpted heads, and the frescoes of 1428, should also be noted.

The choir and the vaulting of the church is late Gothic, while the pillars are embellished by frescoes or Baroque statuary. Several well-carved tombstones of Masters of the Order of St. George are notable, particularly those of Johann Geumann (died 1533) and Johann Siebenhirter (died 1508). Recitals are given in summer on its organ of 1977, by Marcussen.

The road follows the lakeside before turning NE up the valley to (13km) *Radenthein*, there veering SE past two small lakes to (11km)

Afritz, before descending a wooded valley to meet the B94 after 11km, with a view ahead of the *Landskron*. The motorway passing to the N of **Villach** to meet the A2 for Klagenfurt here crosses the B94, which leads directly into the town; see Rte 40A.

A recommended DETOUR is the ascent to the **Landskron**, a height overlooking Villach to the E. The castle on this commanding site had been rebuilt by Khevenhüller, who entertained the Emperor Charles V here. On his death in 1557 his son Bartholomew continued to extend its fortifications, and it became a bastion of Lutheranism in Carinthia. In 1613 it was visited by archdukes Ferdinand and Maximilian, but within 20 years the property was confiscated and handed over to the Catholic Dietrichsteins. The castle was hit by lightning in 1812, and the main roof burned out, and the huge four-storeyed structure was left to disintegrate. In recent years it has been partially rebuilt as a restaurant, its splendid site (fee) providing a wide view over Villach towards the Dobratsch (2166m), and S to the Karawanken range, etc.

For **Villach** and the roads to **Klagenfurt**, see Rtes 40A, and 39, and from **Villach** to **St. Veit**, Rte 38; all these in reverse.

12 Salzburg to Liezen

A. Via Bad Ischl

Total distance, 116km (72 miles). N158. 32km *St. Gilgen*—12km *Strobl* (for **St. Wolfgang**, 7km NW)—12km **Bad Ischl**—B145. 9km **Hallstatt** lies 11.5km S—19km **Bad Aussee**—27km *Trautenfels*, on the B308—14km *Liezen*.

Maps: F&B 4; BEV 48/13–14.

On driving E from Salzburg you approach the *Gaisberg* (1288m), which may be ascended by road (right) for the panoramic view it commands.—After c 20km the small *Fuschlsee* is skirted, prior to entering *Fuschl* itself, dominated to the NE by the *Schober* (1329m). Its *Schloss*, once a hunting-lodge of the Prince-archbishops of Salzburg, later appropriated by Joachim von Ribbentrop (the former Nazi Foreign Minister), and now a hotel, is passed before reaching **St. Gilgen** (3050 inhab.), attractively sited at the NW end of the **St. Wolfgangsee**, overlooked to the S by the *Zwölferhorn* (1522m).

The lake, also locally known as the *Abersee*, is 11km long, 2km wide, and reaches a depth of 114m. Anna Maria Pertl (1720–78), Mozart's mother, was born in St. Gilgen, and his sister Nannerl settled here after her marriage in 1784 to Johann Baptist von Berchtold zu Sonnenberg.
    The B154 leads NE past the little *Krottensee*, to (5km) *Scharfling*, on the *Mondsee*; see Rte 13.

The B158 skirts the S bank of the St. Wolfgangsee, with a view across the lake, above which rises the *Schafberg* (1783m; reached by rack-railway from St. Wolfgang, and commanding a wide view), and passing several camping sites, to reach at 7km a left-hand turning to a ferry across the lake to *St. Wolfgang* itself.
    In view of the congested state of the village, and as access by road is hazardous, it is recommended to park and take the ferry. A further 4km brings you to (left) *Strobl*, beyond which is *St. Wolfgang (2450 resident inhab.).

This village, once attractive, and preserving several 16–17C houses, has been ruined irreparably by an excess of visitors since one of its lakeside inns, the *Weisses Rössl* (first mentioned in 1640) gave its name to an operetta by Ralph Benatzky and Robert Stolz known as 'The White Horse Inn' (1930). Benatzky (died 1957) lies in the local cemetery, as does the actor Emil Jannings (1884–1950).

Nevertheless, the 15C pilgrimage-*Church* dedicated to St. Wolfgang, bishop of Regensburg (972–94), contains a *High altar, completed 1481, which is considered to be the masterpiece of *Michael Pacher*. It was commissioned by the abbot of Mondsee a decade earlier, and has recently been restored.

The predella consists of paintings of the Visitation, and Flight into Egypt (on the reverse are the Fathers of the Church), between which is a carved and gilt representation of the Adoration of the Three Kings. Above this is the central scene of the crowned Virgin kneeling before Christ the King surrounded by angels, while on either side stand St. Wolfgang holding a model of his church, and St. Benedict. The wings display 16 other painted panels, mostly of scenes from the life of Christ, while above are a delicately carved Crucifixion, and miscellaneous saints.

Also of interest are the retable of Thomas Schwanthaler (1676), sculptures by Meinrad Guggenbichler, and an organ of 1629 by Hans Waldburger.

12km ***Bad Ischl** (469m; 13,000 inhab.; 6800 in 1869) lies at the junction of three valleys on a peninsula formed by the Traun and the Ischl, and is surrounded by wooded hills.

Although of ancient foundation, it was only frequented as a watering-place from 1822, its properties being exploited by Dr. Wirer von Rettenbach. It became fashionable after being 'discovered' by Franz Josef's parents; indeed his younger brother, Maximilian, was born here in 1832, and the Emperor was engaged here to Elisabeth of Bavaria in 1853. The artists of the Empire congregated at Bad Ischl in summer: Waldmüller, the Von Alts, Schwind and Makart, Johann Strauss the Younger, and others. Brahms, whose cousin had a villa here, visited it in 1880 and 1882, and occasionally from 1889 to 1896. Here he composed his Tragic and Academic Festival overtures, the C Major Piano Trio, and F Major String Quartet, among other works. Bruckner played the organ in its church; and Lehár, who lived here from 1912 and died here in 1948, composed his 'The Merry Widow' in his villa, now a museum.

King Edward VII visited the place on three occasions, in 1905, 1907 and 1908, hoping to woo the aging Emperor from the German alliance.

Although it has all the amenities of a modern spa, and is surrounded by attractive country, and as such is not a bad spot from which to explore the SALZKAMMERGUT (see Rte 13), it has few monuments of importance. The *Konditorei Zauner* has offered some consolation to travellers both present and past.

Of historical interest is the former **Imperial Villa** or '*Kaiservilla*', situated at the end of a short avenue a few minutes' walk to the N of the town centre, on the far bank of the Ischl. Its contents characterise the man, who, with great imagination, from 1856 passed here the monotonous summer months of several decades of his long life.

Groups are escorted around a series of rooms, the walls of several being entirely covered with the hunting trophies of the animals he had slaughtered: a log-book records that he personally killed 50,000 birds and beasts, including—in round figures—over 18,000 pheasants, 1440 wild boar, 2050 chamois, and 1430 stags. Another room displays paintings of Elisabeth's horses (see also p 317). Here may be seen a sofa and chair (re-covered), the gift of Queen Victoria; an inlaid Chinoiserie chest-of-drawers belonging to Maria Theresia; an electric fan of 1890; a sedan-chair used until 1914; and the desk on which the senile Emperor signed the declaration of war against Serbia in July 1914 after the assassination of the Archduke Franz Ferdinand at Sarajevo, which precipitated the First World War. Here he would work daily from 4.30 am, his bath having been carried into his adjacent spartan bedroom at 3.30; breakfast was at 6.30. Among other mementos of this curious despot are his last hunting-suit, several of his guns, a marble statue of his dog 'Shadow', and the death-mask of his wife.—In the park is the *Marmorschlössl*, one of Elisabeth's favourite refuges from the court, now containing a *Museum of Photography*.

For the road NE to *Gmunden*, and the N half of the *Salzkammergut*, see Rte 13.

Driving S, the road ascends the Traun valley for 9km, with the DACHSTEIN RANGE rising ahead, to a junction, where the B145 continues the ascent to the SE; see below.

The right-hand fork shortly skirts the sombre **Hallstätter See** past (7km) *Gosaumühle* (from which the B166 climbs W to approach the *Gosausee*, 17km SW; see p 178), to (4.5km) *Hallstatt, a picturesque lakeside village of 1100 inhabitants, standing at a height of 508m, which has given its name to an important epoch in Celtic culture known as the Hallstatt Period (1000–500 BC), or Early Iron Age.

The lake itself, 8km long and c 2km wide, is hemmed in, rather oppressively, by mountains rising precipitously from its shore. To the S it is overlooked by the *Krippenstein* (2109m), and to the W by the *Plassen* (1953m). The road along the W bank was only completed in 1890; previously, visitors took the train to the opposite bank and crossed the lake to Hallstatt by ferry. The main buildings of interest are the **Pfarrkirche**, containing a winged *Altar* of c 1515, carved by Lienhart Astl, with charming statues of SS. Barbara and Catherine, while adjacent is the curious *Ossuary*, preserving skulls from the 15C on, often decorated and displaying the name and dates of the deceased, relics from its otherwise overcrowded graveyard.

The interesting **Museum of Prehistory** graphically explains the working of the salt-mines, which over the millennia had made the site famous, for it was not until 1846, when some 2000 graves were systematically excavated by Johann Georg Ramsauer at the lower end of the *Salzberg high valley*, c 350m above the lake level, that any great interest in the archaeology of the area developed. Sections are devoted to this, although many of the more important finds are now displayed in the Natural History Museum, Vienna; others are concerned with the La Tène Period (Late Iron Age; 500 BC to the Roman occupation, c AD 488).

The *Salt-mines* themselves may be visited (April–October) by funicular from the adjacent hamlet of *Lahn* to the *Rudolfsturm*, with the ruins of a castle built in 1284 to protect the mines from incursions by its main competitors in the region, the Prince-bishops of Salzburg (cf. Hallein). The salt itself was from 1607 conveyed in solution, as brine, by forms of canalisation known as *Soleleitungen* as far as *Ebensee* (30km NE of Ischl), where it was evaporated, refined, and transported by barge to *Gmunden*; see Rte 13.

The main route may be regained by skirting the S bank of the fjord-like lake to (4km) **Obertraun**, the point of departure for the excursion to the ice-caves of *Rieseneishöhle*, and the *Mammuthöhle*, approached by cable-car from a point 2km from the village, and piercing the *Dachstein* at a height of 1458m and 1400m respectively. The latter extend into the range for c 30km, only 1.5km of which may be visited. The ascent may be continued to the summit of the *Krippenstein* (2109m), providing a panoramic view over the S half of the Salzkammergut, and of the limestone peaks of the Dachstein massif rising to the SW to the *Hoher Dachstein* (2995m).—From Obertraun the road climbs very steeply (23 per cent) to the head of a pass before descending through the woods to join the B145 at (12km) *Bad Aussee*; see below.

The main road ascends from the junction for Hallstatt to a fine viewpoint dominating the *Hallstätter See* (see above) before turning E to enter Styria at (9km) the PÖTSCHEN PASS (992m), between the

Steinberg (1717m; N) and the *Hoher Sarstein* (1975m), and providing a view NE towards the TOTES GEBIRGE range, with several peaks between 2000 and 2100m, before descending to (9km) *Bad Aussee (659m; 5500 inhab.).

This small resort, lying in a comparatively protected site, preserves several late Gothic houses, and in the *Pfarrkirche St. Paul* some good sculpture; notable among the tombstones is that of Hans Herzheimer (died 1532). The *Spitalkirche* of 1395 contains a painted altarpiece of 1449. Opposite the latter, in the MERANPLATZ, was the home of Anna Plochl (1804–85), the post-master's daughter, who in 1829 married the Archduke Johann (1782–1859)—one of the more sensible of the Habsburgs—at *Brandhof* (c 20km S of Mariazell). She was later created Countess Meran. In the upper town the *Kammerhof* (c 1500) was a former office of the salt-works of the region (now housing a local museum), the director of which lived in the nearby *Hoferhaus*. The *Alpine Garden* is of some interest.

A short EXCURSION can be made to **Altaussee**, 5km N, at the W extremity of its lake, overlooked by the *Loser* (1838m) and to the E by the *Trisselwand* (1755m). The largest Solar-power generating plant in the Alps, with 263 square m of solar modules, was inaugurated on the Loser in 1989. During the Second World War several important works of art were stored by the Germans in salt-mines some 3km W of the village.—6km E of Bad Aussee lies **Grundlsee**, on the N bank of its well-stocked 6km-long lake, encircled by mountains. The lakeside road leads to (5km) *Gössl*, beyond which is the smaller *Toplitzsee*, with two waterfalls, and the *Kammersee* tarn. Beyond rise several peaks of the TOTES GEBIRGE, the highest being the *Grosser Priel* (2525m).

From Bad Aussee the main road leads SE, at 7km passing a right-hand turning for the nearby *Oden See*, before crossing notably attractive country and by-passing several small villages of the Hinterberg plateau, with views SW towards the *Hirzberg* (2052m), part of the Dachstein group, and ahead of the bold GRIMMING MASSIF (2351m).

At (14km) *Bad Mitterndorf* a road (toll) climbs 11km NE to the resort of *Tauplitzalm* (1647m)—also reached by cable-car from *Tauplitz*, 6km E of Mitterndorf, while another road leads S to *Bad Heilbrunn*, at the N end of its reservoir.

After c 10km a minor road climbs left to the perched village of **Pürgg**, where the *Johanneskapelle* contains remarkable late 12C *Frescoes* (restored), showing Byzantine influence; note the battle between cats and mice. The *Pfarrkirche St. Georg* preserves early 14C frescoes in its belfry-porch. The site also provides a fine view W towards the *Grimming* and into the ENNSTAL, to which, regaining the main road, you now descend, at *Trautenfels* meeting the B308, where turn left.

The *Schloss Trautenfels*, built in the 16C, preserves several rooms decorated by the same artists who worked at Eggenberg, near Graz, and it contains a small folk museum.—For the road to *Radstadt*, 65km W, see Rte 12B in reverse, which may be followed by those making the circular tour to either Bad Ischl or Salzburg.

A minor road climbs the DONNERSBACH VALLEY to the SE towards the WÖLZER TAUERN RANGE, passing near several old castles.

The main road leads NE, passing near *Schloss Friedstein* (early 17C), the ruins of *Wolkenstein*, and *Schloss Grafenegg*, before circling E to approach (14km) **Liezen** (659m; 7050 inhab.), a small market and industrial town of little interest in itself, but an important road junction, although less so with the continuing construction of the A9 motorway, entered 5km E. For roads to *Wels*, and **Graz**, see Rtes 18A and B; and also the latter for **Admont**, 20km E of Liezen.

B. Via Radstadt

Total distance, 128km (79 miles). A10 to (29km) the *Golling* exit (see alternative route below)—25km *Radstadt* exit—B308. 6km **Radstadt**—18km **Schladming**—36km *Trautenfels*—14km *Liezen*.

Maps: F&B 4; BEV 48/13–14, 47/13–14.

For the road to **Golling**, see Rte 10.

GOLLING TO RADSTADT VIA ABTENAU (54km, plus 44km if you include the excursion to the Gosausee). The B162 bears left, climbing past (9km) the *Lammeröfen gorges* to (9km) **Abtenau** (715m; 5050 inhab.) with the TEN-NENGEBIRGE RANGE rising to the S. There are several old houses in its triangular Platz, while the church contains Baroque sculptured figures by Simeon Fries, etc.

At 3km beyond is a turning (left) for (15km) *Gosau*, and the lake of **Gosausee**, 7km S, hemmed in by the abrupt heights of the HOHER DACHSTEIN to the SE, rising to 2995m.—The road from Gosau descends E to meet the *Hallstätter See*, at 10km, some 4.5km N of *Hallstatt* itself; see p 176.

From the junction just E of Abtenau, ascend the LAMMERTAL on the B166, the *Salzburger Dolomitenstrasse*, passing through several pastoral villages, to (17km) *St. Martin* (950m), and then descending rapidly to meet the main route after 5km, some 11km NW of *Radstadt*; see below.

From a point some 3km E, just after the road is crossed by the motorway, a minor road climbs a side valley to (12km) the village of *Filzmoos*. 19km beyond, a left-hand turning approaches the lower station of a cable-car to the *Hunerkogel* (2694m), just E of the *Hoher Dachstein* (2995m), the vertiginous wall of which dominates the area. This side road continues E through *Ramsau* (1083m) before regaining the B308.

For the road from Golling to the Radstadt exit, see Rtes 10 and 11.

To the right after the exit from the motorway lies *Altenmarkt im Pongau*, a characteristic village with a church founded in 1074 and rebuilt by 1400, containing a polychromed stone Virgin and Child of 1393, and other items of note.

Radstadt (862m; 4000 inhab.), an ancient town built on a grid plan, and still retaining three of its cylindrical towers and some of its walls (1543). It also contains a HAUPTPLATZ of some character, and a Romanesque and Gothic church. Paul Hofhaimer (1459–1537), organist and composer at the court of Maximilian from 1489, and later at Salzburg, was born here.—Just E of the town stands *Schloss Mauer* (1608).—For the old road S to *Mauterndorf*, see Rte 11.

Continuing E, after 9km you enter the province of Styria, and the road shortly veers SE towards the *Hochwurzen* (1850m), with the wall of the *Dachstein* rearing up to the N to a height of 2995m.—9km **Schladming** (749m; 3900 inhab.), a small textile town where Styrian loden is manufactured, once had important mines, and is now a winter-sports centre. The town retains a Romanesque and Gothic hall-church, but little of its walls, dismantled during the peasant revolts of 1525–26, when it was the scene of massacres and reprisals. Opposite the Rathaus is the former shooting-lodge of Augustus von Saxe-Cobourg-Gotha.

19km *Gröbming*. Its 15–17C church retains a carved Gothic retable of the school of Lienhard Astl, with paintings on the reverse of the wings by artists of the Danube School after the Passion of Altdorfer.

A toll road ascends NW to (11km) the foot of the *Stoderzinken* (2048m); while the so-called *Erzherzog-Johann-Strasse* (closed in winter) leads SE across the WÖLZER TAUERN via the SÖLKER PASS (1788m), descending to (57km) *Murau;* see p 172.

At 7km *St. Martin am Grimming* (left) preserves a good mid 17C carved altarpiece, probably from the Zürn workshops. Beyond, the road leads past the imposing bulk of the *Grimming* (2351m) to (10km) *Trautenfels*, and **Liezen**, 14km further; see last paragraphs of Rte 12A, above.

13 The Salzkammergut

Maps: F&B 4; BEV 48/13–14.

The S half of this area is covered by Rte 12A, while Rte 14 skirts its N perimeter.

This route describes most of the central Salzkammergut, and of course can be combined with the others, depending on your base and/or destination. The circuit starts and ends at Mondsee, but may be followed from any other point. Unfortunately parts of this lake district can become uncomfortably crowded in summer.

The **Salzkammergut**, literally meaning 'Salt Chamber Estate', acquired its name from being crown property, from which the revenues flowed directly into the sovereign's exchequer. The name originally applied only to a pocket of land around the S tip of the Hallstätter See from which salt was extracted, including the Gosau district and the upper Traun valley SW of Ebensee, but because of the competition between the rapacious archbishops of Salzburg (who should have had more than enough with their own salt-workings at Hallein) and the Habsburgs, Maximilian I began to buy out the private shareholders. Thus the crown gradually gained possession of the entire district, including Ischl, and to a certain extent, Aussee, although the latter (being governed by the Hofkammer of Graz) was only formally transferred to the state in 1741. The royal monopoly was tightly controlled, the whole area being treated as a private estate, and as such remained isolated until Franz Josef chose to make Ischl his summer retreat. However, it was only when the Kammergut as such no longer existed that this name was applied, loosely and without specific boundaries, to this region with its unrivalled series of lakes.

Its geological structure is complicated: it is formed of rounded mountains of comparatively soft, clayey rocks alternating with precipitous rocky cliffs and desolate plateaux of hard limestone, which culminate in the S in the mighty Dachstein massif. Most of the area is now part of Upper Austria, although Styria has the Aussee; Salzburg only lays claim to the Fuschlsee and certain banks of the Wolfgangsee and Mondsee. Very roughly it is the area within a radius of 50km centred on Bad Ischl, with Mondsee and Gmunden on the NW and NE perimeter, and with the Dachstein forming its S boundary.

From Mondsee to Gmunden via Scharfling, Weissenbach, Ebensee, and Traunkirchen (63km).

Mondsee lies 1km S of the A1 autobahn some 25km E of Salzburg. The village itself (2150 inhab.), with a number of characteristic lanes, is a pleasant centre from which to explore the district.

It was built near the site of a pile village of 2500–1800 BC, which gave its name to the Mondseekultur. The present village was founded in 748 by Odilio, a Bavarian duke, when the Benedictine monastery was established. Until its dissolution in 1791 this was the oldest surviving in Upper Austria (now Kremsmünster). Its school of illuminators was well known, and it was here that the 'Mondseer Liederbuch' was compiled in the 16C. In the first part of the 17C it was frequently at odds with the peasants of *Wildeneck*, whom it oppressed.

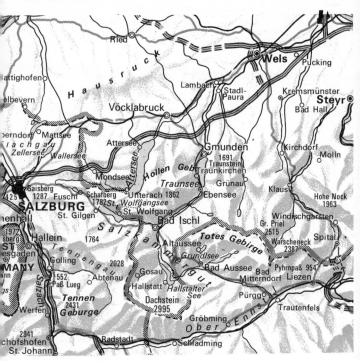

The former *Abbey Church*, now the parish church and replacing
one of 1104, was built in the late 15C, and the exterior baroquised
after 1730, while its two towers were added later. It contains five
black and gilt altars and a pulpit by Meinrad Guggenbichler, and a
high altar by Hans Waldburger. Several tombstones of former abbots
are notable, as are the Roman stones incorporated into the porch
walls. Next to the entrance is a *Museum*, while to the N is an area
undergoing excavation.

Passing a long avenue of limes, you approach the lakeside, with its
erratic boulders, and follow the W bank. The **Mondsee** is 11km long
and 2km wide, dominated by the *Schafberg* (1782m) to the S. After
8km we leave the road to *St. Gilgen* to the right (see Rte 12A), and
veer E to (5km) *Au*, on the *Seeache*, a stream joining the Mondsee
with the **Attersee** (the largest of the Austrian lakes with the exception of the Neusiedler See, the S shore of which is in Hungary; cf.),
being 20km long and about 3km wide, with an area of 47 sq km.

After 2km we fork right along its steep narrow S bank past the
gorge of *Burggrabenklamm* through *Burgau*, and at (7km) *Weissenbach*, where Gustav Klimt spent the summers of 1914–16, turn right;
for *Steinbach*, 4km N on the lakeside, see p 182. The B153 ascends to
a low pass in the HÖLLENGEBIRGE, with the *Grosser Höllkogel*
(1862m) rising to the NE, and the *Leonsberg* (1745m) to the SW,
before climbing down to (14km) *Mitterweissenbach*, on the B145
6km NE of **Bad Ischl**; see Rte 12A.

The road bears NE along the wooded TRAUN VALLEY, following

the ancient line of the *Soleleitung*—occasionally seen from the road—a form of brine conduit constructed with wooden pipes in 1607 to carry the saline flow from Hallstatt (cf.) and Bad Ischl to the lakeside port of Ebensee. To the S rises the *Hohe Schrott* (1839m), and further E the TOTES GEBIRGE, while on approaching (12km) *Ebensee*, the characteristic *Traunstein*, on the far bank of the Traunsee, comes into view.—4km prior to reaching the town a right-hand turning leads 9km to the small lake of *Offensee*.

Ebensee (9000 inhab.), where the earlier evaporating houses stood, is still important for its salt refineries, among other industries, but is otherwise of slight interest.

From the N side of the town a road ascends for 8km to reach the little mountain-girt *Langbathsee*, with its upper tarn a short walk further W. After c 1km this road passes the lower station of a cable-car to the summit of the *Feuerkogel* (1594m).

The main road, constructed only in 1872, which skirts the steep W bank of the **Traunsee* (12km long, and 3km wide; the deepest lake in Austria: 191m), known to the Romans as *Lacus Felix*, commands a good view across to the precipitous E bank and the *Erlakogel* (1575m). It is later dominated by the **Traunstein** (1691m), before reaching, after 4km, the charmingly sited lakeside village of **Traunkirchen**.

Hugo Wolf stayed in 1891–93 in a house which is passed on approaching the promontory. The mid 17C *Pfarrkirche* and cemetery are overlooked by an octagonal tower. Remarkable in the interior is the pulpit known as the **Fischerkanzel* (1753), representing the miraculous draught of fishes.

The road continues to skirt the lake side, which gradually opens out on approaching (8km) **Altmünster** (8550 inhab.), where Gothic *St. Benedikt* has some interesting sculptures, including naive reliefs, and an altarpiece of 1518, in some ways similar to that at Mauer (cf.), and ascribed to the Master of the St. Anne's altar. Brahms visited the town on several occasions, staying with the Miller zu Aichholz family (whose villa stood on a height some 700m NW of the main road passing Schloss Ort); while Wagner composed part of 'Tristan and Isolde' at Schloss Wesendonk at *Traunblick*—the home of Otto and Mathilde Wesendonck.—For the road to *Steinbach*, see below.

After 2km, on approaching Gmunden, turn right to visit the picturesque lakeside **Schloss Ort**, in fact two buildings, the 17C *Landschloss*, and the **Seeschloss* on its island site, reached by a 130m-long wooden foot-bridge, and dating from the 11C, although rebuilt in the 16–17C, when its onion-dome was added; it preserves a triangular courtyard.

The two castles were acquired by Leopold II, Grand Duke of Tuscany, whose son, the Archduke Johann Salvator (a nephew of Franz Josef), renounced his Habsburg title in 1889, adopting the name Ort, and marrying a certain Milly Stubel. The following year he set sail from Chatham for Buenos Aires, but the ship disappeared without trace. Maria Antonia, widow of the Grand Duke Leopold, retired here in 1870, where she died in 1898.

Gmunden (12,650 inhab.), a well-sited and prosperous summer resort at the N end of the lake, of which it commands a fine view, is divided into two by the river Traun (which flows on through Lambach to enter the Danube just E of Linz).

It rose to prominence in the 14C, becoming the Salzamt or administrative headquarters of the salt-mining operations in the Salzkammergut, and the main salt depots stood here. The peasants were defeated nearby on 8 November 1626 during the revolts of that year. Schubert and Vogl lodged for six weeks here with Ferdinand Traweger in June–July 1825, and it is said that the lost 'Gastein Symphony' was partly composed here. Schubert intended to visit the place again during the summer of 1828, but financial embarrassment and ill-health made it impossible. Bela Bartok had piano lessons from Dohnányi at Gmunden in the summer of 1903.

It has several buildings of interest, particularly near the RATHAUSPLATZ, W of which, in the FRANZ-JOSEF-PLATZ, the *Cafe Grellinger* was long a favourite rendezvous. The *Rathaus* itself, with its ceramic carillon, dates from the 16C. From here the Kammerhofgasse leads E past the *Kammerhof* (15C; rebuilt c 1629 and again in the 18C), now housing a local museum displaying archaeological finds, local ceramic ware, and souvenirs of Hebbel and Brahms. Further E is the *Spitalskirche St. Jakob* of 1340, near the bridgehead. The Traungasse leads N to the characteristic MARKTPLATZ, with the *Altes Rathaus* (16C, with a 17C façade) and '*Kapuzinerhaus*' (No. 13; with an 18C façade). To the NW is the 14C *Pfarrkirche*, later baroquised, preserving several tombstones of interest, and a well-carved Adoration of the Magi of 1678 by Thomas Schwanthaler, flanked by statues by Michael Zürn the Younger (1690).

On a hill to the NE, on the far bank of the Traun, stands the *Schloss Cumberland* (1886), where the last Duke of Cumberland (son of George V of Hanover) died in 1923. On the lake itself sails the restored paddle-steamer 'Gisela' (1871).
   A cable-car ascends SE to the viewpoint of *Grünberg* (1004m).

GMUNDEN TO KREMSMÜNSTER (43km). The B120 leads E to (16km) *Scharnstein*, with the ruins of a 12C castle, and the restored late 16C Schloss housing a museum of 'Law and Justice', etc.
   6km S lies **Grünau im Almtal** (2100 inhab.), where the church has a notable high altar (1618), and a finely carved angel (c 1690) by Michael Zürn the Younger.—The wooded ALMTAL may be climbed past the *Wildpark des Herzogs von Cumberland*, where the late Konrad Lorenz undertook some of his researches, to (12km) *Almsee*, surrounded by mountains, beyond which the TOTES GEBIRGE range rises to over 2000m.
   From Scharnstein you can turn NE via (10km) *Pettenbach* and (9km) *Voitsdorf* to *Kremsmünster*, 8km beyond; see p 190.
   The return journey can be made via *Lambach* and *Stadl-Paura* (22km W; see Rte 17); from there following the B144 SW to (24km) *Gmunden*.

The A1 autobahn may be reached 8km NW of Gmunden (providing a rapid return to *Mondsee*, 32km SW), while *Vöcklabruck* lies only 8km further NW on the old main road (B1; see Rte 14).

A recommended route back **from Gmunden to Mondsee via Altmünster, Steinbach, Seewalchen, Unterach, and Pichl** (77km).
   From (4km) *Altmünster* (see above) the road climbs SW via *Neukirchen* and the pastoral AURACH VALLEY to the GROSSALM PASS (829m), descending, with fine views to the SW over the **Attersee**, to (22km) *Steinbach* (4km N of Weissenbach). Mahler spent the summers of 1893–96 here. Behind the Zum Höllengebirge Inn, in the middle of a lakeside camping-site, is a reconstructed summer-house, in which, it is said, he composed his Third Symphony, but it hardly deserves visiting.—The road skirts the lake, passing through several villages to the head of the Attersee between *Schörfling* (near an entrance to the A1), with the nearby *Schloss Kammer* (17–18C; Gustav Klimt painted the avenue of trees approaching it), and (15km) *Seewalchen*, a lakeside resort with a Gothic church. Circling the N end of the lake, the B151 enters (8km) **Attersee** itself, where near the *Church*, containing statues by Meinrad Guggenbichler, the mosaic

pavement of a Roman villa was discovered in 1924. In the vicinity, on an isolated hill, stood a 9C Carolingian palace.

You pass through several lakeside villages on the road along this wooded W shore, with a good view towards the far bank, dominated by the HÖLLENGEBIRGE, rising to 1862m.—13km *Unterach*, at the SW extremity of the lake, was painted by Gustav Klimt, who spent almost every summer between 1901–18 on the Attersee, where Emilie Flöge (1874–1952) had a house.—3km *Au*, beyond which the road veers away from the *Schafberg* (1782m), to the S, passing through *Pichl* and skirting the E bank of the *Mondsee*, with attractive views across the lake, to return to the village of (10km) **Mondsee**; see p 179.

14 Salzburg to Linz

A. Via the A1 autobahn

Total distance, 130km (81 miles). B1 for 8km, then A1 for (17km) the *Mondsee* exit—22km *Attersee* exit—19km *Gmunden* exit—28km *Kremsmünster* exit—26km *Linz* exit—10km **Linz**.

Maps: F&B 1; BEV 18/13–14.

The motorway provides a rapid route to several points from which the N half of the **Salzkammergut** (see Rte 13) may be explored, and is itself an attractive drive. It has a number of good road-side snack-bars and restaurants.

The autobahn shortly follows a ridge N of the *Fuschlsee* (see p 174), with the *Kolomannsberg* (1114m) to the left, to approach the Mondsee exit, with a good view SE of the lakeside village and the *Schafberg* (1782m) rising beyond its far shore.

4km to the N lies *Zell am Moos*, on the E bank of the small *Zeller See*.

The road now makes a circle to the S, with a plunging view over the **Mondsee**, turning N prior to reaching the exit for **Attersee** (3km right), and bearing E above the N shore of the lake near (8km) *Seewalchen*; see last part of Rte 13. Passing (right) the *Alpenberg* (972m), at 11km we reach the exit for **Gmunden**, 8km SE (see Rte 13), or **Vöcklabruck** (see Rte 12B), 8km NW.

At 7km the road crosses the valley of the Traun: **Stadl-Paura** and **Lambach** lie 13km NE; see Rte 14B.—At 19km you reach a point where the important intersection of the A1 and A9 will take place, once the latter motorway, crossing Austria diagonally from NW (near *Passau* in Germany) to *Graz*, and on to *Zagreb* in Yugoslavia, is completed.—2km beyond is the exit for **Kremsmünster** (6km E; see Rte 17), and **Wels** (12km N; see Rte 14B), and the present main road (B138) S from Wels to Graz; see Rte 18.

Continuing NE, the autobahn is joined after 19km by the A25 from Wels, and 7km beyond, you turn onto the A7, descending towards **Linz**; see Rte 19.—The A1 circles round towards the SE for **Vienna**; see Rte 21A.

B.   Via Lambach and Wels

Total distance, 125km (77 miles). B1. 27km *Strasswalchen*—32km
Vöcklabruck—21km **Lambach** (for **Stadl-Paura**)—15km **Wels**—
30km **Linz**.

Maps: F&B 1; BEV 18/13–14.

Passing below the A1, at 8km the road meets a turning for
Seekirchen, 3km N, with a collegial *Church* of ancient foundation,
rebuilt in 1669–79 by G.A. Dario, with marble altars by W.
Hagenauer, and a carved Virgin and Child by Simeon Fries. The
nearby *Schloss Seeburg* dates from the 12C and 14C. For the area
further NW, see p 186.

The B1, which until the laying of the motorway was the main road
between Salzburg and Vienna, shortly passes close to the S bank of
the *Wallersee*, and continues NE, with a view of the *Tannberg* (786m)
to the N and of the extensive *Kobernausser Wald* ahead, to enter
(19km) *Strasswalchen* (5100 inhab.), its late Gothic *Pfarrkirche* with a
high altar by Meinrad Guggenbichler (an early work; 1675). The
road following a ridge, provides some fine views S.

At *Irrsdorf*, 2km SE, the *Church* of 1408 preserves remarkable carved doors,
several sculptures by Guggenbichler, and a late 14C Virgin and Child.

14km *Frankenmarkt*. The Gothic nave of its *Pfarrkirche*, its vaulting
sustained by a central pillar, has been transformed into rococo, but it
preserves (repainted) frescoes by Hans Baldung Grien, a Nativity by
Guggenbichler, and an altarpiece by Altomonte.—At 10km **Gam-
pern** lies 2km right. Its church, has similar vaulting to that at
Frankenmarkt and contains a remarkable carved and painted
Winged-altarpiece by Lienhart Astl (c 1500) or of his school.
You pass a medieval tower at *Timelkam* on approaching (8km)
Vöcklabruck (11,000 inhab.), once walled, with two gate-houses of
1502–03 at either end of its characteristic STADTPLATZ, while in a
suburb to the NE is the *St. Ägidius-Kirche*, built by C.A. Carlone in
1688, decorated with stucco by his brother Giovanni Battista.—There
is a Gothic church with a double nave and fortified tower at
Schöndorf, to the SE.—**Gmunden** lies 16km further SE; see Rte 13.

12km *Schwanenstadt* (3700 inhab.), Roman *Tergolape*, retains a
number of Gothic and Baroque houses, and was the birthplace of
Franz Xavier Süssmayr (1766–1803), the composer and friend of
Mozart. After 9km you come to **Lambach** (3150 inhab.), an old
market town on the Traun, containing several Baroque mansions.

Its centre is dominated by the **Benedictine Abbey**, founded in
1056, and rebuilt in the mid 17C, with an imposing marble entrance
by Jakob Auer (1693). Unfortunately its early *Romanesque frescoes*
(c 1080) are normally only to be seen in a guided tour. Uncovered in
what was the choir of the original church, they were restored in the
1960s, and show pronounced Byzantine influence. Also to be seen
are the 14C *Chapterhouse*, an early 18C *Refectory*, a picture-gallery,
library, and even a *Theatre* (restored in 1983), which was inaugurated by Maria Antonia on 23 April 1770 while on her way to Paris to
become, as Marie Antoinette, queen of France. The *Church*, by
Philiberto Lucchese, contains a monumental high altar, and paintings by Joachim von Sandrart.
Perhaps of more interest—excepting the above-mentioned
frescoes—is the remarkable triangular church (the *Dreifaltigkeitskirche*) of *Stadl-Paura*, 1km away on a small hill, and reached

by a right-hand turning S of the Traun. The approach is spoilt by the presence of a small housing estate at its foot. Built in 1714–22 by Johann Michael Prunner, the church is dedicated to the Trinity, and not only is its ground-plan symbolic, but its towers, doors, altars, organs, and confessionals, etc. are also three in number, while in the dome, surmounted by a triangular cupola, is a fresco of the Trinity by Carlo Carlone.

Some 8km NW of Lambach stands moated *Schloss Würting bei Offenhausen*.

Regaining the B1, continue NE, after c 1km reaching the turning (right) for **Kremsmünster** (see Rte 17) to approach (15km) *Wels*.

  WELS (51,050 inhab.; 11,700 in 1869; 29,550 in 1939), as *Ovilava* the capital of the Roman province of *Noricum*, is now an important market and industrial town, standing mainly on the N bank of the Traun. The old enceinte contains several interesting buildings.

It was at one time the home of Hans Sachs, the cobbler and 'Mastersinger' of Nuremberg, and from 1612 that of Salome von Alt, the ex-mistress of Wolf Dietrich, Prince-archbishop of Salzburg (cf.), while the Emperor Maximilian I died here in 1519. The psychiatrist Julius Wagner-Jauregg (1857–1940), was born here.

In the wide Pollheimerstrasse, immediately W of the old centre, is the municipal *Museum*, containing some archaeological and Roman relics, including a diminutive Roman bronze of Venus. (The line of Roman walls lay approximately along the Schubertstrasse to the N, the Roseggstrasse to the E and just W of the Local-bahnhof.)— Opposite is the medieval *Schloss Pollheim*, in a sad state of disfigurement.—Further S is the *Ledererturm*, the only surviving town gate, giving access to the long but characteristic STADTPLATZ, with several 16–17C houses.

  S of its *Fountain* of 1593 are relics of the 12–14C *Minoritenkirche*, now used as a fire-station! Adjacent is the *Rathaus*, with a Baroque façade of 1748. (It is advisable to enquire at the *Tourist Office* opposite about admission to the church at *Pucking*; see below.)

  The Traungasse leads S to the river-bank, where, a few steps to the W is the well-vaulted **Barbarakapelle** (of the Minorites), containing frescoes of 1480.—Further W is the *Wasserturm* of 1577.—Turning E along the riverside walk, you come to the restored *Kaiserliche Burg*. Of very ancient origin (first mentioned in 776), it was enlarged in the 15C, and it was here that Maximilian I died. Although his cenotaph remains at Innsbruck (cf.), he was buried at Wiener Neustadt, his birthplace. The building is now a museum.—Passing N through gardens, you return to the Stadtplatz near the *House of Salome von Alt*, with its chequered brickwork, and opposite the Gothic *Stadtpfarrkirche St. Johannes der Evangelist*, with Baroque additions to its tower, etc., and preserving a Romanesque W door, some late 14C glass, and Pollheim epitaphs.

  The Schmidgasse, turning right further W, contains several old houses, while further N, in the KAISER-JOSEF-PLATZ, Nos 12 and 56 have façades of 1723 and 1767 respectively.

For roads from Wels to **Graz**, see Rte 18; and from Wels to **Schärding**, Rte 16A in reverse; for **Eferding**, 22km N, see Rte 16B; **Kremsmünster** lies 18km SE; see Rte 17.

5km *Marchtrenk* (9400 inhab.).

A DETOUR of c 14km (there and back) may be made by turning S across the Traun and beneath the motorway, there turning left to the hamlet of **Pucking**, where the interior of the church is covered with mid 15C *Frescoes*, discovered in 1946 and since restored. Enquire first at the Tourist Office in Wels about admission.

At 7km NE of Marchtrenk you pass (left) *Linz airport*, and 4km beyond you can turn left to avoid some of the industrial S suburbs of **Linz**, which is shortly entered; see Rte 19.

15 (Munich) Braunau to Linz: the Innviertel

Total distance, 120km (74 miles). B309. 41km **Ried im Innkreis**.— 25km N137—24km **Wels**—B1. 30km **Linz**.

Maps: F&B 1; BEV 48/13–14.

*Braunau am Inn** (16,300 inhab.), above the S bank of the Inn opposite Bavarian *Simbach*, lies 124km E of Munich, and in the *Innviertel*, an area long in dispute with Bavaria, and which only became definitively part of Austria in 1779.

Adolf Hitler (1889–1945) was born here, the son of Alois Schicklgruber (legitimised as Hitler in 1876), a customs officer who was briefly stationed at Braunau and remained here only another three years.

It retains a long central STADTPLATZ of some character, running from N to S, where there is a gate-house, once commanding a moat, beyond which grew up the Salzburger Vorstadt. Notable is the *'Gnändinger Haus'* of 1530 at No. 32 in the platz, to the W of which are several picturesque old lanes. Dominating the platz is the lofty Baroque helm of 1759 surmounting the noble *Tower* of the **Stadt-pfarrkirche St. Stephan**, a mid 15C Gothic building plastered with tombstones. The interior, with its fine vaulting, contains several 'apostle' capitals and the marble tomb of Bishop Friedrich Mauerkirchner of Passau (died 1485).

To the W are relics of the town walls and barbican; and a short distance to the E, the *Bürgerspital*, with its early 15C church.

At *Ranshofen*, 4km SW, with aluminium factories, is the *Herzoghof*, founded in 788, preserving parts of an Augustinian monastery from 1125–1811. Its church dates from 1651 and contains notable Baroque altars and frescoes.

BRAUNAU TO SALZBURG VIA MATTIGHOFEN (66km). The B310 leads SE, at 8km passing just W of St. *Georgen an der Mattig*, with remarkable mid 17C Baroque altars by Martin and Michael Zürn.—8km *Helpfau-Uttendorf*, where to the NE, the church of St. *Florian* contains a notable if overloaded altarpiece by the Zürn brothers and Thomas Schwanthaler.—Some 4km SW at *Pischelsdorf am Engelbach*, the early 14C church retains good vaulting.—At (5km) *Mattighofen* is a church by F.A. Kirchgrabner of Munich (1775), with a high altar by Schwanthaler.—*Strasswalchen* (see Rte 14B) lies 17km SE on the road to *Mondsee*, 18km beyond.—Follow the road S towards *Mattsee*.—*Lochen*, 4km E of (11km) *Palting*, preserves a notable high altar of 1709, while the carved *winged altar* at **Gebertsham** (c 3km SW of Lochen) is a remarkable work by Gordian Gugg, of 1515–20, with the Crucifixion as its main feature.

The main road shortly crosses a neck of land known as the FLACHGAU, between *Mattsee* (left), the smaller lake of *Graben See*, and the *Obertrumer See*, before entering **Mattsee** itself after 6km. This small summer resort was the birthplace of Anton Diabelli (1781–1858), the music publisher, who in 1821 established his business in Vienna. The 13C collegiate *Church* is that of an abbey traditionally founded c 777 by Duke Tassilo III of Bavaria. Its interior was baroquised in 1700, and contains sculptures from the studio of Guggenbichler, and by Michael Zürn the Younger, and stalls by M. Steinl (1649). Its cloister preserves numerous 15–17C tombstones. Adjacent is the site of a 12C castle.— From here the road continues S towards (24km) **Salzburg**, on approaching it passing near the conspicuous pilgrimage-church of *Maria Plain*; see Rte 9D.

BRAUNAU TO SALZBURG VIA OBERNDORF (63km). The B156 leads S to (25km) *Eggelsberg*, where the hilltop 15C church, with its 72m-high baroquised tower, contains some vaulting of interest, and sculptures by Martin Zürn.—To the W of (3km) *Moosdorf* is an area of swampy plateau with one or two small lakes, where you fork left to (c 4km) **Michaelbeuern**, with the restored *Church* of a Benedictine abbey founded in 977, with a fine high altar by Meinrad Guggenbichler, and paintings by J.M. Rottmayr. Among conventual dependencies are a hall with rococo decoration by F.N. Streicher (1771), while a museum including cult objects is housed in the cloister.

The main road can be rejoined 8km SW, and 8km before entering *Oberndorf an der Salzach*, a riverside frontier-village. Just before this a right-hand turning leads shortly to the pilgrimage-church of *Maria Büchel* (1663), with two disproportionate Baroque towers. The high altar is by Antonio Beduzzi; the paintings in the side altars are by J.M. Rottmayr. At *Oberndorf*, the *Stille-Nacht-Kapelle* was built in 1937 on the site of an earlier church destroyed in 1899, where at Christmas 1818 the carol 'Silent Night, Holy Night' was first sung, with words by Joseph Mohr and music by F.X. Gruber.—From here we bear SE parallel to the Salzach to (19km) **Salzburg**.

Leaving Braunau, the B309 drives due E to (17km) *Altheim*; route continued below.

ALTHEIM TO SCHÄRDING (31km). The B142 bears NE to regain the Inn at (10km) **Obernberg**, an ancient town with a MARKTPLATZ of some character, in which several houses retain their rococo stucco-work by Johann Baptist Modler, notably the *Apothekerhaus*, and *Woerndlehaus*.—3km **Reichersberg**, with its 17C *Augustinian Abbey* founded c 1084. The statue of St. Michael above the fountain in the outer courtyard is by Schwanthaler, while the *Church* contains rococo stucco-work by J.B. Modler, frescoes of 1779, and the red marble tomb of the founder, Werner von Reichenberg, and his family. Numerous tombstones may be seen in the cloisters, and some conventual dependencies may be visited, including a *Refectory* by the Carlone brothers.—After crossing the motorway, **Suben** is entered, where the 18C church of another Augustinian *Abbey* (1162–1787) contains several features of interest, including a charming rococo organ-loft.—The Gothic church of *St. Florian am Inn*, with a Baroque high altar and rococo pulpit, is passed on the S outskirts of *Schärding*; see Rte 16A.

Continuing E from Altheim, the B309 approaches (21km) **Ried im Innkreis** (10,850 inhab.), an old but not now so attractive market town, retaining few streets of any interest, among them the HAUPTPLATZ. The *Church* in the Kirchenplatz contains sculpture by Martin and Michael Zürn, and a group by Thomas Schwanthaler (died 1705), the most influential of a local family of sculptors; also several notable tombstones.

5km NW is the early 18C *Schloss Aurolzmünster*, containing good stucco, as does the parish church.

At 12km the 'old' frontier village of *Haag am Hausruck* lies 2km S, with sculpture by the Schwanthalers in its church (under restoration). The nearby *Schloss Starhemberg*, dating from 1254, was rebuilt in the late 16C.

At 9km the moated *Schloss Aistersheim* lies 5km S.—After 3km you reach the B137 and continue E, at 15km passing a left-hand turning for **Eferding**, 12km NE (see Rte 16B), and veer SE to (9km) **Wels**; see Rte 14B, and for the road onward to (30km) **Linz**.

16   (Regensburg) Passau to Linz

A.   Via Schärding and Wels

Total distance, 109km (68 miles). B137b. 17km **Schärding**—B137.
22km *Zell an der Pram*—40km **Wels**—B1. 30km **Linz**.

Maps: F&B 1; BEV 48/13–14.

Travellers driving SE on the main road from *Nuremberg* and
Regensburg, and then along the Danube valley, may enter Austria by
crossing the river at *Passau*. The autobahn veers S on approaching
Passau, and enters Austria S of Schärding, while the old main road
crosses the Inn at *Schärding* itself. The A8 autobahn, which has
recently been completed, now by-passes Wels and joins the A1
further E.

The old centre of **Passau** itself (32,000 inhab.), dominated by its
Cathedral, lies on a tongue of land at the confluence of the Inn and
Danube. It is also the point of embarkation for river-steamers to Linz
and Vienna. Passau was the Emperor Leopold's HQ prior to the relief
of Vienna in 1683. Customs are passed just beyond its S outskirts.

From here follow the B137b S to (17km) **Schärding** (5750 inhab.),
on the right bank of the Inn, an ancient walled town, referred to in
804 as *Scardinga*. It retains its characteristic STADTPLATZ lined with
multicoloured gabled houses, most of them restored. To the NE of the
Stadtplatz stands the baroquised *Pfarrkirche*, to the NW the *Burg Tor*
of 1583, and to the W the *Schlosspark*, on the site of the moated castle
which here defended the river-crossing, notably in 1809. To the SE is
the 15C *Linzer Tor*, and to the SW extends the Innsbruckerstrasse,
containing several old houses. S of the Innsbruckerstrasse is the early
17C *Sebastianskirche*. Michael Denis (1729–1800), a translator of
Ossian, and chief librarian of the Hofbibliothek at Vienna from 1784,
was born here.—For *St. Florian am Inn*, see p 206.

The B136 leads E onto the plateau of SAUWALD and then descends through *St.
Aegidi* to (30km) *Engelhartszell*; see Rte 16B.

The B137 bears SE from Schärding to (22km) *Zell an der Pram*, where
the *Schloss* contains a Festsaal decorated with frescoes by Christian
Wink (1772) and some trompe l'oeil frescoes of note.—16km beyond,
on joining the B309 from Ried, turn due E to follow the road to **Wels**,
and beyond to **Linz**; see Rte 14B.

B.   Via the Danube Valley

Total distance, 85km (53 miles). B130. 26km *Engelhartszell*—34km
Eferding—B129. 18km **Wilhering**—7km **Linz**.

Maps: F&B 1; BEV 48/13–14.

From **Passau** (see above; Customs) follow the right bank of the
Danube below the plateau of SAUWALD to a point (17km) opposite
Obernzell, on the far bank, with the former castle (17C) of the Prince-
bishops of Passau, and at (2km) *Kasten*, pass below the ancient

fortress of *Vichtenstein* before reaching a point opposite the island rock of *Jochenstein*. The Bavarian border extends some 30km N to Czechoslovakia; see the latter part of Rte 20.

7km **Engelhartszell**, a village dominated by its monastery of *Engelszell* (Cella Angelica), a Cistercian foundation of 1293, suppressed in 1786, and since 1925 in Trappist hands. The mid 18C *Church*, with a rococo portal, contains several altarpieces with paintings by B. Altomonte. More of this artist's work can be seen in the Baroque library, while the tombstone of Eustach and Dorothea Albrechtshaimer is also notable.

The road continues to skirt the Danube, passing several medieval castles or ruins, at (15km) *Schlögen* bearing away from the river and shortly passing near (right) *St. Agatha*, the home of Stefan Fadinger, leader of the peasant revolt of 1626.—12km *Hartkirchen* (left) has frescoes of 1750 in its church.

Riverside **Aschach an der Donau**, 1.5km further E, was the birthplace of Leonard Paminger (1495–1567), the composer, who settled at Passau in 1516. It contains several charactistic old houses along the river, but the 16C Harrach castle—not far from the river to the S of the town—is derelict. (The E wing was built in 1709 by J. Lukas von Hildebrandt; its chapel is said to contain sculptures by Georg Raphael Donner.)

The B131 leads E, crossing the Danube, which may be re-crossed at (12km) *Ottensheim*, with a conspicuous castle, opposite *Wilhering* (see below), or the N bank may be followed to (10km), *Linz*, passing at 4km just N of *Pesenbach*, the church of which contains a notable carved *Altarpiece* of 1495.

Bearing SE, at 7km we enter **Eferding**, an ancient town (3100 inhab.), which in 1367 passed into the hands of the Schaunberg family, and then the Starhembergs, whose *Schloss* (15C and 18C) contains a small museum. To the W is the impressive Gothic *Pfarrkirche* with tombs of members of these families, a well-carved pulpit, and a neo-Gothic high altar, but with bad 19C glass. To the S is the characteristic and colourful STADTPLATZ, close to the SE corner of which is the baroquised *Spitalskirche*, founded by Rudolf von Schifner in 1325, and containing his tomb among others of interest, and ceiling frescoes of c 1430 in a N chapel. Eferding was the scene of a defeat of the peasants during the revolt of 1526.

At (7km) *Alkoven*, the 16C *Schloss Hartheim* lies to the S, with its four-storeyed courtyard; its associations with the Nazi regime are better forgotten.

11km **Wilhering**, a riverside village of 4100 inhab., is dominated by the Baroque belfry of its *** *Abbey Church**. Founded by Cistercians in 1146, it was rebuilt after a fire in 1733. The exuberantly decorated interior, with its rich gilding, Baroque statuary, and the white, pink, grey and terracotta-coloured stucco-work, is one of the more remarkable examples of rococo decoration in Austria. Only the porch and the cloister survive from the original building.

The architect of the massive tower was Matthias Götz of Passau, and the body of the church was designed by Johann Haslinger of Linz. The interior decoration by Martino and Bartolomeo Altomonte is of a high order, remarkable for both its delicacy and unity. Notable too is the sculpture by J.G. Übelhör and J.M. Feichtmayr, the pulpit and choir-organ, both by Nikolaus Rummel, and the main organ. Note the Gothic tombs of Wernhard IV von Schaunberg (died 1267) and Ulrich II von Schaunberg (died 1398) below the organ-loft. Its *Chapterhouse* and *Cloisters* contain 18 paintings of the Life of St.

Bernard of Clairvaux by Altomonte. Other dependencies may also be visited on request.

Continuing E along the right bank of the Danube, **Linz** is shortly entered; see Rte 19.

The organ in the abbey church at Wilhering

17 Lambach to Amstetten via Kremsmünster and Steyr

Total distance, 91km (56 miles). B122. 16km *Sattledt*—6km **Kremsmünster**—10km *Bad Hall*—18km **Steyr**—41km **Amstetten.**

Maps: F&B 1; BEV 48/14.

This attractive cross-country route may be followed as an alternative to the main road E via *St. Florian* and *Enns* (both of which are not far from it), and provides several panoramic views towards the mountains rising to the S. It crosses an area dotted with a number of large square two-storeyed farm-houses or *Vierkanthof*, an attractive feature of the landscape.

Turning right just E of *Lambach* (see Rte 14B), near *Sattledt* both the A9 and the A1 are crossed (see also Rte 18) and, 6km beyond, you descend into the valley of the Krems at **Kremsmünster** (5800 inhab.). The town is dominated by two buildings, those of the **Monastery**, with its *Church*, and its silo-like Observatory, to the E. Together with its dependencies it was restored to celebrate its 1200th anniversary.

The abbey, founded in 777 by Duke Tassilo III of Bavaria, is the oldest in the Austrian Alps after that of St. Peter at Salzburg. Simon Rettenpacher (1634–1706), who left some 6000 Latin poems, was librarian there from 1675; F.X. Süssmayer, the friend of Mozart, was organist there before 1787, when he moved to Vienna. Its famous grammar school was founded in 1549, and in 1804 a boarding school, at which Adalbert Stifter, and several friends of Schubert, including Schober, were educated. The composer visited the school on several occasions, notably with Vogl, who had also been a pupil. It was made baroque between c 1615 and 1712.

To the left, beyond the *Eichentor* (by Jakob Prandtauer; 1732), is the remarkable ***Fish Tank** (or *Fischkalter*; 1691), in fact a series of five water-basins surrounded by antler-embellished arcades, three by C.A. Carlone, with two added in 1717 by Prandtauer.

From the SE corner of the outer courtyard one may approach the *Observatory*; see below.

Passing through the *Brückenturm*, built over the medieval moat, cross the inner Prälaten-Hof to reach (left) the *Church. A mid 13C building in Transitional style, with twin towers (mid 14C, but with Baroque ornamentation), and containing heavy Baroque stucco-work, it was remodelled by C.A. Carlone. Notable are the wrought-iron grille, the mid 16C Brussels tapestries encircling the pillars, and the marble angels carved by Michael Zürn the Younger (1682–85). Note in the Marienkapelle, the *Tomb of Gunther* (1304), with his dog and a wild boar; the Benedict Altar (1713), by J.B. Spaz; and among the paintings, Christ on the Mount of Olives, and The Last Supper, by F.I. Torriani; the Martyrdom of St. Agapitus; and over the high altar, a Transfiguration by Johann Andreas Wolf. The vault paintings are by the brothers Grabenberger.

From the S side of the courtyard you can climb to the **Museum and Kaisersaal* (by C.A. Carlone), with plaster-work by D.F. Carlone, a painted vault by Melchior Steidl, and a Portrait of Karl VI by M. Altomonte, who also painted that of Rudolf I of Habsburg. The first five rooms of the museum contain a variety of paintings, among which are the Endl-Epitaph, by *Wolf Huber*; *Jan Brueghel the Elder*, The Elements; *Michiel Coxie*, The Holy Family; *Jan Gossaert*, The Annunciation; works by *'Kremser' Schmidt*, and *Altomonte*, and *F.G. Bibiena*; *Josef von Fuhrich*, Macbeth and the witches; F. van Valckenborch, Venetian Carnival; and a ceiling with scenes from Ovid's Metamorphoses; and note the Renaissance stove.

The following rooms contain collections of glass; arms and armour; vestments; a curious carved elephant-bone stool (1554); ivories; a disc-cross of 1170–80; the 'Codex Millenarius' (c 800); and a number of cult objects, pride of place being given to the *Tassilo Chalice of gilded copper with niello plaques on a silver background (c 781). Lastly, the **Library**, of three sections, embellished with Italian stucco-work, in which several of its 400 MSS and 792 *incunabula* are displayed, and also musical instruments.

The *Observatory or 'Mathematical Tower' (70m high), a few minutes' walk to the E, is an unusual eight-storey building of 1748–58, accommodating a variety of natural history and scientific collections: in ascending order—Geology, Palaeontology, Mineralogy; Physics; Zoology; Anthropology; Astronomy, including early scientific instruments, among them a 'Tychonic' sextant perhaps used by Kepler. The stairs are embellished by some 240 oval portraits of pupils of this academy for the sons of noblemen. The upper terrace commands a wide view.

The *Kalvarienbergkirche* (1736–38), on a neighbouring hill, and preserving features of interest, is by Johann Michael Prunner.—There is another church of note at *Weigersdorf*, 4km W.

Following the S bank of the valley to the E through *Oberrohr*, with a late 15C church, you turn right at (6km) *Rohr im Kremstal*.

The B139 bears N here for Linz via (10km) *Neuhofen*, birthplace of Marshal Georg von Derfflinger (1606–95), a peasant's son (who was present at the siege of Bonn in 1689, in his 84th year), while *Schloss Weissenberg*, a short distance beyond, once belonged to Marshal Tilly.

4km **Bad Hall** (4050 inhab.), a spa known for its iodine waters since 777, taken by Bruckner, Grillparzer, and Adalbert Stifter, among others. Mahler conducted the local orchestra here at the beginning of his career.—The church at *Pfarrkirchen*, 2km W, dating from 1744–77, contains some remarkable rococo decoration, and frescoes by W.A. Heindl.

Continuing E via (8km) *Sierning*, the road descends into the valley of the Steyr, following its N bank to approach the centre, reached by turning right.

STEYR (38,950 inhab.; 16,600 in 1869), an attractively sited town, the second largest in Upper Austria, lies at the confluence of the Steyr and the Enns. It is of ancient origin, and much of the picturesque older town is well preserved.

To the NE is an industrial district which has grown up with the expansion of the important *Steyr-Daimler-Puch* works, which originated with the earlier Small Arms Factory which produced the Mannlicher rifles (named after their designer, Ferdinand Ritter von Mannlicher; 1848–1904), etc. This caused it to be severely damaged by bombing in 1944, since when it has been rebuilt and modernised.

Its ironworks have flourished for a millennium, and it was known for the manufacture and export of weapons since the 12C, the pig-iron supplied from *Eisenerz* (see Rte 18B) being transported down the Enns valley from *Hieflau*. Its castle, the *Stirapurch* (built by Ottokar of Traungau) was first mentioned in a document of 985. The town and province (Steiermark; Styria) were acquired by Babenberg dukes in 1186, the former being given its statute in 1287, and becoming Habsburg property in 1282. It was a centre of peasant revolts in 1573, 1588 and 1601, which spread widely.

During the Counter-Reformation, numerous Protestant burghers were forced to leave, some of them establishing iron-works elsewhere, as at Solingen. It was three times in the hands of Napoleon. In 1869 Josef Werndl (1831–89) founded the *Österreichische Waffenfabriks-Gesellschaft*, which gave the town much of its more recent prosperity, and it is now an important centre of manufacture of ball-bearings, bicycles, cars, lorries, and tractors. It was also one of the first towns in Europe to be lit by electricity, in 1884.

Among those born here were Johann Mayrhofer (1787–1836), the poet, who leapt to his death from a third floor window of the Book Revision Office during a cholera epidemic in Vienna; Johann Michael Vogl (1768–1840), the singer of lieder. Schubert made his first visit to the town in July 1819, remarking that he thought the surrounding country 'inconceivably lovely'. Sylvester Paumgartner (c 1763–1841), a manager of the iron-works and amateur 'cellist', was at that time the musical patron of Steyr; and at his home—now Stadtplatz 16—regular performances took place. He commissioned Schubert's 'Trout Quintet'.

Approaching the town from the W, the road climbs onto the tongue of land between the two rivers, and you enter the old enceinte by the *Neutor* (1573), at the S end of the *Grünmarkt* (green, i.e. vegetable market) and its broader extension, the *Stadtplatz. There is a municipal *Museum* adjacent to the gate, housed in the early 17C *Innerberger Stadel*, containing a scythe-hammer, a collection of knives, and an 18C Nativity composed of over 400 mechanical figures.

To the right rises the former *Dominikaner-Kirche* (1647), an early Baroque building with late 18C decoration, preserving some good ironwork, stucco, and a rococo pulpit, etc.—You next pass the imposing rococo *Rathaus* (1765–78; by Johann Gotthard Hayberger).

Opposite, at No. 32, is the restored *'Bummerlhaus', a late Gothic edifice (now a bank), the first floor of which—shown on request—preserves a rare wooden ceiling of 1543. The courtyard may also be seen, one of several behind other façades flanking the square. Further N is the late 17C *Leopoldbrunnen*, and beyond, as the platz narrows, are more 16C houses. Follow the Engegasse from here to reach the confluence of the rivers. The Enns bridge (right) provides an attractive view of the gabled riverside houses; the bridge over the Steyr leads to the suburb of *Steyrdorf*. Near steps between the two is a plaque showing the high-water mark of 1572.

The far end of the latter bridge is dominated by the former Jesuit **Michaelerkirche** (1635–77; with a marble high altar of 1766), recently restored, while to the left, abutting the bridge, is the former *Bürgerspitalkirche*, retaining its Gothic crypt.—The Kirchengasse, the Sierningerstrasse (forking left), and the Gleinkergasse (continuing the Kirchengasse), all preserve a number of characteristic old houses (notice for example Nos 1 and 16 in the first, and Nos 14 and 16 in the last of these streets). The street continues up towards the *Alter Friedhof*, with late 16C arcades, on the hill known as *Tabor*. Further NW is the *Schnallentor* of 1613. An 'Industrial Environment' museum is being accommodated in former factory buildings in the riverside Wehrgraben, from which a foot-bridge crosses the Steyr to below the Schloss, to which steps ascend.

On regaining the S bank via the road-bridge, continue uphill to the right through a Gothic arch to the **Schloss**, rebuilt c 1750 by Johann Michael Prunner. The dwarf figures around its fountain, largely carved by J.B. Wuntscher in 1720, are said to be after engravings by Callot.—Adjacent is the *Schlosspark*, while the narrow Berggasse leads S parallel to the lower Stadtplatz (to which flights of steps steeply descend), to approach the *Stadtpfarrkirche Hl. Ägid und Koloman*, rebuilt in the 1880s in a neo-Gothic style, having on several occasions been severely damaged by fire since first built in 1443–1522. It retains an original Gothic doorway. Below the organ-gallery is the tomb of its architect, Wolfgang Tenk (1513). Adjacent is the mid 15C *Margaretenkapelle*, while in the priest's house Bruckner composed on occasions between the years 1886 and 1894.—Here the Pfarrgasse descends to regain the S end of the main square.

Among several interesting Baroque churches in the vicinity of Steyr are *Hl. Andreas* at *Gleink* (3km N), formerly part of a Benedictine abbey, with paintings by Martino Altomonte; that at **Garsten** (6050 inhab.; 3km SW), also at one time Benedictine (its dependencies now a prison), an imposing building by Pietro Francesco Carlone and his son Carlo Antonio, with a good high altar, stuccoes by Giovanni Battista Carlone similar to those at Schlierbach, and frescoes and altar-paintings by Carl von Reslfeld and twin organs in a stuccoed loft.—3km W of Steyr is the hilltop *Christkindl*, a domed building by G.B. Carlone and Jakob Prandtauer (1708), with an attractive pulpit.

This latter is also the address of a Post Office in December, the presence of which as a clearing-house does much to encourage the commercialisation of Christmas by answering letters from Austrian children to 'Christkind', and sending messages of good will to philatelists throughout the world, to the State's profit.

The B337 leads N from Steyr to (21km) **Enns** and the A1 autobahn; see Rte 21.

STEYR TO HIEFLAU (80km). The B115 leads S, following the wooded valley of the Enns to (22km) *Losenstein*, with a ruined castle of 1186, and (22km) *Kastenreith*, where the *Flössermuseum* (open in summer) describes the transport downstream of iron from Eisenerz to Steyr.—The village of *Weyer Markt*, 2km NE in the GAFLENZ VALLEY, preserves several late Gothic and Renaissance mansions from the time its numerous forges flourished.—16km *Altenmarkt bei St. Gallen*, 5km SW of which, above the B117, are the ruins of the 13–15C *Schloss Gallenstein*. *Admont* (see Rte 18B) lies 19km beyond.—The B115 continues SE up the Enns valley to (20km) *Hieflau*, from which the *Gesäuse* (W) and the *Erzberg* (SE), may be visited; see Rte 18B.

The B122 leads E from Steyr, at 16km passing just S of *Weistrach*, where the *Church of 1520 contains remarkable vaulting. After 3km it by-passes *St. Peter in der Au* (left), with a good example of a fortified church joined by a bridge to the adjacent Schloss, with its tower, to (3km) **Seitenstetten Markt**, the site of a Benedictine *Monastery founded in 1112.

The *Church* (1250–1300), rebuilt after a fire, was somewhat awkwardly baroquised between 1677–1706, and restored in 1975. The high altar and pulpit preserve statuary by F.J. Feichtmayr, and it retains a Romanesque chapel. The conventual dependencies were rebuilt between 1718–47 by Josef Munggenast (died 1741) and Johann Gotthard Hayberger, and contain a remarkable *Staircase* decorated with frescoes by B. Altomonte. The *Marmorsaal* has a ceiling-painting of 1735 by Paul Troger and trompe l'oeils by Franz Josef Wiedon; a *Cabinet* of natural history and minerals; an important *Library* with a ceiling by Troger; and a *Summer Refectory* with frescoes by J.I. Mildorfer. Paintings by 'Kremser' Schmidt can be seen in another salon. A collection of sculpture, among them reliefs by J.T. Stammel, and a *Picture-gallery*, containing several canvases of interest, may also be visited.

The road now bears NE to meet the B121 after 15km, some 8km SW of **Amstetten**; see Rte 21B.

A DETOUR may be made by taking the right-hand road at this junction leading past (1km) *Rosenau*, on the hill above which is the conspicuous pilgrimage-church of *Sonntagberg* (704m; view), founded in 1438 but rebuilt in 1706–32 by Prandtauer and Munggenast. It contains grey and mauve frescoes by Daniel Gran, and a high altar and pulpit by Melchior Hefele.

6km further up the valley is the ancient town of **Waidhofen an der Ybbs** (11,300 inhab.), at the confluence of that stream with the Schwarzbach. It lies at the centre of the Eisenwurzen, and received its charter c 1270.

At its N end is the *Schloss* (1407, but modernised in the 1880s by the Rothschilds). Adjacent is the *Pfarrkirche* of 1470, with a baroquised tower. The OBERER STADTPLATZ leads S, with its *Mariensäule* (1665), opposite which are the *Rathaus* and *Stadtturm*, completed in 1542 to commemorate the Turkish defeat in 1532. No. 32 houses the local museum, while off the S end of the platz is the former *Rathaus*, near the 13C *Ybbsturm*. The Freisinger Berg joins the Oberer with the UNTERER STADTPLATZ. At the S end of the platz (No. 22) is the *Altes Rathaus* and beyond this the *Bürgerspitalskirche Hl. Katharina*.

The excursion may be extended up the YBBS VALLEY on the B31, which circles to the SW before ascending to (46km) *Göstling an der Ybbs*, a winter-sports resort, the Gothic church of which has a Baroque belfry by J. Munggenast (1718). To the E rises the *Dürrenstein* (1878m).—From (11km) *Lunz am See*, with its adjacent lake surrounded by mountains, the road continues E, and after 9.5km one may turn left for (4km) *Lackendorf*, from which a cable-car ascends to a view-point (1418m) below the summit of the *Ötscher* (1893m).—From just E of Lunz the B25 climbs NE over a pass to descend to (11km) **Gaming**, an old market village, the site of what was once the largest Carthusian monastery in Austria or Germany, founded in 1330 and suppressed in 1782, the 17C buildings of which preserve a Library (its frescoes restored in 1989); the interior of its Gothic church is baroquised.—For *Scheibbs*, 13km NE in the Erlauf valley, see Rte 21B.

18 Wels to Graz

A. Via Liezen and the Gleinalmtunnel

Total distance, 202km (125 miles). B138. 12km *Sattledt*.
Kremsmünster lies 6km E.—22km **Schlierbach** lies 2km left.—31km *Spital am Pyhrn*—16km *Liezen*—B113. 23km *Trieben*—48km *St. Michael*—A9 autobahn (toll). 50km **Graz**.

Maps: F&B 1, 2; BEV 48/14–15, 47/14–15.

This route closely follows the line of the A9 motorway under construction from a point just W of Wels to just E of Liezen, which will meet that part already completed from St. Michael to Graz.

The B138 leads due S from Wels, crossing the A1 at *Sattledt*, from which point one may make the detour to **Kremsmünster** (see Rte 17), regaining the route 16.5km further S near *Schlierbach*.

20km A chapel at *Inzersdorf* (right) contains a fine carved and gilt Virgin and Child of c 1430.

2km **Schlierbach**, 2km NE, has a notable *Monastery* founded in 1355 for Cistercian nuns, and since 1671 occupied by monks. The Baroque *Church* of which—best seen in a good light—is by Pietro Francesco Carlone and his two sons. The pilasters and walls are covered by carved and gilded wood panels by J.J. Wanscher. Some will consider the interior too overloaded with heavy stucco-work and carved furniture. Less richly decorated are the *Bernardisaal*, with trompe l'oeil frescoes, and the *Library*, both of 1712, with illusionist architectural frescoes in the dome of the latter.

Regaining the main road, continue S through (6km) *Micheldorf*, a centre of scythe making, with a small museum devoted to the industry (Sensenmuseum). On the nearby *Georgenberg* (595m), with its Gothic and Baroque church, are traces of a fortified Celtic camp, Roman temple (1–2C), and Palaeo-Christian sanctuary with a 4–5C apse.—*Schloss Altpernstein*, dating from c 1160, was remodelled in the 16C.

4km *Frauenstein*, 1km E, has a pilgrimage-church preserving a charming carved Virgin and Child with donors beneath her mantle.

After 10km the B138 bears SE away from the *Grosser Priel* (SW; 2515m), which dominates the STRODERTAL, leading SW towards the E flank of the TOTES GEBIRGE range. You soon meet the motorway, which later pierces the spur of *Bosruck* (2009m) by the *Bosrucktunnel* to reach the ENNSTAL E of Liezen, but it is provided with an exit for *Spital am Pyhrn*; see below.

At 13km the B138, following the line of a Roman road, by-passes (left) *Windischgarsten*, once colonised by Slavs (Windischen), and later by Bavarians and Franks.—8km **Spital am Pyhrn**, named after a hospice founded in 1190 by Bishop Otto II of Bamberg, which was replaced by the present *Church* by J.M. Prunner in 1714–30, containing *frescoes* by B. Altomonte in its choir.—To the S of the village is the 15C *St. Leonardi-Kirche*.

The road now climbs between the WARSCHENECK MASSIF (2389m; W) and the *Grosser Pyhrgas* (2244m) to reach (7.5km) the PYHRNPASS (945m), the border between Upper Austria and Styria, descending from there to (8.5km) **Liezen**; see last paragraph of Rte 12A.

From Liezen, the motorway and B113 bear abruptly SE.—At 9km a right-hand turning ascends 8km to *Oppenberg*, where the church contains a remarkable carved Adoration of the Magi of c 1500 (restored), ascribed to the workshop of Erasmus Grasse of Munich.—3km *Rottenmann*, commanded by the castle of *Strechau* (c 1140), with an arcaded courtyard, has a late Gothic church with interesting vaulting.—Continuing up the PALTENTAL you reach (11km) *Trieben*.—*Dietmannsdorf*, 1.5km N, beyond the motorway, has a 12C Romanesque church with Baroque frescoes.

TRIEBEN TO JUDENBURG (48km). The B114 climbs steeply to (9km) *Hohentauern*, its 18C church containing frescoes and sculptures by J.T. Stammel. Beyond, it veers S away from the *Grosser Bösenstein* (2448m), descending the upper valley of the Pölsbach by-pass at 24km the village of *Oberzeiring* (right), formerly important for its silver-mines, and with a *Miners' Church* of c 1100 (Knappenkirche).—The church at (7km) *Pöls*, 1km left, of Romanesque origin, has a Gothic choir and Baroque furniture.—The B96 is met after 5km, some 6km W of *Judenburg*, see Rte 37.

6km *Gaishorn*, the church of which, of 1425, contains sculpture by Stammel.—The road continues to climb, with the EISENERZER ALPEN to the N, here rising to 2125m, while to the S are the SECKAUER ALPEN (2417m), at 11km reaching the SCHOBERPASS (849m). The road then descends the LIESINGTAL to (7km) *Kalwang* (left), where the church has a Nativity by Stammel. More of Stammel's sculpture can be seen in the two churches of (7km) *Mautern*.—A further 18km brings you to *St. Michael*, where *St. Walpurgis* retains some late 13C glass.—For the road SW to **Klagenfurt**, see Rte 37; for **Leoben**, 9km NE, see Rte 18B.

You now join the A9 autobahn (toll for the tunnel), which after c 7km enters the **Gleinalmtunnel** (8290m long) piercing the *Gleinalpe*, here rising to 1831m.—After c 17km the valley of the Mur is entered some 3km S of *Peggau*, for which, and the B67 onward to *Graz*, see Rte 32C. **Graz** itself is entered after 17km; see Rte 33.

B.   Via Admont and Bruck an der Mur

Total distance, 237km (147 miles). B138. 81km *Liezen*—B112. 20km **Admont**—24km *Hieflau*—B115. 16km **Eisenerz**—30km **Leoben**—B306. 12km **Bruck an der Mur**—B335. 54km **Graz**.

Maps: F&B 1, 2; BEV 48/14–15, 47/15.

For the road between Wels and *Liezen*, see Rte 18A.

Bear NE from *Liezen*, and then E down the ENNS VALLEY, with an attractive view ahead of (12km) the hilltop pilgrimage-church of *Frauenberg*, with its two conspicuous bulbous-domed towers. Built in 1683–87 on the site of an earlier church, it contains rich stucco-work, and an altar by J.T. Stammel, among other objects of interest.

After 7km turn right for **Admont** (3100 inhab.) a pleasantly sited market-town, dominated by its famous Benedictine *Abbey*, founded in 1074. The neo-Gothic *Church* (of its predecessor only one Romanesque door survives) was rebuilt in 1734 by Johann Gotthard Hayberger, and again partly rebuilt after a ravaging fire in 1865. It contains a Crib by Stammel.

SE of the church is the wing containing the sumptuous white and gilt *Library, and Museum. Stairs ascend to the former, by Josef Huber, 72m long, erected in 1774. The frescoes in its shallow vaults are painted by Bartolomeo Altomonte. Notable are the statues of carved lime-wood, bronzed (after 1726) by Josef Thaddäus Stammel of Graz (1695–1765). Several of its 1100 MSS and 900 incunabula are displayed, including Luther's Bible (Augsburg 1539, and Frankfurt 1566), a Greek and Latin New Testament edited by Erasmus (Froben; Basel 1516), a Latin Bible of 1481; a German Bible printed by Koberger of Nuremberg (1483), and the Commentaries of Irimbert von Admont, abbot in 1172–77. Some of the bindings do not appear to be well protected from the sun.

On the floor above is a collection of pewter, glass, cult objects, vestments, a bishop's ivory crook and a narwhal's horn; a good collection of 15–16C paintings; paintings of saints by Gottfried Bernard Gotz (1708–74), and among sculptures, a 17C Ecce Homo. There is also an extensive Natural History section, notably rich in insects.

Beyond (5km) *Krumau* the road begins the picturesque descent of the narrowing valley of the foaming Enns, between the *Grosser Buchstein* (2224m; N), and the fractured limestone range rising to the *Hochtor* (2369m), and here known as the *Gesäuse.—9km *Gstatterboden*, where the local hotel terrace commands a fine view S, and which is the starting-point for rambles and ascents of every variety and grade of difficulty.—10km *Hieflau*, where you bear SE up the valley of the ERZBACH, off which at 13km a left-hand turning leads shortly to the tiny *Leopoldsteiner See*, overlooked to the N by the wall of the *Kalte Mauer* (1930m).

3km **Eisenerz** (694m; 10,050 inhab.; 3850 in 1869), a large mining village below the towering *Pfaffenstein* (1871m) preserves an imposing fortified church (1279–1517) with some remarkable interior carving, some of Arragonite form; Near by is a small mining museum.

But the whole area is dominated by the rusty terraced pyramid of the *Erzberg itself, rising in a series of ziggurat-like steps to the SE to a present height of 1465m. It was 1532m until c 1870, since when surface mining has gradually eroded its peak.

The greater part of this mountain is composed of spathic iron-ore (siderite; yielding 32 per cent of iron), which has been quarried from time immemorial. Much of the ore was formerly transported by barge from Hieflau to Steyr, but now it is sent to the blast furnaces of Linz, or Donawitz near Leoben. The site may be visited in groups during weekdays, on application to the offices of the mining company—The VÖEST-Alpine-Montan AG.

The road climbs steeply to (7km) the PRÄBICHL PASS (1232m), commanded to the N by the *Polster* (1910m), providing curious retrospective views, before descending rapidly through the mining-town of *Vordernberg* to (14km) *Trofaiach*. A by-road (right) then leads across to meet the autobahn 5km N of *St. Michael*; see the latter part of Rte 18A.

The main road by-passes (right) industrial *Donawitz* to enter (9km) **LEOBEN** (32,000 inhab.; 11,050 in 1869; 25,500 in 1900), in the Mur valley. The Preliminary Peace of Leoben was signed here on 18 April 1797 between the Austrians and French. Leoben is also known for its Gösser beer.

The older enceinte lies on the neck of a meander of the river, once defended by a glacis. The central HAUPTPLATZ has two fountains and a *Pestsäule* of 1717. Near the latter is the *Rathaus* (16–18C), with its belfry. Opposite is the decorated façade of the *Hacklhaus* (16C and 1680), the *Gasthof Adler*, and the *Schönowitzhaus*. To the NE and NW respectively are the former *Dominikanerkirche*, and the stark façade of the Baroque *Stadtpfarrkirche* (formerly Jesuit) of 1660–65, by P.F. Carlone, behind which was the Jesuit College, now housing the municipal museum. A few steps to the S is the *Mautturm*, a 17C town gate and toll-house defending the bridge-head, on the far bank of which is *Maria am Waasen* (14–15C), with some good glass.—S of the enceinte stands *Hl. Jakob* (16–17C).

In the industrial suburb of **Göss** is the *Church of a former Benedictine abbey, founded in 1020 and secularised in 1782, of Romanesque origin but rebuilt in the 14th and 16Cs, and retaining its 11C crypt. Its vaulting is unusual, while the Bischofskapelle, S of the choir, is one of the earliest Gothic buildings in Styria (completed 1283), preserving contemporary frescoes.

On regaining the main road (B306), bear NE, with the *Hochalpe* (1643m) rising to the S. After c 7km you pass a right-hand turning for *Utsch*, where the church contains a notable fresco (1390) of the Crucifixion.—5km **Bruck an der Mur**, for which, and for the road onward to **Graz**, 54km S, see Rte 32C.

19 Linz

Maps; F&B 1; BEV 48/14.

LINZ, the capital of Upper Austria, the third largest city in Austria (after Vienna and Graz), with a population of 199,900 (49,650 in 1869; 115,350 in 1934), lies on the S bank of the Danube, here dominated by its Schloss, while opposite is the transpontine suburb of *Urfahr*. It is a busy industrial and commercial centre, but its Altstadt preserves several characteristic streets, and it contains two good museums. The surrounding countryside is notably attractive, and within easy reach.

Roman *Lentia* developed into an important trading centre, which belonged to the bishops of Passau from 823 until c 1190, when it was acquired by Leopold V of Babenberg. Owing to its favourable position it continued to flourish, trading in wood, salt, and the iron of Steyr, and it was for a time the residence of the Emperor Friedrich III, who died here in 1493. The place had been fortified, and in 1497 a bridge was built across the Danube. It was frequently at the centre of peasant revolts, and for some decades in the late 16C and early 17C was dominated by Protestants. In 1614 a Protestant confederation held an important general diet here. For several years before 1626 Johann Kepler, the astronomer, taught mathematics at their 'university'. Kepler's 'Harmonices mundi' were published here in 1619. In the peasants' war which started in 1626 it held out against Stefan Fadinger and Christoph Zeller, and became a reactionary bastion of the Counter-Reformation, although it only became the seat of a bishop in 1785. (In 1626 20 waggons full of Protestant books were collected in a four day house to house search, and burned by the Catholic authorities.)

Linz was visited in 1783 by Mozart, passing through from Salzburg to Vienna, who wrote to his father on 31 October: 'On Tuesday, 4 November, I am giving a concert in the theatre here and, as I have not a single symphony with me, I am writing a new one at breakneck speed, which must be finished by that time...'. This was the so-called 'Linz Symphony', K.425. The German traveller Riesbeck found Linz so prosperous at this period 'as to make the Bavarian cities appear like poorhouses in comparison'.

During the Napoleonic Wars it was three times under French occupation, in 1802, 1805, and 1809. In 1812 it was briefly visited by Beethoven, whose brother Johann was an apothecary here. In August 1819 Schubert first visited the place (his friend Josef von Spaun lived here from 1821), while Albert Stadler became secretary of the Linz Musical Society, formed in 1821, which gave Schubert a 'diploma of honour' in 1823. The composer was again in Linz in 1825, staying at Schloss Steyregg, c 5km E. In 1830, under the Archduke Maximilian d'Este, a ring of 32 defensive towers was constructed around the town by the engineer F. Zola, father of the novelist. In 1832 railway lines were laid between Linz and Budweis (now 'YCeské Budejovice) in Bohemia—at first a horse railway, converted to steam in 1873—and to Gmunden, which with the extension of its river-port facilities, made it an even more important hub of communications. Its iron-works expanded, and textile factories were established, and in 1938, chemical works, which made it the target of air-raids during the Second World War.

Johann Michael Prunner (1669–1739), the architect; General Khevenhüller (1683–1744); the controversial essayist Hermann Bahr (1863–1934); and the singer Richard Tauber (1892–1948) were born here; Adalbert Stifter (1805–68) lived here from 1848 until shortly before his death, having been for 15 years an inspector of schools. Anton Bruckner, in 1840–41; Ludwig Wittgenstein, in 1903–06; and Rainer Maria Rilke, in 1891–92, were partly educated here (the last in a 'Commercial School'); and Adolf Hitler attended the Realschule from 1900. The minnesinger Dietmar von Eist (fl. 1139–71) came from a noble family living near Linz, as did his contemporary, the lyric poet known as Der Kürnberger.

The main centre is the HAUPTPLATZ (a short distance S of the *Nibelungen Brücke*), an impressive square surrounded by tall 16–18C houses, in which stands the *Dreifaltigkeitssäule* or *Trinity Column* (1723). To the E of the platz is the *Rathaus*, altered in 1658 and several times since.

The next lane leads to the *Stadtpfarrkirche Maria Himmelfahrt*, originally Gothic, but remodelled in the mid 17C, in which, to the right of the high altar of 1772 is the red marble tomb of the Emperor Friedrich III (containing only his heart). The choir contains paintings by B. Altomonte. In the chapel of St. John Nepomuk (with a statue of that saint by Georg Raphael Donner, of 1723), lies the architect Johann Michael Prunner.

To the S is the Domgasse, flanked by the *Alter Dom* or *Jesuitenkirche*, built in 1669–78 by Pietro Francesco Carlone, and the cathedral from 1785–1909. Notable in the ornate aisleless interior are the St. Aloysius altarpiece by B. Altomonte; the richly carved stalls, from Garsten (cf.; 1633); and the organ by F.X. Krismann (from Engelszell; cf.), on which Bruckner played when cathedral organist (1856–68).

Regaining the Hauptplatz, turn left past the 17C *Weissenwolf palace* and into the Schmidtorstrasse, which leads S to the pedestrian Landstrasse, a busy shopping street.

To the left and right at this junction are the Graben and Promenade, the site of the former moat surrounding the medieval town. Nos 12 (1715) and 32 (1720) on the W side of the LANDSTRASSE, are notable, as are Nos 22 and 30, the town palaces of the abbots of St. Florian (1618), and Baumgartenberg (17C), respectively. On the E, opposite the latter, rise the twin Baroque towers of the

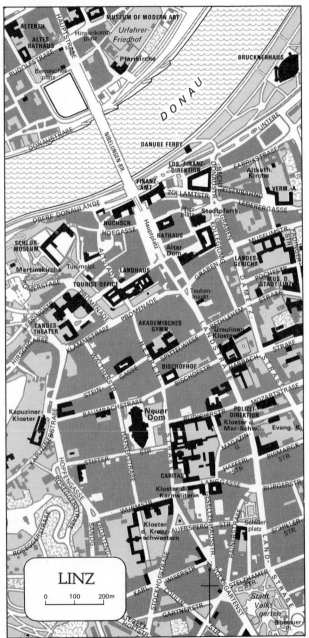

ALTERSH.
ALTES RATHAUS
MUSEUM OF MODERN ART
Hinsenkampplatz
Urfahrer-Friedhof
Pfarrkirche
BRUCKNERHAUS
HAUPTSTRASSE
RUDOLFSTRASSE
Bernaschekplatz
DONAU
DONAUSTRASSE
NIBELUNGEN-BR.
DANUBE FERRY
LDS.-FINANZ-DIREKTION
FINANZAMT
ZOLLAMTSTR.
OBERE DONAULANDE
Hauptplatz
HOCHSCH.
HOFGASSE
ALTSTADT
SCHLOSS-MUSEUM
Martinskirche
Tummelpl.
POMERSTRASSE
LESSINGSTR.
LANDHAUS
TOURIST OFFICE
PROMENADE
PROMENADE
Pfarrplatz
Stadtpfarrk.
RATHAUS
Alter Dom
Taubenmarkt
FABRIKSTRASSE
Altkath. Kirche
VERM.-A.
BLECHTSTRASSE
DONAUSTR.
EISENBAHNG
LEDERERGASSE
KOLLEGIUMG.
GRABEN
MUSEUMSTR.
PADINGERSTR.
LANDESGERICHT
POCHESTR.
MUS. D. STADT LINZ
DAMETZSTRASSE
LANDESTHEATER
HIRSCHGASSE
KLAMMSTRASSE
WALTHERGASSE
AKADEMISCHES GYMN.
HERRENSTR.
SPITTELWIESE
LANDSTRASSE
STRASSE
Ursulinenkloster
KAPUZINERSTRASSE
Kapuziner-Kloster
STEINGASSE
BAUMBACHSTRASSE
HAFNERSTR.
Neuer Dom
BISCHOFHOF
BISCHOFSTR.
HARBACHSTRASSE
MOZARTSTRASSE
RUDIGERSTR.
BETHLEHEMSTR.
POLIZEI-DIREKTION
Kloster d. Mar.-Schw.
Evang. K.
MAGAZING
BISMARCKSTR.
HOPFENGASSE
ROSEGGERSTRASSE
STIFTERSTR.
WURMSTR.
CARITAS
LANGGASSE
HAFFERLSTR.
BURGERSTR.
Kloster d. Karmeliterin
Kloster d. Kreuzschwestern
AUERSPERGSTR.
SANDG.
KROATENG.
KARL
STOCKHOFRSTR.
COULINSTR.
WISERSTR.
GARTNERSTR.
TEGETHOFFSTR.
ESSELHAUSSTR.
RAINERSTRASSE
STELZHAMERSTR.
SCHILLERPLATZ
Schillerplatz
SCHILLERSTR.
LANDSTRASSE
N. VOLKSGARTENSTR.
VOLKSGARTENSTR.
Stadt-Volks-garten
Blümauer Pl.
BAHNHOF

LINZ

0   100   200m

Ursulinenkirche Hl. Michael (1736–72), built by Johann Haslinger. A few steps further S is the *Karmeliterkirche Hl. Josef* (1674–1726), on which J.M. Prunner worked, which preserves painted altarpieces by Carlo Carlone (St. Anne), and M. Altomonte (Holy Family, and St. Albert), etc., while the stucco-work is by D.F. Carlone and P. d'Allio.

For the area W of the Landstrasse, see below.

The Harrachstrasse leads E beside the church to approach the former *Deutschordenskirche* (of the Teutonic Order), now the *Seminarkirche*, built by J.M. Prunner in 1718–25 on the plans of J. Lukas von Hildebrandt. The latter also designed the high altar, with paintings by M. Altomonte. The stucco is by P. d'Allio.

Turning left along the Dametzstrasse (crossed prior to reaching the church) we pass (right) the *City Museum* (Stadtmuseum), containing collections of furniture, models of local costumes, a View of the Hauptplatz in 1774, and a Maquette of the town in 1740. The building (1610; by Francesco Silva), later appropriated by the Jesuits, became a college for Scandinavian students, and received the name *Nordico*. Above the portal are the arms of canonised kings: Knut, Eric, and Olaf.

Further E is the *Elisabethinenkirche*, a mid 18C hospital church by Paul Ulrich Trientl, with a good dome.—Further NE is the *Francisco-Carolinum Museum*, largely devoted to Natural History.

Regaining the Landstrasse, follow the Bischofstrasse (almost opposite the Ursuline church) to the W to cross the Herrenstrasse, to the left in which is the *Barmherzigen-Brüder-Kirche* (Brothers of Charity), with its concave façade, by J.M. Prunner (1743), containing paintings by 'Kremser' Schmidt.—To the right in this street, No. 19 is the Baroque *Bischofshof*, the bishop's residence, and formerly that of the abbot of Kremsmünster, built by Franz Michael Pruckmayr in 1721–26 on the plans of Jakob Prandtauer.

Further W is the all-too-conspicuous bulk of the neo-Gothic new *Cathedral* (Maria Emfängis), erected between 1862–1924 on the plans of Vinzenz Statz, and with a 134m-high steeple. It contains two huge statues of SS Peter and Paul (1663; from Eferding), but is mainly remarkable for its size.—A short walk further W brings you to the *Kapuziner-Kirche* of 1660–61, containing the tomb of Count Raimondo Montecuccoli (died 1680), commander of the Austrian troops at St. Gotthard (cf.).

Turning N, and shortly bearing half-right along the Klammstrasse, you reach the PROMENADE, flanked by the restored S façade of the **Landhaus**. Of the early Renaissance edifice (1571) only the N wing in the Klosterstrasse remains, with its marble portal. The *Planetenbrunnen* of 1582, in an arcaded courtyard to the left of a passageway, is notable. The *Landhauskirche*, formerly that of the Minorites, was baroquised in the mid 18C, and contains a high altar with an Annunciation by B. Altomonte, and paintings by 'Kremser' Schmidt.

Opposite is a 17C mansion housing the *Tourist Office*; while a few steps to the W, on the far side of the Promenade, is the *Landestheater* of 1803, enlarged in 1958 by Clemens Holzmeister.

A short walk NW is the **Martinskirche**, restored in 1948, perhaps the oldest church in Austria, referred to in 799, but probably of pre-Carolingian origin, constructed on Roman foundations. A Gothic choir was added in the late 15C, and the W façade was later changed. It preserves some mid 15C frescoes.

A passage to the E below an arch provides an entrance to the *Schloss*; see below.

A turning left off the Altstadt (leading N from the Tourist Office), the TUMMELPLATZ, leads to the base of a ramp ascending to the **Schloss**, on a low hill overlooking the Danube, a site fortified since at least 799, acquired by Leopold V in 1190, and extended towards the end of the 15C by Friedrich III. It was virtually rebuilt by Rudolf II in the Renaissance style, but was damaged by fire in 1800, after which it was used as a military hospital and barracks, which did not improve it. During the 1960s it was restored to accommodate the provincial *Museum of Upper Austria, an impressively rich collection, tastefully displayed, and in itself well worth a visit to the city.

Rooms on the GROUND FLOOR contain the Archaeological collections, with a number of Bronze Age artefacts, jewellery of the Hallstatt period, and Roman statuettes, glass, and terra-sigillata, etc.—**RR5–6** are devoted to jewellery, etc. from the 7C AD.

FIRST FLOOR. **RR1–2** concentrate on arms and armour; notable also is a Portal from Schloss Hartheim (late 16C).—**RR3–8** display a fine collection of medieval sculpture, some polychromed, among them a Mary of Egypt, and paintings, including a Crucifixion by *Master Hans* (late 15C), a Bavarian Nativity of 1481 (the Eggelsberg altar), and a Scourging of Christ by the *Monogrammist H* (1507); also furniture and fabrics, etc.—**R9** is devoted to 19C Austria, with a display of costumes, etc., and a Portrait of Bruckner by *Hermann Kaulbach*. Also on this floor are an anon. Portrait of Graf Franz Christoph Khevenhüller, and a member of that family playing the flute.—In **RR10–12** are several notable examples of goldsmiths' work; an anon. Portrait of Kepler; *Maulbertsch*, Martyrdom of St. Barbara, and a collection of musical instruments (among them an early 17C lute, by Jakob Langenwalder, and late 17C barytons by Johann Seelos of Linz); also coins and medals.—**R13** is devoted to militaria.

SECOND FLOOR. **RR1–11** contain a notable collection of folk art of the province, with several outstanding pieces of carved and painted furniture, decorative stoves, glass, ceramics, and ironware; costumes and accessories; toys; ex-votos and religious folk art; folk instruments; dolls, puppets, and cribs.—**R12** preserves a pharmacy from Schloss Weinberg, near Kefermarkt, of 1700, etc., while other rooms contain 19C paintings (many from the collection of Walter Kastner), including several good landscapes and portraits, among them a Self-portrait of *Josef Abel* (1764–1818).

RR8–10, in the far wing, are devoted to railways (see History above), and the *Mostmuseum* (with several cider-presses, etc.), while in the courtyards are numerous sepulchral monuments of all periods.

The Hofgasse descends from the Schloss to cross a small platz, off which the Hofberg—in which Nos 4 and 17 are 16C—leads N to the river bank. The Hofgasse continues S past (No. 7) the 17C *Hohenfeld palace* to regain the *Hauptplatz* opposite the Rathaus.

Turning N, one may cross the **Nibelungen Brücke**, spanning the Danube, the near bank of which has been embellished with riverside gardens, in which—to the E—a concert-hall, etc., usually known as the **Brucknerhaus**, was built in 1969–74 by Heikki Siren, a Finnish architect.

The ***Neue Galerie der Stadt Linz** (or *Wolfgang-Gurlitt-Museum*), inaugurated in 1979, is on the first floor of a modern shopping precinct called *Lentia 2000* at Blütenstrasse 15, a turning right off the Hauptstrasse some five minutes' walk N of the bridge.

Among the more important works in the collection are: *Rudolf von Alt*, Venetian scene; *Herbert Boeckl*, Mother and child; *Lovis Corinth*, Negro, and Portrait of Wolfgang Gurlitt; *Albin Egger-Lienz*, The artist's daughter; *Thomas Ender*, View of Gmunden; *Caspar David Friedrich* (1774–1840), Moonscape; *Carl Hofer* (1878–1955), Female portrait; *Klimt*, Birchwood, Portrait of Maria Munk, and several sketches; *Kokoschka*, Father Hirsch, Friends, View of Linz, and Portraits of Marcel von Nemeš, and Theodor Körner; *Anton Lehmden*, View of Linz from the NW; *Franz von Lenbach* (1836–1905), Female portrait; *Max Liebermann* (1847–1935), Self-portrait; *Makart*, Woman in red; *Carl Moll*, The Naschmarkt and Karlskirche, Vienna, in 1894; *Kolo Moser*, Venus in a grotto; *Max Oppenheimer*, Still-life, and The Rosé Quartet; *Josef Rebell*, Neopolitan scene; *Anton Romako*, Haymaking; *Schiele*, Mother and child in a red cloak, View of Krumau, Portrait of Trude Engel, and of Heinrich and Otto Benesch; *E.J. Schindler*, Mill at Bad Goisern; *Franz Sedlacek*, Skiing scene, and The Possessed; *Wilhelm Trubner* (1851–1917), Self-portrait, and The meadow; Drawings by *Alfred Kubin*, and numerous other modern works. It is also the venue for regular exhibitions of contemporary art.

A short distance W of the Hauptstrasse is the lower station of the *Pöstlingberg*-Bahnhof, which ascends to a hill (539m), also approached by a good road, crowned by a Baroque pilgrimage-church of 1738, and providing panoramic views.—The road may be continued to the summit of the *Lichtenberg* (927m), some 14km from Linz, commanding a more extensive view.

8km W of Linz, on the S bank of the Danube, is the remarkable rococo *Church* of **Wilhering**; see Rte 16B. Also within easy reach of Linz is **St. Florian** (c 18km S); see Rte 21B.

20   Linz to Freistadt: the Mühlviertel

Total distance, 42km (26 miles). A7 and B125.

This route may be extended by Rte 23; alternatively a circular excursion through the *Mühlviertel* may be made from Freistadt W to (57km) *Rohrbach*, returning SE to (44km) *Linz*.

Maps: F&B 1; BEV 48/14, 49/14.

The autobahn heading NE is preferable to the B125, which is gained near (c 20km) *Unterweitersdorf*.

The main road continues N via (10km) *Neumarkt im Mühlkreis*, its church containing fine reticulated vaulting of c 1500, and providing attractive views to the W, but it is recommended that you fork right some 2km before the village for (7km) **Kefermarkt**. The late 15C triple-naved Gothic church of *St. Wolfgang* here preserves a remarkable carved lime-wood *altarpiece of 1490–97, which has been ascribed to Martin Kriechbaum of Passau, or Jörg Hüber, influenced by Veit Stoss of Cracow and Michael Pacher (cf. St. Wolfgang). Adalbert Stifter was responsible for its restoration in the 1850s, and it was again restored in 1959.

In the centre stands St. Wolfgang, between SS. Peter and Christopher (the latter an outstanding sculpture), while on the opened wings there are reliefs of the

*Detail of the limewood altarpiece in St. Wolfgang,
Kefermarkt*

Annunciation, Nativity, Adoration of the Magi, and the Death of the Virgin, the
whole surmounted by delicate tracery surrounding figures of the Virgin and
Child flanked by SS. Catherine and Barbara. On either side stand armed figures
of SS. George and Florian. Notable are the remains of mid 16C frescoes, the
tombstones of Christoph von Zelking (died 1491), who commissioned the
altarpiece, and the tomb of Veit von Zelking (died 1559).

Continuing N you pass hilltop *Schloss Weinburg* (restored), with its sugar-
castor tower.

The medieval *Enceinte* of (11km) **Freistadt** (6250 inhab.) is one of
the least spoilt in Austria, and has many interesting features. It is still
surrounded by a moat—now orchards and gardens—and its 14–15C
walls with their gates and towers. At the SW corner of its characteristic central HAUPTPLATZ stands *Hl. Katharina* (1288, with a choir of
1501), the interior of which was baroquised by C.A. Carlone in 1690,
and it contains, in the choir, a Martyrdom of St. Catherine by Adrien
Blomaert. The black and gilt organ-case, and remains of murals,
should be noted.

To the NE of the platz rises the 14–15C *Schloss*, with its tall keep, which houses a regional museum. Note No. 13 Waaggasse, opposite the Post Office.

For the road leading NE; see Rte 23; for that to *Rohrbach*, see below.

The B125 continues N to (16.5km) *Wullowitz*, 1.5km beyond which is the Czech frontier, and the former S border of Bohemia. *České Budějovice* (formerly *Budweis*) lies 38km further N.

From just S of Freistadt, drive NW on the B128, shortly turning left to climb to (5km) **Waldburg**, the church of which has three naive carved and painted winged altars, the high altar (1517) with the Virgin between Mary Magdalen and St. Catherine; the others are dedicated to St. Laurence, and St. Wolfgang.

The main road is regained after 2km, where we continue W.—After 5km another left-hand turning leads shortly to *Schenkenfelden*, with a Gothic church and 17C pillory. On approaching the village, an abrupt left-hand fork ascends to the huge onion-domed *Kalvarienbergkirche* (1712; by J.M. Prunner).

9km *Bad Leonfelden*, a small town overlooked to the NW by the *Sternstein* (1122m), providing a view over both the **Mühlviertel**, and N over Bohemia. To the NW is the extensive Lipenska reservoir, from which the Vltava flows.

An ALTERNATIVE return to **Linz** (27km S) may be made by following the B126, crossing the rolling Mühlviertel hills through (8km) *Zwettl an der Rodl*, with 4km W, the charming village of *Oberneukirchen*.—5km *Hellmonsödt* (left), with a church of 1441 containing a painting by B. Altomonte, and the funerary chapel of the Starhemberg family. Nearby is the *Freilichtmuseum Pelmberg*, or farm museum.—4km *Wildberg*, with a medieval castle rebuilt after a fire in 1665, which in 1198 belonged to Gundaker von Stiria, ancestor of the Starhembergs.—The *Lichtenberg* (927m) rises to the W as you descend the HASELBACH VALLEY to *Linz*.

The B128 continues to run W, over a ridge, roughly parallel to the Czech frontier, 4–5km N, descending into the valley to (17km) *Helfenberg*, near which are the castles of *Revertera* (right; 17C), and *Piberstein* (13C).—The road now winds across the hills to (12km) *Haslach an der Mühl*, its river giving its name to the region (the Mühlkreis). Among remains of fortifications is a gate-tower. The Gothic church has a separate belfry; a weaving museum (Webereimuseum) can be visited.—*Rohrbach in Oberösterreich* lies 7km W (see below).

A recommended DETOUR is that following a minor road N to (10km) **Schlägl**, with a Premonstratensian *Abbey*, founded in 1218 and rebuilt in 1630–40, the church containing sculptures by Johann Worath, a fine organ of 1634, and a collection of vestments. The abbey, recently restored, is said to preserve a good collection of paintings.—From adjacent *Aigen im Mühlkreis* (1.5km N), a track ascends towards the *Bärenstein* (1077m), commanding wide views over the Bohemian forests.—The road continues NW to (18km) *Schwarzenberg im Mühlkreis*, on the German border, overlooked to the N by the *Plöckenstein* (1378m), marking the junction of the frontiers of Austria, Germany, and Czechoslavakia.

Turning S from Schlägl, follow the B127 to (9.5km) **Rohrbach**, with a mid 16C *Rathaus*, and Baroque *Church* of 1700, by C.A. Carlone.

11km S of Rohrbach is high-lying *Altenfelden*, providing a fine view to the E, and with a church founded in 1242.

9km W, at *Lembach im Mühlkreis*, the peasants commanded by Stefan Fadinger fought the first skirmish of the revolt of 1626.—*Putzleinsdorf*, 3km beyond, retains its characteristic market-square.

2km *Neufelden*, with a small Gothic church under restoration, 2km N of which, on a height to the right, beyond a lake, stands the late 10C fortress of *Pürnstein*.—Continuing SE, at 8km a right-hand turning leads 8km to *Untermühl*, commanded by the 13C *Schloss Neuhaus*, with 16–18C additions, dominating a stretch of the Danube.—The river is reached at (16km) *Ottensheim*, with its castle and Flamboyant Gothic church. On the far bank lies *Wilhering* (see Rte 16B).— *Pesenbach* (see also Rte 16B) is c 8km due W of Ottensheim, turning E from which the N bank of the Danube is followed to (10km) *Urfahr*, the N suburb of **Linz**. The *Schloss* is conspicuous, while to the N rises the *Pöstlingberg*; see Rte 19.

21   Linz to Vienna

A.   Via the autobahn; St. Florian, Enns, and Melk

Total distance, 179km (111 miles). A7 for 7km, then A1—9km **St. Florian** exit—5km **Enns** and **Steyr** exit—32km **Amstetten** exit— 22km **Ybbs** and **Wieselburg** exit—20km **Melk** exit—22km **St. Pölten** exit (also for *Lilienfeld*)—at 28km the two branches of the motorway divide, the more northerly being the most direct approach to **Vienna**, 34km further E.

Maps: F&B 1; BEV 48/14–16.

The autobahn provides a pleasant and fast approach to Vienna from the W, commanding several wide views, particularly when crossing the ridge of hills above the S bank of the Danube. A number of exits make the approach to such sites as St. Florian very easy, but there are few places of much interest between Enns and Melk except *Ardagger Stift*, just N of Amstetten, and *Waidhofen*, 25km S of the latter; see Rte 17. Rte 21A can of course be used in conjunction with 21B.

19km (St. Florian exit). Turning right, **Markt St. Florian** (4150 inhab.) lies 3km W, an attractive village dominated by its huge monastery, the domed towers of which are seen as you approach.

The ****Abbey of St. Florian**, in Augustinian hands since 1071, is built over the tomb of St. Florian, who c 304 suffered martyrdom by drowning in the river Enns. Excavations on the site confirm that it was a Christian cemetery in the 5–6Cs. The abbey, rebuilt in the Baroque style from 1686 on the plans of Carlo Carlone, and continued after 1708 by Jakob Prandtauer, is entered from its W side by an ornate portal, decorated with sculptures, above which rises the *Bläserturm*. From the vestibule, *Stairs ascend both left and right, but they should first be seen from the *Eagle Fountain* in the courtyard, from which they have the appearance of an organ-case, with openwork panels surmounted by upper balustrades. Note also the wrought ironwork. These ascend to a series of *State Apartments*, containing good 18C furniture (including the carved 'Turkish Bed' once belonging to Prince Eugene; and that in which Bruckner died, transferred from the Belvedere). A portrait of Bruckner by C.M. Rebel is also displayed here.

Adjacent is the gallery of paintings, outstanding among which is *Albrecht Altdorfer's* colourful ***St. Sebastian Altarpiece** (completed c 1518), consisting of eight panels depicting scenes of the Passion, while on the reverse of the outer wings are four illustrating the Legend of St. Sebastian. The original paintings of the Burial and Resurrection of Christ from the predella are in the Kunsthistorisches Museum, Vienna; the others show SS. Margaret and Barbara, and Abbot Peter Maurer, who commissioned the altarpiece for St. Florian. Two paintings by *Wolf Huber*, and four anon. examples of the Danube School are also notable.

In the centre of the S wing is the *Marble Hall*, with a ceiling by Martino and Bartolomeo Altomonte, dedicated to Prince Eugene's victory over the Turks and including portraits of the prince and of Karl VI at either end of the room, above which are carved trophies.— In the E wing is the *Library*, with ceiling frescoes by B. Altomonte, preserving an important collection of c 1000 MSS and 800 incunabula.

Descend to the courtyard to approach, at the NW corner of the abbey, its *Church*, where in the crypt, below the main organ, is the sarcophagus of Anton Bruckner (1824–96). He was born at neighbouring *Ansfelden*, 14km W, and was a chorister, and later organist, of the abbey (1848–58). The church itself, completed in 1715, with its twin-towered façade, stands on the site of its Gothic predecessor. The white interior is notable for its huge half-columns, joined by arches supporting galleries, above which runs a heavy ornate (and dusty) cornice. The frescoes (1690–95) are by J.A. Gumpp and M.M. Steidl. Remarkable too is the wrought-iron grille by Joseph Messner (1698) below the carved and gilded organ-loft, with its fine *Organ* of 1770–74 by Franz Xaver Krismann; two smaller instruments by Josef Remmer (1691) are seen above the ornately carved choir-stalls.

A *Hunting Museum* may be visited in the *Jagdschloss*, a dependency of the abbey at *Hohenbrunn*, some 2km to the SW.—The road up the IPFBACH VALLEY may be followed to **Steyr**, c 22km S; see Rte 17.

On returning towards the motorway, it is preferable to join the B1 at adjacent *Asten*, and there turn right for (5km) *Enns*. On the W outskirts of Enns, in the suburb of *Lorch*, lay the Roman camp of *Lauriacum*, that of the II Legion; the harbour of their Danube fleet was at *Enghagen*, to the N of the town. (Another camp was sited just E of *Albing*, on the bank of the Danube E of the road to *Heinrichsbrun*.)

Enns (9750 inhab.), sited on a low plateau between the Danube and the river Enns to the E, received its municipal charter in 1212, and is thus the earliest of Austrian cities.

Roman *Lauriacum* stood to the NW; see above. The settlement prospered during the medieval period with the growth of the salt trade, and it was here that the 'iron road' from Eisenerz and Steyr reached the river crossing. The Enns itself formed the frontier between the Eastern March, the area colonised by the Bavarians, and that settled by the Slavs. It was near here that Charlemagne, together with Theodoric and Wagenfried, encamped before driving back the Avars in 791. The river, which here was the boundary between the American and Russian zones of occupation in 1945, is also the dividing line between Upper and Lower Austria.

Florian, a Roman administrator converted to Christianity, was martyred here in 304, being thrown into the river with a millstone tied round his neck. He was later canonised, and was invoked to protect one's own home against fire while burning down that of one's neighbour.

Approaching from the W, bear to the left just before a junction W of the centre to reach **St. Laurenz** (13–15C), built on the site of a Carolingian church, itself constructed over an early Christian basilica (370), when St. Severin, the 'Apostle of Noricum', resided there. Behind the altar a *Roman cella has been excavated, probably from the time of Caracalla. The site of the Roman forum is covered by the cemetery. Adjacent is a *Charnel-house* of 1507.

Forking right, you skirt the medieval enceinte, transferred to this site in 912, the SW wall of which was later rebuilt, partly perhaps by the ransom paid by Richard I (cf.). Entering the old town from the S you pass (left) the **Pfarrkirche Maria Schnee**, formerly that of the Minorites, a Gothic structure completed in 1300, with two aisles, the well-vaulted *Wallseer-Kapelle* of 1345, murals of 1625, and a small cloister.—Here the Wienerstrasse leads into the characteristic HAUPTPLATZ, dominated by the *Stadtturm*, a lookout tower and belfry 56m high, dating from 1568. To the E is the *Rathaus* (1547), also housing the municipal *Museum*, with notable collections of Roman remains, particularly relics of murals.

There are several 16C houses in the Linzerstrasse, leading W, while the Haupthausnerstrasse, descending to the N, leads past the *Tourist Office* (right; enquire regarding admission) to the **Frauenturm** or *Women's Tower*, preserving Gothic murals of 1320–60, and once the chapel of the Hospital of the Knights of St. John. Regrettably the four gate-towers of Enns were demolished in the 1840s.

The motorway may be regained just S of the town. It shortly veers SE and then E, providing several wide views to (33km) the Amstetten West exit (see Rte 21B).—21km *Ybbs an der Donau* lies 3km NW; see Rte 21B.

A further 20km brings you to the exit for *Melk*.

The characteristic riverside town of **Melk** (5050 inhab.), Roman *Namare*, and the *Medelike* of the Nibelungenlied (c 1200), contains a *Rathaus* of 1575, and a *Pfarrkirche* dating from 1481. But the whole is entirely dominated by the huge ochre and white S façade of the famous Benedictine *Abbey of Melk*, with its twin towers and bell-shaped dome, which now stands on the site of the Babenberg stronghold, here commanding an arm of the Danube just S of its main stream.

In 1089 it was handed over by Margrave Leopold II to the Benedictines of Lambach, whose church, destroyed by fire in 1297, was later replaced by a Gothic edifice. In 1702–49 this was rebuilt in the Baroque style from the plans of Jakob Prandtauer and completed by Josef Munggenast. The church has been restored, which the rest of the building deserves.

It is perhaps best approached from the car-park on the hill to the SE of the precinct, from which steps descend past a rococo *Pavilion* by Franz Munggenast to reach the main entrance, flanked by bastions, where the conducted tours begin. Unfortunately the monastery is too often crowded with visitors.

Crossing two courtyards, you ascend stairs at the NW corner of the second to enter a series of rooms with stucco ceilings, containing the treasures of the abbey, among which are several interesting early Views of Melk, and a good altarpiece by *Jörg Breu the Elder* (1502). The *Marble Hall*, in fact painted in red and grey stucco, with a ceiling by Paul Troger (1732), is crossed next, to reach the semi-circular exterior terrace (views; and plunging views; and of the Danube sluices), standing some 60m above the river. It also provides a closer view of the *Towers*, their superstructures rebuilt by Josef Mung-genast after a fire in 1738.

You next enter, in a parallel wing, the *Library*, also with a ceiling by Troger, containing some 300 MSS and 900 incunabula, some of which, with illuminated miniatures, are on display. From here a spiral staircase descends to the **Church**. Notable in its richly embel-lished and gilded interior of yellows and pinks, are its fluted pillars, heavy cornice, and the high altar (completed 1732), by Antonio Beduzzi, with fine statuary by Lorenzo Mattielli of SS. Peter and Paul taking leave of each other, while the central group is by Peter Widerin. The side altars, with their obelisks, date from 1732; the organ-case from 1735. Mozart, aged eleven, played on the organ at Melk. The frescoes are mostly by Rottmayr.

It is thought that the medieval poetess 'Frau Ava' (died 1127; the first known German woman writer) and the 12C poet Heinrich von Melk lived in the vicinity. Maximilian Stadler (1748–1833), the composer, was born at Melk.

For *Schallaburg* and *Mauer*, see Rte 21B; for *Krems*, Rte 22.

Regaining the motorway, continue E to (22km) the exit for **St. Pölten**; see Rte 21B.—After 13km the village of *Kirchstetten*, where W.H. Auden (1907–73) spent 15 summers, is passed (left). The poet is buried in the churchyard; the *Audenhaus* is in the Audengasse. Shortly beyond, the road provides a view (left) of *Schloss Neu-lengbach*, in which in April 1912 Egon Schiele was briefly jailed for 'pornography'. He had lived with Wally Neuzil at Au 48, *Neu-lengbach* from the previous summer.

Another 15km brings you to the 'Knoten Steinhäusl', where the motorway divides into two branches, the northerly shortly crossing part of the WIENERWALD before descending into the valley of the river Wien at 22km, the right bank of which is followed, after c 7km passing (right) *Schönbrunn* (see Rte 25L) on approaching the centre of **Vienna**.

The southerly branch (A21) bears S through the WIENERWALD, with a view (right) of the *Schöpfl* (893m), at 17km reaching the *Alland* exit.

The monastery of **Heiligenkreuz** lies 4km E (see Rte 27) on the B11 descending to *Mödling*, while 3km S is *Mayerling*, on the B305, which descends the charming HELENENTAL to (15km) *Baden*. For this area, see Rte 27.

The A21 shortly begins to climb down through the wooded E slopes of the WIENERWALD, with the belfry of *Perchtoldsdorf* (see Rte 27) conspicuous to the left, to join at 21km the A2, and veering N, enters the S outskirts of *Vienna*; see Rte 25.

B.   Via the B1 and St. Pölten

Total distance, 182km (113 miles). B1. 17km **Enns**—32km **Amstetten**—20km **Ybbs** lies 2.5km N—23km **Melk**—24km **St. Pölten**—66km **Vienna**.

Maps: F&B 1; BEV 48/14–16.

This slower route may of course be combined with Rte 21A and Rte 22.

For the road to the exits for *St. Florian*, and *Enns*, see also Rte 21A.—The B1 crosses *Ebelsberg*, on the Traun, the site of a bloody engagement between Masséna and the Austrians under Hiller, in 1809. Its Schloss exhibits arms from the 1914–18 war. A road junction is reached 6km E of **Enns**, 4km NE of which lies *St. Pantaleon*, where the Pfarrkirche preserves a primitive crypt dating from the 10th or 11C.—*St. Valentin*, 2.5km SW, has a late Gothic church containing some remarkable vaulting, among other features.

13km *Wallsee*, 4km N, overlooking the Danube, was the residence of the Archduchess Marie Valerie (died 1924), daughter of Franz Josef, after her marriage to the Archduke Franz Salvator.

At 3km fork left; the right-hand fork leads 25km SE to *Waidhofen an der Ybbs*; see Rte 17.

At 10km, just beyond the *Amstetten West* entrance to the motorway, the B119 turns left for (3.5km) **Ardagger Stift**, with the 13–14C *Church* of the abbey founded in 1049, and later baroquised, with a tower rebuilt in 1806. Notable are the stained glass in the choir depicting the legend of St. Margaret (c 1230), and the early 13C crypt, while frescoes have been uncovered in the 14C cloister.—The road goes on through *Ardagger Markt* to cross the Danube at 9km, 2km S of *Grein*; see Rte 21C.

2km **Amstetten** (22,000 inhab.; 10,300 in 1900), a small industrial town and railway junction, is of slight interest, except for the *Pfarrkirche St. Stephan*, dating from the 14C. The religious poetess Catharina Regina von Greiffenberg (née Baroness von Seyssenegg; 1633–94), was born close by. It is possible that Turkish raiding parties reached this far west prior to besieging Vienna itself in July 1683.

The B1 later passes under the motorway and runs parallel to it to (20km) a crossroad 2.5km S of **Ybbs an der Donau** (5950 inhab.), a riverside town of some character, preserving several 15C houses, and a late Gothic church provided with a belvedere, and containing a finely carved tomb of an armed knight (1358). It occupies the site of Roman *Adiuvense*, near which in c 837 the Bavarians established the fortress of *Ipsburg*.—N of the town are the hydro-electric works of *Ybbs-Persenbeug* (1957), with locks and a bridge across the Danube to *Persenbeug* on the far bank, for which see Rte 21C.

YBBS TO MARIAZELL (74km). 5km S of the Ybbs crossroads lies *Wieselburg*, with a late Gothic church of two naves and 10C choir, probably one arm of the pre-Romanesque church built around a central cupola.—Here the B25 leads up the ERLAUF VALLEY past *Mühling*, where in 1916 Egon Schiele did part of his military service working as a clerk in a prisoner-of-war camp for Russian officers. The road by-passes (9km) *Purgstall*, with a 16C *Schloss*, and Gothic church, its choir baroquised, and with a high altar of 1783.—6.5km **Scheibbs** (4500 inhab.), once important, with remains of its 16C walls and castle and several old houses near its triple-naved 15C church, which contains Baroque decoration. It was the birthplace of Johann Heinrich Schmel[t]zer (c 1620–80), the composer.—3.5km *Gaming* (see last paragraph of Rte 17) lies c 10km SW.—Forking left onto the B28, the road starts to climb parallel to the N boundary of the *Naturpark Ötscher-Tormäuer*, with the *Grosser Ötscher* (1893m) rising at its S boundary.—At 27km, after reaching a height of 1106m, you meet the B20 from St. Pölten to **Mariazell**, 20km further S; see Rte 21D.

The first left-hand turning E of the Ybbs crossroads leads shortly to *Säusenstein*, its church containing ceiling-paintings by Johann Bergl (1767), and also relics of a Cistercian abbey.—On a height to the NE, above the far bank of the Danube, stands the pilgrimage-church of *Maria Taferl*; see Rte 21C.

Continuing E on the B1, after 7km a road leads left to (3km) riverside **Pöchlarn**, near the confluence of the Erlauf with the Danube, with relics of medieval fortifications, and the residence —in the Nibelungenlied—of the legendary Margrave Rüdiger of

Bechelaren, who here received Kriemhild. The artist Oskar Kokoschka (1886–1980) was born at Regensburger Strasse 29, where a small collection of his work can be seen. The late Gothic *Church* was remodelled in 1766; the waterside *Welserturm* houses a local museum; the *Schloss* dates from 1576. The main road may be regained further E, some 8km from **Melk**, with an impressive view of the monastery on your approach; see Rte 21A.

For the roads to **Krems**, see Rte 22.

Schallaburg (not too well sign-posted) may be approached direct from Melk or *Loosdorf*. The latter lies 6km SE on the B1, with a Gothic church remodelled in the late 16C by Hans Wilhelm von Losenstein, who also built, c 4km SW, the picturesque pile of *Schloss Schallaburg next to a keep dating from c 1104.

Its triangular courtyard is surrounded by Italianate arcades of 1573, the upper storey of which is adorned with terracotta reliefs, hermae, coats of arms, masks, and busts, etc. Its rooms are frequently the site of important exhibitions.

At *Schloss Pielach*, 2km NW of Loosdorf, are restored frescoes by Johann Bergl; and 3km N of Loosdorf lies the village of **Mauer**, the site of a Roman fort (Ad Muri), its *Church*, with a choir of 1427, containing a remarkable carved limewood *altarpiece of c 1515, by an unknown artist.

It depicts the Coronation of the Virgin, below which is an adoring group. Above is Christ on the Cross, and two prophets. The bas-reliefs on the wings, by another hand, show scenes from the life of the Virgin. The Stations of the Cross, and the armed knight to the right of the altar, are notable.

Regaining the B1, continue E, at 7km passing c 4km S of the imposing ruined castle of *Hohenegg* (1594).

12km **ST. PÖLTEN** (53,000 inhab.; 14,500 in 1869; 24,500 in 1900), an industrial town and railway junction, and since 1986 the capital of Lower Austrial, contains several streets, squares, and monuments of interest in its old centre on the W bank of the Traisen.

Its site is that of Roman *Aelium Cetium* (which lay to the N of the Dom), and the Carolingian monastery of *Sancti Hipolyti* gave it its present name. It has been a bishopric since 1785. Jakob Prandtauer (1660–1726) lived here, while the architect Josef Munggenast died here in 1741. Schubert and his friend Franz von Schober visited the town in the autumn of 1821, where of three 'Schubertiads', two took place in the Bishop's palace (cf. Ochsenburg, Rte 21D). Rainer Maria Rilke was sent to the Military Academy here at the age of eleven!

The Hesstrasse leads E into the rectangular RATHAUSPLATZ, its S side flanked by the *Rathaus* of 1575, with an octagonal tower and façade of 1728. In the centre rises the *Trinity Column* of 1767–82 by Andreas Gruber, while at its NE corner stands the Baroque *Franziskanerkirche Hl. Dreifaltigkeit* of 1757–68. At the SW corner of the square is the *Karmeliterinnenkirche* (1708–12; under restoration) by J. Prandtauer, with a concave façade and a high altar by J. Lukas von Hildebrandt. Its dependencies house the *Municipal Museum*, with collections of local interest.

A few steps to the S stands the **Kirche und Institut der Englischen Fräulein** (1715–69), an order founded by Mary Ward (1585–1645). It is attributed to Prandtauer, and the church contains frescoes by B. Altomonte and Paul Troger, while one altar preserves a Virgin and Child by Lucas Cranach the Elder.—Turning left in the Linzerstrasse past its unusual façade, you shortly reach the small RIEMERPLATZ, and then follow the Wienerstrasse to the right, in which are several

18C mansions.—Crossing the HERRENPLATZ, with its *Mariensäule* of 1718, the DOMPLATZ is entered.

Its E side is dominated by the plain exterior of the **Dom 'Mariae Himmelfahrt'**, once the abbey-church of the monastery, a mid 13C pillared basilica, with a S tower of the 16C (N unfinished). The interior was radically transformed into the baroque style by Prandtauer in 1722–50, and is surprisingly rich, with lavish gilding, and a splendid organ surmounted by David with his harp. The vault frescoes and paintings in the nave are by Daniel Gran, Thomas Friedrich Gedon, and B. Altomonte, while the high altar is by Tobias Pock (1658). To the right of the choir is the 12C *Rosenkranzkapelle*.

On the NE side of the Domplatz is the *Bischofshof*, accommodated in part of the 17C monastic dependencies, with a staircase of 1727.— By passing through its arcades one may reach the HOFSTATT further E.—To the N of this small square is the Klostergasse, in which No. 15 was Prandtauer's residence.—Turning S from the square, the Wienerstrasse is regained adjacent to (left) the *Bürgerspital* (1833), opposite which is the former *Franciscan church* of 1507. At No. 41 Kremsergasse is a house built in 1899 by Josef Olbrich for Ernest Stöhr.

At Dr Karl Renner Promenade 22 is the restored *Synagogue* of 1910 together with a collection of Judaica.

For an alternative route to **Vienna**, making the short detour to *Lilienfeld*, and also for the road to *Mariazell*, see Rte 21D.

ST. PÖLTEN TO KREMS (24km); slightly more with the recommended detours. That to Herzogenburg may also be made from Pottenbrunn; see below. The valley of the Traisen here is rich in Bronze Age remains and cemeteries. Follow the B333 to the N, at 10km turning right for (4km) **Herzogenburg** (7300 inhab.), with an Augustinian *Abbey* founded in 1112 and transferred here in 1244. It was largely rebuilt by Prandtauer and Josef Munggenast in 1714–40, although the central part of the E wing was by J.B. Fischer von Erlach. The *Library* and *Art gallery*, mostly 14–15C German paintings, may also be visited. The noble *Church*, lavishly decorated with frescoes and paintings by B. Altomonte, assisted in the choir by Daniel Gran, contains a beautiful gilt and pale green *Organ-case* by Joseph Hanke (1749–52), in which the figure of David in a niche is not a statue but an illusory painting by Domenico Francia, responsible also for several other similar features.—Regaining the main road, you continue N, at 9km reaching the left-hand turning for **Göttweig** (see Rte 22B), usually visited from *Krems*, 5km N, on the far bank of the Danube, to which the road now descends; see Rte 22A.

The B1, on crossing the Traisen, bears NE to (8km) **Pottenbrunn**, where the moated 16C *Schloss* contains a remarkable *Zinnfiguren-museum*, an extensive collection of (flat) tin soldiers.

Among several maquettes are those of the Sieges of Vienna (1683), Belgrade (1717), and Lutzen (1632), and the battles of Mohacs (1526), Wien (1529), and Eger (1634). On the third floor are both flat and round figures, and maquettes of Berg Isel (1809), Kolin (1757), Sacile (1809), Leipzig (1813), and Custozza (1866), and First World War scenes.

After passing *Schloss Wasserburg*, *Herzogenburg* (see above), on the W bank of the Traisen some 5km N, can easily be visited, together with *St. Andrä*, on the E bank, an Augustinian church of 1160, baroquised in 1725–29 and with frescoes by Troger. Bear E from here towards Gutenbrunn.

At 5km a left-hand fork leads 5km NE to **Heiligenkreuz-Gutenbrunn**, with a rococo *Schloss* containing a notable staircase, and frescoes by Paul Troger, while the handsome mid 18C *Kirche Mariae Himmelfahrt* preserves frescoes by Maulbertsch. The

Niederösterreichisches Barockmuseum may also be visited.—The B1 may be regained 6km SE.

At *Perschling* (18km from Pottenbrunn), with a Posthouse of 1825, you pass *Murstetten* (4km SE), in the church of which is the Althan monument by Alexander Colin (1578). After another 10km, turn right at *Mitterndorf*, 1km NW of which is *Schloss Atzenbrugg*, where in c 1820 several 'Schubertiads' took place.—After 4km the left-hand fork off the B1 leads 11km NE to *Tulln*, whence the B14 follows the right bank of the Danube to Vienna via *Klosterneuburg*; see Rte 30.— The B1 continues E, after 9km climbing SE (views over the Danube valley) into the WIENERWALD, with the *Troppberg* (542m) rising to the S, and the *Tulbingerkogel* (494m) to the NE.—At 6km *Mauerbach* lies 3km E, with the early 17C buildings of a former Carthusian monastery, founded in 1313 and dissolved in 1782. It is now a training centre for craftsmen in various fields.

5km *Purkersdorf*, with a *Sanatorium* designed by Josef Hoffmann in 1904 at Weiner Strasse 74. The A2 is met 4km beyond. This is followed along the right bank of the river Wien, passing (right) *Schönbrunn* (see Rte 25L) on approaching the centre of **Vienna**.

C. Via Mauthausen, Grein, and Melk

Total distance, 193km (120 miles). B3. 25km *Mauthausen*—33km *Grein*—45km **Melk**—B1. 24km **St. Pölten**—66km **Vienna**.

Maps: F&B 1; BEV 48/14–16.

Shortly after crossing to the N bank of the Danube, *Steyregg* is entered, where stood a Schloss (1788; demolished 1966) visited by Schubert in 1825, when it belonged to Count Weissenwolff. His wife Sophie Gabriele, Countess Breuner, a contralto, was an enthusiastic supporter of the composer, and held 'Schubertiads' there.

After 22km a left-hand turning climbs in 2km to **KZ Lager**, the former Nazi concentration camp, parts of which have been preserved as a memorial of man's inhumanity to man.

It was the notorious main camp in German-occupied Austria, established in August 1938, and liberated by the 3rd Division of the US Army on 7 May 1945. During this period some 320,000 prisoners (mainly political) were incarcerated here, of whom only 80,000 survived. A museum of photographs and documents may be visited (an explanatory booklet in English is available), and numerous monuments may be seen above the track leading to the 186 steps descending to the 'Wiener Graben', a granite quarry in which over 2000 prisoners were put to work daily.

2km The old centre of the small town of **Mauthausen** itself (4350 inhab.), whose name is regrettably overshadowed by such tragic associations, in fact preserves several attractive features, both near the MARKTPLATZ (to the N of which is the 15C *Church* and 13C circular *Charnel-house*), and on the Leopold-Heindl-Kai, where the *Schloss Pragstein* (1491) houses a local museum.

Immediately to the E a bridge spans the Danube, for **Enns**, 7km SW; see Rte 21A. Keeping to the N bank, the road shortly veers away from the river, here flanked by the fertile MACHLAND, at 5km passing a left-hand turning for (3km) moated *Schloss Schwertberg* (16C).— 5km *Perg* is reached, and 6km beyond, *Arbing*, its church with a turreted tower.

4km **Baumgartenberg**, where S of the railway are relics of the once-influential Cistercian abbey, founded in 1141 by Otto von Machland, devastated during the Hussite wars (1428–32), and suppressed in 1784. The *Church*, entered from the E, contains ornate stucco-work, and intricately carved 17C stalls.—6km SW, at *Mitterkirchen im Machland*, there are concentric earthworks.

On regaining the main road, the first left-hand turning climbs to the picturesque fortress of *Klam, raised in the 12C by Otto von Machland, which in 1487 held out against Mathias Corvinus. August Strindberg lived here in 1895–96. It contains a small museum.

The B3 shortly approaches the Danube, where the thickly wooded valley, known between here and Persenbeug as the STRUDENGAU, narrows. After 11km (from Baumgartenberg) the river is crossed by a bridge to *Ardagger*, on the far bank; see Rte 21B.

2km **Grein** (2800 inhab.), a pleasant riverside village dominated by the *Greinburg*, a castle of 1493, enlarged in the early 17C, and passing to the Saxe-Cobourg-Gotha family in 1823. Its restored three-storeyed courtyard is imposing, and a museum devoted to Danube navigation, etc. may be visited.—In the small STADTPLATZ, the *Rathaus* of 1562 preserves its former salt-warehouse, which in 1790 was converted into a rococo *Theatre*. Adjacent is the 16C *Blumensträussl*, beyond which is the *Pfarrkirche*, a Flamboyant Gothic building with a baroquised belfry, and containing a painting by B. Altomonte.

The next left-hand turning (B119) leads 29km N to *Königswiesen*, in the unfrequented WEINSBERGER WALD, possessing a remarkable late Gothic *Church* containing outstandingly beautiful *vaulting.

The B3 next passes the island of *Wörth* in the Danube, here dominated by the ruins of *Werfenstein*, the legendary home of Ute, Kriemhild's mother, in the Nibelungenlied. The rapids known as the *Strudel* may be seen before passing *St. Nikola an der Donau* to (7km) *Sarmingstein*, with castle ruins.

6km N, at **Waldhausen im Strudengau**, is the *Church* of the former Augustinian monastery of *Silvia Domus*, founded in 1161 and suppressed in 1792. It was built in 1650–93 by Carlo Canavale and Christof Colomba, with remarkable stucco-work by G.B. Carlone, and frescoes by the Grabenberger brothers. The organ of 1677 by Nikolaus Rummel is also notable. The *Pfarrkirche* dates from 1610–12.

The main road continues to skirt the steep wooded banks of the Danube to (15km) *Persenbeug*, opposite *Ybbs* (see Rte 21B), site of hydro-electric works, completed in 1957. The *Schloss*, referred to in 863, was rebuilt in the early 17C, and in 1800 acquired by Franz II; Karl I (1887–1922), the last Emperor of Austria, was born there.

The B3 now bears NE across a meander of the Danube to (7km) *Marbach an der Donau*, with a 16C *Rathaus* and 15C Church. From here a by-road ascends steeply to (3.5km) **Maria Taferl**, a village commanding a wide view and known for its conspicuous twin-towered pilgrimage-*Church* of 1660–1711, on which Georg Gerstenbrand, Carlo Lurago, and Prandtauer worked. Its restored frescoes are by Antonio Beduzzi; the pulpit of 1727, by Matthäus Tempe, is notable.

The main road may be regained by descending to the E, off which a left-hand lane leads shortly to **Schloss Artstetten**, with its four onion-domed towers, rebuilt in the second half of the 16C, and remodelled by Archduke Franz Ferdinand, who with his morganatic wife Sophie Chotek, Duchess of Hohenburg, was assassinated at Sarajevo on 28 June 1914.

As his wife could not be buried in the Imperial vault at Vienna, and as he had stated in his will that he wished to be buried with her in the crypt he had himself prepared at Artstetten, they were discreetly brought by train to Pöchlarn and were ferried across the Danube at midnight during a thunderstorm....

From Marbach the B3 leads up a stretch of the valley known as the NIBELUNGENAU to (12km) *Weitenegg*, with a fine view ahead across the river towards *Melk* on its commanding height above the far bank.

The Gothic church at *Weiten*, 9km up the valley of the same name, preserves notable 14–15C glass; 8km beyond lies *Pöggstall*, also with a Gothic church, containing a carved 15C altarpiece, and with a massive keep to its 16C Schloss.

Schloss Luberegg is passed before reaching (4km) *Emmersdorf*, with several attractive houses and a good church of 1458–1590, beyond which a bridge now spans the Danube, providing access to **Melk**, for which, together with the A1 autobahn, and B1, see Rte 21A. For the road to *Vienna* via **Krems** on either bank of the river, see Rte 22.

D. Via St. Pölten, Lilienfeld, and Hainfeld

Total distance, 206km (128 miles). A1. 117km to the **St. Pölten** exit—B20. 15km for the crossroads 5km N of **Lilienfeld**—B18. 13km *Hainfeld*—19km B11.—8km *Alland*, 2km beyond which is the A21 motorway for (32km) **Vienna**.

Maps: F&B 1; BEV 48/14–16.

For the road from Linz to the St. Pölten exit, see Rte 21A, and for **St. Pölten** itself, Rte 21B.

The B20 leads due S up the TRAISEN VALLEY from the autobahn, passing (left) at 5km **Schloss Ochsenburg**, a late 14C castle of the bishops of St. Pölten, later baroquised.

Schubert and his friend Franz von Schober (who was related to Johann Nepomuk, Ritter von Dankesreither, the then bishop), spent part of the autumn of 1821 here, working on the opera 'Alfonso and Estrella'. Schober, writing to their mutual friend Josef von Spaun, observed that 'At Ochsenburg we were much taken up with the truly beautiful surroundings, and at St. Pölten with balls and concerts; in spite of which we worked hard, especially Schubert, who has done nearly two acts, while I am on the last'.

4km *Wilhelmsburg* is by-passed prior to reaching the turning for *Lilienfeld*, 5km S, beyond which the village of *Traisen*.

Dominating the charmingly sited village of **Lilienfeld** (3000 inhab.) is the Cistercian **Abbey**, founded in 1202 by Leopold VI of Babenberg, with 17C dependencies surrounding its late Romanesque church, completed 1263. The monastery was devastated by fire in 1810, and damaged during the Second World War, but has since been renovated.

The baroquised façade of the *Church*, approached through an outer courtyard, is entered by a Gothic portal. Notable in the interior (83m long, 21m wide, and 24.5m high—the largest in Lower Austria) are its pink and black Türnitz marble Baroque altars, the black and gilt organ-case, and the crossing, below which is the tomb of the founder (died 1230). Also buried here are his daughter Margarete, and Zimburgis von Masovien (died 1429; wife of Duke Ernst der Eiserne, and grandmother of Maximilian I). The painting of the Assumption on the high altar is by Daniel Gran. The octagonal piers with their capitals in the polygonal choir, and the three Baroque altars in the apse, are remarkable. The left aisle is adjoined by a Gothic *Baptistery*; from the right aisle enter the beautiful *Cloister* (1230–60), on the E side of which is the *Chapterhouse*, its vaulting supported by four squat pillars; the octagonal *Lavatory* dates from 1886. To the W of the cloister is a *Refectory* at a lower level. Steps ascend (left) to the charming *Library* of 1700, with colourfully painted flat vaults, and containing some 226 MSS, including abbot Ulrich's 'Concordantiae Caritatis' (1351). One of its abbots was Ladislaus Pyrker, a patron of Schubert, who dedicated three lieder to him.

Lilienfeld gives its name to a method of skiing invented in 1905 by Matthias Zdarsky (1856–1940); a *Skiing Museum* may be visited.

For the road E from the junction 5km N, see below.

LILIENFELD TO MARIAZELL (56km). The B20 continues S up the verdant TRAISEN VALLEY, at 6km forking right, with the *Muckenkogel* (1248m) rising to the E, and W, the *Hohenstein* (1195m), later climbing steeply below the *Tirolerkogel* (1377m; left) to (32km) *Annaberg* (976m), descending, with a view ahead of the grand pyramidal bulk of the *Ötscher* (1893m) to the W, and after 4km meeting the B28 from *Scheibbs*; see p 195. The road again ascends through the hamlet of (8km) *Josefsberg* (1028m), and then climbs down towards (right) the narrow *Erlauf Stausee*, to enter Styria at (7km) *Mitterbach*, where a cable-car, near by, ascends to the summit of the *Gemeindealpe* (1626m).—Further SW is the *Erlaufsee*, a small mountain tarn.

5km **Mariazell** (868m; 1950 inhab.), overlooked from the NE by the *Bürgeralpe* (1266m), reached by cable-car. The large village, both a winter and summer resort, beautifully sited in a wide upland valley surrounded by wooded mountains, may conveniently be termed the 'Lourdes of Austria', although the much older cult of the 'Virgin of Mariazell' or 'Magna Mater Austriae' has been established here since 1157.

In this year Benedictines from the abbey of St. Lambrecht founded a priory, which Margrave Heinrich I of Moravia replaced by a church. By the early 14C it had become an important centre of pilgrimage, Louis I, King of Hungary (died 1382) attributing his victory over the Turks in 1377 to the intervention of its Virgin, and the early Italian painting of the Madonna enshrined in silver, and now in its treasury, was formerly his. Haydn composed the two 'Missa Cellensis' for the church in 1766 and 1782 respectively.

The present **Basilica**, dating from the 14C, was enlarged in 1644–83 by Domenico Sciassia, when it was re-consecrated. The exterior is notable for the Gothic spire flanked by Baroque towers, while the W portal preserves its tympanum of 1438, on either side of which are statues of the founders (Heinrich and Louis). The *interior*, 84m long, has elaborate stucco-work in its vault, sustained by tall square piers. In the centre of the nave is the *Gnadenkapelle*, with a silver altarpiece designed by J.E. Fischer von Erlach (1727), and behind the silver grille, the gift of Maria Theresia and her consort, the venerated 12C image of the Virgin and Child. Beyond the crossing, lit by an oval cupola, is a tall marble column of 1682 surmounted by a 16C image of the Virgin.

The *high altar*, designed by J.B. Fischer von Erlach, is in the form of a large terrestial globe encircled by a snake, the whole covered with silver leaf. Above a group depicting Christ crucified hover angels among clouds, etc. Steps ascend to the *Treasury*, containing a rich collection of cult objects, reliquaries, ex-votos, a carved cedar-wood Cross from Mt. Athos (1531), and statuary. Also notable are the iron grilles to the side-chapels; the organ-loft of 1740, and organ (in part dating from 1689); and the tomb of Card. Mindszenty (died 1975).

For the road to *Mürzzuschlag*, c 50km SE, see p 349, in reverse.

MARIAZELL TO BRUCK AN DER MUR (61km). The B20 continues S, with a view of the *Zeller Staritzen* (1619m) ahead, at 5km forking left, and later climbs past *Brandhof*, where after 1829 the Archduke Johann lived with his wife Anna Plochl (cf. Bad Aussee). A hunting museum may be visited here. To the W rises the *Hochschwab* (2277m); to the E the *Veitschalpe* (1981m). Crossing at 16km the SEEBERGSATTEL (1253m) you descend in zigzags through *Seewiesen* to (15km) *Grassnitz*, with a satellite telecommunication station (1979 by Gustav Peichl). Shortly beyond, *Aflenz*, a small resort, is by-passed to the right. Its 12th and 16C church preserves curious capitals and a Romanesque Crucifix.—7km **Thörl**, with iron-works, and commanded by *Schloss Schachenstein* (1471), has an unusual carved *Calvary* of 1530 in a wayside chapel, and its *Pfarrkirche* contains late 15C frescoes.—You now descend the THÖRLBACH to (12km) industrial *Kapfenberg*, on the B306, and turn right for (6km) **Bruck an der Mur**; for both of which see Rte 32C.

From the junction 5km N of Lilienfeld, the B18 turns E along the valley of the Gölsen, which separates the WIENERWALD from the limestone fore-alps (right), passing through several villages with Gothic and Baroque churches, among them (13km) *Hainfeld*, 7km beyond which the road passes below (right) the ruins of 12C *Araburg*, destroyed in 1683. It was at an inn at Hainfeld that the Social Democrat party was founded in December 1888.

At 10km **Kleinmariazell** lies 2km N, with the former Benedictine *abbey* (founded 1136; dissolved 1782), a Romanesque basilica baroquised in the mid 18C, with frescoes, etc. by Johann Bergl. Its Romanesque N portal is reached by turning left and left again from the main entrance.—A minor road leads NW towards the *Schöpfl* (893m), the highest point in the Wienerwald.

2km beyond this turning, the right-hand fork leads 20km SE to join the A2 motorway S of Baden, at 5km passing S of *Neuhaus*, with a 17C *Schloss*, and (5km) *Pottenstein*, where in the 17C *Zum goldenen Hirschen* died the actor and playwright Ferdinand Raimund (1790–1836). Industrial **Berndorf** (8150 inhab.) is entered 2km beyond.—7km S of Berndorf is the imposing lakeside Gothick Schloss of *Hernstein*, built by Theophil Hansen in 1856–80; adjacent are castle ruins of 1125.

The left-hand fork 2km E of the Kleinmariazell turning climbs NE to **Hafnerberg**, with a restored pilgrimage-church of 1729–35 by Daniel Dietrich, containing notable rococo decoration, pulpit, and an organ of 1767 by A. Pliegler.—On reaching *Alland* there is the choice of turning right past *Mayerling* to (17km) *Baden* via the HELENENTAL; following the B11 to *Mödling* via *Heiligenkreuz*; or joining the A21 motorway for **Vienna**; see the latter part of Rte 21A, and Rte 27.

22 Melk to Vienna via Krems: the Wachau

A. Via the North Bank of the Danube

Total distance, 113km (70 miles). B3. 30km **Dürnstein**—6km *Stein*—
3km **Krems**—31km. **Tulln** lies 3km S—10km *Stockerau*—S3 and
A22. 32km **Vienna**.

Maps: F&B 1; BEV 48/15–16.

On crossing the river at **Melk** (see Rte 21A, and also last part of Rte
21C) you turn right and pass through the narrow craggy defile of the
Danube to Krems known as the *WACHAU, with its occasional
vineyards, and apricot orchards in blossom in early April. Several
small ferries cross the river on this stretch, with its banks followed by
tow-paths. *Schloss Schönbühel* is shortly seen on the far bank, as you
approach (8km) *Aggsbach Markt*.

A lane climbs to (7km) **Maria Laach**, where the late Gothic church contains the
fine tomb of Johann Georg III von Kuefstein (died 1603), by Alexander Colin,
and by the choir wall, that of Anna von Kuefstein; also a painting of the Virgin
(whose right hand has six fingers), and a high altar of 1480.—Some 7km further
N is the *Jauerling* (960m), the highest point of the Wachau (view).

Above the far bank stand the ruins of the castle of *Aggstein* (see Rte
22B) as at 3km the village of *Willendorf* is passed, where in 1906 the
Palaeolithic figure known as the 'Venus of Willendorf' was found,
now in the Natural History Museum, Vienna.—You pass through
Schwallenbach, with a characteristic church tower, and reach (5km)
Spitz an der Donau, an attractive village preserving several 16–18C
houses, overlooked from the SW by the ruined castle of *Hinterhaus*.
The 15C *Church* contains, on the organ-balustrade, carved and
painted figures of Christ and the Apostles of 1380.

At *Oberrana*, above *Mühldorf*, 6km W, is the interesting *Burgkapelle St. Georg*,
of 1125, its crypt preserving primitive capitals.

The valley widens at (3km) *St. Michael*, with a church of ancient
origin, but rebuilt in the mid 15C and altered by Cipriano Biasino in
the 17C, with a crenellated tower, and a cylindrical keep adjacent.
  3km **Weissenkirchen** retains a fortified church approached by
covered steps, and several 16C mansions. Among them is the
Teisenhofer Hof, with a characteristic arcaded courtyard, housing the
Wachaumuseum, with its 18C winepress, and collections of paintings, mostly of local views by local artists. The white wine of the
district, particularly that of the vineyards of *Ritzing*, referred to in
1301, is said to have given its name to Riesling.
  The road now follows a wide bend of the river to (6km) **Dürnstein**,
with a picturesque view of it on the approach. The main road tunnels
below the village (1050 inhab.), which is entered by a left-hand fork.
Its ruined 12C castle, dismantled in 1645 by the Swedes, and from
which town walls extend from the S and W, dominates the place.

Richard I of England, 'Lionheart', 'Coeur-de-Lion', or 'Löwenherz' (1157–99), on
his long journey home after 16 months of crusading, was wrecked at Aquileia,
NW of Trieste. He then decided to cross Carinthia and Austria in disguise to
reach the territory of his brother-in-law Heinrich of Saxony, but near Vienna
was recognised and led before Duke Leopold V of Austria, whom he
had offended at Acre. Leopold, accusing him of the murder of Conrad of

Montferrat, imprisoned him in the fortress of Durnstein from December 1192 until the following March, when he was handed over to the Emperor Heinrich VI. Richard was not released by the latter until March 1194, and then only on the payment of a huge ransom and an oath of vassaldom. That his faithful minstrel Blondel is said to have discovered him here, is a fiction.

At the N end of the narrow Hauptstrasse is the early 17C *Schloss*, now a luxury hotel, its garden providing a fine *view over the Danube. Further S is the former Augustinian **Monastery**, founded in 1410 and rebuilt in 1710–40 by Matthias Steinl and Josef Munggenast after the plans of Prandtauer. The imposing S portal, theatrical cloister, and Baroque tower with its corner obelisks, are notable, the latter, again in pale blue and white, being restored in 1985–87, as were the stucco reliefs embellishing the vault of the *Church*, which contains works by 'Kremser' Schmidt.

A few steps further S is the former *Klarissinnenkloster*, with a choir of c 1300. Beyond, on the far side of the main street, are relics of the former church of *Hl. Kunigunde* (13C), with an adjacent *charnel-house* (14C).

To the SE of the village is the restored *Kellerschlössl*, built in 1714 by Prandtauer for Abbot Übelbacher, with good frescoes and stucco-work, and the extensive cellars of the former abbatial vineyards.

It was at *Loiben*, between Dürnstein—good retrospective views on leaving—and (6km) *Stein*, that the French force, under Mortier, defeated the large Austrian and Russian army, commanded by Kutúsov, on 11 November 1809. This bloody engagement was described by Tolstoy in Book II of 'War and Peace'.

Stein is an ancient walled river-side town. It has fortified entrance-gates at either end of its long Landstrasse, in which are preserved several 16C mansions, and retains a number of charming squares, among them the SCHÜRERPLATZ, and further E, the RATHAUSPLATZ, where Mozart's first cataloguer, Ludwig von Köchel (1800–77) was born. Just E of the latter is the baroquised *Pfarrkirche Hl. Nikolaus* (15C), with an earlier choir, and containing works by Johann Martin Schmidt (1718–1801), better known as 'Kremser' Schmidt, the artist of innumerable religious paintings of variable merit, who had his home at Stein, although born at neighbouring *Grafenwörth*.

Steps climb steeply from its apse to the smaller *Frauenbergkirche* (1380), with a lofty tower (twice painted by Egon Schiele) and providing a distant view of the palatial monastery of *Göttweig* on a height some way S of the river; see Rte 22B. In the MINORITENPLATZ, off the Landstrasse further E, is the 13C *Minoritenkirche*, once used as a tobacco warehouse, and now for exhibitions. Adjacent to the *Kremser Tor* is the *Göttweiger Hof*, with a chapel of c 1300.

Crossing the suburb of *Und*, where the dependencies of an early 17C monastery have been converted into a wine-tasting establishment, gardens are reached. At their NE corner is the late 15C **Steiner Tor**, the W gateway to medieval Krems, surmounted by an octagonal Baroque belfry (1754), flanked by cylindrical towers capped by pepperpot roofs.

KREMS (23,050 inhab., with *Stein*), once apparently famous for its mustard and gunpowder, grew up around a 10C fortress erected at the confluence of the Danube and the small river Krems. Although it has recently been much extended to the E, the old enceinte is relatively unspoilt, and has been the object of tasteful restoration.

The long LANDSTRASSE (largely a pedestrian precinct) bisects the

area from W to E. In it are a number of 16–17C houses, including the
Alte Post (No. 32; 1584), with a charming courtyard. On the S side of
the street is the *Bürgerspitalskirche* of 1470, containing sculptures by
Matthias Schwanthaler (1680); further E is the *Rathaus*, mid 16C but
altered in the 18th.

S of the next intersection is the mid 12C *Göglhaus* (altered in the
early 16C), with its oriel window, beyond which is the DREI-
FALTIGKEITSPLATZ, with a *Trinity Column* of 1738 by J.M. Götz.

Some distance E of the Rathaus is the small MOSERPLATZ.

By turning left just before this you enter the HOHER MARKT, where
No. 1, built in 1722, is occupied by the *Institut der Englischen
Fräulein* (cf. St. Pölten). The *Herkulesbrunnen* dates from 1682.—
From the SW corner of the platz, near the 12C and 16C '*Gozzoburg*'
the short Margarethenstrasse leads into the PFARRPLATZ (another
market-place), flanked by the **Pfarrkirche Hl. Veit**.

Romanesque in origin, but rebuilt in the early Baroque style by
Cipriano Biasino in 1616–30, it contains frescoes by 'Kremser'
Schmidt, and a high altar by Johann Georg or 'Wiener' Schmidt
(1734); others are by M. Altomonte and Maulbertsch. The pulpit and
other furniture is by J.M. Götz; the organ is notable.

From its N side, covered steps ascend to the late Gothic
Piaristenkirche, which dominates the town, with its steeply gabled
roof and turreted W lookout-tower. Its nave and side-aisles are of
equal height; the altarpieces are all by 'Kremser' Schmidt; several
Baroque statues, and also the organ, deserve notice.

From the SW corner of the Pfarrplatz you enter the THEATERPLATZ,
so-named because the former *Dominikanerkirche*, on its N side,
disaffected since 1785, was from 1826 used as a theatre. Built in 1265,
and with a 14C choir, it now accommodates a good **Historisches
Stadtmuseum** (entrance to the W).

Relics of murals will be seen in the vaults. Among the sculptures are examples
from the Mauterner altarpiece of 1625; some curious naked saints being boiled
alive, of c 1520; a model for an altar by Josef Matthias Götz (1739); also a
Portrait of Magdalena Kappler (1544), with on the reverse the Kappler family
tree—a vine; and naive paintings by Andre Stragl (1515), paintings and
engravings by Martin Johann Schmidt ('Kremser' Schmidt; 1718–1801), including a Self-portrait; and sculpture by Jakob Christoph Schletterer (1756). In the
cloister are collections of wood and metal-work, pewter, arms, furniture, glass,
etc., and models of Danube shipping; old views of Krems, and a maquette of the
town of 1745. A *Wine museum*, with old presses and carved butts, is also housed
here, together with small collections of the archaeology of the region, and
modern art, displayed on the first floor.

Crossing the KÖRNERMARKT, with several attractive façades, among
them Nos 4, and 14, the former Dominican library, follow the short
Schmidgasse to regain the *Steiner Tor*.

For **Göttweig**, some 5km S, see Rte 25B. For the road to **Zwettl**, 52km NW, Rte
23, in reverse, and also for the churches of *Imbach* and *Senftenberg*, both of
interest, the former 6km from Krems.

KREMS TO HORN (40km). The B218 leads NE through (4km) *Gneixendorf*, where in 1819 Johann van Beethoven bought the property of
Wassenhof. It was visited by his brother Ludwig (29 September–1
December 1826), just before his last illness, and here he completed
his last Quartet, in F major, Opus 135, and wrote the alternative
finale to that in B flat, Opus 130.—At Stratzing, just to the
NW, was found the so-called 'Tanzenden Venus' or 'Venus von

Galgenberg', a diminitive figure, some 7.2 cm in height, dated c 30,000 BC, now in the Natural History Museum, Vienna.

6km **Langenlois** (6450 inhab.), a town of ancient foundation, and a centre of the local wine trade, lies on the Loisbach stream, to the S of which is the HOLZPLATZ and mid 13C *Pfarrkirche*. From here the *Rathaus* (1728) is passed to reach the characteristic KÖRN PLATZ, with its 16C houses and *Pestsäule* of 1713. Several other façades of interest may be seen in the cross street to the N.—At *Gobelsburg*, c 2km SE, is an 18C *Schloss* containing features and collections of interest, notably of furniture and ceramics. There is an imposing ruined castle at *Kronsegg*, 7km NW, while at *Strass im Strassertal*, some 6km E, is a good church of 1638.

Continuing N from Langenlois on the B34, you climb the KAMPTAL, passing several ruins and the old castle of *Buchberg am Kamp*, restored to house a collection of modern art. After 21km you reach **Gars am Kamp** (3750 inhab.), with a baroquised 13–15C *Church* and Gothic *Charnel-house*, overlooked by the ruins of its 11C and 18C fortress. Franz von Suppé spent the summers of 1876–95 here.—At *Thunau*, to the SW, is a reconstructed 9–10C fortification near an excavated cemetery.—4km **Rosenburg**, a village commanded by its *Schloss* on a thickly wooded height to the SW. Of ancient foundation, it was enlarged in the late 15C, and later given a Renaissance character. It was the scene of a massacre in 1620, and as a base of the 'Horner Bund' it became a centre of Lutheranism in N Austria. It was reconstructed in the mid 19C and is to be restored. The so-called *Turnierhof* or Tilt-yard dates only from the 17C, and was no more than an outer court in which *carrousels* and mock tourneys took place.—For **Altenburg**, 5km NW, see Rte 24A; also for **Horn**, 6km NE.

The B3 leads due E from Krems, at 15km passing 3km SE of the restored *Schloss Grafenegg*, largely neo-Gothicised in the mid 19C, and the venue of occasional exhibitions. Grafenegg was the birthplace of Johann Fischbach (1787–1871), the artist.—The main road later veers SE, with a view on the far bank of the Danube of an atomic power-station at *Zwentendorf*, an expensive folly, for after a referendum it was never put to use. A Roman fort stood in the neighbourhood. Beyond rises the WIENERWALD.

23km *Tulln* lies 3km S, on the right bank of the river, and the roads from here to Vienna—see below—are attractive alternatives to the B3, which after 10km meets the S3 motorway just W of **Stockerau**. For Stockerau and for the road along the N bank of the Danube, see Rte 24A, in reverse.

TULLN TO VIENNA (35–40km, depending on which road is followed). **TULLN** (11,250 inhab.), known as *Comagena* by the Romans, who had a river-port there (and a fort just N of the Pfarrkirche), and as *Tulne* in the Nibelungenlied, to which Attila came to meet his bride Kriemhild, was a Babenberg residence from the 11C. In 1683 it was the rendezvous of the allied forces converging to raise the Turkish siege of Vienna, from which on 9 September they broke camp, and deploying in four widely separated columns, pushed S into the Wienerwald, dislodging Turkish outposts on its crest on the 11th; see also pp 232; 234. Egon Schiele, the artist, was born here (1890–1919), above the railway station where his father was station-master. A museum devoted to the artist is at No. 72 Donaulände.

Among its main surviving monuments are the *Pfarrkirche*, a Romanesque basilica, altered to Gothic in 1486–1513, and baroquised in the mid 18C. Its Romanesque W door includes carved busts of the apostles, and is surmounted by a double-headed eagle grasping Turks' heads in its talons. The spacious interior has ogival vaulting, while the high altar depicts the Stoning of Stephen, by Josef Steiner.—The adjacent polygonal *Charnel-house*, with an apse, and circular interior preserving frescoes, is an imposing late Romanesque edifice of 1260.—The *Minoritenkirche*, rebuilt in the 1730s, has a rococo interior.

There are several alternative roads which may be taken from here: the B213, leading S to meet the B1 at 10km, 12km NW of *Purkersdorf*, providing the most rapid approach to Vienna from the W; and that leading SE through (9km) *Königstetten*, to the E of which climbing right (views) across the WIENERWALD, descending towards Vienna from the NW.

There is also the B14, which leads E through *Zeiselmauer* site of another Roman fort, with a view ahead of *Burg Greifenstein* (12C or earlier, and several times rebuilt) overlooking the Danube, to (21km) **Klosterneuburg** (see Rte 30), skirting the river to enter the capital from the N.

B. Via the South Bank of the Danube, and Göttweig

Total distance, 111km (69 miles). B33. 11km *Aggstein Dorf*—23km *Mautern*. **Göttweig** lies 5km SE.—*Stein* and **Krems** lie on the far bank of the Danube. Descending from Göttweig, the S33 is followed E to (15km) *Traismauer*—B43. 16km *Mitterndorf*—B1. 25km *Purkersdorf*—16km **Vienna**.

Maps: F&B 1; BEV 48/15–16.

From **Melk**, the narrow right or S bank is followed through a stretch of the steep-sided river-valley known as the *WACHAU, while to the E, between the Danube and the Traisen, is a high-lying wooded district known as the DUNKELSTEINERWALD.

6km *Schönbühel*, with a fine Schloss rebuilt in 1821 on the ruins of a 12C fortress, not far beyond which is a late 17C Servite *Monastery*, its chapel with a ceiling-painting by Johann Bergl.

5km *Aggsbach Dorf*, with a Gothic church of 1390, formerly that of a Carthusian monastery.

A right-hand turning ascends to (5km) *Maria Langegg*. The restored church of 1773, with ceiling-paintings by J. von Mölk, which commands a fine view over the Danube, is part of a Servite convent. Some dependencies containing good stucco-work may be visited.

After 2km the ruins of the fortress of **Aggstein** will be seen on a precipitous crag 300m above. An eyrie of the Kuenringer, it was destroyed in 1295 by Albrecht I, and rebuilt by Georg Scheck von Wald in the early 15C, but by the 19C it had disintegrated.

The road goes on through several hamlets of the so-called ANSDÖRFER, before entering (15km) *Rossatz*, amongst its vineyards. On the far bank opposite Rossatz is *Dürnstein*; see Rte 22A.

6km **Mautern** (2900 inhab.), the Roman camp of *Faviana*, and the 'Mutaren' of the Nibelungenlied, with relics of its medieval walls. St. Severin died here in 482, where he had founded a monastery. It was long the site of a bridge over the Danube, and so suffered repeatedly from the passage of foreign armies, among them the Hungarians in 1481, the Swedes in 1654, the Bavarians in 1741, and during the Napoleonic Wars. Among the monuments of its past are a 15–16C 16C castle, a *Pfarrkirche* of 1490, baroquised in 1697, and two Gothic chapels.

For *Stein* and **Krems**, on the far bank, see Rte 22A.

It is recommended to take the road leading SE, climbing steeply to

Göttweig, which may also be approached from Krems, by turning right off the B333 for St. Pölten.

The Benedictine *Abbey of Göttweig stands on a conspicuous hill c 260m above the Danube, and commands an extensive view.

It was founded c 1083 by Altmann, Bishop of Passau, on the site of a Roman camp and temple. The earlier buildings were severely damaged by fires in 1580, 1608, and 1718. Although already baroquised in the mid 17C, in 1719 its rebuilding commenced, partly following the plan of J. Lukas von Hildebrandt, but the ambitious project—as sketched in 1744 by Salomon Kleiner—remained unfinished in 1783.

To the right of the entrance to the precinct stands the *Church*, with its uncompleted classical façade (after 1750). The interior is unattractive, with garish 19C colouring, and perhaps its best feature is the tripartite organ. Its crypt contains the 16C tomb of St. Altmann, the founder. Adjacent to the W is a cloister. Further W is the main entrance to the monastery. The notable staircase (the *Kaiserstiege*; 1738) has a huge fresco by Paul Troger. Several rooms—some attractively panelled or painted—now accommodate collections of religious art, and sculptures by Johann Schmidt, and also miscellaneous collections of early views of the abbey, ivories, tapestries, arms, musical instruments, and books, etc. Among paintings are *Hans Eckl*, Martyrdoms of SS. Catherine, and Barbara; *Altomonte*, Mater Dolorosa; *Martin van Meytens*, Portraits of Maria Theresia and Franz I; numerous canvases by '*Kremser*' *Schmidt*, and portraits of abbots, etc.; and also works by Ludger Tom Ring the Elder, and Paul Troger.

The *Library* and Archives, containing important collections of MSS, incunabula, and prints, may be visited on prior application. The *Stiftskeller* provides a good view towards Krems.

Descending SE from Göttweig, follow the road S to *Herzogenburg* and *St. Pölten* (see Rte 21B), or turning E, take the riverside road to *Wagram ob der Traisen*, crossing that stream to *Traismauer*, preserving relics of the Roman walls of *Augustianis*, and the *Wiener* or *Römertor*, a 16C town gate.—*St. Andrä* lies some 6km S; see p 212.

Bearing SE, skirting the flat TULLNERFELD, with a view E of the nuclear power-station of *Zwentendorf* (see Rte 22A), the B1 is reached after 16km, at *Mitterndorf*. For the road to **Vienna**, see Rte 21B.

23 Freistadt to Krems via Zwettl: the Waldviertel

Total distance, 113km (70 miles). B41. 25km *Karlstift*. **Weitra** lies 21km further NE, and **Gmünd** 11km beyond.—B38. 36km **Zwettl**—B37. 15km *Rastenfeld*—29km *Senftenberg*—8km **Krems**.
Maps: F&B 1; BEV 49/14–15.

From **Freistadt** (see Rte 20) the road leads NE across the lonely FREIWALD, with the *Viehberg* (1112m) rising to the W of (14km) *Sandl*, 6km beyond which, while skirting the Czech border some 5km N, you cross from Upper into Lower Austria.—11km *Karlstift*.

KARLSTIFT TO GMÜND (32km). The B41 climbs NE through wooded hills, later descending into and following the LAINSITZ VALLEY to (21km) **Weitra**, a small once-walled town of 3100 inhabitants, with several houses in the Rathausplatz and Dr Kordik-Platz retaining their sgraffito decoration. Both the town and its dominating *Schloss* (late 16C), were founded by Hadmar II von Kuenring at the beginning of the 13C. To the N is the Gothic *Pfarrkirche*, and by the riverside, the restored *Spitalskirche*.—11km **Gmünd** (see Rte 24A), from which turn c 27km SE to Zwettl via (10km) *Kirchberg am Walde*, where a *Schloss* with a Baroque façade was the temporary residence in exile of Charles X of France and his entourage after the revolution of 1830; it was later frequently visited by the pretender, the Comte de Chambord.

The B38 drives E from Karlstift to reach (17km) *Gross-Gerungs*, 6km beyond which, a right-hand turning leads 7km SE to **Rappottenstein**, on the Kleiner Kamp, dominated by its *Fortress (14–16C)*, with the 12C keep of Rapoto von Kuenring providing a wide view over the WALDVIERTEL, and preserving several features of interest.— Regaining the main road, you pass 5km S of *Schloss Rosenau* (now a hotel), with frescoes by Daniel Gran, and in the chapel one by Paul Troger (both c 1740); there is a small Masonic museum.

Zwettl (11,500 inhab.; 13,600 in 1900) is a small industrial town at the confluence of the Kamp and Zwettl rivers.

It received its charter in 1200, after which the Kuenrings raised its walls, of which several bastions remain. The town was damaged during the Hussite wars (1427), besieged by Matthias Corvinus in 1486, and again in the peasants' revolt of 1595, in the Thirty Years' War, and during the Napoleonic invasions.

At the S end of the enceinte stands the *Pfarrkirche* (13–15C), later baroquised. To the right is the HAUPTPLATZ, with the *Rathaus* (rebuilt 1483, with a façade of 1814). From the adjacent triangular DREIFALTIGKEITSPLATZ, with its *Pestsäule* of 1734, extends the wide Landstrasse, preserving several characteristic houses, at the N end of which is the *Pernerstorferhof*, a 16C tower.

To the S of the centre stand the former *Propsteikirche*, the earliest in the town, with a 13C *Charnel-house*, near the site of the castle; while from near the Rathaus, the Hamerlingstrasse leads N past the mid 15C *Spitalskirche* to approach—beyond the medieval walls—the *Gasthof 'Zum goldenen Stern'* of 1590.

A right-hand turning just N of the railway viaduct follows the KAMP VALLEY NE for 3km to the Cistercian **Monastery of Zwettl**, founded in 1138 by Hadmar I von Kuenring, and occupied by monks from Heiligenkreuz.

A ramp descends to the **Church**, which dates from 1159, with a 90m-high belfry above its granite façade of 1722–27 by Matthias Steinl and Josef Munggenast. The interior, with its slender lofty pillars, was partly baroquised (in 1732–49). Notable are the Gothic ambulatory (1343–48, by Master Johannes); the high altar by Munggenast, with its statues carved by Josef Matthias Götz (1733); the stalls and organ-loft of 1748 (the organ of 1731, by Johann Ignatz Egedacher, has been restored); and the smaller organ opposite the pulpit. In the 2nd chapel of the left-hand aisle is the retable of St. Bernard, by Jörg Breu the Elder, while other altars are embellished with paintings by M. Altomonte, Troger, and both 'Kremser' Schmidt and 'Wiener' Schmidt, with sculptures by Schletterer.

By turning left you enter the colourful early 18C courtyard. Turn left here to approach the granite *Cloister* of 1204–17, with its dissimilar walks and capitals, off which are an octagonal *Lavatory* (1706), and the *Chapterhouse* (c 1180; the earliest extant in Austria), vaulted from a single column supporting a remarkable capital.

The *Library*, (by Munggenast, and decorated by Troger), *Refectory* and

Museum are not always open to the public. Crossing the outer courtyard, another ramp is ascended to reach the exit.

The main road E can be regained at *Rudmanns*, 4km E of Zwettl, just beyond which the left-hand fork leads close to the *Ottenstein reservoir* to (11km) *Rastenfeld*, but a recommended approach is that following the right-hand fork. At 11km this provides an impressive view ahead of *Schloss Rastenberg*, climbing beyond which the B37 is regained.

A DETOUR may be made from this point, by turning N across the dam to visit *Schloss Ottenstein* (12–16C; now a restaurant); for the road beyond to *Altenburg* and *Horn* (c 30km NE), see Rte 24A, in reverse.—Turning back from the Schloss, follow the serpentine road along the S side of the *Dobra Stausee*, that of the dammed Kamp, to (12km) *Krumau*, dominated by its castle, 5km SE of which, after climbing out of the valley, the B32 is reached. (This was not the Krumau known to Egon Schiele, which was near České Budějovice, in Czechoslavakia, where his mother was born.) Turning right and forking left at (6km) *Gföhl*, the main route is regained after 6km, and 5km NW of *Senftenberg*.

From the Rastenfeld or (3km) Rastenberg crossroads, bear SE on the B37 to (9km) *Lichtenau*, with its castle, 6km S of which is the massive 17C *Schloss Albrechtsberg*, and a baroquised Gothic church.

Some 6km SE of the latter, below the ruins of *Hartenstein* (founded by Heinrich von Kuenring c 1190) is the *Gudenushöhle*, where important artefacts of the Magdalenian period were discovered in 1922.

The B37 continues to descend the wooded KREMSTAL to (17km) *Senftenberg*, with a fortified church and ruined castle, some 4km NE of which, at *Dross*, the Schloss chapel contains 14–15C frescoes.

2km *Imbach*, visited from Gneixendorf (cf.) by Beethoven and his nephew Karl on 30 September 1826. It was the site of a 13C Dominican foundation with a double-aisled *Church*, its vault sustained by lofty central pillars. The carved altarpiece (16C) is notable.—*Rehberg*, with castle ruins, is passed before reaching (6km) **Krems**; see Rte 22A.

24 From Vienna to Gmünd

A. Via Horn

Total distance, 139km (86 miles). A22 and S3. 32km **Stockerau** exit—B4. 24km *Ziersdorf*—9km *Maissau*—19km **Horn**—B303. 49km *Schrems* exit—B41. 6km **Gmünd**.

Maps: F&B 1; BEV 48/16, 49/15–16.

Crossing to the left bank of the Danube at Vienna, turn NW, with a view of the *Kahlenberg* and of *Klosterneuburg* (see Rte 30) on the far bank. At 17km you pass (right) **Korneuburg** (9100 inhab.), its neo-Gothic Rathaus with a *Belfry* dating from 1450, a *Trinity Column* of 1747, and to the W, the *Augustinerkirche*, with a columned high altar with a partly trompe l'oeil painting of The Last Supper by Maulbertsch, who also painted the side altars.—See also Rte 31.

Some 8km N stands the hilltop fortress of *Kreuzenstein*. Dating from the 12C, it was destroyed by the Swedes in 1645, and in the late 19C rebuilt for Count

Johann von Wilczek in a feudal style. It contains several collections—furniture, arms, etc.—and may be visited.

The main road veers to the W, at 13km by-passing (right) **Stockerau** (12,700 inhab.), its main street retaining several 17–18C houses, a 17C *Rathaus*, and a *Pfarrkirche* with a lofty Baroque belfry. The poet Nikolaus Lenau (1802–50) spent part of his youth here, and his archives are preserved in the *Niembschhof*.

For the B303, bearing N, see Rte 24B.

Following the B4 to the NW at 9km the right-hand turning leads 3km to *Stranzendorf*, with a church of 1733 built by J. Lukas von Hildebrandt.—8km *Grossweikersdorf*, where the church, after a design by J.B. and J.E. Fischer von Erlach, with a façade of 1835, contains a painting by M. Altomonte on the high altar.—Ignace Joseph Pleyel (1757–1831), the composer, publisher and piano-maker, was born at *Ruppersthal*, 4km W.

4km **Kleinwetzdorf**. Its 17C–early 19C *Schloss*, is 1.5km to the W.

Here is the *Heldenberg*, an exaggerated 'Temple of Fame', glorifying the forces of the Austrian monarchy, with the busts of 142 generals (among them Daun, Laudon, Prince Eugene, and the Archduke Karl), together with statues of F.M. Count Radetzky (1766–1848); Baron Wimpffen (1797–1854), buried here under an obelisk; Franz Josef; and Josef Pargfrieder, an army contractor and admirer of Radetzky, who laid out the park, presumably at the expense of the taxpayer. Pargfrieder had the honour of burying the Field Marshal here, having once helped him out of financial difficulties.

At 4km *Ziersdorf* is reached and, 6km beyond, *Ravelsbach* (left), with a church of 1725 by Prandtauer, under restoration, to enter (3km) *Maissau*, with a picturesque mid 13C castle.

The B35 leads 9km N to **Eggenburg** (3700 inhab.), a high-lying village preserving some 15C walls and with a characteristic HAUPTPLATZ of 16–18C houses. To the W of the *Trinity Column* of 1715, passing the *Pfarrhof*, with a portal of 1537, is the imposing *Pfarrkirche*, with two Romanesque towers, a 14C choir, and a late 15C nave. The pulpit of 1515 is notable.—The *Krahuletz-museum* contains collections of some interest.—At *Wartberg*, 5km E, is a conspicuous 15C church, baroquised in 1730; for *Röschitz*, 4km N of Wartberg, see Rte 24B.—The B303 leading W from Eggenburg to (14km) *Horn* passes through *Kühnring*, ancient *Azzmanswiesen*, founded c 1057, with a *Pfarrkirche*, the chapel of the former castle, rebuilt in the 12C and altered c 1660, and circular *Charnel-house* adjacent.—5km beyond is the hilltop pilgrimage-church of **Maria Dreieichen** (1750; by Leopold Wissgrill), with frescoes by Troger in its cupola and others by Johann Bergl, et al.

From Maissau the B4 climbs and continues NW through woods to (9km) *Harmannsdorf*, with its *Schloss*, baroquised in 1760, shortly after which a turning leads 5km left to *Gars* (cf). The main road later provides a view (right) of *Maria Dreieichen*; see above.

7km **Horn** (6300 inhab.), also with a by-pass, lies at the confluence of two small streams, near which is its *Schloss* (16–19C), and adjacent, the *Höbarth-museum*, with regional and archaeological collections. Beyond the mid 17C *Piaristenkirche*, in the centre of the KIRCHPLATZ, extended by the HAUPTPLATZ, is *Hl. Georg* (1593, with a late 19C spire), near which are several characteristic 16C houses. Further to the SW is the *Pfarrkirche Hl. Stephan*, founded c 1045, and rebuilt c 1440, with baroque chapels, and several other interesting features.—Returning to the Hauptplatz, you can follow the Flor-ianigasse N to the 16C *Thurnhof*, the present *Rathaus*, and then turn right along the Thurnhofstrasse to gain the SCHLOSSPLATZ.

HORN TO ZWETTL (48km). The first part may be considered a

recommended DETOUR from the main route. The B34 leads W to (6km) **Altenburg**, with a remarkable Benedictine *‘Abbey*, founded in 1144, destroyed by the Swedes in 1645, and rebuilt between 1730–33 by Josef Munggenast, among others, and well-restored since the Russian military occupation. It has rightly been compared to Melk and St. Florian in architectural and artistic importance. Notable is the tall tower, embellished with urns and angels. The *Church* is oval in plan, with pink and grey pilasters (some imitation marble), blue pendentives, and gilt capitals; the ceiling-painting, etc. is by Troger; the stucco-work and statuary by Franz Josef Holzinger; the organ of 1775 by Anton Pflügler. Groups are also guided through the colourful *Library*, also with frescoes by Troger, and by J.J. Zeiler; the equestrian monuments and other sculptures should be noted.—Steps descend to a huge *Crypt*, in which the ‘Etruscan’ and Grotesque paintwork at a lower level has been restored.—Another monumental staircase, the *Kaiserstiege* (with frescoes by Troger) and a further series of elaborately decorated rooms—the *Marmortrakt*—may be seen, together with statues of dwarf musicians, etc. Recent excavations have uncovered the early 14C cloister with 15C murals; this had been filled in during the Baroque reconstruction.

4km further W, just beyond *Fuglau*, fork right for (2.5km) *Greillenstein*; see below. The B34 continues ahead above the KAMP VALLEY to (20km) *Schloss Ottenstein*, for which, and the road beyond to *Zwettl*, 18km W, see p 224.—Romantically sited **Schloss Greillenstein**, seat of the Kuefstein family, rebuilt in the 16C and altered in the 17C, has a tall turreted entrance tower flanked by obelisks, carved lions and other statuary, and with crowned negroes on its coat of arms. It contains a small historical museum.—After 5.5km turn right for 5km to regain the B303 11km W of Horn.

The main road from Horn continues NW—one of the main routes between Prague and Vienna—through a rolling, partly wooded district known as DIE WILD, to (14km) *Göpfritz*.

The right-hand fork 3km beyond the village leads 10km NW to **Waidhofen an der Thaya** (5400 inhab.), an ancient fortified town. It has a 16C *Rathaus*, and a richly decorated aisleless Baroque *Church* of 1723, with a remarkable organcase of 1729 by Wenzel Kasparides.—The main route may be regained 10km SW.—There is a Museum devoted to Freemasonry at *Allentsteig*, 5km SW of the junction W of Göpfritz.

8km *Schwarzenau*, on the Thaya, has a large towered and moated late 16C *Schloss* containing good stucco-work of 1732 by G.B. d'Allio.—At 14km the main road by-passes (right) *Schrems*, long a favourite Imperial stopping-place on the highway, at the ‘Zum Weissen Rössl’. Mozart stayed at the Schloss en route to Prague to attend the first performance of ‘Don Giovanni’ (1787).—After 2km turn left to (6km) *Gmünd*.

Gmünd (6400 inhab.), the frontier town, on the river Lainsitz, near which, in the old enceinte, is the long STADTPLATZ. Here, opposite the 16C *Altes Rathaus* (housing a small museum), are two 16C houses with sgraffito decoration; the *Pfarrkirche*, to the NE, dates from the 12–14C. W of the platz is the restored 16C *Schloss*, not far N of which is the JOSEFSPLATZ, and the adjacent border-crossing into Czechoslovakia (Customs, etc.).

Interesting EXCURSIONS may be made to **Weitra**, 16km SW (see Rte 23), and N along by-roads skirting the frontier via (7km) *Neunagelberg* to (6km) *Brand*, with several glass factories. Follow the road N to (10km) *Litschau*, a fortified village possessing an impressive 15–17C castle, and to *Heidenreichstein* (10km E of Brand) which may also be reached via *Eisgarn*, SE of Litschau; see Rte 24B.

B.   Via Retz and Raabs an der Thaya

Total distance, 193km (120 miles). A22 and S3. 32km **Stockerau** exit—24km *Hollabrunn*—4km **Schöngrabern**—7km *Guntersdorf*—B30. 15m **Retz**—6km *Niederfladnitz*—7km *Hardegg*—8km *Riegersburg*—B30. 12km *Geras*—10km **Drosendorf**—13km *Raabs an der Thaya*—16km *Dobersberg*—20km *Heidenreichstein*—19km **Gmünd**.

Maps F&B 1; BEV 48/16, 49/15–16.

For the road to *Stockerau*, see Rte 24A, beyond which you veer N up the GÖLLERSBACH VALLEY, at 6km passing (right) *Sierndorf*, with the early 16C *Schlosskapelle* of the Colloredo family, which contains a fine Renaissance carved stone altarpiece of the Annunciation with carved wood wings, and an oratory housing two busts from the workshop of Anton Pilgram (1516) of Wilhelm von Zelking and Margarete von Sanizell.

Best approached by the by-road leading N to Göllersdorf parallel to the S3, is (5km) *Schloss Schönborn*, completed in 1717 by J. Lukas von Hildebrandt for Friedrich Karl von Schönborn, preserving several interesting features.—Some 7km NE are the extensive ruins of *Schloss Steinabrunn*.

8km *Göllersdorf* has a 16C *Schloss*, and a *Pestsäule* of 1731 designed by Von Hildebrandt, who also baroquised the mid 15C church in 1741.—At *Grossmugl*, 11km E, is a huge tumulus.

9km **Hollabrunn** (10,150 inhab.), also by-passed some 4km N of which, to the right of the road, stands the Romanesque *Church* of *Schöngrabern* (1230). The sculptures on the exterior of its apse are perhaps the most curious of their kind in Austria, and have been the subject of learned controversy.

On the S side—at a lower level—stand Adam and Eve; to the E, the offerings of Cain and Abel; and to the N, David slaying the lion. The imagery of the upper reliefs is more complex, but deserves detailed study. The interior contains several capitals and frescoes of interest.

SCHÖNGRABERN TO RETZ VIA PULKAU (34km). The B303 is followed to the NW to (11km) *Roseldorf* (9km E of Eggenburg; see Rte 24A), where you turn right to (5km) **Röschitz**, where in the *Ludwig-Weber-Keller* are some extraordinary carved reliefs dating from the 1920s.

The characteristic village of **Pulkau** lies just W of crossroads 6km N. Its 15C *Heiligblut-Kirche*, in the centre, contains an early 16C altarpiece of interest by a local sculptor, while on the hill to the N stands the Romanesque and Gothic *Pfarrkirche*, with an unusual 13C *Charnel-house* (view).—From the crossroads, follow the B35 through (3km) *Schrattenthal*, with an attractive late Gothic chapel and ruined castle. The nearby *Schafberg* (500m) commands a fine panorama over the WEINVIERTEL, the WALDVIERTEL to the W, and N into Czechoslovakia.—**Retz** lies 6km beyond; see below.

4km *Grund*, 3km E of which, at *Wullersdorf*, is a church altered by Prandtauer and Josef Munggenast.—3km NE of Wullersdorf stood *Schloss Immendorf*, set alight by the retreating SS troops. Klimt's paintings of Jurisprudence, Medicine and Philosophy originally commissioned for the Aula of Vienna University (cf.) and evacuated here for safe-keeping during the Second World War, were destroyed, as was his 'Schubert at the piano' and several other works belonging to the Lederer family.—For *Mailberg*, 6km further NE, see Rte 31.

3km *Guntersdorf*, with a 14C church and Renaissance *Schloss* with a notable courtyard.

The B2 continues N via (6km) *Jetzelsdorf* to reach the Czech border 6km beyond, at *Kleinhaugsdorf* (Customs, etc.).—*Znojmo* lies 16km beyond; at 80km NW is the motorway from Brno to **Prague**, 123km further NW.

From Guntersdorf follow the B30 NW through vineyards to (15km) **Retz** (4350 inhab.), an ancient town which received its charter in 1295, and the centre of the local wine trade. It preserves parts of its four-square fortifications, at the SE corner of which is the *Schloss*, altered in the 17C.

The central HAUPTPLATZ contains several monuments and fountains, the *Sgraffitohaus* (1576), the castellated *Verderberhaus* (late 16C) built over a passageway, and towards the W end of the platz, the *Rathaus*, with its imposing tower heightened in 1572, a 14C chapel, and local museum. Below is the uninvitingly styled *Ratskeller*, from which the extensive cellars beneath the town may be visited.

Passing below the Verderberhaus, the *Znaimer Tor* is reached, a town gate beyond which (right) are the *Stiftshof* (1701) and adjacent *Pfarrkirche* (13C; later baroquised), containing paintings by M. Altomonte and Leopold Kupelwieser. Not far distant is an 18C windmill.

Bearing NW, after 6km *Niederfladnitz* is entered, from which you can cut across country to the W to (21km) *Geras*, see below. Some 3km to the E of Niederfladnitz is the hunting-lodge of *Karlslust* (1794), built for Karl Fürst Auersperg.—The recommended route is that continuing NW to (4km) *Merkersdorf*, to the E of which, in the forest, are the ruins of the 12–15C castle of *Kaja*.

3km **Hardegg an der Thaya**, in a deep valley adjacent to the Czech frontier, is commanded by an imposing *Fortress* (restored), with four towers. It contains a museum devoted to the Emperor Maximilian of Mexico (1832–67), brother of Franz Josef, a collection of arms, and the Khevenhüller crypt. The village church retains a cross carved from the mast of the frigate 'Novara' in which Maximilian sailed to Mexico where he was later assassinated.

The road circles close to the border before veering SW to (8km) **Riegersburg**, with an early 18C *Schloss*, in 1735 enlarged by J.E. Fischer von Erlach, containing collections of ecclesiastical art, and an exhibition devoted to 18C residences in the Waldviertel, etc.

12km **Geras**, with a Premonstratensian *Abbey* founded in 1153, and rebuilt in 1625 after its destruction in 1619. It was altered by Josef Munggenast in 1740, and some rooms contain frescoes by Troger; the ceiling-painting in the Library is by Winterhalter (1805). Cultural courses are held here.

Turning NW again, you approach (10km) **Drosendorf**, its upper village lying within a strongly fortified outcrop on a meander of the Thaya, with 12C *walls*, town gates, a *Schloss* rebuilt in the 17C, and an attractive STADTPLATZ, where the baroquised *Martinskirche* of 1464 stands. The 16–17C *Altstadt-Pfarrkirche*, to the E of the enceinte, contains frescoes by Lukas Stipperger.

The river is followed SW to *Eibenstein*, before bearing W, and at 10km passing (left) a turning for adjacent *Kollmitzdörfl*, below which the Thaya is dominated by the ruined fortress of *Kollmitzgraben*, in another meander of that river.

3km **Raabs an der Thaya**, a small riverside village, is entirely commanded by its rock-crowned *Castle* (largely 16C); its church is 13–15C.—9km *Karlstein*, with a 15–16C castle overlooking the Deutsche Thaya, is passed, and 7km beyond you enter **Heidenreichstein** (5300 inhab.), with a massive moated *Fortress* (13–15C) in the centre of the village.

Litschau lies 12km beyond, in this NW corner of the country, while *Brand* is 10km E, for which, and for **Gmünd**, 19km SW by the main road, see Rte 24A.

25 Vienna

A.   General

'This city, the capital of the empire, and residence of the imperial family, is so remote from England, has been so imperfectly described by writers of travels, and is so seldom visited by Englishmen, that I should have presented my readers with a minute account of its public buildings and curiosities...' wrote Dr Charles Burney, who, travelling downstream on the Danube, disembarked, and spent the first half of September 1770 in Vienna. The following pages will attempt to right his omission, for while it was never on the track beaten by the Grand Tourist, and two centuries have seen many changes, it is still one of the great cultural centres of Europe.

VIENNA (Wien) was for several centuries the Imperial capital, and is now the capital of the Republic of Austria. Its present estimated population is 1,487,600 approximately 20 per cent of that of the whole country. Since 1921 it has formed a separate province or *Land*, with extended boundaries established in 1954. It already had 1,162,600 inhabitants a century ago, although the population of the inner city has meanwhile dropped from 72,700 to 19,500. It reached its highest number (2,083,600) in 1910. Its area is 414 sq km (160 sq miles), with a circumference of 133km, which is divided into 23 districts or *Bezirke*; see p 242. Although population density in general is 3690 per sq km, this varies widely between districts, from 975 per sq km in *Donaustadt* (Vienna 22) to 25,831 per sq km in

Margareten (Vienna 5). Its mean height above sea level is 171m (560ft), and its centre (Stephansplatz) lies at 48° 12' latitude, and 16° 22' longitude. Its lowest point is 151m; its highest is 542m, at the Hermannskogel in the sandstone hills of the Wienerwald, with its woods and vineyards, rising to the W and NW. To the E, the older centre or *Altstadt* is skirted by the Donau Kanal or Danube Canal, a branch of the Danube, which, here canalised in 1870–77, flows from NW to SE a short distance beyond. Further E, beyond the river, the plain of the Marchfeld stretches towards the Carpathians.

Its position of strategic importance as a bulwark against the East has been frequently recognised, not only by Metternich, who remarked that 'Asia begins at the Landstrasse' (SE of the older nucleus). Because of its position it has been the focus of immigration from all parts of the Habsburg Empire, and later of the Austro-Hungarian monarchy, which has produced that charming combination of races, the 'Viennese'. It should be remembered that it was the capital of an Empire which at its fullest extent contained over 40,000,000 people. When the Turkish menace evaporated after the raising of the siege of Vienna in 1683 the city experienced a period of rapid growth, with the erection of numerous Baroque palaces. It later flourished as a centre of musical culture, particularly from 1781 (when Mozart settled in Vienna) to 1828, the year Schubert died.

It has since remained a bulwark of European civilisation, a city with many remarkable museums and notable monuments. It is steeped in historical and cultural associations, preserves an alluringly relaxed atmosphere, and has—in addition—unusually attractive environs within easy reach of its centre. Vienna was extensively damaged during the Second World War (although not as severely as many German cities); some 21,000 houses were destroyed or made uninhabitable, and it looked distinctly shabby for some years after a decade of Allied occupation. It was then disorganised by the construction of its underground system, now being extended.

The renewed prosperity of Vienna has expressed itself in several obtrusive buildings which have been the subject of political scandal. Nevertheless many streets retain their individuality and the patina of its illustrious past, occasionally revealing charming anachronisms. Where will one see black-costumed chimney-sweeps; where else see so many citizens carrying their musical instrument cases ... two sides only of a many faceted city that come to mind. Although Sir Thomas Browne once wrote that 'Cholical Persons will find little Comfort in *Austria* or *Vienna*', the author, for one (with his tincture of irascibility), found a great deal.

Roman *Vindobona* was established among a Celtic population probably during the latter half of the 1C AD, and legionaries built a walled camp on the bank of the *Danubius*, which is circumscribed by the present Kramergasse and Rotgasse on its SE side, the Naglergasse and Graben on its SW side, and the *Tiefer Graben* on the NW. Its garrison included 1000 British cavalry (the civilian settlement stood astride the Rennweg, E of the Salesian church.) This was by 114 superseded by the camp at *Carnuntum* (cf.; some 40km E), although it remained a fortress of importance against the incursions of the Germanic Marcomanni, among other tribes. They were defeated in 178 by Marcus Aurelius, who is presumed to have died at Vindobona two years later. Partly destroyed by fire in 395, it was shortly after abandoned by the Romans, and by the middle of the 5C was in the hands of the Ostrogoths. The town is referred to in a document of 881 as *Weniam*.

Soon after the defeat of the Hungarians on the Lechfeld in 955, the border province was given to Leopold I of Babenberg, Heinrich Jasomirgott (1141–77), a later member of the house, transferring his seat to Vienna from the

Leopoldsberg, commanding it to the N. It was referred to by Walther von der Vogelweide, the court poet, in the last decade of the 12C, while the minnesinger Reinmar der Alte was also at the Babenberg Court at this time. The Hospital of the Holy Ghost, the first institute of its kind in Vienna, was established in 1208 by Master Gerhard, Duke Leopold's physician, served by an order of monks from Montpellier. Municipal privileges were granted to the town in 1221, which expanded, first to the SE, later filling up the area surrounded by its early 13C walls, said to have been erected with part of the proceeds of the ransom paid by Richard I of England, who was captured en route from the Crusades (cf. Dürnstein), and released in 1194. It was visited by Frederick II Hohenstaufen in 1237, who had his nine-year-old son Conradin elected 'King of the Romans' here.

With the defeat in 1278 at the Battle of Marchfeld of Ottokar of Bohemia, usurper of the duchy, Vienna became the seat of Rudolph of Habsburg, and remained the capital of that dynasty until its demise in 1918. During the reign of Rudolph IV, the 'Stifter' (1356–65; so-called for having founded so many monasteries), the cathedral was enlarged and the University founded. Meanwhile, from 1235, the Minorites, Dominicans, Augustinians, and Heironymites, followed by the Franciscans and several other religious orders, infiltrated the town, which by 1480 had become the seat of a bishop—being previously dependent on the Bavarian see of Passau—and from 1772, of an archbishop. Here, in 1515 Maximilian I entertained Ladislaus, king of Bohemia and Hungary. Vienna also saw several of the marriages of the Emperor's grandchildren, whereby Bohemia, Moravia, and Hungary were integrated into the Empire ('Bella gerant alii, tu felix Austria nube; Nam quae Mars aliis, dat tibi regna Venus', or 'Let others wage war for a throne—you, happy Austria, marry; the lands that others are given by Mars, you receive from Venus'). From 26 September to 14 October 1529 it was besieged by the Turkish troops of Sultan Suleiman the Magnificent, which were successfully repulsed and dispersed by Count Niklas Salm. (The 'Danube Chain', with which the Turks held their vessels in position, now embellishes the Cour d'Angoulême of the Hôtel des Invalides, Paris.)

In 1551 Ferdinand I established the Jesuits here, in an attempt to eradicate the Protestant heresy; its first Anabaptists had been burnt in 1524. The bigoted religious ordinances promulgated during the reigns of Ferdinand II and III also radically demoralised and impoverished the social fabric of Vienna, precipitating an exodus of its Protestant citizens, even though, for a brief period while Matthias was emperor, influenced by Bishop Melchior Khlesl, there was some recognition of Protestantism. It was an irreparable loss, and left deep and permanent marks on her character.

Vienna was visited by Sir Philip Sidney in 1573 and in 1577, when he acted as official emissary of Queen Elizabeth. Edward Wotton was acting as secretary to the embassy in 1574–75. From 1573–88 the botanist Carolus Clusius made his home in Vienna, having been invited there from the Netherlands by Maximilian II. After the death of his father in 1576, Rudolf II shifted the seat of government from Vienna to Prague, a process completed by 1583.

During the Thirty Years' War Vienna was menaced in 1619 and 1644 by Bohemian and Swedish armies respectively commanded by Count Matthias Thurn, and Gen. Torstensson. (It should be remembered that what has been referred to as members of 'the Celtic fringe' were frequently in the service of the Habsburgs at this and later periods—among them John Gordon, Walter Butler, Walter Leslie and Walter Devereux, who were responsible for the assassination of Wallenstein in 1634, and received some of his confiscated estates in reward.)

In 1669 some 3000–4000 Jews were expelled from the capital. In 1679 some tens of thousands died in a devastating plague, which had previously more than decimated the population, both in 1349 and 1588. But an equally serious and continuing menace was that of the Turks, who in mid July 1683 surrounded the city with an army said to have numbered as many as 200,000, but probably around 90,000, under the command of the Grand Vizier Kara Mustafa.

The main Turkish attack was on the outwork known as the *Burgbastei*, to the W of the Hofburg, where on 12 August a mine demolished part of the earthworks and filled the moat. But this attack and several others were beaten off during the following days. The beleaguered garrison, commanded by Count Ernst Rüdiger von Starhemberg, numbered about 15,000. As a precautionary measure they had first set light to the suburbs to form a glacis prior to retiring behind its defences. Meanwhile, the Emperor Leopold had been drumming up support. By early September several allied armies were converging on Vienna. Duke Charles of Lorraine's combined forces, which included Bavarian,

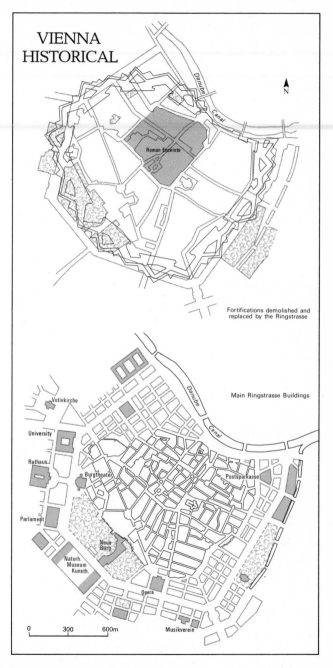

VIENNA
HISTORICAL

Danube Canal

N

Roman Enceinte

Fortifications demolished and
replaced by the Ringstrasse

Danube Canal

Main Ringstrasse Buildings

Votivkirche

University

Rathaus

Burgtheater

Postsparkasse

Parlament

Neue
Burg

Naturh.
Museum
Kunsth.

Opera

Musikverein

0   300   600m

Franconian, Swabian, and Saxon contingents, together with cavalry supplied by Hanover (largely a bodyguard for Duke Ernst August's two sons, including the future George I of England), made up an Imperial Army of almost 50,000, which was supported by the last-minute arrival of 18,000 Poles under Jan Sobieski. The allied commanders rendezvoused at Tulln before leading their relieving armies on a two-day march through the Wienerwald. The battle commenced early on 12 September, with the combined forces descending from the Leopoldsberg and the heights to the NW towards the Turkish camp like 'a stream of black pitch'. The Ottoman front soon collapsed, and the besieging army melted away, Kara Mustafa escaping in the confusion as night fell; he was later strangled on the orders of the Sultan. Not expecting such instant victory, Leopold hurriedly left his HQ at Dürnstein, reaching Vienna in time to attend the Te Deum in the cathedral the following day. Among those who entered Vienna for the first time was the 20-year-old Prince Eugene of Savoy. On the 19th Leopold left for his temporary capital at Linz.

It is claimed that the first coffee-house in Vienna was opened immediately after the victory by a certain Georg Franz Kolschitzky (1640–98), using the sacks of coffee-beans left by the Turks, but in fact coffee had become a fashionable drink among the aristocracy some decades earlier, when it was imported by Armenian merchants.

Edmund Halley, the astronomer, visited Vienna in 1703, when he was presented with a diamond ring from the Emperor's finger; he had recently advised the imperial engineers on the fortification of Trieste.

The fortifications of the city were repaired and strengthened, and a wall, known as the *Linienwall* or Line Wall, was constructed to protect the suburbs then being rebuilt. The city at this time had a population of 100,000. The following decades saw the erection of the *Karlskirche* by Fischer von Erlach, and the *Upper* and *Lower Belvederes*, built for Prince Eugene (who had meanwhile undertaken several successful campaigns against the Turks) by Lukas von Hildebrandt, who was also the architect of the *Imperial Chancery* in the Ballhausplatz. The palace of *Schönbrunn* was completed in 1750 for Maria Theresia, where in 1762 young Mozart performed before the Empress. In 1766 her reforming son, Joseph II, threw open the *Prater* to the public. Some fine vistas and townscapes in Vienna were painted during 1758–61 by Bernardo Bellotto, then resident here.

As well as Haydn, Mozart, and the young Beethoven, the 'Vienna School' of music during this period also included such less well-known but notable figures as Monn, Wagenseil, Dittersdorf, Schenk, Albrechtsberger, Pleyel, and Czerny, all of whom were born either in Vienna or Lower Austria; while also from Habsburg lands came Mysliweczek, George Benda, Dussek, Johann Stamitz, Koželuch, Weigl, Wranitzky, Wenzel Müller, and Gyrowetz, to mention only a few. The numerous aristocratic households in Austria could, therefore, call on plenty of talented composers for their entertainment. The Vienna Theatre Almanac of 1794, describes the lively 'street' music of the city at this time: 'During the summer months ... one will meet serenaders in the streets ... at all hours.... They do not, as in Italy or Spain, consist of a vocal part simply accompanied by a mandolin or guitar ... but of trios, and quartets (most frequently from operas) of several vocal parts, of wind instruments, often an entire orchestra, and the most ambitious symphonies are performed ... and no matter how late at night they take place ... people soon appear at their open windows and within a few minutes the musicians are surrounded by a crowd of listeners who rarely depart until the serenade has come to an end.'

Mozart died in Vienna in December 1791, after a residence of ten years. By then the population had grown to c 235,000. The French occupied Vienna twice, from 12 November 1805–13 January 1806, and in 1809 (on which occasion Stendhal was among the French commissariate). On 12 May 1809 Napoleon installed himself at Schönbrunn. On the 22nd the French were defeated at *Aspern* and *Essling* by the Archduke Karl's Austrian army. On 31 May Joseph Haydn died in his house in the western suburbs of Vienna. On 6 July the tables were turned by Napoleon's victory at adjacent *Wagram*, and the French occupied the city until 19 November. On 2 April 1810 Napoleon married Maria Louise, the daughter of the Emperor Franz. From 16 September 1814 to 19 June 1815, the prestigious *Congress of Vienna* took place; it was an attempt to settle the political state of Europe, under the presidency of Metternich (referred to by Grillparzer as 'a very great diplomat but not a great statesman'). On 25 January 1815 Beethoven (who had settled in Vienna in 1794, and was to remain there until his death in 1827) conducted a concert of his works before the assembled dignataries, presumably including Castlereagh, Talleyrand, Alexander I of Russia, Friedrich Wilhelm III of Prussia, Nesselrode, Hardenberg, W. von

Humboldt, et al, but not yet Wellington, who only reached Vienna on 3 February. (Sir Thomas Lawrence was also in Vienna, commissioned to paint the portraits of the assembled heads of state.) On 7 March Wellington learnt of Napoleon's escape from Elba, which put a fairly abrupt end to the dancing, while plans rapidly matured for a joint offensive by the Powers. Wellington set off for Brussels on 29 March.

From 1815, the following 30-odd years, often referred to as the '*Biedermeier*' period (after a fictitious naïve poet named Gottlieb Biedermaier), were described by Edward Crankshaw as 'a comfortable, middle-class age with an emphasis on decency and cosy cheerfulness and a strong philistine tinge: the philistinism was partly masked by an enthusiasm for music and the theatre'. Politics were forbidden ground; censorship, and the activities of the ubiquitous and officious secret police were the rule. It was part of the system perfected by Metternich.

In 1830 severe flooding of the Danube during the thaw caused heavy mortality.

But, inevitably, by attempting to stifle nationalism and suppressing any form of liberalism, Metternich was digging his own grave, and with the outbreak of revolution in 1848 he was forced to escape to London. The insurrection was severely repressed by the stiff-necked Prince Alfred Windischgrätz, who in early November bombarded the city and established martial law (not lifted until 1853).

On 2 December 1848 the 18-year-old Franz Josef's accession was proclaimed. The young emperor, still dominated by his mother, the Archduchess Sophie, and swayed by Archbishop Rauscher, his philosophy tutor, signed a Concordat with Rome, one of several retrograde steps he was to take, abrogating the sensible reforms of Joseph II. Censorship was re-established.

In 1857 demolition of the old fortifications and glacis started. On their site a series of monumental buildings were planned to flank the *Ringstrasse*, and other districts expanded rapidly. Its population, including the suburbs, had risen from c 330,000 in 1840 to about 490,000 by 1859, the first year of a modern census. It is interesting to note that in 1820 only 13,550 of its inhabitants had been born *outside* the city; by 1846 this figure had risen to over 131,000. And during the period 1827–47, although the population of Vienna (including the outer suburbs) had increased by 45 per cent, the increase in housing was only 1.4 per cent. The crowded city was ripe for a revolution.

In 1893 the old *Linienwall* was razed, and replaced by the *Gürtel*, a wide thoroughfare, which included the *Stadtbahn* or City Railway. By this time— taking in the outlying suburbs—the population had increased to over 1,350,000. Meanwhile, in 1867, a compromise agreement made Budapest the capital of the Eastern half of the Empire (a blow to imperial pride from which it took Vienna some time to recover).

The first of the Ringstrassenstil buildings to go up (see Rte 25F) was the *Votivkirche* (1856–79), by Ferstel, the architect of the adjacent *University*. In the next three decades a dozen or more structures were erected, including the *Opera-house* (1869), the *Burgtheater* (1888), the *Rathaus* (1872–82), the *Parliament* building (1873–83), the *Musikverein* (1867–69), and several museums. In 1873 took place the Vienna Universal Exhibition. In spite of the dead weight of much academic architecture, reactions to banality were never far below the surface.

But it was a notable period for music and the arts. Brahms first visited Vienna in 1862 and remained there from 1871 until his death in 1897. Bruckner had lived there since 1864, and died there in 1896 in a 'grace and favour' lodge in the grounds of the Belvedere. Hugo Wolf lived in Vienna from 1875 until his death in an asylum in 1903. Between 1897 and 1907 Mahler was Director of the Vienna Opera, dying in Vienna 1911. Richard Strauss's 'Der Rosenkavalier' was performed for the first time in Vienna in 1911.

A new generation of artists, architects, and designers began to make an impact, breaking away from the sterile influence of the *Akademie der bildenden Künste*, and *Künstlerhaus*. Among the more influential was Gustav Klimt, elected president of a group known as the Secessionists, who held their second exhibition in Joseph Olbrich's new *Secession building* in November 1898. This stood near the Linke Wienzeile, where in the following year Otto Wagner's apartment blocks were to display their astonishing façades. Another notable architect (and designer) was Josef Hoffmann; Kolo Moser, and Adolf Loos were also important figures at this time. The next generation of artists was dominated by Egon Schiele, who died aged 28 of Spanish influenza in 1918, and Oskar Kokoschka. Among other influential figures of the period were Sigmund Freud (1856–1939); and the writer Arthur Schnitzler (1862–1931); Karl Kraus (1874–1936, publisher from 1899—and largely the author—of the satirical journal 'Die Fackel', The Torch, of which 922 numbers appeared); Hugo von Hofmannsthal (1874–1929); and Stefan Zweig (1882–1942), whose autobiography, and 'Josephine Mutzenbacher', describe the fin-de-siècle city.

The Jewish population of the capital had between 1870 and 1890 risen from 40,200 (6.6 per cent of the total) to 118,500 (8.7 per cent); by 1881 61 per cent of the doctors in Vienna were Jews, and they were also strongly represented in the legal profession, from which they had been excluded until 1862. In 1910 almost 25 per cent of the inhabitants of the 1st, 2nd, and 9th Districts were Jewish.

By 1910, by which date the transpontine suburb of Floridsdorf had been incorporated within the city limits, Vienna's population had grown to over 2,000,000. Before the rapid rise of Berlin, Vienna had been the third largest of European capitals, after London and Paris. By the end of the First World War, and with the dissolution of the Habsburg monarchy, Vienna was a 'glorified but bedraggled rehabilitation centre', thronged with refugees, ex-soldiers, and civil-servants from all four corners of the disintegrating Empire. Only gradually was stability regained, although there were riots in Vienna in June–July 1927, when the Palace of Justice was burnt out. The Socialist municipality provided numerous large blocks of tenements in an attempt to solve the housing problem, including the *Karl Marx Hof* in the N suburbs. In February 1934 some of these provided excellent fortresses for the Vienna Socialists, who had staged a general strike, when defending themselves from the officious reactions of Major Emil Fey (one of Dollfuss's deputies, he committed suicide four years later), who ordered up the artillery. The Socialist Mayor was imprisoned, and the fascist element was triumphant. On 25 July 1934 Nazi conspirators stalked into the Chancery in army uniforms, and shot Dollfuss dead.

On 13 March 1938 Adolf Hitler and his Gestapo drove into Vienna, with all its consequences. One was the liquidation of over 50,000 Viennese Jews who had not previously sought exile abroad, and it has been estimated that some 100,000 Viennese were used as cannon-fodder on various fronts. There was of course considerable resistance to the Nazi regime in the capital. Between 1938 and 1945 some 2700 Viennese were sentenced to death for their part in this resistance; another 16,500 were murdered in concentration camps; 9700 met their end in Gestapo prisons; and at least another 6400 died in normal prisons. Vienna experienced several air raids between September 1944 and the following April, the most serious of which was on 12 March 1945, when the Opera-house was hit. Under shell-fire during the Battle of Vienna the cathedral was set alight. As the Russians marched in, the artist Carl Moll committed suicide. By 12 April the city was virtually liberated by the Third Ukranian Army. The following day the Burgtheater was severely damaged.

But it was not for several weeks that the four Allied powers were allotted sectors of the city, the First District being also under quadripartite control: the period of the 'four men in a jeep'. The area E of the Danube Canal and a segment to the S remained in Russian hands; a sector on either side of the latter was under British control; the N of the city was occupied by the Americans; while an area to the W was held by French forces.

On 6 October 1945 Beethoven's 'Fidelio' was again performed in provisional quarters in the Theater an der Wien, where its first performance had taken place during Napoleon's occupation of the city. Very gradually the rubble was cleared, and a semblance of order restored, but food rationing continued for some years, as did the occupation. The partially restored cathedral was re-opened in April 1952; the Burgtheater inaugurated in October 1955, and the Opera-house in the following month. In 1953 Nikolaus Harnoncourt's 'Concentus Musicus' ensemble was formed. Meanwhile, on 15 May 1955 the *State Treaty* was signed in the Belvedere Palace, re-establishing Austrian independence, and affirming the principal of Permanent Neutrality.

In the 37 years which have since elapsed a great deal of modernisation has taken place. Vienna has been provided with a *U-Bahn*, or Underground-railway system; a series of autobahns to facilitate entry and exit; a new *Airport* at *Schwechat*, beyond its SE outskirts; several hospitals (sic; see p 326); extensive industrial installations, including oil-refineries, have been built, and the regulation of the Danube continues. The restoration of damaged or derelict buildings progresses and new structures are continually rising up—several of them aesthetically unacceptably to most Viennese—and the struggle continues...

Among those born in Vienna or in the immediate neighbourhood were artists Rudolf von Alt (1812–1905), Carl Moll (1861–1945), Gustav Klimt (1862–1918), Kolo Moser (1868–1918), and Richard Gerstl (1883–1908); architects Joseph Emanuel Fischer von Erlach (1693–1742) and Otto Wagner (1841–1918); the writers and dramatists Johann Nestroy (1801–62), Arthur Schnitzler

(1862–1931), Hugo von Hofmannsthal (1874–1929), and Stefan Zweig (1881–1942); the composers Georg Christoph Wagenseil (1715–77), Matthias George Monn (1717–50), Carl Ditters von Dittersdorf (1739–99), composer, violinist and friend of Haydn, Carl Czerny (1791–1857), pianist and composer, who studied under Beethoven and Clementi and who taught Liszt, Franz Schubert (1797–1828), Johann Strauss, father (1804–49), and son (1825–99), Alexander Zemlinsky (1871–1942), composer, conductor and brother-in-law of Schönberg, Arnold Schönberg (1874–1951), Anton von Webern (1883–1945), Alban Berg (1885–1935), and Ernst Křenek (1900–) who still lives in Vienna; and in their various fields: Wenzel Kaunitz (1711–94), statesman; Fanny Elssler ((1810–84), dancer; Alfred Adler (1870–1937), psychiatrist; Ludwig Wittgenstein (1889–1951), philosopher.

Employment of Time. A good deal of Vienna may be seen in a minimum of five days by the energetic, but this will only allow a cursory glance at the contents of some of the more important museums and monuments. With the information given below and by using the index, visitors should have little difficulty in choosing and following their own itineraries. The leaflet 'Museums: Vienna', obtainable from Tourist Offices, indicates any changes in opening times.

The first day should perhaps be devoted to a general tour of the old centre, the *Altstadt*, densely packed with objects of interest, starting from the *Opera-house*, and this area is covered in Rtes 25A and B. The second day can be spent visiting the *Kunsthistorisches Museum* (Rte 25E), but some may prefer to spend two separate mornings there. Day three (but not a Friday) could include the museums of *Military History*, and of the *Belvedere* (starting with the Upper): Rte 25K. Day four might be *Schönbrunn* in the morning—starting early—(Rte 25L) and the *Historical Museum of the City*, near the *Karlskirche*, in the afternoon: Rte 25I. The fifth day could then be devoted to the buildings of the *Hofburg* (including at least the Great Hall of the National Library, and the Schatzkammer) and the collections of the *Neue Burg* (musical instruments; arms and armour, etc.), or the adjacent *Ethnological Museum*, or parts of the *Natural History Museum*. Of course there are also the *Albertina*, the *Academy of Fine Arts*, and the *Museum of Applied Arts*; buildings associated with composers, or *Freud*, and the *Josephinum*. Depending on the time of year, the *St. Marxer Friedhof* and/or the *Zentralfriedhof* (Rte 25N) could be included, if visited early in the day, or late afternoon.

Hours of Admission to the principal Museums, Collections, etc.

With certain exceptions, they are *closed on Mondays* and on *National holidays*. Almost all are open daily from 10.00–15.00 or 16.00. The times listed are subject to alteration. A *Museum Pass* of 14 coupons is available for places marked (M), the number of coupons taken depending on the category of the museum. (On presentation of their credit cards, Eurocard and Mastercard holders have a limited opportunity to gain free admission to 19 national museums and collections in Vienna.)

NAME AND ADDRESS	OPEN
Academy of Fine Arts	10.00–14.00
(bildenden Künste)	Wed. 10.00–13.00; 15.00–18.00
Schillerplatz 3(M)	Sat.; Sun. 9.00–13.00
Albertina Collection of Graphic Arts	Wed. 10.00–16.00
Augustinerstrasse 1 (M)	Fri. 10.00–14.00
	Sat., Sun. 10.00–13.00
Applied Arts (angewandte Kunst)	Wed.–Mon. 11.00–18.00
Stubenring 5 (M)	
Arms and Armour	10.10–16.00; closed Tues.
(Hofjagd-und Rüstkammer)	Sat., Sun. 9.00–16.00
Neue Burg, Heldenplatz (M)	
Belvedere	10.00–16.00
Österreichische Galerie	Sun. 9.00–16.00
(19–early 20C art)	
Prinz-Eugen-Strasse 27 (M)	
Baroque Museum, and *Lower*	
Belvedere (Medieval art),	
Rennweg 6a	

Cathedral Museum Stephansplatz 6	Wed.–Sat. 10.00–18.00 Sun. 10.00–16.00
Clock Museum (Uhrenmuseum) Schulhof 2 (M)	Tues.–Sun. 9.00–16.30
Clock and Watch collection at Geymüller-Schlossl Pötzleinsdorfer Strasse 102 (M)	by prior arrangement Tues.; Wed. 11.00–15.30 closed Dec.–Feb.
Court Tableware and Silver (Hoftafel-und Silberkammer) Michaelerplatz, Hofburg (M)	Tues.–Fri; Sun. 9.00–13.00
Doll and Toy Museum Schulhof 4	Tues.–Sun. 10.00–18.00
Ephesus Museum Neue Burg; Heldenplatz (M)	Mon.–Wed., Fri. 10.00–16.00 Sat., Sun. 9.00–16.00
Ethnological Museum (Für Völkerkunde) Neue Burg; entrance near Burgring (M)	10.00–13.00; closed Tues. Wed. 10.00–17.00 Sun. 9.00–13.00
Folklore, Austrian Laudongasse 15 (M)	may be closed for renovation
Historical Museum of the City of Vienna Karlsplatz (M)	Tues.–Sun. 9.00–16.30
Hofburg; Imperial Apartments Michaelerplatz, Hofburg	Mon.–Sat. 8.30–12.00; 12.30–16.00 Sun. 8.30–12.30
Josephinum Währingerstrasse 25	Mon.–Fri. 9.00–15.00
Kunsthistorisches Museum (Fine Arts) Maria-Theresien-Platz (M)	Tues.–Fri. 10.00–16.00 or 18.00 (in summer) Sat., Sun. 9.00–18.00 parts open Tues., Fri. 19.00–21.00
Lower Austrian Museum (Niederösterr. Landesmuseum) Herrengasse 9	9.00–17.00 Sat. 9.00–14.00 Sun. 9.00–12.00
Military Museum (Herresgeschichtliches) Arsenal, Objekt 18 (M)	10.00–16.00 closed Fri., but open Mon.
Modern Art (Moderner Kunst) Liechtenstein Palace, Fürstengasse 1 (M)	Wed.–Mon. 10.00–18.00
Musical Instruments Neue Burg; Heldenplatz (M)	may be closed for renovation.
National Library: Great Hall (Nationalbibliothek: Prunksaal)	11.00–12.00; closed Sun. 10.00–16.00 and to 13.00 on Sun. during exhibitions
Natural History (Naturhistorisches) Maria-Theresien-Platz	9.00–18.00; closed Tues.
Schönbrunn, Schloss *Apartments* *Coach collection* (Wagenburg) (M)	8.30 or 9.00–16.00, 17.00, or 17.30 (guided) 10.00–16.00, or 17.00
Technology and Science (Technisches) Mariashilfer Strasse 212 (M)	Tues.–Sun. 9.00–16.30
Teutonic Knights, Treasury of the (Deutschen Ordens), Singerstrasse 7	10.00–12.00; 15.00–17.00, except Tues. and Sun.
Treasury (Schatzkammer) Hofburg, Schweizerhof (M)	Mon; Wed.–Fri. 10.00–16.00, Sat., Sun 9.00–16.00 or 18.00

Principal houses, etc., with associations, which may be visited:

Beethoven: Pasqualatihaus, Mölker   Tues.–Sun, 9.00–12.15; 13.00–16.30
Bastei 8 (M)
(also Probusgasse 6; Döblinger
Hauptstrasse 92, etc.)

Brahms: Haydngasse 19 (M)   Tues.–Sun. 9.00–12.15; 13.00–16.30

Central Cemetery (Zentralfriedhof)   7.00–18.00 or 19.00
Simmeringer Hauptstrasse 234   Nov.–Feb. 8.00–17.00
(graves of Beethoven, Brahms,
Schubert, Gluck, Hugo Wolf,
Schoenberg, et al)

Grinzing Cemetery (grave of Mahler)

Habsburg Burial Vault (Kaisergruft)   9.30–16.00
Neuer Markt

Haydn: Haydngasse 19 (M)   Tues.–Sun. 9.00–12.15; 13.00–16.30

Hietzing Cemetery (graves of Alban
Berg, Grillparzer, Klimt, Otto Wagner,
et al)

Sigmund Freud: Berggasse 19   9.00–15.00

Mozart: St. Mark Cemetery (Friedhof   7.00–18.00 or 19.00
St. Marx) Leberstrasse 6   Nov.–March 9.00 until dusk
'Figard-Haus', Domgasse 5 (M)   9.00–12.15; 13.00–16.30

Schubert: Nussdorfer Strasse 54 (M)   Tues.–Sun. 9.00–12.15; 13.00–16.30
(birthplace)
Kettenbrückengasse 6 (last residence)   9.00–12.15; 13.00–16.30
(M)

Schubertpark, Währinger Strasse
(original graves of Beethoven, and
Schubert)

Strauss, Johann (the younger),   Tues.–Sun. 9.00–12.15
Praterstrasse   13.00–16.30

Otto Wagner, Döblergasse 4   Mon.–Fri. 9.00–12.00
Otto Wagner, metro station, Hietzing   Tues.–Sun. 9.00–12.15; 13.00–16.30
(M)

In addition to the collections, etc., listed above, there are numerous other sites of lesser or more specialised interest, among them: the *Austrian Film Museum*; a *Museum of Harnesses and Saddlery*; of *Pathological Anatomy*; *Tobacco Museum*; *Viticultural Museum*; *Streetcar Museum*; *Prater Museum*; and even an *Undertaker's Museum* (Bestattungsmuseum). Not far from Vienna is the *Harrach Collection* at Rohrau; see p 337.

There are also several guided tours available, for example of the *Opera-house*; *Rathaus*; *Parliament*; *St. Stephan's Cathedral*; the *Urania Observatory*; and the church of *Am Steinhof*. All these tours are listed in the leaflet entitled 'Museums: Vienna', available from Tourist Offices, but see below.

N.B. As visitors to Vienna may find it difficult to obtain seats at short notice for several well-publicised forms of entertainment, the following advice may be found useful.

Advance bookings for the *State Opera*, the *Volksoper*, the *Burgtheater*, and *Akademietheater* are made by writing to the Österreichischer Bundestheaterverband, Goethegasse 1, A-1010 Vienna.

For *Musikverein* concerts: Gesellschaft der Musikfreunde, Dumbastrasse 12, A-1010 Vienna.

For the *Konzerthaus*: Wiener Konzerthausgesellschaft, Lothringerstrasse 20, A-1030 Vienna.

Sung mass by the Vienna Boys' Choir and members of the Hofmusikkapelle in the *Imperial Chapel* (Burgkapelle), on each Sunday and religious holiday from September to June: the Hofmusikkapelle, A-1010 Vienna (at least 8 weeks in advance).

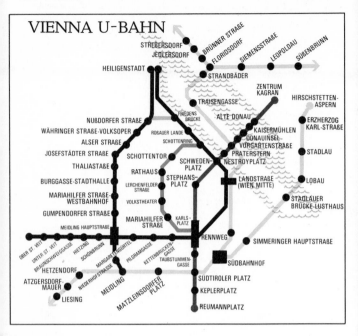

The *Spanish Riding School*; Wednesday and Saturday performances may only be booked through a booking or travel agency; tickets for Sunday performances may be ordered from the Spanish Riding School itself, Michaelerplatz 1, A-1010 Vienna. Training sessions (daily except Sunday and Monday) from Josefsplatz, door 3, A-1010 Vienna—no prior reservation necessary. The adjacent stables can be visited between 14.00 and 16.00 on Wednesday and Saturday, and from 10.00–12.00 on Sunday when there is *no* performance; they may be visited from 12.15–12.45 when there is a performance.

The province of Vienna is divided into 23 districts or **Bezirke**, few of which have any significance for the tourist. When referred to as postal districts they are written A–1010, A–1020, A–1030, etc.

1 or I	*Innere Stadt* (the old centre, within the Ring)
2 or II	*Leopoldstadt* (E of 1, between the Danube Canal and the river)
3 or III	*Landstrasse* (SE of 1, and extended SE by 11)
4 or IV	*Wieden* (S of 1, and extended S by 10)
5 or V	*Margareten* (SW of the latter)
6 or VI	*Mariahilf* (N of the latter, and extended N by 6–9, all E of the Gürtel)
7 or VII	*Neubau* (W of the Maria-Theresien-Platz)
8 or VIII	*Josefstadt* (W of the Rathaus)
9 or IX	*Alsergrund* (NW of the Schottenring)
10 or X	*Favoriten* (the S suburb, beyond 4)
11 or XI	*Simmering* (E of 10, in which is the Zentralfriedhof)
12 or XII	*Meidling* (W of 11 and 5)
13 or XIII	*Hietzing* (the SW suburb with 23 extending beyond Schönbrunn)

B. The Inner City: East of the Kärntner Strasse and Rotenturmstrasse

The **Kärntner Strasse** (the old thoroughfare leading S from the centre towards Carinthia) in fact starts a short distance S of the Ringstrasse. To the N of their intersection stands the *Opera-house* or *Staats-Oper*, while in the *Opernpassage*, the pedestrian subway adjacent, is a *Tourist Information Office*. The subway continues S to the *Karlsplatz Underground*: see Rtes 25H and 25I.

The **OPERA-HOUSE**, less pretentious than its counterpart in Paris, begun in the same year, was originally constructed in 1861–69, and was the first major building on the Ringstrasse. Its architects were August von Siccardsburg and Eduard van der Nüll, the latter being largely responsible for its decoration. Neither lived to see its inauguration on 25 May 1869 with a performance of 'Don Giovanni', for Van der Nüll had shot himself, and Siccardsburg died of a stroke some months later.

On 12 March 1945 the building received a direct hit during an American air-raid, and much of it was burnt out, only the S façade, with its portico or loggia, the lobby, central staircase, first floor *Foyer* with its frescoes by Moritz von Schwind depicting scenes from 'The Magic Flute', and the *Imperial Tea Salon*, were saved. The scenery and costumes for 120 operas were destroyed. Its reconstruction on the original lines, but with technical modernisation, was entrusted to Erich Boltenstern, Otto Prossinger, and Ceno Kosak, and the new Opera-house was inaugurated on 5 November 1955 with a performance of 'Fidelio', conducted by Karl Böhm. It was the subject of a painting by Kokoschka in 1956.

Among great directors during previous decades was Gustav Mahler (1897–1907)—the censor prevented him from putting on Strauss's 'Salome' here in 1905, which was first performed in Austria at Graz in May 1906, with the composer conducting; his 'Rosenkavalier', with Roller's costumes and settings, received its first performance at Dresden, although its Viennese première took place in the same year (1911) under Franz Schalk. Other past directors include Felix Weingartner (1908–11, and 1935–36); Richard Strauss (1919–24); Clemens Krauss (1929–34). In 1957–64 Herbert von Karajan (died 1989) was lionised. Claudio Abbado took up this exacting post in 1986. Among several famous conductors of the resident Vienna Philharmonic Orchestra have been Hans Richter, Bruno Walter, Wilhelm Furtwängler, Hans Knappertsbusch, and Joseph Krips.

Among the rooms which may be visited during the intervals of performances or during conducted tours, which take place during

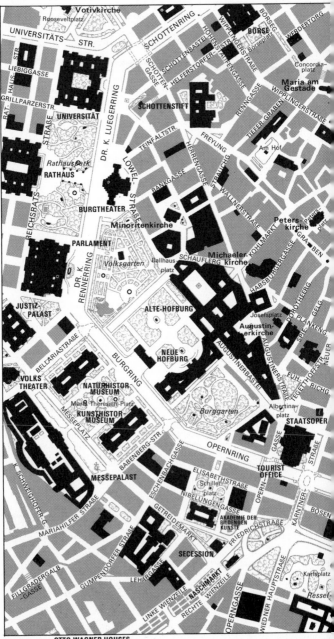

OTTO WAGNER HOUSES

CENTRAL VIENNA

0   100   200   300   400m

PRATER

HEINRICHSGASSE
Rudolfsplatz G.
GOLDSDRFG.
SALZGRIES
HQ.-STR.
SALZTOR BR.
VORLAUF
STR.
MARC AURELSTR.
DONAU
OBERE-DONAU-STRASSE
MARIEN BR.
SCHWEDEN-BR.
ASPERN BR.
ASPERN BR.

Morzinplatz
Ruprechtskirche
Synagogue
Schwenden-pl.
FRANZ-JOSEFSKAI
Jul. Raabplatz

TUCHLAUBEN
Hoher Markt
ROTENTURMSTRASSE
FLEISCHMARKT
WIESINGERSTR.
REGIERUNGS-GEBÄUDE
POSTSPARKASSE

BRANDSTÄTTE
ERZBISCH. PALAIS
SONNENFELSGASSE
BÄCKERSTRASSE
POSTGASSE
ROSENBURSEN-STR.

Stephansplatz
St. Stephan
WOLLZEILE
SCHULERSTRASSE
Jesuiten-kirche
DOMINIKANERBASTEI
HOCHSCHULE F. ANGEW. KUNST
STUBENRING

KÄRNTNER STRASSE
SINGERSTRASSE
ZEDLITZ-STEI
STUBENBA-STL-GASSE
ÖSTERR. MUS. F. ANGEW. KUNST
WEISKCHN-STR.
VORDERE ZOLLAMTSSTRASSE

MARKT
HIMMELPFORTGASSE
LIEBENBGG
PARKRING
AIR TERMINUS
AM HEUMARKT

JOHANNESGASSE
SEILERSTÄTTE
WEIHBURGGASSE

ANNAG
KRUGERSTRASSE
SCHWARZENBERGSTR.
SCHELLINGGASSE
HEGELGASSE
Stadtpark
Stadtpark
MINT

WALFISCHGASSE
SCHWARZENBERGSTRASSE
SCH. HEGELSTEG
JOHANNESGASSE
BEATRIXGASSE

MAHLERSTRASSE
SCHUBERTRING
Beethovenplatz

KÄRNTNER RING
KÜNSTLERHAUS
AKADEMIE-DORFERSTRASSE
KONZERTHAUS
GER-
SCHWARZENBERGPLATZ
AM HEUMARKT
SALESIANERGASSE
REISNERSTRASSE

MUSIKVEREIN
LOTHRIN-
STRASSE
MAROKKANERG.

park
HISTOR MUSEUM WIEN
Schwarzenberg-platz
ZAUNERGASSE
NEULINGGASSE

Karlskirche
SCHWARZENBERG PALACE   LOWER BELVEDERE

afternoons when no rehearsals are on (enquire at W side of the building), are the *Marmorsaal*, and *Gobelinsaal*, with the 'Magic Flute' tapestries designed by Rudolf Eisenmenger. The new auditorium, less sumptuous than the old, holds some 2200 people, including 550 standing. The auditorium together with the huge stage, is the venue of the traditional 'Opera Ball', which takes place each year on the Thursday prior to Ash Wednesday, when the *jeunesse dorée* perspire to the sound of violins. The opera season generally lasts from September until the following June.

No. 1 in the Kärntner Ring is the old-established *Bristol Hotel*, British HQ after 1945. Further E, on the S side of the street, stands the *Imperial* (No. 16), patronised by Richard Wagner in his heyday (1875), and in which Hitler stayed after the Anschluss. It was built in 1867 as a palatial residence for the Duke of Württemberg and converted in 1873 to accommodate VIPs visiting Vienna for the Universal Exhibition of that year. It has been restored and modernised since the post-war occupation.

Keeping the Opera-house on your left, continue up the once exclusive but now inelegant KÄRNTNER STRASSE (here a pedestrian precinct), which has always been one of the main thoroughfares of the city. A *Tourist Information Office* is on its W side (No. 38).

At 3A Annagasse, to the right, is the **Annakirche**, dating mainly from 1629–32, although founded earlier. Its interior of pink and grey marble contains frescoes by Daniel Gran, a good organ-loft, and notable statuary.—At No. 4 in the same street is the *Kremsmünsterhof*, a 17C building with a façade of c 1700; No. 8, the *Deybelhof* or *Täuberlhof*, in 1666–76 housing a drawing school, has a façade of c 1730 probably designed by a pupil of J. Lukas von Hildebrandt; while No. 14 (17C, but remodelled in 1814) is known as the *Haus 'Zum blauen Karpfen'* (of the Blue Carp). No. 5 is the S entrance of 1768 of the buildings housing the Imperial Household Records, a director of which in 1832–56 was Franz Grillparzer.

Returning to the Kärntner Strasse, you pass at No. 37 the *Malteserkirche*, a Gothic church with a façade of 1806–8, belonging to the Knights Hospitallers.

At Nos 5 and 5A Johannesgasse, the next street to the right, is the *Questenberg-Kaunitz palace* (after 1701), in which Talleyrand resided during the period of the Congress of Vienna. No. 15 is the *Savoysches Damenstift* (from 1688, with a lead statue by F.X. Messerschmidt), once a retreat for noble ladies. No. 8, the *Ursulinenkirche und kloster* (1665–75) contains a collection of Religious Folk Art.

Parallel to the N is the Himmelpfortgasse, in which No. 8—housing the Ministry of Finance—was the former *Winter palace of Prince Eugene, built by J.B. Fischer von Erlach in 1697–98, and later extended to the W by J. Lukas von Hildebrandt. The *Staircase*, decorated by Giovanni Giuliani, is remarkable for its Atlantes by Mattielli. It also contains several richly embellished rooms.—No. 13, the *Erdödy-Fürstenberg palace*, dates from c 1724.

At the corner of the Himmelpfortgasse and Seilerstätte stood the *Hungarian Crown Inn* (Zur ungarischen Krone), at which Mozart played billiards; it was later frequented by Schubert and his circle. Off the N side of the Himmelpfortgasse leads the Rauhensteingasse, where on the site of No. 8 stood, until the late 1840s, the house where Mozart lived from September 1790 until his death on 5 December 1791. It was here that 'The Magic Flute' and his Requiem were composed. Mozart's death may have been hastened by the bleeding that his physicians induced as a remedy for rheumatic fever.

On regaining the Kärntner Strasse, at No. 26 you pass the shop of *J. and L. Lobmeyr*, on the upper floor of which is a notable *Glass Museum*.

Founded in 1823 by Josef Lobmeyr (1792–1855), the business was carried on by his sons Josef (1828–64), and notably, Ludwig (1829–1917). Their sister Mathilde married August Rath (1832–1925), whose descendants, including Stefan (1876–1960) and Hans Harald (1904–68), inherited the establishment. At the turn of the century Josef Hoffmann, Kolo Moser, and Alfred Roller were designing for them, and later Adolf Loos.

In 1908 Adolf Loos designed the so-called 'Kärntner Bar', a diminutive establishment in a turning to the left of the Kärntner Strasse.

No. 29–30 in the street was long the 'Erzherzog Karl' hotel, at which Weber, Richard Wagner, and many other famous visitors to Vienna lodged.

The Weihburggasse leads right to the FRANZISKANERPLATZ, and its *Church*, rebuilt in 1603–11 on the site of a late 14C monastery; it contains an over-elaborate altar.—At the far end of the street is the Seilerstätte, where No. 3 is the *Palais Coburg*, which until the construction of the Ringstrasse, stood on one of the town bastions, relics of which may be seen beyond in the *Coburg-Bastei*.

Turning N from the Franziskanerplatz, you reach the Singerstrasse, preserving several old mansions, including at No. 17, the former *Rottal palace* of c 1750, built on the site of a hospital.—In the adjacent Grünangergasse (named after the 'Anker Tavern', frequently visited by Schubert and his friends), No. 4 is the *Fürstenberg palace*, of 1720. No. 16 Singerstrasse is the *Neupauer-Bräuner palace* of 1715–16, opposite which the narrow Blutgasse (with a courtyard at No. 3) leads shortly to the Domgasse, in which No. 5, a 17C house, was the residence of Mozart in 1784–87, formerly with its main entrance at No. 8 Schulerstrasse, parallel to the N. It is commonly known, incorrectly, as the '**Figaro-Haus**', for it was 'Der Schauspieldirektor'—not 'The Marriage of Figaro'—which he composed here. Here he also gave lessons in composition to Thomas Attwood (1765–1838), in 1785 and to young Johann Nepomuk Hummel (1778–1837). Stephen Storace visited Mozart there. His sister, Anna Storace, was the original Suzanne in 'The Marriage of Figaro'. It contains material associated with the composer. An earlier tenant, Albert Camesina, was responsible for the stucco-work in one room; a latter tenant was J.B. Lampi the Elder, the portrait-painter.— Also notable in this street is No. 6, the *Kleiner Bischofhof* (1760–61).

Regaining the Singerstrasse (at its corner with the Blutgasse stood Bogner's Coffee-house, another haunt of the Schubert circle), and turning W, you reach (right; No. 7) the ***Church of the Teutonic Order**, or *Deutschordenskirche*, an early 14C building dedicated to St. Elisabeth, but largely baroquised in 1720–25. The carved organ-loft, and carved and painted altar from Malines (early 15C; which until 1808 was in Danzig), and several of the monuments (among them those of Jobst von Wetzhausen, Erasmus von Starhemberg, Guido von Starhemberg, and Josef Philippe von Harrach), are of interest.

A lift from near the adjacent courtyard (in which a plaque records that Mozart briefly lived here in the spring of 1781, while Brahms also resided here in 1863–65) ascends to the ***Treasury of the Order of the Teutonic Knights** (Schatzkammer des Deutschen Ordens), one of the more interesting smaller collections in Vienna. This has been its home since 1807.

Well-displayed here are numerous documents, including Henry IV's renewal of an annual grant of 40 silver marks; a gold Bull of Frederick II (1221); several seals, coins, medals, and crucifixes, and the Grandmaster's insignia (1500); chalices, goblets, and cutlery; chocolate sets; a Dog with a goose in its jaw (1570), and a Welcoming dog (1556), both made in Nuremberg; mounted silver relief of Maximilian I; rock-crystal objects; a 'Viper's tongue credence'; jewellery; maces and other weapons, some of Persian origin; miniature portraits of Grandmasters and Knights of the Order; a silver shelf-clock from Augsburg (1640); two silver filigree banqueting dishes (17–18C); armour of c 1620; Regalia of the last Grandmaster (from 1894–1923), the Archduke Eugene (died 1954); glass; funeral helmet; votive-picture of Konräd von Stuchwitz of c 1480, and a painting of the Coronation of the Virgin by the Trinity (c 1450).

No. 5 Singerstrasse is the *Churhaus* or Curate's House (rebuilt 1738–40, on the site of a seminary founded in 1618), providing a view of the S façade of the cathedral.

By continuing W, you reach the STOCK-IM-EISEN-PLATZ, at the junction of the Kärntner Strasse and the Graben, further W (see Rte 25C). It is named after a nail-studded stump which has stood there from 1533 if not earlier, said to have been one in which journeymen blacksmiths hammered a nail for good luck before furthering their career elsewhere. Almost opposite the W front of the cathedral stands the recent glass and mirror fronted *Das Neue Haas Haus* (1987–91),

The Stephansplatz, by Rudolf von Alt

by Hans Hollein (born 1934), which has come in for much well-deserved criticism.

To the N is the STEPHANSPLATZ, dominated by the *Stephansdom, or **Cathedral of St. Stephen**. Prior to entering the cathedral it is worth descending into the Underground Station to visit *St. Virgil's Chapel*, in fact the crypt of the former cemetery chapel of Maria Magdalena, excavated when the subway was constructed. Adjacent are artefacts discovered at this time. The churchyard was not finally removed from the area until 1783.

The most obvious exterior features of the cathedral are the huge steeply pitched roof of yellow, green, and black tiles in chevron, and depicting the Imperial double-headed eagle, and the towering steeple rising to a height of 137m (the spire of Salisbury is 123m; that of Strasbourg is 142m) and the W façade with its two 'Heidentürme' (64m high), or towers of the Heathens.

The cathedral, dedicated to Stephen, the first king of Hungary (1000–38), canonised in 1083, originated in a small Romanesque church just outside the medieval walls consecrated in 1147, but burnt in 1193 as was its successor in 1258. This was replaced by another, of which parts of the present W front are relics. In the first decades of the 14C the late Romanesque apses were demolished, and the church was extended to the E by a Gothic choir with three apses (modelled on that of Ratisbon). This was consecrated in 1340, after which the nave was widened and two chapels were adjoined to the façade. The S tower, known to the Viennese as the 'Steffl', dates from 1365–1433, but the N tower, begun in 1450, was never completed, being crowned by a copper Renaissance cupola in 1556 (replaced since the original melted in 1945). The gable of the *Singertor* (near the SW corner of the building) by Hans Puchsbaum, dates from 1450, but the seven others were added in the 1850s, when the fabric was 'restored', for the spire had also been severely damaged in a storm.

On 12 April 1945 the cathedral was set on fire, and among other parts of the edifice the carved-wood roof of the nave was burnt out, and the 'Pummerin' bell, cast in 1711 from Turkish guns left on their retreat from Vienna in 1683, fell from the N tower and was shattered. The bell was replaced in April 1952, when the whole building was re-opened for services; its restoration continued for over a decade, but among the total losses were the main organ and the Gothic choirstalls.

Here in 1515 took place the double wedding of the grandchildren of Maximilian I with the children of Ladislas, king of Hungary and Bohemia. Haydn was a choirboy here in 1740–49, and here on 4 August 1782 Mozart married Constanze Weber. In 1916 the obsequies of Franz Josef were celebrated in the cathedral.

EXTERIOR. Several details of the Romanesque W front, with the so-called *Giant's Door* (*Riesen-Tor*) deserve notice, including the sculpture of Samson and the lion, while a number of tombstones from the once circumjacent cemetery have been placed against its exterior, here and elsewhere. By circling the building in an anti-clockwise direction, you pass first the *Singertor*, preserving a well-sculpted depiction of the Conversion of St. Paul in its tympanum, while below (right) stands Duke Rudolf IV, the Founder. To the left is the damaged tombstone of the minnesinger Neidhart von Reuenthal (died 1334). Skirting the wall of the 18C Sacristy, you pass the S entrance below its tower and several Renaissance tombstones, to reach, behind its S apse, some restored 15C frescoes, etc. The main features of the N façade are a baroquised Gothic pulpit from which Johann Capistran preached against the Turks in 1451. Nearby is an area riddled with catacombs, and the *Bischofstor*, with early 16C sculptures in its porch.

Notable in the picturesque INTERIOR—107m long, and with a nave 39m high—covered with reticulated vaulting, are the 18 massive pillars with their numerous statues below Gothic canopies, together

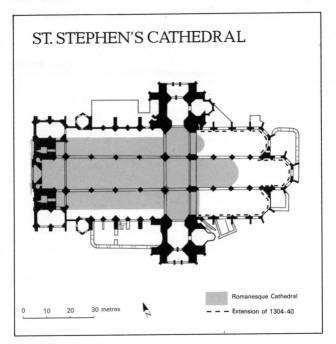

ST. STEPHEN'S CATHEDRAL

	Romanesque Cathedral
- - -	Extension of 1304-40

0   10   20   30 metres

with several Baroque altars. The Reiger organ dates from 1991. In the
Kreuzkapelle (left), with a fine wrought-iron gate, is the *Tomb* (1754)
of Prince Eugene of Savoy (1663–1736). Adjacent is the *Cenotaph* of
the humanist Johannes Cuspinian (1443–1529), with his two wives,
and children. On the N side of the nave is the *Pulpit* of c 1510,
depicting the four Fathers of the Church, by Anton Pilgram, whose
half-figure peers from below its stairs. Another bust of Pilgram may
be seen below the Gothic *Organ-loft* abutting the N transept wall.
The entrance to the *Catacombs* below the cathedral is a few paces
beyond, with the Habsburg intestines preserved in bronze boxes.

Unfortunately, the *Choir* can usually only be visited in a group. In
the N apse is a fine carved and gilt winged retable from Wiener
Neustadt of 1447, and to the left of this is the *Cenotaph of Duke
Rudolf IV*, the Founder. The high altar (behind which is some glass of
1340, restored) is by J. Pöck (1647); the altarpiece, of the Stoning of
Stephen, is by Tobias Pöck. In the S apse is the red marble *Tomb of
the Emperor Friedrich III* (died 1493), by Niklas Gerhaert van
Leyden, completed in 1513 by Michael Tichter. In the *Katherinen-
Kapelle*, off the S transept, is a well-carved Gothic *Font* of 1481.

On the W side of the square, Stephansplatz 10, is a *Jewish Welcome Service*,
which can give more information about Martin Buber (1878–1965), Theodor
Herzl (1860–1904), and other influential Jews in Vienna, only a few of whom
have been referred to in these pages, together with other associations, etc.

Immediately to the NE of the cathedral is the *Archbishop's Palace*,
dating from 1630–40, and replacing an earlier building. Abutting it to

the E is the ***Dom Und Diözesanmuseum**, on the first floor, approached by turning into a passage-way.

Several of the more interesting cult objects are to be found in the first room to the right, among them: 1, a 3C Roman cameo Seal, reworked in 1365; 2, an illuminated Carolingian Gospel (late 9C); 3, a portative altar, with enamel plaques of c 1170–80; 7 and 8, two Syrian glass flasks, of 1280 and 1310; 9, Shroud of Rudolf IV, of Persian manufacture and with Islamic motives, but of Chinese cotton; 10, Portrait of Prince Rudolf IV (1365); 13, a Pastoral staff of 1515; 14 and 15, Monstrances of 1482 and 1515; 16, the Pazifikale reliquary (1514); 18, the St. Andrew's Cross reliquary (c 1440); and 25, the many-branched Leopold reliquary (1592): note the alligators at its base.

Among the collection of paintings and sculptures are: 48, Epitaph of Johannes Geus (1440; ascribed to the *Albrechtsmeister*); 49, the Hornperger votive-altar from Maria am Gestade (1462); 50, *Lucas Cranach the Younger*, Ecce Homo (1537; from the Rochuskirche); 53, Christ derided (early 16C); 54, *Hans Schaufelein*, The Ober St. Veit altarpiece (1507), closely copying sketches by Dürer; 59, a carved and polychromed Deposition of c 1340; 64, the Schutzmantelmadonna (1430), opening to display the Trinity; 72, relief of the Carrying of the Cross (1523; note background); 75, *Jan van Hemessen*, Deposition; *Karel Škreta*, Blessing of bread by St. Nicholas of Tolentino; *Rottmayr*, Glory of Karl Borromeo; 78, *Unterberger*, Virgin and Child with St. Anthony, and 85, Avenging angels; 79, *Tanzio de Varallo*, St. Catherine of Siena; 80, *Jan van Kessel*, Virgin and Child in a garland; 81, Calvary with St. Veronica; 83, *Maulbertsch*, Golgotha; 84, *Troger*, Martyrdom of St. Cassian; 88, *Josef Keller*, three sketches; also 17C carved ivory plaques. It is expected that other objects will be added to the collection in the future.

The second turning to the left off the Rotenturmstrasse, skirting the *Archbishop's Palace*, leads to the *Hoher Markt* (see Rte 25C); that to the right (Lugeck) is continued by the Sonnenfelsgasse (left) in which Nos 1 and 3 are two mansions of interest, the former of 1793; the latter with a façade of 1721 masking a 15C building. Note also Nos 15 and 19 in the same street.

Parallel to the S is the Bäckerstrasse, in which No. 7, with an 18C façade, has a Renaissance courtyard, its arcade unfortunately built in. No. 8, the *Seilerpalace*, dates from 1722, in which Mme de Staël lived in 1808. No. 16, of 1712, was once an eating-house known as the 'Schmauswaberl', which served left-overs from the Court to the students of the adjacent **Akademie der Wissenschaften** (Science; founded 1847), recently restored, once the main building of the neighbouring (Jesuit-controlled) *Alte Universität* of 1753–55, by Jean-Nicolas Jadot de Ville-Issey (born at Lunéville in 1710). Its main entrance is in DR-IGNAZ-SEIPEL-PLATZ (named after the Austrian Chancellor—a priest—in 1922–24, and 1926–29).

The *Ceremonial Hall* was severely damaged by fire in 1961, but the destroyed ceiling-frescoes by Gregorio Guglielmo have since been reproduced. Here, late in 1813, took place the memorable first performances of Beethoven's 'Battle Symphony', Opus 91, and 7th Symphony, Opus 92, in which Salieri, Hummel, Meyerbeer, Spohr, and Moscheles played in the orchestra, conducted by the composer.

The N side of the square (in which Schubert boarded at No. 1 in 1808–13, when with the Vienna Boys' Choir) is dominated by the *Universitätskirche*, or **Jesuitenkirche** (1623–31), with a pink and green interior, Salomonic pillars, Baroque pulpit, and a trompe-l'oeil fresco of a dome by Andrea Pozzo (1705).

By skirting the W side of the church, and then turning left, you approach at the end of a lane the *Heiligenkreuz Court*, rebuilt after 1660, but retaining features from the 12–13C, and again trans-formed in the 18C, on the S side of which is the richly decorated chapel of *St. Bernard*, with an altarpiece by Martino Altomonte.—

Robert Schumann lived at No. 7A in the neighbouring Schönlatern-gasse in 1838–39.

By passing behind the apse of the Jesuit Church and turning left you approach the main *Post Office* (Hauptpostamt). A few paces to the S is the *Dominikanerkirche* (1631–34), replacing a 13C building, and with a lavishly decorated interior (often shut).—To the E of the Post Office is the *Postsparkassenamt* (that of the Post Office Savings Bank), with its main entrance vestibule on its E side. It is one of the more remarkable buildings designed by Otto Wagner, dating from 1904, and restored in the 1970s. It retains several of its original features, although the hall has been 'modernised'.

For the Stuben-Ring, a short distance beyond, see Rte 25J.

On regaining the W side of the Post Office, follow the *Fleischmarkt* to the W, passing (right) a turning to the *Schweden-Brücke*, a bridge spanning the Danube Canal to the beginning of the Praterstrasse (see Rte 25N). You shortly reach a small *Greek Orthodox Church* dedicated to St. Barbara (rebuilt 1858 and its interior repainted in the 1980s). It was once part of a Jesuit monastery, but was given to the Greek community of Vienna by Maria Theresia in 1775. Adjacent is the *Griechenbeisl*, a famous old inn, with a 13C tower in its courtyard, perhaps part of the medieval walls. Franz Hauer (1866–1914), a former proprietor, was a patron of the arts. No. 15 in the Fleischmarkt (the old meat market, its name documented since 1285), a house of 1718, was the birthplace in 1804 of Moritz von Schwind, the artist, and a friend of Schubert. No. 9, with a façade of c 1700, is of Renaissance foundation; No. 1 is a restored building of 1909–10 by Arthur Baron.

Continuing W, you soon reach the Rotenturmstrasse (descending towards the *Marien-Brücke*), in which George Borrow lodged in May 1844 before taking the Danube ferry to Budapest on his Balkan tour.

Turn left to regain the *Stephansplatz*. For the *Ruprechtskirche* and *Hoher Markt*, a short distance further W, see Rte 25C.

C. The Inner City West of the Kärntner Strasse and Rotenturmstrasse

Immediately behind the *Opera-house* (see Rte 25B), at No. 4 Philar-monikerstrasse, stands the plushy and genteel **Hotel Sacher**.

It was erected in 1876 for Eduard Sacher, a sophisticated caterer whose father, Franz, had in 1832 made his name by confecting a type of chocolate-cake for Metternich, which has since done much to promote the name of the establishment; it enjoyed a great reputation under the management of the eccentric cigar-smoking Anna Sacher (until 1929), usually surrounded by midget bull-dogs. In earlier epochs Billroth would invite Brahms there for an oyster breakfast as a special treat. During the Allied occupation from 1945 it was a British Senior Officers' Club.

To the W is the ALBERTINAPLATZ. To the NW is a fountain of 1869 (the *Danubius* or *Albrechtsbrunnen*; truncated after bomb damage) by Johann Meixner and recently restored, putting back in their place the statues which originally stood here, which had been stored away for several decades. To the N of this starts the Augustinerstrasse: see p 271.

Turn N along the Tegetthoffstrasse towards the NEUER MARKT (known as such since 1234, and in the 18C the site of Court sleigh-riding), on the W side of which is the *Kapuzinerkirche* and *****KAISER-GRUFT**, the *Imperial Burial Vault*.

This lies below the Baroque church of 1622–32, with a façade of 1935–36, founded by the consort of the Emperor Matthias. Steps descend from a passage to the vaults, in which the sarcophagi of the House of Habsburg from 1633 to 1916 lie; that of *Karl I* is empty, for he was buried in Madeira, where he died in 1922, although Zita, his wife, was buried here in 1989. The only other exception is Ferdinand II (died 1637), who was buried at Graz. Among the more interesting examples of funerary sculpture are those of *Elisabeth Christine* (1691–1750), and *Karl VI* (1685–1740; parents of Maria Theresia), by Balthasar F. Moll; that of *Joseph I* (1678–1711), by J. Lukas von Hildebrandt; *Franz Stephan* (1708–65), and *Maria Theresia* (1717–80), also by Moll; *Franz Josef* (1830–1916), on a plain marble plinth; on either side lie those of *Elisabeth* (1837–94), and their son *Rudolf* (1858–89); *Maria Louise* (1791–1847; consort of Napoleon); that of their son, the Duc de Reichstadt (1811–32; cf. Schönbrunn), was transferred to a site near the tomb of his father in the Dôme des Invalides, Paris, in 1940); *Maximilian of Mexico* (1832–67); and *Ferdinand I* (1793–1875; abdi-cated 1848). *Gräfin Füchs* (died 1754), confidante of Maria Theresia, was condescendingly allowed to be buried here.

In the centre of the square is the **Donner-Brunnen**, a fountain set up in 1739 and named after its designer, Georg Raphael Donner, depicting Providence surrounded by naked figures (which offended the Empress) personifying tributary rivers of the Danube: the Traun, Enns, Ybbs, and March. The lead original of this bronze copy of 1873 may be seen in the Baroque Museum at the Belvedere.

No. 4 Neuer Markt is the former *Rauchmiller palace*, of 1665, with a façade probably designed by J.E. Fischer von Erlach. This square was the site of the famous early 19C ballroom known as the *Mehlgrube* or Flour Pit.

Here we may turn W along the Plankengasse to cross the Spiegelgasse, where at their junction stood *Silbernes Coffee-house* from 1808. No. 21 in the latter street occupies the site of a house in which Grillparzer died in 1872 (see p 302); in 1823 Schubert, staying with his friend Schober, composed his B Minor or 'Unfinished Symphony' at No. 9; it was first performed in 1865!

To the left, facing its PLATZ, is the restored façade of the **Lobkowitz palace** (1685–87; by G.P. Tencala), with a portal and upper floor by J.B. Fischer von Erlach (1709–11). The first semi-professional perfor-mance of Beethoven's Third, or 'Eroica', Symphony, took place here, although it had had an earlier amateur performance at the house of Würth, the banker. It was Prince Franz Joseph Maximilian Lobkowitz (1772–1816), who was a patron of the composer. The *Austrian Theatre Museum* is now housed here.

Between No. 17 in this street and the next parallel street, the Dorotheergasse, stands the **Dorotheum**, the Austrian equivalent to Christie's or Sotheby's, which as a pawn shop stood here from 1788, replacing an earlier establishment in the Annagasse, and it still provides a pledge and loan service.

The present neo-Baroque buildings of the auction-house date from 1898–1901, but the premises have been modernised recently. It is named after a chapel and convent dedicated to St. Dorothy which previously stood on the site. The Dorotheum also has a banking service with 24 branches (15 of which are in Vienna), and their clients may bid on a credit basis.

At Nos 18 and 19 in the Dorotheergasse stand two *Protestant Churches*, the latter erected in 1784 by Gottlieb Nigrelli. Nos 11, 10, and 9 in the street are the former *Nako, Dietrichstein*, and *Starhemberg palaces*, the last of them by Domenico Martinelli.

Follow the Stallburggasse (with the *Stallburg* itself to the left: see p 271), before turning right up the Bräunerstrasse, at No. 3 in which Johann Nestroy was born in 1801, while Grillparzer lived at No. 11, a Classical Revival building of 1783 by Ferdinand von Hohenberg, in 1832–35. Nos 7 and 8 were the former *Walterskirchen* and *Cavriani palaces*.

You soon reach the GRABEN, an animated esplanade which until the 13C formed part of a moat outside the medieval fortifications. Its main feature is the convoluted Baroque **Dreifaltigkeitssäule** (or Trinity Column), popularly known as the *Pestsäule*.

It is a memorial in thanksgiving for the end of a particularly pestilential plague which scourged Vienna and its environs in 1679; the number of victims has been variously estimated between at least 75,000 and as high as 150,000. (The last outbreak of plague in Vienna was 1713). It was erected in Salzburg marble in 1687–93 from a design by Ludovico Burnacini, assisted by J.B. Fischer von Erlach, with sculptures in gilded copper by Paul Strudel, Rauchmiller and others. At its base kneels its donor, Leopold I. Two fountains were added in 1804. It was freely copied in numerous other towns of Austria.

At No. 11 in the Graben stands the former *Bartolotti-Partenfeld palace*, designed by J. Lukas von Hildebrandt and built by Franz Janggl in c 1720. No. 10 was erected by Otto Wagner, (also partly responsible for Nos 14 and 15). Nos 13 and 16 were designed by Adolf Loos; No. 30 by Josef Hoffmann.

The Graben extends E towards the *Stephansplatz*; see p 247.

Mozart completed his 'Entführung aus dem Serail' began 'Figaro', and composed the 'Haffner' Symphony in a third floor apartment on the site of Graben 8 (September 1781–July 1782). Anton Diabelli (1781–1858), the music publisher, had his offices in the Graben, as also did Tobias Haslinger.

Off its N side stands the **Peterskirche**, on the site of perhaps the oldest church in Vienna. It was rebuilt in its present form in 1702 to the design of Gabriele Montani, followed in 1703–08 by J. Lukas von Hildebrandt, but was not completed until 1733, while between the obliquely set towers is a porch added in 1751–53 by Andrea Altomonte. The interior of the drum dome was painted by J.M. Rottmayr; also notable are the organ-case, the pulpit (by M. Steinl), and the galleries.—The *Parsonage*, No. 6 Petersplatz, was probably also by Montani.

Off the SW end of the Graben leads the *Kohlmarkt*; see p 259.

A few steps to the W is the TUCHLAUBEN (the cloth arcades), in which Nos 5, 8, 11, 19, and 23 have features of interest, particularly No. 19, on the first floor of which, the so-called 'Neidhart' frescoes of c 1400 were uncovered in 1979, and have been restored.

The Philharmonic Society's headquarters were at Tuchlauben 12 from 1822, at the sign of the 'Red Hedgehog', later the frequent haunt of Brahms, while on the second floor above the 'Blue Hedgehog' (Nos 16–18) lived Schubert from mid February 1827 until moving to Kettenbrückengasse in September 1828; see p 298. In 1781 Mozart lived briefly in the family home of his future wife at what is now Tuchlauben 6, before moving to the Graben; see above.

The street leads to the HOHER MARKT, a rectangular square on the site of the forum of Roman *Vindobona*, relics of which may be seen by descending steps at No. 3 on its SW side.

From its SW corner leads the BAUERNMARKT. Grillparzer was born in No. 10 (1791); it has since been transformed. The last execution to take place in the Hoher Markt was in 1703, but a pillory remained here until 1848. The *St. Joseph's Fountain* was erected by J.E. Fischer von Erlach in 1729–32. At its E end is the jacquemart *'Anker Clock'* (1911; recently restored), designed by Franz Matsch.

The Judengasse leads NE, with a view (right) of the tower-shaped studio of the architect Josef Kornhäusel, built above the **Synagogue** (1825–27) which he also designed, on an elliptical plan, with its entrance at No. 4 Seitenstettengasse, descending towards Rabensteig. It was restored in 1963 by Otto Niedermoser after desecration in 1938. Part of the *Max Berger collection* of Judaica may be seen here. (There were still c 220,000 Jews in Austria in 1938, a high proportion in Vienna. By May 1939 only 121,000 remained, most had emigrated. By 1946 only 5000 survived in Austria.) Adalbert Stifter lived in the vicinity in 1842–48.

A few paces further N in the Judengasse is the oft-restored **Ruprechtskirche**, a relic of the earliest documented church in Vienna, said to have been founded in 740, of which the aisle and lower part of the tower are 11C.

Bearing W along Sterngasse, you pass (left; No. 3) the *Wiener Neustädter Hof* (1734); adjacent to its entrance, mounted on the wall, is a cannonball fired into beleaguered Vienna by the Turks in 1683.

The Marc-Aurel-Strasse is shortly reached, leading down from the Tuchlauben to the MORZIN-PLATZ, skirting the Danube Canal, and the site of an earlier bastion of the city's defensive wall. Here stood the *Hotel Metropol*, HQ of the Gestapo in Vienna in 1938–45. The steps descending from the Ruprechtskirche served as a background to several scenes in the film, 'The Third Man' (1949).

By turning left and then right along the Salvatorgasse, you pass (left) the notable Renaissance *Portal* (c 1520–30) of the 14C chapel of the *Old City Hall* (or Altes Rathaus; see below). At the end of the street is the church of **Maria am Gestade**, which at an earlier period stood on a bluff overlooking the river. Although referred to as early as 1158, the present building, dating from 1394–1414, was thoroughly restored in the 19C. Its most obvious feature is the tower with its elaborate openwork lantern, damaged in both Turkish sieges. A grille in the interior precludes the close perusal of its glass and paintings, etc. The canopy, with its pendant keystones above the W door, and the upper gallery, will be noted.

Both Nos 3 and 5 Am Gestade, opposite, date from the 16C, while No. 3 Schwertgasse, which you follow, known as that 'Zu den 7 Schwerten' (of the Seven Swords), was rebuilt in 1720–30.

At No. 18 in the TIEFER GRABEN, a short distance further W, on the site of the NW fosse of the medieval walls, lived Mozart and his father in 1775; Beethoven briefly resided in the same street in 1800.

By turning left into Wipplingerstrasse (in which, on the site of No. 16, Mozart lived from mid 1788 to September 1790), you approach (left) No. 8, the **Altes Rathaus** (used as such until 1885), which, extended several times previously, received its elaborate façade in 1699. The portals of both Nos 6 and 8 are by J.M. Fischer (1781). Part of the building now contains a *Museum of Austrian Resistance to Fascism* in its several forms from 1934 until 1945. Remarkable is the *Andromeda Fountain* of 1741, by Georg Raphael Donner, in its courtyard.

Opposite, at No. 7, is the entrance (largely sculpted by Lorenzo Mattielli) of the former **Bohemian Court Chancery** (Böhmische

Hofkanzlei), transferred from Prague to Vienna in 1627. The edifice
was constructed by J.B. Fischer von Erlach in 1708–14, and enlarged
by Matthias Gerl in 1751–54. It now accommodates two of Austria's
supreme courts.

Passing through its courtyards, the JUDENPLATZ is reached, in
which an inscription on the 15C Haus 'Zum grossen Jordan' (No. 2;
the name of a former owner) refers to a pogrom against the Jews of
this quarter in 1421. A plaque on Nos 3 and 4 refers to Mozart's
residence in 1783 and 1785 in houses on this site.—At No. 5
Jordangasse, leading E, died J.B. Fischer von Erlach, in 1723.
Nestroy resided in the same building in his youth.

By briefly following the Kurrentgasse from the S corner of the
square, and turning right, you reach the entrance of the *Horologi-
cal Museum (Uhrenmuseum), at Schulhof 2. (Beware of calling it the
'Hurenmuseum', as has been heard!)

The museum was opened in 1921, and is largely based on the extensive
collections of Rudolf Kaftan (1870–1961, who was its curator until his death),
and of Baroness Maria von Ebner-Eschenbach, the novelist (1830–1916). The
collections were partly paid for by donations from manufacturers of tinned food,
and of arms (Skoda). Closed during 1944–64, it was then re-inaugurated, the
collection having been overhauled and re-arranged. Some 1000 exhibits of all
periods are displayed in 15 rooms of the former *Obizzi palace* (from 1690, but a
much older building). Time should be allowed to give the clocks and watches
the detailed perusal they deserve, even by the non-specialist. A well-illustrated
explanatory catalogue in English is available. See also the *Geymüller Collection*; Rte 26A.

Among the more remarkable time-pieces may be mentioned the movement of
a turret-clock from the cathedral, of 1699; a 'Monstrance clock' of c 1680;
several mid 18C long case clocks (by Nicholas Lambert, and Henry Batherson,
London, among others); a selection of pendant, turnip, and pocket watches—
the museum owns over a thousand—a number by Abraham Breguet (1747–
1823); early 19C Viennese mantel clocks; bracket clocks; travelling clocks;
picture clocks; pillar-clocks; and automata.

At No. 4 Schulhof is a *Doll and Toy Museum*, displaying Vaclav Sladsky's
collection of c 600 dolls, some dating back to the 1830s.

At No. 8 Schulhof is the late 17C *Collalto palace*, with a façade of
1808; that fronting AM HOF dates from 1715–25. Mozart gave a
concert here in October 1762, aged six.

On the E side of the square, surmounted by a series of statues, is
the **Church of Am Hof**, also known as that 'of the Nine Choirs of the
Angels', built in 1386–1403, and replacing an earlier chapel, but its
interior was baroquised in 1607–10. One chapel was later embellished by a fresco by Maulbertsch. The Baroque façade by C.A.
Carlone was added in 1662.

Among historic events which have taken place in this square was
the promulgation of Franz I's abdication as Holy Roman Emperor
(August 1806). The *Mariensäule* (with a pedestal by Carlone) dates
from 1667, replacing one erected in 1646 to fulfil a vow made by
Ferdinand III when the Swedes under Tortenssen were threatening
the city during the Thirty Years' War.

The façade of the mansion at No. 12 dates from c 1730; the
Markleinsches Haus (No. 7; 1727–30), with fire-engine garages
below, is named after its first owner. Designed by J. Lukas von
Hildebrandt, it replaced the residence of J.A. Liebenberg, the mayor
of Vienna during the Turkish siege of 1683. This was itself the
successor of a castle of the Babenbergs, which originally stood on the
site, whence the name 'at the Court' (Am Hof).—Some Roman
remains may be seen below No. 9.

At No. 10 stood the *Zeughaus* or **Arsenal of the Civic Guard** in the

16C, and from 1685 the fire wardens kept their equipment there. It is now the headquarters of the city's Fire Department, and contains a *Firefighting Museum*. The building itself, with its carved trophies and crowned double-headed eagle, was radically remodelled in 1731–32 by Anton Ospel, while the statues on its façade are by Lorenzo Mattielli.

Cross the Bognergasse at the SW side of Am Hof into the Irisgasse, there turning right along the Naglergasse (where a tavern called 'Zum Schloss Eisenstadt' was frequented by Schubert and his friends in 1827). Flanked by several ancient buildings, this narrow street follows the line of the Roman fortifications of *Vindobona* at their W limit.

Detail from The Freyung, by Bernardo Bellotto

In the Wallnerstrasse, parallel to the W, No. 4 is the *Esterházy palace* (c 1695, but later remodelled), containing 18C decoration, in the chapel of which Haydn gave occasional concerts.—No. 6 is the former *Palffy palace*, and No. 8 the former *Caprara-Geymüller palace* (c 1698; by Domenico Rossi, but changed in the early 18C), in which Grillparzer met Kathi Fröhlich, his 'eternal fiancée'.

From the former *Montenuovo palace*, adjacent, at the corner of Strauchgasse, followed to the right, you reach the S end of the triangular **Freyung** opposite the *Tiefer Graben* (see above). Freyung means the right of asylum, granted to the Scots Church (see below). It is embellished by a *Fountain* of 1846 by Schwanthaler.

No. 2 is the *Ferstel palace* (1856–60; restored since 1975), the building of the former National Bank of Austria and later of the Austro-Hungarian Bank, and until 1877 of the Stock Exchange or Börse. Its E entrance is now connected by a smart shopping *Arcade* (reopened 1981) to Herrengasse 17; see below.

On the SW of the Freyung stands the *Harrach palace* of c 1690, probably designed by Domenico Martinelli. It was severely damaged in 1944, and its thorough restoration is projected. The important Harrach art collections may be seen at *Rohrau*; see Rte 29.—At No. 4 Renngasse, leading NE, stands the *Schönborn-Batthyány palace* (1699–1706), by J.B. Fischer von Erlach. The first public performance of a work by Schubert took place in a house opposite, in 1819.

On the N side of the Freyung No. 7 was erected in 1774 as the priory for the **Schottenkirche** (*Scots Church*), which dominates this side of the square.

The *Schottenkirche* and *Schottenhof*, the Church and Court of the Scots, owe their origin to the Babenberg duke Heinrich II Jasomirgott (1141–77), who in 1155 founded a Benedictine monastery for Scottish (or more likely, Irish) monks. The humanist Chelidonius was abbot of the monastery in the early 16C. It was virtually rebuilt in 1643–48 by the Allios and Silvestro Carlone, but suffered severely in a fire on 14 July 1683, during the siege, and its present appearance is largely due to a 19C reconstruction. Its dependencies were rebuilt by Joseph de Podinger in 1828–35, following the design of Josef Kornhäusel, and contain a notable *Library*.

Below the high altar is the tomb of Count Starhemberg (died 1701), defender of Vienna in 1683; General Khevenhüller (1683–1744) is also buried here. The *Schottenaltar* (1469–75; of 19 panels, some containing early views of Vienna), among other paintings, is regrettably rarely on view, but may be seen by the persistent, or on Saturday at 14.00.

Young Stendhal, when with the French commissariat, attended Haydn's memorial service here on 15 June 1809, when Mozart's Requiem was performed, which moved him to write 'Lettres sur Haydn', his first published book (1814). Haydn's friend, Marianne von Genzinger, whose husband was Esterházy's personal physician, lived in apartments of the Schottenstift; Moritz von Schwind attended the Schotten grammar school; while Liszt had a pied-à-terre at the far end of its courtyard in 1869–86.

Before turning S along the Herrengasse, you can visit, at No. 3 Schottengasse (leading NW) the *Melker Hof*, built in 1769–74, with an early 16C chapel containing a 12C cross originally in the Ruprechtskirche. The property, owned by the abbey of Melk since 1439, is just E of the **Mölker Bastei**, forming the NW corner of the city's earlier defensive wall. Steps immediately to the N ascend left to approach the Schreyvogelgasse, in which No. 10 is a typical bourgeoise residence of its period (1804). Just to the N, at Mölker Bastei 8, is the so-called *Pasqualatihaus*, of 1798, named after its owner. It was sporadically Beethoven's residence during the years 1804–15, and his apartments on the 4th floor are reached by a winding stair.

It now contains several relics of the composer, including a 5-pedal piano by Andreas Streicher (1761–1835) of 1821; portraits of his father (1712–73); Johann, his nephew (1776–1848); of Beethoven in 1804, by *J.W. Mähler*; *J.B. Lampi*, Portrait of Andreas Razumovsky (1752–1836), of J.B. von Pasqualati (1733–99); a pastel of Amalie Sebald; *Franz Klein*, Bust of Beethoven (1812; see p 64), and Mask taken from life (1811–12).

In adjacent rooms is a collection of drawings and paintings by the poet *Adalbert Stifter* (1805–68).

Below, to the W, is the *Ringstrasse*, with the *University* beyond; see Rte 25F. You can get back to the Herrengasse by turning S and then left along the Teinfaltstrasse.

At Freyung 4 stands the **Kinsky palace** (1713–16), built by J. Lukas von Hildebrandt for Count Philipp Laurenz Daun (1669–1741), whose son, Count Leopold (1705–66), fought against Frederick the Great during the Seven Years' War. The façade and *Staircase* are notable, but it has been recently commercialised, after serving as a British Officers' Club in 1945–55.—Adjacent, at Herrengasse 23, is the former *Porcia palace*, several times altered since its erection in 1546 in the Renaissance taste.

At Bankgasse 2, the next right-hand turning, is the *Batthyány palace* (1695), beyond which, at Nos 4–6, is the *Hungarian Embassy*, composed of the former *Strattmann-Windischgrätz palace* (designed by J.B. Fischer von Erlach) together with the *Trautson palace*, which were given a uniform arcade by Franz Anton Hillebrand in 1784.

Turning N off the Bankgasse is the Schenkenstrasse, in which No. 4 accommodates the offices and library of the British Council.

Beyond the Hungarian Embassy, at No. 2, on the S side of the Bankgasse, is the *Liechtenstein winter palace*, originally by Enrico Zuccalli and Domenico Martinelli (1694–1706), and later changed by Antonio Riva and Gabriel de Gabrielli, the latter probably responsible for the Minoritenplatz entrance. The interior stucco-work by Santino Bussi, and sculptures by Giovanni Giuliani, are notable.—For the neighbouring *Burgtheater*, see Rte 25F.

On the N side of the nearby MINORITENPLATZ is the former *Starhemberg palace* (mid 17C, but later remodelled), in which Graf Rüdiger von Starhemberg died in 1701. It now houses government offices, as do several other mansions in the area. At No. 3 is the *Dietrichstein palace*, a 17C building remodelled in 1755 by Franz Hillebrand, and now housing offices of the Federal Chancellor and the Foreign Office.—For the *Chancellor's Office* (Bundeskanzleramt), further S in the Ballhausplatz, see p 265.

The Gothic **Minoritenkirche** (under restoration), that of the Friars Minor (and since 1784 of the Italian colony in Vienna), was begun before 1339 and completed some decades later, succeeding an early 13C building. The spire of the tower was decapitated during the Turkish siege of 1683. Later baroquised in part, it was remodelled by Ferdinand von Hohenberg in 1784–89. Its most interesting external features, apart from the tombstones against its W wall and the varying designs of the small rose-windows above, is the tympanum of the W portal, of 1350, in which an armed figure points towards Christ on the cross.

The interior is of little interest, and would be improved by the removal of an early 19C mosaic copy on its N wall of Da Vinci's Last Supper, a confection by Raffaelli of Milan, apparently commissioned by Napoleon for the Louvre, and later acquired by Franz II. In the S aisle is a Monument to Metastasio, of 1855 (see below), in which the figures of Salieri, Mozart, and Haydn appear.

Turning E from the square along the Landhausgasse, you return to the Herrengasse. On the far side is the *Café Central*, a favourite rendez-vous at the turn of the century and since, and said to have been patronised by Leon Trotsky among other influential intellectuals.

At Herrengasse 13 is the **Landhaus**, or *Palace of the Lower Austrian Diet*, with a *Chapel*, probably by Anton Pilgram, dating from 1513–16. The edifice was largely rebuilt in 1837–48 by Ludwig Pichl. The Landhaus was a hot-bed of revolution in 1848 (when troops were ordered to fire on demonstrators assembled outside), and the headquarters of the council which in October 1918 set out to establish the Republic of Austria.

At No. 9 stands the **Niederösterreichisches Landesmuseum**, housed in the former *Mollard-Clary palace* (1689).

It contains several rooms on two floors, largely devoted to the geology, flora, and fauna of the province; models of farm buildings, and agricultural imple-ments; painted chests and rustic furniture; costumes; ceramics; folk art, etc. On the SECOND FLOOR are collections of religious paintings and sculptures, notable among which is a group of the Ascension (after Dürer), of c 1515; a polychromed St. Catherine (1510); the Roggendorfer Altar (1500); *Master of the Winkler-Epitaphs*, Christ on the Mount of Olives, and Crucifixion; also a bust of Haydn by *Anton Grassi* (1802), and works by *Josef Schwemminger, Johann Peter Krafft*, and *Waldmüller*. It is expected that the museum will be considerably extended and modernised during the next decade.

Herrengasse 8 was the site of the riding-school of Prince Liechtenstein, in 1872 converted into a concert-hall by Ludwig Bösendorfer, the piano manufac-turer, and demolished in 1913 (Ignaz Bosendorfer had established his firm in Vienna in 1828); Liszt, Anton Rubinstein, and numerous other virtuosi per-formed there.

Herrengasse 7, restored since severely damaged in 1944, the former *Modena palace*, a 16C building remodelled in 1811 by Ludwig Pichl and Giocomo Quarenghi, houses the *Ministry of the Interior* (Innenministerium).—No. 5, the *Wilczek* (or *Lembruch*) *palace*, was built before 1737, probably after a design by Anton Ospel.

We now reach the **Michaelerplatz**, providing a good view towards the *Michaeler Trakt* (or Wing) of the Hofburg; see Rte 25D. In striking contrast is the N side of the platz, dominated by the **Looshaus**, a remarkable yet controversial building for its time. Commissioned in 1910 for the department store of Goldman and Salatsch, Adolf Loos' design caused a storm of criticism on its completion the following year, and even the aged Franz Josef—who had little enough taste, anyhow—was indignant on seeing 'windows without eyebrows'. The entrance has been restored recently. Two Roman buildings have been discovered below the Platz, which will be on view once excavations are completed.

On the E side stands the **Michaelerkirche*, which received its present façade, by Ferdinand von Hohenberg, in 1792. Parts of the church date back to the early 13C, while the choir is of 1327–40, after which it was frequently remodelled. The archangel above its porch is by Lorenzo Mattielli, while the dark interior contains a number of notable monuments, including that of Georg von Liechtenstein in armour (1548) against a pillar of the crossing, and several Trautson tombs. The late Baroque high altar is by Jean-Baptiste d'Avrange (1781); behind it is a large alabaster relief representing the Fall of the Angels. The Baroque organ, by J. David Sieber, is also remarkable, and the church is the venue of occasional recitals.—On the S exterior wall, seen from an alley, is a relief of the Mount of Olives (1494).

Pietro Metastasio, the poet (1698–1782), who was buried in the crypt of the Michaelerkirche, and who had come to Vienna in 1730, died at No. 11 in the adjacent **Kohlmarkt** (leading NE to the Graben), a street of ancient origin, leading from the Porta Decumana of Roman *Vindobona*, but the medieval charcoal-sellers' stalls have given way to less grimy establishments. In the garret of the same house lived Haydn c 1750–55, who was at this time a pupil of Nicola Porpora (1686–1768), a resident of Vienna from 1752/3–57. Chopin lodged at No. 9 from November 1830 until the following July. Here is the shop of *Freytag & Berndt*, with a comprehensive collection of maps and guides, above which is the print-shop of *Artaria*, established in 1782 by Carlo Artaria (1747–1808). Domenico Artaria (1775–1842) was a music-publisher, as was Matthias. Opposite are the long-reputed café-konditorei of *Demel* and at No. 16 the bookshop *Manz*, with a façade designed by Adolf Loos in 1912.

For the route S from the Michaelerkirche to the *Albertinaplatz*, passing the *Stallburg* (left) and the *Winter Riding School* (right), see p 270.

D. The Hofburg

The **HOFBURG**, the former Imperial Palace of the Habsburgs, is an extensive series of buildings erected over the centuries, as sprawling and lacking in unity as the diverse parts of the Empire which until 1918 were controlled from it: it is nevertheless one of the more important sights of Vienna, and contains several museums of great interest.

Its long history begins c 1275, when Ottokar II Přemysl, the Bohemian Duke of Austria from 1251, chose to construct a fortified camp outside the medieval walls of the city, in which, at *Am Hof*, the Babenberg Residence stood. This was taken over in 1278 by Rudolph I of Habsburg on the death in battle of his adversary, and was enlarged and strengthened. The fort stood on the site of the present Swiss Court or *Schweizer Hof*. Part of the moat, which lay without its NE corner, may be seen from the SE corner of the present Inner Courtyard, '*In der Burg*', or immediately to the left on entering the precinct from the *Michaelerplatz*; see above.

On the SW side of the *Swiss Court*, at each corner of which once stood a tower, stands the *Burg Chapel* (founded in 1296 by Albrecht I), itself radically altered after 1447 by Friedrich III, and several times since. In 1525 a number of accretions were destroyed by a ravaging fire, and after 1533, when Ferdinand I decided to make Vienna his court, much reconstruction and rebuilding was inaugurated. A defensive bastion had already, in 1531, been laid out just to the W (to which another was added further W in 1659, which crossed the present course of the Ringstrasse). Several of Ferdinand's 12 surviving children were accommodated in a 'Nursery Wing', later extended as the *Leopoldine Wing*, by Giovanni Lucchese and G.P. Tencala, on the W side of the 'In der Burg' court. The *Swiss Gateway* also dates from this period (1552–55). Gardens were laid out to the E (later the *Summer Riding School*), and on the site of the *Josefsplatz*, to the SE, was the exercise ground for the imperial horses. Not far to the E stood the stables (the *Stallburg*; after 1558).

Under Maximilian II and Rudolph II, the '*Amalia Residence*' (so-named after it had been the quarters of Wilhelmina Amalia of Brunswick, widow of Joseph I) was built by Pietro Ferabosco between 1575–1611 at the N end of the 'In der Burg'. This court was at that time used as a tilt-yard. More important works

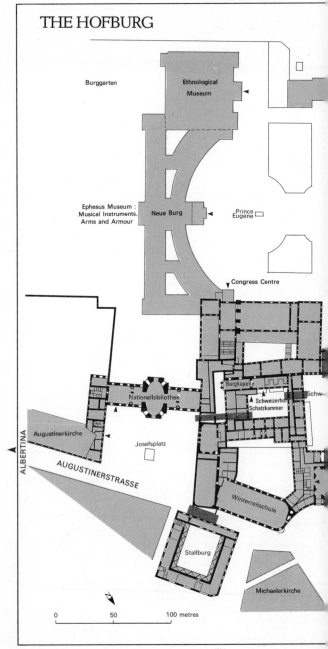

THE HOFBURG

Burggarten

Ethnological Museum

Ephesus Museum :
Musical Instruments,
Arms and Armour

Neue Burg

Prince
Eugene

Congress Centre

Burgkapelle

Schweizerhof

Schw—

Nationalbibliothek

Schatzkammer

Augustinerkirche

Josefsplatz

ALBERTINA

AUGUSTINERSTRASSE

Winterreitschule

Stallburg

Michaelerkirche

N

0   50   100 metres

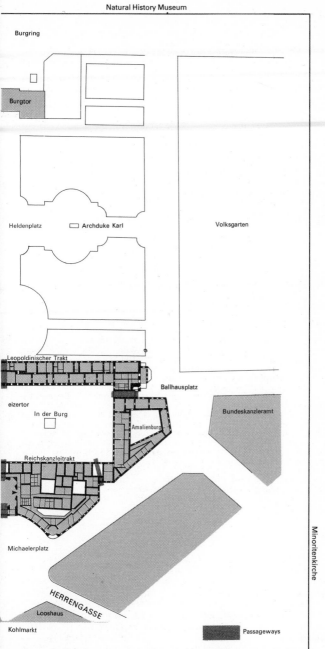

Natural History Museum

Burgring

Burgtor

Heldenplatz   Archduke Karl

Volksgarten

Leopoldinischer Trakt

Ballhausplatz

eizertor

In der Burg

Bundeskanzleramt

Amalienburg

Reichskanzleitrakt

Michaelerplatz

Minoritenkirche

HERRENGASSE

Looshaus

Kohlmarkt

Passageways

were carried out under Karl VI, starting in 1712 when a gateway was replaced by a Triumphal Arch designed by J. Lukas von Hildebrandt. This stood between the SE corner of the court and the Michaelerplatz, and was demolished in 1728 to make way for the *Reichskanzleitrakt* (or *Empire Chancery Wing*), closing the courtyard, which was erected to the design of J.E. Fischer von Erlach and virtually completed by 1730. Two groups of sculpture by Lorenzo Mattielli were commissioned, but in 1735 funds ran out and work on the project was halted.

The building of the neighbouring *Winter Riding School*, also by Fischer von Erlach, was finished just in time. The adjacent building, which became the 'Old Burgtheater', was demolished to make way for Ferdinand Kirschner's adaptation of Fischer von Erlach's design for the *Michaelertor* and *Michaelertrakt* (Michael's Gateway and Wing), erected between 1889–93; see below.

Until 1683 (when it was pulled down because it was thought to offer an inflammable target for the Turks), an Opera-house, by Burnacini, a wooden structure which accommodated 5000 and opened in 1666 on the occasion of Leopold I's marriage, stood on a site just SE of the Chapel. In its place, from 1723, rose the 'Court Library'. Further S stood the Augustinian *Church* (1330–49), with a later choir, abutting the monastic dependencies on the city ramparts, adapted as a palace in 1745–47 by Louis de Montoyer (1749–1811), which became that of Duke Albert von Saxe-Teschen (1738–1822), later remodelled by Josef Kornhäusel, and restored in 1947–52 after war damage. For the duke's collection of graphic art (thus known as the 'Albertina') still housed in the building, which is not in fact part of the Hofburg proper, see p 272.

The *Neue Hofburg* extends at right-angles from the *Alte Burg* (or Old Palace), and is the only part completed of an elaborate and ill-conceived project to form a vast symmetric 'Imperial Forum' on the site of the *Heldenplatz*. The defensive bastions were razed in 1809–12; the site of the parade-ground was later levelled and drained, and in 1821–24 an outer gate, at first retaining the name *Burgbastei*, was erected. In 1862–63 the rampart was also removed and the outer moat filled in, to make way for the Ringstrasse: see Rte 25F.

Gottfried Semper's plan of 1869 was to build *two* huge hemicycles, which would be joined to the two museums already projected by triumphal arches over the Ringstrasse, and in 1885 foundations were being dug for the southernmost wing. Karl von Hasenauer, in charge of the immense project, died in 1890, and Friedrich Ohmann took over from 1899–1907, concentrating on the completion of the Corps de Logis, which never found favour, either with the Emperor or his subjects. What could one possibly do with such a 'white elephant'? Any further ideas for a forum were vetoed by Franz Josef himself in April 1913. The massive 'Neue' Hofburg remained a supererogatory torso, one with few attractions, and certainly no one wished to live in it.

It was then decided to transfer to its marble halls the several Imperial collections overflowing from the already overcrowded Kunsthistorisches Museum and Natural History Museum, including the *Musical Instruments* (in 1916), the *Ethnological collection* (1928), and in 1934 the *Arms and Armour*. In 1947 the *Picture Archives* of the National Library were moved to its upper floor, and in 1966 the new *Reading Rooms* of the Library were inaugurated, as part of a general project. In 1977 it was the turn of the *Ephesus Museum* to be displayed in these palatial surroundings, and no doubt there will be further changes. It must be admitted that the Neue Hofburg looks better after its recent cleaning.

Meanwhile, in the years after 1958 the several late 19C halls between the Hofburg and the new wing were converted to accommodate a *Congress Centre*, which, as with the new premises of the Library, are fitted out with the latest devices and facilities.

A variety of government offices and departments have been housed in several other sections of the Hofburg, which in many respects is now put to good use, and remains a hive of activity.

For the buildings to the N and E of the **Michaelerplatz**, see p 257–58. The view of this entrance to the Hofburg, particularly when approached from the Kohlmarkt, is one of the more impressive, although by no means the oldest part of the complex; see above.

In the centre is the **Michaelertor** or *Gateway* (1889–93), above which, to a height of 37m, rises its cupola, and from which curve two wings. That to the S ends below J.E. Fischer von Erlach's smaller dome above the *Winter Riding School* (1729–35), which with its original façade was duplicated when the N wing was erected by Ferdinand Kirschner: few would realise that the latter was built a century and a half later.

On a site just S of the gateway stood the old *Burgtheater*, from 1741 until demolished in 1888. Three of Mozart's operas had their first performances there: 'Die Entführung aus dem Serail' (16 July 1782), 'Le nozze di Figaro' (1 May 1786), and 'Cosi fan tutte' (26 January 1790); 'Don Giovanni' also received its first Viennese performance here (7 May 1788), although first performed at Prague the previous 29 October.

Each balustrade of the Michaelertor is embellished with a globe surmounted by an eagle, trophies, etc., and above the central gate are figures of Wisdom, Justice, and Strength; while in niches at the base of each pavilion are fountain groups representing military and

Photograph of Franz Josef

naval power. Below the gateway are other groups depicting four Labours of Hercules. All six groups are by different sculptors. On entering the gateway you find yourself below a huge rotunda, the so-called '*Octagon*', dimly lit by eight oval windows, and containing several sententious statues of emperors.

From this point the **Hoftafel-und Silberkammer**, and the **Kaiserappartements**, or *Imperial Apartments* of the palace, may be visited. The former preserves the *Imperial Tableware and Silver Treasury*, including the apple-green Sèvres service given to Maria Theresia, his future mother-in-law, by the future Louis XV; a Meissen service of flowers on a white background (1775); and the Vienna Porcelain Manufacture series (1820), with its exquisitely painted panoramic views. Also displayed are a glass service by Lobmeyr; a silver Travelling-set (Paris, 1718); a Jardinière given to the Empress Elisabeth by Queen Victoria; Franz Josef's *vermeil* banqueting service, among a resplendent array of plate, candelabra, gilt centre-pieces (including one produced in Milan, and another in the form of a rocky landscape, of c 1740, from Vienna).

The *Imperial Apartments* may be visited in a group, but they are mainly of interest for the insight they provide into the character of those obliged to reside in such surroundings: no wonder 'Sisi' preferred to avoid the place! But as Richard Ford observed of its finer equivalent at Madrid: 'Nothing is more tiresome than a palace, a house of velvet, tapestry, gold, and bore...'. Some 20-odd rooms of the State Chancery and Amalia Wings are seen. Among their more notable contents are the several ornate stoves of various periods (mostly fired from parallel corridors), and 17C tapestries, mostly from Brussels. Among the few rooms of interest are: a reception-room containing three large encaustic paintings of 1833–37 by J.P. Krafft depicting scenes from the life of Franz I—entering Vienna after the Battle of Leipzig; alighting at the Swiss Gate; and appearing to his (devoted) subjects after an illness in 1826—the Bohemian glass chandelier should also be noticed. The *Audience-chamber*, with portraits of Ferdinand I, Franz II, and Franz Josef aged 55, and aged 85, with the high desk at which the Emperor stood to receive visitors personally (some 250,000 are estimated to have been granted audience here between 1848 and 1916); the *Conference-room*, with two portraits by Winterhalter, of the Empress Elisabeth ('Sisi') aged 28, and of Franz Josef aged 35; the latter's *Bedroom* (in which his wooden bath-tub was placed, there being no bathroom in his apartments; cf. Schönbrunn, and Bad Ischl), with battle scenes (Novara, Custozza, etc.), and a painting of the emperor aged two with his imperious mother, the archduchess Sophie; a small *Salon* devoted to his brother, the Emperor Maximilian of Mexico (shot in 1867), with a painting of his wife Charlotte (daughter of Leopold I of Belgium), who died mad in 1927.

A corridor leads to the **Amalia Wing**, with the *Living/Bedroom of the Empress Elisabeth* (whose iron bed was removed from the room every morning), with a portrait of Franz Josef aged 20; her *Dressing-room* (in which she took her daily Swedish gymnastic exercises, which caused consternation and provoked criticism at the inflexible court), with paintings of her favourite horses ('Flick' and 'Flock'), and dogs; of her palace at Corfu, and of herself on horseback in England. A large *Drawing-room* contains landscapes, and the adjacent room commemorating the Empress (assassinated at Geneva on 10 September 1898, aged 61, by the Italian anarchist Luigi Luccheni), has a painting of the Imperial couple hunting in Silesia (by E. Adam; 1882).

Beyond an anteroom displaying decorative paintings by the School of Meytens are apartments occupied by Tsar Alexander I during the Congress of Vienna. The *Red Drawing-room*, with red-ground Gobelins tapestries presented to Joseph II by Marie-Antoinette, his sister, with designs by Boucher, is crossed before you enter the *Study of Karl I*, the last emperor, and then the *Dining-room*. From the exit, stairs descend to the N end of the Amalia Wing opposite the Ballhausplatz. Here turn left through the Löweltor to enter the 'In der Burg' courtyard.

No. 2 **Ballhausplatz** (no entry) is the main entrance to the *Office of the Austrian Federal Chancellor*, or **Bundeskanzleramt**, and also of the *Foreign Office* (Aussenministerium), which, although not part of the Hofburg proper, may conveniently be described here.

It was built near the site of an earlier Royal Tennis-court (*jeu de paume*) by J. Lukas von Hildebrandt in 1717–21 at the suggestion of Count Sinzendorf, Lord Chancellor to Karl VI, and was at that time abutting one of the city bastions. From within its walls the destiny of Europe was partially shaped for about a century by Prince Wenzel Kaunitz (1711–94) from 1753, and Count Metternich (1773–1859; Prince from 1813), whose office and residence it was from 1809 to 1848. Here the latter guided several meetings during the Congress of Vienna (1814–15), and from here he made his way to exile in England at the Revolution of 1848, to be replaced by Prince Felix Schwarzenberg (1800–52).

After the disintegration of the monarchy in 1918 it was occupied by the Foreign Office and by Chancellors, notable among whom were Ignaz Seipel (1876–1932) in 1922–24 and 1926–29; it was here on 25 July 1934 that Engelbert Dollfuss was assassinated by Nazis in an attempted *putsch*. Here Wilhelm Miklas received Germany's ultimatum in March 1938 before the invasion of Austria; and from here Kurt Schuschnigg broadcast his farewell address to the nation. It was hit in an Allied air-raid in September 1944 and severely damaged. In 1945 Karl Renner (1870–1950), State Chancellor in the First Republic, became Federal President, with Leopold Figl as Federal Chancellor until 1953, since when the latter office has been held by Julius Raab (1953–61), Alfons Gorbach (1961–64), Josef Klaus (1964–70), Bruno Kreisky (1970–83), Fred Sinowatz (1983–86), and Franz Vranitzky (1986–).

An extension, housing the **Austrian State Archives**, is in the adjacent *Minoritenplatz*, where a number of important historical documents and treaties, etc., are occasionally on view.

From the 'Octagon' of the Michaelertor you enter the '**In der Burg**' courtyard, passing two earlier groups of the Labours of Hercules, by Lorenzo Mattielli; two more embellish the *Schauflertor*, at the NE corner of the court. To the left is the moat of the 13C fort; see History, above.

The main point of interest on this S side is the **Schweizertor** or *Swiss Gateway*, of 1552–53, painted maroon, with its decorative features and inscription gilded. Note the rollers for the chains of a former drawbridge, which are still in place. The whole, together with the interior vault, was restored after 1945.

In the centre of the courtyard (now a parking lot) stands a *Monument to Franz II* (1846); to the right is the *Reichskanzleitrakt* or *Chancery Wing*, the Imperial Apartments which have been described above; ahead is the Amaliaburg façade, adjacent to which is the *Löweltor*, leading to the Ballhausplatz; see above. Here too is the so-called 'Eagle's Staircase', ascending to the offices and residence since 1946 of the Federal President, installed in the former apartments of Maria Theresia. This extends along the *Leopoldine Wing* (left), dating from 1681 and replacing its predecessor destroyed by fire in 1668, which had in turn been an extension of Ferdinand I's

'Nursery Wing'; see History. The national flag flies from the roof of this wing when the Federal President is in the capital.

A passage at the SW corner of the court leads to the *Heldenplatz*; see p 273.

Passing through the Swiss Gateway, you enter the **Schweizerhof** or *Swiss Court* (named after the Swiss Guards who once did duty here), and the site of the oldest part of the palace. To the left is a *Fountain* of 1552, beyond which is the remarkable *Säulenstiege* or *Column Staircase* of c 1780. At the opposite side of the courtyard is the entrance to the ****SCHATZKAMMER**, the **Imperial Treasury**. It was first opened to the public in 1871, and was re-inaugurated here in 1986 after a thorough restoration of the premises. Although the remarkable collection of 'Crown Jewels' can be seen again, there has been some criticism of the lighting and labelling.

The Imperial Crown

Steps ascend from the lobby to the first of a series of rooms containing Keys to the Treasurey, tabards or coats or arms, and heraldic devices.—**R2** Portrait of Karl VI; bronze Bust of Rudolf II by 'Adriaen de Vries (Prague, 1607): the *Imperial Orb* (1612–17) and *Sceptre of Matthias* (1615); and the sapphire-surmounted *Crown of Rudolf II* (Prague, 1602), intended as the Austrian Imperial Crown after 1804, but never so worn.—**R3** the *Imperial mantle* designed by *Philipp von Stubenrauch* (1830) and first worn by Franz II; the *Robes* *of the Order of St. Stephan* (1764), and of *St. Leopold* (1836), and *Vestments of the Order of the Iron Crown* (Vienna, 1815–16).—**R4** *Lombardo-Venetian robes* (1838).—Passing through R9 (see below) turn left into **R5**, devoted to the Napoleonic period, with *Gérard's* Portrait of Marie Louise; the *Cradle of the Roi de Rome* (1811); Marie Louise's *Jewel-box* (1810; by *Biennais* and *Dupré*), embellished with Napoleonic bees; and the Sceptre and other regalia of Maximilian of Mexico (1832–67).—**R6** Imperial baby-clothes and Christening robes, including those of Franz Joseph and his siblings.—**R7** a remarkable *Emerald vessel of 2680 carats (the *Smaragdgefäss*), cut by *Dionysio Miseroni* in 1641; the *Crown of Stephan Bocskay* of Transylvania (Turkish, 1605), a gift of the Sultan Achmed I; also its Case; the *'La Bella' Hyacinth* (1687) set in an Imperial Double-Eagle; the *Hungarian Opal* (1600); a 492 carat Aquamarine; a gold *Family-tree* from which chalcedony intaglio portraits are suspended (1725–30); the *Golden Rose* (1819; by *Giuseppe Spagna*); and collections of cameos, onyx, opals and quartz.—**R8** *Agate bowl* (? Constantinople, 4C); a Narwhal horn; bronze busts of Maria Theresia and Franz Stefan of Lorrain (by *Matthäus Donner*; 1750).

The corridor is the first of five rooms devoted to **Ecclesiastical Treasure**, including in **RI** a Mariensäule (Augsburg, c 1675) by *Philipp Küsel*; and a collection of richly woven chasubles, mitres, and other vestments.—**RII** Reliquary crosses, including that of Ludwig the Great of Hungary (1326–82); several chalices, monstrances, and other cult objects; and a notable late 16C reliquary Casket by *Joris Hoefnagel*.—**RIII** rock-crystal crucifix from the Saracchi workshop (Milan, c 1600); gilt and jasper candlesticks from the workshop of Ottavio Miseroni, c 1620.—**RIV** St. Eustace Reliquary (Augsburg, c 1660) by *Hans Otto*; several ivory reliefs; *Christ between the two thieves* (Schwäbisch Hall, c 1626), carved by *Leonhard Kern*; the *nail reliquary*, sustained by two angels (Augsburg, mid 17C); a monstrance by *Zacharias Frill* (Vienna, 1701).—**RV** Bust reliquaries by *Joseph Moser* and his workshop (Vienna, 1760–79), and a collection of rosaries.

Turn left through RR6 and 5 to enter **RR9–12**, displaying the **Regalia of the Holy Roman Empire**, with a gold lamé *Coronation mantle* (mid 17C); *Alb* (Palermo, 1181); silk *Dalmatic* (Sicilian, early 12C); leggings, shoes, and gloves; the *'Eagle' Dalmatic* (c 1300); the *Imperial Cross* (c 1024, with a base of 1352), on the reverse of which are niello plaques depicting eleven apostles; the *lance*, possible of Lombardic origin (8C); the *Imperial Crown* (second half of the 10C), octagonal, encrusted with pearls and precious stones, and with enamel plaques. The brow-plate is surmounted by a cross, behind which is a single arch. The original crown is probably the work of a West German goldsmith, but had early 11C additions. Its leather case, with iron mountings, was made at Prague c 1350; the *Imperial Gospels* (Aachen, late 8C, with a cover of c 1500 by *Hans von Reutlingen*; the *Stephansbursa*, an early 9C reliquary, richly encrusted with gems; the *'Sabre of Charlemagne'* (late 9C or early 10C, possibly of Hungarian origin), and probably booty from the Avars; the *Mauritian Sword*, dating from between 1198 and 1218, with its (earlier) scabbard; a ceremonial *Sword of Investiture* (Palermo, before c 1220) with filigree work and cloisonné enamels, etc., and worn by Frederick II at his coronation in Rome; the *Imperial Orb* (Cologne ?, late 12C); the leather boxes for other objects displayed were made in Nürnberg between 1495 and 1518; two paintings from the studio of Martin van Meytens the Younger of the Coronation of

Joseph II at Frankfurt in March 1764, as described by Goethe in 'Dichtung und Wahrheit' (book 5); the *robes and regalia of Franz I* (Vienna, 1763–64), the only complete set of the Holy Roman Emperor's private vestments preserved, and worn at his coronation.—**R13** contains several coats of arms and other heraldic paraphernalia.—**R14** Portraits (including copies) of a number of Burgundian dukes, and including Mary of Burgundy, first wife of Maximilian I; also of Maximilian, by *Bernhard Strigel*; a charming *brooch* (Netherlands, 1430–40) showing lovers in a garden; the *Sword of Maximilain I* (Hall in Tirol, 1496), by *Hans Sumersperger*; the *Burgundian Court Goblet* of rock crystal mounted in gold, and partly enamelled (between 1453 and 1467)—**R15** is devoted to the *Order of the Golden Fleece*, with robes, collars, potences, tabards, etc., and the *Cross of the Order* (French, early 15C).—**R16** contains a rich display of altar-frontals, pluvials, copes, etc., from which you make your exit.

Since 1948 several apartments in this courtyard (in the 19C the residential quarters of Franz II, and later of the Crown Prince Rudolph) have accommodated the *Federal Bureau for the Protection of Monuments (Bundesdenkmalamtes)*, responsible—among other things—for the impressive work of restoration and preservation of so much of Austria's architectural heritage.

On the SW side of the courtyard is the mid 18C '*Ambassador Staircase*', by J.-N. Jadot, ascending to the entrance of the ***Burgkapelle** or *Hofmusikkapelle*, the chapel of the Hofburg, mainly dating from 1447–49, but with its interior several times altered since, when box-like balconies were added, and in 1802 further neo-Gothic modifications took place. The whole of the interior was renovated in 1977, and its statues restored.

Although the composers and organists Heinrich Isaac, Paul Hofhaimer, and Ludwig Senfl formed part of Maximilian I's musical retinue, none of them spent much time in Vienna, and it was not until after 1619 that there was any permanent Imperial Court Music Chapel here, when two of Giovanni Gabrieli's disciples succeeded as directors of music. Wolfgang Ebner (1612–65) was organist from 1637, succeeded by Alessandro Poglietti (died 1683) from 1661. Several emperors, including Ferdinand III, Leopold I, Josef I, and Karl VI, took a keen interest in its activities, some composing in their own right, while among later directors Heinrich Schmelzer (1679–80), and particularly Johann Josef Fux (1715–40), were notable. Gottlieb Muffat (1690–1770), trained by Fux, became a Court organist there in 1717. Other musicians who visited or performed in the chapel during this period were Froberger, Bononcini, and Caldara, and at a later date, Antonio Salieri (1750–1825), who had lived in Vienna from 1766. The position of Court Composer was revived in 1696, and incumbents included Wagenseil, Gluck, and Mozart; among organists was Albrechtsberger. Schubert, who had been a member of the Boys' Choir in 1808–12, was unsuccessful when applying for a conductor's post. Bruckner was Court Organist from 1868.

The *Boys' Choir* was disbanded in 1918, but re-instituted in 1924 and, under the enthusiastic directorship of Joseph Schnitt, became an important cultural institution emulating the choir of King's College, Cambridge.

Services in the chapel are conducted each Sunday and at Church festivals at 9.25am from mid September to late June, when (usually) classical church music, advertised in advance, is well performed by the Court Musicians and by one of the four Boys' Choirs (others may be on tour). Standing room, which is limited, is free, but seats may be reserved (see p 239).The music is frequently interrupted by the Mass, as in the original performances; and for most of the 'audience' the choir and orchestra will be out of view in an upper gallery, not that this affects the fine acoustics. See also *Augustinerkirche*, below.

From the SE corner of the Swiss Court passages lead past the chapel courtyard, providing a glimpse of its apse, to reach the JOSEFSPLATZ. In the centre stands an equestrian *Monument to Joseph II*, by Franz Anton Zauner (1807), looking away from the imposing façade of the *Great Hall* of the *National Library*, above the centre of which is the marble quadriga of Minerva riding down Envy and Ignorance, by Lorenzo Mattielli. The two façades were added in the same style by Nikolaus Pacassi c 1767. At the SW corner is the main entrance to the Library; on its S side is the masked entrance to the *Augustinerkirche*; while to the N is that of the *Redoutensäle*, with the entrance to the *Winter Riding School* below.

The several departments of the **AUSTRIAN NATIONAL LIBRARY** (*Die Österreichische Nationalbibliothek*) are spread among the buildings of the Hofburg, with the main entrance in the SW corner of the Josefsplatz, and with the entrance to the main *Catalogue Room* (*Kataloghalle*) and main *Reading Room* in the Heldenplatz façade of the Neue Burg.

Formerly the *Imperial Court Library*, it had its origins in the collections of such Habsburg connoisseurs as Albrecht III, Friedrich III, and Maximilian I. Maximilian II invited Hugo Blotius to be its keeper, a position he held from 1575–1608. Work began on a building to house these collections shortly after the siege of Vienna of 1683, prior to which the MSS from Leopold I's library, the archives of the Imperial Chancery, and the contents of the Schatzkammer (see above) had been removed to Passau for their safe-keeping.

The original plan was superseded in 1722 by an edifice designed by Johann Bernhard Fischer von Erlach, completed by his son Josef Emanuel in 1726, and this is still the main object of architectural interest to the visitor. Gottfried van Swieten (1733–1803), Mozart's patron, was Librarian from 1781.

This is approached from the entrance vestibule by ascending a staircase (left) by Nikolaus Pacassi (1780), the walls of which were embellished by a number of Roman inscriptions. The magnificent tripartite Baroque * *Hall of State** or *Prunksaal* is 77.7m long, 14.2m wide, and 19.6m high, with an oval cupola 29.2m high, containing allegorical ceiling paintings by Daniel Gran apotheosising Karl VI. Its capacity is c 200,000 volumes, and it originally contained c 90,000 (mainly 16–17C works), including 15,000 from the library of Prince Eugene acquired in 1736, displayed in the central oval. (Mathematics and Sciences were bound in yellow; Law, Theology and hagiography in blue; and other subjects in red.) At his death the prince left some 15,000 printed books, c 500 volumes and cartons of prints (now in the Albertina), and 237 MSS.

The marble statue of Karl VI in the centre, and those of other Habsburg monarchs, etc., are by Paul and Peter von Strudel.

It has been suggested that it served as a model for the great Library at Coimbra in Portugal, commissioned by Karl VI's brother-in-law, João V, possibly in rivalry, while it has similarities in style with several monastic libraries in Austria built during the same epoch.

The *old Reading Room*, previously the library of the abutting Augustinian monastery, with a ceiling fresco by Johann Bergl, was still the main reading-room until 1967.

The holdings of the National Library (in 1983) are over 6.6 million items, including in the Manuscript and Incunabula Collection some 39,000 MSS, almost 8000 incunabula, and 223,000 autographs. Among these are the 'Vienna Genesis' (mid 6C); the 'Vienna Dioskurides' (c 512); the 'Tabula Peutingeriana'; the illuminated 'Le coeur d'amour épris' (c 1460; for King René d'Anjou); the Ambras Book of

Hours (1517), etc. The MSS of five important medical treatises by Gerhard van Swieten were acquired in 1987.

The *Cartographical collection*, with 222,000 maps and atlases, and 247,000 geographical and topographical illustrations, and 142 globes, is in the same building. The *Music Collection* (Musiksammlung) comprises 45,000 MSS and 98,000 musical scores; the Hoboken Archive; 61,000 photostats of musical MSS; and an extensive collection of gramophone and tape recordings. These are preserved in Augustiner-Bastei 6, the S extension of the Hofburg, with its entrance in Augustinerstrasse 1; and also the *Papyrus Collection*, originating in that of Archduke Rainer (from El Fayoum, Egypt). Here also is the entrance to the *Albertina*; see below.

The *Department of Prints, Portraits, and Photographs* may be found on the upper floor of the Neue Burg, while the *Theatrical Collections* (entrance in the Michaelerplatz) contains some 1,378,000 autographs, play bills, stage models, and associated material. The National Library also houses an *Institute of Restoration* (of books and MSS), apart from the administrative offices of the Austrian Bibliography.

The N wing of the Josefsplatz comprises what was the *Court Theatre* of c 1700, with its two rococo halls, the larger intended for performances of opera, the smaller for burlesques and masquerades, etc.

These were remodelled as ballrooms in 1744 by Jean-Nicolas Jadot, but they continued to be used for chamber operas and concerts, and among the latter were some in which Beethoven performed (in 1795–96), while the masques and balls that took place during the Congress of Vienna caused the Prince de Ligne to remark unfairly, with some sarcasm: 'Le congrès danse, mais il ne marche pas', which provoked a humourless reaction from Metternich. Here in March 1842 Otto Nicolai inaugurated Philharmonic Concerts, which continued under his baton until 1847. Several first performances of the waltzes of Johann Strauss the Younger were heard here in the middle of the century.

At an angle to this wing stands the **WINTER RIDING SCHOOL** (1729–35), home of the *Spanish Riding School* or *Spanische Reitschule*, designed by J.E. Fischer von Erlach. The *Riding Hall* itself, with a capacity of c 1100, is 55m long, 18m wide, and 17m high, and is surrounded by 46 columns, between which and from an upper gallery, the audience may view the equestrian performance (see p 242). At the N end is the former Emperor's Box, above which is an equestrian portrait of Karl VI, surmounted by suitable trophies, etc.

A tablet confirms that the Imperial Riding-school had been established in 1735 for the instruction and training of young nobles and for the training of horses for *haute école* and war, under the supervision of Count Althan. Earlier, several extravagant carousels, etc. took place here, while in July 1848 it served for a meeting-place for the first constitutional assemblies—doubtless talking a lot of horse sense—after the revolution of that year.

The *Lippizaner* stallions pass from their stables across the street through a narrow passage to enter the hall, mounted by their soberly dressed trainers (*Bereiter*), wearing coffee-coloured riding-tails and bicorne hats. They then go through their complicated paces, accompanied by music. Previously a small band would play, but in recent years the music is taped—much of it sounding out of place in the Baroque surroundings.

A variety of trots and steps including the '*passage*' or Spanish step, and '*piaffe*' (trotting on the spot with lowered hind-quarters), side-stepping, etc., are displayed, together with curvetting, among other exercises *off* the ground. But as Edward Crankshaw has observed: 'The cabrioling of the pure white Lippizaners is, by all our standards, the absolute of uselessness. The horses, fine, beautiful, and strong, are utterly divorced from all natural movement, living their lives in an atmosphere of unreality with every step laid down for them and no chance whatsoever of a moment's deviation. And so it was with the 19C Habsburgs.'

Before 1918 the performances were only attended by the emperor's guests, but from the turn of the century his subjects had also been admitted to watch the routine training of the horses on two mornings a week (*Morgenarbeit*). From 1920 all performances were open to the public, and soon became a popular attraction. In March 1945 the horses were transferred from Vienna to St. Martin, near Schärding, and then to Wels (while the stud from *Piber*, which had been evacuated to Hostau in Czechoslovakia in 1942, was moved to Upper Austria, where it remained until 1947), a redeeming action supervised by General Patton—himself a keen horseman—on the intervention of Colonel Alois Podhajsky, then the director of the school. The Riding School itself returned from Wels to the Stallburg in 1955.

The *Lippizaners* stem from a Spanish breed and also a Neapolitan strain, crossed with horses from the Carso plateau near Trieste, and in 1810 with an Arab grey. They are named after the stud established in Lipic (now in Yugoslavia) by the Archduke Karl in 1580, although Maximilian II already had a stud at Kladrub in Bohemia. They are born dark, but on maturing turn white, usually before their 7th or 10th year. The main stud is at *Piber* in W Styria (cf.). At the age of 3¾ the stallions are brought to Vienna, and are first stabled at the *Hermes Villa* in the Lainzer Tiergarten (cf.) before being moved to the adjacent stables, which only accommodates 65 mounts. Their training takes about four years, but some stallions are sold after the first year.

The *Imperial Stables*, or the **Stallburg** (on the E side of the street), was originally erected as a residence for the King of Bohemia, who, prior to its completion, succeeded as Maximilian II. From 1564 it housed the riding and coach horses of successive emperors, and since 1700, the Lippizaners. The Renaissance courtyard was radically restored in 1955–60, when the arcades, which had been bricked up for almost two centuries, were re-opened. Parts of the building had previously housed court officials, and during the reactionary Metternich era, his 'Cypher Office'; also, at an earlier period, the art treasures and library of the Archduke Leopold William. At the N end of the block stands the *Alte Hofapotheke*, or former *Court Dispensary*, of 1746, since 1976 leased out although state-owned.

The '**Neue Galerie**' *of the Kunsthistorisches Museum*, installed in the Stallburg in 1967, has been moved to the Upper *Belvedere* (see Rte 25K).

On the E side of the JOSEFSPLATZ is the *Pallavicini palace* (No. 5), erected in 1783–84 by Ferdinand von Hohenberg, with a portal and statues by F.A. Zauner. Adjacent is the *Pálffy palace* (c 1575), with a Renaissance façade, restored after war damage, and now used as a venue for cultural events.

The Augustinerstrasse continues S, alongside the *Augustinerkirche*, and passing (left) the LOBKOWITZPLATZ (see Rte 25C) before reaching the ALBERTINAPLATZ; see below.

The **AUGUSTINERKIRCHE**, or Church of the Augustinian Friary (1330–38), that of a monastery founded in 1327, was baroquised during the 17C, and its tower was erected in 1652. In 1784–85 the internal accretions were removed by Ferdinand von Hohenberg, and its Gothic structure revealed, although the Baroque pews remained in the central aisle. It was restored after bomb damage in the Second World War but deserves a further renovation.

It was long considered the parish church of the Court as opposed to the Imperial Chapel (or *Burgkapelle*; see above). The sung Mass on Sunday (programme advertised; collection) is more easily attended than that in the Burgkapelle.

Among marriages celebrated here were those of Margarita Teresa of Spain to Leopold I (1666); Maria Theresia and the future Franz I (1736); Maria Antonia

(Marie Antoinette) to the future Louis XVI (1770; by proxy); Maria Louise and Napoleon (1810; the Archduke Karl acting as proxy); and Franz Josef to Elisabeth of Bavaria (1854).

One of the most striking monuments is the pyramidal *Cenotaph of Maria Christine* (1742–98; daughter of Maria Theresia, and wife of Duke Albert; see Albertina, below), by Canova, completed in 1805. Her tomb is in the Kaisergruft. To the right before reaching the choir is the *Georgkapelle*, containing a monument to Leopold II; here were buried Gerhard van Swieten (died 1772), Maria Theresia's physician (and the father of Mozart's patron, Gottfried van Swieten), and Marshal Daun (1705–66). Habsburg *hearts* are also preserved here.

Skirting the E wall of the church you reach the entrance to the Albertina.

The *ALBERTINA State Collection of Graphic Art, named after its founder, Duke Albert of Sachsen-Teschen (1738–1822), in whose palace it was housed, is without doubt one of the most important and extensive collections of its kind. To the original collection, later extended to contain c 22,000 drawings and 230,000 engravings, were added (in 1919–20) some 250,000 works of art housed in the Print-room of the Imperial Library. In exchange, the Cartographic collections of the Albertina were handed over to the Library. Numerous duplicates were sold during the following decade, and from the proceeds new acquisitions were made, particularly in the contemporary field. It now preserves over 44,000 drawings and water-colours, and over a million examples of printed graphic art. Among numerous special collections are miniatures; architectural drawings; artists' sketchbooks; caricatures; illustrated books; landscapes and townscapes; posters, etc., apart from numerous examples of early wood-engraving blocks. Its Library and Archives are invaluable to researchers.

While the Albertina mounts a constant flow of well-catalogued *Exhibitions*, it should be emphasised that no 'permanent selection of masterpieces' is on regular view—although several reproductions are—owing largely to their delicate nature. Scholars wishing to see works that are not on display should apply to the *Study Hall* (Studiensall; 3rd floor).

Duke Albert, son of the Elector Frederick Augustus of Saxe, King of Poland, and the Austrian Archduchess Josepha, in 1766 married Maria Christine, a daughter of Maria Theresia. Soon after, he acquired the Durazzo collection (30,000 items) in Venice, while during his term of office as Vice-Governor of the Austrian Netherlands (1780–92) he further enriched his treasures, and in 1786 he was given a substantial number of works of graphic art by his sister-in-law, Marie Antoinette. Much of the important collection of Prince Charles de Ligne was acquired at auction in Vienna in 1794, soon after the duke's return to the capital, where after 1796 he devoted himself to improving his collection, almost entirely so after the death of his wife in 1798. A lot of Dürer drawings were transferred to him from the Court Library (originally acquired by Rudolf II in Prague c 1589), while a collection of Dürer prints were secured in Rotterdam in 1800; several other important purchases were made during succeeding years.

Among collections transferred from the Print Room were the 290 portfolios gathered by Prince Eugene of Savoy, assisted by Pierre Jean Mariette, who entered his service in Vienna in 1717, although the prince had already started collecting when in London in 1712. Working more systematically, Adam von Bartsch (1757–1821) acquired very substantial collections of the graphic work of Rembrandt, Callot, and Della Bella, among others, but in 1818 he stressed that its works should be available 'to art collectors and scholars, to painters seeking advice, to engravers and apprentices in the graphic arts, desirous of practising...'. He added that 'admission shold be refused to idlers merely wishing to look at the pictures as a pastime...', an over-protective attitude which now appears excessively élitist. The process of adding to the treasures of the Print Room was continued by his son and successor, Friedrich Bartsch.

The building, restored since severely damaged in 1945, also houses the *Austrian Film Museum*, and important collections of *Papyrus*, largely collected by the Archduke Rainer, and the *Department of Music* of the National Library; and also a *Goethe Museum*, with a comprehensive collection of first editions, portraits, and other souvenirs of the great German poet and his epoch.

Steps immediately S of the Albertina ascend to a terrace on the site of a former bastion, on which is an equestrian *Statue of Archduke Albrecht*, victor of Custozza (1866), by Kaspar von Zumbusch. See also the *Albrechtsbrunnen*; p 250.

By bearing right around the base of this promontory, with a view ahead of the rear of the *Opera-house* (see Rte 25B), a ramp is passed before reaching the SE entrance of the shady **Burggarten**, the promenade of the Imperial family and the upper ranks of the Court from c 1820 until 1918. Its E side is flanked by extensive *Palm-houses* and other hot-houses (1902; by Friedrich Ohmann); on its N side is the S façade of the *Neue Burg*, near which since 1953 has stood Viktor Tilgner's *Statue of Mozart* (1896), which formerly embellished the Albertinaplatz.

Following the S side of the palace, with the *Kunsthistorisches Museum* on the far side of the Burgring (see Rtes 25E and F) you approach the classical **Burgtor** (or Äussere Burgtor; 1821–24; completed by Peter von Nobile), converted in 1934 to become Austria's *War Memorial to the Unknown Soldier*.

From here there is a panoramic view across the **Heldenplatz** (the Heroes' Square) towards the façade of the *Leopoldine Wing* of the Hofburg.

To the N is an equestrian statue of the victor of Aspern, the *Archduke Karl* (1771–1847), who was also the Austrian commander at Wagram. To the S, is an equestrian monument of *Prince Eugene of Savoy* (1663–1736). Both these sculptures are the work of Anton Dominik Fernkorn (1859, and 1865, respectively).

The Heldenplatz—unfortunately too often crowded with parked cars and buses—can of course be as easily approached from the 'In der Burg' courtyard by the *Burgpassage*, where a section of wall has been uncovered, which was once the base of the *Widmertor*, the gateway-tower of the 13C fortress; see History. Between the Burgpassage and the Neue Burg is a loggia, and the façade of the *Neuer Saal*, now part of a **Congress Centre**.

This Centre was formed in recent decades by modifying and utilising several halls suitable for meetings, small exhibitions, and commercial or international conferences. Since 1969 the Centre has been run by a private company, the Hofburg-Kongresszentrum Betriebsgesellschaft, and all modern facilities are provided in an opulent setting, where—in the season—balls are also held.

From a central point in the Heldenplatz you get a view NW towards the prominent towers of the *Rathaus*, seen above the *Volksgarten*; see Rte 25F.—To the SW rise the domes of the *Natural History Museum*, and *Kunsthistorisches Museum*; and to the SE, the huge hemicycle of the **NEUE BURG** (see History), completed on the eve of the First World War, with its immense colonnade, recently cleaned, below which stand statues representing historical personages of the monarchy over the centuries. In the centre, above an entrance porch, is a balcony from which on 13 March 1938 Hitler proclaimed the *Anschluss*, or forcible annexation or—as some have put it—the 'rape' of Austria, only Russia, Mexico, Chile, and China protesting. Later that day Cardinal Innitzer greeted the Führer and promised him all support.

The porch now serves as the main entrance to the *Catalogue* and main *Reading-room* of the National Library (see p 269), and—also housed in this central hemicycle—to the *Ephesus Museum*; the collection of *Arms and Armour*; and collections of *Musical Instruments*; see below. At the W end of the Neue Burg is the *Ethnological Museum*; see p 276.

The **Ephesus Museum** is the name given to the collection of relics apparently given by the Sultan to Franz Josef in gratitude for the excavations undertaken by Austrian archaeologists at *Ephesus* (in Turkey) during the years 1895–1908. They were installed here in 1977/8, and are well displayed on tubular supports.

Steps to the left of the entrance vestibule ascend past an *altar of Artemis* (2nd half of the 4C BC) to a hall in the E hemicycle in which a maquette of the site (1:500) is exhibited. The main objects are the remains of a colossal *Frieze* in high relief in memory of Lucius Verus, erected at the end of the war against the Parthians in AD 165; also several carved capitals. At the far end of the wing is part of an *Octagon*, on either side of which are two *Charioteers*. On returning through this area, you mount steps to pass a number of busts, and a restored bronze statue of an *Athlete*, a Roman copy of a Greek original of 340–330 BC; a reconstructed Theban *Sphinx*; a marble *Child with a duck* (3C BC); a bronze *Hercules and the Centaur* (2C BC), and a five-armed lamp. Steps descend to an area preserving further artefacts and relics excavated on the island of *Samothrace* in 1873–75 by A. Conze. These include objects from the Arsineoion rotunda, the Propylon of the Temenos, Ptolemaion, and Hìeron, etc.

The extensive and remarkable ***Collection of Arms and Armour** (*Hofjagd-und Rüstkammer*) of the *Kunsthistorisches Museum* is housed in the W hemicycle of the Neue Burg, and comprises several once-dispersed collections, assembled in chronological order. It concentrates on particular examples of armour and weapons which are of historical interest as having been associated with specific members of the Habsburg dynasty, its generals, courtiers, and officials, and includes ceremonial and jousting armour. The arms and armour of the rank and file can be seen in the *Arsenal* (cf.), and in the *Armoury* at *Graz*. A subsidiary collection is displayed at *Ambras*, near Innsbruck.

Several cases of hunting weapons are passed prior to entering **RI** (AD 500–1480), in which are two *Habsburg Family Trees* painted on canvas in 1497 and 1507 and designed as wall-hangings. A section here explains the art of engraving armour, and inlaying, etc., and another is devoted to children's armour. Other notable objects are the horned or crested helmet of Albert von Prankh (mid 14C); the 'Hundsgugel', two helmets with pointed snout-shaped visors (Milan; c 1400); the armour of Friedrich I von der Pfalz (Milan; 1450); and the goat-mounted helmet of Georg Kastriota (Skanderbeg) von Albanien (1460).—**RII** (1480–1500): the armour of Archduke Siegmund of Tyrol (by the great armourer Lorenz Helmschmid of Augsburg; 1485); of Maximilian I (L. Helmschmid; 1480); ditto, 1492; of Philip the Handsome (by the same; 1495–1500); also a suit by Hans Prunner of Innsbruck (1489); of Ferdinand V of Aragon (Master IP; 1495), and horse-armour of Friedrich III.

Gallery A: Jousting-armour of Maximilian I, etc.—**RIII** (1500–30): Costume-armour of Wilhelm von Roggendorf (Kolman Helmschmid; 1525), and another suit made by the same (1510) for Andreas von Sonnenberg; a suit made for Maximilian I by Francesco da Merate in Arbois (1508); black fluted armour of Johann Friedrich von Sachsen

(Hans Ringler; Nuremberg, 1530); costume-armour of Karl V (by Hans Rabeiler; Innsbruck, 1512); a fluted and skirted example for the same by Konrad Seusenhofer (Innsbruck, 1514); skirted costume armour with a grotesque helmet, of Albrecht von Brandenburg (1526); fluted armour with a mask-helmet, of Ulrich von Württemberg (1525–30); another of the same date, for Wolf Dietrich von Hohenems; and a snout-shaped visor of Ferdinand I (Hans Seusenhofer; 1526–29).

The series of rooms continues the display of arms and armour, many of them exquisitely embellished, produced during the reigns of Karl V, Ferdinand I, Maximilian II, the Archduke Ferdinand of Tyrol, Rudolf II, the Archduke Leopold V (whose richly worked wheel-lock of 1628 is remarkable), and the period of the Thirty Years' War. These are followed by displays in several more rooms, covering the reigns of Ferdinand II and III, and Leopold I, the Turkish Siege of Vienna in 1683 (including booty from the Turkish camp), etc.

The *Great Colonnade* displays a chronological arrangement of various types of hand firearms (c 1000 examples), often elaborately decorated or damascened, together with hunting weapons, garnitures and accoutrements, court swords, etc.—The *Gallery Franz Josef* contains arms from 1720 to 1916, including a pair of guns made by Kaspar Zelner and Georg Keiser, which belonged to Prince Eugene of Savoy; several hunting guns used by the penultimate emperor; and firearms belonging to the crown-prince Rudolf, and to Franz Ferdinand, himself a crack shot.

The **·Collection of Ancient Musical Instruments** (*Sammlung alter Musikinstrumente*) of the *Kunsthistorisches Museum*, at present under restoration, is accommodated in the SW wing of the Neue Burg. Among the exhibits are several earlier collections (including that of the Archduke Ferdinand of Tyrol at Ambras, and that of the Marchesi Obizzi at Castello Catajo near Padua), also the instruments acquired or inherited by the *Gesellschaft der Musikfreunde* over the years, together with numerous individual instruments with special associations. The collection is, therefore, one of great historical and musicological significance. They are not infrequently used in performances requiring period instruments, and occasional concerts are given in the Marble Hall of this wing.

Sections are devoted to different types of instruments: among the *Keyboard instruments* are several clavichords, dating from the late 17C to the second half of the 18C; the earliest cembalo is dated Venice 1559, made by Joseph Salodiensis, while a fine example is that by Shudi and J. Broadwood, London 1775, once owned by *Haydn*. Among the spinets are an Italian example of the 16C; a Biderman spinet (Augsburg; 17C); and one by Christoph Bock of Vienna (1804). There are a number of *hammerflügels* or grand pianos, by such makers as Ignatz Kober, Ferdinand Hofmann, Johann Schantz, and Anton Walter, in Vienna, and by J.A. Stein, in Augsburg, together with the Erard piano-forte presented to *Beethoven* in 1803, and a Broadwood of 1807. Later examples are those of the Vienna manufacturers Joseph Brodmann, Conrad Graf, J.B. Streicher, Ludwig Bösendorfer, et al. Individual instruments include the square piano by Walter used by *Schubert* when staying with his friend the artist W.A. Rieder; the grand piano by Graf, presented to *Robert* and *Clara Schumann* as a wedding present in 1839, and later donated by *Brahms* to the Gesellschaft der Musikfreunde; a piano used by *Hugo Wolf*, and *Mahler's* Bluthner, etc.

Also of interest are the upright piano or 'clavicytherium' of Leopold I, a combined spinet and regal (Augsburg; 1587); a 'hausorgel', a 'sewing'-piano, and several other hybrid instruments, and a harmonium of 1859 owned by *Liszt*. Note also the wax Bust of Haydn.

Among *Stringed instruments* are several 15C examples which evolved from the medieval rebec, etc., together with violas da gamba, and violas da braccio, an Italian example of c 1500 being one of the oldest surviving. Notable are the Venetian violin by Ventura Linarolo (1581), the violoncello by Dorigo Spilman (Padua; c 1590), an early consort of three viols by Antonio Ciciliano (Venice; c 1520); a lira da braccio by Giovanni d'Andrea (Verona; 1511); the baryton of Magnus Feldlen (Vienna; 1656), and another example by D.A. Stadlmann of Vienna (1732), and a viola d'amore by Matthias Thir (Vienna; 1779), both of which are said to have belonged to *Haydn*; and a quartet of instruments by Francisco Geissenhof of Vienna. Also of interest are the lira da gamba of Vendelinus Tieffenbrucker of Padua (2nd half of 16C), the single-stringed marine trumpet, the hurdy-gurdy, and—a curiosity—a tortoiseshell violin of 1749.

Among *Plucked instruments* are a remarkable cithern or zither by Girolamo de Virchi (Brescia; 1574), once in the collection of Ferdinand of Tyrol; a lute by Georg Gerle (Innsbruck; c 1580); lutes by Hans Frei (early 16C): converted late Renaissance instruments; a bass 'lautencister' of 1500; several 17C Italian guitars; and a Renaissance harp, together with more modern instruments.

Notable among the *Brass instruments* are an engraved trumpet made for the Archduke Ferdinand by Antoni Schnitzer (Nuremberg; 1581), with its original mouthpiece; and six silver trumpets by Franz and Michael Leichamschneider of Vienna (1741; 1746), made for Maria Theresia; two trumpets by Hanns Gayer of Vienna (1690), and a variety of other horns.

Numerous *Woodwind instruments* are displayed, including a complete set of 21 recorders; 16C krummhorns or cromornes; dulcians; serpents; a bass-flute of 1501; oboes, flutes, clarinets, bassoons, oboes d'amore, etc., while among the curiosities is the 'Tartölten', a set of five dragon-faced shawms, probably from the Tyrol (16C).

A small section is devoted to musical toys, and miniature instruments, while several tapestries depicting early instruments may also be seen. Among recent acquisitions are a lute of 1580, a trombone of 1557 (the second oldest known), and *Lanner's* violin, a clavichord by Anton Röhmer of Graz (1774), and a Baroque lute by Blasius Weigert of Linz (1740).

The **'Ethnological Museum** (*Museum für Völkerkunde*), situated at the W end of the Neue Burg, unfortunately displays only a very small proportion of its extensive collections at any one time, although it is the venue for important temporary exhibitions.

Among the permanent displays (on the ground floor) are those of *Benin Bronzes*, including some Portuguese figures, and carved ivory objects; and part of the *Oriental collection*, including ceramics; cloisonné, jade, ivory, and lacquer objects; 10–15C celadon ware; netsukes; pipes; arms and armur; kimonos and other costumes, including Chinese womens' shoes for binding their feet; furniture; musical instruments; agricultural implements, etc. On the FIRST FLOOR, is the section devoted to Aztec art, including a Quetzalfeather and gold *Headdress*, a feather fan, and a feather shield, probably given to Cortés, and passed on by the Emperor Karl V to his nephew, Ferdinand II of Tyrol, which were listed in the inventory of the Ambras collection from 1595. Also to be seen are a number of objects of jade and obsidian of the Zapotec culture, and U-shaped yokes (Tajin culture); and in a separate section, artefacts from Polynesia collected by Captain James Cook (1728–79).

E.   The Kunsthistorisches Museum

The *** *KUNSTHISTORICHES MUSEUM** is without doubt one of the world's greatest collections. Only a proportion is accommodated in the monumental building at No. 5 Burgring, including the main collections of *paintings, Classical art, Egyptian antiquities, sculpture, decorative art* and *objets d'art*, and *coins and medals*. Its collections of *musical instruments, arms and armour*, the excavations from *Ephesus*, etc., are displayed in the Neue Burg, while the *Crown Jewels* and *Ecclesiastical Treasures* are conserved in the *Schatzkammer* of the Hofburg. *Coaches and carriages* may be seen at *Schönbrunn*. In addition to these dispersed sections are the important collections at *Schloss Ambras*, just S of Innsbruck: for all of which see the index. A good, illustrated, general 'Guide to the Collections', published for the museum by Verlag Christian Brandstätter, is available at the bookstall.

This enormous collection, even more remarkable for the general quality of the exhibits than for the actual quantity accumulated, owes its origins to the acquisitive proclivities of Friedrich III, and notably Ferdinand I, together with their successors. Certain portions had been previously dispersed among various archdukes, some being held at Graz, at Laxenburg, in the Belvedere palace, and in parts of the Hofburg, near the gates of which, with the planning of the Ringstrasse, two new buildings were to be erected in which they might be assembled and shown to advantage. Their architect was Karl Hasenauer, whose plans were modified by Gottfried von Semper, and work started in 1871. The structures were virtually completed by 1880. That to the N was to be a *Natural History Museum*, while a space between the two was reserved for the Maria Theresia Monument; see Rte 25F. The two buildings almost exactly mirror each other, although the *Kunsthistorisches Museum* is slightly deeper. Both contain two interior courtyards, and above the centre block of each main façade rises an octagonal dome flanked by four subsidiary turrets. No expense was spared with their internal decoration, on which the foremost artists were employed, while the costliest materials were used in providing a suitably sumptuous framework in which to display the Imperial collections, at the same time exemplifying Franz Josef's taste.

Additional works, including the 'Este Collection', formerly housed in the Obizzi castle near Padau, and the bequest of Gustav von Benda, in 1932, have extended its range. Its contents were largely evacuated during the Second World War, when the museum itself suffered bomb damage. In 1949 several clocks and scientific instruments in the Dr Alphonse de Rothschild collection were donated.

The interior of the dome contains medallions of the several emperors who indulged themselves in collecting, among them Maximilian I, Karl V, Rudolph II, Karl VI, and Franz Josef, together with Archdukes Ferdinand II, Albrecht VII, and Leopold Wilhelm. On the landing of the elaborate staircase is a sculpted group of Theseus and the Centaur by *Canova*, while the lunettes are decorated with depictions of great artists by *Makart*, and in certain spandrels are paintings of 'the evolution of art' by *Gustav Klimt* and his brother *Ernst*, and *Franz Matsch*.

Regrettably very few of almost 800 tapestries which once embellished the Imperial palaces are at present on display in the museum;
others may be seen at Schönbrunn and in the Hofburg.

Steps (right) ascend from the entrance vestibule to the GROUND or
MEZZANINE FLOOR, and the first of several rooms (**RRI–VIII**) devoted
to **Egyptian Antiquities**, containing clustered columns of red granite
from Aswan (18th Dyn.; bases and capitals modern); torso of a young
woman (3C BC); sarcophagus of Nesshutfêne, and cover—note
female form; lid of the sarcophagus of Queen Khedebnityerbone; a
rare elephant statue; and several reliefs. A number of exhibits were
found during Austrian excavations near Giza in 1912–29, but the
Seated figure of the priest Khaihapi (c 1250 BC) was unearthed in
Vienna in 1800 on the site of the Roman encampment of
Vindobona.—Jewellery; funerary stelae; and mummified crocodiles,
cats, ibises, and falcons, representing their associated deities.—
Additional figures of gods, and several uschebtis.—Another section
is devoted to funerary rites, with a number of mummies, canopic jars,
and funerary masks.—Two seated statues of the lion-headed goddess Sekhmet (18th Dyn.); Statuettes of Isis, Ptah, Osiris, Horus, Apis,

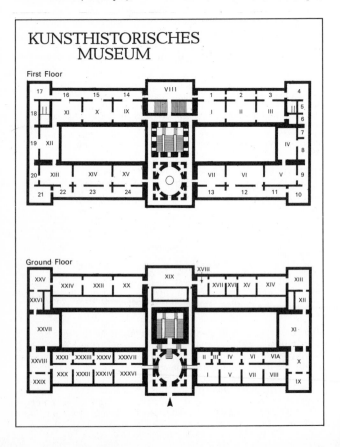

KUNSTHISTORISCHES
MUSEUM

and Bastet; Horemheb with the god Harendotes; Bust of a youth; Statue of Sebekemsauf (a stout administrator of c 1700 BC); a Stone lion falling upon a calf; Seated baboon; Heads of Sesostris III (12th Dyn.), and Thutmosis III (18th Dyn.); faience Statuette of a hippopotamus; and a collection of ceramics and amulets.—Tomb of Prince Kaninisut of Giza (5th Dyn.), and several mummies, stelae, amulets, and further examples of jewellery, signet rings, etc.; also the 'Reserve head' of a man (4th Dyn.).—Artefacts from Săyg, above Aswan.—Collection of wooden head-rests, and one of alabaster (2450 BC); bronze objects; libation vessels, etc.

Part of the collection of Egyptology is closed to the public but can be seen by appointment for those with a specialist interest.

RIX Cyprus. Ceramics; a Throned goddess; votive statue of a priest (c 500 BC) and votive statuettes; several carved capitals; and the so-called Treasure of Jupiter Dolichenus, discovered near *Mauer* in Lower Austria in 1937, including a statue of that god standing on a bull, etc.

RX–XVIII Greek and Roman Antiquities. Among sculptures are a bronze statue of an athlete (late 5C BC), a late 16C cast of a Roman original, found in 1502 on the *Magdalensberg*, Carinthia; the Sarcophagus of the Amazons (late 4C BC); and a marble Head of Aristotle (a Roman copy of a Greek original of the 4C BC).—Several Roman tombstones, and busts; Sarcophagi depicting a lion hunt late 3C; a triple-headed sphinx; Mosaic uncovered in 1815 from a villa near *Salzburg* of the 4C AD of the legend of Theseus and Ariadne, displaying a maze.—Greek bronze statuettes, and armed figurines, both from the Archaic and Classical periods, and including a notable Apollo (early 5C BC); Roman and Greek armour, including miniature pieces.—Etruscan bronze objects, including funerary urns with sculpted male and female reclining figures (3–2C BC); hand-mirrors of engraved bronze, and bronze figurines; also a collection of bronze helmets; Black Etruscan pottery; and a storage-vessel with a frieze displaying centaurs, of 600 BC.—A notable collection of Greek vases; a quadriga on wheels; Tanagra figurines; Greek and Roman jewellery (4–3C BC), including the onyx cameo of a Ptolemaic royal couple (? 278 BC).—A remarkable collection of cameos, including the so-called 'Gemma Augustea', depicting the Pannonian Triumph of Tiberius (end of 1C BC); an Eagle holding a palm branch and oak wreath (27 BC); also a lion (1C AD); Roman glass, and bronze figurines; a marble Bust of Julia Mamaea, mother of Alexander Severus; ceramic plaques, and small mosaics; silver torques and buckles; Greek and Roman jewellery; bronze table-legs; an enamelled bronze flask (late 2C, from Pinguent, now Pazin, in Yugoslavia); a mask of Silenus; several portrait busts of Roman emperors, including Marcus Aurelius (died AD 180 in Vienna), and Septimius Severus (proclaimed emperor at Carnuntum in 193), and silver platers from *Carnuntum* (1C BC–2C AD).—Roman glass, rings, seals, and buckles; marble Portrait-bust of Eutropius (late 5C AD), among others, found at Ephesus; and several mummy portraits from Alexandria; Byzantine ivory plaques personifying Rome, and Constantinople.

Early Christian Antiquities. Early Christian objects from the 4–5Cs; Coptic fabrics; Germanic buckles and jewellery (4–8Cs); and a notable Monogram Cross from Aquileia (5C); Byzantine and Slav jewellery; several treasures found in the Empire, including the hoard discovered at *Untersiebenbrunn* in the Marchfeld (5C), and that of *Şimleul*, in Transylvania.—Byzantine silver treasure from *Zalesie*

(Galicia; 6–7C); the necklace of *Olesko* (Galicia); silver bowls, and plated silver objects; gold jewellery from Bulgaria (9C); and the gold treasure of *Nagyszentmiklós* (Romania; late 9C), including a notable jug with its representation of an armed knight.

Ascending left from the entrance vestibule, you enter the first of a series of rooms devoted to **Sculpture and Decorative Arts**. Many of the objets d'art assembled here came from the collections of Rudolf II, and the Archduke Leopold Wilhelm; those of the Archduke Ferdinand II remain largely at *Schloss Ambras*, near Innsbruck (cf.). Notable are an ivory plaque depicting St. Gregory with scribes (? Lotharingian; late 9C); an ivory box (12C); an Olifant (? Salerno; 11C); several carved ivory and wood coffers, some octagonal, by the Embriachi (14–15C); Byzantine ivories; a steatite icon depicting the Death of the Virgin (late 10C); Byzantine gems (10–14C), and cameos (13–14C); several remarkable rock crystal jugs and bowls, and of amethyst; an Aquamanile or water-jug in the form of a griffon (circle of Roger of Helmarshausen, Lower Saxony; early 12C); a bronze 'Püsterich' or fire-blower in the form of squatting figure (N Italian; early 12C); Communion plate and chalice from Stift Wilten (near Innsbruck; c 1160–70), and another chalice from St. Peter's Salzburg, of the same date; the reliquary-cross of Ludwig of Hungary, and a reliquary-monstrance; the so-called 'Natternzungen-Kredenz' or 'Vipers' tongues credence' (German; mid 15C), in fact fossilised sharks' teeth; Scandinavian or N German drinking-horns (14–15C); a series of Nottingham alabasters (late 14C); and a late 14C Venetian games-board.

An extraordinary collection of **Clocks and Automata**, many constructed in Augsburg, including several Astronomical clocks (notable being one of brass from Bohemia, of the late 16C), a monstrance-clock, fob-watches, a *Tischuhr* or pendulum-clock, a clock on an elephant base; *Säulenuhr* or column-clocks, a *Kugellaufuhr* or ball-operated clock, from Prague (late 16C); and a series of quadrants, armillary spheres, astrolabes, and compasses, etc. Clock of Diana and a centaur, by *Melchoir Mair* (Augsburg; c 1605); a Parrot-automata; automata of the Triumph of Bacchus, sitting on a barrel-clock (c 1605); of Minerva; a Bell-tower; a Turkish horseman; a Ship (1585); and numerous bronze instruments, together with a model of a Galley in ivory (1626).

Carving and Sculpture. Carved boxes (late 15C); reliquary bust (St. Cassian ?; S Tyrol; late 14C); the 'Krumauer Virgin' (? Prague; c 1400); a Virgin and Child carved by *Tilman Riemenschneider* (c 1495), and several other late Gothic Virgins, etc.; a series of silver-gilt drinking vessels (1500–1600), including the so-called Maximilian Goblet (Nuremberg; c 1510), and the Dürer Goblet, designed by that artist, whose father was a goldsmith (Nuremberg; c 1500); a bronze Bust of Maximilian I by *Jörg Muskat* (1450–1527); the Allegory of Vanity (by *Gregor Erhart*; c 1500), three figures of carved and painted wood, of naked male and female youths, and an old hag, back to back; the 'Wiener Musterbuch', or artist's pattern book of tinted drawings (Bohemia; early 15C); the 'Ambraser Hofjagdspiel', 54 of 56 mid 15C playing-cards from the Upper Rhine; carved wood and gilt covered bowls (Upper Rhine; c 1500); carving of a Falconer, ascribed to Hans Syfer (c 1495).

Italian Renaissance. *Desiderio da Settignano*, marble Bust of a laughing boy (Florence, c 1464); *Antonio Rossellino*, Plaque of the Madonna and Child (marble; c 1465); *Francesco Laurana*, marble

Portrait-bust of a young woman, probably Isabella d' Aragón (c 1488?); Bust of Matthias Corvinus (Italian; 1480) and several bronze figures.

More bronze figures and plaques, mostly from Padua, including a number by *Andrea Riccio* (c 1470–1532); *L'Antico* (Pier Jacopo Alari-Bonacolsi; c 1460–1528), Bronze and gilt Venus Felix (c 1500), and other figures or busts; *Tullio Lombardi*, marble relief of busts of a young couple as Bacchus and Ariadne (c 1500).

German Renaissance. Cameos and medallions (mid 16–17C); the Seal of Charles V (or Karl V), with the device PLUS ULTRA; several mounted Bezoars; a display of carved and engraved rock crystal bowls, goblets, etc., some from the Saracchi workshop at Milan; jasper, lapis lazuli, and celadon bowls, etc.; three Commedia dell'Arte figures of Murano glass (c 1600).

Carved figures, including boxwood Adam and Eve, by *Conrad Meit* (c 1480–1550); carved and mounted Seychelles coconuts; carved wooden plaques depicting the battles of Charles V (S German; late 16C); *Christoph Weiditz* (1500–59), pearwood figures of Adam and Eve (Augsburg ?; c 1600); Charles V's drinking-glass (1522); plaques by *Hans Daucher* (1486–1538) of Maximilian as St. George, and of the Judgement of Paris; plaques of the Flight into Egypt (early 16C); The Fall of Man (*Monogrammist I.P.*; c 1520); 'draughts-board' (actually for the game of *Langer Puff*) and 32 carved playing pieces, by *Hans Kels the Elder*, c 1537; alabaster plaque of Maximilian and Charles V (Augsburg; 1529); and marble relief of Ferdinand I (? Augsburg; c 1525).

Mannerist bronzes. *Leone Leoni*, bronze bust of Charles V, and plaque of the same; also bust of Mary of Hungary, c 1555; head of Carlo Borromeo; *Pompeo Leoni*, head of a bust (provided by Balthaser Moll) of Philip II of Spain; *Benvenuto Cellini*, gold salt-cellar, partly enamelled, on an ivory base, made in Paris in 1540–43 for François I and presented by Charles IX to the Archduke Ferdinand II of Tyrol in 1570.

French Mannerists. The St. Michael Goblet, similarly presented to the Archduke Ferdinand of Tyrol; several cameos, including a rosary-cameo; an onyx pitcher; Limoges enamels, and plates by *Pierre Raymond*. Painted and engraved glass from Innsbruck (late 16C); several mounted objects bearing ostrich-eggs, corals, and shells; a pelican (Ulm; 1583); drinking-horn by *Cornelius Gross* of Augsburg; goblet of Ferdinand II (Innsbruck; 1583); ceramic figures by *Christoph Gantner* (late 16C); figures of pilgrims to Santiago by *Leonhard Umbach* (Augsburg; late 16C); objects from the China trade, including jades; cabinets from Augsburg (late 16C), including a coin-box of ebony with gilt bronze figurines; ironstone objects of the second half of the 16C.

Cabinet of stone intarsia from Prague (1600); Florentine mosaic plaques; carved and gilt jug and bowl, by *Christoph Jamnitzer* of Nuremberg (1563–1618); examples of the intricate work of *Nikolaus Schmidt*, *Christoph Lencker*, and *Friedrich Hillebrandt*; *Adrien de Vries* (1545–1626), bronze bust of Rudolf II (Prague; 1603); several glyptics from the workshop of *Andrea Masnago* of Milan, among other cameos; jewellery; onyx, heliotrope, jasper, prase, and other hardstone vessels.

Carved objects of rhinoceros horn; carved plaques by *Georg Schweigger* (1613–90); turned and carved ivory objects, plaques, and figures, some by *Leonhard Kern* (1588–1662); jewellery and celadon and rock-crystal objects.

Carved horn dish by *J.M. Maucher* (1645–1700); ivory goblets; *Matthias Steinl* (c 1645–1727), ivory equestrian figure of Leopold I trampling a Turk; also equestrian figures by the same artist of Joseph I, and Karl VI; *J.B. Hagenauer*, Prometheus; *Matthias Rauchmiller* (or *Jakob Auer*), Apollo and Daphne; and several other ivory reliefs, by *Ignaz Elhafen* (Innsbruck; 1658–1715) among others, and also equestrian figures; *J.-B. Lemoyne*, bust of Marie Antoinette (1771); the centre-piece of Duke Karl Alexander of Lorraine, and candle-sticks, by *P.J. Fonson* (1755); *F.X. Messerschmidt* (1736–83), busts of Joseph II (1767), and of Gerhard van Swieten; carved wood figures of Prince Joseph II and Maria Theresia; the toilet-set and breakfast-service of Franz I, by *A.M. Domanek* (1713–79).

FIRST FLOOR. **Paintings**. In general the *German, Dutch, Flemish* and *English Schools* are displayed in a series of rooms in the E WING of the building; the *Italian, Spanish* and *French Schools* are in the W wing; see p 286. The former are described first, commencing at RVIII.

Some important paintings may not be on display, being under restoration, on exhibition elsewhere, or moved from the room indicated (perhaps to the *Sekundärgalerie*—see p 288): only recently has the remarkable collection of paintings by Bernardo Bellotto been sent up to the Second Floor, for example. Only a selection of the paintings in the collection have been listed.

RVIII, *Jean Fouquet*, Gonella, court fool at Ferrara; *Jan van Eyck*, Cardinal Niccolò Albergati, and Jan de Leeuw, the goldsmith; *Van der Weyden*, Triptych of the Crucifixion, Diptych of the Virgin and Child and St. Catherine; *Van der Goes*, Diptych of the Fall of Man, and Deposition; *Gerard David*, Nativity, Triptych of the St. Michael's altarpiece, with the Virgin and Child with an angel and donor, and with the Baptist and the Evangelist on the side panels (on the reverse of which are Adam and Eve), The goldsmith Jacques Cnoop the Younger; *Isenbrandt*, Rest on the Flight into Egypt; *Patinir*, Martyr-dom of St. Catherine, and Baptism of Christ; *Herri Met de Bles*, The Baptist preaching, Calvary, and others; *Jan de Beer*, Martyrdom of St. Matthew, and of St. Sebastian; *Lucas I van Valkenborch*, Land-scape with a smelting scene, and others, Triptych of the St. John's altarpiece, and Adam and Eve; *Van Orley*, The St. Thomas and St. Matthew altarpiece, Portrait of a youth, and The Circumcision; *Coeke van Aelst*, Rest on the Flight into Egypt; *Master of the Aachen altarpiece*, The Deposition; *Quinten Massys*, St. Jerome; *Michiel Sittow*, Portrait of a princess, probably Catherine of Aragon, and Nativity; *Bartholomäus Bruyn the Elder*, Card. Bernhard Clesius, and three other male portraits; *Juan de Flandes*, Juana la Loca (the Mad), who was married to Philip the Handsome, by the *Master of the Magdalen Legend*; also by Jan de Flandes, Carrying the Cross, and Crucifixion; *Master of the Female Half-lengths*, Rest on the Flight into Egypt, and A young girl, ascribed to the same; *Jan Gossaert (Mabuse)*, Male portrait, St. Luke painting the Virgin, and Virgin and Child; *Joos van Cleve*, Nativity, Triptych of the Virgin and Child, and saints, Death of Lucrezia, Virgin and Child with a rosary, and Eleonore of France (sister of Charles V and wife of François I).

Cabinet 14, adjoining: *Jacob Cornelisz*, The Hieronymous altar-piece; *Geertgen van Haarlem*, Deposition, and History of the relics of the Baptist; *Bosch*, The road to Calvary; *Van Heemskerck*, altar-wings with donors; *Anthonis Mor van Dashorst*, Anna of Spain, and Antoine Perronet de Granvelle, governor of the Low Countries; *Adriaen Thomas Key*, Male, and Female, portraits.

RIX *Ivan Valkenborch*. The Four Seasons; *Jan Massys*, Lot and his daughters; *Michiel Coxie*, The Fall of Man, and the Expulsion from Paradise; *Frans Floris*, Portrait; *Momper*, Mountain landscape; *Pieter Aertsen*, Rustic feast and Market-scene; *Pourbus the Elder*, Portrait of a Knight of Santiago; *Joachim Bueckelaer*, Market scenes; *Floris*, Liveryman; *Lucas I van Valckenborch*, May, and Harvesting.

RX Pieter Brueghel the Elder, Children's games, Fight between Carnival and Lent, Death of Saul, The Tower of Babel, The Road to Calvary, The Return of the hunters, The gloomy day, Return of the herd, Massacre of the Innocents, The conversion of Paul, Rustic wedding, Village dance, The nest-robber; *after Brueghel*, The feast of St. Martin; *Pieter Brueghel the Younger*, Winter landscape; *Jan Brueghel the Elder*, Visiting the peasants, and several flower pieces.

Cabinet 15: *Dürer*, Virgin and Child (1503), Virgin and Child (1512), Young Venetian girl, Youth, with Avarice (a hag with her cash) on the reverse, Martyrdom of the ten thousand Christians under Sapor, king of Persia, Adoration of the Trinity, Portrait of Johann Kleberger, Maximilian I (1519); *Schongauer*, Holy Family; *Baldung Grien*, The three ages of woman, and Death, and Male portrait; *Barthel Beham*, The arbitrator, and Woman with a parrot; *Georg Pencz*, Clean-shaven man, and Bearded man.

Cabinet 16: *Holbein the Elder*, Virgin and Child, and Virgin and Child with a pomegranate; *Burgkmair*, Male portrait (1506); *Martin Schaffner*, Man with a rosary; *Leonhard Beck*, St. George and the dragon; *Hans Maler*, The Archduke Ferdinand, aged 17, and Male portrait; *Bernhard Strigel*, The family of Maximilian I, The Holy genealogy; *Amberger*, Ulrich Sulczer of Augsburg, Christoph Baumgartner, and several other portraits; *Lukas Furtenagel*, Hans Burgkmair the artist, and his wife; *Cranach the Elder*, Crucifixion, St. Jerome; *Altdorfer*, The beheading of St. Catherine, Entombment, and Resurrection of Christ (from the predella of the St. Sebastian altarpiece at St. Florian; cf.), Adoration, Virgin and Child; *Wolf Huber*, Crucifixion, The humanist Jakob Ziegler, Allegory of the Redemption; *H. Mielich*, Portrait of Hanns Mädl.

RXI, adjoining: *Frans Snyders*, Fishmarkets, the first with figures by *Van Dyck*, the second with figures by *Cornelis de Vos*; *Abraham Janssens*, Venus and Adonis; *Peter Thys*, The Archduke Leopold Wilhelm; *Jacob van Oost the Elder*, Adoration of the Shepherds; *Jordaens*, The Feast of the Bean; Pietà, one of several large paintings by *Gaspard de Crayer*.

Cabinet 17 (SE corner of the building): **Cranach the Elder**, Adam and Eve, with Christ and Mary on the reverse, Christ's farewell to the holy women, The Margrave Casimir von Brandenburg-Kulmbach, Lot and his daughters, Paradise, The road to Calvary, two versions of Judith with the head of Holofernes, Old man and girl, Staghunt, The princesses Sibylla, Emilia, and Sidonia von Sachsen, Flagellation of Christ, *Cranach the Younger*, Male and Female portraits; *Altdorfer*, Lot and his daughters. In a display case are: *Berhard Strigel*, Maximilian I, Ludwig II of Hungary as a boy, *Master of the history of Frederick and Maximilian*, Beheading of the Baptist; *Wolf Huber*, Christ appearing to Mary; *Altdorfer*, Holy Family; *Hans Maler*, Archduke Ferdinand.

Cabinet 18: **Hans Holbein the Younger**, Portraits of Dirck Tybis, Courtier of Henry VIII and his wife, Jane Seymour, An English lady, Young merchant, Dr John Chambers, physician to Henry VIII; *François Clouet*, Charles IX of France, and a full-length portrait of the same; *anon. French* Male portraits, and of a Young girl; *Corneille* de Lyon, A youth; *Hans von Aachen*, Rudolf II; *Joseph Heintz the Elder*, Rudolf II; *Jan Brueghel the Elder*, Landscape, and Village street; *Jakob Seisenegger*, Charles V and his dog, The Archduke Ferdinand of Tyrol; and Allegories by *Bartholomäus Spranger*.

Water, by Giuseppe Arcimboldo

Cabinet 19: *Giuseppe Arcimboldo*, Summer, Winter, Fire, and Water; *Hans von Aachen*, Bacchus, Ceres, and Amor; *Jan Brueghel the Elder*, Studies of dogs; *Spranger*, Minerva triumphant, Venus and Adonis; *Gysbrecht Lytens*, Winter landscape with gypsies; and Landscapes by *Momper*, and *Savery*; *Jan Brueghel the Elder*, Forest scene, Aeneas in the underworld, Landscape with Christ tempted, Adoration of the Magi, Crucifixion, Riverside scene, Waggons attacked (with figures by *Sebastian Vrancx*), Landscape with a hermit, Flower-pieces, Temptation of St. Anthony; *Pieter Brueghel the Elder*, Storm at sea; *Paul Bril*, Landscapes.

RXII Van Dyck, Study of a female head, Portrait of an artist, possibly Paul de Vos, Young field officer in gilded armour, Holy family, Jan de Mortfort, Samson and Delilah, Jacomo de Cachiopin, P. Carolus Scribani S.J., A youth, Nicholas Lanier, Master of the King's Music, The apostles Simon, Philip, and Jude, Female portrait, Prince Karl Ludwig von der Pfalz, Prince Ruprecht von der Pfalz (of the Palatinate) with a dog, Portrait of a Lady, The Marquis Francisco de Moncada, Thomas Howard, Earl of Arundel (Ambassador to Vienna in 1636), and his wife, and several allegorical and religious paintings.

Cabinet 20, the first of three rooms devoted to the art of **Rubens**, of which the museum contains an extensive collection, among them a Self-portrait, Helen Fourment wrapped in a fur (known as 'Das Pelzchen'), Medusa's head, Landscape (damaged) with Philomon and Baucis.

RXIII *Rubens*, The Ildefonso altarpiece, The meeting of Ferdinand of Hungary and the Cardinal Infante Ferdinand after the Battle of Nördlingen; St. Jerome wearing his cardinal's hat, The Holy Family under an appletree, Maximilian I in armour, and Charles the Bold (both after earlier portraits or medals), also of St. Theresa of Ávila, The festival of Venus, and The hunt of Meleager and Atalante.

RXIV *Rubens*, The miracles of St. Francis Xavier, and of St. Ignatius, together with preliminary sketches for both, The Archduke Albrecht VII and his wife Isabella Clara Eugenia (daughter of Philip II of Spain), Isabella d'Este (after Titian), Girl with a flag (also after Titian), Dying Christ between Mary and John, The Annunciation, Cimon and Ephigenia, Pipin and Bega, Mary Magdalen and Martha, The four continents.

Cabinet 21 (NE corner of the building), largely devoted to *David Teniers the Younger*, two paintings of the Archduke Leopold Wilhelm in his Gallery at Brussels, Shooting birds in Brussels, The Sacrifice of Isaac, and several smaller works; *Snyders*, Still-life with cat; *Peeter Neefs the Younger*, Interior of Notre-Dame at Antwerp; *David Ryckaerts III*, The witch; *Gerard Seghers*, Virgin and Child with St. John; *Robert van der Hoecke*, Skating near Brussels; View near Ostend.

Cabinet 22: *Anthonie Palamedesz*, Group of friends; *Hendrick Avercamp*, Skating scene; *Wolfgang Heimbach*, Candle-lit banquet; *Mierevelt*, Young woman; *Esias van de Velde*, Dinner-party in a park; *Frans Hals*, Tielemann Roosterman, and other male portraits; and Landscapes by *Salomon van Ruysdael* and *Van Goyen*.

Cabinet 23: **Rembrandt**, Male and Female portraits, The artist's mother as the prophetess Hanna, Self-portrait of 1652, Self-portrait wearing fur, chain and earring, Titus reading, small Self-portrait, *Van Mieris the Elder*, The doctor's visit, The cavalier; *Metsu*, Girl and officer; Noli me tangere; *Gerard ter Borch*, Peeling an apple; *Pieter de Hooch*, Mother and child with a maid; *Gerard Dou*, The physician, Girl with a lantern, Woman watering plants; and several Landscapes by *Wouwerman, Jakob van Ruisdael*, and *Aert van der Neer*.

Cabinet 24: Several genre paintings by *Adraien van Ostade*, and *Jan Steen*; *Jan Vermeer*, Allegory of Painting, or The Artist in his studio; *Raeburn*, William Law of Elvinston; *Gainsborough*, Suffolk landscape; *Reynolds*, Study for a female portrait; *Joseph Wright of Derby*, the Rev. Basil Bury Beridge; *Lawrence*, Diana Sturt, Lady Milner; *Kneller*, Female portrait.

RXV, *Rembrandt*, Paul the apostle; *Hals*, Female portrait; *Melchior d'Hondecoeter*, Birds; *Nicolaes Maes*, Portrait of Sara Ingelbrechts; *Dirck van Santvoort*, Male and Female portraits; *Bartholomeus van der Helst*, Female portrait; *Ludolf Backhuysen*, The harbour at

Amsterdam; *Jan Wynants*, Landscape with hunters; *Van Goyen*, Seascape near Dordrecht; *Salomon van Ruysdael*, May festival; *Jacob van Ruisdael*, The Great Forest; *Adriaen van de Velde*, Vertumnus and Pomona.

W WING: *Italian, Spanish, and French Schools.*

RI Several works by *Bassano*; *anon. Brescian* Portrait of a young lady; *Moretto*, St. Justina with a unicorn; *Bartolomeo Passarotti*, Family portrait; *Perugino*, two paintings of the Madonna and Child with saints, Baptism of Christ, St. Jerome; *Sebastiano del Piombo*, Card. Ridolfo Pio; *Raphael*, The Madonna in the meadow, St. Margaret and the dragon; *attrib. Raphael*, Holy Family and St. John; *Del Sarto*, Lamentation of Mary, Tobias and the angel; *Parmigianino*, Young lady, Malatesta Baglione ?, Self-portrait in a convex mirror, Cupid shaping his bow; *Correggio*, Jupiter and Io, Abduction of Ganymede.

Cabinet 1: *Cosmè Tura*, Christ sustained by angels; *Pisanello*, The Emperor Sigismund; *Antonello da Messina*, Madonna and Child with saints; *Gozzoli*, Madonna and Child with saints; *Giovanni Bellini*, Presentation in the Temple; *Marco Basiati*, The calling of the son of Zebedee; *Mantegna*, St. Sebastian; *Sebastiano del Piombo*, Male portrait; *anon. Venetian* Portrait of a youth wearing a hat (c 1510).

Cabinet 2: *Palma Vecchio*, Profile of a young woman, and two Female portraits, Madonna and Child with saints, Diana and Callisto, The visitation of Mary; *Catena*, Man holding a book; *Giovanni Bellini*, Lady at her toilet; *Pordenone*, The musician; *Giorgione*, Portrait of a youth, Young woman (Laura?), Three philosophers; *Studio of Giorgione*, Adoration of the Shepherds.

RII Titian, Violante, Lucrezia and Tarquin, Girl wearing a fur, Isabella d'Este, Margravine of Mantua, Jacobo Strada, Benedetto Varchi, Palma, the physician, Pope Paul III, Danae, Fabrizio Salvaresio, Johann Friedrich von Sachen (of Saxony), Ecce Homo, Madonna and Child with saints, Lavinia, the artist's daughter ?, The Gypsy Madonna, Madonna with the cherries, etc.

RIII *Bordone*, several Female portraits, and Allegories; *Tintoretto*, Venus and Adonis; *Veronese*, Judith with the head of Holofernes, Lucrezia, Susanna and the elders, Lot and his daughters fleeing from Sodom, Christ and the Samaritan at the well, Woman with a stork, *anon. Venetian* Male portrait of 1538.

Cabinet 3: *Cariani*, The Visitation of Mary; several remarkable Male portraits by *Lorenzo Lotto*, notably A Youth, Man holding a golden claw, Man in red, St. Dominic preaching, Madonna and Child with saints, *Bernardino Licinio*, Ottaviano Grimani, and Male portrait.

Cabinet 4: largely devoted to the work of *Bassano*, beyond which are **Cabinets 5** and **6**, the latter containing *Moroni*, Man with a letter, and Alessandro Vittoria, the sculptor.

Cabinet 7: *Ambrogio de Predis*, Profile of Maximilian I; *Bernardino Luini*, St. Jerome, while **Cabinet 8** displays several Portraits by *Tintoretto*.

RIV Tintoretto, Susanna and the elders, and more Portraits, among them Lorenzo Soranzo, Youth in gilded armour, Sebastiano Venier, St. Jerome, Marco Grimani, and a series of panoramas of Old Testament scenes, etc.; *Cagnacci*, Death of Cleopatra; *Annibale Carracci*, Venus and Adonis; *Daniele Crespi*, Joseph's dream; *Guercino*, St. John the Baptist; *B.G. Lupicini*, Mary and Martha;

Vasari, Death of Peter the Martyr; *Empoli*, The bath of Susanna; *Guido Reni*, The Baptism of Christ, and several other representative works by the artist.

Cabinet 9: *Bronzino*, Maria de Medici, Holy Family, *anon. Florentine* Female portrait (c 1550–60); *Salviati*, Male portrait; *Sánchez Coëllo*, Anne of Austria, and Elisabeth of Valois, both queens of Spain, and the Infante Don Carlos; *Juan Pantoja de la Cruz*, Infante Philip, armed.

Cabinet 10, at the NW corner of the building: *Antonio de Pereda*, Allegory of Mortality ?; *Carreño*, Carlos II of Spain; *Del Mazo*, The artist's family; **Velázquez**, Philip IV of Spain, and a half-length of the same, Infante Balthasar Carlos, Infante Philip Prosper, three portraits of Infanta Margarita Teresa, Isabella of Spain, Infanta Maria Teresa.

Cabinet 11: *Sassoferrato*, Madonna and Child; *Salvator Rosa*, Asträa; *Annibale Carracci*, Christ and the Samaritan at the fountain; *Poussin*, Capture of Jerusalem by Titus.

RV, *Terbrughen*, Lute-player; *Ribera*, Christ disputing in the Temple, Carrying the Cross; *Simon Vouet*, Mary and Martha, Judith with the head of Holofernes; *Jean Valentin de Boulogne*, Moses; *Gentileschi*, Mary Magdalen, Rest on the Flight into Egypt; *Herrera*, The blind hurdy-gurdy player; *Preti*, Doubting Thomas, The calling of Matthew; *Caravaggio*, David with the head of Goliath, Madonna of the rosary.

RVI 253, *Guercino*, Return of the prodigal son; *Empoli*, The bath of Susanna; *Guido Reni*, Baptism of Christ; *Pompeo Batoni*, Return of the prodigal son; *Domenico Fetti*, Moses and the burning bush; *Luca Giordano*, A beggar, The archangel Michael, The macaroni eater; *Giandomenico Tiepolo*, Venetian mail-boat; *Magnasco*, Washerwomen.

Cabinet 12: *Bernardo Strozzi*, The Doge Francesco Erizzo, and other works; *Johann Heinrich Schönfeld*, The halt at the inn; *Fetti*, The Flight into Egypt, and smaller paintings.

Cabinet 13: *G.-B. Tiepolo*, St. Catherine of Siena, and other works; *Guardi*, Dominican miracle; Venetian scenes; *Canaletto*, Venetian scenes; *Bellotto* (see below), Mounted hussars.

RVII, *Mengs*, Princess Maria Ludovika, Virgin and Child with angels; *Joseph-Silfrède Duplessis*, Christoph Willibald von Gluck playing a spinet; *Largillière*, Boucher d'Orsay; *Rigaud*, Philipp Ludwig Wenzel Graf Sinzendorf (1617–1742); *Giacomo Ceruti*, The 'cellist; *Johann Zoffany*, The Archduchess Maria Christine; *Batoni*, Joseph II with his brother, later Leopold II; *G.-B. Pittoni*, The mathematician, Joseph II and the Grand duke Leopold of Tuscany, The return of the prodigal son; *Solimena*, Deposition; Judith with the head of Holofernes, Karl VI and Graf Gundaker Althann, Boreas carrying off Oreithyia; *G.-B. Tiepolo*, Hannibal recognises the head of his brother Hasdrubal, Brutus and Aruns; *Anton von Maron*, Elisabeth Hervey, Marchioness of Bristol; *David*, Napoleon crossing the St. Bernard pass.

SECOND FLOOR. Several subsidiary collections are accommodated here, including (in **R13**) a series of remarkable townscapes by **Bernardo Bellotto** (1721–80; a nephew of Canaletto, and often— confusingly—so-called in Austria), which have recently been moved up here, but which on no account should be overlooked. Among them are: Vienna from the Upper Belvedere palace; The Freyung, Vienna, from the NW, and from the SE; The Mehlmarkt, Vienna; The

Dominikanerkirche, Vienna; Schönbrunn from the N, and S; three views of Schlosshof, near Marchegg (see Rte 29).

RR1–12 comprise the so-called 'Sekundärgalerie', in which a number of paintings of comparatively secondary interest and importance or by comparatively minor artists may be seen, displayed as in former centuries (cf. those painting in Cabinet 21), but which is normally only open to the public on Fridays. Among them are several works by *Luca Giordano, Guido Reni, Giorgione, Tom Ring, Van Kessel, Balthasar Denner* (1685–1749), and two series depicting The Months, by *Lucas I van Valckenborch*, and *Bassano*; also genre scenes by *Teniers the Younger*. Among individual paintings are *Matthias Gerung*, The Mompelgard altarpiece; the *Hoogstraeten Master*, Virgin and Child with SS. Catherine and Barbara; the *Frankfurt Master* (fl. 1490–1515), Adoration of the Kings; *Pourbus the Elder*, Portrait of Jan van Hembyze; *Lorenzo Lippi*, Christ and the Samaritan; and *Murillo*, John the Baptist as a child.

Cartoons by *Jan Vermeyen* (1500–59) for the 'Tunis Campaign of Charles V' series of tapestries hang in adjacent corridors.

Also to be seen on this floor—displayed in three rooms—is the *** Collection of Coins and Medals**, one of the world's largest, containing almost 500,000 items, only 4500 of which are on show.

On the walls is a series of c 1100 small portraits of historical interest, some two-thirds of which are originals collected by the Archduke Ferdinand of Tyrol at Ambras. Sections are devoted to orders and decorations of all periods, and to the Brettauer Collection of over 7000 coins and medals relating to the history of medicine.

Franz I did much to build up the collection, and on his death the Abbé Joseph Eckhel (died 1798), a famous numismatist, acted as conservator. While primarily of interest to the specialist, some time may be spent to advantage in perusing the exhibited examples of this art. Several early coin and medal cabinets are also preserved.

Of interest to the specialist, and accommodated in the basement at the W end of the building, are the reliefs from the (reconstructed) **Heroon of Gölbaşi-Trysa** (S Turkey). Found in 1841 by Schöborn, in 1882–83 this quadrangular funerary enclosure was excavated and transferred to Vienna. A model of the mausoleum is shown adjacent.

F.   From the Marie-Theresien-Platz to the Votivkirche

It was on 20 December 1857 that the minister concerned, Alexander von Bach, received a hand-written communication from Franz Josef, which began to this effect: 'It is My Will that the extension of the inner city of Vienna, with due regard to its suitable connection with the suburbs, should be taken in hand as soon as possible, and that attention should also be paid to the regulation and embellishment of My Residence and Capital. I therefore give My permission to dismantle the circumvallation and fortifications of the Inner City, together with its surrounding ditches'. On 31 January 1858 proposals for this scheme were invited and 85 were eventually submitted. The design by *Ludwig Förster* was accepted, with August von Siccardsburg, and Eduard van der Nüll as runners-up (cf. Opera-house). However, numerous changes were later made to the initial plan.

Demolition of the ramparts facing the Danube canal was started immediately, and a boulevard was laid out along the quay. Most of the bastions were razed—some being blown down with explosives—by 1864, and their sites, with the former glacis, levelled to form the Ringstrasse, 57m wide and 4km long, which on 1 May the following year was sufficiently advanced to be ceremonially opened to traffic by being circled by the Emperor and Empress in their carriage. From then on the grandiose buildings planned rose rapidly, one of the first being the Opera-house; see Rte 25B. Although the Vienna Stock Exchange crash of 1873 put a temporary stop to credit in the private sector of the boom, the State intervened, and the erection of public buildings continued.

The several sections of the **Ringstrasse** were later given different names, which, reading clockwise from the Opera, are now: *Opernring*, *Burgring*, *Dr Karl-Renner-Ring*, and *Dr Karl-Lueger-Ring* (both previously Franzensring and then Ring des 12 November), *Schottenring*, followed by the *Franz Josefs Kai*, before continuing SW as *Stubenring*, *Parkring*, *Schubertring* (formerly Kolowratring), and *Kärntner Ring*.

The **Maria-Theresien-Platz** lies immediately SW of the Burgring, flanked to the N by the *Natural History Museum* (see below), and S by the *Kunsthistorisches Museum*; see Rte 25E. To the W is the façade of the *Messepalast*; to the E the *Burgtor*, and beyond, the *Heldenplatz*; see p 273.

In the centre of the square rises the **Monument to Maria Theresia**, designed by *Hasenauer*, with bronze sculptures by *Kaspar von Zumbusch*, and unveiled in 1888, depicting the Empress at the flattering age of 35, enthroned on a tall plinth and clutching in her left hand a sceptre and the scroll of the Pragmatic Sanction.

She is defended by equestrian statues of her generals: Gideon Ernst Laudon (1716–90), Otto Ferdinand Traun (1677–1748), Leopold Daun (1705–66), and Ludwig Andreas Khevenhüller (1683–1744). Below her are her chancellor, Wenzel Anton Kauniz (1711–94), and her physician, Gerhard van Swieten (1700–72), while among the several other figures Gluck, Haydn, and young Mozart can be distinguished (not that the Empress particularly appreciated any of them).

The **Messepalast** was formerly the *Imperial Stables*, built in 1721–25, partly from the designs of J.B. Fischer von Erlach, but altered in 1850–54. It was long the venue for the Vienna Trade Fair, but recently it has been restored in part, as it deserves, for temporary exhibitions of Modern art, etc.—For districts further W, see Rte 25 O.

The **NATURAL HISTORY MUSEUM** (Naturhistorisches Museum) is complementary in style to the Kunsthistorisches Museum, which its main entrance faces; for its architectural history see the first few paragraphs of Rte 25E.

It was inaugurated in 1889, and comprises eight main departments: *Mineralogy-petrology*; *Geology-palaeontology*; three *Zoological* departments—vertebrates, insects, and invertebrates; *Botany*; *Anthropology*; and *Prehistory*. Additional space will become available with the construction of floors in the two interior courtyards.

On the lower floor, **RR1–5** (right of entrance vestibule) contain the *Mineralogical collections*, including precious and semi-precious stones, among them a topaz from Brazil weighing 117kg and a 'bouquet' of c 1760, composed of 1200 diamonds and 1500 other precious stones. The latter was presented by Maria Theresia to her consort, the founder of the Imperial Collection, who in 1748 had purchased the cabinet of a Florentine collector containing c 30,000 specimens of minerals, and shells, etc.—In **R5** is an extensive collection of *Meteorites*.

RR11–15 are devoted to the **Prehistoric collections*, including (in **R11**) a replica of a small but fleshy female figure carved in limestone known as the *'Venus' of Willendorf* (in the Wachau; cf.), variously estimated to date from c 15,000 to 25,000 BC: the original is more closely guarded. A more recent acquisition is the so-called *'Venus von Galgenberg'* or the *'Tanzenden Venus'*, a diminutive figure (7.2cm in height) radio-carbon-dated c 30,000 BC. It was found at Stratzing, near Krems. Also conserved here are collections of gold objects from Romania, while notable in **R13** are an engraved Urn from *Sopron*; a reconstructed Funeral waggon; and a bronze Bull of 5C BC.—**R14** contains important collections of artefacts of the *Hallstatt Culture* (8–5C BC), including jewellery, arms, implements, buckets, and leather bags.

On the staircase is *Franz Messmer*'s Portrait of Franz Stephan I (1773), surrounded by directors of the Imperial Collection. The *Zoological* and *Botanical* departments, housed on the upper floor, were founded in 1796 and 1803 respectively, by Franz II, although very considerably extended since. The *Library* and *Herbarium* are open to visitors.

Immediately to the W stands the *Volkstheater* of 1887–89, in front of which is a monument to the playwright Ferdinand Raimund (1790–1836).—A few paces further NW is the **Trautson palace** (Museumstrasse 7), designed by J.B. Fischer von Erlach and erected from 1710 by C.A. Oettel for Prince Johann Leopold Trautson. In 1760 it was acquired by Maria Theresia as a residence for her newly created Royal Hungarian Bodyguard. It now houses the *Ministry of Justice*. The staircase, with Atlantes by Giovanni Giuliani, is notable.

The composer Joseph Lanner (1801–43) was born at Mechitaristengasse 5, a short distance W; while Johann Strauss the Younger (1825–99) was born in an earlier building at Lerchenfelderstrasse 15, to the NW.

Follow the Auerspergstrasse to the N, in which No. 1 is the **Auersperg Palace** (formerly the Weltz-Rofrano palace) of c 1706, altered in 1721 and again in the 19C. Gluck conducted Prince von Sachsen-Hildburghausen's private orchestra here on first settling in Vienna in 1751.—Beethoven composed part of his 'Missa Solemnis' at adjacent Trautsongasse 2.

Turning E, we pass (right) the **Palace of Justice** (1875–81), its entrance at Schmerlingplatz 10.

It was burnt out during the disturbances of 15 July 1927, precipitated by a jury's acquittal of right-wing extremists. During the subsequent demonstration the building was set alight, and the police fired into the crowd, killing 86 (including five police officers) and wounding many more. The *Heimwehr* took full advantage of the event, further aggravating the tension between political parties.

You now approach (left) the **Parlament**, a Greek Revival structure, suitably embellished with a quantity of quadrigae, by Theophil Hansen (1873–83; also architect of the concert-hall of the Musik-verein, and of the Stock Exchange).

It was formerly the seat of the polyglot *Imperial Diet*. Karl Kundermann's colossal *Pallas Athene Fountain* was put up in front of it in 1902. The Parlament now accommodates both the *National Council (Nationalrat;* of 183 members), the lower house of the bi-cameral parliament, and the *Federal Council (Bundesrat;* 63 members), the former elected by universal suffrage for a four-year term, the latter being members delegated by the Federal states to serve in the upper house, together constituting the *Federal Assembly* or *Bundes-versammlung*.

Among several monuments in the vicinity is one to Viktor Adler

(1852–1918), architect of the Austrian Social-Democrat Party, who had once observed of that machinery of administration, the Civil Service, that it was 'despotism mitigated by muddle', also translated as 'absolutism tempered by slovenliness'!

Parts of the interior of the Parlament building may be visited from No. 3 Karl-Renner-platz on weekdays from 11.00–15.00 when not in session. Much of it was reconstructed after war damage, and in 1974–77 attic storeys were added to provide more bureaucratic space.

For the *Volksgarten* and *Burgtheater*, on the E side of the RING-STRASSE here, see below.

By bearing left along the N façade of the Parlament building and then right, the neo-Gothic (plus some neo-Renaissance) **Rathaus**, or *City Hall* is approached. It was built in 1872–82 to the design of the Würtemberger, Friedrich von Schmidt (1825–91). The main features of its E façade are the 100m-high central tower surmounted by the *Eiserner Rathausmann*, a copper figure of a knight, and its four subsidiary towers, below which is a range of open galleries and ground-floor arcades.

This building is the seat of both the mayor and governor of Vienna, but as Vienna is composed of both a City and a State, their functions are united in the person of the mayor (*Bürgermeister*); the offices of the City Council and the Assembly are also here. The main courtyard is the venue for concerts in the summer; there are also six smaller courtyards.

Perhaps the most famous and energetic—but anti-semitic—Bürgermeister was Karl Lueger (1844–1910), who although elected to that position in 1895, was unable to carry out his functions until 1897 as Franz Josef repeatedly refused to confirm the appointment.

Of particular importance (and often overlooked by visitors), is the *Wiener Stadt-und Landes-bibliothek*, with its extensive archives and collections of MSS and musical scores (especially rich in those of Schubert, many of them previously acquired by Nicolaus Dumba). This is approached from its NE corner, while the *Musiksammlung* is located at Rathausstrasse 11, near its NW corner.

A *City Information Office* (*Stadtinformation*; not a tourist post) is to be found in the Schmidhalle, supplying statistical data and information on public services and administration, etc.

Among the statues in the adjacent *Rathauspark* are those of Joseph Lanner; Johann Strauss the Elder; Ferdinand Georg Waldmüller, the artist; Karl Renner, the statesman; J.B. Fischer von Erlach; and Ernst Mach (1838–1916), the physicist whose name is associated with high-speed motion.

Facing the N end of the gardens is the S façade of the **Universität**, a neo-Renaissance building of 1873–84 by Heinrich von Ferstel.

Previously in the inner city (see p 249), the *University*, founded in 1365, is the oldest German-speaking university after that of Prague (1348). After being in Jesuit hands from 1623, it was reformed in 1752 by Gerhard van Swieten (Maria Theresia's physician). In 1777 its extensive *Library* was established.

Klimt's designs commissioned in 1894 for the ceiling of the *Aula* were not accepted: they were thought to be too 'advanced' and establishment critics viciously attacked them; see p 228.

At the N end of the University building, the Ringstrasse veers NE; see Rte 25G.

To the NW rear the two 99m-high openwork spires of the **Votivkirche**, an essay in the French Gothic style by the versatile Heinrich von Ferstel, erected between 1856–79 and started before the Ringstrasse project was initiated. It was apparently built by public subscription in gratitude for young Franz Josef's escape from an assassination attempt by János Libényi, an Hungarian tailor (18 February 1853).

Its unremarkable interior contains in the baptistry the marble *Renaissance Monument* (formerly in the Dorotheerkirche) of Count Niklas Salm (died 1530), commander in Vienna during the first Turkish siege (1529); a 15C Flemish altarpiece; and in the N transept, a huge painting by Gustave Doré of Christ leaving the Praetorium (1867–72).

Turning back on our tracks, we may cross to the E side of the Dr Karl-Lueger-Ring opposite the University, a short distance to the E of which, on one of the bastions not razed, stands the so-called *Pasqualatihaus*, one of Beethoven's many residences; see p 256.

The **Burgtheater**, a few paces S, facing the Rathaus, was designed in 1874–88 by Gottfried Semper and Karl von Hasenauer, and largely rebuilt and modernised in 1950–55 after being gutted by fire on 12 April 1945.

It superseded the original Hofburgtheater founded in the Hofburg in 1776 and closed in 1881, which was held in high repute for its acting during the 19C, particularly under its director from 1815, Joseph Schreyvogel (1768–1832). Together with the Akademie-Theater (Vienna 3; Lisztstrasse 1; which concentrates on contemporary drama) it is state-owned, and is run on a repertory basis (season from 1 September to 30 June).

On the stairways are frescoes by Gustav and Ernst Klimt, and Franz Matsch; portraits of famous actors and actresses hang in its 30m-long foyer.

Immediately to the S is the **Volksgarten**, laid out in 1819–23 on the *Burgbastei*, demolished on Napoleon's orders in 1809 (and translated in some brochures as 'Common Gardens' as opposed to the genteel Burggarten; p 273. It provides a fine display of roses in May/June.

To the left of its N entrance is a *Monument to the Empress Elisabeth*; in the centre, a *'Temple of Theseus'* (1820–23), designed by Peter von Nobile in imitation of the Theseion at Athens, and built to house Canova's Statue of Theseus, which now adorns the main staircase of the Kunsthistorisches Museum. Further S is a *Monument to Grillparzer*, while adjacent to the Heldenplatz is the former *Cortisches Kaffeehaus*, also by Nobile, at which Lanner and Strauss played. For the *Heldenplatz* itself see p 273.

G.   North of the Schottenring

From the *Freyung* (see Rte 25C) follow the Schottengasse N to reach the SCHOTTENRING. Below this intersection is the underground station of the *Schottentor*; to the NW, the *Votivkirche*; see above.

Turn right here and cross Hessegasse; Anton Bruckner lived in No. 7 (on the far side of the Schottenring) between 1877 and 1895, before he moved to an apartment provided for him in a lodge of the Belvedere (cf.; also Währinger Strasse 41, below). Most of his works were composed here.

Further E, at No. 14 Schottenring, was born Stefan Zweig (1881–1942; author of the autobiographical 'The World of Yesterday'). Beyond is the **Stock Exchange** or *Börse*, a large building of 1872–77 by Theophil Hansen.—At the far end of the street is the *Ringturm*, a modern building overlooking gardens skirting the Danube Canal, here crossed by the *Augarten-Brücke*; see Rte 25M.

Obere Donaustrasse 5, some minutes' walk to the N on the far side of the canal, was the birthplace of Arnold Schönberg (1874–1951).—Otto Wagner's *Schützenhaus* or lock-house, of 1906/7, is seen across the canal to the E.

Cross the street immediately beyond the Börse to approach the SCHLICKPLATZ, dominated by the ugly *Rossauer-Kaserne*, a brick barracks of 1869 in the 'Arsenal style' (see Rte 25K).

Continuing N, the Berggasse is soon reached, at No. 19 in which, to the left, was the ***Apartment of Sigmund Freud** (1856–1939), in which he lived and practised from 1891 to 1938, before emigrating to London. (Four of his sisters died at Auschwitz.)

The family apartments were entered from door No. 5 on the mezzanine floor, while No. 6, opposite, was the entrance to his consulting-room, and that of Anna Freud (from 1923), and now a *Museum*, opened in 1971. Here are displayed his couch and a large number of curious objects in their original positions, including Freud's collection of small Egyptian and Classical antiquities, which clutter up the shelves, together with numerous photographs, books, and other memorabilia; an informative Catalogue is available. Dr Viktor Adler (1852–1918), founder of Austria's Social Democrat Party, was a previous tenant.

At Liechtensteinstrasse 11, the next street to the W, lived Friedrich Hebbel (1813–63) from 1857 until his death.

On retracing your steps and turning diagonally left·along Servitengasse, you reach at No. 9 the fine **Servitenkirche**, built by Carlo Canevale in 1651–77, and the first church in Vienna to have an oval nave. It was the only church in the then suburbs to survive the Turkish siege of 1683. Here was buried the imperial general Prince Ottavio Piccolomini (died 1656). Its stuccoes are by G.B. Barbarino.

Bearing NW along Grünetorgasse, and turning right on reaching Porzellangasse, the **Liechtenstein Palace** is approached, its entrance at Fürstengasse 1. Built by Domenico Egido Rossi and Domenico Martinelli between 1690–1711, it has since 1979 accommodated the **Federal Museum of Modern Art**, however much out of place it appears in such surroundings. The most notable feature of the building is the monumental *Staircase* ascending from the central vestibule, and the *Marmorsaal*, decorated by Andrea Pozzo.

Near the entrance is a sculpture by *Wotruba*, and two hideous Heads by *Rudolf Hausner*, etc. Among the more important paintings to be seen are: *Max Oppenheimer* ('Mopp'; 1885–1954), Portrait of Franz Blei; *Richard Gerstl* (1883–1908), The Schönberg family in 1908; *Schiele*, Portrait of Eduard Kosmack, and The Embrace; *Klimt*, Portrait of Adele Bloch-Bauer, and The appletree; *Kokoschka*, Landscape with a girl; *Alexej Jawlensky* (1864–1941), Self-portrait, and others; *Picasso*, Harlequin with crossed hands; Bust of Fernande (1907); Seated woman with a green shawl; Dancing girl and seated man; *F. Botero*, The house of Raquel Vega; *Wolfgang Herzig*, The party; and representative works by *Ben Nicholson, Magritte, Léger, Kupka, Ernst Fuchs, Anton Lehmden, Max Ernst, Arik (Erich) Brauer, Christian Schad*, and *Albert Paris Gütersloh* (1887–1973).

At Marktgasse 40, some few minutes' walk to the N, to the E of the Liechtensteinstrasse, is the *Lichtentaler Pfarrkirche* (1712–18), where Schubert was baptised; later he sang in the choir and was organist here. The existing organ is that on which he played; and he composed his first mass for this church, aged 17.

No. 54 Nussdorferstrasse, parallel to and W of the Liechtensteinstrasse, with its galleried courtyard, was the **Birthplace of Franz
Schubert** (31 January 1797), with a small museum devoted to the
composer. His father came from Moravia, and his mother from
Austrian Silesia; so he may be considered as a 'typical' Viennese. In
1801 the family moved to Säulengasse 3, leading W off the Nussdorferstrasse a few paces S of No. 54. Here they lived for the next 17
years; on the ground floor was their school. See also Kettenbrückengasse 6, p 298.

For the district further N, see Rte 26A.

The route may be extended to visit the so-called **Schubertpark**, some 15
minutes' walk to the W (approached by turning left at the W end of the
Säulengasse and then, after crossing the Gürtel, right along Schulgasse). Here,
on the E wall, at the SW corner of the small park (the former Währing District
Cemetery), are the original graves of both Schubert and Beethoven (who died
on 19 November 1828, and 26 March 1827, respectively). Their remains were
exhumed and transferred to the Central Cemetery in 1888; see Rte 25N. Also
first buried here were the artist J.B. Lampi the Elder, Nestroy, and Grillparzer.

By following the Währinger Strasse (the parallel street to the N) to
the E, and re-crossing the Gürtel, you have a view S of the mammoth
new Allgemeine Krankenhaus, a hospital commenced in 1972,
already outmoded and still unfinished, and the subject of almost
universal criticism on numerous accounts. The former general hospital had been inaugurated in 1784, in a building of 1699 adapted for
the purpose. You shortly pass (left) the *Volksoper* (1898), the People's
Opera-house.

Passing Währinger Strasse 41, in which Bruckner lived in 1868–76,
we eventually reach (right), at No. 25, the **Josephinum**, founded in
1785 by Joseph II as a military Academy of Surgery and Medicine.
The building, started in 1783 by Isidor Canevale, preserves among
other objects of more specialist interest, a collection of *Wax Ana-
tomical Models*, used by student army surgeons at a time when the
dissection of corpses was not customary.

The models—1192 specimens in all—were made in Florence in 1775–85 under
the supervision of the anatomists Felice Fontana and Paolo Mascagni. In
adjacent rooms are the important Medical Library, MSS Collection, Picture
Archives, and *Museum*, the latter containing early surgical instruments, and
numerous objects associated with the great names of the Vienna Medical
School of the 19C and early 20C (see p 326).

Among other medical museums in Vienna are that of *Pathological Anatomy*,
housed in the cylindrical '*Narrenturm*' (1784; by Canevale)—the 'Fools' Tower'
of the *Allgemeine Krankenhaus* (entrance at Spitalgasse 2, some minutes to the
W of the Josephinum, said to be the first institution in Europe specifically for
mental patients, and in occupation until 1870. Also of professional interest is the
Elektro-pathological Museum, at Selzegasse 19, some distance W of the West
Bahnhof.

The building opposite the Josephinum is now the premises of the *French
Institute*; it was formerly the Dietrichstein or Clam-Gallas palace.

You shortly reach (right) Schwarzspanierstrasse, where No. 15 stands
on the site of the house, demolished in 1903, in which on 26 March
1827 Beethoven died.

From here on the 29th his coffin was conveyed to the Pfarrkirche in the
Alserstrasse, the funeral being attended by an immense crowd. Among his pall-
bearers were Hummel, and Kreutzer; among his 36 torch-bearers were Raim-
und, Czerny, and Schubert, as well as Grillparzer, who had written the funeral

oration. His body was buried in the Während District Cemetery (see above), and in 1888 removed to the Central Cemetery; see Rte 25N.

The Ringstrasse is shortly regained.

H. From the Schillerplatz to the Schwarzenbergplatz

A few minutes' walk SW of the Opera-house, off the S side of the Opernring, is the SCHILLERPLATZ.

At No. 3, on the W side of the square, in a building of 1872–76 by Theophil Hansen, is the *ACADEMY OF FINE ARTS (Akademie der bildenden Künste), on the second floor of which (stairs to the right of the entrance vestibule) is its collection of paintings, while its *Library* also contains important collections of drawings, engravings, and water-colours, including those of Austrian flowers made by Moritz Michael Daffinger (1790–1849).

The academy was originally founded in 1692 by Leopold I, while among the directors of the art gallery, from 1829, was Waldmüller. One young aspirant for admission to the academy was Adolf Hitler, who was twice refused, which had its repercussions. Schiele was accepted in October 1906 and left in April 1909.

Among the more notable paintings are *Hieronymus Bosch's* great Triptych of The Last Judgement; *Gentile da Fabriano*, Coronation of the Virgin; *School of Botticelli*, Madonna and Child with angels; *Hans Baldung Grien*, Rest on the Flight into Egypt; *Antwerp Mannerist*, Triptych of the Deposition; *Van Cleve*, Holy Family; *Lucas Cranach the Elder*, The Holy Family; St. Valentine with donor; The Stigmata of St. Francis; Death of Lucrezia; Old lecher and girl; *Dirk Bouts*, Coronation of the Virgin; *Ambrosius Holbein*, Death of the Virgin; *Hans Pruckendorfer*, The Holy Family in a wood; *Hans Maler (?)*, Portraits of Moritz Welzer and his wife; *Jan Cornelisz Vermeyen*, Male portrait; *Murillo*, Boys playing dice; *Cornelis Saftleven*, The duet; *Brent Fabritius*, Self-portrait; *J. van Ruisdael*, Woodland scene; *Jan Fyt*, Still lifes; *Rachel Ruysch*, Flower paintings, etc.; *Jordaens*, Portrait of his daughter Elisabeth; *Pieter Codde*, A social gathering; *Van Dyck*, youthful Self-portrait (1614); *Adrien Brouwer*, Sand-dunes; *Gaspar de Crayer*, Female portrait; *Johann Heinrich Schönfeld*, Classical fantasy view; *Karel Dujardin*, Italian landscape; *Ph. Wouwerman*, The hold-up; *Pieter de Hooch*, Dutch family in a courtyard; *Herman van Swanevelt*, Landscapes; *Jan Asselijn*, several Landscapes; *Rembrandt*, Portrait of a young girl (1632); *Jan van Goyen*, Harbour scene; *G.A. Berckheyde*, The Town Hall, Amsterdam; *Guardi*, several Venetian scenes; *P. Moreelse*, Young woman; *Daniel Gran*, Allegory; *Pierre Subleyras*, Portrait of Virginia Parker Hunt, and The artist's studio; *Samuel van Hoogstraaten*, Still life; *A. Pijnacker*, Landscapes; and several sketches by *Rubens*, including the Apotheosis of James I (for the ceiling of the Banqueting House, Whitehall). Also works by *Preti*, *Jacob Duck*, *Jan Weenix*, *Maulbertsch*, and two small landscapes by *Claude Lorrain*.

For the area to the S, see Rte 25I.

Turning E, you shortly reach and cross the Operngasse and then the Kärntner Strasse to skirt the N side of the KARLSPLATZ. On the S side of the street are the *Jugendstil* or *Art Nouveau* **Stadtbahn Pavilions**, designed by Otto Wagner in 1894–96, which were dismantled during work on the new underground system, and restored and rebuilt in 1978.

The dome and columns of the *Karlskirche* are conspicuous to the S, for which see Rte 25I.

The next building of importance (at No. 5 Karlsplatz) is the **Künstlerhaus**, of 1865–68, by A. Weber, several times extended, restored in 1968, and containing extensive art exhibition halls.

The private exhibition society, a bastion of the Establishment, was founded by August von Siccardsburg in 1861. Together with the Academy of Fine Arts (see above), it exerted a virtual stranglehold on the artistic life of Vienna during the second half of the 19C. The re-election of Eugene Felix, its conservative president, in 1896, precipitated a strong reaction among several of its younger artists and architects, and in the following April an independent society known as the *Vereinigung bildender Künstler Öesterreichs*, or *Secession*, was formed, with Gustav Klimt elected as president.

All but 17 of the 40 founding members were also members of the Künstlerhaus, and the committee of the latter, on passing a motion of censure on the break-away group, merely provoked numerous resignations, amongst them Klimt himself, and also Josef Maria Olbrich, Carl Moll, Kolo Moser, and Josef Hoffmann, and even, eventually, Otto Wagner. The first exhibition given by this new association took place in the Horticultural Society building in the Parkring in the spring of 1898, when it was even visited by Franz Josef: Rudolf von Alt, in his capacity of honorary president, greeting the philistine emperor. See also *Secession Building*, Rte 25I.

Nevertheless, in recent years, under a more enlightened directorship, the Künstlerhaus has been the venue of several remarkable exhibitions, not specifically of paintings.

Adjacent stands the red and yellow *Haus der Gesellschaft der Musikfreunde*, usually referred to as the **Musikverein** (Music Society), built by Theophil Hansen in 1867–69, with alterations in 1911. Its '*Goldener Saal*', (restored since a Russian shell pierced its coffered ceiling, and renovated recently), the largest of three concert-halls, is remarkable both for its sumptuous decoration and for its acoustic properties, and is the home of the Vienna Philharmonic Orchestra. The small *Brahms Saal* was inaugurated in 1870 with a recital by Clara Schumann.

The *Musikfreunde* (the Society of the Friends of Music), founded in 1812, possesses an important *Library* of musical MSS, particularly those of Brahms (director in 1872–75), including his own collection of over 2000 volumes of music, and extensive archives, and exhibitions of these are occasionally held. Most of the musical instruments in its collection are on permanent loan to the *Sammlung alter Musikinstrumente*, in the Neue Burg; (cf.). Schubert, who was a member of its committee, dedicated his great C Major Symphony to the Gesellschaft, receiving from them a fee of 100 guilders.

The Lothringenstrasse continues E, passing (right) the *Historical Museum of the City of Vienna* (see Rte 25I) to reach the N extension of the SCHWARZENBERGPLATZ; see Rte 25J.

I. From the Secession Building to the Karlskirche and Historical Museum

The Operngasse leads S from the W side of the Opera-house, shortly skirting the W end of the Karlsplatz, and after passing (right) a sculptured bronze group of the *Triumph of Mark Antony*, by Arthur Strasser (1899), reaches the ***SECESSION BUILDING**.

Erected in six months by Josef Olbrich (with financial assistance from Karl Wittgenstein), it has a gilded bronze openwork cupola, or rather sphere, of laurel leaves and berries, and has been nicknamed the 'Golden Cabbage' (by the stall-holders of the neighbouring market) and the 'Mahdi's Tomb', and other less complimentary titles. On its façade is carved the inscription 'Der Zeit ihre Kunst, der Kunst ihre Freiheit' (To every age its art, to art its freedom), in the portentous words of Ludwig Hevesi. The bronze doors, designed by Georg Klimt, are replicas of the originals.

The Secession Building by Joseph Olbrich

It remains a landmark in the history of Austrian culture. Built as a counter-blast to the exhibition halls of the *Künstlerhaus* (see above), it soon became a symbol of the whole *Art Nouveau* or *Jugendstil* reaction to the established artistic scene, the first phase of which lasted some eight years. In its fifth exhibition (1899) Aubrey Beardsley's work was shown; in its eighth (1900), the productions of Charles Rennie Mackintosh and his circle were first displayed in Vienna; the 18th (1903) was entirely devoted to Gustav Klimt.

The Secession Building was provisionally restored after extensive war damage (although the dome was not hit), and was re-inaugurated in January 1986 after a thorough reconstruction by Adolf Krischanitz, its re-gilded cupola again resplendent. Klimt's ***'Beethoven' Frieze**, also restored, has been placed along three sides of a newly excavated basement room, where it may be seen to advantage. Almost 27m long, it was painted for the 14th exhibition of the Secession in 1902. Facsimiles of his sketches are also displayed. Regular exhibitions of the works of contemporary artists continue to be held here.

To the SW extends the **Naschmarkt** or produce market, built over the river Wien, and flanked by the Linke Wienzeile and Rechte Wienzeile, to the N and S respectively.

At No. 6 in the former is the **Theater an der Wien**, built in 1797–1801 by Franz Jäger. At the E entrance in Millöckerstrasse, is the so-called *Papageno Gate*, decorated with a group depicting the plumed characters invented by Emanuel Schikaneder (1751–1812), its first director, and the librettist of Mozart's 'The Magic Flute' (Die Zauberflöte). He also produced 'Don Giovanni', 'Die Entführung aus dem Serail', and 'La Clemenza di Tito'. Its interior has been several times remodelled, and the whole was restored in 1960–62, after having been the temporary home of the State Opera in 1945–55.

Schikaneder had arrived in Vienna in 1785 as an actor and singer, and subsequently became an impresario. In 1803 he engaged Beethoven—who was to live on the premises—to write an opera, which here received its first, and unsuccessful, performance on 20 November 1805, under the title 'Fidelio'. Its first librettist, Joseph Sonnleithner, was young Grillparzer's uncle. Beethoven's Violin Concerto (1806) was written for Franz Clement (1780–1842), the violinist and conductor at the theatre. Several other works by Beethoven received their first public performances here: at a benefit concert of 22 December 1808, no less than the 5th and 6th Symphonies, the G Major Piano Concerto, the Choral Fantasia (Opus 80), with four shorter pieces as make-weights, were played. Spohr was concert-master here in 1812, and Lortzing in 1846–49. Johann Strauss's 'Fledermaus' received its first performance here, in 1874.

In 1822–23 Beethoven lived in rooms at Laimgrubengasse 22, not far to the W.

Continuing along the LINKE WIENZEILE, you reach at No. 38 the first of Otto Wagner's two *Apartment blocks*, built in 1898–99, which brought the architect some notoriety, with its golden medallions, swags, and sprays (by Kolo Moser); No. 40, adjacent, is the so-called *Majolika Haus*, with its elaborate rose, green, and blue floral ornamentation in ceramic tiles. Recently restored, they are best seen from the S side of the market-place.

A short distance further W, beyond the Kettenbrückengasse Underground Station, is the site of a crowded 'Flea Market' on Saturdays, although recently infiltrated by professionals.

By turning left (S) along Kettenbrückengasse (named after a suspension bridge over the Wien built in 1828, which previously stood here), you reach at No. 6, near its far end, the *Schubert's Sterbehaus*, that in which the composer died. His small room was opposite the entrance to the apartment on the second floor; another room contains a piano and desk belonging to his brother Ferdinand.

On 1 September 1828 Schubert moved to Ferdinand's newly built apartment for a change of air, for he had been unwell. Here, by the 26th, he had completed his final revisions to his last three piano sonatas, and later, the String Quintet, and in October, The Shepherd on the Rock (Der Hirt auf dem Felsen). In early October he was well enough to walk to Eisenstadt with his brother and two friends, to visit Haydn's grave. On the last day of that month he was taken ill, probably by another bout of an endemic typhoid infection. On 12 November he wrote to his friend Schober: 'I am ill; I have eaten nothing for eleven days and drink nothing and I totter feebly and shakily from my chair to my bed and back again ... If I take anything I bring it up again at once.' He also requested the loan of more novels by Fenimore Cooper, and to hear Beethoven's C sharp minor Quartet, Opus 131, which was performed here by friends, and the last music Schubert ever heard. By the 14th he was bedridden. But between delirious attacks he corrected the proofs of the second part of the 'Winterreise', and talked to his friends. On the 19th, at 3 o'clock in the afternoon, he died, turning his face to the wall with the words, 'Here, here is my end'. He was aged 31 years, nine months, and 19 days. His funeral took place on the 21st, and he was interred in the *Währing District Cemetery* adjacent to Beethoven, who had pre-deceased him by 18 months; his remains were transferred to the Central Cemetery in 1888; see Rte 25N. The total estimated value of his assets was 63 florins. (By way of comparison, Beethoven was able to leave 9000 florins to his nephew.)

By turning left into Margaretenstrasse, and then shortly right along Waaggasse, the WIEDNER HAUPTSTRASSE is reached, in which No. 32 was the residence of Christoph Willibald Gluck (born 1714), where he died on 15 November 1787 (cf. Central Cemetery). Antonín Dvořák once lodged at No. 7, and Jean Sibelius (in 1890–91, when a pupil of Goldmark and Robert Fuchs) at No. 36 in this street.

To the N, on the E side of the Wiedner Hauptstrasse, stands the *Paulanerkirche* (1627–51), rebuilt after 1683, with a notable organ, and Baroque decoration. The ceiling frescoes are attributed to Carlo Carlone.

A few minutes' walk to the SE, at Favoritenstrasse 15, is the main entrance in its long façade of the **Theresianum**, designed by Ludovico Burnacini, built in 1687–90 on the site of an imperial summer seat, and restored several times. Lady Mary Wortley Montagu attended a performance, in the gardens, of an opera by Fux. Maria Theresia established the *Theresianische Akademie* here in 1746, with a school of imperial administration for impecunious nobles, etc. The *Diplomatic Academy* was re-established here in 1964.

At Argentinierstrasse 30a, the parallel street to the E, stands the **ORF-Funkhaus**, or *Broadcasting-house*, the original foyer of which was designed by Clemens Holzmeister in 1935, but the buildings have been considerably extended since.

By bearing along Gusshausstrasse, leading off the Favoritenstrasse just E of the Paulanerkirche, and forking left into Karlsgasse, you

The Karlskirche

pass at No. 4 the site of a house in which Johannes Brahms (born at Hamburg in 1833) lived from 1871, and died on 3 April 1897.

The street leads back to the **Karlsplatz**, passing left the *Technical University* building of 1816–18.—Further W is the obtrusive eau-de-Nil façade of its modern extension and adjacent block, on which perch sculpted owls.

To the E, the gardens are dominated by the ****KARLSKIRCHE** (1716–39), one of the outstandingly original buildings of Austria—indeed one of the more remarkable in Europe—and the masterpiece of Johann Bernard Fischer von Erlach, but completed by his son Josef Emanuel from 1723. Both Lukas von Hildebrandt and Ferdinando Galli-Bibiena had submitted projects.

It is a richly articulated oval edifice in the Baroque style, with a wide façade, and surmounted by a massive copper dome, with its high drum and lantern. The centre of the façade is occupied by a Corinthian portico, with a relief by Giovanni Stanetti in the tympanum depicting the cessation of the plague of 1713. Above is a statue of St. Charles Borromeo, to whom the votive church is dedicated.

THE KARLSKIRCHE

0   5   10 metres

On either side rise colossal *columns* in imitation of Trajan's Column in Rome (for which the architect had a penchant), with spiral reliefs of the life of Borromeo by Johann Christoph Mader, Johann Baptist Staub, and Jakob Schletterer. They terminate in turrets below which are platforms decorated with gilded eagles by Lorenzo Mattielli, an attractive feature.

The *interior* contains frescoes by J.M. Rottmayr, with trompe l'oeil paintings by

Gaetano Fanti, and others by M. Altomonte, D. Gran, and Sebastiano Ricci (an Assumption). The glazed 'boxes' are notable. Georg Matthias Monn (1717–50) was for some years its organist. In March 1902 Gustav Mahler and Alma Maria Schindler were married here. It survived seven bombs which fell around it during the Second World War.

To the W is a sculpture entitled 'Hill arches' (1978) by Henry Moore; immediately NE stands the *Historical Museum*; while a short distance E is the SCHWARZENBERGPLATZ; see Rte 25J.

The ****HISTORICAL MUSEUM of the City of Vienna** (*Historisches Museum der Stadt Wien*) was inaugurated here in 1959, and provides a remarkable collection of objects relative to the history and culture of the city, and also a notable collection of paintings, displayed in a series of open-plan sections on three floors.

The GROUND FLOOR is primarily concerned with the history of the area from the Hallstatt period up to and including medieval Vienna, with collections of pottery, terra-sigillata, figurines, inscriptions, jewellery, arms, and other artefacts excavated from the site of *Vindobona*. Also several sandstone statues and 14C glass, from the cathedral; a number of bosses and carved and polychromed plaques (late 15C); examples of armour, including a series of late 15C tournament helmets, and five paintings by the *Master of the Friedrichsaltar* (1447).

FIRST FLOOR. *Josef Hickel* (1736–1807), Portrait of Joseph II; a series of blue and white pastel plaques by *Jean Pillement*; mid 18C Vienna porcelain and porcelain figures; *Josef Kreutzinger*, Portraits of Carlo Artaria (1747–1808), and Alois J. Liechtenstein (1759–1805); 'bird's-eye' Plan of Vienna of c 1776; and a Maquette of the inner city by *Eduard Fischer* (1852–54); *F.X. Messerschmidt* (1732–83), Grotesque busts; *Meytens*, Portraits of Maria Theresia (1744) and of Franz I (1740); *J. Kupetzky* (1667–1740), Karl VI (1716); Freemason's regalia, etc. of 1780; *Johann Christian Brand* (1722–95) Landscapes; *Paul Troger* (1698–1765), Pietà; *Franz Christoph Janneck* (1703–61), Self-portrait; *Jacob van Schuppen* (1670–1751), Self-portrait; several canvases by *Maulbertsch, Troger, M. Altomonte*, and *Rottmayr*, including a Self-portrait by the latter; *Johann Adam Delsenbach* (1687–1765), Views of Vienna (1740); works by *Johann Georg Platzer* (1704–61) and *Johann Martin* ('Kremser') *Schmidt* (1718–1801), miniature portraits of artists, including Johann Georg Schmidt, Angelica Kauffmann, Troger, and Maulbertsch.

A circular plan of Vienna by *Augustin Hirschvogel* (1548), together with its original copper plates; *Hans Guldemund*, View of Vienna surrounded by Turkish tents (1529); *Daniel Suttinger* (1640–90), Plan of the inner town in 1683; *Franz Geffels*, View of the Siege; *anon.* Portrait of Kara Mustafa; a fine collection of arms, armour, turbans, pennants, and shields; The entrance of the Marquis de Mirepoix into Vienna on 12 October 1738; *Bonifaz Wolmut*, Plan of Vienna in 1547; Engravings of panoramas and bird's-eye views by *Matthäus Merian the Elder* (1593–1650) and the *Younger*, by *Georg Matthäus Vischer* (1628–96), *Folbert van Alten-Allen, Hoefnagel* (1683), *Domenico Cetto* (1690), and *Joseph Mulder* (1686); *anon.* Views of 1632; *Josef Kreutzinger* (1757–1829), Portrait of Alois Josef Liechtenstein; *Gabriele Beyer*, Portrait of the architect Wilhelm Beyer; *anon.* painting of a Meeting of the Freemason's Lodge in Vienna in 1790, including Mozart and Schikaneder.

Engravings of Street-vendors, etc.; armorial and memorial plaques; brass weights and measures; carved and inlaid chests; Armour of Rudolf II by *Anton Pfeffenhauser* (Augsburg; 1575), and of

Maximilian II, and the Archduke Matthias; maquettes with tin soldiers; pennants; a chess-board; and a collection of silver-gilt objects.

Stairs ascend to the SECOND FLOOR: *Johann Martin Fischer* (1740–1820), several marble busts; a reconstructed 'Pompeian room' from the Caprara palace (1798), and a Vienna porcelain Vase; desk by *Joseph Haupt* (1805); *Laurenz Janscha* (1749–1812), View of the Prater in 1800; painted and engraved glass by *Anton Kothgasser*, and *Gottlob Samuel Mohn*; also porcelain; a dinner-service with views, dated 1801; porcelain view from the Belvedere (1821).

Views of Vienna during the Napoleonic occupation; several portraits by *Johann Baptist Lampi the Elder* (1751–1830) including that of Josef von Weinbrenner; *Johann Nepomuk Höchle* (1790–1835), several paintings of the campaigns of 1815; a bronze Bust of Metternich in 1810, and a section devoted to the Congress of Vienna in 1814–15; small Portrait of the Duke of Reichstadt (1834); *Rudolf von Alt* (1812–1905), The Stephansplatz in 1834; *Franz Scheyerer* (1762–1839), View towards Mödling; Views by *H. Neefe*; *Alois von Saar* (1779–1861), View of Grinzing; *Anton de Pian*, The Dom in 1824; several objects of mother-of-pearl; a reconstruction of Grillparzer's Library, etc., from Spiegelgasse 21, together with mementoes, and portraits of him by *Waldmüller* (1844), and *Amerling* (1856).

Another section is devoted to the **Biedermeier period**, with cards and games, albums, etc. of the era. *L. Fertbauer*, Kaiser Franz and his family (1826); *Peter Fendi* (1796–1842), The sad tidings; *Johann Endletsberger* (1782–1850), The greeting; *Franz Alt* (1821–1914), The garden; Interiors by *N. Moreau, Friedrich Loos* (1797–1890), et al; Portraits by *Josef Danhauser* (1805–45), including one of Franz von Schober; *Franz Eybl* (1806–80), Portraits of Moritz Graf Fries the Younger, of Franz Wipplinger, the artist (1804–47), and of Karl Gross; *Philipp Steidler*, Portrait of Joseph Lanner, and the latter's giraffe piano.

Prints depicting the plays of Nestroy, and Raimund, etc., plans of Vienna and its districts, street scenes, etc., *Johann Michael Neder* (1807–82), Viennese scenes, and two Self-portraits; wax portrait-bust by *Franz Gaul the Elder*; *Johann Baptist Reiter* (1813–90), several portraits, and other paintings; *Friedrich Amerling* (1803–87), Self-portrait of 1855, etc.; *Friedrich Loos*, View of Vienna in 1845.

A section is concerned with the capital during the **Revolution of 1848**, with a collection of swords, and paintings by *Franz Schams* of the Academic Legion, and by *Heinrich Hollpein* of Arrested revolutionaries.

Ferdinand Georg Waldmüller (1793–1865), Self-portrait of 1845, and The Dachstein, and Portraits of J.J. Schwartz von Mohrenstern and his wife, and of Elise Höfer; *August von Pettenkofen* (1822–99), Viennese scenes; postcards of the operetta, and theatre; a contour plan of Vienna in 1858; *Josef Feid* (1806–70), The Arsenal in 1860; *Josef Langl*, Bird's eye view of Vienna in 1873; Early photographs of Vienna, from 1858; *Franz Seifert* (1866–1951), Bust of Hugo Wolf (1899); *Hans Makart* (1840–84), Portrait of Franziska Charlemont (1878), and other works; *Hans Temple*, The Fine Arts Committee (1897); *Ernst Klimt* (1864–92), Standing boy; Maquette of Vienna with the Ringstrasse, by *Erwin Pendl* (1897–98).

The following section is devoted to the architect *Otto Wagner* (1841–1918); also *Max Oppenheimer* (1885–1954), Portrait of Adolf Loos in 1910; a reconstructed sitting-room from Loos' residence at

Bösendorferstrasse 3; *Emil Jakob Schindler* (1842–92; father of Alma Mahler), The Prater, and The mill at Plankenberg; *Richard Gerstl* (1883–1908), Portrait of Arnold Schönberg in 1907–8, also Self-portrait, and of his Mother, and Daughter; *Max Kurzweil* (1867–1916), Woman in a yellow dress; *Egon Schiele* (1890–1918), Self-portrait, The artist's bedroom, Portraits of Ida and Arthur Roessler, A sunflower, and Portrait of Schiele in 1907 by *Max Oppenheimer*; *Otto Wagner*, Dr Karl Leuger's mother-of-pearl armchair (1904); silver plaques and other objects designed by *Josef Hoffmann* (1870–1956), and *Kolo Moser* (1868–1918); *Arnold Schönberg*, Portrait of Alban Berg in 1910; *Wilhelm List* (1864–1918), Woman in white; *Gustav Klimt* (1862–1918), Portrait of Emilie Flöge (1902), Pallas Athene, and Love (1895); *W.V. Krausz*, Portrait of Arthur Schnitzler; *Fritz Wotruba* (1907–75), Sitting youth, Bust of Robert Musil; *Carl Moll* (1861–1945), Self-portrait, and Anna Moll writing; *Josef Dobrowsky* (1889–1964), Portrait of J.M. Hauer, the composer; *Josef Humplik* (1888–1958), Busts of Anton Webern (1928) and Karl Kraus (1920); *Herbert Boeckl* (1894–1966), Anatomy; *Ernst Fuchs* (1930–), Child with an angel; *Anton Lehmden* (1929–), Anti-aircraft tower at Arenbergpark (1953), View of Vienna (1960–62); *Rudolf Hausner* (1914–), The arc of Odysseus; *Oskar Kokoschka* (1886–1980), Vienna from the Wilhelminenberg; *Franz Sedlacek* (1891–1945?), Winter scene, and The chemist; *G.T. Kempf-Hartenkampf*, (1871–1964), Female portrait; *Rodin*, Bust of Gustav Mahler in 1909; and, near the head of the stairs: *Angelica Kauffmann* (1741–1807), Portrait of Josef Johann Graf Fries (1787), and *Heinrich Friedrich Füger* (1751–1818), Portrait of Johann Hunczovsky.

J.   From the Schwarzenbergplatz to the Stubenring

Just N of the intersection of the SCHWARZENBERGPLATZ and the Lothringerstrasse stands an equestrian *Statue of Prince Karl Philipp zu Schwarzenberg* (1771–1820), the allied commander at the Battle of Leipzig (1813), while to the NE stood the former *Officer's Club* or *Casino* of 1863 by Ferstel, which has been rebuilt in the original neo-Renaissance style after severe war damage, to preserve the appearance of the square. For its S extension, see Rte 25K. A few paces to the E stands the *Konzerthaus*, a complex of three concert-halls, dating from 1913. Here also is the experimental *Akademie-theater*.

Continuing NE along the Lothringerstrasse (built over the river Wien)—in No. 6 of which Karl Kraus (1874–1936), the author and journalist, lived from 1912 until his death—you pass (left, in a small platz to the N) a *Monument to Beethoven* of 1880, by Kaspar von Zumbusch, to approach a hotel block overlooking the E end of the Johannesgasse, with the Stadtpark beyond.

Salesianergasse 12, a few minutes' walk to the SE, was the birthplace of Hugo von Hofmannsthal (1874–1929), the poet, playwright, and librettist. Mary Vetsera also lived in this street, discreetly observed by Count Taaffe's secret police, prior to the dénouement at Mayerling (cf.).

To the E of this street is an enclave containing several embassies, among them the Italian, British (at Reisnerstrasse 40), and Russian, with the characteristic *Russian Orthodox Church* of 1893–99 adjacent, at Jaurésgasse 2. The

British ambassador's Residence is at neighbouring Metternichgasse 6; adjacent is the *Anglican Church* of 1875.—Josef Hoffmann lived from 1939–56 at Salesianergasse 31–33, a short distance N.

At Am Heumarkt 1, facing the SE side of the Stadtpark, is the *Hauptmünzamt* or *Mint* (1835–38; by Paul Sprenger), where a collection of minting stamps may be seen.

The **Stadtpark** itself was laid out on either bank of the river Wien by Josef Selleny and Rudolf Siebeck, and inaugurated in 1862, while Friedrich Ohmann designed the steps and walks adjacent to its Underground station. It also contains a small lake, and is embellished with several monuments and statues (of Schubert, Bruckner, Johann Strauss the Younger, and Hans Makart, among others), while near its SW corner is the *Kursalon*, typical of its period (1867).

At Stubenring 5, beyond the N end of the park, is the *MUSEUM OF APPPLIED OR DECORATIVE ART* (*Österreichisches Museum für angewandte Kunst*), founded in 1864, and housed on its completion in 1871 in a neo-Florentine Renaissance building by Heinrich von Ferstel, to which an extension was added in 1906–08. Unfortunately the canalised river Wien flows beneath its site, and subsidence has recently caused some damage to the structure, which has necessitated underpinning, etc., and certain sections may be temporarily closed. It is also the venue for occasional exhibitions. The Library and collection of Art Prints is of importance, as is the Wiener Werkstätte Archive.

Several rooms on the GROUND FLOOR contain notable collections of *furniture* and *objets d'art*, including cloisonné Limoges enamels from Göss; fabrics from Melk (1300) of gold filigree, made in England; an illuminated missal (English 1270–80); an Abbot's seat from Admont (early 13C); a good collection of 16–17C Venetian glass; 16C jewellery; Locks from Heiligenkreuz (16C); Palissy ware; clocks and astronomical instruments; a mid 16C Spanish bargaño; and Venetian furniture; a 17C dolls' house; 16C inlaid cabinets; ivories; silk hunting-scenes; hard-stone vases, etc. from Milan; a late 16C Tyrolese door; silver-gilt and painted glass; pewter; tapestries, etc.; and in the central courtyard, a collection of Italian majolicas.

Rooms in the extension are devoted to *Islam and the Orient*, including a wooden section from a mimbar (Cairo; 1296); Coptic textiles; an extensive collection of Oriental carpets, and Egyptian carpets, including an early 16C example in silk, and another depicting hunting scenes; a Portuguese carpet; prayer-rugs. Also ceramics and glass, many examples from China, and Chinese bronzes; ceramic figures (7–8C); T'ang porcelain (8–9C); a Celadon vase (10C); bronzes, and enamelled vases, etc.; lacquer-work; and a Head of Buddha (late 15C), rusted iron, once gilt.

Another section is concerned with the decorative arts of Europe in the 17–18Cs, including White Meissen ware of 1715 (founded 1710); polished hard-stones; an intarsia table from the Old University (1735), with folding chairs; carved cupboard from the Law-courts, depicting the Judgement of Solomon (1700); a Meissen bear of 1732, by *J.G. Kirchner*; Meissen porcelain of Oriental influence, and also figures; The 'Eger-cabinet' (1723); Habsburg medallions, etc.; Viennese porcelain of 1718; porcelain figures from Zwettl; Bohemian glass; intarsia panels by David Roëntgen (1779).

Stairs ascend to the FIRST FLOOR, with a section devoted to the Biedermeier period: a Hunting-service from the Augarten manufactory, founded by Du Paquier in 1718, and from 1744 the Imperial porcelain factory; glass by *Loetz* (from 1898); Biedermeier glass and porcelain painted by *Gottlob Samuel Mohn* (died 1815), and *Anton Kothgasser* (1769–1851); Venetian dish of painted glass (early 16C); black and gilt painted glass; Viennese ceramics (14–15C); glazed and coloured panels from a 16C stove from the cathedral; and a collection of stoves (*Kachelofen*); Viennese porcelain decoration from the Dubsky palace in Brno (1746), etc.

Other collections include *Jugendstil* furniture, among them examples designed by *Josef Hoffmann*, *Kolo Moser* (desk of 1903–04), and *Otto Wagner*; a first volume of the 'Ver Sacrum' (1898), its cover designed by *Alfred Roller*; *Klimt*, cartoons for the decoration of the dining-room of the Palais Stoclet in Brussels (1905–09); also bentwood furniture by *Michael Thonet*, and glass by *Ludwig Lobmeyr*, etc.

Encouraged by Charles Rennie Mackintosh (1868–1928; whose work, together with others of the 'Glasgow School' had been exhibited at the Secession Building in 1900), and following the example set by Charles Robert Ashbee's Guild of Handicraft, Hoffmann, Moser, and Fritz Waerndorfer established the short-lived but influential *Wiener Werkstätte* in the summer of 1903. Waerndorfer lost his fortune in the enterprise, and in 1914 emigrated penniless to the United States. In 1906 the *Wiener Keramik-Werkstätte* was set up, under the direction of Dagobert Peche and Michael Powolny.

Next to the museum is the *Academy of Applied Art* (attended by Kolo Moser in 1893–95, and by Kokoschka in 1904–09; both taught there later). Beyond it is the huge building erected in 1909–13 to house the *War Office*. Opposite is an equestrian *Statue of Marshal Radetsky* (1766–1858) by Kaspar von Zumbusch, just W of which is the façade of the *Postsparkassenamt*; see p 250. The STUBENRING ends at the JULIUS-RAAB-PLATZ, beyond which the Danube Canal is spanned by the *Aspernbrücke*. For the district to the N and E, see Rte 25M.

In the LANDSTRASSER HAUPTSTRASSE, SE of the museum, is the *Wien-Mitte Railway and Underground-station*, *City Air Terminal* and bus terminus. No. 4 in the street is the *Elisabethinenkirche* (1710; but reconstructed in 1743–49 by F.A. Pilgram, after a flood), its convent preserving an 18C pharmacy.—Some minutes' walk beyond, at No. 45, is the oft-remodelled *Rochuskirche* (of St. Roch), with a façade of 1721 by Anton Ospel. Between the two, leading from No. 28 to Ungargasse 13, is the restored *Sünnhof* (1823), now in part the 'Biedermeierhotel'. The frieze on No. 110 Landstrasser Hauptstrasse should be noted. No. 138 was Kolo Moser's home from 1905–18.

Here the Rasumofskygasse leads NE; Robert Musil lived at No. 20 between 1921 and 1938, before leaving for Switzerland. No. 23 is the former *Rasumofsky palace*, built in 1806–07 by Louis de Montoyer for the Russian ambassador and patron of Beethoven, Andreas Kyrillovich, Prince Rasumofsky (or Razumovsky; 1752–1836). Restored after being gutted by fire in 1814, it now houses the *Federal Institute of Geology*.—Friedensreich Hundertwasser's 'ÖKO-Hauses', colourful if eccentric dwelling-houses (1983), are at Kegelgasse 36–8 and Löwengasse 41–3.

At Kundmanngasse 19, a short distance to the E, is the *Bulgarian Cultural Institute*, recently installed in the former home of Ludwig Wittgenstein (1889–1951, at Cambridge), built in a stark style by Paul Engelmann to the specifications of the author of the 'Tractatus logicophilosophicus' in 1926, and now surrounded by a high wall.

From a point just to the NE, the *Rotundenbrücke* crosses the Danube Canal, providing an alternative approach to the *Prater*; see Rte 26M.

At Weissgerberstrasse 13, to the N, is the *KunstHaus Wien*, installed in a former *Thonet* furniture factory, converted by F. Hundertwasser, and containing his own paintings, together with a display area for modern art exhibitions.

K. The Belvedere; and the Military Museum

On the W side of the SCHWARZENBERGPLATZ stands the *French Embassy*, a notable Art Nouveau building by Chédanne, completed in 1909. To the S of the main square is a large *Fountain*, the jets of which partly mask the *Monument* erected by the Russians in 1945 to commemorate their occupying army.

Behind this, with its main entrance to the E, at Rennweg 2, is the *Schwarzenberg palace*, built in 1697–1704 to the design of J. Lukas von Hildebrandt, and altered in 1720–23 by J.B. Fischer von Erlach, whose work was completed by his son, who laid out the gardens. Regrettably its ceiling frescoes, by Daniel Gran, were virtually destroyed during the Second World War, since when the building has been tastefully restored. Part of it has been converted to accommodate a luxury hotel and restaurant. Permission may be given to visit the main halls, some containing good plasterwork, while several still lifes, and canvases by Rubens, embellish some walls.

On the far side of the Rennweg, No. 3 is the former *Palais Hoyos*, now the *Yugoslav Embassy*. It was designed by Otto Wagner (1889), who once lived here. Nos 1 and 5 were also designed by Wagner; the latter was Gustav Mahler's residence in 1898–1909. Adjacent is the **Gardekirche** or *Guards' Chapel* (1755–63) by Nikolaus Pacassi, which was adopted by the Polish Life Guards and by the end of the 19C had become the unofficial Polish Church in Vienna.

At Rennweg 6 is the entrance to the *Unteres (Lower) Belvedere* (see below), before entering which you can visit, at No. 10, the *Salesianerinnenkirche* (1717–30; by D.F. dell' Allio), with frescoes by G.A. Pellegrini in its conspicuous dome.

A short distance to the S, at Mechelgasse 2, is the entrance to the *Botanischer Garten*, established here in 1754 as a garden of medicinal herbs at the suggestion of Gerhard van Swieten, and later converted to a more general botanical garden by Nikolaus Joseph von Jacquin (1727–1817).

At Jacquingasse 8, further E, Richard Strauss built a villa on a plot of land given to him in exchange for the MSS score of 'Der Rosenkavalier', which he had presented to the National Library. He lived there intermittently between 1924–c 1940).

Although the more attractive approach to the **Lower Belvedere** is from the Upper, it is more convenient to describe its contents here (its history is given on p 308). It accommodates two museums, the first of which, the *ÖSTERREICHISCHES BAROCKMUSEUM*, devoted to Austrian Baroque art, is entered from a vestibule approached either from the Rennweg or the gardens.

Notable are *Martin van Meytens* (1695–1770), The Family of Graf Nikolaus Pálffy von Erdöd, and Portrait of Maria Theresia as Queen of Hungary (1741), and of Johann Christoph von Bartenstein; *Christian Seybold* (1703–68), Self-portrait, and Portrait of a young girl; *Jakob van Schuppen* (1670–1754), Portrait of Parrocel; *Johann Kupetzky* (1667–1740), Self-portrait, and Portrait of Guido Starhemberg; *Franz Xaver Messerschmidt* (1736–83), bronze Busts of Franz I, and of Maria Theresia; *Johann Michael Rottmayr* (1654–1730), Tarquin and Lucrezia; *Martino Altomonte* (1659–1745), Susanna and the elders; *Daniel Gran* (1694–1757), Sketches for ceiling-frescoes; *Paul Troger* (1698–1762), Christ on the Mount of Olives, and other similar subjects; *Giovanni Giuliani* (1663–1744), wood sculptures of St. Sebastian and St. Roch; *Johann Lukas Kracker* (1717–79), St. Andrew; *Johann Martin Schmidt* ('Kremser Schmidt'; 1718–1801), Dream of St. Martin, and other similar subjects; and works by *Franz Xaver Carl Palko*, and *Franz Anton Palko* (1724–76, and 1717–76, respectively), including a portrait of Carl Joseph Batthyany in 1760 by the latter.

The central MARBLE HALL, with its white plaques, has a ceiling by *Altomonte* depicting the Triumph of Prince Eugene, and the original lead figures from the Neuer Markt Fountain (1739; cf.) by *Georg Raphael Donner* (1693–1741). Notable is the carved Christ by *Johann Peter Schwanthaler the Elder* (1720–95) in the adjacent room. Note the bronze and marble plaques by Donner. *Franz Anton Maulbertsch* (1724–96) is represented by a Martyrdom of St. Andrew, a Crucifixion, and several other martyrdoms, and allegorical subjects, also a Self-portrait of 1767; *Johann Christian Brand* (1722–95), Landscapes, including four Views from Laxenburg, and a battle scene; also two Landscapes by *Anton Faistenberger* (1663–1708).

GROTESQUE HALL, with grotesque Busts by *Messerschmidt*.—RED MARBLE GALLERY, with white stucco-work: Busts of Franz I, and Maria Theresia, by *Messerschmidt*, and also by *Balthasar Ferdinand Moll* (1717–85); gilt bronze Bust of Josef Wenzel, Prince Liechtenstein.—CABINET DORÉ. *Balthasar Permoser* (1651–1732), marble Apotheosis of Prince Eugene (1721), its posture disliked by the Prince!; also several lacquered cabinets, Chinese bowls, medals, etc. The last room contains works by *Vinzenz Fischer* (1729–1810); and *Martin Knodler*, Laying the foundation-stone for the Temple of Concord at Laxenburg in 1745.

The **Orangery** (1720; but virtually rebuilt after the Second World War) next door houses *****Medieval Austrian Art**, including works by the *Master of the Albrechtsaltar*, Joachim and the angel, etc.; *Master of the Votive-panel of St. Lambrecht*, Christ carrying the cross; *Master of the Schloss Liechtenstein*, Nativity, Presentation in the Temple; a carved Crucifix from the Tyrol (1160–80); *The Salzburg painter of 1390*, Nativity; *Master of the Friedrichaltar*, The three kings; *Lienhard Scherhauff* (?), Adoration; *Conrad Laib*, Crucifixion (1449); Tyrolean 'Wiltener Calvary' (1420–30); Epitaph of Alexius Funck with donors (1522); *Michael Pacher* (died 1498), Pope Sixtus being led away from St. Laurence, Marriage of the Virgin, and a Flagellation; *Urban Görtschacher*, Ecce Homo (1508); *Rueland Frueauf the Elder* (died 1507), Male portrait (c 1490), a Crucifixion, Christ on the Mount of Olives, and several other fine works; *The Habsburg Master*, Adoration of the three kings (1500); *Hans Siebenburger*, Crucifixion, with donors (1478); *Master of the St. Veit Legend*, Martyrdom (in an oven) of St. Veit (1480); *Master of the St. Oswald Legend*, Recovery of the relics (1470); *Master of the Wiener Schottenaltar*, Deposition, and Adoration of the Magi; stone Statues of St. Ambrose and St. Augustine; *Master of the Divisio Apostolorum*, Nativity, with SS. Joachim and Anne; *Master of Mondsee*, Mary in the Temple, and Flight into Egypt; *Marx Reichlich*, The Visitation; the Donau Altarpiece, and the Wiener Schnitzaltar (c 1440); also several wood sculptures, some polychromed; and a carved plaque of the Fall of Man, by *Master I.P.* (1521).

You can walk S, ascending gently through the **Gardens**, with their fountains and waterfalls, to reach the *Upper* Belvedere. This is also approached by the Prinz-Eugen-Strasse, climbing SE from the W side of the Schwarzenbergplatz. The street is also followed by the line D tram, in the direction of Südbahnhof.

The **˙˙BELVEDERE**, built by J. Lukas von Hildebrandt for Prince Eugene of Savoy (1663–1736), consists of two separate buildings, between which, on a gentle slope, lie the main terraces of its gardens. The lower palace was the first erected, a modest single-storey building of 1714–16, while the *Upper Belvedere* was in construction between 1721 and 1723. Dominique Girard, a pupil of Le Nôtre, was lent to Eugene by Max Emmanuel of Bavaria, and was busy laying out its gardens between 1717–19. Although Montesquieu considered the façade 'in bad taste: a mass of fancy bits and pieces', it was nevertheless, with its (green) copper roof and white stucco walls, frequently reproduced in engravings; some one hundred were printed by Salomon Kleiner of Augsburg between 1731 and 1740.

To the S, shaped to conform with the apex of the site, was a large *Pièce d'eau* in which small gondolas floated. It reflected the S façade, the three storeys of its central section balanced by lower pavilions with squat cupolas at its four octagonally-shaped corners.

Unfortunately the gardens were adjacent to a Salesian nunnery, 'so that a person cannot walk in it, without being overlooked'. They also contained an *Orangery* (see above) and a small zoo, while the palaces themselves were filled with fine furniture and paintings as befitted the Prince, whose library of 15,000 books, 237 MSS, and c 500 volumes and cartons of prints were eventually disposed of to the Nationalbibliothek and the Albertina.

These had impressed Lady Mary Wortley Montagu, who visited the *Lower Belvedere* in 1717, and remarked that the library was well chosen, and that the prince would not admit any edition 'but what are beautiful and pleasing to the eye … [many] pompously bound in Turkey leather'. As he once told St. Saphorin, the English minister: 'I have more than enough books not to be bored.' In 1752 the palace was acquired by the royal house, and in 1770 was the site of a fête in honour of Maria Antonia's engagement to the Duke de Berry, who in 1774 succeeded to the French throne as Louis XVI. In 1779 its park was opened to the public.

The Belvedere contained the *Imperial Picture Gallery* from 1781 to 1891, when it was transferred to the new Kunsthistorisches Museum, and in 1904 it was occupied by the Archduke Franz Ferdinand, whose assassination at Sarajevo on 28 June 1914 possibly spared the Austrians an emperor to whom were attributed the traits of 'callousness and cruelty of an Asian despot'.

Since 1923 the upper building has housed the so-called *Österreichische Galerie* or *Austrian Gallery of paintings* (from the early 19C)—see below—while the lower building and the Orangery have accommodated important collections of *Baroque* and *Medieval Austrian art*, respectively; see above. Damaged by American bombs in the Second World War, the buildings were re-opened to the public in 1953 after repair and restoration. On 15 May 1955 the *Austrian State Treaty* was signed here (by Macmillan, Dulles, Molotov, Pinay, and Figl), by which the country regained her independence after a decade of occupation by the Allied powers. The official opening of the Strategic Arms Limitation Talks (SALT) took place here on 16 April 1970.

Anton Bruckner lived for the last 16 months of his life in a lodge of the Belvedere. He died on 11 October 1896.

The *View N from its main entrance is particularly fine, and for this reason it is recommended that the Upper Palace is visited first. An alternative approach is that from the Landstrasser Gürtel, further S.

The palace containing the **˙˙ÖSTERREICHISCHE GALERIE**, is entered from the centre of its N façade, first passing through the *Garden Room*; the ceiling of this vestibule is sustained by four Atlantes, with stucco-work from the workshop of Santino Bussi.

The 19C European paintings which since 1967 had been displayed in the 'Neue Galerie' at the Stallburg (cf.) have been transferred to the Belvedere. At the time of writing only a selection of the following are on view in the NE octagon on the first floor. Among them are: *Caspar David Friedrich*, Rocky Landscape near Dresden; *Millet*, Self-portrait; *Corot*, Portrait of Mme Legois; *Delacroix*, Jacob wrestling with the angel, and Bowl of Flowers; *Daumier*, Sancho Panza; *Courbet*, Self-portrait (wounded, or asleep), Young Girl, and Landscape near Ornans; *Manet*, Woman in a fur; *Rodin*, Eve, and busts of Henri de Rochefort-Luçay, and of Gustav Mahler; *Piotr von Michalowski*, Austrian hussar; *Anselm Feuerbach*, Self-portrait; *Arnold Böcklin*, Marine idyll; *Toulouse-Lautrec*, Woman on a pillow; *Renoir*, two Nudes, and a bronze Mother and child; *Monet*, Fishing on the Seine near Poissy, The Garden at Giverny, and The Chef (M. Paul); *Degas*, Harlequin threatens Columbine; *Pissarro*, The rue de Gisors, Pontoise; *Wilhelm Trübner*, Female portrait; *Wilhelm Leibl*, Portrait of the Gräfin Rosine Treuberg, and Head of a peasant girl; *Max Liebermann*, The artist's daughter; several works by *Lovis Corinth*; *Cézanne*, Still life; *Van Gogh*, Self-portrait, Landscape near Auvers, and Still life (bottles); *Picasso*, Catalan landscape (1897); *Edvard Munch*, Double portrait, Park in Kösen, Midnight sun, and Bathers; *Giovanni Segantini*, 'Die bösen Mütter'; *Max Slevogt*, Portrait of Eva Steinbarth; also characteristic paintings by *Géricault*, *Lépine*, and *Eva Gonzalez*.

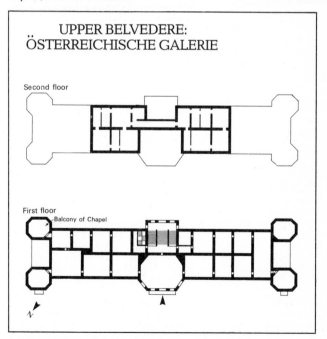

UPPER BELVEDERE: ÖSTERREICHISCHE GALERIE

Second floor

First floor

Balcony of Chapel

N

GROUND FLOOR rooms to the left of the entrance (occasionally closed) contain: *Angelica Kauffmann* (1741–1807), Portrait of the Gräfin Merveldt, and several other works; *Friedrich Heinrich Füger*

(1751–1818), Self-portrait; and of his wife, brother and son; *Barbara Krafft* (1764–1825), Anton von Marx and family; *Johann Peter Krafft* (1780–1856), The artist's daughter writing, and several family portraits, also detailed sketches of Franz I entering Vienna after the Battle of Leipzig (the finished version is in the Imperial Apartments of the Hofburg); *Johann Baptist Lampi the Elder* (1751–1830), Caroline and Zoë Thomatis; Two children; and Graf Nicolai; *Josef Rebell* (1787–1828), Classical landscapes; *Josef Fischer* (1769–1822), View of Vienna from Nussdorf; *Josef Anton Koch* (1768–1839), Berner Oberland landscape; *Josef Kreutzinger* (1757–1829), Portraits of Ferdinand Kinsky; and Eva Passy. The NE rotunda contains several sketches by *Moritz von Schwind* (1804–71).

To the right of the vestibule are a further series of rooms, in which note the ceiling of the NW rotunda.

Steps ascend to the FIRST FLOOR and the domed red *Marble Hall*, two storeys high, in which the Austrian State Treaty was signed (see above), providing a fine view N over the gardens (as painted by Bernardo Bellotto in 1669; see p 287) with the Karlskirche and Schwarzenberg Palace to the left, the dome of the Salesianerinnenkirche to the right, and in the centre, the spire of the Stephansdom, with the Leopoldsberg in the distance.

Among the more interesting canvases on this floor are: *Franz Eybl* (1806–80) Woman in a blue dress, Male portrait, Portraits of Franz Wipplinger, and of Herr and Frau Nadassy, and The smithy; *Friedrich von Amerling* (1803–87), Portraits of Franz Stober, of a Child, of his Mother, Girl with a green-ribboned hat, Kaiser Franz in uniform (1834), Boy fishing, Rudolf von Arthaber and his children; Robert Theer, and Amalie Klein.

Ferdinand Georg Waldmüller (1793–1865), The artist's mother; Self-portraits (aged 35 and 54); The artist's second wife, Catharina von Kondelka; Roses; and smaller portraits; of the Wife of Joseph von Stadler, of Frau Antonie Schaumburg; and several realistic Landscapes.

Moritz Michael Daffinger (1790–1849), several miniature portraits, including The artist's wife, and of the Duke de Reichstadt (1831); *Johann Baptist Reiter* (1813–90), Portrait of Barbara Meyer, and Boy reading; *Rudolf von Alt* (1812–1905), two Views of the Stephansdom; *Hans Makart* (1840–84), Frau Carl von Piloty, and other works; *Anton Romako* (1832–89), Portrait of Mathilde Stern, of the Empress Elisabeth in 1883, and other works; *Leopold Kupelwieser* (1796–1862), several Portraits; *Karl Moll* (1861–1945), the Naschmarkt in 1894; *Friedrich Loos* (1797–1890), Landscapes; and representative works by *August von Pettenkofen* (1822–89), *Carl Schuch* (1846–1903), *Carl Schindler* (1821–42), *Theodor von Hörmann* (1840–95), *Peter Fendi* (1796–1842), *Thomas Ender* (1793–1875), *Friedrich Gauermann* (1807–62), *Moritz von Schwind* (1804–71; the friend of Schubert), and *Adalbert Stifter* (1805–68; better known as a poet), Roofs in Vienna. A view of the chapel may be glimpsed in the SE rotunda.

Stairs ascend to the SECOND FLOOR, notable on which are the paintings by *Gustav Klimt* (1862–1918), *Egon Schiele* (1890–1918), and *Oskar Kokoschka* (1886–1980). Among works by the former are Portraits of Joseph Lewinsky; Sonja Knips (in a pink dress); Judith I (1901); Johanna Stande; Woman with a hat and boa; Woman's head; Fritza Riedler; Adele Bloch-Bauer I; The kiss; Adam and Eve; The bride; Watersnakes I; Field of poppies; House at Attersee; Farm-house; Alley in the park at Schloss Kammer; and several Flower-pieces.

Among canvases by *Schiele*: Death and the maiden; Portraits of Dr Hugo Koller; of Edith, his wife, seated (the first of his paintings to be acquired by an Austrian museum; Hofrat Haberditzl was director at that time); of Viktor Ritter von Bauer; of Eduard Kosmack; of Herbert Rainer (as a child); The artist's family, naked; Windowscape; Sunset; Woman with two children; Four trees.

Paintings by *Kokoschka* include Portraits of Ernst Koesster; of Carl Moll, the artist; The artist's mother; View of Prague; Still life with mouse; The Tigerlöwe; The revenue officer; also note his Bust by *Alfred Hrdlicka*.

Other works of interest are: *Franz Jaschke* (1862–1910), a pointill-ist View of Vienna; *Max Kurzweil* (1867–1916), Portraits of children, and of Mira and Bettina Bauer; *Fritz Silberbauer* (1883–1975), Portrait of his son; *Wilhelm Thöny* (1888–1949), Don Giovanni, etc.; *Josef Dobrowsky* (1889–1964), Winter scene; *Herbert Boeckl* (1894–1966), Portrait of Prof. Bruno Grimschitz, and others; *Broncia Knoller* (1863–1934), Mother sewing; *Kolo Moser* (1868–1918), Portrait of Franz Dangl; *Theodor Krämer* (1897–1958), Portrait of Theodor von Hörmann, the artist, and other works; *Richard Gerstl* (1883–1908), Laughing man; *Fritz Schwarz-Waldegg* (1889–1942?), Self-portrait; *Oskar Laske* (1874–1951), The Ship of Fools; *Albert Paris Gütersloh* (1887–1973), The artist's daughter; and examples of the art of *Anton Kolig* (1886–1950), *Franz Wiegele* (1887–1945), and *Max Oppenheimer* ('Mopp'; 1885–1954).

From the S front of the palace you skirt the *Pièce d'eau* to the E of which is the lodge in which Bruckner died (see History) and the walled *Alpengarten*, where in summer months there is an extensive collection of alpine plants. Eventually the LANDSTRASSER GÜRTEL is reached. The S Gate of the Belvedere gardens is notable.

To the SW is the *Südbahnhof*, or *Southern Railway Station*; to the SE, the *Schweizer Garten*, in which, facing the Arsenalstrasse, is the **Museum des 20. Jahrhunderts**, or *20C Museum*, founded in 1962, which is a pendant to the Museum of Modern Art (see Rte 25G). Concentrating on exhibitions of contemporary art, it is housed in an adaptation by Karl Schwanzer (1918–75) of his steel and glass 'Austria Pavilion', constructed for the Brussels Fair of 1958.

Beyond the gardens rears the brick-built quadrangular complex of the **Arsenal** (1849–55), erected immediately after the Revolution of 1848 in apprehension of future uprisings, and subsequently enlarged.

Passing through the main entrance in the centre of the NW wing, you reach the ***MILITARY MUSEUM**, or *Heeresgeschichtliches Museum* block (Objekt 18), built in a mock Romano-Byzantine style by Ludwig von Förster and Theophil Hansen in 1850–56. Under the inspired curatorship of Johann Christoph Allmayer-Beck much was done to modernise the display of the collections, illustrating the history of the Imperial Army (and Navy).

The central domed room on the FIRST FLOOR is devoted to the *Order of the Golden Fleece*. To the left is a gallery displaying relics of the Thirty Years' War (1618–48), including the Battle of Lützen (1632), with engravings by *Jacques de Gheyne* (1565–1629); 12 canvases by *Snayers*; a copy of *Van Dyck*'s Portrait of Wallenstein; a

series of Turkish muskets and maces (17C); a painting of the Relief of Vienna by Sobieski in 1683, and other material devoted to that epoch. *Johann Kupetzky* (1667–1740), Portrait of Prince Eugene, and another equestrian portrait, together with the prince's funeral hangings.

A section is devoted to the War of the Spanish Succession (1708–13), and to Marshal Starhemberg (died 1737); *Jean Pierre Bredael the Younger*, The battles of Villaviciosa, and Zaragoza; Turkish tent; Russian Folding-chair made in Tula; other sections are concerned with Franz I, and Bathyány; and The Seven Years' War (1756–63), with Prussian Grenadier and Fusilier caps, together with several paintings of cavalry by *J.C. Brand* (1722–95).

To the right of the central block is a second gallery devoted to 19C campaigns; to the Archduke Karl (1771–1847), with a Montgolfier balloon captured in 1796 at Würzburg; captured French Republican ensigns, etc.; *J.P. Krafft* (1780–1856), The battle of Aspern; souvenirs of the Duc de Reichstadt; Radetzky's sabre; and numerous Uniforms, including those of an Hungarian Hussar General, and of Franz Josef (1854); also a Prussian breech-loading needle-gun of 1841.

The W wing of the GROUND FLOOR contains later 19C uniforms; Franz Josef's Order of the Garter, marshal's baton, and personal uniforms; Bodyguards' uniforms, and those of 1913–14; also the Graef and Stift Car (1910), in which Franz Ferdinand and his morganatic wife Sophie Chotek von Chotkowa were travelling when assassinated by Gavrilo Princep at Sarajevo on 28 June 1914, in which is seen the bullet-hole of the shot which killed his wife. Adjacent is displayed the blood-stained uniform the Archduke was wearing at the time (cf. Artstetten).

Several paintings of the 1914–18 war as seen through the eyes of Austrian artists are passed before reaching a section in which a number of heavy artillery pieces are shown, including an 80-tonne Howitzer used at St. Quentin, and on the Italian front; a Turret of the fortress of Przemysel, manufactured in 1894 by Skoda of Pilsen; a pierced Belgian gun-turret; anti-aircraft guns, and mortars; a 30.5cm steel plate from a Battle-cruiser (1913); a model of a Tank designed by Gunter Barstyn before 1911, but never taken up; and the equipment of mountain troops, largely used on the Italian front, etc.

The E wing illustrates the exploits of the *Austrian Navy* (when Pola, near Trieste, was the site of their main base and Naval Academy). Among the exhibits are 18C and early 19C Ship models; River-boats; a model of 'SMS Novara', which carried the Emperor Maximilian to Mexico, having been converted to steam in 1862; of the iron-clad frigate which in 1866 rammed Italian men-of-war at the Battle of Lissa (near Dubrovnik); a section devoted to Weyprecht and Payer's Polar expedition to Franz Josef's Land in 1872–74; model of a Torpedo, designed by Robert Whitehead (who had been employed at Trieste from 1848, and from 1856 at Fiume) in 1872; and the 7m-long half-section (at 1:25) of the 'Viribus Unitis', the Austrian flag-ship in c 1911, etc.

For the *St. Marxer Cemetery*, to the E, circled by the motorway, see Rte 25N.
    Some distance SW, on the Reumannplatz (Favoriten Strasse) are the Jugendstil swimming-pools of **Amalienbad** (1923–26; by Otto Nadel and Karl Schmalhofer), restored in 1980–86.

The most pleasant return to the centre from the Army Museum is by walking through the Belvedere Gardens; see above.

L. Schönbrunn; and the Technical Museum

The most convenient approach is by the Underground from *Karlsplatz*, direction Hütteldorf, making your exit at either Schönbrunn or Hietzing, the palace being between the two stops. By car, follow the Linke Wienzeile from the Karlsplatz to the Schlossbrücke, there turning left.

Some distance beyond is the *Hofpavillon Hietzing (by Otto Wagner; 1898) a private railway station for the palace, recently restored, its octagonal 'waiting-room' with remarkable panelling and metalwork.

The *PALACE OF SCHÖNBRUNN, which once stood well beyond the city limits, was the summer residence of the Habsburgs, the Hofburg being their winter home.

The property was originally a hunting-lodge known as the *Katterburg*, which became the residence of Ferdinand III's widow after 1657, but was destroyed during the Turkish siege of 1683. In 1696 J.B. Fischer von Erlach was commissioned to erect a summer palace on the site of the present Gloriette (see below), but economic considerations necessitated a change of site to near the S bank of the river Wien. This palace was completed by 1730, the central section of which was occupied by Joseph I, and on his death his widow, Wilhelmina Amalia, passed the summers there. Alterations were made by the architect's son, Josef Emanuel, and further changes by Nikolaus Pacassi were carried out after 1743, commissioned by Maria Theresia, whose favourite residence it was. (She had a penchant for keeping windows open, which froze her courtiers, only allowing her hypochondrical and eccentric minister Wenzel Anton Kaunitz (1711–94) to close them while in audience.)
    Modifications were made by Johann Aman in 1817, while in 1808 a system of irrigation for its gardens had been laid out. In both 1805 and 1809 it was Napoleon's HQ while in Vienna, and in due course it became the principal residence and virtual prison of his son, the Duc de Reichstadt (or Roi de Rome 1811–32), who died here of phthisis. Here also died Franz Josef, during the night of 20 November 1916, aged 86. Karl, the last Habsburg emperor, made his statement of renunciation here, on 11 November 1918, before leaving for Eckartsau in the Marchfeld (cf.).
    Together with its outbuildings, it received substantial damage during the Second World War, immediately after which it served as the Russian HQ, and later that of the British. Restored, it has been the scene of several state receptions since the signing of the State Treaty in 1955, and is now, with its gardens, one of the more popular sights in the immediate vicinity of the capital.

To the W of the main entrance, flanked by obelisks, is the *Theatre (1747), designed by Pacassi, but elaborately decorated by J.F. von Hohenberg in 1767. It was restored in 1979–80, and is the venue for occasional chamber-opera performances; it is also the home of the *Max Reinhardt School of Dramatic Art*.
    A few paces beyond the SW corner of the courtyard is the entrance to the *Wagenburg or *Carriage Museum*, in which numerous coaches and sleighs surviving from the Imperial era, and which formed part of the collections of the Kunsthistorisches Museum, have been assembled after restoration. Since 1974 they have been displayed in what is virtually a new building. Also to be seen are several gorgeous coachmen's liveries; red velvet and gold embroidered harnesses and other accoutrements and trappings, stirrups and buckles. All objects are suitably labelled, and the catalogue is informative.

SCHONBRUNN: PALACE AND GARDENS

To Gloriette

To Gloriette

To Zoo

Neptune Fountain

To Roman Ruins and
Schöner Brunnen

To Hothouse

To Hietzing Gate

From main gate

To Meidling Gate

N

0   20   40 metres

To Coach Museum

Among notable vehicles are the 'Imperialwagen' of 1763 (or earlier), the central richly carved and gilt rococo compartment of which is suspended by velvet-covered leather straps from the shafts (and last used at the coronation of Karl I as King of Hungary at Budapest in 1916); the Carousel-carriage of Maria Theresia (1742); a ceremonial State carriage (by Jacquin of Paris; 1805); the Prince of Schwarzenberg's State carriage (1809); the Harrach Diligence of 1780; the Duke of Reichstadt's Phaeton (1811–12); Crown-prince Rudolf's Vis-à-vis (1860); a Berline of 1735–40; the Coronation Landau built by Ulmann of Vienna in 1816, painted dark green. Here are Franz Josef's personal Coupé (by Carl Marius; Vienna 1887); the Coach of Prince Joseph Wenceslas of Liechtenstein; and the Imperial Hearse (1876–77), last used at the funeral of Franz Josef in 1916; also several ceremonial litters, notably one of red leather, dated 1705 (which transported the Austrian Archduke's hat from Klosterneuburg to the Hofburg). Also sedan-chairs; and several Sleighs, including Maria Theresia's Carousel-sleigh (c 1740); bell-harnesses, etc.; the charming painting by Charles Herbel of c 1690 depicts similar sleighs in use. On a landing is a collection of paintings of the Empress Elisabeth's horses and dogs, mostly by Wilhelm Richter (1824–92).

From the main *Entrance Vestibule* of the **Palace** itself, the ochre-coloured façade of which is 175m long, groups are escorted around several suites of rooms.

The *Chapel*, of 1700, in the E wing, is normally only open on Sundays. It contains a painting by Paul Troger above the main altar, and a ceiling fresco by Daniel Gran.

The restored murals in the so-called '*Bergl-Zimmer*' rooms to the left of the entrance, painted in 1769–77 by Johann Wenzl Bergl (1718–89), a Bohemian artist of exotic landscapes, may be seen on request; they also contain an exhibition explaining the architectural history of the palace.

Stairs to the right ascend to the **State Apartments** (**RR1–15**), preserving several notable stoves, Bohemian glass chandeliers, and family portraits.—**R4** (*Franz Josef's Study*) contains a portrait of the future emperor on horseback, aged five; his *Bedroom*, adjoining, with the simple iron bed in which he died, has a portrait of the Crown Prince Rudolf, by *Hans Canon*, and the Emperor on his deathbed, by *Franz von Matsch*; also a French Mirror-clock (1795), and Augarten porcelain.—**RR6–12** overlook the *Kammergarten*, the private garden of the imperial family, beyond which **R13**, at the SW corner, is Maria Theresia's attractively decorated *Breakfast-room*, containing embroidery, possibly the work of the empress and her daughters.

The *Ceremonial Apartments* (**RR16–25**) are entered next, with the *Mirror Room*, in which Mozart and his sister Nannerl (aged six and nine respectively) played before the Empress in October 1762; three other rooms follow, embellished with decorative landscapes by *Josef Rosa* of 1760–69, also a Portrait of Maria Theresia aged 45, by *Van Meytens*. Notable is the round *Chinese Room* (**R20**), with its marquetry floor, black lacquer panels, and collection of blue and white Chinese vases. Cross the *Great Gallery* (**R41**), with its fluted pilasters, gilt decoration by Albert Bolla, and ceiling frescoes by Gregorio Guglielmi (1760), that to the E being a copy of the original, destroyed in 1945.—**R40** contains a painting by *Van Meytens* of a Carousel in the Winter Riding-school of the Hofburg on 2 January 1743.

R24, adjacent, a *Ceremonial Hall*, has several canvases of interest, among them a large portrait of Maria Theresia by *Van Meytens*; the Banquet following the wedding of Prince Josef and Princess Isabella of Parma in the Augustinerkirche (October 1760); and a Concert in the Redoutensaal of the Hofburg, in which Mozart and his father may be discerned near the lower right-hand corner. The room also provides a good view of the Gloriette.

From **R25**, the *Blue Chinese Drawing-room*, with Chinese papers and Florentine scagliola tables, enter **R26**, the *'Vieux-Laque-Zimmer'*, with a marquetry floor, decorated c 1770 with black lacquer panels, and containing *Pompeo Battoni*'s Portrait of 1771 of Franz Stephan of Lothringen (or Lorrain), consort of Maria Theresia, and also a portrait of their daughter-in-law, Ludovica, the wife of the Archduke Leopold of Tuscany, and their children, by *Anton von Maron*.—**R27**, the so-called *Bedroom of Napoleon*, in which the Duc de Reichstadt, his son by Marie Louise, died, is embellished with 18C Brussels tapestries, and lacquer screens.

Passing through the *Porcelain Room* (formerly Maria Theresia's Study), you enter the *'Millionen-Zimmer'* (**R29**: so-called in reference to its reputed cost), its walls providing 60 rococo rosewood frames for some 260 Persian and Indian miniatures of c 1627, several depicting life at the Mogul court.—Off this is a small *Breakfast-room*, preserving Augarten porcelain.—**R30** displays several more 18C Brussels tapestries.—**R34**, in which Franz Josef was born, contains a parade bed, and pastels by *Jean-Etienne Liotard* (who had visited Vienna on three occasions; in 1743–45, 1762 and 1777); while **R35**, adjoining, preserves several miniature portraits (including copies) of members of the family, including a Self-portrait, among others, by the Archduchess Maria Christine, herself a gifted artist.

The **'Park** was laid out in 1705 by Jean Trehet of Paris. It was modified in 1765 by Adrian van Steckhoven, a Dutch landscape-gardener, whose design was executed by J.F. von Hohenberg, also responsible for a number of its buildings and embellishments. Its main features are the long avenues of trees clipped to form tall hedges flanking the colourful parterre, and the dominating **Gloriette** on the hill-crest to the S, its central portico flanked by two wings (1775), and providing an extensive view.

At the foot of the steep slope is the *Neptune Fountain* (1780), by F.A. Zauner, a short distance to the E of which are the artificial 'Roman Ruins'. A few paces NE of the latter is the site of the 'Schöner Brunnen' or 'beautiful fountain' which gave the palace its name, transformed into a grotto in which the nymph Egeria (by Wilhelm Beyer) dispenses water from a pitcher.

To the W of the Neptune Fountain is a *Palm-house* of 1882 (recently restored), near which is a *Botanical Garden* of 1848. Close by is the *Tiergarten* or *Menagerie*, a Baroque octagonal pavilion of 1752 by Jean-Nicolas Jadot, preserving ceiling frescoes by Gregorio Guglielmi. A 'Butterfly House', in the *sonnenuhrhaus* (1906) can also be visited.

Just N of the *Hietzing Gate* (near the Palm-house) is the *'Kaiser-stöckl'*, built in 1770 for Prince Kaunitz, and which long remained the summer residence of the Minister of Foreign Affairs. To the S is the *Parish Church* (from 1607), containing paintings by Rottmayr.

No. 101 Hietzinger Hauptstrasse was the Studio of Egon Schiele from October 1912 until his death in 1918, although he died (31 October) in his mother-in-law's apartment at No. 114, opposite. His wife, Edith Harms, had died three days earlier, both having caught Spanish influenza in the epidemic which had dispatched Klimt eight months before.

The Maxingerstrasse (in which at No. 18 Johann Strauss lived until 1878 and composed the 'Fledermaus') leads S uphill from the church. Off this street is the Gloriettegasse, in which No. 9 was the residence of Katharina Schratt, the actress and confidante of Franz Josef from 1886; the Emperor would not infrequently call on her at 7.00 for breakfast. No. 14–16; the 'Villa Primavesi', was designed by Josef Hoffmann in 1913–15; the architect of No. 21, the 'Villa Schopp' (1901–02), was Friedrich Ohmann. Alban Berg lived at nearby Trauttmansdorfgasse 27, now the home of the *Alban-Berg-Gesellschaft*, where his rooms on the ground floor may be visited.

Further S is the **Hietzinger Cemetery**, with the graves of *Franz Grillparzer* (1791–1882) and *Kathi Fröhlich*; the dancer *Fanny Elssler* (1810–84); *Gustav Klimt* (1862–1918; group 5, number 194/5); *Otto Wagner* (1841–1918; group 13, number 131), the elaborate canopied tomb designed by himself, but an early work; Chancellor *Engelbert Dollfuss* (1892–1934); *Kolo Moser* (1868–1918; group 16, number 14); F.M. *Franz Conrad von Hötzendorf* (1852–1925), chief-of-staff of the Imperial Staff in 1906–11 and 1912–17; *Katharina Schratt* (1853–1940; see above); *Alban Berg* (1885–1935; group 49, number 24), with a plain wooden cross; and *J.-B. Cléry* (1759–1809), last valet-de-chambre to Louis XVI in the Temple prison, Paris, who later served Mme Royal in exile in Vienna.

A short distance to the W is the *ORF-Zentrum* on Küniglberg, the home of Austrian Television, a complex of buildings by Roland Rainer (1970).—For the area W and SW of this, see Rte 26C.

The **Museum of Technology** (*Technisches Museum für Industrie und Gewerbe*), Mariahilfer Strasse 212, is a few minutes' walk NW from the Schönbrunn Underground Station. Inaugurated in 1918, its main entrance is on its S façade, while adjacent to the W is an exterior display of railway locomotives. It must be admitted that several of the collections, while containing objects of great interest, deserve a more modern form of display, which will no doubt be provided eventually. Meanwhile, you can see numerous sections devoted to the history of industrial development in Austria, and to the contributions of Austrian engineers, and inventors. Among many other objects here are the Typewriter of *Peter Mitterhofer* (1864); the petrol engine of *Siegfried Marcus* (1887), and automobile of 1888; the low-pressure turbine of *Viktor Kaplan* (1919); the screw propellor of *Josef Ressel* (1827); and the rack-and-pinion or mountain railway of *Carl von Ghega*.

Among the collections are those concerned with mining, and salt-mining; the production of Bohemian glass; early agricultural implements and machinery (including a Scythe smithy of 1758), and milk production; the timber trade, and woodworkers' tools, from the circular-saw of 1816 to the bent-wood furniture of *Michael Thonet* (1796–1871); blast-furnaces; models of drilling-rigs; hydraulic steam-presses (by John Haswell; 1862); silver-plating techniques; the manufacture of cutlery; machines for minting, and printing; water-wheels; electric motors, etc. Among automobiles is a Lohner-Porsche of 1900; among the trains, an Ajax locomotive (by Jones, Turner, and Evans) of 1841; and numerous train models.

FIRST FLOOR. Sections are concerned with the chemical industry (also displaying a pharmacy of 1720); weights and measures; clocks (including an astronomical clock of 1555); stone and building technology; machines for spinning; weaving; photo-printing; paper-making; etc.

SECOND FLOOR. Musical instruments, including the *old* organ from the Burgkapelle played on by Bruckner, and automata; the technology of bridge-building; a section devoted to data-processing, including a Baroque writing-machine by Friedrich von Knaus of 1760; models of flying machines; and lastly, a **Postal Museum**, also containing stage coaches, etc.

M.   North-East Vienna and the Prater

This sub-route may be conveniently divided into three sections: the **Augarten**; the **Donaupark**; and the **Prater**. The first is approached by crossing the Danube Canal by the *Schwedenbrücke* (see Rte 25B), following the old Taborstrasse N. This shortly passes (right) the *Kirche der Barmherzigen Brüder* (of the Brothers of Charity; 1622–52), whose monastery and hospital were founded in 1614; both have been repeatedly rebuilt, and the church contains paintings by Daniel Gran, among other Baroque artists.

The street is one of the main thoroughfares of the district of *Leopoldstadt*, formerly (since 1622) the Jewish quarter of Vienna (although the original ghetto was closed down in 1670), in which, in 1938, it was estimated that there were c 180,000 Austrian Jews. It next passes (left) the *Karmeliterkirche* (1623; restored after 1683), since 1783 known as that of *St. Joseph*.—At Karmelitergasse 9 is a *Circus and Clown Museum*, and a district museum.—A short distance beyond, to the left, is the *Pfarrkirche St. Leopold* (1722–24; by Anton Ospel), on the site of an earlier church.—Fritz Kreisler (1875–1962), the violinist, was born at Grosse Schiffgasse 21, several streets to the W.

Slightly further N is the Obere Augartenstrasse, in which No. 40 is the restored *Grassalovics palace*, by Isidore Canavale, housing the offices of the *Vienna Tourist Board*. To its NE extends the *Park* laid out in 1650, re-designed in 1712 by Jean Trehet, and in 1775 opened to the public, on the bridle-paths of which Stendhal galloped in 1809, when with the French army of occupation. In dependencies of the early 18C *Augarten palace* is the famous **Vienna Porcelain Manufactory**, originally established in 1718 by Claudius du Paquier (died 1751), a Dutchman, but nationalised in 1744. He was assisted by an artist-artisan or two, enticed from Meissen. It was administered from 1784–1805 by C. Sögel von Sorgenthal, and from 1805–27 by Matthias Niedermayer, but the factory was forced to close between 1864–1922 due to competition from Bohemia. The flower-painters Joseph Nigg (1782–1863) and Franz Xaver Petter (1791–1866) taught at the art school attached to the establishment.

Another building has been the home since 1948 of the Vienna Boys' Choir; see p 268.—At Scherzergasse 1A, off the E side of the park, is a museum devoted to the sculptor Gustinus Ambrosi (1893–1975).

The U1 Underground from *Karlsplatz* or *Stephansplatz* (direction Zentrum Kagran) crosses the Danube Canal and Danube, the Kaisermühlen stop being that for the **Vienna International Centre**, to the N of the Wagramer Strasse, otherwise known as *VIC*, or *UNO-City*. Construction of the centre began in 1973 to the design of Johann Staber; it was inaugurated in 1979 to accommodate several international organisations previously dispersed throughout the capital.

Among them are the *International Atomic Energy Agency* (IAEA), the *UN Industrial Development Organisation*, the *Narcotics Control Board*, etc. The centre has extra-territorial status. It also contains an *International Congress Center*. Guided tours are provided through the complex, the main features of which are four Y-shaped towers (120, 100, 80, and 60m in height, respectively) with concave façades, having—the brochures claim—24,000 windows, hopefully aiding perceptive vision.

Adjacent is the recently inaugurated **Austria Center** a triangular complex of conference halls on three main levels and providing 6500 square metres of exhibition space.

Close by is the *Donauturm*, a tower 252m high, with a restaurant and viewing terrace; beyond is a park, and some distance further NW, an *Islamic Centre*, its *Mosque* (1975–79) with a 20m-diameter dome, and 32m-high minaret.

The old or *Alte* arm of the **Danube**, which flowed to the E, has been converted into a lake, while the *Neue Donau* channel has been cut parallel to the older course, excavated in 1870–75 as part of the 'Regulation of the Danube' after a series of destructive inundations. The river previously meandered through an area of low wooded islands in its bed, further SE forming the district known as the *Lobau*.

Just S of the Reichsbrücke, on the W bank of the river, is the landing-stage of the Danube ferries, or *Donau-Dampfschiffahrts-Gesellschaft*; see p 99.

It succeeded a company founded in 1829 on a privilege granted to John Andrews and Joseph Pickard, two Englishmen who were the first to build a steamboat on the river, with an engine by James Watt.

The **PRATER**, lying between the Danube Canal and the river itself, is conveniently approached by the above-mentioned Underground, making your exit at the Praterstern stop, there turning SE towards the Hauptallee. The Praterstern can also be reached on foot from the Schwedenbrücke via the Praterstrasse, at No. 54 in which Johann Strauss the Younger composed his 'Blue Danube' waltz in 1867, and now a museum. The PLATZ is dominated by a *Column* erected in 1886 to commemorate the victory of Wilhelm von Tegetthoff (1827–71) over the Italian fleet at the Battle of Lissa in 1866; cf. the Army Museum.

The Prater had its origins in an Imperial game preserve, which was opened to the public in 1766, and although this wooded area later became the preserve of less desirable denizens, it was long the favourite promenade of the populace, whether pedestrian or in their fiacres, while more fashionable society remained in their liveried carriages. Known as the Praterfahrt, it was the Viennese equivalent to the Bois de Boulogne at Paris, but now has as little to commend it.

Restaurants, beer-halls, and amusement arcades flourished, and the area developed into a general fairground. Here was held the Universal Exhibition of 1873, and here in 1896–97 the **Riesenrad**, or *Giant Ferris Wheel*, 54m in diameter, designed by an English engineer named Hitchins, was erected by the firm of Walter Basset. Restored after war damage, it figured in the film 'The Third Man' (1949), in which Orson Welles played the part of 'Harry Lime'. Adjacent is the *Planetarium* of 1964, also housing the *Prater Museum*, with mementoes of the 'Würstelprater' in its heyday (there were no less than 54 taverns and restaurants there in 1846).

To the N of the 5km-long chestnut-lined HAUPTALLEE are exhibition-grounds, a hippodrome, and stadium, etc. At its far end, beyond the Gürtelautobahn which spans the park, is the so-called *Lusthaus*, an octagonal Pleasure Pavilion, formerly a hunting-lodge, remodelled in 1782 by Isidore Canavale, and now a café-restaurant.

N. South-East Vienna

From the SCHWARZENBERGPLATZ (see Rte 25J) the Rennweg, leading SE, is followed by the 71 tram, passing (left; No. 91) the
Waisenhauskirche or *Orphanage Church*, by Thaddäus Karner. In
December 1768, Mozart, aged twelve, conducted his first mass here,
in the presence of Maria Theresia, on the occasion of its consecration.

Prior to passing below the Gürtelautobahn, turn right under a
railway-bridge and then left along the Leberstrasse, to reach the *St.
Marxer Friedhof, the deconsecrated cemetery in which *Mozart*
received a third-class funeral, attended by his friend *Johann Georg
Albrechtsberger* (also buried there, in 1809). Mozart was buried in an
unmarked grave on 6 December 1791, aged 35. The very approximate site of his interment, with a pathetic *monument*, is to the left of
the shady main walk, at some distance from the entrance, surrounded by lilac-bushes. *Diabelli* was buried here in 1858. Among
others were the sculptor *Georg Raphael Donner*, and the artists
Daffinger and *Fendi*, and *Josef Kornhäusel*, the architect, before
their graves were transferred to the Central Cemetery.

The Rennweg is continued by the Simmeringer Hauptstrasse, with a
view (left) of the four prominent brick *Simmering Gasometers* (1899;
recently restored) each almost 38m high and 65m in diameter.

At some distance after passing below a railway bridge, is the main
entrance to the **ZENTRALFRIEDHOF**, or *Central Cemetery of
Vienna*, inaugurated in 1874, and several times enlarged since. A

GRÄBERGRUPPE 32A

1 Beethoven

2 Brahms

3 Gluck

4 Lanner

5 Mozart (monument only)

6 Schubert

7 Johann Strauss the Elder

8 Johann Strauss the Younger

9 Suppé

10 Hugo Wolf

11 Schoenberg

from Entrance

general plan (by Freytag & Berndt) of its ramifications should be available at the main gate.

The main walk leads towards the domed *Dr Karl Lueger Memorial Church*, by Max Hegele, commemorating the influential mayor of Vienna from 1897–1910, who is buried there. On approaching this, you reach (left) *•Section* or **Gräbergruppe 32A**, with the graves of many famous men transferred from other cemeteries in the capital.

Prominent is a *monument to Mozart* (see above), adjacent to which lie *Schubert* and *Beethoven*; and behind the latter, *Hugo Wolf*; a few paces beyond is *Gluck*. In the segment to the left of Beethoven lie *Suppé*, and *Johann Nestroy*, the actor and playwright, together with *Eduard von Bauernfeld*, the playwright. To the right of Schubert lie *Brahms*, and *Johann Strauss the Younger*; and beyond the former, *Lanner*, and *Johann Strauss the Elder*.

The section on the far side of the main walk (14) contains the graves of *Peter Fendi*, *Hans Makart*, *Friedrich von Amerling*, and *Rudolph von Alt*, among artists; *Josef Hoffmann*, the architect and designer; and *Theodor Billroth*, the surgeon.

Adjoining Section 32A, but nearer the church, is a triangular area (Section 32C) in which lie *Arnold Schönberg* (who died in Los Angeles); *Egon Wellesz*; *Fritz Wotruba*, the sculptor; *Franz Schmidt*, the composer; *G.W. Pabst*, the film director; *Julius Wagner-Jauregg*, the psychiatrist; and *Lotte Lehmann*, the singer.—In Section 14C, opposite, lie the composer *Hans Pfitzner*; the politicians *Ignaz Seipel*, *Julius Raab*, and *Leopold Figl*; and *Anton Wildgans*, the poet.

In a sunken circle facing the church lie *Karl Renner*, and other presidents of the Second Republic.

Among many other famous men buried here are *Arthur Schnitzler*, playwright; *Adolf Loos*, architect; *Ludwig Bösenforfer*, the piano manufacturer; *Karl Goldmark*, and *Antonio Salieri*, composers; *Peter Altenberg*, the poet; *Viktor Adler* the politician; and *Eduard Hanslick*, the music-critic.

Opposite the main entrance is the *Crematorium* (1922; by Clemens Holzmeister), enclosed in the walls of the long-abandoned Renaissance palace of *Neugebäude*, of 1569–76, further N, long used as a powder-magazine. There is a project to restore the building.

O.   South-West Vienna

This area is best covered in two parts. The S section can be approached from the SW corner of the *Kunsthistorisches Museum* (see Rte 25E), by following and ascending MARIAHILFER STRASSE, a long commercial and shopping street of slight interest in itself, passing (right at No. 2) a *Museum* devoted to *Tobacco*, and smoking.—At No. 1B Emilie Flöge and her sister established in 1904 a 'fashion salon' on the premises of the 'casa Piccola café', its interior designed by Kolo Moser and Josef Hoffmann, but which is no longer in existence.—At No. 24 (right) is the **Stiftskirche** or *Garnisonskirche*, of 1739, possibly designed by J.E. Fischer von Erlach, but later modified.—On the far side of the street, No. 45 was the birthplace of the playwright Ferdinand Raimund (1790–1836).

The Stiftgasse (right, skirting the church) leads shortly to the Siebensterngasse, on the far side of which, to the right, is the **Spittelberg** or Old Hospital Hill, once with an equivocal reputation, which has recently been tastefully restored and is now a pedestrian precinct. Mozart is said to have come here to play skittles.

Continuing along Mariahilfer Strasse, you reach (left, at No. 55) the **Mariahilf Kirche** (1686–89; probably by Sebastiano Carlone), replacing an earlier church destroyed in 1683. A *Statue of Haydn* stands before it; see below.

The next street to the left leads down to a huge and practically indestructible *flak tower*, one of several remaining in Vienna, its platform once the emplacement of German anti-aircraft guns, and the tower itself now accommodating the *Haus des Meeres*, an *Aquarium*.—At neighbouring Gumpendorfer Strasse 54 lived Viktor Adler (1852–1918), the politician, from 1905 until his death.

At Mariahilfer Strasse 70 is a bank, the entrance and main hall of which was designed by Adolf Loos. No. 88 (right) is the entrance to the **Bundessammlung alter Stilmöbel**, the former *Court Furniture Repository*, which still provides appropriate period furniture (whether Biedermeier or Jugendstil) when required by the Federal Government. The warehouse contains several pieces of interest, and may be visited by joining a guided group (Tuesday–Friday 9.00–16.00, Saturday 9.00–12.00).

At some distance further W, the Webgasse turns left, off which, by bearing right, and then left, you reach, at 19 Haydngasse, **Joseph Haydn's House**, acquired with the profits of his visits to London, and in which he lived from 1797 until his death on 31 May 1809, and composed 'The Creation', and 'The Seasons', among other works. It now houses a small museum devoted to the composer, and also, on the second floor, a *Memorial room to Brahms*, with his Portrait by Carl Jagemann (1860), and writing-desk, and paintings of his apartment by Wilhelm Nowak.

On returning uphill to the Mariahilfer Strasse and turning left, the GÜRTEL is reached. This ring road was laid out after 1890 when the early 18C outer fortifications of Vienna, known as the Linienwall, were demolished. Alfred Adler (1870–1937, Aberdeen), the psychologist, was born at No. 208 Mariahilfer Strasse.—To the NW is the *West-Bahnhof*, one of the main railway termini, replacing an earlier station damaged during the Second World War.

Four streets further N, and to the W, is the *Stadthalle*, a Civic Centre (completed 1974), a complex of several large halls, sports arenas, and pools, etc., designed by Roland Rainer.—To the E of this point, in the Kaiserstrasse, is the *Erika-Kino*, one of the earliest cinemas.—Gustav Klimt died at neighbouring Westbahnstrasse 36.

A short distance SW of the railway station is the conspicuous dome of *Maria vom Siege* (1868–75), also known as the *Fünfhauser Kirche*, by Friedrich von Schmidt, a concentric red-brick building with two spires, built to the specifications of Josef Rauscher, the reactionary Card.-Archbishop.

To cover the N half of this route, follow the Josefstadt Strasse W from just SW of the *Rathaus* (see Rte 25F), shortly passing (left) Lange Gasse, No. 34 in which, the *Haus 'Zur heiligen Dreifaltigkeit'* is a Baroque building of 1697 preserving an old *Bakery*, and *Baking museum*.—The home of Vienna's *English Theatre*, established in 1963, is at Josefsgasse 12, to the S, off Lange Gasse.

No. 21 Josefstädter Strasse was once Gustav Klimt's studio.

No. 26 is the **Theater 'In der Josefstädt'**, with a long tradition—since 1788. In 1822 Beethoven composed his overture 'The Consecration of the House' for the opening of the new theatre, designed by

Josef Kornhäusel. From 1924 until 1935 it was directed by Max Reinhardt.

At Piaristengasse 28, to the S, lived the film director Fritz Lang (1890–1976) during the decade 1909–19.—At Döblergasse 4 (a turning off the Lerchenfelder Strasse) was Otto Wagner's last home (1912), recently opened to the public, and containing an information centre concerned with his work.

No. 39 Josefstädter Strasse was the former *Strozzi palace*, in part of which lived the artist Friedrich von Amerling during the years 1828–41.—On the site of Strozzigasse 22 was born the artist Ferdinand Georg Waldmüller (1793–1865).

Turning right at the Theater 'In der Josefstädt', you soon come to a small square flanked (left) by the **Piaristenkirche**, in front of which stands a *Plague-column* of 1713. Its façade received its present form in 1860, but the church, also known as *Maria Treu*, was commenced in 1716, and is said to follow an earlier plan of J. Lukas von Hildebrandt, but it was not completed until 1753. The *Interior* contains some remarkable frescoes by Maulbertsch. Bruckner passed his final exams on its organ, in 1861.

To the W, at Hamerlingplatz 3, is the shop of the *Kartographisches Institut*, where a variety of maps and plans of Austria may be bought.

A few minutes' walk S, at the junction of the Albertgasse and Lerchenfelder Strasse, stands the *Altlerchenfelder Pfarrkirche* (1848–61; completed by Van der Nüll), with frescoes by Joseph von Führich, completed by L. Kupelwieser and E. von Engerth.

Continuing N from the Piaristenkirche, you reach the Laudongasse, in which (right) at Nos 15–19, is the *Museum of Austrian Folklore* (*Österreichisches Museum für Volkskunde*), since 1917 housed in the former *Schönborn Palace* (1706–11), designed by J. Lukas von Hildebrandt on the site of an older building.

Unfortunately the display is somewhat cramped, and only a small proportion of the extensive collection is on view. This includes models of farms, agricultural implements, including yokes, scythes and scythe-shields, from S Tyrol; reconstructed panelled and beamed rooms; furniture—some painted—from several provinces; ovens and stoves (including one with circular green tiles, and another in the form of a peasant woman); ceramics; metalware; wood-carvings; costumes; textiles; copper and ceramic moulds; wedding-crowns; hair-work; painted glass; lamps; spits; hand-mills; salt-miners' bottles; clocks; spoon-holders; sledges; and what not.

On the SECOND FLOOR the display continues with Bavarian costumes; head-dresses from the Danube valley, with silver and gold thread; tradesmen's signs; moulds for gingerbread, and ex-votos; ex-votos of iron, wood, painted, and of wax; also a wax-taper house of 1789 from Graz; musical instruments; masks and masquerades; Christmas cribs; religious folk-art; sculptures, including a triple-faced Trinity, and a 'Palmesel' or figure of Christ on ass-back, used on Palm Sunday processions; and more furniture.

At Skodagasse 11, a short distance W, lived the artist Rudolf von Alt (1812–1905) from 1841 until his death, as well as his father, Jakob (1789–1872).

By turning E, and then left, you reach the Alser Strasse, with (No. 17; right) the *Dreifaltigkeitskirche*, or *Trinity Church*, a building of the Franciscan order of 1685–1727, by an unknown architect, in which the funeral service for Beethoven was held (29 March 1827; see p 294.

Opposite are the extensive dependencies of the **Allgemeines Krankenhaus** or **General Hospital** (1783–84), a project initiated by Joseph II, and in the late 19C closely connected with the famous Vienna School of Medicine.

Among those who worked there was Theodor Billroth (1829–94), the surgeon, and a friend of Brahms (and dedicatee of the Opus 51 String Quartets), who often met at his home at No. 20 in the street. Other names of influential specialists associated with the hospital are Karl Rokitansky (1804–78), Ferdinand Hebra (1816–80), the dermatologist; Ignaz Semmelweis (1818–65), the gynaecologist; Ernst Ritter von Brücke (1819–92), the physiologist; Joseph Skoda (1805–81), the diagnostician; Richard Freiherr von Krafft-Ebing (1840–1902), author of 'Psychopathia sexualis'; Theodor Meynert (1833–78); and many more.

For the *Museum of Pathological Anatomy* in the '*Narrenturm*', and other medical museums, see the *Josephinum*, a short walk to the NE.

Gustav Mahler (1860–1911) died at Mariannengasse 20, to the N of and parallel to the Alser Strasse; while further N, at Lazarettgasse 14, was the site of the asylum in which Hugo Wolf spent the last four years and four months of his life and died, on 22 February 1903.

Turning E along the Alser Strasse, and shortly following the Universitätstrasse (in which No. 12 is an early building by Otto Wagner: note cornice), with the *Votivkirche* on your left and the *University building* to your right, you reach the Ringstrasse at the *Schottentor*; see Rtes 25F and G.

26 Short Excursions from Vienna

The NW, W, and SW suburbs are more conveniently visited by car, preferably accompanied by a good map-reader, and are described in three sections.

A. The 19th District of Döbling, including Grinzing, Heiligenstadt, and Nussdorf

A separate excursion can be made by those interested in clocks to the **Geymüller-Schlossl** (Pötzleinsdorfer Strasse 102, a continuation of Währinger Strasse—see Rte 25G—but normally closed in winter). The Währinger Strasse is continued by the Gersthofer Strasse, in which, at No. 55, Béla Bartók resided in 1905–06. The mansion, situated on the edge of the Vienna Woods, was erected in 1808 for the banker, Geymüller, who also had a town house in Wallnerstrasse. It was restored after 1947 by Dr Franz Sobek (died 1976; former director of the National Printing Works), and left with its contents to the state in 1965. These include a collection of 170 clocks. It is therefore complementary to the *Uhrenmuseum* (see p 254), although a dependency of the Museum of Applied Arts.

Driving N along Nussdorfer Strasse (see Rte 25G), the GÜRTEL is crossed to follow the Billrothstrasse to the NW, in which, at No. 68, Hugo Wolf lived intermittently in the house of the Köchert family during the years 1885–94. This leads towards the former village of

Grinzing, with its much rebuilt late Gothic *Parish-church* surmounted by a Baroque helm.

The whole area, surrounded by vineyards on the lower slopes and ridges of the *Kahlenberg* (484m, and rising further W to the *Hermannskogel*; 542m) has for some decades been almost entirely devoted to the exploitation of the folklore of the *Heurigen* (see p 105), accompanied by 'Schrammel Musik'. This music, named after its creators, Johann and Joseph Schrammel (1850–93, and 1852–95, respectively), has since c 1878 been produced by a quartet of instruments, usually two violins, an accordion—previously a clarinet—and a guitar. It is better to avoid the place in the evenings when it becomes very crowded, although certain comparatively secluded spots may still be discovered away from the centre.

From the church, the Mannagettagasse leads to the entrance of the **Grinzing Cemetery**, in which lie *Gustav Mahler* (1860–1911; group 7, row 2; tombstone designed by Josef Hoffmann), and *Alma Mahler-Werfel* (1879–1964; group 6, row 6); *Heimito von Doderer* (1896–1966), the author; the architects *Heinrich von Ferstel* (1828–83), and *August von Siccardsburg* (1813–68); the artist *Leopold Kupelwieser* (1796–1862); *Arnold Rosé* (1863–1946), of the Rosé Quartet and Mahler's brother-in-law; and *Paul Wittgenstein* (1887–1961), the one-armed pianist brother of Ludwig, the philosopher.

At Cobenzlgasse 30, in the village centre, is the *Trummelhof*, a Baroque mansion standing on a Roman site; while in Grinzinger Strasse 64, further E, both Beethoven (in 1808) and Grillparzer lodged, the former objecting to the poet's mother listening to him playing the piano.—Albert Einstein lived at No. 70 in 1927–31.—Alma Mahler (see above) resided at Steinfeldgasse 2 (now an embassy), a short distance to the S. During her widowhood she was the mistress of Kokoschka. She then married Walter Gropius, the architect, in 1915, and then in 1929, Franz Werfel, the author.

At Probusgasse 6, parallel to and N of Grinzinger Strasse, in the suburb of **Heiligenstadt**, Beethoven wrote in 1802 his pathetic 'Heiligenstadt Testament', when despairing of his increasing deafness. He also stayed briefly at adjacent Pfarrplatz 2, in 1817. *St. Jakobskirche*, originally 10C, stands on a Roman site. In 1817, and again in 1824, Beethoven lived at Kahlenberger Strasse 26, a short distance NE, in *Nussdorf*.

Further NE in Hackhofergasse, No. 17 is the *Zwettl Hof*, built by Josef Munggenast in 1730–31; the chapel contains a painting by Altomonte. No. 18 in the same street was a residence of Emanuel Schikaneder (cf.), and later, of Franz Lehar.

For an extension of this route, and for Josefsdorf and Leopoldsberg, on the Kahlenberg, see Rte 26B below.

The return towards the centre may be made along the Heiligenstädter Strasse, flanked to the E by the **Karl-Marx-Hof**, an extensive housing project designed by Karl Ehn and built in 1927–34, providing 1600 apartments. It was a centre of resistance to the authoritarian regime of the diminutive Dollfuss (assassinated 25 July 1934 in a Nazi *putsch*), during whose absence from Vienna his assistant, Emil Fey, chose to shell this tenement fortress (12 February 1934), and the Social Democrats were obliged to surrender to reactionary forces.

At 92 Döblinger Hauptstrasse, to the W (approached by turning right along Barawitzkagasse just before the railway bridge, and then turning left) is the so-called 'Eroica-Haus', in which Beethoven lived in 1803–04 when composing his Third Symphony, Opus 55.

No. 96 in this street is the **Villa Wertheimstein**, built for Rudolf von
Arthaber in 1834–35 by Ludwig Pichl, with frescoes by Moritz von
Schwind. The villa also contains a memorial-room to Eduard von
Bauernfeld, the playwright, who died in 1890 in a cottage in the park.
Here also is a small viticultural museum.

It was long the home of Josephine von Wertheimstein (died 1894) and her
daughter 'Franzi' (died 1907), who here presided over their literary salon, at
which Ferdinand von Saar (1833–1906), the author, and the young Hugo von
Hofmannsthal, were often present. Anton Rubinstein gave recitals here.
  At No. 22 Nusswaldgasse, leading W from the N end of the Döblinger
Haupstrasse, is the house built in 1925 by Josef Hoffmann for Sonia Knips.

The GÜRTEL is regained a short distance to the S.

B. Kahlenberg

The thickly wooded hills to the N of Vienna may be approached with
ease from *Grinzing* (see Rte 26A), by continuing NW along the
COBENZLGASSE, which winds through the beech-woods to a T-junction, at which turn right along the HÖHENSTRASSE to **Kahlenberg**
(484m; views), with the small *Josefskirche*, rebuilt after 1683. Here
mass was celebrated by the allied commanders at dawn on the 12
September of that year before leading their forces down towards the
Turkish hordes encamped around the capital; see p 232; 234. The
cemetery contains the tomb of the Prince de Ligne (1735–1814). The
cells of the monastery here had been turned into a fashionable hotel
in the late 18C, in which Mme Vigée-Lebrun, the portraitist, was a
resident in 1795.
  Continuing along the road, which later descends towards *Klosterneuburg* (see Rte 30), you soon reach a right-hand turning to
approach the **Leopoldsberg** (425m). This, the NE spur of the *Wienerwald*, which here rises abruptly over the Danube, provides extensive
views over the city, and to the E, over the *Marchfeld*, and the
battlefields of Aspern and Wagram. In the distance are the *Little
Carpathians*, beyond the Czechoslovak border. A Babenberg fortress
built c 1100 by Leopold III (see Klosterneuburg) once stood here; it
was destroyed by the Turks in 1529. The *Church*, with its two towers,
painted by Rudolf von Alt in 1833, when it looked almost derelict, has
been restored several times (after 1683, and 1945). A narrow lane
descends steeply to meet the main road at *Kahlenbergerdorf*, a short
distance N of *Nussdorf*; see Rte 26A.
  Alternatively, you can return to the above-mentioned T-junction,
and by continuing ahead through the woods, past several roads
leading back into the city, you eventually descend to meet the main
road from the W (A1) at *Hütteldorf*; see Rte 26C.

C.   Western Suburbs

Several monuments may be visited to the W of the city, and a tour of these is outlined below. The No. 48A bus also follows the same route to the *Am Steinhof church*, but its interior may only be visited in a group, and enquiry should be made in advance as to times of admission (normally Saturday at 15.00).

From just N of the *Volkstheater* (Rte 25F) you follow the Neustiftgasse W, after crossing the GÜRTEL continuing W along the Koppstrasse for some distance before forking left to join the Flötzersteig, and then right along the Spiegelgrundstrasse to the main entrance in the Baumgartner Höhe of the *Psychiatrisches Krankenhaus der Stadt Wien*. Hidden some distance behind the main buildings of the asylum, on the Gallitzinberg, stands the *Kirche am Steinhof, with its conspicuous copper dome, built in 1904–07 by Otto Wagner, with glass windows designed by Kolo Moser and mosaic work by Remigius Geyling.

Devotees of Otto Wagner's architecture may wish to visit the two villas he built in Hüttelbergstrasse in 1885–86 and 1912–13 (Nos 26 and 28, respectively). These are approached by continuing W from the Flötzersteig, briefly following the Linzer Strasse, and then turning right up the Hüttelbergstrasse; see also last paragraph of Rte 26B.

The Linzer Strasse continues W, off which the Mauerbachstrasse forks right through *Hadersdorf*, just beyond which (left) is the late 17C *Schloss Hadersdorf*, now a hotel, built for General Gideon Laudon, containing frescoes by Johann Bergl.

From the Hüttelbergstrasse turning you can cross to the S bank of the river Wien, following it to the E as far as the *Kennedy Brücke*, prior to reaching *Schönbrunn*.

It was at Hadikgasse 72, just to the N, that Richard Wagner lived in 1863–64, while composing 'The Mastersingers', and where on 6 February 1864 he and Brahms first met.

Turn right (S) and then fork right to follow the Lainzer Strasse SW, skirting an area (right) described on p 318–19.

After some distance, the Veitingergasse turns right. To the W, between this street and the Jagdschlossgasse (left; which brings one back to the Lainzer Strasse), is an area known as the **Werkbundsiedlung**, a modest collection of villas and terrace houses designed in 1930–31 by Viennese and guest architects (including *André Lurçat*, at Veitingergasse 87, 89, 91, and 93). Their aim was to produce a model suburban estate. *Josef Hoffmann* was responsible for 79, 81, 83, and 85 in Veitingergasse; *Adolf Loos* for Woinovichgasse 13, 15, 17, and 19, and *Richard Neutra* for No. 9 in the same street; and *Clemens Holzmeister* for Jagicgasse 8 and 10. The houses on the estate have been restored.

Further W is the hillside **Ober-St. Veiter Friedhof**, where Egon Schiele (1890–1918) is buried (group B, row 10, 15/6), with a tombstone of Benjamin Ferenczy.

Continuing S on the Lainzer Strasse, you reach a T-junction at Feldkellergasse, there turning right and shortly bearing right, to follow the Hermesstrasse to the entrance of the **Lainzer Tiergarten** (parking). It may also be reached by a No. 62 bus from the Opernring, later changing to 60B.

The entire park is open to the public from the Sunday before Easter to the beginning of November; the area around the *Hermesvilla* is open all year round.

This part of the Vienna woods, or *Wienerwald*, was acquired as an Imperial game-preserve in 1557, and from 1782 work commenced with the erection of an encircling wall, 24km long. The park was opened to the public in 1919, and in 1941 became a protected reserve, some species being kept in enclosures, while since 1981 the villa's stables have provided summer quarters for the Lippizaner stallions of the Spanish Riding School. The *Kaltbründlberg* (508m), its highest point (almost due W of the Hermesvilla), commands a panoramic view.

The **Hermesvilla** itself was built in 1882–86 by Hasenauer as a retreat for the Empress Elisabeth. Restored in the 1970s after suffering dilapidation, it is now used for occasional exhibitions, although some 20 rooms, retaining their fin-de-siècle decoration, furniture and works of art, may also be visited.

From here, return to the main road at the E end of the Hermesstrasse.

An extension to the route—only recommended to those specifically interested in contemporary architecture—is that to the so-called **Wotruba Church** (or *Zur Heiligsten Dreifaltigkeit*), built on the St. Georgen-Berg in 1974–76 to the design of the sculptor Fritz Wotruba (1907–75), consisting of some 152 irregularly placed modular cubes. Many will be disappointed with the resulting concretion, although the view from it is good. It may be approached by driving SW along the Speisinger Strasse and turning W on reaching the Maurer Lange Gasse, which it overlooks from the S.

From the Hermesstrasse crossroads turn NE and follow the Hetzendorfer Strasse to the E to reach at No. 79 (right) the **Schloss Hetzendorf**. Originally a hunting-lodge built by Sigismund Graf Thun in 1694, it was remodelled in 1712 by J. Lukas von Hildebrandt and further altered in 1743 by Nikolaus Pacassi. The palace, which now accommodates the *Vienna Fashion School*, contains good stucco-work, a notable 'Japanese Salon', some frescoes by Daniel Gran, and Gustav Klimt's smock.

By turning NW down the Schönbrunner Allee, directly opposite its entrance, the S bank of the Wien is regained, just before which turn right towards the centre, following the road to the Karlsplatz.

27 Perchtoldsdorf; Heiligenkreuz; Mayerling; Baden; Mödling

A pleasant excursion may be made by following the route described, starting from the MATZLEINSDORFER PLATZ (at the S end of the Wiedner Hauptstrasse; see p 299), from where the Triester Strasse ascends SW to (right) the Gothic monument known as the **Spinnerin am Kreuz**. This was erected in 1452, replacing an older column which indicated the S limit of the city's jurisdiction. Just beyond it stood the scaffold—it was the equivalent to London's Tyburn—in use from 1311–1747, and again from 1805 until the last public execution in 1868.—In the neighbouring Windtenstrasse is the 67m high red brick *Favoriten Water Tower* (1899, but redundant by 1910), recently restored, an interesting example of industrial archaeology, which can be visited on prior application. The road descends gently to join the autobahn A21, which shortly bears W.

Taking the second exit, turn right towards the centre of the suburban village of **Perchtoldsdorf** (or *Petersdorf*; 13,450 inhab.) in which the most prominent landmarks are the steep-roofed and turreted keep of 1465 and the adjacent *Church* of 1340. In 1683 the Turks massacred the people as they left the church, even though a ransom had already been paid. Close to the late 15C *Rathaus* is a *Plague-column* of 1713 designed by J.B. Fischer von Erlach.

The village has associations with Gluck, who spent some summers towards the end of his life at Weinergasse 22, and with Hugo Wolf, who stayed on several occasions at the villa of the Werner family (at Brunnergasse 24), where he composed some 115 songs. Franz Schmidt also stayed here and died, in 1939, at Lohnsteinstrasse 4. The artist Ferdinand Georg Waldmüller (1793–1865) was born here.—For *Mödling*, 5km S, see below.

Turning N for just over 1km, and then left along the Kaltenleutgebner Strasse, which follows the narrow valley (unfortunately in danger of further disfigurement owing to the uncontrolled exploitation of its limestone quarries and cement-works, etc.) you cross the straggling village of *Kaltenleutgeben*, to approach, 10km beyond, a road junction. Turning left through *Gruberau* and down another valley, and later crossing below the A21 motorway, at 8km **Heiligenkreuz** is reached.

The *Monastery* was founded in 1133 by Leopold III. In the main arcaded courtyard is a *Pestsäule* of 1737 and a *fountain* of 1739, both by Giovanni Giuliani (1663–1744), who died and was buried here. The Romanesque *Church* (12–13C), with an interior of Cistercian severity, has a large early Gothic choir, unfortunately spoilt by neo-Gothic altars of 1885. The stalls were carved by Giuliani; the organ on the N wall dates from 1804. On this organ, in June 1828, Schubert and a friend played the two fugues that Schubert had composed the previous day. Groups are guided round the *cloister*, with its nine-sided *lavatory*; the *chapterhouse*, once the burial-place of the Babenberg family, including the last duke, Friedrich II (died 1246), and with Baroque murals; and the *sacristy*, containing good marquetry.

By driving W, and turning left, you reach (4km) the hamlet of **Mayerling**, which during the night of 29/30 January 1889 was the scene of the sensational suicides of Rudolf, the unstable and dissipated 29-year-old crown prince, and the 17-year-old Baroness Mary Vetsera. Their bodies were discovered together in what was then Rudolf's hunting-lodge. The scandal was played down by Count Taaffe (Franz Josef's chief minister, and of Irish extraction), who with Baron Krauss, the head of Vienna's police, arranged for the girl's body to be spirited away to Heiligenkreuz, held upright in a coach by her two uncles, the Baltazzi brothers, sons of Levantine bankers, and there she is buried. The lodge was later demolished on the instructions of Franz Josef, and a Carmelite nunnery erected on its site.

The excursion may be continued by driving SE through the delightful scenery of the Schwechat valley, here known as the *HELENENTAL, later passing between two hilltop castle ruins—those of Rauhenstein, and Rauheneck, the latter triangular in plan, below which Kornhäusel's *Schloss Weilburg* (1823) once stood.

Passing through an aqueduct, we enter (15km) **Baden** (23,150 inhab.), Roman *Aquae*, its sulphurous waters have long been resorted to.

Although frequented during previous decades, Baden had a new lease of life as a spa in 1813–43, after the ravaging fire of July 1812. Many of the new buildings erected were designed by Josef Kornhäusel. It was patronised by Franz II during this period, and its numerous ochre-coloured façades help to preserve its 'Biedermeier' atmosphere. Constanze Mozart frequently visited the place, and Beethoven spent several summers here. Among the composer's visitors here, were Carl Maria von Weber in 1823, and the English conductor Sir George Smart in 1825. During the 1914–18 war it was the Austrian military HQ, and that of the Russians during the decade of occupation, 1945–55. It was the birthplace of Max Reinhardt (born Goldmann, 1873–1943), the theatrical designer and producer; Wenzel Müller (1767–1835), the composer of Singspiele; and Moritz Gottlieb Saphir (1795–1858), the critic, died here, as did the music critic Eduard Hanslick (1825–1904). Sacher-Masoch describes his six months' submission here to Baroness Fanny Pistor in 'Venus in furs'.

One of Beethoven's lodgings may be visited at Rathausplatz 10, a few paces W of the central *Hauptplatz*, with its *Plague-column* of 1718. Tsar Peter the Great stayed at Frauengasse 8, leading S, in 1698. In 1791 Mozart composed his 'Ave Verum' (K.618) for the late 15C *Stephanskirche*, to the NE, its tower surmounted by an onion-dome. Several notable villas may be seen on the wooded hillside N of the town.—At *Kottingbrunn*, 6km S, beyond the motorway, is a moated Renaissance Schloss.

Bearing NE, at 7km, after skirting *Pfaffstätten*, with the vinous dependencies of the *Lilienfeldhof*, and winding through the vineyards on the E slope of the WIENERWALD, here rising to the *Anninger* (675m), we enter **Gumpoldskirchen**, a village of 3000 inhab., reputed for its wines and Heurigen. Its *Rathaus* dates from 1559, and it preserves an over-restored *Castle* of the Teutonic knights.

At *Guntramsdorf*, 3km E, is a Schloss in the style of J. Lukas von Hildebrandt, in the garden-pavilion of which are charming frescoes of 1720 by Jonas Drentwett.

5km ***Mödling** (19,300 inhab.), an old town retaining some characteristic corners, has a *Rathaus* of 1529 in its central *Schrannenplatz*. Beethoven spent the summers of 1818 and 1819 at Hauptstrasse 79, to the E. To the S is the 15C church of *Hl. Ägyd*. To the W, at a higher level, stands *St. Othmar*, a fortified church of 1454–1523, its interior restored after 1690. Note the 'goat of arms' on its apse. Adjacent is a circular Romanesque *Charnel-house* surmounted by a Baroque dome, and containing 13C frescoes. The knotted columns of its portal are remarkable. A cemetery of the Avars has been excavated in the neighbourhood.

Footpaths ascend NW through the woods from near the church to the over-restored but well-sited *Schloss Liechtenstein*, preserving some medieval walls of the former residence of the minnesinger Ulrich von Liechtenstein (1199–1275).

Mödling was also the home of Arnold Schönberg in 1918–24 (Bernhardgasse 6; the address of the *Internationale Schönberg Gesellschaft*), and of Webern in 1918–32 (Neusiedler Strasse 58); the latter lived from 1932 until shortly before his death in 1945 (cf. Mittersill) at *Maria Enzersdorf*, 2km N.

Cross this village to regain the motorway at the point you left it.

28 Laxenburg, Eisenstadt, and the Neusiedler See

Total distance, 162km (101 miles). A2 motorway for c 15km—4km
Laxenburg—6km *Münchendorf*—B16. 9km *Ebreichsdorf*—17km.
B59. 4km **Eisenstadt**—B52. 16km **Rust**—6km **Mörbisch**—18km
Donnerskirchen—B304. 21km *Parndorf*—B10. 7km *Bruck an der
Leitha*—27km *Schwechat*—12km **Vienna**.

Maps: F&B 1; BEV 48/16–17.

This excursion may of course be extended by the exploration of the area E of the
Neusiedler See, known as the *Seewinkel*; or by following the road NE from
Parndorf to *Kittsee*, etc.

Follow the road SW from the centre (see Rte 27), and continue S on
the motorway, turn off for the village of *Laxenburg**, with several
18C mansions, the residences of courtiers, among them Kaunitz, and
Countess Wilhelmina Auersperg. The *Church* of 1693–1726 by Matthias Steinl contains a notable pulpit.

The former Imperial country seat consists of a complex of buildings, including the **Neues Schloss**, by Nikolaus Pacassi (c 1752),
birthplace of the crown prince Rudolf in 1858. In 1796 the Archduke
Alexander had been killed here by an exploding firework. Tastefully
restored after its Russian occupation, since 1972 it has been the HQ
of the *International Institute for Applied Systems Analysis* (IIASA).—
To the S is the **Altes Schloss**, of c 1381, rebuilt after 1683 by Ludovico
Burnacini and previously moated. Tastelessly restored, it now contains the *Austrian Film Archives*. It reminded Montesquieu of a
dovecote when he saw it in 1728.

A small fee is charged to enter the shady *Park*, laid out in the
English taste, in which, surrounded by a lake, stands the mock
medieval *Franzenburg* of 1796–1836, built for Franz II. Its restoration
is projected.

The road shortly veers SE to join the B16 just before *Münchendorf*.—
9km *Ebreichsdorf*, with a 13–14C *Schloss*, some 7km SW of which is
Pottendorf, with a notable church of 1716 attributed to J. Lukas von
Hildebrandt, and a 12–18C *Schloss*; 12km SE is the pilgrimage-
church of *Loretto* (1651–59).

You approach a range of low hills, the LEITHAGEBIRGE, with the
Sonnenberg (484m) at its W end, which you circle, passing (right)
Grosshöflein, where an arcaded mansion may be seen (right)
Hauptstrasse 37, to (21km) *Eisenstadt** (10,100 inhab.) the provincial
capital of the Burgenland, and long a favourite seat of the once-
influential Esterházy family. It was the birthplace of the composer
Josef Weigl (1766–1846), but is better known for its associations with
Haydn.

On entering the town from the W the *Kalvarienberg* is passed
(right), a curious ecclesiastical 'folly', built by a Franciscan in 1711.
Adjacent is the **Bergkirche**, in which Joseph Haydn (1732–1809) was
re-interred in 1820. He was originally buried in the Hundsturm
cemetery in Vienna, but later Prince Nikolaus II Esterházy, prompted
by a remark by Adolphus Frederick, Duke of Cambridge, moved his
body here. His *Mausoleum*, built in 1932, lies to the left of the W
entrance to the church, in which is the 'Haydn' organ of 1743.

Before reaching the Schloss, turn left into the Unterbergstrasse,
where you can visit, at No. 6, the *Austrian Jewish Museum* (open mid

Portrait of Haydn by George Dance, 1794

May to late October; at other times by appointment), recently installed in a building of the Ghetto established here in 1671, and which was only suspended in 1938. There are a number of Jewish cemeteries and former synagogues surviving in Burgenland, details of which can be supplied to those interested. The old *Jewish Cemetery* lies some few minutes' walk to the N.

Adjacent to the E is the **Landesmuseum, a notable collection concentrating on the archaeology, ethnography and folk-art of the Burgenland, attractively installed in an imaginatively restored mansion formerly owned by Sandor Wolf. The Celtic artefacts and Roman sarcophagi and mosaics are remarkable.

The ochre façade of **Schloss Esterházy** (previously painted grey and pink), with grotesque masks in the courtyard, stands four-square on the N side of its platz. Its towers were originally surmounted by onion-domes.

The late 17C edifice, designed by Carlo Martino Carlone for Prince Paul Esterházy (1635–1713), with its early 19C modifications, is primarily of interest for its associations with Haydn, who was employed as Kapellmeister by Prince Nikolaus Joseph Esterházy from 1762 to 1790, when the prince died, and when the composer was first invited to London by Johann Peter Salomon, the impresario. Lord Nelson and the Hamiltons, together with Cornelia Knight, the authoress, visited Haydn at Eisenstadt in September 1800, and his D minor Mass was later known as the 'Nelson Mass'. However, Haydn would have spent much of his time at the palace of Esterháza (as it was then known), some 45km SE, in Hungary.

The *Schloss*, which may be visited, contains several rooms of slight interest, among them two halls in which operas and concerts took place (and still do in the season). The building still belongs to the family, who do little to preserve it although it deserves restoration. Canova's seated statue of Leopoldine Esterházy (1805) is notable. Opposite is a range of *Stables*, now partly a restaurant, and with extensive wine cellars.

The composer resided from 1766–78 at Haydngasse 21, a street just E of the Schloss, now a *Haydn Museum*, but also with rooms commemorating Liszt (cf. Raiding) and the dancer Fanny Elssler (a daughter of Haydn's valet-de-chambre and copyist). Haydn's home was severely damaged by ravaging fires in 1768 and 1776, after both being rebuilt at Esterházy's expense. In c 1772 Ignace Joseph Pleyel was his lodger and pupil.—Further down the street is the *Franziskanerkirche* (1386; rebuilt 1629, with a belfry of 1778), containing the Esterházy vault. A new—largely educational—museum has been installed at Haydngasse 1.—There are several houses of interest in the Hauptstrasse, parallel to the S, with the *Rathaus* of 1648 and a *Plague-column* of 1713.—Further S is *St. Martin* (1460), denominated a cathedral in 1960, but of slight interest.

For the road to *Graz*, see Rte 32B.

5km S of the town is the crossroads for *Klingenbach* (8km SE; Customs), the frontier post for **Sopron**, formerly Ödenburg.

Bearing SE 2.5km S of Eisenstadt, at 11km you pass (left) the stone-quarries of *Römersteinbruch* before entering **Rust**, an attractive vinous village of 1700 inhab. plus numerous storks. It retains several 17C houses in its Hauptstrasse, while its RATHAUSPLATZ is dominated by the picturesque *Fischerkirche*, the 12–16C church of local lake fishermen, containing some Romanesque frescoes, and an organ of 1705.

The desolate and reed-encircled **Neusiedler See**, which extends to the E, is a slightly saline lake between 7 and 15km wide, and 36km from N to S, with an area of 320 sq km (124 sq miles). It is nowhere more than 3m deep, and is largely fed by subterranean springs; it has no outflow, and loses most of its water by evaporation. Indeed on some rare occasions (lastly in the 1860s) it has virtually dried up, but normally it is the haunt of wildfowlers, wind-surfers, and other amphibious sportsmen, and of skaters in winter. It is also an important bird sanctuary, with a biological station. From its far bank extends the *puzta*, the Hungarian steppes, while its S shore is Hungarian territory.

6km S of Rust lies the rustic frontier village of **Mörbisch** (2350 inhab.), at right-angles to the main street of which are a number of low whitewashed houses with their maize-festooned galleries. The road stops 1.5km further S, until recently overlooked by the 'Iron Curtain', or 'Eiserner Vorhang'.

Turning N from Rust, circle to the NE through *Donnerskirchen*, with its late 17C fortified church on the S slope of the LEITHAGEBIRGE, on which remains of the Hallstatt period have been found. The road, running some 3–4km N of the lake, passes through several villages, among them *Purbach*, with three town gates, *Breitenbrunn*, with a fortified tower of c 1650, and *Jois*, providing the best view over the Neusiedler See. At 16km crossroads are reached 3km NW of *Neusiedl am See*, with a museum of bygones at Kalvarienbergstrasse 40.

The reed-weaving villages of the fenny SEEWINKEL, between the E bank and the Hungarian frontier, may be explored from here, among them, 13km SE, **Halbturn**, with the former Harrach hunting-lodge or *Schloss*, built by J. Lukas von Hildebrandt in 1710, and recently restored. It contains a fresco by Maulbertsch, and is the site of important temporary exhibitions, largely from the imperial collections.—5km further SW, at **Frauenkirchen**, is a large pilgrimage-church, rebuilt in 1695–1702 by Francesco Martinelli, and containing good plasterwork. There is a Jewish cemetery nearby.—Not far, beyond is the characteristic village of *St. Andrä*.—Most of its meres lie between this village and the Neusiedler See.

At (5km) *Parndorf*, turn left to return directly to Vienna; see below.

The B10 continues NE to (10km) *Gattendorf*, where it bears SE to reach the Hungarian frontier (Customs) 14km beyond. *Budapest* lies 184km further SE.— 12km NE of Gattendorf lies **Kittsee**, the birthplace of the violinist Joseph Joachim (1831–1907), with an *Ethnographical museum* in its *Altes Schloss*. You meet the B9 4km beyond, and turn left for (7km) *Hainburg*; see Rte 29. **Bratislava**, formerly *Pressburg*, lies 5km to the E, just beyond the Czech border (Customs, etc.).

Bearing NW from Parndorf, **Bruck an der Leitha** (7200 inhab.) is reached after 7km. This was a frontier-post between Austria and Hungary during the dual-monarchy, and it was in the barracks here that Hazek's 'good soldier Schwejk' received his military training! It preserves some 13C walls, and a Gothic keep rebuilt by J. Lukas von Hildebrandt.

For *Rohrau*, 9.5km NE, see Rte 29.

The main road continues NW, by-passing several villages, while a continuation of the motorway from Vienna is being constructed further N. After 16km you pass S of Vienna's *Schwechat airport* (right), and then an area of oil refineries, later skirting *Schwechat* itself before entering the SE suburbs of **Vienna**; see Rte 25N.

29 Vienna to Hainburg (for Bratislava); the Marchfeld

Total distance, 49km (30 miles). B9. 17km *Schwechat* airport—5km *Fischamend*—19km **Petronell-Carnuntum**. **Rohrau** lies 6km S.— 4.5km **Bad Deutsch-Altenburg**—3.5km **Hainburg**.

The excursion may of course be extended—as described—by turning N through the Marchfeld to **Marchegg**, returning from there to Vienna; or alternatively by bearing SE to *Kittsee*; see above.

Maps: F&B 1; BEV 48/16–17.

The A4 autobahn provides a more rapid route from the centre to **Schwechat airport** (*Flughafen*), first passing the extensive refineries of *Österreichische Mineralölverwaltung* (ÖMV), to reach *Fischamend Markt*, with its Romanesque and Renaissance belfry, and its *Church*, formerly containing Maulbertsch's 'The Last Supper'. The road follows the tree-bordered S bank of the Danube, passing *Wildungsmauer*, with a Filialkirche of 1230 of some interest, at 18km, on approaching **Petronell**, reaching a lay-by (left). A track leads right for a short distance past (right) the remains of the early 2C *Roman Amphitheatre II*, which would have accommodated c 25,000 spectators. Some 500m further S, beyond a railway-line, is the *Heidentor*, the ruins of either a funerary monument or triumphal arch.

Returning to the main road, continue E to reach the village, with (right) a picturesque circular Romanesque *Chapel* (12C).—To the N of the road are the excavated remains of the site of **Carnuntum**, founded c AD 72 as the capital of Roman *Pannonia*, which thrived for the next three centuries. A lane leads to *Schloss Traun*, rebuilt c 1673 and preserving several interesting features including the frescoed Festsaal. It contains the *Donau-Museum*, devoted to the natural history of the Danube. An 'Archaeological Park' is planned for the whole area, together with the restoration of its museum, etc., but this may take a decade to complete.

6km to the S lies the village of **Rohrau**, where the birthplace of Joseph Haydn (31 March 1732–1809) and Michael Haydn (1737–1806) has been converted into a museum; their parents lie in the village cemetery. Their humble home burned down in 1899 and has been virtually rebuilt. (A painting of it in 1829, by Wilhelm Kröpsch, is in the Gesellschaft de Musikfreunde, Vienna.) A short distance further S stands *Schloss Rohrau*, the country seat of the Harrach family, surrounded by a moat. (Haydn's mothers was employed as cook here.) Several times modified, it received its present façade, by Andreas Zach, in c 1770. It contains the remarkable *Harrach Collection* of paintings, moved here from their palace in Vienna and opened to the public in 1970 (10.00–17.00, except Monday, from April to October).

Stairs ascend to the right of the inner courtyard to a series of rooms on the first floor. Among the more important paintings displayed are several battle scenes of the Thirty Years' War, possibly by *Peeter Snayers*, including views of Vienna and Pressburg; *Solimena*, Old Testament and Allegorical scenes; Virgin and Child; St. Januarius of Naples; and Alois Thomas Harrach when viceroy of Naples; *Salvator Rosa*, Martyrdom of St. Bartholomew; *Bernardo Cavallino*, Feast of Absalom; F.C. Thaller (previously ascribed to *Anton Grassi*), *Bust of Haydn*, showing pock-marks; *Luca Giordano*, Isaac and Jacob; Moses in the bullrushes; *Ribera*, St. Bartholomew; Joseph; and an Immaculate Conception; *Carreño*, Portraits of Maria Anna of Spain, and Carlos II; *F. de Palacios*, Still-lifes (1648); *Monsù Desiderio* (François Didier Nomé), five fantastic Architectural compositions; *The Master of the Female Half-lengths*, The concert; *Monogrammist MS of 1570*, Female portrait of a member of the Harrach family; *Ambrosius Benson*, two panels; *Bernard Strigel*, Male portrait; two paintings by followers of Bosch; *Domenico Brandi*, Cattle, and Goats; *D. Feti*, The goldsmith; *Nicolo Maria Rossi*, Viceroy Harrach at Naples; The Royal Palace at Naples; and Corpus Christi in Naples; *Mattia Preti*, Solomon and the Queen of Sheba; *Stanzione*, Massacre of the Innocents; *Vaccaro*, Death of Lucretia; terracotta mid 19C Busts of the Harrach girls; *Michele di Ridolfo*, Madonna and Child with St. John; *H. Bloemaert*, St. Jerome; *School of Quentin Massys*, Triptych of the Crucifixion (in the Chapel); two sculpted figures from the Convent of the Descalsas Reales, Madrid, presented to F.B. Harrach; *Mengs*, Nativity; *Terbruggen*, Mater Dolorosa; a MS Prayer by St. Teresa de Ávila; *Jan van Bylert*, St. Irene extracting arrows from St. Sebastian; *Rigaud*, Portrait of F.B. Harrach (1698); a collection of inlaid furniture of c 1750, and Bohemian glass; *Cornelis de Vos*, Female portrait; *D. Teniers*, the Archduke Leopold and Harrach in the Royal Gallery; *Franz Franken II*, The studio; *Van Dyck*, two Children's heads, and Sketch for a Deposition; a Scene signed by *W. van Herp*; *Pieter Brueghel the Younger*, The Seven works of Mercy; collections of pewter, and tortoiseshell, and a brass and ebony Desk of c 1700 (? from Antwerp), and Clock; Landscapes by *Nicolas Berchem*, and *J. Wouverman*; *Pannini*, two Classical scenes; *Pompeo Batoni*, Susanna and the Elders; *Claude Joseph Vernet*, four Landscapes; *Johann Kupetzky*, Portrait of Alois Thomas Harrach.

Among the more notable members of the illustrious family were Ernst Adalbert (1598–1667); Ferdinand Bonaventura (1636–1706), who collected paintings in Spain, and founded the collection; Alois Thomas (1669–1742), Viceroy of Naples in 1728–33, who collected Italian paintings; and Friedrich August (1696–1749), who collected in Brussels.

From Petronell, the main road shortly crosses the site of the permanent Roman camp, laid out in AD 73 and destroyed c 400, and then (left) *Amphitheatre I*, probably built for the garrison.

Turning left on entering adjacent **Bad Deutsch-Altenburg**, a small spa on the site of Roman *Aquae Pannonicae*, you pass the 17C *Schloss* (containing a collection of Africana), to reach the Romanesque and Gothic *Church*, with its circular *Charnel-house*. The *Museum Carnuntum* (under restoration) contains a good collection of bronze artefacts, statuettes, fibulae, lamps, ceramics, silver, enamels, jewellery, mosaics, coins, sepulchral monuments, and statuary, including a Bust of Julia Domna (193–211), wife of Septimius Severus. A *Mithraeum* has been reconstructed here, and in the garden there are other remains of the Roman occupation.

The main road climbs past a bridge spanning the Danube (see below) to enter **Hainburg**, a partially walled town of 5750 inhab., retaining two *Town gates*, and overlooked to the S by the ruins of its castle, where in 1252 Ottokar II of Bohemia married Margarete von Babenberg. In the HAUPTPLATZ is a *Mariensäule* of 1749, and a *Fountain* commemorating Haydn's schooldays here (1737–40). The hill of Braunberg, to the N, is noted for its spring flora.

To the E rise the *Little Carpathians* and **Bratislava**, formerly *Pressburg*, conspicuous just beyond the Czech border, 10km to the E (Customs, etc.).—Off this road, at 7km, just beyond *Wolfsthal*, with a 17–19C Schloss, the right-hand fork leads 5km to *Kittsee*; see Rte 28.

Returning to the bridge, you can cross the Danube onto the MARCHFELD, a low-lying but rich alluvial plain.

Some 10km to the W on the N bank, approached by the first left-hand turning, lies **Eckartsau**; its *Schloss* was the former Kinsky hunting-lodge on which both J. Lukas von Hildebrandt and J.E. Fischer von Erlach worked. It was reconstructed for the Archduke Franz Ferdinand, but its frescoes by Daniel Gran, and sculpture by Lorenzo Mattielli survived both this and the Russian occupation. Here, during four months of the winter of 1918–19, subsisted Karl, the last Habsburg (died 1922), the Empress Zita (died 1989), and their family, before being escorted into exile by Lt-Col Edward Lisle Strutt.—8km W lies *Orth*; see below.

Driving N from the bridge, at 8km you pass (right) *Schloss Engelhartstetten* at **Niederweiden**, built by J.B. Fischer von Erlach in 1694, to which an oval room was added by Nikolaus Pacassi, decorated by Pillement.—Forking right here, you approach neighbouring *Schloss Schlosshof, an austere edifice erected in 1725–29 by J. Lukas von Hildebrandt for Eugene of Savoy, and in 1755 enlarged by Maria Theresia, who had bought it from his niece, Victoria. It was after she had attended a performance of Gluck's opera 'Le Cinesi' here in September 1754 that the composer was invited to Vienna to take up the post of her *Kapellmeister*.

The palatial building later accommodated an army riding-school, which hardly improved its appearance, but it has been thoroughly restored to commemorate the 250th anniversary of Prince Eugene's death (1736). The *Chapel* is notable. The Schloss was several times painted by Bellotto; see Kunsthistorisches Museum, Vienna.

Continuing NW, you enter (c 9km) **Marchegg**, preserving remains of its fortifications on the bank of the river March, which here forms the frontier with Czechoslovakia. Its ochre-coloured *Schloss*, last modified in 1733, contains a large *Hunting Museum* (*Jagdmuseum*), in which several rooms are devoted to the flora and fauna of the region, while a series of prints by Stradarnus (1580) is notable.

19km N of Marchegg lies **Stillfried**, populated in Palaeolithic times, and in the Roman period a base of Marbod, chief of the Marcomanni.—8km further N, at *Dürnkrut*, the decisive 'Battle of the Marchfeld' took place in 1278, in which Rudolf von Habsburg, founder of the dynasty, defeated Ottokar II P'Yrzemysl of Bohemia, who was slain in the mêlée. Ottokar had defeated the Hungarians here in 1260.—Several excavations have taken place recently of Bronze Age sites, among others, in the vicinity of neighbouring *Waidendorf-Buhuberg.*

From Marchegg turn due W across the Marchfeld to (15.5km) *Obersiebenbrunn*, with a pavilion of 1728 by J. Lukas von Hildebrandt in the gardens of its *Schloss*, containing restored frescoes by Jonas Drentwett.—A further 12km brings you to **Deutsch Wagram**, the site of the bloody battle of 5–6 July 1809, where a small museum may be visited.

Napoleon, whose army had received reinforcements after his recent discomfiture at Essling (see below), with corps commanded by Oudinot (promoted Marshal after the battle), Davout, Masséna (created Prince d'Essling the following year), Bernadotte, Marmont, Bessiéres, Macdonald, and Eugéne de Beauharnais, amounting to 160,000 men and 584 cannon, defeated the army of the Archduke Karl, with 110,000 men and 452 cannon. Their respective losses were in the region of 34,000 and 50,000.

A road leads 10km due S across an area where most of the manoeuvring and fighting took place, to *Gross Enzersdorf*, just W of which lie the villages of *Essling* and **Aspern**. Between them, on 21–22 May 1809, took place the battle (known as Essling by the French, but as Aspern and Essling by the Austrians) in which Napoleon was defeated by the Archduke Karl, and in which Marshal Lannes, Duc de Montebello, was mortally wounded. The Austrian losses were some 23,000 dead and wounded, almost one-third of their army; those of the French amounted to c 44,300, including prisoners, nearly half their whole force.

Georg Raphael Donner (1693–1741), the sculptor, was born at Aspern, not to be confused with *Asparn*; see Rte 31.

At *Orth*, 13.5km SE of Gross Enzersdorf, the 16C *Schloss* contains an *Apiarian museum* (Bee-keeping) and another devoted to Danube fisheries.

From either Deutsch Wagram or Aspern roads lead through the transpontine suburbs of Vienna (see Rte 25M) to approach its centre.

30 Klosterneuburg

The excursion may be made with ease from central Vienna, either by following Rte 26B, or by taking the direct B14 N, skirting the suburb of *Nussdorf* (Rte 26A) and crossing the narrow stretch between the *Leopoldsberg* and the *Danube*.

The upper town of (13km) **KLOSTERNEUBURG** (23,000 inhab.) is dominated by the twin spires of its Augustinian abbey church, approached by forking left off the riverside road, and entered from the RATHAUS PLATZ. The UNTERER STADTPLATZ, in which are several 16–17C houses, lies some distance N, on the far side of the Kierlingbach.

Johann Georg Albrechtsberger (1736–1809), the musical theorist who taught Beethoven counterpoint, was born here.

The *Abbey was founded by Margrave Leopold III (canonised 1485), and the church was consecrated in 1136, just before his death.

Donato Felice dell' Allio's project for the mid 18C rebuilding of Klosterneuburg (by Joseph Knapp, 1744)

Additional dependencies, erected c 1220 by Duke Leopold VI, were demolished in the 18C; the relics of these buildings may be seen some short distance to the N of its SW entrance. By the mid 16C the abbey was virtually Protestant, under its Humanist provost Peter Hübner, and his successor Leopold Hintermayr; while among other cultivated canons of the period was Andreas Weissenstein. Only 16 or so canons now reside there; there were 47 only a few decades ago, but under the enterprising direction of its present abbot, the buildings and its treasures are tastefully preserved.

Near the entrance is the *Stiftskeller*, selling the produce of its vineyards, etc., still an important source of income. (Between this and a point not far beyond the church stood a Roman fort.)

Near by is a Gothic *Chapterhouse* (from near Horn), which has been re-erected here; adjacent is the *Chapel of St. Sebastian*, rebuilt in 1974 to house the restored *Albrecht altarpiece*. This remarkable work, named after its donor Duke Albrecht, formerly embellished the Carmelite church of Am Hof in Vienna. It consists of 24 panels, and dates from 1437–39. In one of them, depicting Joachim and Anne, is the oldest extant view of Vienna as a background (cf. the Schottenaltar, p 256). Other paintings of interest are also displayed. Adjacent is the 15C *Cooperage*, containing a colossal wine cask holding over 56,000 litres (12,000 gallons).

The **Church**, which was begun in 1114 on the site of a previous building, has two towers, the S dating from 1390–1592, with a Renaissance superstructure; the other, by J.B. Carlone (1638–44), Gothic in form. Both were extensively remodelled by Friedrich von Schmidt (architect of Vienna's Rathaus) after 1879, and are now without character. The interior dates from a restoration of 1636–42, and the organ, by Johann Freundt—in a case by Michael Schmidt—is of the same epoch, utilising the pipes of its predecessor; the *Choir* dates from 1714–30. The frescoes in the vault are by Johann Georg Greiner (1689); those in the cupola by Rottmayr; the high altar, by Matthias Steinl (1728), has a painting of the Death of the Virgin by Johann Georg Schmidt; the marble *pulpit*, and the *stalls*, with the coats of arms of the Habsburg provinces, are also notable.

Steps descend to the *cloister*, built on part of the site of the Roman fort, with a *lavatory* of 1185. Adjoining it is the former *refectory*, containing lapidary collections—bread being turned to stones—and a branched bronze candelabrum of 1125, a mutilated French Virgin of c 1300, and the original statues of the founder and his wife, of c 1400, which previously embellished the façade of the church, and which have been replaced by copies.—Adjacent is the *St. Leopold Chapel*, in which some early 17C frescoes of the life of that saint have been uncovered; note the painted stucco ceilings, and glass of 1330–1400.

Beyond a grille of 1677 is displayed the *Verdun altarpiece*, completed in 1191 by Nicolas of Verdun, with two wings of gilded copper and 51 blue enamel plaques, reconstructed after the original had been damaged by fire in 1330. Relics of St. Leopold are preserved in a shrine of 1936.

Steps descend to a restored courtyard, in the NW corner of which is a late Gothic double oriel, part of the duke's residence, now housing archives, and the abbot's house. Passing through an archway, the church is regained.

From the side of the church we reach the entrance (by Kornhäusel) to the Baroque monastic dependencies planned by Karl VI and started in 1730. Designed by Donato Felice d'Allio, they were intended to have four large courtyards and no less than nine domes, but with the death of the emperor in 1740 the project languished, and only two domes were completed, the larger surmounted by a reproduction of the crown of the Holy Roman Empire; the other with that of the Archduke of Austria. The actual archducal crown has been preserved in its *Treasury* since 1616.

The uncompleted *Grand Staircase* (Kaiserstiege) ascends to the right of the oval entrance vestibule, above which is the *Library* (normally no admission, but which contains c 1250 MSS and 850 incunabula), to the S Wing. This accommodates several state rooms, with good plasterwork ceilings and notable stoves; also Brussels tapestries (scenes from Télémaque; the story of the Queen of Sheba, etc.) and dessus de portes. The fresco in the oval dome of the *Marble Hall* is by Daniel Gran (1749).

Also displayed are parts of the original Verdun altarpiece; the *Genealogical Tree of the Babenbergs*, by Hans Part (1492), with topographical views, and depicting wives of the family in the wings; MSS with miniatures illustrating the history of the Babenbergs (1491); *Rueland Frueauf the Younger*, Crucifixion; The Legend of St. Leopold (1505); Scenes from the life of the Baptist; and representative paintings of the Danube School; Italian bronzes, and a lead group of Mercury, by *G.R. Donner*.

On the SECOND FLOOR is a collection of statues, including a Pietà of 1380; Gothic paintings, among them the Magdalen altarpiece of 1456; a good Crucifixion; a Virgin and Child of 1460; reliquaries; Neapolitan filigree work; silver and gold thread altar-frontals; ivories; and a 12C writing-case.

Among more recent works are several 19C views of Klosterneuburg, some by *Friedrich Loos*, and 20C views, some by *Egon Schiele* (1906), who received part of his education in the school (*Obergymnasium*) attached to the abbey. Schiele was born at *Tulln*, 22km W, in 1890; see Rte 22A.

Franz Kafka (1883–1924) spent the last months of his life in a sanatorium at *Kierling* (3km W), nursed by Dora Dymant.—Nikolaus Lenau (1802–50) is buried in the cemetery at *Weidling*, 2km SW of Klosterneuburg.

31   The Weinviertel

Maps: F&B 1; BEV 48/16, 49/16.

The **Weinviertel**, as its name implies, is an area of rolling hills in part clad with vines, extending N and NE of Vienna towards the Czech frontier. Its W half is covered by Rte 24B. The district between *Matzen* and *Gänserndorf* (13km NE of Deutsch-Wagram; see Rte 29) is also the centre of the Austrian oilfields, apart from several other smaller areas of exploitation further N near *Zistersdorf* and *Neusiedl an der Zaya*.

It is planned to continue the Nordautobahn (A22) from Vienna to the Czech frontier E of Laa an der Thaya, passing W of Mistelbach. Meanwhile, several circuits may be made off the dull main B7 (from Vienna to Brno), which leads NE from the capital through *Floridsdorf*, later driving through more attractive rolling country to (61km) *Poysdorf*, 14km from the border, en route passing through

(18.5km) *Wolkersdorf*, and 17.5km beyond, by-passing (right) *Schrick*.

At **Niedersulz**, 7km SE of Schrick, is an attractive *Farm museum*, together with several reconstructed South Moravian peasant houses (the *Südmährischen Hof*).

At *Gaiselberg*, a hamlet near *Zisterdorf* (see above), 12km NE, are huge concentric earthworks.

SCHRICK TO LAA AN DER THAYA (31km). The B46 forks NW to (7km) **Mistelbach** (10,250 inhab.), with a *Church* of 1502 preserving a number of interesting tombstones. A circular Romanesque *Charnel-house* with a sculpted tympanum stands adjacent. The *Schloss* (1725) contains a museum of local interest, while frescoes by Maulbertsch may be seen in the library of the *Pfarrhof*.

At **Asparn an der Zaya**, 7km W, the 13–15C *Schloss* and its park is the site of a *Museum of Prehistory* (closed Monday). Near by, in the *Minoritenkloster*, is a *wine museum*.—The church at *Michelstetten*, 4km further W, has 13C murals, while in the entrance to *Schloss Loosdorf*, 7.5km NW of Asparn, is the notable Renaissance monument to Adam von Gall (1574). The porcelain collection here was destroyed by the Russians.

The main road may be regained NE of Asparn (not to be confused with *Aspern*; see Rte 29) and 8km NW of Mistelbach, and followed past *Staatz*, dominated by castle ruins, to (18km) **Laa an der Thaya**, the frontier village, with remains of 13–15C fortifications in its NE suburbs. The Romanesque and Gothic church has a notable high altar of 1745 by Ignaz Lengelacher depicting the Martyrdom of St. Veit.

You can return to Vienna on the B6, at 18km crossing the *Leiser Berge*, rising to 491m, passing (1km W after a further 6km) *Ernstbrunn*, with a picturesque Baroque *Schloss*. Some distance further W, perhaps best approached from Nursch, is *Schloss Glaswein*, containing hunting-scenes painted by Franz Greipel (1769). A scarped hill just E of *Oberleis* was once fortified. The road continues S to (23km) *Korneuburg*; see Rte 24A.

ALTERNATIVELY, follow the B45 due W from Laa. At 17km we pass 4km N of *Mailberg*, with a *Schloss* of 1594 and 1762, containing a museum devoted to the Knights of Malta, and with 15–16C sculptures and several good tombstones in its church. Leopold II fought and lost a battle here in 1082 against the Czechs and Bavarians.—The B45 continues W to meet the B2 at (11km) *Jetzelsdorf*; see Rte 24B.

From Schrick the B7 continues N to (18km) *Poysdorf*, with a church of 1648, 4km beyond which a left-hand turning leads past the romantically sited ruined castle of *Falkenstein*. The adjacent village has a picturesque *Pfarrkirche* and a street of cellars (*Kellergasse*).

The next right-hand turning off the B7 circles to the E, leading you across a sequestered district bounded by the Czech frontier, before bearing S through *Hohenau* and continuing S parallel to the river March through *Dürnkrut* and *Stillfried* (see p 339). At *Angern* it veers SW via *Gänserndorf* towards *Vienna*.

6km N of this turning lies the frontier village of *Drasenhofen*, 4km beyond which is the actual Czech border (Customs, etc.).

At *Mikulov*, formerly *Nikolsburg*, 2km N in Czechoslovakia, Franz Josef signed the armistice in 1866 after the defeat of F.M. Benedek at *Königgrätz* by von Moltke, with his superior breech-loading rifles. The site of the battle, also known as *Sadowa*, was at present-day *Hradec Králové*, some 143km NE of *Brno*, the former capital of Moravia, which is 52km N of Mikulov. The following Peace of Prague was to exclude Austria from the German League. Joseph Sonnenfels (1732–1817), the radical reformer of Jewish parentage, was born at Nikolsburg.

32   Vienna to Graz

A.   Via the A2 autobahn

Total distance, 196km (122 miles).

Maps: F&B 1,2; BEV 48/16, 47/25–16

The motorway, completed in 1985, provides an attractive and fast route between the two cities, and it has sufficient exits for approaching some of the more interesting sights—notably **Vorau**—to be seen on or near the old main road; see Rte 32C. The S half of Rte 32D may be reached with ease by turning down the Pinka valley to *Oberwart*.

Well-engineered, the A2 crosses the mountainous BUCKLIGE WELT in a series of viaducts and tunnels, gradually climbing above the B54 (in the Pitten valley), before descending beyond *Hartberg* into Styria. It is particularly recommended in winter.

B.   Via Eisenstadt, Bernstein, and Güssing

Total distance, 258km (160 miles). B16. 50km **Eisenstadt**—S4. 42km *Oberpullendorf*—27km *Bernstein*—B50 and then B57. 48km **Güssing**—13km *Heiligenkreuz*—B307. 50km *Gleisdorf*—A2. 28km **Graz**.

Maps: F&B 1, 2; BEV 48/16, 47/15–16.

Not the most rapid road, but one that traverses almost the length of the elongated frontier province of **Burgenland**. Follow the first part of Rte 28 to **Eisenstadt**, or the direct and slightly shorter B16, which skirts the E side of the park of *Laxenburg*.

From the junction 4km SW of Eisenstadt, follow the S4 SW.

At 15km you reach an exit for *Mattersburg* (left), a market town reputed for its strawberries, with an early 15C church in a fortified cemetery, and a Jewish cemetery (one of several surviving in Burgenland; and 3km W, *Forchtenau*, a village commanded by *Schloss Forchtenstein*, crowning a spur below the ROSALIEN-GEBIRGE, here rising to 748m.

A winding road ascends to the fortress, approached by a bridge across a dry moat cut out of the rock, built in the early 14C, and in the 17C provided with bastions. It passed to the Esterházy family in 1622, and their portraits can be seen in the picture gallery; collections of arms and armour are also on display.

Regaining the main road, you continue S over a pass at the 'waist' of Burgenland, here a mere 6km across, with the ÖDENBURGER GEBIRGE (606m) to the E, its crest marking the Hungarian frontier, and *Sopron*, formerly *Ödenburg*, beyond. To the SW rise the hilly BUCKLIGE WELT, and to the SE the vineyards of the red Blaufränkischer; while beyond the border extends the Hungarian plain or *puzta*.

17km *Weppersdorf*, 3km NW of which is the 12–17C moated

Schloss Kobersdorf; 3km NE is *Lackenbach*, with a Jewish cemetery; at *Landsee*, c 6km W, are castle ruins.

11km E, to the S of the B62, lies **Raiding**, birthplace of Franz Liszt (1811–86, at Bayreuth), with mementoes of the composer, who last visited his birthplace in 1881. Only three (restored) rooms of the original building remain of the more extensive farm dependencies, which were mysteriously burnt down in 1945. The B62 can be regained 4km NE and 8km W of *Deutschkreutz*, with an Esterházy *Schloss* rebuilt in 1625, since 1966 the property of the artist Anton Lehmden. There is a border-crossing to *Sopron*, to the NE.

Continuing S, with a view (left) of the 13C keep of *Landsee*, you enter *Stoob* after 8km, which has a school of pottery.—4km beyond, *Oberpullendorf*, with a 17C Schloss, is by-passed, the main road circling to the W.

The B61 leads 11km S to the frontier village of *Rattersdorf* (customs). Szombathely lies 25km further S in Hungary.—The main route is rejoined 10km W, beyond Lockenhaus.

At 12km a left-hand turning leads 3km to *Lockenhaus*, its mid 17C church with a richly decorated high altar; above stands the *Burg* (1254), with a Gothic hall. To the S rises the *Geschriebenstein* (884m; the highest point in Burgenland), part of the GÜNSER GEBIRGE, which extends into Hungary.

15km **Bernstein**, with a finely sited 13C fortress (views), rebuilt in the early 17C, and owned by the Bathyány family from 1644–1864, after which it was briefly in the hands of Edward O'Egan, their Irish factor. The Rittersaal contains good 17C Italian plaster-work. Since 1953 it has been partly a hotel. Veering S again over the hills, at 7km you pass near (right) *Mariasdorf*, with a striking late Gothic church.

The left-hand turning here leads 5km up to *Stadschlaining*, a charming village, with 15C walls and a Gothic and Baroque church containing a neo-classical high altar (restored). It is dominated by its 13C *Schloss*, rebuilt in the mid 15C by Andreas Baumkircher who, having revolted against Friedrich III, was later beheaded at Graz. Some rooms contain stucco-work of c 1700.—The church at *Neumarkt im Tauchental*, just beyond, contains a 2C funerary monument and a Roman relief in its porch.

The main road shortly by-passes (right) *Jormannsdorf*, with a 17C Batthyány *Schloss*, and (left) the small spa of *Bad Tatzmannsdorf*, where a 'typical' Burgenland village has been reconstructed.—9km *Oberwart*, a small industrial town in the PINKA VALLEY.—At *Burg*, 10km beyond *Grosspetersdorf*, 11km SE, is a complex of earthworks dominating a meander of the Pinka. There is another crossing to *Szombathely* 13km E of Grosspetersdorf.—5km beyond Oberwart a right-hand turning leads 16km W across country—crossing the motorway—to *Hartberg*, on the direct road to *Graz*; see Rte 32C.

The B57 descends the STREMBACH VALLEY via (14km) *Stegersbach*, with a local museum, to (9km) *St. Michael in Burgenland* (left).

A circuit to the E can be made to (10km) *Kohfidisch*—just N of crossroads—with what was a fine 18C *Schloss*, there turning SE to (12km) **Eberau** (left), abutting the Hungarian border, to the S of which is its ancient moated *Schloss* in a 'Grand Meaulnes' setting.—3km *Gaas*, with the pilgrimage-church of *Maria Weinberg* (1524; later baroqueised) nearby.—At (3km) *Moschendorf* you turn W, and N of **Heiligenbrunn**, above which, in the woods, are a number of charming and characteristic wine-cellars (some built into the hillside), mostly constructed of daub and wood, and thatched. The main route is regained at (16km) Güssing.

9km **Güssing** (3900 inhab.), formerly *Németújvár*, where the church of the *Franziskanerkloster* contains the Batthyány crypt (1648), which holds the lead coffin of Prince Karl Batthyány (1697–1772), by

Balthasar Moll. The brick and stone *Batthyány Schloss*, on a commanding height, is under restoration. Here Clusius, the botanist, was entertained by Balthasar Batthyány, and he published his 'Stirpium Nomenclator Pannonius' at Güssing in 1583.

Bearing SW, the B307 is met at (13km) *Heiligenkreuz im Laftnitz-, tal*. For the road to *Graz*, 74km W, see Rte 35 in reverse; for **Graz** itself, Rte 33.

C. Via Wiener Neustadt and Hartberg

Total distance, 195km (121 miles). A2. 54km **Weiner Neustadt**—B54. 65km **Vorau** lies 11.5km W.—14km *Hartberg*—34km *Gleisdorf*—A2. 28km **Graz**.
Maps: F&B 1, 2; BEV 48/16, 47/15–16.

The motorway leads S, at 27km passing the exit for **Baden** 5km W; see Rte 27.

At 23km you turn off for **Wiener Neustadt** (35,000 inhab.; 39,350 in 1939), a busy industrial town, the old centre of which contains a few monuments of interest.

It was founded in 1194 by Leopold V of Babenberg as a frontier fortress to guard against Magyar incursions, and its walls were said to have been partly paid for by Richard Lionheart's ransom (cf. Dürnstein). It was the fortified base of Friedrich, Duke of Austria (died 1246). The town flourished during the reign of Friedrich III, who in 1477 made it the seat of a bishopric (transferred to St. Pölten in 1785). A decade later it surrendered to Matthias Corvinus after a long siege, but four years later it was recaptured by Maximilian I, who had been born in its castle in 1459. The town resisted the Turks in 1529, but was severely damaged by fire in 1834. In 1752 the Schloss was converted into a military academy, which gave the town a certain cachet.

In the summer of 1821 Beethoven, on an excursion from Baden, was arrested nearby, and it was only after Anton Herzog, the director of music, had confirmed that it was indeed the famous composer, and no tramp, that he was released, and sent home in the burgomaster's coach!

Johann Schenk (1753–1836), who had taught Beethoven counterpoint soon after his arrival in Vienna, was born here, and also Nikolaus Pacassi (1716–90), the architect; the poet Heinrich von Neustadt (fl. 1300), later practising as a physician in Vienna; and the composer Josef Matthias Hauer (1883–1959).

During the later 19C the town developed several industries, including the building of locomotives, and these, together with armament factories, made it the target of bombing during the Second World War, after which it was under Russian occupation.

The Duchess of Angoulême lived in exile at *Schloss Frohsdorf* (c 10km S, near Lanzenkirchen) from 1844 until her death in 1851. The Comte de Chambord, her nephew, died there in 1883. It was severely damaged by the Russians during their occupation.

At the SE corner of the quadrangular enceinte stands the **Burg**, the site of the former fortress, with the restored *Georgskapelle* (1449–60), by Peter von Pusika, with its emblazoned façade and statue of Friedrich III. Below the high altar are the remains of the Emperor Maximilian I (1459–1519), transferred here from Wels, where he died. A museum devoted to the military academy may be visited. It was here that F.M. Benedek (1804–81) was shamefully allowed to be court-martialled in the presence of Franz Josef, who required a scapegoat after the defeat of Königgrätz (Sadowa; 1866).

The letters A E I O U here and elsewhere in the town, can be interpreted as 'Austriae est imperare orbi universo' (it falls to Austria to rule over the whole globe), the arrogant motto of Friedrich III, an alternative form being 'Austria erit in orbe ultima', while the German version is 'Alles Erdreich ist Österreich untertan'.

From the BURGPLATZ opposite, the narrow Kesslergasse leads N to the arcaded HAUPTPLATZ, with a *Mariensäule*, and *Rathaus* dating from the late 16C. From its NW corner, enter the DOMPLATZ, in the centre of which rises the **Stadtpfarrkirche** (13–15C), the cathedral from 1468 until 1784, with, on its S side, the late Romanesque *Brautor*. Several statues and tombstones in the interior are notable, together with the cenotaph of Cardinal Khlesl (died 1630). To the NW is the former *Bishop's palace*.

Turning right from the NE corner of the platz, and then left, the apse of *St. Peter an der Sperr* (14C; now an exhibition hall) is passed to approach the Jesuit church of *Hl. Leopold* (1737–43), and the *Museum*, preserving among other objects the so-called Cor-vinusbecher, a huge 15C silver-gilt and enamel tankard, and Gospels of 1325.—Some distance further N, in a park, is an impressive wayside *Cross* of 1384, by Michael Chnab.

Returning S by the main thoroughfare further E, you pass near (left) the *Deutschordenskirche*, and a few steps E (opposite the Ungargasse, leading right into the Hauptplatz) the **Neu-klosterkirche**, founded in 1250, and after 1444 the church of a Cistercian convent. Here is the remarkable *Tomb of the Empress Leonor (Eleanor) of Portugal* (died 1467), the wife of Friedrich III and mother of Maximilian I. It was probably carved by Niklas Gerhaert von Leyden, or one of his pupils. Among the paintings are works by Solimena, M. Altomonte, and Michael Unterberger.—A few minutes' walk to the W of the Burg is the *Kapuzinerkirche*, 13C, but much altered.

Driving S up the PITTEN VALLEY, the B54 closely follows the motor-way (see Rte 32A), at 16km passing (left) *Seebenstein*, with a *Schloss* rebuilt in the 17C, containing several collections, including land-scapes by Gauermann, and a Virgin and Child carved by Tilman Riemenschneider.—Bronze Age tombs have recently been excavated at *Pitten*, to the NE.

The wooded hills of the BUCKLIGE WELT are soon entered, and you pass near the folly (left; 1826) of *Türkensturz*, and near *Thernberg* (to the E), with a ruined castle, a *Schloss* of 1774, and a notable 12C church. A right-hand turning leads 4km W to *Feistritz am Wechsel*, with a restored *Schloss* of 1684, altered in the early 19C. To the SW rises the *Hochwechsel* (1743m).

After 14km you reach *Mönichkirchen*, just before crossing into Styria at the WECHSEL-PASS (980m), and descending SE, with the *Hochkogel* (1314m) to the right. At 11km you will by-pass (right) *Pinggau*, in the upper valley of the Pinka.—Some 11km further SE lies *Pinkafeld*, in the valley colonised by Germans in the mid 9C.

The main road bears SW, with a view (right) of the medieval *Schloss Thalberg*, to reach, at 10km, the exit for *Vorau*.

The Augustinian * *Abbey of Vorau** lies 11.5km W in a side valley of the JOGLLAND, with the *Masenberg* (1261m) rising to the S, and the *Wildwiesen* (1254m) to the W. Above the town, approached by a tree-lined avenue, stands the impressive and colourful abbey, founded in 1163, but completely rebuilt between 1625 and the mid 18C, and restored after war damage. The highly decorated interior of the **Church**, entirely covered with paintings and frescoes, contains a notable pulpit, and a richly gilt high altar by Matthias Steidl (1704), while in the Sacristy are frescoes by Johann Cyriak Hackhofer (1675–1731), who died there. The huge double-organ and organ-loft is remarkable. Off the three-storey *Cloister* opens the **Library** (1725–33) which preserves numerous MSS and incunabula in its rococo shelves.—The *Marktkirche* also has frescoes by Hackhofer.

The main road continues S to (14km) **Hartberg**, at the foot of the vine-clad *Ringkogel* (789m; right), with relics of its walls, a 13–18C *Church* with a massive Baroque belfry, and high altar by Hackhofer, adjacent to which is a well-preserved *Charnel-house* (c 1200).—The Roman villa of *Löffelbach* has been excavated W of Hartberg.—Some 3km W stands *Burg Neuberg*, rebuilt in the 16C.

An entrance to the motorway lies not far SE of Hartberg.

At 3km a right-hand turning leads to (12km) **Pöllau**, sacked by the Turks in 1532, where within the enceinte of an earlier castle stood an Augustinian abbey (1504–1785), with 17–18C dependencies. Its domed church (1701–08), by Joachim Carlone, contains frescoes by Matthias von Görz, born here in 1670.— 5km NE is the Gothic pilgrimage-church of *Pöllauberg* (late 14C), with fluted piers, and a notable Baroque altar.

The B54 undulates to the SW to (15km) *Kaibing*, 3km NW of which is the remarkably sited 14–17C *Schloss Herberstein*, one of several former fortresses in the area.

17km *Gleisdorf* (5100 inhab.), is of slight interest.

15km NW lies industrial **Weiz** (8400 inhab.), an old town, where, by the HAUPTPLATZ, is the *Taborkirche*, several times rebuilt, last in the mid 18C, containing frescoes by J.A. von Mölk. Several 16C houses, and the riverside mid 16C *Schloss Ratmannsdorf* are noteworthy. Here also is the pilgrimage-church of *Weizberg*, by Josef Hueber (1757–76), built under the direction of J.A. von Mölk.

The old road (B65) leads from Gleisdorf to *Graz*, 26km W, but the recommended approach is by the A2 motorway, entered just W of the town. Bear right after 19km to enter **Graz** from the SE; see Rte 33.

D.   Via the Semmering Pass and Bruck an der Mur

Total distance, 209km (130 miles). A2. 65km—S6 and B306. 33km *Semmering*—14km *Mürzzuschlag* (also by-passed)—43km **Bruck an der Mur**—S35 and B335. 54km **Graz**.

Maps: F&B 1, 2; BEV 48/15–16, 47/15.

For the road to **Weiner Neustadt**, which is by-passed (left) at 54km, see Rte 32C.

To the W rises the **Hohe Wand** (1132m), and beyond, to the SW, the *Schneeberg* (2076m), the nearest peak to Vienna over 2000m. The Hohe Wand, with a precipitous wall of rock on its S side, is best approached by turning off the motorway for *Wöllersdorf* and turning right beyond *Stollhof*. The summit may also be reached by lift from Grünbach, further W.

After 11km turn off the motorway onto an expressway to by-pass the industrial town of *Neunkirchen* (10,750 inhab.), and ascend above the SCHWARZA VALLEY to the SW.

At 16km **Gloggnitz** (6250 inhab.) is by-passed. It has an imposing former Benedictine priory, and a *Pfarrkirche* completed in 1961 by Clemens Holzmeister. To the S stands the Romantic *Schloss Wartenstein*, in part dating back to the 11–12Cs, remodelled in 1645, but largely destroyed by the French in 1809.

At Gloggnitz on 1 April 1945 Karl Renner, the ex-Chancellor of Austria (in 1918–20), living there in retirement, met the occupying Russian troops to offer his services in setting up a provisional civil administration in the liberated country prior to the fall of Vienna.
Ludwig Wittgenstein taught in the elementary schools of *Otterthal* (c 10km S) and adjacent *Trattenbach*, among others, during the years 1920–26.

After 6km the improved road begins to climb through a craggy gorge. It passes (left) the pilgrimage-church of *Maria Schutz*, and ascends, in several steep zigzags, below (right) the *Sonnwendstein* (1523m), to the pass and watershed at (10km) **Semmering** (985m), both a summer and winter resort. From here the road descends gently into Styria.

A road over the Semmering, completed in 1728, took the place of the ancient bridle-path, and was itself replaced by a new road constructed in 1839–42. The Semmering railway, the first of the great Alpine railways, connecting Vienna with Trieste (completed in 1854), climbed in a series of loops and minor tunnels over brick-built viaducts designed by Karl von Ghega (1802–60) to reach the main tunnel below the pass.

To the S rises the *Stuhleck* (1782m). At 6km the left-hand fork by-passes **Mürzzuschlag** (10,750 inhab.), birthplace of Viktor Kaplan (1876–1934), inventor of a turbine, of interest for the *Ski Museum* at No. 3 Wiener Strasse. Brahms composed his 4th Symphony during 1884–85 at No. 2 in that street.

MÜRZZUSCHLAG TO MARIAZELL (51km). The B23 ascends the MÜRZTAL to the NW to (12km) **Neuberg an der Mürz**, at the foot of the SCHNEEALPE (*Windberg*; 1903m), where the imposing 15C *Church* of the Cistercian monastery, founded in 1327, with three naves of equal height, contains a high altar of 1611, and a mid 14C carved Virgin and Child.—The road continues past *Mürzsteg*, with a former hunting-lodge of Franz Josef (now a summer residence of the Austrian President), to (25km) the *Lahnsattel* (1015m), overlooked by the Göller (1766m), and descends to *Mariazell*; see Rte 21D.

The main road continues to descend the partly industrialised MÜRZ-TAL past (15km) *Krieglach* (5150 inhab.), where the poet Peter Rosegger (1843–1918) died. He had a summer villa there. The church of 1376 contains a fresco of The Last Judgement, dated 1420.
    At 12km *Kindberg* (6250 inhab.), with several 17–18C houses in its platz, is by-passed, and 4km beyond, *Allerheiligen im Mürztal*, with a well-vaulted 15C church, is also passed before you reach the turning to (9km) **Kapfenberg**, an industrial town of 25,700 inhab. (3750 in 1880), now by-passed.
    6km **Bruck an der Mur** (15,050 inhab.), Roman *Poedicum*, another small industrial centre, lies at the confluence of the Mürz and the Mur. Of its fortress of *Landskron* on the Schlossberg, built by Ottokar of Bohemia in 1268, only the clock-tower survived a ravaging fire in 1792. Below it is the *Minoritenkirche* (13C, with late 14C frescoes). Further W is the spacious HAUPTPLATZ, with its *Mariensäule*, and wrought-iron *well-canopy*. At its NE corner is the *Kornmesserhaus* (1505), with late Gothic arcading, and elaborately decorated loggia. Behind the classical façade of the *Rathaus* stands the *Pfarrkirche* (13–15C), with a wrought-iron door of 1500.—Some distance W is the Gothic *Ruprechtskirche*, with good early 15C frescoes of The Last Judgement.

For the road to **Klagenfurt** via *St. Veit*, see Rte 37; and for that to *Eisenerz*, the *Gesäuse*, and **Admont**, Rte 18B, in reverse.

The S35 turns S to follow the windings of the Mur, at 26km passing (right) *Schloss Rabenstein*, well-sited on a crag, rebuilt in the 17C, and now a hotel. After a further 7km the *Lurgrotte* cave is passed (left), and 1km beyond, *Peggau*, overlooked by the *Schöckl* (1445m), before meeting the A9 motorway which has pierced the *Gleinalmtunnel* to the NW.

A recommended DETOUR may be made from here, by crossing to the W bank of the Mur and turning S at *Kleinstübing* to visit the *Österreichisches Freilichtmuseum, or *Open-air Museum*, one of the finest of its kind. It is a collection of almost 80 re-erected farm-buildings—barns, mills and forges, together with their furniture and implements—transferred here from their original sites throughout Austria, and laid out in roughly geographical order: those of the Burgenland lie near the entrance; those of the Vorarlberg stand at the W end of the valley. An interesting Catalogue, with a brief English explanation, is available. Plenty of time should be allowed. It is normally open from 9.00–16.00 daily, except Monday, from 1 April to 31 October.

Continuing along this side road, we shortly reach *Gratwein*, 3km W of which lies **Rein**, with a notable Cistercian *Monastery*, founded in 1129, sacked by the Turks in 1480, rebuilt in the 17th and early 18C, and restored since flood damage in 1975. The *Church*, with an external organ-loft, is by Johann Georg Streng (1738–47), and its impressive interior contains frescoes by J.A. von Mölk, a high altarpiece by 'Kremser' Schmidt, the grave of Ottokar III of Styria (died 1164), and the red marble tomb of Ernst der Eiserne (died 1424; the 'Iron Duke', and grandfather of Maximilian I).

On regaining Gratwein, bear SE and then fork right for (2.5km) **Strassengel**, with a remarkable Gothic *pilgrimage-Church*, its fine octagonal belfry surmounted by an openwork steeple. It preserves 14–15C stained-glass in the choir, and an expressive carved tympanum of the Deposition above its S doorway. The main road may be regained a short distance E, just before you enter the outskirts of *Graz*.

The A9, entered 3km S of Peggau, provides the best approach to the centre of (17km) **Graz** also by-passed by a tunnel to the W.

33 Graz

Maps: F&B 2; BEV 47/15.

GRAZ (243,150 inhab.; 116,750 in 1880; 199,600 in 1923), the ancient capital of Styria, a university town, and industrial centre, is the second city in size of Austria. Strategically sited at the S end of the narrow Mur valley, it acquired its name from the ancient fort (Slav *gradec*; as in Belgrade, or Beograd) which once stood on the *Schlossberg*, rising just N of the medieval enceinte. It is an animated city, with a remarkable Museum, a unique Arsenal, and several fine buildings (apart from neighbouring *Schloss Eggenberg*), and characteristic older quarters.

Its ancient history is vague, for it was by-passed by the Romans, who preferred Leibnitz (*Flavia Solva*; c 35km S) as a base, and it was not properly settled until the early 12C. In 1164 it was acquired by Ottokar III of Styria, and later passed to the Babenbergs, becoming a possession of Albrecht of Habsburg in 1283. After 1379 it became the chief residence of the Leopoldine line, of which the Archduke Friedrich V later became Emperor as Friedrich III (1440–93), who was a great benefactor of the town. It was menaced by Turkish incursions in 1480 and again in 1532, after which its fortifications were strengthened by Italian architects, which made it a bastion against the infidel.

The Archduke Karl II inherited Innerösterreich in 1564, and in 1585 founded a University there (at which Kepler taught in 1594–98), which the Jesuits converted into a bastion of the Counter-Reformation. The University was zealously supported by Karl II's eldest son, the Archduke Ferdinand, who, when elected Emperor in 1619, moved to Vienna, as Ferdinand II. His younger son, Leopold Wilhelm, built up an important collection of paintings, which later passed to the Emperor Leopold, his nephew. In 1640, in the face of possible Turkish invasion, an arsenal was established here to furnish an army of volunteers who would reinforce the professional army. Although decimated by plague, notably in 1680, the town revived, and once the Turkish threat was over, with their defeat at Vienna in 1683, it again flourished.

In 1784 its fortifications were razed, and it was unable to resist Napoleon's troops. In 1813 Louis Napoleon, ex-king of Holland, was resident in Graz. The enlightened Archduke Johann (1782–1859, in Graz), in disgrace after his morganatic marriage in 1829 (cf. Bad Aussee), settled in Graz, and did much to develop it into a cultural and technical centre. Beethoven had been elected an honorary member of the Musik-Verein of Styria in 1822, for he had had musical associations with Graz for a decade, after allowing his compositions to be played at charity concerts in aid of the local Ursuline nuns.

In 1844 a railway was inaugurated between Graz and Koflach (40km W), with its lignite mines. This gave a further boost to its growing industrial activity, which caused it to be the target of air attack during the Second World War, since when the city has yet again expanded and continues to prosper. It is the home of Druck, the academic publishers; and is reputed for its Puntigam and Reininghaus beers.

At one time it was a popular place of retirement for pensioned civil servants and military men (including F.M. Benedek, in 1881; cf. Wiener Neustadt). Among those born at Graz were Johann Bernard Fischer von Erlach (1656–1732), the architect; Joseph Anton Stranitzky (1676–1726), the actor and theatrical director; the sculptor Josef Thaddäus Stammel (1695–1765); Johann Nepomuk Malzel (1772–1838), the inventor of the metronome in 1817; Anselm Huttenbrenner (1794–1868), the friend of Schubert; Friedrich Loos (1797–1890), the artist; the Archduke Franz Ferdinand (1863–1914, died at Sarajevo); and Karl Böhm (1894–1981), the conductor. Leopold Sacher-Masoch (1836–95) received part of his education at Graz. Busoni studied composition here from 1876, before moving to Vienna.

From the *Hauptbrücke*, the northerly of the two central bridges over the Mur, the Murgasse leads E, while the Neutorgasse leads SE to the main museums, see Rte 33B. Conspicuous is the **Franziskanerkirche**, with a mid 14C choir, a nave of 1520, and a solidly based belfry of 1636. Behind it is a warren of alleys, once the precinct of butchers.

A few steps brings one to the N end of the triangular HAUPTPLATZ, surrounded by tall 16th or 17C mansions with characteristic stucco decoration. In the centre is a statue of Archduke Johann, while the S side is taken up by the 19C *Rathaus*. A good view may be had from its SW corner of the *Clocktower* (1588), with its huge face, on the *Schlossberg* to the N.

There are several alleys leading E to the adjacent FÄRBERPLATZ from the Herrengasse, in which Nos 3, 7, 9, and 11 are notable. The S side of the street is flanked by the **Landhaus**, seat of the provincial government, erected by Domenico dell'Allio in 1557–65, and containing the *Rittersaal* of a previous building, altered in the mid 18C, and containing stucco-work by P.A. Formentini, as does the *Landhausstube*.

The ***Courtyard**, with three stages of arcades (one wing of which dates from 1890), is notable, as is the cast-iron *well-canopy*, etc.—On the S side is the ****Zeughaus** or **Arsenal**, built in 1643–45 by Antonio Solari, consisting of four floors, largely unaltered since the 17C, which houses over 29,000 examples of contemporary or earlier arms, including 3300 suits of armour (among them several remarkable fluted or engraved examples); over 7800 firearms; over 5000

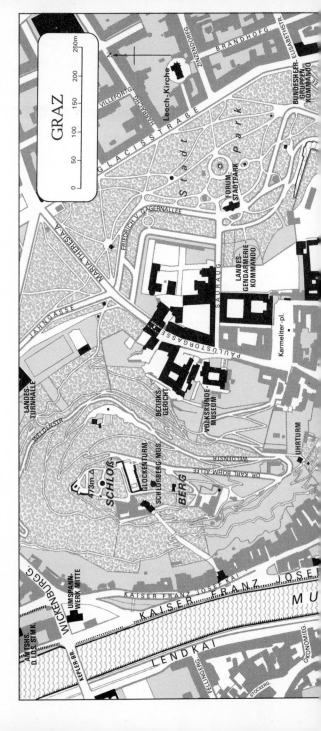

halberds, etc.; 2275 swords and sabres, etc.; cavalry cuirasses, and lobster-tailed helmets, powder-flasks, shields, and miscellaneous accoutrements available to the Styrian mercenaries, obviously burnished and protected, and no longer the 'rusty old armour' referred to in one guide of the turn of this century.

Regaining the Herrengasse, you pass the *Stadtpfarrkirche* (15–16C), later baroquised, and at the end of the street turn left past the *Mariensäule* of 1671 in the Opernring, on the site of earlier fortifications. To the right is the *Opera-house*, a neo-Baroque building of 1899.

Turn left again to skirt the STADT PARK, laid out in 1869, before bearing W along the Erzherzog Johann-Allee to re-enter the old enceinte at the *Burgtor*. It will be noticed that several corner-buildings in the old town are canted, and faced with triple columns.

Most of the several *University buildings* lie E of the park, while a few minutes' walk NE brings you to the **Leechkirche**, founded by Leopold VI Babenberg, rebuilt in the late 13C, with belfries of 1500, and containing 13–14C glass.

The *Burg*, considerably altered over the centuries, was the Imperial palace. It retains an unusual double spiral staircase (1499) and additions were made in the 1950s.

Immediately to the S rises the **Cathedral of Hl. Ägydius** (St. Giles), built between 1438–62 on the site of a Romanesque church. Several Baroque additions were later made, and the interior was also redecorated while in Jesuit hands (until 1786). It contains several features of interest, among them a new organ-loft incorporating its rococo predecessor by Veit Köninger (1772) to hold the organ by J.G. Klais of Bonn, completed in 1978. Against a right-hand pillar is the tomb of Count Cobenzl, with a lead medallion of 1741 by G.R. Donner. On either side of the choir entrance are the late 15C bridal chests of Paolo Gonzaga of Mantua, used as reliquaries.

Adjacent to the S is the **Mausoleum of Ferdinand II** (1578–1637), an extravagant Baroque edifice of 1614–38 designed by Giovanni Pietro de Pomis. It is a cruciform building with a lofty copper dome and cylindrical E tower; it is adjoined by a tomb-house, also with its cupola, and was completed by Pietro Valnegro. The interior decoration and high altar are early works designed by J.B. Fischer von Erlach. In the crypt is the sarcophagus of the Emperor's parents, bearing recumbent effigies, but only his mother, Maria von Bayern (died 1608) is interred here; his father, the Archduke Karl (died 1590) was buried at Seckau.

Opposite is the *Jesuitenkollegium* (1572), and the original *University building* (1607–09).—Turning N, cross the adjacent FREIHEITS PLATZ, with (right) the *Schauspielhaus*, a theatre in the classical style by Peter von Nobile (1825), built on the site of the Baroque theatre (by Josef Huber), burnt down in 1823. (It is said that the performance in Graz of Marlowe's 'Dr Faustus' in 1608 was the earliest on the Continent.)—Continue to climb N to enter the KARMELITERPLATZ, there turning left.

The path ascending to the W below an arch leads to the *Clocktower* on the *Schlossberg*, while the right-hand turning ascends to the *Paulustor* (1614), passing (left) steps to the *Styrian Folk-Museum*, containing reconstructed rooms in a former Capuchin convent, etc.

Descending the Sporgasse, you pass (left) at the corner of the Hofgasse the *Palace of the Teutonic Order* (1621; by Peter Valnegro), with an early Renaissance courtyard, opposite which (No. 21) are steps ascending to the *Stiegenkirche St. Paul im Walde* (1619–27).

On regaining the Hauptplatz, turn right along the Sackstrasse (with the *Erzherzog Johann Hotel* at No. 3–5), in which stand the mid 17C *Herberstein palace* (No. 16), containing a notable staircase, and art gallery (four paintings by Schiele may be seen on application), and the *Attems palace* (by Andreas Stengg; 1702–05; No. 17). Beyond, past a small square, is the *Alter Münz*, or *Mint* (1690; No. 22), and further on the Franz Josef Kai, off which a funicular ascends to the *Schlossberg*, with remains of its ancient fortifications, razed in 1809, and the *Glockenturm* of 1588.

By turning down the Schmiedgasse (leading S from the Hauptplatz), and then right along the Landhausgasse, you reach (left) at Raubergasse 10 (completed in 1674 by Domenico Sciassia) the entrance to the *Mineralogical* and *Natural History collections* of the Joanneum, the collections of art being found at Neutorgasse 45, the parallel street to the W.

The **LANDESMUSEUM JOANNEUM** (named after Archduke Johann, its founder; see history) is one of the more impressive and extensive of provincial museums. Rooms to the right on the GROUND FLOOR are devoted to the medieval period. Notable are a Crucifixion by *Wölfel von Neumarkt* (c 1370); the epitaph of Ulrich Reichenecker (c 1410); the carved so-called Virgin of Admont I, with the dead Christ (1400); votive-painting of Ludwig I of Hungary (1430); a retable of the Crucifixion (c 1410); bust and reliquary· of St. Oswald (1400); a carved Virgin and Child with her protective mantle (1436); the retable of St. Martin (1440); parts of altarpieces, one depicting the Massacre of the Innocents (1478), and another of the Murder of Becket, by *Michael Pacher*; carved Styrian Archangel Michael (1430), *School of Michel Erhart*, a carved Magdalen (1490); a carved St. Sebastian (Styrian; 1500); the Virgin of Mondsichel (1530), showing pre-Baroque carving; *Monogrammist AA*, carved and painted altarpiece of 1518, and portrait of the dead Maximilian I (1519); an altarpiece of 1525; *Master of the Bruckner Martinstafel*, Martyrdom altarpiece (1520); St. Martin with donors (1518); *Marx Reichlich*, Dispersal of the Apostles (1490); fragment of a Styrian altarpiece depicting the Magi (1490); *School of Cranach*, the Maria-zeller Wunderaltar (1512); and numerous other Styrian altarpieces and carved statues, etc.

Steps ascend from the main vestibule past two good Tombstones to **R1** *Pieter Brueghel the Younger*, Kermis, and two paintings of The Triumph of Death; *Hans Cranach*, Lucrezia; *Lucas Cranach the Elder*, The Judgement of Paris; *Herri Met de Bles*, Landscape with the Flight into Egypt; *Momper*, two Landscapes; *Battista Dossi*, Hercules and the Pygmies.—**R2** Equestrian scenes by *P. Wouwerman*, and *Dirk Stoop*; *Gillis Remeeus*, Lute-player.—**R3** *Feti*, David and Goliath.—**R4** *Franz Floris*, Bacchanal; *Spranger*, Mars, Venus and Amor, and Venus, Ceres, and Bacchus; *Cornelis de Vos*, Diana and Acteon; *Martin de Vos*, Self-portrait.—**R5** *Anon.* Portraits of Georg Primbsch von Königsbrun (1694), and Anna Katharina von Primbsch (1672); *Stammel*, carved Fallen angel.

Steps ascend to **R6** *Rottmayr*, Abraham and Isaac; gilt Baroque statues by *Veit Königer*, and *Stammel*, including—by the latter—SS. Joachim and Anna.—Steps descend to **R7**, with several works by *Johann Heinrich Schönfeld* (1609–84); *Rottmayr*, Ecce Homo; *M. Altomonte*, Deposition, the Magdalen, and two paintings of St. Jerome; *J.G. Edlinger*, Old man; *Martin von Meytens*, Male portrait;

Ph.F. von Hamilton (1664–1750), four Birds; *Maulbertsch*, Christ on the Mount of Olives; works by *'Kremser' Schmidt*; and Landscapes by *M.J. Schinnagl, J.G. Glauber*, etc.

R8 displays a series of smaller works by Baroque artists, including *Maulbertsch*, Holy Family, and Christ at the house of Emmaeus; and examples of the art of *Carlone, M. Altomonte*, and *Paul Troger.—***R9** *'Kremser' Schmidt*, Self-portrait, Holy Family, and several small religious and allegorical canvases.—**R10** *J.C. Brand*, Landscape; *J.B. Lampi*, Portrait of Elisabeth Wilhelmine von Würtemberg; works by *Pillement*, and small paintings by *Norbert Grund* (1717–67).

To the left of the entrance vestibule is a series of rooms displaying (in **R2**) musical instruments, including zithers, and a Clavichord of 1727.—**R5**, a Cabinet of inlaid wood of 1760; Portraits of Franz I, Maria Theresia, and Josef, the crown prince, etc.—**R4** Pastel portraits.—**R6**, with a painted ceiling from Schloss Burgstall, dated 1592.—**R7** Boiseries from Schloss Radmannsdorf (1564).

R1 *Ironwork: with a remarkable collection of locks, grilles, keys, handles, knockers, shop-signs, etc.

FIRST FLOOR. **R8** (left) the silver-gilt neck-ring of Albrecht III (1365–95); portrait of Friedrich III, crowned, and of his wife, Eleanor of Portugal, together with the body of their marriage-wagon, of c 1450; collections of ecclesiastical furniture and cult objects.—**R9** furniture; early 14C ironwork; and illuminated MSS.—**R10** a silver-gilt tankard from Augsburg (the 'Steirischer Landschaden-bundbecher'), perhaps the work of *Hans Schaller*, a gift of the province to the Archduke Karl II on the occasion of his marriage to Maria of Bavaria in 1571, and other goldsmiths' work; ivories; a cross-bow; an iron table of 1589; a double Litter of c 1595 belonging to Sigismund Báthory and his wife the Archduchess Maria Christina; stamped leather cases and bindings.—**R11** furniture, scientific instruments, clocks, and a portrait of Siegmund von Dietrichstein (1480–1533).—**R12** celestial globe of 1693 by *V. Coronelli*; painted boxes and chests; ceramics and glass; pewter, and more furniture.—**R13** stoves; ebony chests, one with stone inlay.—**R14** (a domed hall), is devoted to Franz II and his brothers, among them the Archduke Johann.—**R15**, with a notable iron door; more ceramics, much of it from Nuremberg, and 18C Krüge (pewter-lidded tankards); a prayer-table; inlaid desks, seal-presses, etc.—**RR16–19** contain collections of engraved glass; stoves; 18C inlaid furniture, including Grandfather clocks; figurines for Christmas cribs; a carved sacristy cupboard of c 1700; some Jewish furniture; and an 18C Pharmacy from Radkersburg.—**RR20** and **24** are at present closed.—**R25** displays panelling; and **R23**, Ironwork, plaques, grilles, chests (note the locks), candelabra, a 16C oven, etc.

Other sections contain Costume collections, and Oriental collections, etc.

On the W bank of the Mur, a short distance N of the Hauptbrücke, stands the *Mariahilf-Kirche* (1611), by G.P. de Pomis (died 1633, and buried here), with Baroque towers added in 1744 by Josef Hueber. Adjacent is a cloister, and the Minoritensaal of 1700, by J. Carlone.— A few steps to the SW is the church of the *Barmherzigen Brüder* (1740; by Johann Georg Stengg), containing features of interest.

The Annenstrasse leads c 3km W (best approached by car or tram No. 1) to *Schloss Eggenberg*, with a shady park in which peacocks stalk. It is an imposing four-square edifice with corner towers, built around an arcaded courtyard of three storeys during the years

1625–35 for Johann Ulrich von Eggenberg by G.P. de Pomis. Several modifications were made by Count Herberstain in the mid 18C. Restored after a brief Russian occupation, it now accommodates several collections, the most interesting being the *Archaeological section* of the Joanneum, including important artefacts of the Hallstatt period. Notable is the bronze ritual *Strettweg Chariot* (or 'Strettweger Wagen'), dating from the 7C BC, and found near Judenburg. An extensive *Numismatic collection* may also be seen.

On the floor above is the *Hunting Museum*, with a series of paintings by Johann Georg Hamilton (1672–1737), among other objects. A number of state rooms may be visited (in groups, at each hour), many with stucco decoration by Alessandro Serenio (1668–82), ceiling-frescoes by Hans Adam Weissenkircher, and wall-tapestries by J.B.A. Raunacher (1757). Notable are the *Prunksaal*, and the Chinese cabinets.

Among other EXCURSIONS in the immediate vicinity of Graz are those to *Strassengel*, and *Rein*, to the NW (see last paragraphs of Rte 32C); and 7km NE (on the B72 to Weiz), the pilgrimage-church of *Maria Trost*, by Johann Georg and Andreas Stengg (1714–25), some of the rich interior decoration of which is by Josef Schokotnigg.—At *Forst*, 6km beyond, a left-hand turning leads 6km to St. *Radegund*, whence a cable-car ascends to the summit of the *Schöckel* (1445m), commanding panoramic views.

For roads from Graz to **Vienna**, see Rte 32, in reverse; for **Klagenfurt**, Rte 36; and for *Ehrenhausen*, and *Heiligenkreuz*, Rtes 34 and 35 respectively.

34   Graz to Ehrenhausen (for Maribor, Zagreb, or Ljubljana)

Total distance, 47km (29 miles). B67. 44km to the crossroads for *Ehrenhausen*, 3km W; this is also rapidly approached by the A9 autobahn.

Maps: F&B 2; BEV 47/15–16.

This route can be combined with Rte 35 to provide a pleasant excursion in this SE corner of Austria.

The B27 leads S from the W bank of the Mur, after 7km crossing the A2 motorway, and then (left) the airport of *Graz-Thalerhof*, to follow the wide valley to (6km) *Kalsdorf*, 2km E of which, on the far bank, is *Fernitz*, with a 16–17C pilgrimage-church of earlier foundation, later baroquised, its choir vaulted from a central column.

Continuing S, with a view (left) of *Schloss Weissenegg*, at 9km *Wildon* is entered, overlooked from the S by the *Schlossberg*, with its ruined castle, Tycho Brahe is said to have made astronomical observations here.

11km **Leibnitz**, 2km SW, with a population of 6650, and a centre of the local wine trade, grew up near the Roman town of *Flavia Solva* (c AD 70), founded to the SE, between *Wagna* and *Landscha*, with remains of a lattice of streets, an *Amphitheatre*, and a museum.

Many more remains may be seen embedded in the walls of *Schloss Seggau* (11–17Cs) on the hill W of Leibnitz, together with mosaics. On the nearby hill of *Frauernberg*, to the S, adjacent to the Baroque pilgrimage-church, the foundations of a temple of Isis have been discovered.

Some 17km SW, on the road to *Deutschlandsberg* (see Rte 36B) is *Gleinstätten*, with a restored Schloss of 1556.—W of *Grossklein*, S of this road, is an extensive area of tumuli of the Hallstatt period.

11km S of the turning for Leibnitz is that for (right) **Ehrenhausen**, a village with a mid 18C *Church* by Johann Fuchs, with a notable belfry and façade adorned with sculptures.—On a height above stands the *Eggenberg Mausoleum*, by G.P. de Pomis, dating from 1610 (Ruprecht von Eggenberg died the following year), the interior decoration of which is by J.B. Fischer von Erlach (1690). The nearby *Schloss* (16C) preserves its 12C keep.

EHRENHAUSEN TO EIBISWALD (35km). The B69 leads W towards the *Kreuzberg* (633m), crossing vineyards and shortly veering SW to (15km) *Leutschach*, among hop-gardens. To the S rises the *Possruck* (964m), which is extended to the W by further ranges of hills forming the Yugoslav frontier. At 6km the 12C fortress of *Arnfels* is passed, 3km N of which, at *St. Johann im Saggautal*, is a good mid 18C church by Johann Fuchs.—Several tumuli, known as *Heidengrä- ber* or pagan tombs, can be seen in this valley as you approach (14km) *Eibiswald*; see Rte 36B.

THE EHRENHAUSEN CROSSROADS TO BAD RADKERSBURG (34km). Some 3km NE of this junction lies *St. Veit am Vogau*, with a pilgrimage-church of 1748 by Josef Hueber.

The B69, leading E, skirts the Yugoslav frontier, here formed by the river Mur. On the far bank, at (13km) *Mureck* it passes an old castle. You meet the B66 (see Rte 35) after a further 13km, and 3km before entering *Halbenrain*, with a 16– 17C *Schloss* preserving part of an earlier fortress.—6km **Bad Radkersburg** (1850 inhab.), a frontier village of some character, has remains of its bastions, several 16–17C houses in its Hauptplatz, with a *Mariensäule*, and a *Rathaus* with a tall octagonal tower. In a little square to the S is late 15C *Maria Hilf*, with a mid 17C tower. The courtyard of the *Freyspurghof*, Langgasse 27, dates from 1583. To the W of the latter is the 15C *Stadtpfarrkirche*.

4km S of the Ehrenhausen crossroads, on the S bank of the Mur, the B67 passes *Spielfeld*, with a *Schloss* of ancient foundation, 2km beyond which is the Yugoslav frontier (Customs).

Maribor (*Marburg*) lies 16km further S, and **Zagreb** 121km beyond. *Ljubljana* lies 127km SW of Maribor.

35   Graz to Heiligenkreuz (for Budapest)

Total distance, 77km (48 miles). A2. 27km *Gleisdorf* exit—8km B65. 11km **Riegersburg** lies 13km S.—13km *Fürstenfeld*—18km *Heiligenkreuz*. **Budapest** is 192km further E.

Maps: F&B 2; BEV 47/15–16.

The main road itself is of slight interest, but the excursion off it via *Riegersburg*, combined with the sub-routes described above, give a good idea of this SE corner of the country.

The A2 is followed S and then E to beyond *Gleisdorf*, where the B65 is continued to the E to (11km) *Ilz*. The motorway turns N slightly further E.—For the road S from Ilz, see below.

13km **Fürstenfeld** (6050 inhab.), formerly fortified, with relics of bastions, the mid 16C *Grazer Tor*, and a square HAUPTPLATZ, is the centre of this wine-growing region, but the town has been much rebuilt since 1945. Just beyond, you cross the *Lafnitz* into the S extremity of Burgenland. 18km *Heiligenkreuz*, the frontier village (Customs, etc.).—For **Güssing**, 12km N, see the latter part of Rte 32B.

At *Mogersdorf*, c 7km SW, the *Battle of St. Gotthard* (1 August 1664) took place, in which the Turks under Ahmed Köprülü were defeated by forces commanded by Count Raimondo Montecuccoli (1608–80, Linz). They were pushed back across the river Raab and many of the janissaries were drowned.—From here turn W up the RAAB VALLEY via (8km) *Jennersdorf* to (24km) *Feldbach* (see below) via *Fehring*, with a fortified church and *tabor*, or entrenched camp. There is a colony of artists at *Neumarkt an der Raab*, just SE of Jennersdorf.

ILZ TO BAD RADKERSBURG (59km). The B66 leads S, passing near (left) *Schloss Hainfeld*, once the home of Joseph Freiherr von Hammer-Purgstall (1774–1856), the Orientalist; it also gave its name to a book by Basil Hall, entitled 'Schloss Hainfeld, or a Winter in Lower Styria' (1836).—Climbing over a ridge, you get a fine view ahead of (13km) *Riegersburg*, a huge basalt crag rising some 200m from the valley floor, and surmounted by a redoubtable fortress, which through the centuries, and as recently as 1945, has held at bay its besiegers. Its present form dates from 1613, and in 1648 it was inherited by Katharina Elisabeth, Countess Galler (née Wechsler), known as the 'Gallerin'. She indulged herself, and made the place even more formidable. Since 1822 it has belonged to the Liechtenstein family, who partly restored it, and several sectors of the castle may be visited. It of course commands an extensive view.

Climbing over another ridge, with good retrospective views, we descend into the RAAB VALLEY past *Schloss Kornberg* (right) to (10km) **Feldbach** (4050 inhab.), the busy little market-town with relics of a fortified *tabor* around its church. There was a great witch-hunt here in the 1670s. Turn right 2km E for (11km) **Bad Gleichenberg** (left of the road), an attractively sited spa, its waters known to the Romans, from which the main road may be regained further S.—At 6km you are c 15km W of the *Dreiländerecke*, a hill marking the meeting of the Hungarian, Yugoslav, and Austrian frontiers.—At 13km the B69 is met 2km from *Halbenrain*, for which, and for *Bad Radkersburg*, 5km beyond, see the latter part of Rte 34.

36 Graz to Klagenfurt

A. Via the Packsattel and Wolfsberg

Total distance, 141km (87 miles). A2. 47.5km *Packsattel* exit—at 9.5km is the exit for (7km) *Twimberg*—B70. 13km **Wolfsberg**—32km **Völkermarkt**—26km **Klagenfurt**.

Maps: F&B 2; BEV 47/14–15.

The recently completed motorway provides an excellent route—much faster and shorter than the old road (see below)—crossing the Packalpe range in a series of viaducts and tunnels. It also provides several attractive and extensive views both on the ascent and descent.

GRAZ TO WOLFSBERG VIA KÖFLACH (95km). The B70 bears S and then veers SW before circling NW and ascending to (36km) *Voitsberg* (10,950 inhab.), with open-cast lignite mines. 5km beyond is **Köflach** (12,000 inhab.), also with lignite mines. Its *Church*, by Domenico Sciassia (1643), contains frescoes by J.A. von Mölk (1775).—3km N lies *Piber*, with a 13C church with an octagonal crypt, and Roman sculpted stones in its apse wall. It is better known for its Lippizaner stud-farm; see p 271.—The B70 ascends SW from Köflach towards the PACKALPE range, after 25km, just beyond *Pack*, reaching the watershed at the **Packsattel** (1169m; views). From here the road descends into Carinthia, with a view (left) of the dividing range of the KORALPE, rising to 2140m at the *Grosser Speikkogel*.—14km *Waldenstein*, with a 16C castle and earlier keep. The LAVANTTAL is entered 4km further on at *Twimberg*.—7km N is the spa of **Bad St. Leonhard** (5000 inhab.), with a fortified 14C *Church* preserving contemporary glass, a high altar of 1646, and a Virgin and Child of c 1340.—The main road threads the gorge of the Lavant to the S, with the SAUALPE (*Ladingerspitze*; 2079m) to the W, to (13km) **Wolfsberg**); see below.

The autobahn is met 9km S of Graz, where you turn SW and then NW, later climbing gradually out of the valley of the Kainach and entering the first of several short tunnels. To the N and NW rise the GLEINALPE and STUBALPE ranges; to the SW, the KORALPE, dividing Styria from Carinthia, pierced by a tunnel just before the **Packsattel** exit at 38.5km. Although the W end of the tunnel provides a fine view towards the SAUALPE, a more extensive panorama may be obtained from the pass itself, 2km N, at 1169km.

The motorway continues W, with views into the LAVANTTAL, and is extended by a stretch following the W side of the valley to meet the B70 some 12km S of Wolfsberg, provided with an exit.

At 9.5km leave the motorway and climb down steeply to meet the road to *Bad St. Leonhard* (see above) 3km N of *Twimberg*, before reaching which you pass below a remarkable viaduct of the A2, and thread the narrow gorge of the Lavant.

At 13km you enter **Wolfsberg** (28,100 inhab.), the main town of the valley, founded in the 11C by the bishops of Bamberg, and remaining their property until 1759.

At the N end of the town on the W bank is the 16C *Drei-faltigkeitskirche*; to the S the *Schloss Bayerhofen*, rebuilt 1566–83, and long a centre of Protestantism. On the E bank, dominated by the 13–16C fortress, rebuilt in a neo-'Tudor' style in the mid 19C, is the HOHER PLATZ, with several 16C houses and a *Mariensäule* of 1718. The *Stadtpfarrkirche Hl. Markus* (13–14C) preserves its Romanesque W door, several 15–16C tombstones of interest, a carved Lion of St. Mark, and a painting of that saint by 'Kremser' Schmidt, while the *Annenkapelle* contains a notable Virgin and Child.

The motorway from Wolfsberg has been continued to the SW, avoiding the pass NE of *Griffen*, and will later by-pass Völkermarkt.

9km *St. Andrä*, on the B70, was from 1228–1859 the seat of the Prince-bishops of Lavant, whose Baroque *Schloss* is now a Jesuit convent; their church is a large plain building of 1687; the *Pfarr-kirche* was once a cathedral.

At 3km S of St. Andrä, also by an exit from the motorway, a left-hand turning leads 6km to the village of **St. Paul im Lavanttal**, on a height above which is the Benedictine *Abbey*, founded in 1091 and rebuilt in the early 17C. The *Church of c 1200*, with two towers, has notable Romanesque carving in the tympanums of the S and W doors, several capitals and tombs of interest, and relics of late 15C frescoes depicting its founders, etc. The modern organ is an unfortunate addition. The *Library* and collections of cult objects may be visited.—For *Lavamünd*, 12km beyond, see Rte 36B.

The main road climbs out of the LAVANTTAL to (8km) a pass at 708m, below the *Griffner Berg* (left), and descends past (4km) *Griffen*, birthplace of the author Peter Handke (1942–), commanded by its ruined castle, referred to as early as 1160. There is an exit for Griffen from the motorway.—At *Greutschach*, 6km NW, is a fortified church of 1236.

2km *Enzelsdorf*, just N of which stands **Stift Griffen**, a Pre-monstratensian foundation of 1236, suppressed in 1786. The church stands among 18C conventual dependencies and contains good tombs, including the Epitaph of Elisabeth Kolmitz (died 1538); the pulpit and plasterwork are notable, as is the charming little organ.

The adjacent 13–14C *Alte Pfarrkirche* has 13C frescoes and carved wooden reliefs of the Passion (1525).

At *Haimburg*, 4km W of Enzelsdorf, the Gothic church has vault frescoes of 1473 in its choir, and a remarkable painted linen Lenten hanging of 1504.—The road ascends to (8km) **Diex** (1153m), with a well-preserved fortified church.

7km **Völkermarkt** (10,850 inhab.), on a plateau above the N bank of its large reservoir, formed by the dammed river Drau (or Drava in Yugoslavia), has a pleasant HAUPTPLATZ, with both old (arcaded) and new *Rathäuser*, just E of which is the *Stadtpfarrkirche Hl. Magdalena*, with octagonal pillars, good vaulting, 14C frescoes, and a carved Pietà of the early 15C.—In the N suburb stands *Hl. Ruprecht*, with an 11C tower, surmounted by a mid 19C octagon, and a 12C *Charnel-house*.

8km S lies *Eberndorf*; see Rte 36B.

The B82 turns NW through attractive country just beyond Völkermarkt for (16km) *Brückl*; *Hochosterwitz*, 7km beyond; and 7km further W, **St. Veit**; see Rte 38. There is a notable 14–15C pilgrimage-church at *Hochfeistritz*, in the hills to the E some 5km N of Brückl.

26km **Klagenfurt**; see Rte 39A.

B.   Via Eibiswald and Lavamünd

Total distance, 157km (97 miles). A2. 17km *Lannach* exit—B76. 12km **Stainz**—31km *Eibiswald*—B69. 42km *Lavamünd*—B80. 29km **Völkermarkt**—B70. 26km **Klagenfurt**.

Maps: F&B 2; BEV 47/14–15.

Although the B70 drives directly SW from Graz, the motorway is recommended, after 17km turning off through **Stainz**, just right of the road, reputed for its wines. It has a large 17C *Church*, by Domenico Sciassia, that of a former Augustinian abbey founded in 1228, with good stucco-work in its vault. Its dependencies, converted into a *Schloss* in 1825, and acquired by Archduke Johann in 1840, now accommodate the *Folklore collections* of the Joanneum in Graz, with farm furniture and utensils, and agricultural equipment in general.

10km *Wildbach*, 3km right, is where in September 1827 a 'Schubertiad' was held by members of the Pachler family in the presence of the composer.

2km **Deutschlandsberg** (7600 inhab.), to the W, with an 18C church, HAUPTPLATZ, and overlooked by a 12–16C *Schloss*, is passed, to approach (right at 4km) *Schloss Hollenegg*, an attractive building of 1577, preserving parts of an earlier fortress, which may be visited. The oval church, rebuilt in 1778, contains rococo decoration and 14–17C tombstones.

5km *Schwanberg*, with a *Schloss* of 1581, its interior baroquised. At 7km further on, the Renaissance *Schloss Burgstall* lies 1km left.

4km *Eibiswald*, where you meet the B69 from *Ehrenhausen* (see Rte 34), and turn right to begin the long ascent, via *St. Oswald ob Eibiswald*, of the E flank of the KORALPE range. The Yugoslav frontier lies c 4–5km to the S, here following the crest of the POSSRUCK RANGE.

At 26km the KOGLERECK PASS is reached at 1349m, with the *Hühnerkogel* (1522m) marking the border to the S, before making the steep descent in a series of zigzags to the valley floor at (16km) **Lavamünd** (348m; 3800 inhab.), at the confluence of the Lavant and the Drau (Drava in Yugoslavia). There is a border-crossing 6km SE (Customs) for *Dravograd*, 4km beyond.

LAVAMÜND TO VÖLKERMARKT VIA BLEIBURG (43km). A by-road (B81) circles to the S from the S bank of the Drau up the JAUNTAL to (18km) **Bleiburg** (6200 inhab.), an old frontier town, dominated by a huge Renaissance *Schloss* containing a fine library, a 15C *Church* with good reticulated vaulting, and a *Pestsäule* of 1724.—The road continues SW below the *Kordeschkogel* (2126m), to the S, to (9km) **Globasnitz**, a village of some charm, with 16C frescoes and a notable high altar in its church, and a Gothic *Charnel-house*. Several houses contain Roman stones in their walls; while on the wooded *'Hemmaberg* (843m; views) are remains of a Celto-Roman temple (150 BC) and 5–6C Palaeo-Christian remains. A good hill-road ascends to a parking-place, from which a ten-minute walk further uphill will bring you to the site, where some 35 square m of mosaics are preserved.—Turning NW from Globasnitz, you approach (7km) **Eberndorf** (5650 inhab.), the main town of the JAUNTAL, with a 14C *Stiftskirche* and separate 15C belfry, the remains of an Augustinian abbey, which passed to the Jesuits in 1604. The crypt, and several other features, including the red marble tomb of Christoph Ungnad (died 1490), are of interest.

There are a number of small lakes in the vicinity, including the *Klopeinersee* to the NW, adjacent to which is the village of *St. Kanzian*; while to the S rise the foothills of the KARAWANKEN RANGE, marking the frontier with Yugoslavia, and here rising to 2126m at the *Kordeschkogel* (SE), 2139m at the nearer *Hochobir*, and 2238m at the *Hochstuhl*, further to the SW, and S of Klagenfurt.—The B70 is reached at **Völkermarkt**, 8km N of Eberndorf; see Rte 36A.

For **St. Paul im Lavanttal**, 11km NE of Lavamünd, see Rte 36A.

We fork left and follow the DRAU VALLEY to the W, after 15km veering NW near *Schloss Weissenegg* and into more open country to approach (14km) **Völkermarkt**; see Rte 36A.—*Eberndorf* lies 8km S; see above.

Klagenfurt lies 26km further W (see Rte 39A), approaching which you get a good view of the frontier range of the KARAWANKEN rising to the S.

37 Bruck an der Mur to Klagenfurt via St. Veit

Total distance, 165km (102 miles). B116. 12km **Leoben**—B306. 14km *St. Michael*—B336. 17km. **Seckau** lies 7km NW.—5km *Knittelfeld*—20km **Judenburg**, by-passed, lies 2km E.—B96. 23km *Scheifling*—B83. 27km **Friesach**—8km *Pöckstein*, for **Gurk** (14km W.)—19km **St. Veit**—20km **Klagenfurt**.

Maps: F&B 2; BEV 47/14–15.

Much work is being done to improve the main road between *Bruck* and *Judenburg*, which will ease the congestion of this industrial area.

For **Bruck an der Mur**, see Rte 32D. Drive W up the valley, at 12km by-passing industrial **Leoben** (30km NW of which is *Eisenerz*; for both see Rte 18B), and 14km beyond, you pass through *St. Michael* (see p 196) and cross the A9 motorway. This tunnels below the GLEINALPE, to the SE, here rising to 1831m.

At 15km a right-hand turning leads shortly to *St. Marein bei Knittelfeld*, with a remarkable church of 1075–1140, altered in the 15C.

A DETOUR is recommended to the imposing *Monastery of Seckau 7km NW, with the *Seckauer Zinken* (2397m) in the background. Founded in 1140 by Augustinian canons, and the seat of a bishop (now at Graz) from 1218–1782, it passed into Benedictine hands in 1883. Its dependencies, surrounded by ramparts, and with notable octagonal corner towers, were rebuilt in the late 16C by Berhard de Silvo, but P.F. Carlone was responsible for its long W façade (1625). The W front of the *Church* was drastically altered in 1892, when the towers were rebuilt. The interior dates from the mid 12C, but it was reconstructed after a fire in 1259.

It is a Romanesque pillared basilica, with heavy cubical capitals, above which the roof is supported by lofty late Gothic vaulting, fanning out from the bare walls. Among notable features are the carved wood group of the Crucifixion (c 1200); the carving of the Coronation of the Virgin by the Trinity in the *Bischofskapelle*; the *Mausoleum* of the *Archduke Karl II*, by Alessandro de Verda (1587–1612), the marble tomb sculptured by Sebastiano Carlone; and in the *Sakramentskapelle*, a 12C alabaster relief of the Virgin and Child, probably of Venetian workmanship.

Regaining the main road, **Knittelfeld**, a small industrial town of 14,150 inhab., can be by-passed, with *Schloss Spielberg* (mid 12C, but rebuilt in 1570) not far to the W.

From *Zeltweg*, left at 6km, the B78 climbs S to the *Obdachersattel* to enter the upper LAVANTTAL (see Rte 36A), overlooked to the E by the *Ameringkogel* (2186m), the N spur of the PACKALPE RANGE.

A by-pass now crosses the flat-bottomed valley N of **Judenburg** (11,200 inhab.), which may be entered from the NE or (14km) W. It is an ancient town, sited on a terrace of glacial debris above the Mur, and still preserves some of its original walls.

It is said to have been named after a colony of Jewish merchants once based there but massacred in 1312, which is possible, but it is also known that a family called Jud lived in the vicinity. The Middle High German poet Gundacker von Judenburg (fl. 1300) was presumably a native. It was also known for its stained-glass works during the medieval period. It was ravaged by fire in 1841. The designer Michael Powolny (1871–1954) was born there.

The central HAUPTPLATZ is dominated by a lofty *belfry* of 1449–1515, adjacent to which is the early 16C *Pfarrkirche*, containing mid 18C statues of the Apostles carved by J. Nischwitzer, and a Virgin and Child of c 1420 by Hans von Judenburg.—In the Kasernengasse, leading E from the Platz, are relics of a 17C Jesuit church and college.—On the far bank of the river stands the 12C *Mag-dalenenkirche*, preserving 14C frescoes and 14–15C glass.

To the E are the *Neu-Liechtenstein Schloss* of 1650, and the ruins of a 12C castle at a higher level, the ancestral home of Ulrich von Liechtenstein.

Another of his residences, in which that minnesinger died in 1276, was at *Frauenburg*, above *Unzmarkt*, passed (right) 15km W of Judenburg, as the road circles to the S to (4km) *Scheifling*. See p 172 for the UPPER MUR VALLEY, to the W.

Turning SE ascend to (6km) the PERCHAUER SATTEL (995m) and descend to (6km) *Neumarkt in Steiermark*, with a restored 12C *Forchtenstein* stronghold.

14km SW, in a sequestered valley, lies the former Benedictine abbey of **St. Lambrecht**, founded in 1096, but largely rebuilt in 1639–44 by D. Sciassa. The interior of its imposing *Church* (1430) was baroquised, but retains earlier sculptures and frescoes which are of interest. The *Peterkirsche* (1424) retains a winged altar by the Master of the St. Lambrechtaltar; also notable is the Romanesque *Charnel-house* (1148), while the village contains several old houses and catle ruins.

Continue S past (right) *St. Marein bei Neumarkt*, its Romanesque and Gothic church preserving several sculpted Roman stones in its walls.—Carinthia is entered just prior to (12km) ***Friesach** (7050 inhab.), also by-passed, an ancient fortress-town guarding the narrow valley, and retaining stretches of its defensive walls, and also, on its NE and E sides, a wide *Moat*.

On the *Petersberg*, to the W—approached by steps ascending from N of the central HAUPTPLATZ—stand the considerable remains of its 11–12C castle and church, possibly of Carolingian origin, etc.—Just N of the characteristic platz, with its Renaissance *Fountain* (1563), stands the Romanesque and Gothic *Stadtpfarrkirche*, unfortunately restored in the 19C, but containing several good sepulchral monuments and some early 14C glass.—Further N, beyond the moat, is the sober *Dominikanerkirche* and convent, founded in 1217, containing sculptures of interest.—To the S of the town are relics of the *Deutschordenskirche Hl. Blasius*, reached by turning right past the kitchen of the adjacent hospital.

A DETOUR may be made up the METNITZ VALLEY to the NW, to (12km) *Grades*, where above the village, with its 16–17C *Schloss*, and *Pfarrkirche*, is a fortified and well-buttressed 15C church dedicated to *St. Wolfgang*, with a notable carved winged altar of 1522, and decorated vaulting.—2km beyond is **Metnitz**, where the church contains carved and gilt statues of the Apostles by B. Prandstätter of 1746, conspicuous against its white walls. Both the choir, and the adjacent *Charnel-house* preserve frescoes, in the latter some of the Dance of Death (c 1500). To the N rises the KUCHALPE (1770m), to the SW, the *Mödringberg* (1693m).

Continuing S from Friesach, at 8km *Pöckstein* (or Böckstein) is reached, with a Baroque *Schloss* of 1780, once the property of the Prince-bishops of Gurk, and built by J.G. Hagenauer.

For the excursion to **Gurk**, 14km W, see Rte 38.

Soon you pass (left) *Althofen*, with a fortified tower and several old houses on a hill above the more modern town (4250 inhab.), and after bearing SW out of the valley, the road descends to (19km) **St. Veit an der Glan**, for which, and for its environs, and for the road to *Villach*, see Rte 38.

The widened main road leads S into the ZOLLFELD, rich in relics of the Roman occupation of the area, at 13km reaching the exit for **Maria Saal**, conspicuous on a hill to the left, and for *Karnburg* (right); see Rte 38.—The road shortly enters the N suburbs of **Klagenfurt** (see Rte 39A), with a view ahead of the KARAWANKEN RANGE, marking the Yugoslav frontier, rising to 2238m at the *Hochstuhl*.

38   St. Veit and Environs

Maps: F&B 2; BEV 47/14.

*St. Veit an der Glan (12,000 inhab.), a charmingly sited market-town at the N end of the ZOLLFELD, was the residence of the dukes of Carinthia from the 12C until 1518, when, under the Emperor Maximilian I, Klagenfurt became the capital of the province. The 13C poets Heinrich and Ulrich von dem Türlîn may have been born here. There are a number of sites and monuments to be seen in its vicinity, and it is a pleasant centre from which to explore this area.

The rectangular plan of the medieval town is obvious, and several stretches of its *walls* are still extant. To the E and W of the central street-crossing is the UNTERER PLATZ extended to the W by the wider *HAUPTPLATZ, flanked by a number of attractive 16C houses, and containing the *Florianibrunnen* of c 1676, a *Pestsäule* of 1715, and the *Schlüsselbrunnen* (1566; in which antique marble from *Virunum*—see below—has been incorporated). Between the latter two is the *Rathaus* of 1648, with a Baroque façade, a courtyard retaining sgraffito-work, and a rococo assembly-room on its first floor.

To the S of the Platz is the **Pfarrkirche**, Romanesque in origin, with Gothic vaulting and choir. Its mid 18C high altar, the organ, and the tombstones on its exterior wall, are notable, and likewise the *Charnel-house*, in which a carved Carolingian stone has been incorporated.—To the NE of the *Unterer Platz* is the *Zeughaus* (1529), the old arsenal, preserving its Gothic arcade and tower, and housing the local museum.

5km NW of St. Veit, on the lower slope of a hill rising to 1246m, stands the imposing 16C *Schloss Frauenstein*. To the NE are the hilltop ruins of the castle of *Taggenbrunn*.

Karnburg; Maria Saal; Magdalensberg; Hochosterwitz.

An interesting EXCURSION of c 60km may be made to the S and E of St. Veit by following the B94 SW to (7km) *Liebenfels*, with the extensive ruins of its castle, where you turn left and left again to (5km) the hamlet of *St. Peter am Bichl*, where the wall of its church preserves an ancient tombstone and two carved Carolingian stones from the palace at Karnburg (see below) above the entrance.—5km E, and skirting the S slope of the *Ulrichsberg* (1015m), you pass the ancient *Mons Carantanus*, where there are several early Christian remains and where a temple dedicated to Isis Noraia once stood.—In the village of **Karnburg** itself, the restored *Church, with its 14C steeple, is a 9C foundation, where c 814 Louis le Débonnaire is said to have established the administrative headquarters of Carinthia. In the walls, and in those of the abutting chapel, are numerous Roman sculpted stones. Some 100m NW of the church stood the so-called *Fürstenstein* (now in the museum at Klagenfurt), on which its dukes were formally enthroned until 1414.

Turning right and then left, you shortly cross the B83 and ascend to the conspicuous church of **Maria Saal** c 2.5km E, one of the most remarkable churches in Carinthia.

It was rebuilt in the mid 15C within a fortified enceinte, on the site of a church founded c 767 by St. Modestus, who was sent here on an evangelising mission by Bishop Virgil of Salzburg. Until the foundation of Gurk, in 1072, it was a cathedral.

Its S wall incorporates several Roman inscribed or sculpted stones, notable among which is the covered waggon drawn by a pair of horses, and also the *Keutschacher Tombstone* (c 1510; by Hans Valkenauer), depicting the Coronation of the Virgin. In the S porch is a relief of Romulus and Remus being suckled by the she-wolf. The lattices of vaulting of varying design are memorable, as are the organ-loft and organ of 1735 (by Martin Jäger), pulpit, and high altar

(1714, with a charming Virgin and Child of 1425). In the N apse is the carved and gilt *Arndorfer Altar* (c 1520), guarded by armed statues of St. Florian and St. George; in the S apse is the Retable of St. George (1526), with his dragon.—Opposite the entrance is the octagonal *Charnel-house*, with relics of murals, one of which, St. Michael weighing souls, is now preserved in the church.

Descending to the old road rather than the new main road, we shortly skirt an *Open-air museum* of reconstructed Carinthian farmbuildings, and turn right. At 3km we pass the *Herzogstuhl*, a back-to-back seat made of inscribed Roman stones, where until 1615 further ceremonies took place when Carinthian dukes took office (cf. Karnburg, above). The first turning to the right after the railway bridge soon brings you to the site of *Virunum*, where slight traces remain of a forum, theatre, amphitheatre, and grid of streets, but the town has been pillaged for its stone over the centuries.—2km *St. Michael.*

Here we turn right and after 2km fork left to climb steeply up the flank of the **Magdalensberg** (1059m), passing (right) near the summit the site of the extensive *Excavations* of an important Roman settlement between 15 BC and AD 45. By the later date it had been superseded by that of *Virunum*; see above.—On the summit of the hill is a fortified site, in which stands a *Church* of 1500 replacing a Romanesque building, which in turn was erected on the foundations of a temple dedicated to Mars Katobius. It contains an altarpiece which includes a finely carved figure of St. Helen. The hill commands fine panoramic views.

On descending to the main road, turn right to (3km) *St. Donat*, where the S wall of the *Pfarrkirche* incorporates several Roman stelae and sculptures: one a female figure with a head of Celtic origin added.—Here you turn NE to approach the extraordinary site of *Burg Hochosterwitz*, a fortress perched on an isolated rock of triassic limestone rising 160m above the valley floor. It was built by Georg Freiherr von Khevenhüller during the years 1570–86 (when it was a Protestant refuge) on the foundations of an earlier castle. The ascending ramp spirals to its summit (views), passing through 14 defensive gates; within the enceinte is a collection of arms, and a restaurant.

On descending, continue N (with retrospective views), and shortly meet a main road, there turning left, and after 2km right, to approach *St. Georgen am Längsee*, with the 17C dependencies of a Benedictine foundation of 1003, now in part an hotel. Skirting the neighbouring lake, the B83 is reached 6km NE of *St. Veit.*

The circuit of the Wimitzer Berge; Gurk (c 90km).

Follow the B83 NE and N to (19km) *Pöckstein* (see p 364), there forking left onto the B93, leading up the GURKTAL to (10km) **Strassburg**, a small but ancient town (2550 inhab.), burned down in 1180 after two sieges, for harbouring Hermann of Ortenburg, who had pretentions to the bishopric of Gurk. The restored *Schloss* (12C and 18C) was a residence of the bishops of Gurk until 1787. It was damaged by fire in 1856, but preserves a Romanesque chapel and late 17C arcaded courtyard. The late Gothic *Pfarrkirche* contains several features of interest.

Just W of the town, a lane forking right ascends to the charming hilltop village church of **Lieding**, with a curious carved tympanum over its *W door* of an angel, lion, and dragon. The nave is

Romanesque, the choir Gothic, with mid 14C glass, and an exuberant Baroque high altar. Below the choir is a crypt; in the cemetery, a Gothic *Charnel-house*.

4km **Gurk**, a small village, is dominated by its ***Cathedral**, an imposing Romanesque basilica of 1150–1220, with its twin towers surmounted by Baroque sugar-castor domes of 1680.

A convent was founded by Gräfin Hemma von Friesach-Zeltschach (died 1045), which after 1645 was occupied by Benedictines. Augustinian canons were established here by the archbishop of Salzburg in 1072, thus usurping the dominant position that *Maria Saal* (see above) had previously held. Its first bishop was Günther von Krapfeld (1072–90), who was buried here.

The richly articulated apses should be inspected before entering by the W portal, in the porch of which are mid 14C frescoes, and relics of carved, polychromed, and gilt woodwork of c 1220. The nave was covered by reticulated vaulting in the late 16C. An important series of Romanesque murals may also be seen in the *Bischofskapelle* (reached by a spiral staircase in the S tower), recently restored.

Notable is the Baroque *pulpit* of 1741, designed by G. and A. Bibiena (well known for their theatrical designs), on which a Protestant pastor is shown being precipitated by the Catholic Church triumphant; also the lead *Pietà*, sculpted by G.R. Donner, and his last work (1741). The richly gilt high altar of 1632 is by Michael Hönel, to the right of which is a fresco of c 1380 depicting the Old men of the Apocalypse and the Conversion of St. Paul; to the left is a St. Christopher of c 1250. Further W on the N wall is a relief of Samson slaying the lion (c 1200).

Steps descend into the large *Crypt* below the choir, sustained by a forest of white marble columns; the tomb of Hemma, the founder, is here.—A treasured Lenten hanging of 1458 is displayed at the appropriate season.

Good late 13C frescoes may be seen in the *Charnel-house* of *Pisweg*, 4km S.

4km *Zweinitz* (right) contains 14C frescoes in its church apse, and others of 1425 of the Adoration of the Magi.—At the head of the valley to the NW rises the *Mödringberg* (1693m).

6km *Altenmarkt* (right), the fortified late Gothic church of which, with good vaulting, contains a fresco by Thomas von Villach of the Virgin with the mantle (c 1450), and an early 16C carved Crucifixion.—At 4km a right-hand turning leads 4km to *Deutsch-Griffen*, also with a fortified church, containing mid 15C frescoes.

The main road climbs SW and then S, to approach (c 20km) *Feldkirchen* (see below), just prior to which turn left to meet the B94 22km W of *St. Veit*.

FROM ST. VEIT TO VILLACH (49km).The B94 drives SW past (7km) *Liebenfels* (see p 365), following the valley of the GLAN, at 8km passing the ruined castle of *Glanegg* before reaching (8km) **Feldkirchen in Kärnten** (12,150 inhab.), with a *Pfarrkirche* of ancient foundation.

Here you turn SW to skirt the S bank of the *Ossiacher See* (11km long, and 1.5km wide) to (11km) **Ossiach**, a lakeside village providing a good view of the *Gerlitzen* (1909m) dominating the far bank. The Benedictine *Abbey* was founded by 1028, and partly demolished in 1816; other dependencies now accommodate an hotel. The colourful interior of the *Church*, baroquised by 1749, with frescoes by J.F. Fromiller, is also notable for a carved altarpiece of 1505 depicting the Virgin and Child with SS. Catherine and Margaret. The organ-loft is of 1700, and organ concerts are given here in summer. A plaque commemorates the pianist Wilhelm Backhaus (1884–1969), who died at Ossiach.

9km *St. Andrä*, at the far end of the lake, is dominated to the S by the fortress of **Landskron** (see p 174), shortly beyond which you meet the B83 from Klagenfurt, to enter the NE outskirts of **Villach** (see Rte 40A), with a view ahead of the *Dobratsch* (2166m), and to the S, the KARAWANKEN RANGE, rising to 2143m at the *Mittagskogel*, marking the Yugoslav frontier.

39   Klagenfurt to Villach (for Udine, Venice, and Trieste)

A.   Via the A2 autobahn

Total distance, 38km (23 miles).

Maps: F&B 2; BEV 47/13–14.

KLAGENFURT (87,300 inhab.; 27,150 in 1880), the capital of Carinthia since 1518, lies near the centre of a wide basin bounded by hills, and interspersed with small lakes, the largest of which, the *Wörther See*, lies 3km W, with which it was connected by the *Lend Canal*, cut in 1527. Some 25km to the S rises the rugged KARAWANKEN RANGE, forming the natural frontier with Yugoslavia. It is surrounded by some extremely attractive country, and it is only hoped that its lakes will not be irretrievably spoilt by over-exploitation.

It grew up near a tower guarding a ford of the river *Glan* during the time of Duke Hermann von Spanheim (1161–81), and in the mid 13C it was given its charter by his son Duke Bernhard von Spanheim, and encircled by walls. Being a centre of trade, '*Chlagenvurt*' was a focus of Turkish and Hungarian incursions during the 15C, and although it survived the worst excesses of peasant revolts and the Counter-Reformation, it was in 1514, and again in 1535, ravaged by fire. In 1518 the Emperor Maximilian I established it as the provincial capital, and a new town was later laid out on the plans of Domenico d'Allio.

It was occupied on several occasions during the Napoleonic Wars, firstly by Masséna, and in 1809 its walls were razed, to be replaced by a square 'ring' road. It suffered some damage from bombing during the Second World War, and from May 1945 was the HQ of the occupying forces in the British zone. The only British War Cemetery in Austria is just W of the town; see below.

Among its natives were Emanuel Herrmann (1839–1902), claimed to be the inventor of the post card; Robert Musil (1880–1942), author of 'The Man without Qualities'; and the artist Herbert Boeckl (1894–1966). The composer and organist Isaac Posch died here c 1623.

Its *airport* is a short distance to the NE.

The S half of the old town is laid out on a grid plan, in which is the central NEUER PLATZ, distinguished by its huge **Lindwurmbrunnen**, or *Dragon Fountain*, commemorating the fabulous beast which haunted the district in ancient times when it was a wild morass: a rhinoceros skull found in the area, and now in the museum, partly served as a model. It was sculpted by Ulrich Vogelsang from 1590, and in 1636 the mace-swinging giant was added by Michael Hönel, together with its railings. It now serves as a symbol of the city.

The W side of the Platz is taken up by the *Neues Rathaus*, the former Orsini-Rosenberg palace (16C–mid 17C). From its N side the Kramergasse leads diagonally into the narrow ALTER PLATZ, in which several houses retain their arcaded courtyards, and with a *Trinity Column* of 1680 opposite the *Altes Rathaus* (1600). Continuing N you reach the HEUPLATZ, with the *Florianidenkmal* (1781; by J.G. Hagenauer), to the SW of which stands the *Stadtpfarrkirche Hl. Egyd* (St. Giles) with its lofty tower. It is documented in 1335, but was rebuilt in 1692, and contains frescoes by J.F. Fromiller (in the choir), and J.A. von Mölk.

Turning SW, and re-passing the W end of the ALTER PLATZ, where No. 30, *Zur Goldenen Gans* (the 'Golden Goose'), with a façade of 1600, survived the great fires, you reach the court of the **Landhaus**, dominated by its two seven-storey towers surmounted by bulbous domes. The building, by Anton Verda (1574–81), preserves on the first arcaded landing the *Grosser Wappensaal*, decorated with frescoes by Josef Ferdinand Fromiller (c 1740), and emblazoned with the arms of some 665 members of the Carinthian Estates.

The Ursulinengasse leads NW to the *Theatre* of 1808, altered in 1910, W of which in gardens, are relics of fortification.

To the W of the Landhaus is the busy HEILIGENGEISTPLATZ, with its 14C *Church*. To the S of this square is the BENEDIKTINER PLATZ, with the former *Franziskanerkirche* (early 17C), later in Jesuit hands.

From the SE corner of the NEUER PLATZ, a few paces S brings you to the **Pfarrkirche Hl. Peter und Paul**, now unattractively sited among modern buildings. It was erected by Protestants towards the end of the 16C, and in 1604 passed to the Jesuits, who added the choir in 1665. The whole was restored after a fire in 1723, and in 1787 it was raised to cathedral rank. The high altar, flanked by columns, contains paintings by Daniel Gran (1752).—There is a *Diocesan Museum* at No. 10 in the adjacent Lidmanskygasse.

Some few minutes' walk to the SE, to the E of the *Landesregierung* building, is the ***Landesmuseum für Kärnten**, the Museum of the province of Carinthia, with several of its larger archaeological relics on display in the garden.

The entrance is on the E side of the building, on the FIRST FLOOR of which are zoological, botanical, and geological collections.—SECOND FLOOR: R'K' contains Roman statuary, stelae, and a mosaic of Dionysus or Bacchus from *Virunum*, found in 1898.—R'N' is devoted to the Bronze Age, and the Hallstatt culture, with a number of equestrian statuettes, and a model of a waggon and horses from *Frög* (S of Velden); also statuettes from *Gurina*, and *Virunum*, and fragments of murals; ceramics, jewellery, glass, coins, fibula and buckles, etc. excavated at *Magdalensberg* (cf.).—R'Q' Relief ('Hortus conclusus') from Maria Saal (cf.; early 16C), and Lock and key from the same (early 15C); and an altarpiece from St. Veit (second half of 16C) and another of the Death of the Virgin, from Ossiach (1500).—R'R' The painted Paola Gonzaga reliefs (1477) from her marriage chest, after a design by Mantegna; and glass from the chapel of Landskron (1570).—RR'S–T' contain collections of arms and armour, including the ceremonial Sword of Johann Siebenhirter (1499), of the Order of the Knights of St. George at Millstatt, founded by Friedrich III in 1469; and pewter.—R'U' Panoramas by Markus Pernhart (1824–71), and early naive views of Klagenfurt by Karl Kremser.—R'V'

Collections of Carinthian costumes.—**RR'W–Z'** Folk Art; furniture, musical instruments, etc.—On the landing are examples of woodcarving and metalwork from the province; also of interest are several hollowed-out lake boats.

The Adler Gasse leads N to the KARDINAL PLATZ (see below), with its *Obelisk* of 1807, from the N side of which the Burggasse leads back to the Neuer Platz, in which No. 8 (by J.A. Verda; 1586–1600), known as the **Burg**, was built as a Protestant college.

Its first floor now accommodates the **Landesgalerie**, comprising several rooms of paintings, mostly by Carinthian artists, including works by *Herbert Boeckl*, and a Portrait of Boeckl by *Arnold Clementschitch* (Villach 1887–1970), and the latter's Self-portrait; also a Self-portrait of *Emanuel Fohn* (Klagenfurt 1881–1966); and *Franz Wiegele* (Nötsch, W of Villach, 1887–1944), Mother and Child, and Reading girl. It is the venue of frequent temporary art exhibitions.

Some minutes' walk NE from the Kardinal Platz brings you to the **Bischöfliche Residenz** (1776; by N. Pacassi), built for the Archduchess Marianna (1738–89), adjacent to which is the *Elisabethinenkirche*, in the crypt of which is her tomb, with a group of the Crucifixion by Balthasar Moll. A small museum is devoted to this enlightened and philanthropic daughter of Maria Theresia, who was closely connected to the Masonic lodge 'Zur wohltätigen Marianna', founded in Klagenfurt c 1783. Among influential members were Franz Josef von Enzenberg, Franz von Herbert (descended from the English family of that name), and Franz Salm, Bishop of Gurk, who died in 1822, a cardinal. The bishop was also a great mountaineer and promoted the eventual ascent of the Grossglockner, in 1800.

About 3km W, just S of the Villacher Strasse, is the only *British and Commonwealth War Cemetery* in Austria, containing 589 burials, including remains moved from several small plots in the country.

For the road S to the frontier, see Rte 39D.

The A2 autobahn leads due W from Klagenfurt, at some distance above the N bank of the deep **Wörther See**, 17km long, and 1.5km wide—warm in summer and often iced over in winter—and commanding a number of good views S across the lake towards the *Pyramidenkogel* (846m) and beyond to the rugged KARAWANKEN RANGE, the *Hochstuhl*, its highest peak, and the *Mittagskogel*, further W, rising to 2238m and 2143m respectively. The S bank of the lake was occupied by Yugoslavia from 1918–20, when after a plebiscite it was re-united with Austria.

Several exits provide rapid access to its lakeside resorts; see Rte 39B. Ahead, beyond Villach, rises the *Dobratsch* (2166m).

At 33km a by-pass circles to the N of Villach (to join up with the A10), here overlooked (right) by the *Landskron*; see last paragraphs of Rte 11.

It is planned to extend the A10 to the SE, to the *Karawankentunnel*, which will pierce the range to enter Yugoslavia just W of *Jesenice*, to provide a rapid route from the NW to *Ljubljana* and on to *Zagreb*.

Perhaps the easiest entrance to **Villach** is 2.5km SW, at *Maria Gail*; see Rtes 40A, and 39D. Beyond this exit, the motorway continues SW to reach the Italian frontier (Customs), joining up with the new autostrada (A23; completed in 1986) from Venice and Udine.

The B83 leads W through *Arnoldstein*, where there are remains of a Benedictine abbey founded in 1107 but burnt down in 1886.

At *Seltschach*, 3km S, the 14C church contains good Gothic altarpieces. The neighbouring peak of *Ofen* (1509m) marks the meeting of the Yugoslav, Italian, and Austrian frontiers. Just E of the peak is the little-used *Wurzen-pass* (1073m), providing a crossing into Yugoslavia just W of *Kranjska Gora*; but a better approach is via *Tarvisio*, in Italy.

At 3km the B111 turns right to follow the GAILTAL; see Rte 40C.

At **Thörl**, 2km beyond this turning, the *Pfarrkirche* has remarkable frescoes of c 1470 by Thomas von Villach.—The Italian frontier is reached after 3km (Customs).

B.   Via Pörtschach and Velden

Total distance, 40km (25 miles). B83. 13km **Pörtschach**—10km **Velden**—17km **Villach**.

Maps: F&B 2; BEV 47/13–14.

The lakeside road skirts the N bank of the **Wörther See** (see above) and passes through several villages strung out along its shore which are now threatened with over development.

At c 11km a right-hand turning ascends steeply to (5km) **Moosburg**, to the W of which are two small lakes, overlooked by a 16C *Schloss*, now an hotel, and a ruined keep in which Arnulf von Kärnten was born c 853. The village church incorporates several Roman stones in its wall; a carved stone of the Carolingian epoch can be seen in the cemetery wall. The descent towards (3km) *Pörtschach*, further W, provides a wide *View* S.

2km **Pörtschach** (2500 inhab. out of season), where at its 16C *Schloss Leonstein* (now a very pleasant hotel), to the right of the now too busy main road, Brahms stayed during the summers of 1877 to 1879, there composing in part his 2nd Symphony, and Violin Concerto, and the G Major Violin Sonata Opus 78.

At 10km **Velden** (7400 inhab.), a popular resort at the W extremity of the *Wörther See*, is reached, beyond which the road veers N below the motorway to approach **Villach**; see Rte 40A.

C.   Via Maria Wörth and Velden

Total distance, 43km (27 miles). 16km *Maria Wörth*—10km **Velden**—17km **Villach**.

Maps: F&B 2; BEV 47/13–14.

Turning SW from Klagenfurt, follow the S bank of the **Wörther See** (see above) past (5km) *Maiernigg*, where in 1902, after his marriage to Alma Schindler, Gustav Mahler acquired a property. Here during the next four summers he composed his Symphonies 5, 6, 7, and 8.

11km **Maria Wörth**, a small resort on a lakeside promontory. Covered steps ascend to the Gothic *Pfarrkirche*, from 1151 the church of an abbey founded in 884, of which the Romanesque S portal and crypt survive. It contains Baroque furniture. Adjacent is a late 13C *Charnel-house*; while on a hillock at a lower level is the *Rosenkranzkirche*, with late 12C frescoes.

To the SW rises the *Pyramidenkogel* (846m), providing attractive panoramic views over the area, approached by a road from *Reifnitz*, 2km E of Maria Wörth; but see the parallel road via *Viktring*; Rte 39D.—The lakeside road passes through *Dellach* and (6km) *Auen*, where in the Waldhaus am See (a wooden house on the shore) Alban Berg spent the summers from 1932 until his death in 1935.

On approaching (4km) **Velden** (see above) you pass a *Schloss* built in 1590 for Bartholomäus Khevenhüller, now an hotel.

An alternative road from VELDEN TO VILLACH is that turning SW to (4km) *Rosegg*, near which a large Celtic grave-field has been excavated. After crossing to the S bank of the Drau, and in 7km turning left to *Egg*, on the circular *Faaker See*, continue W via *Maria Gail*; see below.

D.   Via St. Jakob im Rosenthal and Maria Gail

Total distance, 52km (32 miles). B91. At 5km *Viktring* lies 2km right—8km—B85. 19km *St. Jakob im Rosental*—8km—B84. 10km *Maria Gail*—2km **Villach**.

Maps: F&B 2; BEV 47/13–14.

Driving S from Klagenfurt, turn right after 5km for **Viktring**, with a former Cistercian *Abbey*, founded in 1142, with 18C dependencies, including a three-storeyed *Cloister*. It is now a school, and under restoration. The *Church* was partly demolished in 1847, but some good glass of c 1400, and a high altar of 1622, are preserved in its Gothic choir.

A by-road leads W to (8km) the small *Keutschacher See*, from which you can ascend the *Pyramidenkogel* (846m) for the view, or continue W, at 7km turning left for (5km) *St. Egyden*, where the church contains good mid 15C sculpture. The main route can be regained c 7km SE at *Maria Elend*.

Regaining the B91 from Viktring, climb S, shortly passing a turning (left) for the Gothic and Baroque pilgrimage-church of *Maria Rain*, and another to *Schloss Hollenburg* (16C), with a Renaissance court-yard, and providing a plunging view into the ROSENTAL, and towards the KARAWANKEN RANGE, rising to the SW to 2237m at the *Hochstuhl*. A very similar *view is obtained from the main road as you circle S over the Drau, here dammed.

At 8km turn right.

The road ahead by-passes **Ferlach** (3km E; 7600 inhab.), once reputed for its gunsmiths, and ascends the LOIBLBACH VALLEY to reach at 13km the N entrance to the *Loibltunnel* (Customs), here piercing the range below the old pass (the road over which being constructed in 1728), to enter Yugoslavia 57km N of *Ljubljana*.

The B85 follows the S bank of the Drau parallel to the KARAWANKEN RANGE to (16km) *Maria Elend*, where the Gothic and Baroque pilgrimage-church has a charming carved altarpiece of 1515 depicting the Virgin and Child between SS. Roch and Sebastian.—The road passes through *St. Jakob im Rosental*, and shortly crosses the site of the motorway under construction to extend the A10 to the

Karawankentunnel, which will provide a rapid entrance into Yugo-slavia just W of *Jesenice*.

At 11km turn right to circle the wood-girt *Faaker See*. From the far bank (with a view S of the ruined fortress of *Finkenstein* on the Karawanken, in which the Emperor Maximilian I lived for some years when a boy) turn NW below the A2 to (10km) **Maria Gail**.

The fine view from the Gothic **Church* is marred by the modern funerary chapel. The church has several sculptures on its exterior wall, a restored altarpiece of c 1520, and faint frescoes of 1300, among other features.

The E suburbs of **Villach** are shortly entered; see below.

40 Villach to Lienz (for Cortina, or Kitzbühel)

A. Via Spittal, Obervellach, and Winklern (for the Grossglockner road)

Total distance, 114km (70 miles). B100. 38km **Spittal an der Drau**—10km B106.—20km *Obervellach*—30km *Winklern*. **Heiligenblut** lies 28km N.—N107. 16km **Lienz**.

Maps: F&B 2; BEV 47/12–13.

VILLACH (52,700 inhab.; 11,300 in 1869), although well sited on the Drau, and within easy reach of some magnificent scenery, is not a town of great attraction. It is largely devoted to industry and the wood trade, and has become an even more important hub of road and rail communications since the motorway connecting it with Italy has been completed (1986). The spa complex of *Warmbad* lies to the SW of the town.

The Roman settlement near its mineral springs (*Villa ad aquas*) had by the 9C become *Uillah*, also called 'statio bilachiniensis', where in 1955 a cache of 164 Roman gold coins were discovered. In 1007 it was given by Heinrich II to the diocese of Bamberg, from which it was acquired by Maria Theresia in 1759. It flourished during the medieval period, and had a Jewish community, who lived without the walls in *Judendorf*, to the SW, where in two excavated graves in their cemetery remains of golden hairnets have been found.

It was rebuilt after a destructive earthquake in 1348 (being not far from the Friuli region in Italy, where in May and September 1976 widespread damage was done by earthquakes with their epicentre NW of Udine), while in 1524 and in 1679 it was ravaged by fire. The Emperor Charles V stayed briefly as a guest of the Khevenhüller when passing through in 1552. It was here that he induced the Fuggers to provide him with more credit, the famous 'Loan of Villach'.

Between 1809 and 1814 it formed part of the short-lived Kingdom of Illyria, and was occupied by the French. Several monuments were destroyed during its liberation in 1813; and very severe damage was caused by air-raids during the Second World War, since when the rebuilt town has expanded greatly.

The older part of the town, which was originally walled, lies on the S bank of the Drau, centred on the long HAUPTPLATZ, with a *Trinity Column* of 1739, and several 16C houses. No. 18 was the home from 1502 to 1534 of the father of Theophrastus Paracelsus (1493–1541), who was a local doctor. No. 26, formerly a Khevenhüller residence, and now the *Post Hotel*, was rebuilt after a fire in 1679, and again in 1949 after bomb damage. It was occupied by British officers during the years 1945–52, and had been known as the 'Gasthaus zur Post' in 1748, if not earlier.

The platz is dominated to the SW by the **Stadtpfarrkirche Hl. Jakob**, with its semi-detached 95m-high *belfry*, only joined to the main edifice in the 19C. Several 16C tombstones are embedded in the exterior wall of the 14–15C church, notable for its plain piers and vaulting, and for the numerous *tombs and epitaphs* of the Leininger, Khevenhüller, and Dietrichstein families (Sigismund Dietrichstein, a confidant of Maximilian I, married a natural daughter of the emperor, Barbara von Rottal). Although the texts of some have been shown to have Protestant overtones, they were not desecrated as some ecclesiastics had ordered. The carved stone *pulpit* (1555), with its Tree of Jesse, is notable.

At No. 38 in the narrow Pfarrgasse is the *Stadtmuseum*, with archaeological and Roman collections of interest, and Gothic panels by such local artists as Thomas von Villach (late 15C), and Friedrich von Villach (c 1435).

Some distance SE, between the road leading to *Maria Gail* (see Rte 39C) and the river, stands the twin-towered *Stadtpfarrkirche Hl. Peter*, or *Heiligenkreuz-Kirche* (1726–44), with a pulpit and high altar of some interest, and notable for its heavy cornices.

A toll-road climbs steeply to the W to approach the summit of the VILLACHER ALPE, which rises further W to 2166m at the *Dobratsch*, and which commands a wide *·View*.

For the **Landskron**, and the road to **Millstatt** via *Radenthein*, and for **Ossiach**, see the latter parts of Rtes 11 and 38 respectively, in reverse. For the road to *Tarvisio*, in Italy, see the latter part of 39A.

The B100 leads NW up the Drau valley, roughly parallel to the recently completed motorway, to (38km) **Spittal**; see Rte 11.

4km beyond Spittal, a left-hand turning leads to the hillside hamlet of **St. Peter im Holz**, which partly occupies the site of Roman **Teurnia**, only slight remains of which may be seen to the N, in the valley. Here are the foundation of an early Christian basilica (5C), and a *Museum* protecting a well-preserved mosaic pavement, and containing several Roman and Palaeo-Christian inscribed and sculpted stones, excavated in 1908, when the site was discovered by chance.

At 10km we fork right past *Möllbrücke*, the fortified Gothic *Pfarrkirche* of which contains a notable carved altarpiece of 1510; another by the same local sculptor can be seen in the church at *Rappersdorf*, to the N.

The road follows the MÖLLTAL to the NW, between the *Reidbock* (2822m) to the N, and the *Salzkofel* (2498m) to the W, with a view, high up on the right, of the railway-line leading from the Tauerntunnel.

9km *Kolbnitz*, where on the isolated hillock of *Danielsberg* stands a small Romanesque church on the site of a Roman temple of Hercules.—Funiculars ascend NE from here to the high-lying reservoirs between the *Reidbock* and *Reisseck* (2965m).—The road continues past several villages to (9km) *Stallhofen*, where the Gothic pilgrimage-church of *Maria Taxi* retains a rococo high altar, and frescoes by J.F. Fromiller in a domed chapel.

To the E is seen the characteristically roofed medieval keep of *Schloss Oberfalkenstein*.

In the early 16C *Pfarrkirche* of (2km) **Obervellach**, once the administrative seat of gold and silver mines exploited in the vicinity, is a *triptych* by Jan van Scorel of 1520.—The nearby *Schloss Trabuschen* contains frescoes by J.F. Fromiller.—On a spur to the NW rises *Burg Groppenstein* (15C; with a 12C keep).

9km N lies *Mallnitz*, a winter-sports centre, adjacent to which is the S exit of the *Tauerntunnel*, piercing the range below a peak at 2832m. Cars may here entrain on the regular shuttle-service (*Autoverladung*) to *Böckstein*, adjacent to *Badgastein* on the far side of the *Hohe Tauern*; see p 148.—To the NE rises the *Ankogel* (3246m), approached by cable-car; to the NW is the *Geiselkogel* (2974m).

From Obervellach bear W up the MÖLLTAL, and then veer SW, passing several hamlets, later overlooked by the *Zellinkopf* (2695m) to the NW, while to the S rises the *Hochkreuz* (2704m). Beyond (22km) *Rangersdorf* you get a fine view of the mountains to the W behind (8km) *Winklern*, among them the *Schleinitz* (2905m), and further to the NW, in the SCHOBERGRUPPE, the *Petzeck* (3283m).

At *Winklern* (965m), with its watchtower, the B107 turns right up the MÖLLTAL to (28km) **Heiligenblut**, and the S entrance to the *Grossglockner* toll-road, for which see Rte 8C, in reverse.

Turn left and start to climb in zigzags to the ISELSBERGPASS (1204m), with magnificent *Views* S towards the jagged LIENZER DOLOMITEN RANGE (*Grosser Sandspitz*; 2772m), and to the DEFEREG-GENGEBIRGE to the W of Lienz, rising to 2943m at the *Gölbner*. Descending in long zigzags, at 11km you meet the B100 5km E of **Lienz**, in its wide valley, for which see Rte 40B.

B. Via Spittal and the Oberdrautal

Total distance, 110km (68 miles). B100. 38km **Spittal an der Drau**— 10km *Möllbrücke*—23km *Greifenburg*—18km *Oberdrauburg*— 21km **Lienz**.

Maps: F&B 2; BEV 47/12–13.

For the road to *Möllbrücke*, see Rte 40A.

Here bear W, shortly circling S up the DRAU VALLEY, passing (right) *Sachsenburg*, with remains of its fortifications, and old houses.—At c 15km *Gerlamoos* lies to the right, its church preserving frescoes of c 1470 by Thomas von Villach.—Pass through the old village of *Steinfeld*, with a Renaissance *Schloss* to approach (8km) *Greifenburg*, with a mid 12C castle, remodelled in 1485.

Several small churches in the area preserve frescoes, among them those at *Berg*, to the right at 5km. To the S rises the *Reusskofel* (2371m). After 8km the isolated 12C keep of *Stein* is seen on a height to the left.

5km. At *Zwickenberg*, a high-lying hamlet to the right—an ascent of 5km—the church contains a notable early 16C high altar, a Baroque Virgin of the Rosary, suspended from the vault, and a fresco of St. Christopher (c 1500).

1km *Oberdrauburg*, to which the B110 descends from the *Gailbergsattel*, 350m above (left) from *Kötschach*; see Rte 40C.—The road veers NW to enter the East Tyrol.

13km. The two churches at *Lavant*, 2km S—near which are

Palaeo-Christian remains, and 6–7C walls—contain features of interest.

As the valley widens, you get a good view SW of the jagged LIENZER DOLOMITEN, rising to the *Grosser Sandspitze* (2772m), the DEFEREGGENGEBIRGE (*Gölbner*; 2943m), and the *Schleinitz* (2905m), rising N of Lienz.

At 2km fork left; the right-hand fork leads to the B107, zigzagging NE to the ISELSBERGPASS (1204m) and *Winklern*, for *Heiligenblut*; see Rte 40B.—To the right of the road is the site of the mid 1C Roman settlement of *Aguntum*, destroyed c 600, with a small museum of relics.

5km **Lienz** (11,650 inhab.; 2500 in 1869), a largely modern town, well sited at a junction of several valleys at the confluences of the Isel and the Drau, with the picturesque LIENZER DOLOMITEN rising to the S, is the capital of the East Tyrol.

Although its Roman predecessor—*Aguntum*—lay a short distance to the E (see above), it is likely that *Schloss Bruck*, guarding the entrance to the Isel valley, was built on the site of a Roman citadel. This was chosen by the Counts of Görz as their residence, and on the death of the last count, Leonhard, in 1500, it passed by inheritance to the Emperor Maximilian I, who sold it in 1501 to Baron Michael von Wolkenstein-Rodenegg. It was later famous for its brass foundry. It was ravaged by at least six fires during the centuries—in 1444, 1598, 1609, 1723, 1798, and 1825—and much of what remained in its centre was destroyed in four air-raids towards the end of the Second World War.

The centre of activity just N of the railway station is the HAUPTPLATZ, on the S side of which is the 16C *Liebburg*, now the *Rathaus*, with two onion domes. The Muchargasse, leading W from the adjacent JOHANNESPLATZ, passes the late Gothic *Franziskanerkirche*, with 15C frescoes. Crossing the NEUER PLATZ, continue W along the Schweizergasse, at No. 33 in which Albin Egger-Lienz, the artist, lived in his youth.

At the end of this street, by a *Dominican church*, turn right across the Isel, and then left to ascend to the *Stadtpfarrkirche St. Andrä, a mid 15C edifice, with a choir rebuilt and baroquised after a fire in 1738, and abutted by a tall belfry. The interior preserves frescoes of several periods, the latest being by J.A. von Mölk (1761). Notable are the red marble tombs of Graf Leonhard von Görz (1506/7), and of Michael von Wolkenstein (died 1523), and his wife, by Christoph Geiger. The organ-case dates from 1618, but the organ itself has been restored recently. The high altar is by J.A. Zoller (1761). Several statues are by Johann Paterer. The octagonal crypt contains a carved Pietà of c 1400.

Recent excavations have revealed that the church was erected on the site of an early Christian basilica of the 5C. The *Cemetery-chapel* by Clemens Holzmeister (1925) is decorated with frescoes by Albin Egger-Lienz (1868–1926), who is buried here.

A few minutes to the E is Gothic *St. Michael*, with interesting vaulting, and four carved busts by Paterer (c 1730).

Some distance to the W of the Dominican church stands **Schloss Bruck**, a castellated fortress on a wooded hill, built c 1280, with an imposing keep, and which was enlarged in the 16C and 18C. Its *Chapel* preserves frescoes by Simon von Taisten (c 1490), and in the apse, others by Nikolaus Kentner (c 1452). The castle also houses a *Museum* in which several works by Egger-Lienz are displayed, but it is otherwise of comparatively slight interest.

A cable-car from *Gaimberg*, N of the town, ascends to the *Zettersfeld* (1820m), below the *Steinermandl* (2213m), providing a fine view S towards the LIENZER DOLOMITEN.

For the B108 leading NW up the ISEL VALLEY to (22km) **Matrei** (and *Obermauer* to its W), and the TAUERNTAL, at the far end of which is the S entrance of the *Felbertauerntunnel* for *Mittersill*, see Rte 7, in reverse.

LIENZ TO ARNBACH (33km), for *Cortina* or *Bressanone* (Brixen) in the PUSTERTAL. Bearing SW, follow the B100 parallel to the Upper Drau, with a good view of the LIENZER DOLOMITEN to (11km) *Thal* (right), with two churches, the upper of which, *St. Korbinian*, contains three remarkable late 15C altarpieces devoted to the life of that saint, to Mary Magdalen, and the Passion. The keystones of its vault are also notable, while one wall depicts scenes from the life of Christ and of the Last Judgement, by Andreas Peurweg (1589). The Crucifixion group in the choir dates from 1490.

6km *Mittewald an der Drau*, 2km N of which is *St. Justina* (1500; later baroquised), with a carved and painted altarpiece of the School of Friedrich Pacher.—On the far flank of the side-valley lies *Ried*, its church with a carved altarpiece showing the Coronation of the Virgin, by Peter Peisch (1517). To the NW rises the *Gölbner* (2943m).

9km *Strassen*, with two churches of interest, the octagonal *Dreifaltigkeitskirche* containing frescoes by F.A. Zeiller in its cupola (1768); *St. Jakob*'s has frescoes of c 1460 by Jakob Sunter.—The by-road continues to *Tessenberg*, where the church has frescoes of 1500 and a carved altar of 1510.

The main road, joined from the left by the B111 from *Kötschach* (see Rte 40C), in 4km enters *Panzendorf*, with churches containing late 15C frescoes by Simon von Taisten, and overlooked by the ruins of the 12–16C *Schloss Heimfels*. The covered *Bridge* of 1781 is notable.—*Sillian*, at 1003m, is soon reached, with an altar of c 1520 by Peter Peisch at *St. Peter unter Heinfels*, and then *Arnbach*, the frontier village (Customs), between (left) the *Helm* (2433m), and (right) a spur of the DEFEREGGENGEBIRGE (2436m).

At 17km *Cortina* lies 32km to the S.–The S49 continues W via (27km) *Brunico* (Bruneck), to meet the motorway between the *Brenner Pass* and *Bolzano* (Bozen) at 31km, 6km N of *Bressanone* (Brixen) in Italy; see Rte 5.

C. Via Kötschach

Total distance, 114km (70 miles). B83. 18km—B111. 30km *Hermagor*—31km **Kötschach**—B110. 14km *Oberdrauburg*—B100. 21km **Lienz**.

Maps: F&B 2; BEV 47/12–13.

For the road to the turning beyond *Arnoldstein*, see the latter part of Rte 39A.

Here turn right and then past (left) a turning for *Thörl* (see p 371). The road shortly veers N onto the far bank of the Gail to (9km) *Nötsch*, to the NE of which rises the *Dobratsch* (2166m), with the lead-mining village of *Bleiberg-Kreuth* on its NW flank. Continue W above the floor of the GAILTAL, with a view ahead of the *Spitzegel* (2118m), and of the KARNISCHE ALPEN extending to the W, its crest forming the frontier with Italy.—21km *Hermagor*.

Here the B87 turns NE up a side valley, crossing the GAILTALER ALPEN via the KREUZBERG PASS (1077m) to (28km) *Greifenburg* (see Rte 40B), at 19km passing a turning (right) to the narrow *Weissensee*.

7km. At *Schlanitzen*, c 5km S (beyond which the *Trogkofel* rises to 2279m), the church has a notable carved and painted altarpiece of 1485.

15km *Grafendorf*, above which, in the church of *St. Helena am Wieserberg*, are frescoes of c 1300 and c 1500.

9km **Kötschach** (3600 inhab.), a pleasantly sited small town with a notable *Church*, rebuilt in the early 16C, with the frescoes (1499; by

Nikolaus Kentner) of the earlier building in its choir. The unusually intricate vaulting is remarkable.

For the road continuing W, see below.

From Kötschach climb N through *Laas*, its early 16C church with similar vaulting to the above, to the GAILBERG PASS (982m) descending in a series of steep zigzags (views) to (14km) *Oberdrauburg*, for which and for the road on to **Lienz**, 21km NW, see Rte 40B.

14km S of Kötschach is the PLÖCKENPASS (1360m) on the Italian frontier (Customs), whence the road descends to *Paluzza* and (33km) *Tolmezzo*. The remains of the defensive system of this frontier pass during 1915–17 are preserved.

KÖTSCHACH TO PANZENDORF (56km). The B111 continues up the valley, here the LESACHTAL, dominated by the KARNISCHE ALPEN to the S, and to the N by the LIENZER DOLOMITEN, at 29km reaching *Maria Luggau*, with the pilgrimage-church of *Maria Schnee*, completed 1544 but baroquised c 1736, just beyond which the East Tyrol is entered.—At 10km the high-lying village of **Obertilliach** (1450m) has a *Church* by Franz Xaver de Paula Penz (1764), with frescoes by J. and A. Zoller, while the *Nikolauskapelle* has frescoes by Simon von Taisten (late 15C).—At 7km the road crosses the KARTITSCH SATTEL (1526m), and descends into the PUSTERTAL, reaching the B100 2km E of *Panzendorf*.—**Lienz** lies 28km NE of this junction, for which see Rte 40B.

INDEX

Topographical names are printed in Roman or **Bold** type; the names of notable people are in *Italics*; subjects are CAPITALS. Sub-indexes are included for Graz, Innsbruck, Linz, Salzburg, and Vienna. Many Schlösser are listed separately under Schloss. The abbreviations A., P., and S. indicate Architect, Painter or Sculptor, respectively.

ATLAS SECTION

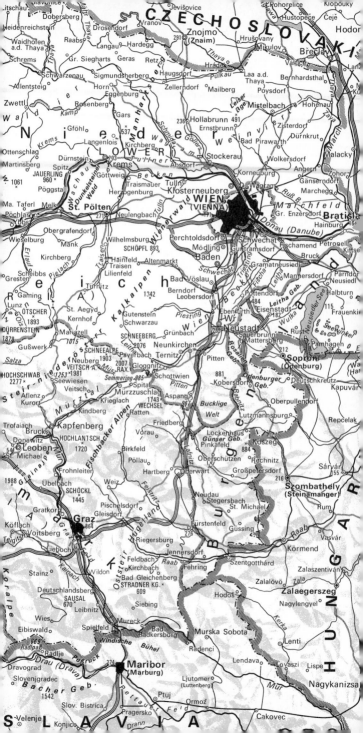

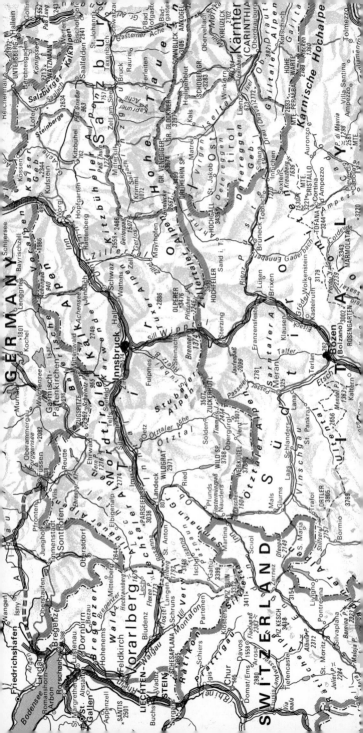

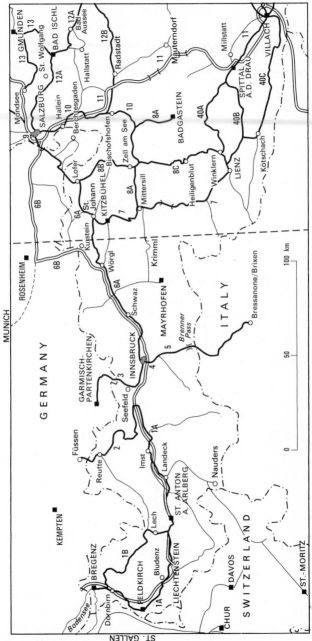